D0457125

THE

OXFORD BOOK OF

SCIENCE FICTION STORIES

THE OXFORD BOOK OF SCIENCE FICTION STORIES

Edited by
TOM SHIPPEY

Oxford New York
OXFORD UNIVERSITY PRESS
1992

Oxford University Press, Walton Street, Oxford OX2 6DP
Oxford New York Toronto
Delhi Bombay Calcutta Madras Karachi
Petaling Jaya Singapore Hong Kong Tokyo
Nairobi Dar es Salaam Cape Town
Melbourne Auckland
and associated companies in
Berlin Ibadan

Oxford is a trade mark of Oxford University Press

British Library Cataloguing in Publication Data
Data available

Library of Congress Cataloging in Publication Data
The Oxford book of science fiction stories/edited by Tom Shippey.
p. cm.
Includes bibliographical references.
1. Science fiction, English. 2. Science fiction, American.
I. Shippey, T. A.
PR1309.S3097 1992 823'.0876208—dc20 92–9512
ISBN 0–19–214204–6

Typeset by Best-set Typesetter Ltd., Hong Kong
Printed in the United States of America

ACKNOWLEDGEMENTS

The number of people who have lent or given me books, magazines, and advice since I first stumbled on science fiction in January 1958 is now beyond recall. I am especially grateful to Dr James Bradley for his entirely convincing notion of 'fabril literature' (which I hope he will develop at length); to Michael Walshe, Peter Weston, and Mike Dickinson for operating a free-trade area in books over many years; and to the science fiction fan-clubs of Birmingham and Leeds, of Leeds and Oxford Universities, for giving me repeated platforms and continuous contention.

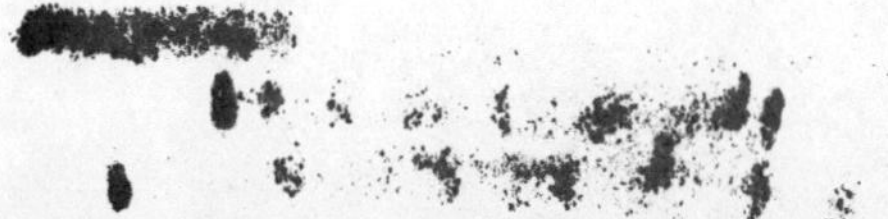

CONTENTS

INTRODUCTION

I

A revealing way of describing science fiction is to say that it is part of a literary mode which one may call 'fabril'.[1] 'Fabril' is the opposite of 'pastoral'. But while 'the pastoral' is an established and much-discussed literary mode, recognized as such since early antiquity, its dark opposite has not yet been accepted, or even named, by the law-givers of literature. Yet the opposition is a clear one. Pastoral literature is rural, nostalgic, conservative. It idealizes the past and tends to convert complexities into simplicity; its central image is the shepherd. Fabril literature (of which science fiction is now by far the most prominent genre) is overwhelmingly urban, disruptive, future-oriented, eager for novelty; its central image is the 'faber', the smith or blacksmith in older usage, but now extended in science fiction to mean the creator of artefacts in general—metallic, crystalline, genetic, or even social.

The first story in this collection, H. G. Wells's 'The Land Ironclads', sets up the opposition made above with Wells's usual uncanny prescience. The story brings into confrontation two countries, two armies, two ways of life, two kinds of human being. It does this, one should note, at the expense of immediate contemporary relevance. By 1903 British readers were quite used to stories predicting future war, but they were nearly always told the identity of the combatants: Britain and Germany, Britain and France, white races versus non-white ones, etc.[2] Wells's story says only 'the invader', 'the defender'; and from the data in the story it is impossible to identify either side more accurately. The defenders—rural outdoorsmen with an adventurous pioneering element—might be Australians, or Boers; the invaders could be any industrialized European nation. But the point of the story (fabril literature,

[1] As far as I am aware, this word has never been used in print. I owe it to Dr James Bradley, of the University of British Columbia, who coined word and concept in his study of early Germanic smithcraft.

[2] See I. F. Clarke, *Voices Prophesying War, 1763–1984* (New York, 1966; reprinted Oxford, 1992), and the anthologies by Michael Moorcock, *Before Armageddon* (London, 1975) and *England Invaded* (London, 1977).

science fiction included, tends much more to the sharp, unexpected, but summarizable point than more accepted literary genres) is stated quite clearly in its last, heavily ironic sentence: that although there is a sentimental bias against machines and the users of machines, a cult of the healthy, simple, and untrammelled, making machines for a particular purpose is nevertheless a fully human activity too—not one which should simply be dismissed, in war, as vaguely unsporting or, in peace, as socially degrading.

Wells wrote many years later that when he died his epitaph would have to be 'I told you so. You *damned* fools',[3] and there is an evident irony in the fact that no one in authority, at least, took any notice of his clear vision of the stalemate of trench warfare broken by the use of the tank, though the *Strand* magazine (whether prophetically or reproachfully) did reprint the story in November 1916, twelve months before the battle of Cambrai. On the whole, though, Wells's story and Wells's point were lost on educated British readers. They continued to reject the values of 'fabril', a reaction obvious for instance in E. M. Forster's avowedly anti-Wellsian story 'The Machine Stops', written in 1908 but not published until twenty years later. But science fiction no longer needed to depend on classically educated readers. It could find, or create, its own constituency, a process that has gone on with accelerating force throughout the century. And in that process it could afford to ignore, or reject, not only an established readership, but also many established literary attitudes or conventions.

Thus, there is no absolute need (in the science fiction *short story* at least) for a hero, heroine, or central figure. There is none in the Wells story, where the central interest, as the title indicates, is on a *thing*. Several other stories in this collection are also named after things (see Le Guin, Niven, Spinrad, and Schenck), and though some of them do have central figures and even 'heroes', or a heroine, others do not. Meanwhile other stories in the collection, however they are titled, do not in fact centre on a person or a personal experience but on an object, a technique, or on the implications of an object or a technique. There is an individual domestic tragedy in 'Raccoona Sheldon's' 'The Screwfly Solution', but the

[3] In the 'Preface' to the 1941 reprint of his novel *The War in the Air* (London, 1908).

foreground of that story is arguably there only to exemplify and to personalize the background; the story's centre is not Anne, Alan, and Amy but 'the screwfly solution' itself, a scientific technique used against humans instead of for them. Similarly, though Tom Disch's 'Problems of Creativeness' has a very clear central figure, and David Brin's 'Piecework' again presents a clearly foregrounded heroine, both stories are actually using individuals to make much wider, though perhaps antithetical, points: in Disch's case, maybe, that individual perception cannot overpower system failure, in Brin's (more clearly, and more in agreement with Wells) that even what appears to be a profoundly dehumanizing technology can be used for good as well as for ill. Science fiction authors have been reluctant to concede the non-necessity of a central figure, Theodore Sturgeon, for instance, asserting that 'A science fiction story is a story built around human beings, with a human problem and a human solution, which would not have happened at all without its scientific content';[4] but there is an element in this of wary defensiveness against established literary opinion, as well as of truth. Nearly all the stories in this collection have human beings in them. But one at least does not (Clarke); and in the rest human beings are by no means always central (see Weinbaum, 'Smith', Sterling, or the arguable case of Le Guin).

What, then, has science fiction had to offer to its human readers? Whatever it is, it has been enough for the genre to make its way to a prominent, if not dominant place in popular literary culture despite every kind of literary misunderstanding or discouragement. A very basic answer must be, Truth. Not every science fiction story, of course, can 'come true', indeed (Cambrai notwithstanding), probably none of them do, can, or ever will. Just the same, many of them (perhaps all of them, in some way or another) may be trying to solve a question for which many people this century have had no acceptable answer. Brian Aldiss has argued boldly that 'Science fiction is the search for a definition of [humanity] and [its] status in the universe which will stand in our advanced but confused state of knowledge';[5] and this definition has immediate relevance to a clutch of stories in this collection (Campbell, Simak, van Vogt,

[4] The definition is given by 'William Atheling Jr.' (i.e. James Blish) in *The Issue at Hand: Studies in Contemporary Magazine Science Fiction* (Chicago, 1964), 14.

[5] See Brian Aldiss, with David Wingrove, *Trillion Year Spree: the History of Science Fiction* (London, 1986), 25. I have altered Aldiss's 'mankind . . . his'.

Miller, Aldiss himself, Martin, or McAuley). There is a less obvious connection between Aldiss's dictum and a number of other stories. Take Clarke's, for instance, the only story in the collection entirely about alien races, with no 'people' in it at all. How can this be part of a 'definition of [humanity]'? But as soon as that question is put, the answer is clear. Clarke's aliens—who have just experienced a war ended by a weapon of mass destruction, whose secret cannot be kept, and which puts them all at risk from guilt and from future retaliation—are self-evidently an analogue of Clarke's readers in 1951; and his point is the need (desire, yearning) for some alternative mode of development, some science of the mind, from which humanity may at present be debarred as naturally as his handless aliens are debarred from becoming blacksmiths. And yet his aliens solve their problem; perhaps humans could make an analogous breakthrough too. The story makes assertions about humanity even though no humans are there. It also in a sense extends the notion of the maker, the 'faber', to a race and a situation paradoxically 'pastoral'. Aldiss's definition of science fiction, and my own categorization of it, survive at least this test.

The same could be said more extensively about the rather large number of 'social' science fiction stories in this collection—those that present a society both like and unlike our own and ask us to accept that the changes, however horrible, are plausible (see, for instance, 'Padgett', Pohl, Ballard, Harrison, Disch, or Spinrad). To take one particular example, what has Gene Wolfe's story about the future reintroduction of slavery, 'How the Whip Came Back', to say about humanity? Here we find a highly personalized story about one woman in a critical place at a critical time. But central though she undoubtedly is, the story is really asking every individual reader whether he or she would be proof against a similar temptation to enslave, *given the altered circumstances laid out in the story*: perhaps most of all the altered world-picture created by robots. Sal the secretary is not a human being nor a central character in the story, but the story would not work without her (it). And behind the story, the circumstances, and the individual question there lurks a metathesis not stated but not really invisible either: that there is no such thing as unvarying human nature or immutable morality. Instead, good and evil are socially defined, and people will do whatever they can get away with, economics and technology permitting. This thesis is not proved by Wolfe's story, indeed it is clear within the story that there is/will be resistance to it (as exemplified by the deluded but not defeated Pope). In other stories the thesis comes over more forcefully, as through the violently ironic endings of Ballard or Harrison. But whichever way the authors tilt the balance, it is clear they are engaging in a similar activity: searching, as Aldiss says, for a definition of humanity *which will stand*, given the depressing insights gained during the twentieth century.

Could Aldiss's argument be extended further, for instance to the apparent 'adventure stories' also represented in this collection (e.g. Schmitz, Le Guin, or Gibson)? Once more, an argument could be made out via the insights of cultural anthropology and the profound effect this has had on American science fiction especially, and particularly as mediated via Ursula Le Guin (the daughter of the two great American anthropologists Alfred and Theodora Kroeber). One might note also the deep urge within several stories to transform the 'soft sciences' into 'hard sciences' and so make their practitioners appropriately 'fabril' as well (see 'Padgett', Brin, and parodically Schenck). But enough has perhaps been said to indicate that science fiction, while full of argument, disagreement, and even rebuttal (Simak and Aldiss, 'Padgett' and McAuley, Brin and *Brave New World*), nevertheless has become in some ways a collective mode, with a shared set of doubts and questions, and even a recoverable if hidden agenda. To go back to the notion of 'fabril': what science fiction has been doing over the decades of this century has been steadily to extend the perceived boundaries of Culture (technology, government, social organization, all seen as affecting—if not absolutely determining—the way human beings act and feel), while at the same time becoming more and more aware of the immense scale of Nature, against which human beings are set and against which they are ultimately powerless.[6] Of this long and vital debate many themes may be seen to be components, all well-represented in this anthology: the nature of intelligence, the nature of civilization, the essentials of humanity, the possibility of super-humanity, the relationship (or otherwise) of theology and morality, the freedom (or otherwise) of the individual within history.

[6] No author has quite managed to challenge this last statement, though one can see the urge to try in van Vogt in this collection, and in works by, in particular, Bruce Sterling elsewhere.

It has been said already in this Introduction that what science fiction has had to offer many readers is Truth. That must seem a most implausible assertion if Truth is taken to mean a single, final solution. If, however, the assertion is taken to mean that science fiction readers have felt able to believe that science fiction authors were addressing them seriously, and trying to explain facts as they saw them and not as more established literary genres would like them to be, then it carries immediately a great deal more force. One might add that the doubts over other branches of literature and their teachers that appear here and there in this anthology ('Padgett', Disch, and Schenck) are not entirely friendly: many science fiction authors feel the 'soft sciences' have let them down both personally and generically. One has to say also in the end that a great reinforcement to the field's sense of iconoclastic inner knowledge has come, this century, through war. Wells foresaw trench stalemate in 1903; 'atomic bombs' appeared in science fiction in 1936;[7] we may never come upon the ICE, icebreakers or 'black ice' of Gibson's universe, or the tanglefoot 'ground-circuits' of Kipling's, but either suggestion has at least more probability than the alternative dimly accepted by other literary genres—that perhaps things will stay more or less the same. It is the repeated and dramatic failure of that prediction this century that has given science fiction so much of its appeal.

II

Do science fiction authors have the literary technique to give proper expression to the undoubted power of their concepts? The view that they do not is a common one, and in it there is a certain truth, as also a certain blindness. The truth stems from the fact that for many years science fiction, and especially the short story in science fiction, was a genre for amateurs and for autodidacts. One might respond to this by saying that almost all authors, classical ones included, were amateurs once; there have never been many who, like Dickens, became commercial successes so early that they could afford to live by writing from the outset. But science fiction,

[7] See Isaac Asimov (ed.), *Before the Golden Age: A Science Fiction Anthology of the 1930s* (London and New York, 1974), 858.

with its multiplicity of magazines demanding copy and its highly participatory readership, was from the late 1920s onwards a genre that gave considerable opportunity for the 'fan' who wrote a story or two, saw them well-received, and went on to become a success within the field, with or without giving up his day-job. The backgrounds of such authors might be very varied—'Cordwainer Smith' was a political scientist and military adviser, Harry Harrison a gunnery-instructor sergeant turned commercial artist, Hilbert Schenck a professor of engineering, while 'Raccoona Sheldon' worked for the Pentagon. Skilled and able as they were, few would have had very much of a literary education. By contrast science fiction, from 1910, was also a fertile field for the professional writer who compensated for a quarter-cent-a-word pay-scale by amazing feats of productivity, like Edgar Rice Burroughs with his scores of 'Tarzan', 'Pellucidar', and 'John Carter' novels, or Will F. Jenkins (better known in science fiction as 'Murray Leinster'), who is estimated to have written and sold more than fifteen hundred stories in his fifty-year career. None of the latter group is represented in this anthology, because (questions of literary quality apart) a quarter-cent a word seems to have acted as a profound discouragement against the idea of a *short* story: the six-part serial or the 25,000-word novelette were the preferred modes of Burroughs and his successors. Just the same, the influence of the penny-a-liners was strong on the amateurs. The idea of the technically crafted short story, the story to match Conrad or Joyce, Stevenson or Hardy, was absent even as a goal for decades of development.

The contrast can be seen in this collection, for instance, by comparing Kipling's careful and assured handling of multiple voices in his 1912 story with the three that follow it, by Williamson, Weinbaum, and Campbell, all three setting up a kind of frame and then retiring thankfully into the haven of the first-person narration: a technique which takes the short story back almost to its ancestor, the oral anecdote. A further contrast could be made between these three stories and the immensely more sophisticated 'I'-narration of Gibson's 'Burning Chrome' fifty years later, where the first person is no longer an easy refuge but a major feature of the 'cyberpunk' effect. Nevertheless, one could honestly concede that the science fiction short story has been for all practical purposes unaffected by the techniques of 'modernism' ever since it left its long gestation as 'scientific romance' (largely in Britain), crossed the Atlantic, and entered the domain of 'the pulps'. To that extent the criticisms of Kurt Vonnegut, or of the writers associated with the 'New Wave' of the 1960s and 1970s, have some truth.[8]

Yet they ignore, and literary criticism has for the most part done the same, science fiction's corresponding self-taught strengths, especially in the field of the short story. All authors in the genre realize that science fiction has one particular, unshared problem: the need to set out the 'rules of the game', the precise and novel nature of each story's individual universe before or as well as getting on with telling the story itself. If a science fiction story did not have something strange and unknown about it, it would not be science fiction;[9] but it is impossible to expect any reader to know in advance what this unknown element is. The reader has to be given some clues (often considerable clues) about how to decode the story, and this takes finite time and space that may all too easily detract from or slow up the narration. With science fiction there is always a problem of information, and there are more and less sophisticated ways of solving it. A common but relatively unsophisticated one is shown by 'Lewis Padgett', noted even by other science fiction authors[10] for his proneness to getting a story going, introducing some element of doubt or paradox, and then halting the action in order to deliver the 'lecture' that is a major part of his story's point. Harrison's 'A Criminal Act' follows a similar trajectory (though there the 'lecture' is a debate); Niven's 'Cloak of Anarchy' baits its hook with a colourful, unexpected image before breaking off to give a brief history of transportation that sets the scene for the central fable of technology, civilization, and the flawed insights of Ron Cole, the fabril anti-hero; even in 1990 David Brin continues the time-honoured science-fiction device of excerpts from future

[8] Vonnegut has created an affectionate parody of the professional science fiction writer, 'Kilgore Trout', in several novels, including *God Bless You, Mr. Rosewater* (New York, 1965), and *Slaughterhouse-Five* (New York, 1969). Trout's technical writing skill is rated especially low. For 'New Wave' criticisms, see several of the author's linking commentaries in *The Best Science Fiction of J. G. Ballard* (London, 1977).

[9] The 'something strange and unknown' is the *novum*, a term used and defined by Darko Suvin in *Metamorphoses of Science Fiction: On the Poetics and History of a Literary Genre* (New Haven, Conn., 1979). See further my 'Preface: Learning to Read Science Fiction' in Tom Shippey (ed.), *Fictional Space: Essays on Contemporary Science Fiction* (Oxford, 1991).

[10] His technique was commented on by Blish, see 'Atheling', *Issue at Hand*, 90 and more supportively in Aldiss, *Trillion Year Spree*, 225–6.

publications, just to transmit economically the 'rules' of his particular game. Techniques like these, simple or complex, are essential for science fiction, especially short science fiction. If they appear inartistic according to 'modernist' principles of indirectness, then that is part of the nature of the genre.

The genre has, however, learned, and learned intelligently, how to turn potential weakness into strength. Science fiction often excels at the 'open' ending and the story poised forever between alternative explanations, both a product of the necessity of shifting from foreground to background, from story-line to required interpretive information. 'Raccoona Sheldon's' 'The Screwfly Solution' is a powerful case in point. If examined closely it consists of almost twenty different interlocking sections in under nine thousand words—carefully distinguished typographically in the original magazine publication, and again here. Rather more than half of these are part of the story's 'foreground' (at least seven of them form the main story-line centred on Alan, four of them are excerpts from letters by Ann, one is an excerpt from a diary by Amy, and a final one consists of an unexpected shift to first-person narration by Ann alone). But there are six more sections—seven if one counts the quotation from Schönweiser—that are traditional science fiction 'background': announcements in a newspaper, interviews, reports or clippings from *Nature*, with one of the reports further subdivided into a majority and a minority version. What is the purpose of this extreme, but still genre-traditional, multiplicity of viewpoints? Clearly, it is to offer multiple alternative explanations for the plague of 'femicide' that is the story: a religious conviction, an airborne plague, an exaggeration of something genuinely present in masculine sexual response, a functional pathology, an alien pheromone trap. The story gains its power from being at once a feminist nightmare and an account of an experiment, from saying simultaneously that the impulse to murder women is internal/real and external/science fictional. But though 'The Screwfly Solution' is an extreme case of skill and sophistication, it is an extreme case of a tendency towards multiple viewpoint very widely present (cf. Kipling, Miller, Le Guin, Harrison, and Schenck, in the last of which typography is again used here to mark off sections).

Further results of the peculiar science fictional problem of foreground and background, story-line and information, include the powerful development of ironic endings, and the ability to tell what one might call a 'non-story', a story of frustration, a story where, in a sense, nothing happens. Ironic endings are a product of the frequent gap between an ignorant, time-bound character and an omniscient, trend-indicating narrator. Spinrad's Mr Harris does not understand the final gesture of the Japanese Mr Ito in sending him a *fake* fake gold brick (i.e. a real one). That is because he, Harris, is trapped in a viewpoint which accepts American decline and cannot perceive the value of American ideals, or American artefacts; to the American reader of 1973 (and still of the 1990s), it is Harris's viewpoint that is alien and the disaster of his incomprehension perfectly clear (perhaps still becoming clearer). In the same way Pohl's Mr Burckhardt finds out, but forgets, that he is merely a creature to be played on by media professionals; no reader in a consumer society can avoid the thought that we are all in some way Burckhardts. Elsewhere, with Niven or Martin or Kipling, it is the characters who 'come upon a knowing' at the end of the story that the reader may, or may not, be prepared to accept. Or the story may close with a moment of silent horror or incomprehension as an argument is thrown into violent reverse, as in Harrison or Aldiss. But all these endings are ironic, and all are to one degree or another 'open': the reader has to take them away and think about them, part of the 'fix' that science fiction delivers.

The same foreground/background gap allows development of the 'non-story' or 'anti-story', the science fiction equivalent of the modernist, Joycean, non-narrative 'prose fiction'. Is the ending of Disch's 'Problems of Creativeness' an 'epiphany', as Joyce would have put it? It is certainly not a conventional ending to a conventional love-story, though there is a love-affair between Birdie and Milly lurking inside the story as memory and as potential. But the potential is aborted, or contraceived, just like the baby the Revised Genetic Testing Act will not allow the lovers to have. Disch's fiction shows how a story can fail to take place, as social requirements overpower individual passion, as background information ironizes the ignorant central character. In Ballard's 'Billennium', too, a breakout is frustrated; what the characters cannot see is that their tiny failure is their world's gigantic intellectual error in miniature. One might say something similar of a second 'failed romance' (this time interlaced with a successful inhumanity) in Gibson's multiple-flashback 'I'-narration 'Burning Chrome'.

It is not difficult, from the stories in this anthology, to argue strongly for the science fiction short story as a highly progressive mode whose authors have reached levels of technical ability in handling information well above those of writers in conventional genres. Yet it could also be argued (from what has been said just above) that, technical ability or no, and regardless of the interest of its concepts, science fiction remains at bottom a depressingly entropic mode. From its beginnings to now (see Pollack or McAuley) its practitioners are ready to imagine apocalypse and the total extinction of humanity; when they do include scenes of beauty, or indulge in pastoral (see Simak, Schmitz, or McAuley again), it is always with some ruinous qualification, like the eight warships poised to obliterate Noorhut—Grimp, lorel, werrets, and all—in Schmitz, or the fat moths pushing out of the butterfly girl's mouth in McAuley. In his study of romance Northrop Frye identified 'themes of descent' in which 'charms and spells hold one motionless; human beings are turned into subhuman creatures, and made more mechanical in behaviour; hero or heroine are trapped in labyrinths or prisons':[11] to which one could say, yes, see specifically Le Guin (the suspended animation relativity-trap journey), Disch (man turned masked guerilla), Miller (Manue trapped in breathlessness on Mars). Behind many stories one may see the entropic vision of Lukyan the Liar in Martin's 'The Way of Cross and Dragon', a vision that convinces Father Damien the Knight Inquisitor even in his victory. Does science fiction tend inevitably towards the ironic mode, a mode in which (in Frye's terms) 'we have the sense of looking down on a scene of bondage, frustration or absurdity'?[12]

If such a charge were to stick, it would at least make a change from the accusations once levelled at science fiction of being 'mere escapism', a literature of wish-fulfilment alone. Actually, science fiction contains stories of every shade from the naïvest optimism (none included here, but see van Vogt for an approach to it) to the most luxurious gloom (again, none included here, but see Sterling or Pollack for an approach to it). The common factor across the entire range of attitudes, from optimism to pessimism, from wish-fulfilment to deepest irony, is perhaps this. Whatever one's theories

[11] Northrop Frye, *The Secular Scripture: A Study of the Structure of Romance* (Cambridge, Mass. and London, 1976), 129.

[12] Northrop Frye, *Anatomy of Criticism: Four essays* (Princeton, NJ, 1957), 34.

about the genre, the very existence of science fiction is intimately connected with a growing popular awareness not only of scientific data (note the fascination with radium in Williamson, 1928), not only of scientific theories (note Le Guin not needing to explain the relativity-trap in 1964), but of the mingled power and weakness of scientific method itself. Recent history has convinced almost all science fiction's readers that modern knowledge of the universe is much more powerful than ancient; but, by the same token, it will be much less powerful than some future, alien, or potential state. This has given the field its mingled pride and humility—humility in the scenes of 'bondage, frustration, or absurdity' that inevitably involve its readers, pride in the awareness that even if one cannot avoid them, one can understand them.

Nor has this mixture of hope and frustration been, for many authors and many readers, a matter of intellectual persuasion or literary artifice alone. It has, instead, often reached the level of belief, one might even say of faith. At the end of Stanley Weinbaum's 'A Martian Odyssey', the hero is asked about the mysterious Martian crystal with the power of destroying diseased tissue and leaving healthy tissue unharmed: '"it might be the cancer cure they've been hunting for a century and a half." "Oh that!" muttered Jarvis gloomily . . . "Here it is."' Weinbaum was dying of cancer when he wrote those words, and probably knew it.[13] He saw his salvation in science fiction, even if he also knew he would not live to see it.

III

One final claim that may be made for science fiction is that it has been, if not the most inclusive, then the most characteristic literary genre of the twentieth century. Did science fiction exist at all before the last hundred years? Nearly all commentators have argued that it did, pointing back to ancestors as various as *Gulliver's Travels* and the floating island, or the voyage to the Moon described by Lucian in the second century AD. In this there is a strong element of a quest for respectable ancestry, generated precisely by uneasy awareness

[13] See Sam Moskowitz (ed.), *A Martian Odyssey and other classics of science fiction by Stanley G. Weinbaum* (New York, 1962), 10.

of novelty. But one may concede that there has no doubt always been in the human race an impulse towards speculation about the unknown, and also, less recognized, an impulse towards glorification of the 'faber', the maker. Both these impulses have at different times been strongly reinforced by new awareness of the conquest of the unknown by technology, whether geographical (as with More's *Utopia* of 1516) or astronomical (as with Kepler's Moon-vision of 1634), or, indeed, more broadly scientific, as with Mary Shelley's *Frankenstein* of 1818, for which Brian Aldiss has made a powerful case (see note 5 above) as being the great originator of modern science fiction. Yet there are two tests one may apply which point to a later date, in fact to the last decade of the nineteenth century, as a critical turning-point. One is public acceptance and the creation of a market. The other is continuing non-historical interest among modern readers. Both tests look to reception rather than to production as delimiters of science fiction.

To take the second one first, it can be said that only H. G. Wells (not Mary Shelley, certainly not George Griffith, not even Jules Verne) is still widely read by science fiction fans for their own amusement only and is still a strongly perceptible influence on modern authors. Wells's clutch of stories from the 1890s—*The Time Machine, The Island of Dr Moreau, The Invisible Man, The War of the Worlds*—all generated whole and continuing sub-genres of imitators, their influence still evident in this collection from Campbell to Le Guin and beyond. Wells, naturally, did not invent his works out of nothing. There was a history behind him of recent, intense speculation about technology and war—for which see note 2 above—and an ancestor-genre of 'scientific romance', especially well-developed in Britain.[14] Nevertheless, Wells changed the field, and the market. It is interesting that there already was a market for the fantastic short story, and for serial fiction, in the new magazines of Britain and America, led by the *Strand* (founded in 1891) and followed by such imitators as *Pearson's*, which serialized *The War of the Worlds* in 1897, or the *Pall Mall*, which serialized *The War in the Air* eleven years later. These magazines, and many others, both satisfied and stimulated an appetite for fantastic fiction, and for science fiction.

Despite this popularizing role, most of what they printed in this

[14] See Brian Stableford, *Scientific Romance in England, 1890–1950* (London, 1985).

genre is unsatisfactory for the modern reader. One can only say that nineteenth-century readers were too easy to shock. London could be destroyed by a volcano! The seat of government might have to move to Manchester! Perhaps electricity won't work one day! Refrigerators could destroy the ice-storage industry! All these plots, and others of the same kind, are to be found in Sam Moskowitz's excellent and well-titled collection *Science Fiction by Gaslight.*[15] None seems to have much potential for development in modern terms, but works of that nature did create an attitude. They made people think about change. And as the pace of change accelerated *in individual lives* all through the later nineteenth and twentieth centuries—steamships, trains, the electric telegraph, 'wireless', the cinema, germ-theory and the microscope (the last three all translated into short stories by Kipling)—so a market, if still a restricted one, was created for fiction that predicted, mediated, and revelled in change.

Major reinforcement was given to this in the USA especially by, successively, the Edisonian string of inventions, the aeroplane, the idea of space travel, and first the idea and then the fact of nuclear power. *The War of the Worlds* created one immediate and indignant riposte in *Edison's Conquest of Mars* by Garrett P. Serviss, serialized in twenty-six instalments in the *New York Journal* in 1898. From 1912 onwards a string of magazines published by Frank A. Munsey, and including *Argosy* and *All-Story Weekly*, launched authors like Edgar Rice Burroughs on an eager readership.[16] There is no doubt that what they produced is science fiction (still read, still imitated or re-created), though as pointed out above it was rarely short, the natural mode of the penny-a-liner being not surprisingly the 25,000 word novelette or better still the eight-part serial. Yet this era laid the foundations, and created the literary conventions, for the modern age of science fiction, which was inaugurated in April 1926 by the first issue of *Amazing Stories*, edited by Hugo Gernsback, and swept on first by the appearance of the rival magazine *Astounding Stories* in January 1930, and then by the appointment of John W. Campbell to the editorship of *Astounding* in September 1937.

From then on it is easy to follow the development of science

[15] Sam Moskowitz (ed.), *Science Fiction by Gaslight: A History and Anthology of Science Fiction in the Popular Magazines, 1891–1911* (Cleveland, Ohio, 1968).

[16] See Sam Moskowitz (ed.), *Under the Moons of Mars: A History and Anthology of 'The Scientific Romance' in the Munsey Magazines, 1912–1920* (New York, 1970).

fiction from this anthology, with its stories by Williamson (from *Amazing* 1928), by Campbell (from before his editorial period), and by several of the authors whom Campbell developed—a group that included Isaac Asimov, Robert Heinlein, and Theodore Sturgeon, besides those represented here. Even authors who were not published by Campbell and who wrote for his later competitor magazines (such as *Galaxy* or *Fantasy and Science Fiction*) would acknowledge his influence, for good or ill.

Quite what this influence was is now hard to say, though Campbell's 'participatory' relationship with his authors was famous: it extended to giving them plots, themes, and scenarios, as well as refusing to print what they wrote until it fitted his direction.[17] Few would deny, though, that a major influence was Campbell's unflagging belief that science fiction *was going to happen,* and that the process could be hastened by writers (and editors). Sometimes his belief led him to disaster: Campbell was responsible, among much else, for the launch of Scientology on the world as L. Ron Hubbard moved from being a run-of-the-mill *Astounding* author of the 1940s to becoming a guru-figure who insisted his science fictional notions were true. At other times Campbell and his authors showed a Wellsian prescience. It has already been remarked that 'atomic bombs' were a recognized concept in science fiction from the 1930s (indeed, from well before). Famously, in an *Astounding* story of March 1944 Cleve Cartmill described an atomic bomb and mentioned the critical mass of uranium-235: the editorial offices were visited by military intelligence, convinced some breach of security must have taken place. But rather more significantly, Robert Heinlein had, in a long story in the same magazine three years before (May 1941), got the mechanics of nuclear weapons completely wrong but predicted with some accuracy the political dilemma such weapons would cause, as well as the seeming inevitability of a future Cold War.[18] On the whole, the Cartmill–Heinlein opposition gives a good image of science fiction's relationship with future reality and its potential as a predictor. Predictively speaking, if you publish thousands of stories about the future, one or two

[17] Campbell printed a famous and much-anthologized story by Tom Godwin, 'The Cold Equations', in *Astounding* (Aug., 1954). It is said that Campbell made Godwin write the story seven times, until he produced an ending *in which the heroine died.*

[18] See further my article 'The Cold War in Science Fiction, 1940–1960', in Patrick Parrinder (ed.), *Science Fiction: A Critical Guide* (London and New York, 1979), 90–109.

will later approximate to reality (when everyone will forget the thousands of misses). But what is much more significant than the occasional coincidental flash is the steady, cumulative creation of a mindset, and a readership, that is accustomed to change and ready to accept that technological change will inevitably bring social and political change as well.

The overall effect of that attitude spreading in society is impossible to quantify. Did science fiction put men on the Moon? Certainly a high proportion of NASA scientists, technicians, and administrators were long-term readers of science fiction: they knew space travel was possible when the general public and its elected representatives did not. Arthur Clarke's career is neatly paradigmatic. He began as a radar instructor with the RAF during the Second World War; foresaw global TV, satellite transmission, and the geosynchronous orbit as early as 1945; and in the middle of his immensely successful career in science fiction (in 1967) wrote a moving story of a non-believing politician converted to space research too late.[19] One can only repeat that part of the fabril mentality is to believe that physical problems have physical solutions, and that these *could* be found even if they have not been. If they had been, of course, we would once more be outside the field of science fiction.

Science fiction, one may conclude, is not an accurate predictor in detail, nor does it have a privileged relationship with reality. On the other hand, it is peopled with acute observers who take a long view. In this anthology one can see the impact of nuclear power, very early, in 'Padgett' and van Vogt. Space travel is a major prop, if not a major theme, in perhaps one story in three. Alien life is accepted unquestioningly in about the same proportion. Other major themes include artificial intelligence, in half-a-dozen stories from Campbell on, with Gibson pre-dating 'virtual reality' by some years; genetic engineering in several stories from 'Cordwainer Smith' on; and world overpopulation in the three stories by Ballard, Harrison, and Disch, seen in each case, fabril-style, as a physical or social problem in which moralizing is irrelevant. Yet this brief rundown of themes totally misses, for instance, Wolfe, Niven, and

[19] The story is 'Death and the Senator', first printed in *Analog* (May, 1961) and reprinted in Clarke's *Tales of Ten Worlds* (New York, 1962). Clarke's autobiographical account of his career in radar is *Glide Path* (New York, 1963).

Spinrad, and has little to do with the central points of a dozen other stories. Science fiction is inherently unpredictable. Its authors are committed (with exceptions)[20] to the belief that unpredictability is as true of the future as it has been of the recent past.

IV

The remarks above make it easier to declare the aims and limits of this anthology. It follows the model set up by other Oxford collections of genre fiction such as *The Oxford Book of English Ghost Stories* (1986) or *The Oxford Book of English Detective Stories* (1990). That is to say, it is chronologically presented; no author provides more than one story; and the overriding aim is to give an impression of the range, vitality, and literally quality of a genre. In one way this volume faces an even greater challenge than its predecessors, one of scale. It includes stories from a dozen magazines, and there have been of course literally scores of others.[21] Many of these were ephemeral, but one at least, *Astounding* (retitled *Analog* in 1960), has carried on printing its four or five stories an issue, fifty stories a year, from 1930 to the present. The number of science fiction stories published in English this century will probably not rise to a hundred thousand, but is certainly deep into the tens of thousands. Calculation will show that the chance of any two people 'perming' the same thirty stories from, say, thirty thousand, makes astronomical numbers look small. No selection, then, can be perfect. Furthermore, many major authors and influential concepts have had to be left out simply because they do not figure in the field of the short story—the premier field for science fiction, but with strong competition, especially in some periods, from both the full novel and the novella or novelette. This selection confines itself also to stories written in English, not in ignorance of the fact that there are worlds elsewhere,[22] but in the conviction that Anglo-American

[20] The urge to make history into a hard science governed by mathematics is strong. See my entry on 'History in SF', in Peter Nicholls (ed.), *The Encyclopaedia of Science Fiction* (London, 1979), 283–4.

[21] Peter Nicholls's *Encyclopaedia* lists 167 English language science fiction magazines on p. 258.

[22] For which see Neil Barron (ed.), *Anatomy of Wonder: A Critical Guide to Science Fiction* (2nd edn., New York and London, 1981).

science fiction has been by far the most powerful branch of the genre, and quite enough for any one selection to cope with.

What this selection can claim is that it provides a fair sample of the best the field can offer. It is possible to follow the development of the genre (subject to the qualification over length above) from these pages alone. Yet no story has been chosen to fill a gap or provide a specimen. Most important, perhaps, is a kind of serendipity inherent in selection from such a rich field. Many comparisons of theme and substance, of subgenre and technique, have been made fleetingly in the preceding pages. Far more arise out of combinations or juxtapositions not made or not seen. I would be pleased if this anthology were to 'convert' previous non-readers of science fiction into exploring the field more widely. But even enthusiasts who have read and collected steadily will find some stories they have missed and, by seeing familiar items unfamiliarly juxtaposed, may discover new insights about science fiction as a whole. Science fiction is an underrated genre, its drives and impulses often unrecognized. Over the years, and entirely by their own efforts, its authors have created the devoted and participatory readership which, collectively, they deserve. I hope this anthology may help to make that achievement more widely recognized and, in institutions of literary education, more sympathetically, but more analytically, understood.

THE LAND IRONCLADS

H. G. WELLS

1

The young lieutenant lay beside the war correspondent and admired the idyllic calm of the enemy's lines through his field-glass.

'So far as I can see,' he said at last, 'one man.'

'What's he doing?' asked the war correspondent.

'Field-glass at us,' said the young lieutenant.

'And this is war!'

'No,' said the young lieutenant; 'it's Bloch.'

'The game's a draw.'

'No! They've got to win or else they lose. A draw's a win for our side.'

They had discussed the political situation fifty times or so, and the war correspondent was weary of it. He stretched out his limbs. 'Aaai s'pose it *is*!' he yawned.

Flut!

'What was that?'

'Shot at us.'

The war correspondent shifted to a slightly lower position. 'No one shot at him,' he complained.

'I wonder if they think we shall get so bored we shall go home?'

The war correspondent made no reply.

'There's the harvest, of course. . . .'

They had been there a month. Since the first brisk movements after the declaration of war things had gone slower and slower, until it seemed as though the whole machine of events must have run down. To begin with, they had had almost a scampering time; the invader had come across the frontier on the very dawn of the war in half-a-dozen parallel columns behind a cloud of cyclists and cavalry, with a general air of coming straight on the capital, and the defender horsemen had held him up, and peppered him and forced him to open out to outflank, and had then bolted to the next position in the most approved style, for a couple of days, until in the afternoon, bump! they had the invader against their prepared lines of defence. He did not suffer so much as had been hoped and expected: he was coming on, it seemed, with his eyes open, his scouts winded the guns, and down he sat at once without the shadow of an attack and began grubbing trenches for himself, as though he meant to sit down there to the very end of time. He was slow, but much more wary than the world had been led to expect, and he kept convoys tucked in and shielded his slow-marching infantry sufficiently well to prevent any heavy adverse scoring.

'But he ought to attack,' the young lieutenant had insisted.

'He'll attack us at dawn, somewhere along the lines. You'll get the bayonets coming into the trenches just about when you can see,' the war correspondent had held until a week ago.

The young lieutenant winked when he said that.

When one early morning the men the defenders sent to lie out five hundred yards before the trenches, with a view to the unexpected emptying of magazines into any night attack, gave way to causeless panic and blazed away at nothing for ten minutes, the war correspondent understood the meaning of that wink.

'What would you do if you were the enemy?' said the war correspondent, suddenly.

'If I had men like I've got now?'

'Yes.'

'Take those trenches.'

'How?'

'Oh—dodges! Crawl out half-way at night before moonrise and get into touch with the chaps we send out. Blaze at 'em if they tried to shift, and so bag some of 'em in the daylight. Learn that patch of ground by heart, lie all day in squatty holes, and come on nearer next night. There's a bit over there, lumpy ground, where they could get across to rushing distance—easy. In a night or so. It would be a mere game for our fellows; it's what they're made for. . . . Guns? Shrapnel and stuff wouldn't stop good men who meant business.'

'Why don't *they* do that?'

'Their men aren't brutes enough; that's the trouble. They're a crowd of devitalized townsmen, and that's the truth of the matter. They're clerks, they're factory hands, they're students, they're civilized men. They can write, they can talk, they can make and do all sorts of things, but they're poor amateurs at war. They've got no physical staying power, and that's the whole thing. They've never slept in the open one night in their lives; they've never drunk anything but the purest water-company water; they've never gone short of three meals a day since they left their feeding-bottles. Half their cavalry never cocked leg over horse till it enlisted six months ago. They ride their horses as though they were bicycles—you watch 'em! They're fools at the game, and they know it. Our boys of fourteen can give their grown men points. . . . Very well——'

The war correspondent mused on his face with his nose between his knuckles.

'If a decent civilization,' he said, 'cannot produce better men for war than——'

He stopped with belated politeness. 'I mean——'

'Than our open-air life,' said the young lieutenant.

'Exactly,' said the war correspondent. 'Then civilization has to stop.'

'It looks like it,' the young lieutenant admitted.

'Civilization has science, you know,' said the war correspondent. 'It invented and it makes the rifles and guns and things you use.'

'Which our nice healthy hunters and stockmen and so on, rowdy-dowdy cowpunchers and negro-whackers, can use ten times better than——*What's that?*'

'What?' said the war correspondent, and then seeing his companion busy with his field-glass he produced his own: 'Where?' said the war correspondent, sweeping the enemy's lines.

'It's nothing,' said the young lieutenant, still looking.

'What's nothing?'

The young lieutenant put down his glass and pointed. 'I thought I saw something there, behind the stems of those trees. Something black. What it was I don't know.'

The war correspondent tried to get even by intense scrutiny.

'It wasn't anything,' said the young lieutenant, rolling over to regard the darkling evening sky, and generalized: 'There never will be anything any more for ever. Unless——'

The war correspondent looked inquiry.

'They may get their stomachs wrong, or something—living without proper drains.'

A sound of bugles came from the tents behind. The war correspondent slid backward down the sand and stood up. 'Boom!'

came from somewhere far away to the left. 'Halloa!' he said, hesitated, and crawled back to peer again. 'Firing at this time is jolly bad manners.'

The young lieutenant was uncommunicative for a space.

Then he pointed to the distant clump of trees again. 'One of our big guns. They were firing at that,' he said.

'The thing that wasn't anything?'

'Something over there, anyhow.'

Both men were silent, peering through their glasses for a space. 'Just when it's twilight,' the lieutenant complained. He stood up.

'I might stay here a bit,' said the war correspondent.

The lieutenant shook his head. 'There's nothing to see,' he apologized, and then went down to where his little squad of sun-brown, loose-limbed men had been yarning in the trench. The war correspondent stood up also, glanced for a moment at the business-like bustle below him, gave perhaps twenty seconds to those enigmatical trees again, then turned his face toward the camp.

He found himself wondering whether his editor would consider the story of how somebody thought he saw something black behind a clump of trees, and how a gun was fired at this illusion by somebody else, too trivial for public consumption.

'It's the only gleam of a shadow of interest,' said the war correspondent, 'for ten whole days.'

'No,' he said presently; 'I'll write that other article, "Is War Played Out?"'

He surveryed the darkling lines in perspective, the tangle of trenches one behind another, one commanding another, which the defender had made ready. The shadows and mists swallowed up their receding contours, and here and there a lantern gleamed, and here and there knots of men were busy about small fires.

'No troops on earth could do it,' he said. . . .

He was depressed. He believed that there were other things in life better worth having than proficiency in war; he believed that in the heart of civilization, for all its stresses, its crushing concentrations of forces, its injustice and suffering, there lay something that might be the hope of the world; and the idea that any people by living in the open air, hunting perpetually, losing touch with books and art and all the things that intensify life, might hope to resist and break that great development to the end of time, jarred on his civilized soul.

Apt to his thought came a file of the defender soldiers and passed him in the gleam of a swinging lamp that marked the way.

He glanced at their red-lit faces, and one shone out for a moment, a common type of face in the defender's ranks: ill-shaped nose, sensuous lips, bright clear eyes full of alert cunning, slouch hat cocked on one side and adorned with the peacock's plume of the rustic Don Juan turned soldier, a hard brown skin, a sinewy frame, an open, tireless stride, and a master's grip on the rifle.

The war correspondent returned their salutations and went on his way.

'Louts,' he whispered. 'Cunning, elementary louts. And they are going to beat the townsmen at the game of war!'

From the red glow among the nearer tents came first one and then half-a-dozen hearty voices, bawling in a drawling unison the words of a particularly slab and sentimental patriotic song.

'Oh, *go* it!' muttered the war correspondent, bitterly.

2

It was opposite the trenches called after Hackbone's Hut that the battle began. There the ground stretched broad and level between the lines, with scarcely shelter for a lizard, and it seemed to the startled, just-awakened men who came crowding into the trenches that this was one more proof of that inexperience of the enemy of which they had heard so much. The war correspondent would not believe his ears at first, and swore that he and the war artist, who, still imperfectly roused, was trying to put on his boots by the light of a match held in his hand, were the victims of a common illusion. Then, after putting his head in a bucket of cold water, his intelligence came back as he towelled. He listened. 'Gollys!' he said; 'that's something more than scare firing this time. It's like ten thousand carts on a bridge of tin.'

There came a sort of enrichment to that steady uproar. 'Machine-guns!'

Then, 'Guns!'

The artist, with one boot on, thought to look at his watch, and went to it hopping.

'Half an hour from dawn,' he said. 'You were right about their attacking, after all. . . .'

The war correspondent came out of the tent, verifying the presence of chocolate in his pocket as he did so. He had to halt for a moment or so until his eyes were toned down to the night a little. 'Pitch!' he said. He stood for a space to season his eyes before he felt justified in striking out for a black gap among the adjacent tents. The artist coming out behind him fell over a tent-rope. It was half-past two o'clock in the morning of the darkest night in time, and against a sky of dull black silk the enemy was talking searchlights, a wild jabber of searchlights. 'He's trying to blind our riflemen,' said the war correspondent with a flash, and waited for the artist and then set off with a sort of discreet haste again. 'Whoa!' he said, presently, 'Ditches!'

They stopped.

'It's the confounded searchlights,' said the war correspondent.

They saw lanterns going to and fro, near by, and men falling in to march down to the trenches. They were for following them, and then the artist began to get his night eyes. 'If we scramble this,' he said, 'and it's only a drain, there's a clear run up to the ridge.' And that way they took. Lights came and went in the tents behind, as the men turned out, and ever and again they came to broken ground and staggered and stumbled. But in a little while they drew near the crest. Something that sounded like the impact of a tremendous railway accident happened in the air above them, and the shrapnel bullets seethed about them like a sudden handful of hail. 'Right-ho!' said the war correspondent, and soon they judged they had come to the crest and stood in the midst of a world of great darkness and frantic glares, whose principal fact was sound.

Right and left of them and all about them was the uproar, an army-full of magazine fire, at first chaotic and monstrous, and then, eked out by little flashes and gleams and suggestions, taking the beginnings of a shape. It looked to the war correspondent as though the enemy must have attacked in line and with his whole force—in which case he was either being or was already annihilated.

'Dawn and the dead,' he said, with his instinct for headlines. He said this to himself, but afterwards by means of shouting he conveyed an idea to the artist.

'They must have meant it for a surprise,' he said.

It was remarkable how the firing kept on. After a time he began to perceive a sort of rhythm in this inferno of noise. It would decline—decline perceptibly, droop towards something that was comparatively a pause—a pause of enquiry. 'Aren't you all dead yet?' this pause seemed to say. The flickering fringe of rifle-flashes would become attenuated and broken, and the whack-bang of the enemy's big guns two miles away there would come up out of the deeps. Then suddenly, east or west of them, something would startle the rifles to a frantic outbreak again.

The war correspondent taxed his brain for some theory of conflict that would account for this, and was suddenly aware that the artist and he were vividly illuminated. He could see the ridge on which they stood, and before them in black outline a file of riflemen hurrying down towards the nearer trenches. It became visible that a light rain was falling, and further away towards the enemy was a clear space with men—'our men?'—running across it in disorder. He saw one of those men throw up his hands and drop. And something else black and shining loomed up on the edge of the beam-coruscating flashes; and behind it and far away a calm, white eye regarded the world. 'Whit, whit, whit,' sang something in the air, and then the artist was running for cover, with the war correspondent behind him. Bang came shrapnel, bursting close at hand as it seemed, and our two men were lying flat in a dip in the ground, and the light and everything had gone again, leaving a vast note of interrogation upon the night.

The war correspondent came within bawling range. 'What the deuce was it? Shooting our men down!'

'Black,' said the artist, 'and like a fort. Not two hundred yards from the first trench.'

He sought for comparisons in his mind. 'Something between a big blockhouse and a giant's dishcover,' he said.

'And they were running!' said the war correspondent.

'*You'd* run if a thing like that, with a searchlight to help it, turned up, like a prowling nightmare in the middle of the night.'

They crawled to what they judged the edge of the dip and lay regarding the unfathomable dark. For a space they could distinguish nothing, and then a sudden convergence of the searchlights of both sides brought the strange thing out again.

In that flickering pallor it had the effect of a large and clumsy black insect, an insect the size of an ironclad cruiser, crawling obliquely to the first line of trenches and firing shots out of port-holes in its side. And on its carcass the bullets must have been battering with more than the passionate violence of hail on a roof of tin.

Then in the twinkling of an eye the curtain of the dark had fallen again and the monster had vanished, but the crescendo of musketry marked its approach to the trenches.

They were beginning to talk about the thing to each other, when a flying bullet kicked dirt into the artist's face, and they decided abruptly to crawl down into the cover of the trenches. They had got down with an unobtrusive persistence into the second line, before the dawn had grown clear enough for anything to be seen. They found themselves in a crowd of expectant riflemen, all noisily arguing about what would happen next. The enemy's contrivance had done execution upon the outlying men, it seemed, but they did not believe it would do any more. 'Come the day and we'll capture the lot of them,' said a burly soldier.

'Them?' said the war correspondent.

'They say there's a regular string of 'em, crawling along the front of our lines.... Who cares?'

The darkness filtered away so imperceptibly that at no moment could one declare decisively that one could see. The searchlights ceased to sweep hither and thither. The enemy's monsters were dubious patches of darkness upon the dark, and then no longer dubious, and so they crept out into distinctness. The war correspondent, munching chocolate absent-mindedly, beheld at last a spacious picture of battle under the cheerless sky, whose central focus was an array of fourteen or fifteen huge clumsy shapes lying in perspective on the very edge of the first line of trenches, at intervals of perhaps three hundred yards, and evidently firing down upon the crowded riflemen. They were so close in that the defender's guns had ceased, and only the first line of trenches was in action.

The second line commanded the first, and as the light grew, the war correspondent could make out the riflemen who were fighting these monsters, crouched in knots and crowds behind the transverse banks that crossed the trenches against the eventuality of an enfilade. The trenches close to the big machines were empty save for the crumpled suggestions of dead and wounded men; the defenders had been driven right and left as soon as the prow of a land ironclad had loomed up over the front of the trench. The war correspondent produced his field-glass, and was immediately a centre of enquiry from the soldiers about him.

They wanted to look, they asked questions, and after he had announced that the men across the traverses seemed unable to advance or retreat, and were crouching under cover rather than fighting, he found it advisable to loan his glasses to a burly and incredulous corporal. He heard a strident voice, and found a lean and sallow soldier at his back talking to the artist.

'There's chaps down there caught,' the man was saying. 'If they retreat they got to expose themselves, and the fire's too straight. . . .'

'They aren't firing much, but every shot's a hit.'

'Who?'

'The chaps in that thing. The men who're coming up——'

'Coming up where?'

'We're evacuating them trenches where we can. Our chaps are coming back up the zigzags. . . . No end of 'em hit. . . . But when we get clear our turn'll come. Rather! Those things won't be able to cross a trench or get into it; and before they can get back our guns'll smash 'em up. Smash 'em right up. See?' A brightness came into his eyes. 'Then we'll have a go at the beggars inside,' he said. . . .

The war correspondent thought for a moment, trying to realize the idea. Then he set himself to recover his field-glasses from the burly corporal. . . .

The daylight was getting clearer now. The clouds were lifting, and a gleam of lemon-yellow amidst the level masses to the east portended sunrise. He looked again at the land ironclad. As he saw it in the bleak, grey dawn, lying obliquely upon the slope and on the very lip of the foremost trench, the suggestion of a stranded vessel was very strong indeed. It might have been from eighty to a hundred feet long—it was about two hundred and fifty yards away—its vertical side was ten feet high or so, smooth for that height, and then with a complex patterning under the eaves of its flattish turtle cover. This patterning was a close interlacing of portholes, rifle barrels, and telescope tubes—sham and real—indistinguishable one from the other. The thing had come into such a position as to enfilade the trench, which was empty now, so far as he could see, except for two or three crouching knots of men and the tumbled dead. Behind it, across the plain, it had scored the grass with a train of linked impressions, like the dotted tracings sea-things leave in sand. Left and right of that track dead men and wounded men were scattered—men it had picked off as they fled back from their advanced positions in the searchlight glare from the invader's lines. And now it lay with its head projecting a little over the trench it had won, as if it were a single sentient thing planning the next phase of its attack. . . .

He lowered his glasses and took a more comprehensive view of the situation. These creatures of the night had evidently won the first line of trenches and the fight had come to a pause. In the increasing light he could make out by a stray shot or a chance exposure that the defender's marksmen were lying thick in the second and third line of trenches up towards the low crest of the position, and in such of the zigzags as gave them a chance of a converging fire. The men about him were talking of guns. 'We're in the line of the big guns at the crest, but they'll soon shift one to pepper them,' the lean man said, reassuringly.

'Whup,' said the corporal.

'Bang! bang! bang! Whir-r-r-r!' it was a sort of nervous jump, and all the rifles were going off by themselves. The war correspondent found himself and the artist, two idle men crouching behind a line of preoccupied backs, of industrious men discharging magazines. The monster had moved. It continued to move regardless of the hail that splashed its skin with bright new specks of lead. It was singing a mechanical little ditty to itself, 'Tuf-tuf, tuf-tuf, tuf-tuf,' and squirting out little jets of steam behind. It had humped itself up, as a limpet does before it crawls; it had lifted its skirt and displayed along the length of it—*feet*! They were thick, stumpy feet, between knobs and buttons in shape—flat, broad things, reminding one of the feet of elephants or the legs of caterpillars; and then, as the skirt rose higher, the war correspondent, scrutinizing the thing through his glasses again, saw that these feet hung, as it were, on the rims of wheels. His thoughts whirled back to Victoria Street, Westminster, and he saw himself in the piping times of peace, seeking matter for an interview.

'Mr—Mr Diplock,' he said; 'and he called them Pedrails.... Fancy meeting them here!'

The marksman beside him raised his head and shoulders in a speculative mood to fire more certainly—it seemed so natural to assume the attention of the monster must be distracted by this trench before it—and was suddenly knocked backwards by a bullet through his neck. His feet flew up, and he vanished out of the margin of the watcher's field of vision. The war correspondent grovelled tighter, but after a glance behind him at a painful little confusion, he resumed his field-glass, for the thing was putting down its feet one after the other, and hoisting itself further and further over the trench. Only a bullet in the head could have stopped him looking just then.

The lean man with the strident voice ceased firing to turn and reiterate his point. 'They can't possibly cross,' he bawled. 'They——'

'Bang! Bang! Bang! Bang!'—drowned everything.

The lean man continued speaking for a word or so, then gave it up, shook his head to enforce the impossibility of anything crossing a trench like the one below, and resumed business once more.

And all the while that great bulk was crossing. When the war correspondent turned his glass on it again it had bridged the trench, and its queer feet were rasping away at the further bank, in the attempt to get a hold there. It got its hold. It continued to crawl until the greater bulk of it was over the trench—until it was all over. Then it paused for a moment, adjusted its skirt a little nearer the ground, gave an unnerving 'toot, toot', and came on abruptly at a pace of, perhaps, six miles an hour straight up the gentle slope towards our observer.

The war correspondent raised himself on his elbow and looked a natural enquiry at the artist.

For a moment the men about him stuck to their position and fired furiously. Then the lean man in a mood of precipitancy slid backwards, and the war correspondent said 'Come along' to the artist, and led the movement along the trench.

As they dropped down, the vision of a hillside of trench being rushed by a dozen vast cockroaches disappeared for a space, and instead was one of a narrow passage, crowded with men, for the most part receding, though one or two turned or halted. He never turned back to see the nose of the monster creep over the brow of the trench; he never even troubled to keep in touch with the artist. He heard the 'whit' of bullets about him soon enough, and saw a man before him stumble and drop, and then he was one of a furious crowd fighting to get into a transverse zigzag ditch that enabled the defenders to get under cover up and down the hill. It was like a theatre panic. He gathered from signs and fragmentary words that on ahead another of these monsters had also won to the second trench.

He lost his interest in the general course of the battle for a space altogether; he became simply a modest egotist, in a mood of hasty circumspection, seeking the furthest rear, amidst a dispersed multitude of disconcerted riflemen similarly employed. He scrambled down through trenches, he took his courage in both hands and sprinted across the open, he had moments of panic when it seemed madness not to be quadrupedal, and moments of shame when he stood up and faced about to see how the fight was going. And he was one of many thousand very similar men that morning. On the ridge he halted in a knot of scrub, and was for a few minutes almost minded to stop and see things out.

The day was now fully come. The grey sky had changed to blue, and of all the cloudy masses of the dawn there remained only a few patches of dissolving fleeciness. The world below was bright and singularly clear. The ridge was not, perhaps, more than a hundred feet or so above the general plain, but in this flat region it sufficed to give the effect of extensive view. Away on the north side of the ridge, little and far, were the camps, the ordered wagons, all the gear of a big army; with officers galloping about and men doing aimless things. Here and there men were falling in, however, and the cavalry was forming up on the plain beyond the tents. The bulk of men who had been in the trenches were still on the move to the rear, scattered like sheep without a shepherd over the further slopes. Here and there were little rallies and attempts to wait and do—something vague; but the general drift was away from any concentration. There on the southern side was the elaborate lace-work of trenches and defences, across which these iron turtles, fourteen of them spread out over a line of perhaps three miles, were now advancing as fast as a man could trot, and methodically shooting down and breaking up any persistent knots of resistance. Here and there stood little clumps of men, outflanked and unable to get away, showing the white flag, and the invader's cyclist infantry was advancing now across the open, in open order but unmolested to complete the work of the machines. Surveyed at large, the defenders already looked a beaten army. A mechanism that was effectually ironclad against bullets, that could at a pinch cross a thirty-foot trench, and that seemed able to shoot out rifle-bullets with unerring precision, was clearly an inevitable victor against anything but rivers, precipices, and guns.

He looked at his watch. 'Half-past four! Lord! What things can happen in two hours. Here's the whole blessed army being walked over, and at half-past two——

'And even now our blessed louts haven't done a thing with their guns!'

He scanned the ridge right and left of him with his glasses. He turned again to the nearest land ironclad, advancing now obliquely to him and not three hundred yards away, and then scanned the ground over which he must retreat if he was not to be captured.

'They'll do nothing,' he said, and glanced again at the enemy.

And then from far away to the left came the thud of a gun, followed very rapidly by a rolling gunfire.

He hesitated and decided to stay.

3

The defender had relied chiefly upon his rifles in the event of an assault. His guns he kept concealed at various points upon and behind the ridge ready to bring them into action against any artillery preparations for an attack on the part of his antagonist. The situation had rushed upon him with the dawn, and by the time the gunners had their guns ready for motion, the land ironclads were already in among the foremost trenches. There is a natural reluctance to fire into one's own broken men, and many of the guns, being intended simply to fight an advance of the enemy's artillery, were not in positions to hit anything in the second line of trenches. After that the advance of the land ironclads was swift. The defender-general found himself suddenly called upon to invent a new sort of warfare, in which guns were to fight alone amidst broken and retreating infantry. He had scarcely thirty minutes in which to think it out. He did not respond to the call, and what happened that morning was that the advance of the land ironclads forced the fight, and each gun and battery made what play its circumstances dictated. For the most part it was poor play.

Some of the guns got in two or three shots, some one or two, and the percentage of misses was unusually high. The howitzers, of course, did nothing. The land ironclads in each case followed much the same tactics. As soon as a gun came into play the monster turned itself almost end-on, so as to minimize the chances of a square hit, and made not for the gun, but for the nearest point on its flank from which the gunners could be shot down. Few of the hits scored were very effectual; only one of the things was disabled, and that was the one that fought the three batteries attached to the brigade on the left wing. Three that were hit when close upon the guns were clean shot through without being put out of action. Our war correspondent did not see that one momentary arrest of the tide of victory on the left; he saw only the very ineffectual fight of half-battery 96B close at hand upon his right. This he watched some time beyond the margin of safety.

Just after he heard the three batteries opening up upon his left he became aware of the thud of horses' hoofs from the sheltered side of the slope, and presently saw first one and then two other guns galloping into position along the north side of the ridge, well out of sight of the great bulk that was now creeping obliquely towards the crest and cutting up the lingering infantry beside it and below, as it came.

The half-battery swung round into line—each gun describing its curve—halted, unlimbered, and prepared for action. . . .

'Bang!'

The land ironclad had become visible over the brow of the hill, and just visible as a long black back to the gunners. It halted, as though it hesitated.

The two remaining guns fired, and then their big antagonist had swung round and was in full view, end-on, against the sky, coming at a rush.

The gunners became frantic in their haste to fire again. They were so near the war correspondent could see the expression of their excited faces through his field-glass. As he looked he saw a man drop, and realized for the first time that the ironclad was shooting.

For a moment the big black monster crawled with an accelerated pace towards the furiously active gunners. Then, as if moved by a generous impulse, it turned its full broadside to their attack, and scarcely forty yards away from them. The war correspondent turned his field-glass back to the gunners and perceived it was now shooting down the men about the guns with the most deadly rapidity.

Just for a moment it seemed splendid, and then it seemed horrible. The gunners were dropping in heaps about their guns. To lay a hand on a gun was death. 'Bang!' went the gun on the left, a hopeless miss, and that was the only second shot the half-battery fired. In another moment half-a-dozen surviving artillerymen were holding up their hands amidst a scattered muddle of dead and wounded men, and the fight was done.

The war correspondent hesitated between stopping in his scrub and waiting for an opportunity to surrender decently, or taking to an adjacent gully he had discovered. If he surrendered it was certain he would get no copy off; while, if he escaped, there were all sorts of chances. He decided to follow the gully, and take the first offer in the confusion beyond the camp of picking up a horse.

4

Subsequent authorities have found fault with the first land ironclads in many particulars, but assuredly they served their purpose on the day of their appearance. They were essentially long, narrow, and very strong steel frameworks carrying the engines, and borne upon eight pairs of big pedrail wheels, each about ten feet in diameter, each a driving wheel and set upon long axles free to swivel round a common axis. This arrangement gave them the maximum of adaptability to the contours of the ground. They crawled level along the ground with one foot high upon a hillock and another deep in a depression, and they could hold themselves erect and steady sideways upon even a steep hillside. The engineers directed the engines under the command of the captain, who had look-out points at small ports all round the upper edge of the adjustable skirt of twelve-inch iron-plating which protected the whole affair, and who could also raise or depress a conning-tower set about the portholes through the centre of the iron top cover. The riflemen each occupied a small cabin of peculiar construction, and these cabins were slung along the sides of and before and behind the great main framework, in a manner suggestive of the slinging of the seats of an Irish jaunting-car. Their rifles, however, were very different pieces of apparatus from the simple mechanisms in the hands of their adversaries.

These were in the first place automatic, ejected their cartridges and loaded again from a magazine each time they fired, until the ammunition store was at an end, and they had the most remarkable sights imaginable, sights which threw a bright little camera-obscura picture into the light-tight box in which the rifleman sat below. This camera-obscura picture was marked with two crossed lines, and whatever was covered by the intersection of these two lines, that the rifle hit. The sighting was ingeniously contrived. The rifleman stood at the table with a thing like an elaboration of a draughtsman's dividers in his hand, and he opened and closed these dividers, so that they were always at the apparent height—if it was an ordinary-sized man—of the man he wanted to kill. A little twisted strand of wire like an electric-light wire ran from this implement up to the gun, and as the dividers opened and shut the sights went up or down. Changes in the clearness of the atmosphere, due to changes of moisture, were met by an ingenious use of that meteorologically sensitive substance, catgut, and when the land ironclad moved forward the sights got a compensatory deflection in the direction of its motion. The rifleman stood up in his pitch-dark chamber and watched the little picture before him. One hand held the dividers for judging distance, and the other grasped a big knob like a door-handle. As he pushed this knob about the rifle above swung to correspond, and the picture passed to and fro like an agitated panorama. When he saw a man he wanted to shoot he brought him up to the cross-lines, and then pressed a finger upon a little push like an electric bell-push, conveniently placed in the centre of the knob. Then the man was shot. If by any chance the rifleman missed his target he moved the knob a trifle, or readjusted his dividers, pressed the push, and got him the second time.

This rifle and its sights protruded from a porthole, exactly like a great number of other portholes that ran in a triple row under the eaves of the cover of the land ironclad. Each porthole displayed a rifle and sight in dummy, so that the real ones could only be hit by a chance shot, and if one was, then the young man below said 'Pshaw!' turned on an electric light, lowered the injured instrument into his camera, replaced the injured part, or put up a new rifle if the injury was considerable.

You must conceive these cabins as hung clear above the swing of the axles, and inside the big wheels upon which the great elephant-like feet were hung, and behind these cabins along the centre of the monster ran a central gallery into which they opened, and along which worked the big compact engines. It was like a long passage into which this throbbing machinery had been packed, and the captain stood about the middle, close to the ladder that led to his conning-tower, and directed the silent, alert engineers—for the most part by signs. The throb and noise of the engines mingled with the reports of the rifles and the intermittent clangour of the bullet hail upon the armour. Ever and again he would touch the wheel that raised his conning-tower, step up his ladder until his engineers could see nothing of him above the waist, and then come down again with orders. Two small electric lights were all the illumination of this space—they were placed to make him most clearly visible to his subordinates: the air was thick with the smell of oil and petrol, and had the war correspondent been suddenly transferred from the spacious dawn outside to the bowels of this apparatus he would have thought himself fallen into another world.

The captain, of course, saw both sides of the battle. When he raised his head into his conning-tower there were the dewy sunrise, the amazed and disordered trenches, the flying and falling soldiers, the depressed-looking groups of prisoners, the beaten guns; when he bent down again to signal 'half speed', 'quarter speed', 'half circle round towards the right', or what not, he was in the oil-smelling twilight of the ill-lit engine-room. Close beside him on either side was the mouthpiece of a speaking-tube, and ever and again he would direct one side or other of his strange craft to 'concentrate fire forward on gunners', or to 'clear out trench about a hundred yards on our right front'.

He was a young man, healthy enough but by no means sun-tanned, and of a type of feature and expression that prevails in His Majesty's Navy: alert, intelligent, quiet. He and his engineers and his riflemen all went about their work, calm and reasonable men. They had none of that flapping strenuousness of the half-wit in a hurry, that excessive strain upon the blood-vessels, that hysteria of effort which is so frequently regarded as the proper state of mind for heroic deeds.

For the enemy these young engineers were defeating they felt a certain qualified pity and a quite unqualified contempt. They regarded these big, healthy men they were shooting down precisely as these same big, healthy men might regard some inferior kind of native. They despised them for making war; despised their bawling patriotisms and their emotionality profoundly; despised them, above all, for the petty cunning and the almost brutish want of imagination their method of fighting displayed. 'If they *must* make war,' these young men thought, 'why in thunder don't they do it like sensible men?' They resented the assumption that their own side was too stupid to do anything more than play their enemy's game, that they were going to play this costly folly according to the rules of unimaginative men. They resented being forced to the trouble of making man-killing machinery; resented the alternative of having to massacre these people or endure their truculent yappings; resented the whole unfathomable imbecility of war.

Meanwhile, with something of the mechanical precision of a good clerk posting a ledger, the riflemen moved their knobs and pressed their buttons. . . .

The captain of Land Ironclad Number Three had halted on the crest close to his captured half-battery. His lined-up prisoners stood hard by and waited for the cyclists behind to come for them. He surveyed the victorious morning through his conning-tower.

He read the general's signals. 'Five and Four are to keep among the guns to the left and prevent any attempt to recover them. Seven and Eleven and Twelve, stick to the guns you have got; Seven, get into position to command the guns taken by Three. Then we're to do something else, are we? Six and One, quicken up to about ten miles an hour and walk round behind that camp to the levels near the river—we shall bag the whole crowd of them,' interjected the young man. 'Ah, here we are! Two and Three, Eight and Nine, Thirteen and Fourteen, space out to a thousand yards, wait for the word, and then go slowly to cover the advance of the cyclist infantry against any charge of mounted troops. That's all right. But where's Ten? Halloa! Ten to repair and get movable as soon as possible. They've broken up Ten!'

The discipline of the new war machines was business-like rather than pedantic, and the head of the captain came down out of the conning-tower to tell his men. 'I say, you chaps there. They've broken up Ten. Not badly, I think; but anyhow, he's stuck.'

But that still left thirteen of the monsters in action to finish up the broken army.

The war correspondent stealing down his gully looked back and saw them all lying along the crest and talking fluttering congratulatory flags to one another. Their iron sides were shinning golden in the light of the rising sun.

5

The private adventures of the war correspondent terminated in surrender about one o'clock in the afternoon, and by that time he had stolen a horse, pitched off it, and narrowly escaped being rolled upon; found the brute had broken its leg, and shot it with his revolver. He had spent some hours in the company of a squad of dispirited riflemen, had quarrelled with them about topography at last, and gone off by himself in a direction that should have brought him to the banks of the river and didn't. Moreover, he had eaten all his chocolate and found nothing in the whole world to drink. Also, it had become extremely hot. From behind a broken, but attractive, stone wall he had seen far away in the distance the defender-horsemen trying to charge cyclists in open order, with land ironclads outflanking them on either side. He had discovered that cyclists could retreat over open turf before horsemen with a sufficient margin of speed to allow of frequent dismounts and much terribly effective sharpshooting; and he had a sufficient persuasion that those horsemen, having charged their hearts out, had halted just beyond his range of vision and surrendered. He had been urged to sudden activity by a forward movement of one of those machines that had threatened to enfilade his wall. He had discovered a fearful blister on his heel.

He was now in a scrubby gravelly place, sitting down and meditating on his pocket-handkerchief, which had in some extraordinary way become in the last twenty-four hours extremely ambiguous in hue. 'It's the whitest thing I've got,' he said.

He had known all along that the enemy was east, west, and south of him, but when he heard land ironclads Numbers One and Six talking in their measured, deadly way not half a mile to the north he decided to make his own little unconditional peace without any further risks. He was for hoisting his white flag to a bush and taking up a position of modest obscurity near it until some one came along. He became aware of voices, clatter, and the distinctive noises of a body of horse, quite near, and he put his handkerchief in his pocket again and went to see what was going forward.

The sound of firing ceased, and then as he drew near he heard the deep sounds of many simple, coarse, but hearty and noble-hearted soldiers of the old school swearing with vigour.

He emerged from his scrub upon a big level plain, and far away a fringe of trees marked the banks of the river.

In the centre of the picture was a still intact road bridge, and a big railway bridge a little to the right. Two land ironclads rested, with a general air of being long, harmless sheds, in a pose of anticipatory peacefulness right and left of the picture, completely commanding two miles and more of the river levels. Emerged and halted a few yards from the scrub was the remainder of the defender's cavalry, dusty, a little disordered and obviously annoyed, but still a very fine show of men. In the middle distance three or four men and horses were receiving medical attendance, and nearer a knot of officers regarded the distant novelties in mechanism with profound distaste. Every one was very distinctly aware of the twelve other ironclads, and of the multitude of townsmen soldiers, on bicycles or afoot, encumbered now by prisoners and captured war-gear but otherwise thoroughly effective, who were sweeping like a great net in their rear.

'Checkmate,' said the war correspondent, walking out into the open. 'But I surrender in the best of company. Twenty-four hours ago I thought war was impossible—and these beggars have captured the whole blessed army! Well! Well!' He thought of his talk with the young lieutenant. 'If there's no end to the surprises of science, the civilized people have it, of course. As long as their science keeps going they will necessarily be ahead of open-country men. Still. . . .' He wondered for a space what might have happened to the young lieutenant.

The war correspondent was one of those inconsistent people who always want the beaten side to win. When he saw all these burly, sun-tanned horsemen, disarmed and dismounted and lined up; when he saw their horses unskilfully led away by the singularly not equestrian cyclists to whom they had surrendered; when he saw these truncated Paladins watching this scandalous sight, he forgot altogether that he had called these men 'cunning louts' and wished them beaten not four-and-twenty hours ago. A month ago he had seen that regiment in its pride going forth to war, and had been told of its terrible prowess, how it could charge in open order with each man firing from his saddle, and sweep before it anything else that ever came out to battle in any sort of order, foot or horse. And it had had to fight a few score of young men in atrociously unfair machines!

'Manhood *versus* Machinery' occurred to him as a suitable headline. Journalism curdles all one's mind to phrases.

He strolled as near the lined-up prisoners as the sentinels seemed disposed to permit, and surveyed them and compared their sturdy proportions with those of their lightly built captors.

'Smart degenerates,' he muttered. 'Anæmic cockneydom.'

The surrendered officers came quite close to him presently, and he could hear the colonel's high-pitched tenor. The poor gentleman had spent three years of arduous toil upon the best material in the world perfecting that shooting from the saddle charge, and he was enquiring with phrases of blasphemy, natural in the circumstances, what one could be expected to do against this suitably consigned ironmongery.

'Guns,' said some one.

'Big guns they can walk round. You can't shift big guns to keep pace with them, and little guns in the open they rush. I saw 'em rushed. You might do a surprise now and then—assassinate the brutes, perhaps——'

'You might make things like 'em.'

'What? *More* ironmongery? Us? . . .'

'I'll call my article,' meditated the war correspondent '"Mankind *versus* Ironmongery", and quote the old boy at the beginning.'

And he was much too good a journalist to spoil his contrast by remarking that the half-dozen comparatively slender young men in blue pyjamas who were standing about their victorious land ironclad, drinking coffee and eating biscuits, had also in their eyes and carriage something not altogether degraded below the level of a man.

FINIS

FRANK L. POLLACK

'I'm getting tired,' complained Davis, lounging in the window of the Physics Building, 'and sleepy. It's after eleven o'clock. This makes the fourth night I've sat up to see your new star, and it'll be the last. Why, the thing was billed to appear three weeks ago.'

'Are *you* tired, Miss Wardour?' asked Eastwood, and the girl glanced up with a quick flush and a negative murmur.

Eastwood made the reflection anew that she certainly was painfully shy. She was almost as plain as she was shy, though her hair had an unusual beauty of its own, fine as silk and coloured like palest flame.

Probably she had brains; Eastwood had seen her reading some extremely 'deep' books, but she seemed to have no amusements, few interests. She worked daily at the Art Students' League, and boarded where he did, and he had thus come to ask her with the Davis's to watch for the new star from the laboratory windows on the Heights.

'Do you really think that it's worth while to wait any longer, professor?' enquired Mrs Davis, concealing a yawn.

Eastwood was somewhat annoyed by the continued failure of the star to show itself and he hated to be called 'professor', being only an assistant professor of physics.

'I don't know,' he answered somewhat curtly. 'This is the twelfth night that I have waited for it. Of course, it would have been a mathematical miracle if astronomers should have solved such a problem exactly, though they've been figuring on it for a quarter of a century.'

The new Physics Building of Columbia University was about twelve storeys high. The physics laboratory occupied the ninth and tenth floors, with the astronomical rooms above it, an arrangement which would have been impossible before the invention of the oil vibration cushion, which practically isolated the instrument rooms from the earth.

Eastwood had arranged a small telescope at the window, and below them spread the illuminated map of Greater New York, sending up a faintly musical roar. All the streets were crowded, as they had been every night since the fifth of the month, when the great new star, or sun, was expected to come into view.

Some error had been made in the calculations, though, as Eastwood said, astronomers had been figuring on them for twenty-five years.

It was, in fact, nearly forty years since Professor Adolphe Bernier first announced his theory of a limited universe at the International Congress of Sciences in Paris, where it was counted as little more than a masterpiece of imagination.

Professor Bernier did not believe that the universe was infinite. Somewhere, he argued, the universe must have a centre, which is the pivot for its revolution.

The moon revolves around the earth, the planetary system revolves about the sun, the solar system revolves about one of the fixed stars, and this whole system in its turn undoubtedly revolves around some more distant point. But this sort of progression must definitely stop somewhere.

Somewhere there must be a central sun, a vast incandescent body which does not move at all. And as a sun is always larger and hotter than its satellites, therefore the body at the centre of the universe must be of an immensity and temperature beyond anything known or imagined.

It was objected that this hypothetical body should then be large enough to be visible from the earth, and Professor Bernier replied that some day it undoubtedly would be visible. Its light had simply not yet had time to reach the earth.

The passage of light from the nearest of the fixed stars is a matter of three years, and there must be many stars so distant that their rays have not yet reached us. The great central sun must be so inconceivably remote that perhaps hundreds, perhaps thousands of years would elapse before its light should burst upon the solar system.

All this was contemptuously classed as 'newspaper science' till the extraordinary mathematical revival a little after the middle of the twentieth century afforded the means of verifying it.

Following the new theorems discovered by Professor Burnside, of Princeton, and elaborated by Dr Taneka, of Tokyo, astronomers succeeded in calculating the arc of the sun's movements through space, and its ratio to the orbit of its satellites. With this as a basis, it was possible to follow the widening circles, the consecutive systems of the heavenly bodies and their rotations.

The theory of Professor Bernier was justified. It was demonstrated that there really was a gigantic mass of incandescent matter, which, whether the central point of the universe or not, appeared to be without motion.

The weight and distance of this new sun were approximately calculated, and, the speed of light being known, it was an easy matter to reckon when its rays would reach the earth.

It was then estimated that the approaching rays would arrive at the earth in twenty-six years, and that was twenty-six years ago. Three weeks had passed since the date when the new heavenly body was expected to become visible, and it had not yet appeared.

Popular interest had risen to a high pitch, stimulated by innumerable newspaper and magazine articles, and the streets were nightly thronged with excited crowds armed with opera-glasses and star maps, while at every corner a telescope man had planted his tripod instrument at a nickel a look.

Similar scenes were taking place in every civilized city on the globe.

It was generally supposed that the new luminary would appear in size about midway between Venus and the moon. Better informed persons expected something like the sun, and a syndicate of capitalists quietly leased large areas on the coast of Greenland in anticipation of a great rise in temperature and a northward movement in population.

Even the business situation was appreciably affected by the public uncertainty and excitement. There was a decline in stocks, and a minor religious sect boldly prophesied the end of the world.

'I've had enough of this,' said Davis, looking at his watch again. 'Are you ready to go, Grace? By the way, isn't it getting warmer?'

It had been a sharp February day, but the temperature was certainly rising. Water was dripping from the roofs, and from the icicles that fringed the window ledges, as if a warm wave had suddenly arrived.

'What's that light?' suddenly asked Alice Wardour, who was lingering by the open window.

'It must be moonrise,' said Eastwood, though the illumination of the horizon was almost like daybreak.

Davis abandoned his intention of leaving, and they watched the east grow pale and flushed till at last a brilliant white disc heaved itself above the horizon.

It resembled the full moon, but as if trebled in lustre, and the streets grew almost as light as by day.

'Good heavens, that must be the new star, after all!' said Davis in an awed voice.

'No, it's only the moon. This is the hour and minute for her rising,' answered Eastwood, who had grasped the cause of the phenomenon. 'But the new sun must have appeared on the other side of the earth. Its light is what makes the moon so brilliant. It will rise here just as the sun does, no telling how soon. It must be brighter than was expected—and maybe hotter,' he added with a vague uneasiness.

'Isn't it getting very warm in here?' said Mrs Davis, loosening her jacket. 'Couldn't you turn off some of the steam heat?'

Eastwood turned it all off, for, in spite of the open window, the room was really growing uncomfortably close. But the warmth appeared to come from without; it was like a warm spring evening, and the icicles were breaking loose from the cornices.

For half an hour they leaned from the windows with but desultory conversation, and below them the streets were black with people and whitened with upturned faces. The brilliant moon rose higher, and the mildness of the night sensibly increased.

It was after midnight when Eastwood first noticed the reddish flush tinging the clouds low in the east, and he pointed it out to his companions.

'That must be it at last,' he exclaimed, with a thrill of vibrating excitement at what he was going to see, a cosmic event unprecedented in intensity.

The brightness waxed rapidly.

'By Jove, see it redden!' Davis ejaculated. 'It's getting lighter than day—and hot! Whew!'

The whole eastern sky glowed with a deepening pink that extended half round the horizon. Sparrows chirped from the roofs, and it looked as if the disc of the unknown star might at any moment be expected to lift above the Atlantic, but it delayed long.

The heavens continued to burn with myriad hues, gathering at last to a fiery furnace glow on the skyline.

Mrs Davis suddenly screamed. An American flag blowing freely from its staff on the roof of the tall building had all at once burst into flame.

Low in the east lay a long streak of intense fire which broadened as they squinted with watering eyes. It was as if the edge of the world had been heated to whiteness.

The brilliant moon faded to a feathery white film in the glare. There was a confused outcry from the observatory overhead, and a crash of something being broken, and as the strange new sunlight fell through the window the onlookers leaped back as if a blast furnace had been opened before them.

The glass cracked and fell inward. Something like the sun, but magnified fifty times in size and hotness, was rising out of the sea. An iron instrument-table by the window began to smoke with an acrid smell of varnish.

'What the devil is this, Eastwood?' shouted Davis accusingly.

From the streets rose a sudden, enormous wail of fright and pain, the outcry of a million throats at once, and the roar of a stampede followed. The pavements were choked with struggling, panic-stricken people in the fierce glare, and above the din arose the clanging rush of fire engines and trucks.

Smoke began to rise from several points below Central Park, and two or three church chimes pealed crazily.

The observers from overhead came running down the stairs with a thunderous trampling, for the elevator man had deserted his post.

'Here, we've got to get out of this,' shouted Davis, seizing his wife by the arm and hustling her toward the door. 'This place'll be on fire directly.'

'Hold on. You can't go down into that crush on the street,' Eastwood cried, trying to prevent him.

But Davis broke away and raced down the stairs, half carrying his terrified wife. Eastwood got his back against the door in time to prevent Alice from following them.

'There's nothing in this building that will burn, Miss Wardour,' he said as calmly as he could. 'We had better stay here for the present. It would be sure death to get involved in that stampede below. Just listen to it.'

The crowds on the street seemed to sway to and fro in contending waves, and the cries, curses, and screams came up in a savage chorus.

The heat was already almost blistering to the skin, though they carefully avoided the direct rays, and instruments of glass in the laboratory cracked loudly one by one.

A vast cloud of dark smoke began to rise from the harbour, where the shipping must have caught fire, and something exploded with a terrific report. A few minutes later half a dozen fires broke out in the lower part of the city, rolling up volumes of smoke that faded to a thin mist in the dazzling light.

The great new sun was now fully above the horizon, and the whole east seemed ablaze. The stampede in the streets had quieted all at once, for the survivors had taken refuge in the nearest houses, and the pavements were black with motionless forms of men and women.

'I'll do whatever you say,' said Alice, who was deadly pale, but remarkably collected. Even at that moment Eastwood was struck by the splendour of her ethereally brilliant hair that burned like pale flame above her pallid face. 'But we can't stay here, can we?'

'No,' replied Eastwood, trying to collect his faculties in the face of this catastrophic revolution of nature. 'We'd better go to the basement, I think.'

In the basement were deep vaults used for the storage of delicate instruments, and these would afford shelter for a time at least. It occurred to him as he spoke that perhaps temporary safety was the best that any living thing on earth could hope for.

But he led the way down the well staircase. They had gone down six or seven flights when a gloom seemed to grow upon the air, with a welcome relief.

It seemed almost cool, and the sky had clouded heavily, with the appearance of polished and heated silver.

A deep but distant roaring arose and grew from the south-east, and they stopped on the second landing to look from the window.

A vast black mass seemed to fill the space between sea and sky, and it was sweeping towards the city, probably from the harbour, Eastwood thought, at a speed that made it visibly grow as they watched it.

'A cyclone—and a waterspout!' muttered Eastwood, appalled.

He might have foreseen it from the sudden, excessive evaporation and the heating of the air. The gigantic black pillar drove towards them swaying and reeling, and a gale came with it, and a wall of impenetrable mist behind.

As Eastwood watched its progress he saw its cloudy bulk illumined momentarily by a dozen lightning-like flashes, and a moment later, above its roar, came the tremendous detonations of heavy cannon.

The forts and the warships were firing shells to break the water-spout, but the shots seemed to produce no effect. It was the city's last and useless attempt at resistance. A moment later forts and ships alike must have been engulfed.

'Hurry! This building will collapse!' Eastwood shouted.

They rushed down another flight, and heard the crash with which the monster broke over the city. A deluge of water, like the emptying of a reservoir, thundered upon the street, and the water was steaming hot as it fell.

There was a rending crash of falling walls, and in another instant the Physics Building seemed to be twisted around by a powerful hand. The walls blew out, and the whole structure sank in a chaotic mass.

But the tough steel frame was practically unwreckable, and, in fact, the upper portion was simply bent down upon the lower storeys, peeling off most of the shell of masonry and stucco.

Eastwood was stunned as he was hurled to the floor, but when he came to himself he was still upon the landing, which was tilted at an alarming angle. A tangled mass of steel rods and beams hung a yard over his head, and a huge steel girder had plunged down perpendicularly from above, smashing everything in its way.

Wreckage choked the well of the staircase, a mass of plaster, bricks, and shattered furniture surrounded him, and he could look out in almost every direction through the rent iron skeleton.

A yard away Alice was sitting up, mechanically wiping the mud and water from her face, and apparently uninjured. Tepid water was pouring through the interstices of the wreck in torrents, though it did not appear to be raining.

A steady, powerful gale had followed the whirlwind, and it brought a little coolness with it. Eastwood enquired perfunctorily of Alice if she were hurt, without being able to feel any degree of interest in the matter. His faculty of sympathy seemed paralysed.

'I don't know. I thought—I thought that we were all dead!' the girl murmured in a sort of daze. 'What was it? Is it all over?'

'I think it's only beginning,' Eastwood answered dully.

The gale had brought up more clouds and the skies were thickly overcast, but shining white-hot. Presently the rain came down in almost scalding floods and as it fell upon the hissing streets it steamed again into the air.

In three minutes all the world was choked with hot vapour, and from the roar and splash the streets seemed to be running rivers.

The downpour seemed too violent to endure, and after an hour it did cease, while the city reeked with mist. Through the whirling fog Eastwood caught glimpses of ruined buildings, vast heaps of debris, all the wreckage of the greatest city of the twentieth century.

Then the torrents fell again, like a cataract, as if the waters of the earth were shuttlecocking between sea and heaven. With a jarring tremor of the ground a landslide went down into the Hudson.

The atmosphere was like a vapour bath, choking and sickening. The physical agony of respiration aroused Alice from a sort of stupor, and she cried out pitifully that she would die.

The strong wind drove the hot spray and steam through the shattered building till it seemed impossible that human lungs could extract life from the semi-liquid that had replaced the air, but the two lived.

After hours of this parboiling the rain slackened, and, as the clouds parted, Eastwood caught a glimpse of a familiar form half-way up the heavens. It was the sun, the old sun, looking small and watery.

But the intense heat and brightness told that the enormous body still blazed behind the clouds. The rain seemed to have ceased definitely, and the hard, shining whiteness of the sky grew rapidly hotter.

The heat of the air increased to an oven-like degree; the mists were dissipated, the clouds licked up, and the earth seemed to dry itself almost immediately. The heat from the two suns beat down simultaneously till it became a monstrous terror, unendurable.

An odour of smoke began to permeate the air; there was a dazzling shimmer over the streets, and great clouds of mist arose from the bay, but these appeared to evaporate before they could darken the sky.

The piled wreck of the building sheltered the two refugees from the direct rays of the new sun, now almost overhead, but not from the penetrating heat of the air. But the body will endure almost anything, short of tearing asunder, for a time at least; it is the finer mechanism of the nerves that suffers most.

Alice lay face down among the bricks, gasping and moaning. The blood hammered in Eastwood's brain, and the strangest mirages flickered before his eyes.

Alternately he lapsed into heavy stupors, and awoke to the agony of the day. In his lucid moments he reflected that this could not last long, and tried to remember what degree of heat would cause death.

Within an hour after the drenching rains he was feverishly thirsty, and the skin felt as if peeling from his whole body.

This fever and horror lasted until he forgot that he had ever known another state; but at last the west reddened, and the flaming sun went down. It left the familiar planet high in the heavens, and there was no darkness until the usual hour, though there was a slight lowering of the temperature.

But when night did come it brought life-giving coolness, and though the heat was still intense it seemed temperate by comparison. More than all, the kindly darkness seemed to set a limit to the cataclysmic disorders of the day.

'Ouf! This is heavenly!' said Eastwood, drawing long breaths and feeling mind and body revived in the gloom.

'It won't last long,' replied Alice, and her voice sounded extraordinarily calm through the darkness. 'The heat will come again when the new sun rises in a few hours.'

'We might find some better place in the meanwhile—a deep cellar; or we might get into the subway,' Eastwood suggested.

'It would be no use. Don't you understand? I have been thinking it all out. After this, the new sun will always shine, and we could not endure it even another day. The wave of heat is passing round the world as it revolves, and in a few hours the whole earth will be a burnt-up ball. Very likely we are the only people left alive in New York, or perhaps in America.'

She seemed to have taken the intellectual initiative, and spoke with an assumption of authority that amazed him.

'But there must be others,' said Eastwood, after thinking for a moment. 'Other people have found sheltered places, or miners, or men underground.'

'They would have been drowned by the rain. At any rate, there will be none left alive by tomorrow night.

'Think of it,' she went dreamily, 'for a thousand years this wave of fire has been rushing towards us, while life has been going on so happily in the world, so unconscious that the world was doomed all the time. And now this is the end of life.'

'I don't know,' Eastwood said slowly. 'It may be the end of human life, but there must be some forms that will survive—some micro-organisms perhaps capable of resisting high temperatures, if nothing higher. The seed of life will be left at any rate, and that is everything. Evolution will begin over again, producing new types to suit the changed conditions. I only wish I could see what creatures will be here in a few thousand years.

'But I can't realize it at all—this thing!' he cried passionately, after a pause. 'Is it real? Or have we all gone mad? It seems too much like a bad dream.'

The rain crashed down again as he spoke, and the earth steamed, though not with the dense reek of the day. For hours the waters roared and splashed against the earth in hot billows till the streets were foaming yellow rivers, dammed by the wreck of fallen buildings.

There was a continual rumble as earth and rock slid into the East River, and at last the Brooklyn Bridge collapsed with a thunderous crash and splash that made all Manhattan vibrate. A gigantic billow like a tidal wave swept up the river from its fall.

The downpour slackened and ceased soon after the moon began to shed an obscured but brilliant light through the clouds.

Presently the east commenced to grow luminous, and this time there could be no doubt as to what was coming.

Alice crept closer to the man as the grey light rose upon the watery air.

'Kiss me!' she whispered suddenly, throwing her arms around his neck. He could feel her trembling. 'Say you love me; hold me in your arms. There is only an hour.'

'Don't be afraid. Try to face it bravely,' stammered Eastwood.

'I don't fear it—not death. But I have never lived. I have always been timid and wretched and afraid—afraid to speak—and I've almost wished for suffering and misery or anything rather than to be stupid and dumb and dead, the way I've always been.

'I've never dared to tell anyone what I was, what I wanted. I've been afraid all my life, but I'm not afraid now. I have never lived; I have never been happy; and now we must die together!'

It seemed to Eastwood the cry of the perishing world. He held her in his arms and kissed her wet, tremulous face that was strained to his.

The twilight was gone before they knew it. The sky was blue already, with crimson flakes mounting to the zenith, and the heat was growing once more intense.

'This is the end, Alice,' said Eastwood, and his voice trembled.

She looked at him, her eyes shining with an unearthly softness and brilliancy, and turned her face to the east.

There, in crimson and orange, flamed the last dawn that human eyes would ever see.

AS EASY AS ABC

RUDYARD KIPLING

The ABC, that semi-elected, semi-nominated body of a few score persons, controls the Planet. Transportation is Civilization, our motto runs. Theoretically we do what we please, so long as we do not interfere with the traffic and all it implies. Practically, the ABC confirms or annuls all international arrangements, and, to judge from its last report, finds our tolerant, humorous, lazy little Planet only too ready to shift the whole burden of public administration on its shoulders.

'With the Night Mail', *Actions and Reactions*

Isn't it almost time that our Planet took some interest in the proceedings of the Aerial Board of Control? One knows that easy communications nowadays, and lack of privacy in the past, have killed all curiosity among mankind, but as the Board's Official Reporter I am bound to tell my tale.

At 9.30 a.m., 26 August, AD 2065, the Board, sitting in London, was informed by De Forest that the District of Northern Illinois had riotously cut itself out of all systems and would remain disconnected till the Board should take over and administer it direct.

Every Northern Illinois freight and passenger tower was, he reported, out of action; all District main, local, and guiding lights had been extinguished; all General Communications were dumb, and through traffic had been diverted. No reason had been given, but he gathered unofficially from the Mayor of Chicago that the District complained of 'crowd-making and invasion of privacy'.

As a matter of fact, it is of no importance whether Northern Illinois stay in or out of planetary circuit; as a matter of policy, any complaint of invasion of privacy needs immediate investigation, lest worse follow.

By 9.45 a.m. De Forest, Dragomiroff (Russia), Takahira (Japan), and Pirolo (Italy) were empowered to visit Illinois and 'to take such steps as might be necessary for the resumption of traffic and *all that that implies*'. By 10 a.m. the Hall was empty, and the four Members and I were aboard what Pirolo insisted on calling 'my leetle godchild'—that is to say, the new *Victor Pirolo*. Our Planet prefers to know Victor Pirolo as a gentle, grey-haired enthusiast who spends his time near Foggia, inventing or creating new breeds of Spanish-Italian olive-trees; but there is another side to his nature—the manufacture of quaint inventions, of which the *Victor Pirolo* is, perhaps, not the least surprising. She and a few score sister-craft of the same type embody his latest ideas. But she is not comfortable. An ABC boat does not take the air with the level-keeled lift of a liner, but shoots up rocket-fashion like the 'aeroplane' of our ancestors, and makes her height at top-speed from the first. That is why I found myself sitting suddenly on the large lap of Eustace Arnott, who commands the ABC Fleet. One knows vaguely that there is such a thing as a Fleet somewhere on the Planet, and that, theoretically, it exists for the purposes of what used to be known as 'war'. Only a week before, while visiting a glacier sanatorium behind Gothaven, I had seen some squadrons making false auroras far to the north while they manœuvred round the Pole; but, naturally, it had never occurred to me that the things could be used in earnest.

Said Arnott to De Forest as I staggered to a seat on the chart-room divan: 'We're tremendously grateful to 'em in Illinois. We've never had a chance of exercising all the Fleet together. I've turned in a General Call, and I expect we'll have at least two hundred keels aloft this evening.'

'Well aloft?' De Forest asked.

'Of course, sir. Out of sight till they're called for.'

Arnott laughed as he lolled over the transparent chart-table where the map of the summer-blue Atlantic slid along, degree by degree, in exact answer to our progress. Our dial already showed 320 m.p.h. and we were two thousand feet above the uppermost traffic lines.

'Now, where is this Illinois District of yours?', said Dragomiroff. 'One travels so much, one sees so little. Oh, I remember! It is in North America.'

De Forest, whose business it is to know the out districts, told us that it lay at the foot of Lake Michigan, on a road to nowhere in particular, was about half an hour's run from end to end, and, except in one corner, as flat as the sea. Like most flat countries nowadays, it was heavily guarded against invasion of privacy by forced timber—fifty-foot spruce and tamarack, grown in five years. The population was close on two millions, largely migratory between Florida and California, with a backbone of small farms (they call a thousand acres a farm in Illinois) whose owners come into Chicago for amusements and society during the winter. They were, he said, noticeably kind, quiet folk, but a little exacting, as all flat countries must be, in their notions of privacy. There had, for instance, been no printed news-sheet in Illinois for twenty-seven years. Chicago argued that engines for printed news sooner or later developed into engines for invasion of privacy, which in turn might bring the old terror of Crowds and blackmail back to the Planet. So news-sheets were not.

'And that's Illinois,' De Forest concluded. 'You see, in the Old Days, she was in the forefront of what they used to call "progress", and Chicago——'

'Chicago?' said Takahira. 'That's the little place where there is Salati's Statue of the Negro in Flames? A fine bit of old work.'

'When did you see it?' asked De Forest quickly. 'They only unveil it once a year.'

'I know. At Thanksgiving. It was then,' said Takahira, with a shudder. 'And they sang MacDonough's Song, too.'

'Whew!' De Forest whistled. 'I did not know that! I wish you'd told me before. MacDonough's Song may have had its uses when it was composed, but it was an infernal legacy for any man to leave behind.'

'It's protective instinct, my dear fellows,' said Pirolo, rolling a cigarette. 'The Planet, she has had her dose of popular government. She suffers from inherited agoraphobia. She has no—ah—use for crowds.'

Dragomiroff leaned forward to give him a light. 'Certainly,' said the white-bearded Russian, 'the Planet has taken all precautions against crowds for the past hundred years. What is our total population today? Six hundred million, we hope; five hundred, we think; but—but if next year's census shows more than four hundred and fifty, I myself will eat all the extra little babies. We have cut the birth-rate out—right out! For a long time we have said to Almighty God, "Thank You, Sir, but we do not much like Your game of life, so we will not play."'

'Anyhow,' said Arnott defiantly, 'men live a century apiece on the average now.'

'Oh, that is quite well! I am rich—you are rich—we are all rich and happy because we are so few and we live so long. Only *I* think Almighty God He will remember what the Planet was like in the time of Crowds and the Plague. Perhaps He will send us nerves. Eh, Pirolo?'

The Italian blinked into space. 'Perhaps,' he said, 'He has sent them already. Anyhow, you cannot argue with the Planet. She does not forget the Old Days, and—what can you do?'

'For sure we can't remake the world.' De Forest glanced at the map flowing smoothly across the table from west to east. 'We ought to be over our ground by nine tonight. There won't be much sleep afterwards.'

On which hint we dispersed, and I slept till Takahira waked me for dinner. Our ancestors thought nine hours' sleep ample for their little lives. We, living thirty years longer, feel ourselves defrauded with less than eleven out of the twenty-four.

By ten o'clock we were over Lake Michigan. The west shore was lightless, except for a dull ground-glare at Chicago, and a single traffic-directing light—its leading beam pointing north—at Waukegan on our starboard bow. None of the Lake villages gave any sign of life; and inland, westward, so far as we could see, blackness lay unbroken on the level earth. We swooped down and skimmed low across the dark, throwing calls county by county. Now and again we picked up the faint glimmer of a house-light, or heard the rasp and rend of a cultivator being played across the fields, but Northern Illinois as a whole was one inky, apparently uninhabited, waste of high, forced woods. Only our illuminated map, with its little pointer switching from county to county, as we wheeled and twisted, gave us any idea of our position. Our calls, urgent, pleading, coaxing or commanding, through the General Communicator brought no answer. Illinois strictly maintained her own privacy in the timber which she grew for that purpose.

'Oh, this is absurd!' said De Forest. 'We're like an owl trying to work a wheat-field. Is this Bureau Creek? Let's land, Arnott, and get hold of some one.'

We brushed over a belt of forced woodland—fifteen-year-old maple sixty feet high—grounded on a private meadow-dock, none too big, where we moored to our own grapnels, and hurried out through the warm dark night towards a light in a verandah. As we neared the garden gate I could have sworn we had stepped knee-

deep in quicksand, for we could scarcely drag our feet against the prickling currents that clogged them. After five paces we stopped, wiping our foreheads, as hopelessly stuck on dry smooth turf as so many cows in a bog.

'Pest!' cried Pirolo angrily. 'We are ground-circuited. And it is my own system of ground-circuits too! I know the pull.'

'Good evening,' said a girl's voice from the verandah. 'Oh, I'm sorry! We've locked up. Wait a minute.'

We heard the click of a switch, and almost fell forward as the currents round our knees were withdrawn.

The girl laughed, and laid aside her knitting. An old-fashioned Controller stood at her elbow, which she reversed from time to time, and we could hear the snort and clank of the obedient cultivator half a mile away, behind the guardian woods.

'Come in and sit down,' she said. 'I'm only playing a plough. Dad's gone to Chicago to—Ah! Then it was *your* call I heard just now!'

She had caught sight of Arnott's Board uniform, leaped to the switch, and turned it full on.

We were checked, gasping, waist-deep in current this time, three yards from the verandah.

'We only want to know what's the matter with Illinois,' said De Forest placidly.

'Then hadn't you better go to Chicago and find out?' she answered. 'There's nothing wrong here. We own ourselves.'

'How can we go anywhere if you won't loose us?' De Forest went on, while Arnott scowled. Admirals of Fleets are still quite human when their dignity is touched.

'Stop a minute—you don't know how funny you look!' She put her hands on her hips and laughed mercilessly.

'Don't worry about that,' said Arnott, and whistled. A voice answered from the *Victor Pirolo* in the meadow.

'Only a single-fuse ground-circuit!' Arnott called. 'Sort it out gently, please.'

We heard the ping of a breaking lamp; a fuse blew out somewhere in the verandah roof, frightening a nest full of birds. The ground-circuit was open. We stooped and rubbed our tingling ankles.

'How rude—how very rude of you!' the maiden cried.

'Sorry, but we haven't time to look funny,' said Arnott. 'We've got to go to Chicago; and if I were you, young lady, I'd go into the cellars for the next two hours, and take mother with me.'

Off he strode, with us at his heels, muttering indignantly, till the humour of the thing struck and doubled him up with laughter at the foot of the gangway ladder.

'The Board hasn't shown what you might call a fat spark on this occasion,' said De Forest, wiping his eyes. 'I hope I didn't look as big a fool as you did, Arnott! Hullo! What on earth is that? Dad coming home from Chicago?'

There was a rattle and a rush, and a five-plough cultivator, blades in air like so many teeth, trundled itself at us round the edge of the timber, fuming and sparking furiously.

'Jump!' said Arnott, as we bundled ourselves through the none-too-wide door. 'Never mind about shutting it. Up!'

The *Victor Pirolo* lifted like a bubble, and the vicious machine shot just underneath us, clawing high as it passed.

'There's a nice little spit-kitten for you!' said Arnott, dusting his knees. 'We ask her a civil question. First she circuits us and then she plays a cultivator at us!'

'And then we fly,' said Dragomiroff. 'If I were forty years more young, I would go back and kiss her. Ho! Ho!'

'I,' said Pirolo, 'would smack her! My pet ship has been chased by a dirty plough; a—how do you say?—agricultural implement.'

'Oh, that is Illinois all over,' said De Forest. 'They don't content themselves with talking about privacy. They arrange to have it. And now, where's your alleged fleet, Arnott? We must assert ourselves against this wench.'

Arnott pointed to the black heavens.

'Waiting on—up there,' said he. 'Shall I give them the whole installation, sir?'

'Oh, I don't think the young lady is quite worth that,' said De Forest. 'Get over Chicago, and perhaps we'll see something.'

In a few minutes we were hanging at two thousand feet over an oblong block of incandescence in the centre of the little town.

'That looks like the old City Hall. Yes, there's Salati's Statue in front of it,' said Takahira. 'But what on earth are they doing to the place? I thought they used it for a market nowadays! Drop a little, please.'

We could hear the sputter and crackle of road-surfacing machines—the cheap Western type which fuse stone and rubbish into lava-like ribbed glass for their rough country roads. Three or four surfacers worked on each side of a square of ruins. The brick and stone wreckage crumbled, slid forward, and presently spread out into white-hot pools of sticky slag, which the levelling-rods smoothed more or less flat. Already a third of the big block had been so treated, and was cooling to dull red before our astonished eyes.

'It is the Old Market,' said De Forest. 'Well, there's nothing to prevent Illinois from making a road through a market. It doesn't interfere with traffic, that I can see.'

'Hsh!' said Arnott, gripping me by the shoulder. 'Listen! They're singing. Why on the earth are they singing?'

We dropped again till we could see the black fringe of people at the edge of that glowing square.

At first they only roared against the roar of the surfacers and levellers. Then the words came up clearly—the words of the Forbidden Song that all men knew, and none let pass their lips—poor Pat MacDonough's Song, made in the days of the Crowds and the Plague—every silly word of it loaded to sparking-point with the Planet's inherited memories of horror, panic, fear, and cruelty. And Chicago—innocent, contented little Chicago—was singing it aloud to the infernal tune that carried riot, pestilence and lunacy round our Planet a few generations ago!

> Once there was The People—Terror gave it birth;
> Once there was The People, and it made a hell of earth!

(Then the stamp and pause):

> Earth arose and crushed it. Listen, oh, ye slain!
> Once there was The People—it shall never be again!

The levellers thrust in savagely against the ruins as the song renewed itself again, again and again, louder than the crash of the melting walls.

De Forest frowned.

'I don't like that,' he said. 'They've broken back to the Old Days! They'll be killing somebody soon. I think we'd better divert 'em, Arnott.'

'Ay, ay, sir.' Arnott's hand went to his cap, and we heard the hull of the *Victor Pirolo* ring to the command: 'Lamps! Both watches stand by! Lamps! Lamps! Lamps!'

'Keep still!' Takahira whispered to me. 'Blinkers, please, quartermaster.'

'It's all right—all right!' said Pirolo from behind, and to my horror slipped over my head some sort of rubber helmet that locked with a snap. I could feel thick colloid bosses before my eyes, but I stood in absolute darkness.

'To save the sight,' he explained, and pushed me on to the chart-room divan. 'You will see in a minute.'

As he spoke I became aware of a thin thread of almost intolerable light, let down from heaven at an immense distance—one vertical hairsbreadth of frozen lightning.

'Those are our flanking ships,' said Arnott at my elbow. 'That one is over Galena. Look south—that other one's over Keithburg. Vincennes is behind us, and north yonder is Winthrop Woods. The Fleet's in position, sir'—this to De Forest. 'As soon as you give the word.'

'Ah no! No!' cried Dragomiroff at my side. I could feel the old man tremble. 'I do not know all that you can do, but be kind! I ask you to be a little kind to them below! This is horrible—horrible!'

When a Woman kills a Chicken,
Dynasties and Empires sicken,

Takahira quoted. 'It is too late to be gentle now.'

'Then take off my helmet! Take off my helmet!' Dragomiroff began hysterically.

Pirolo must have put his arm round him.

'Hush,' he said, 'I am here. It is all right, Ivan, my dear fellow.'

'I'll just send our little girl in Bureau County a warning,' said Arnott. 'She don't deserve it, but we'll allow her a minute or two to take mamma to the cellar.'

In the utter hush that followed the growling spark after Arnott had linked up his Service Communicator with the invisible Fleet, we heard MacDonough's Song from the city beneath us grow fainter as we rose to position. Then I clapped my hand before my mask lenses for it was as though the floor of Heaven had been riddled and all the inconceivable blaze of suns in the making was poured through the manholes.

'You needn't count,' said Arnott. I had had no thought of such a thing. 'There are two hundred and fifty keels up there, five miles apart. Full power, please, for another twelve seconds.'

The firmament, as far as eye could reach, stood on pillars of white fire. One fell on the glowing square at Chicago, and turned it black.

'Oh! Oh! Oh! Can men be allowed to do such things?' Dragomiroff cried, and fell across our knees.

'Glass of water, please,' said Takahira to a helmeted shape that leaped forward. 'He is a little faint.'

The lights switched off, and the darkness stunned like an avalanche. We could hear Dragomiroff's teeth on the glass edge.

Pirolo was comforting him.

'All right, allra-ight,' he repeated. 'Come and lie down. Come below and take off your mask. I give you my word, old friend, it is all right. They are my siege-lights. Little Victor Pirolo's leetle lights. You know *me*! I do not hurt people.'

'Pardon!', Dragomiroff moaned. 'I have never seen Death. I have never seen the Board take action. Shall we go down and burn them alive, or is that already done?'

'Oh, hush,' said Pirolo, and I think he rocked him in his arms.

'Do we repeat, sir?' Arnott asked De Forest.

'Give 'em a minute's break,' De Forest replied. 'They may need it.'

We waited a minute, and then MacDonough's Song, broken but defiant, rose from undefeated Chicago.

'They seem fond of that tune,' said De Forest. 'I should let 'em have it, Arnott.'

'Very good, sir,' said Arnott, and felt his way to the Communicator keys.

No lights broke forth, but the hollow of the skies made herself the mouth for one note that touched the raw fibre of the brain. Men hear such sounds in delirium, advancing like tides from horizons beyond the ruled foreshores of space.

'That's our pitch-pipe,' said Arnott. 'We may be a bit ragged. I've never conducted two hundred and fifty performers before.' He pulled out the couplers, and struck a full chord on the Service Communicators.

The beams of light leaped down again, and danced, solemnly and awfully, a stilt-dance, sweeping thirty or forty miles left and right at each stiff-legged kick, while the darkness delivered itself—there is no scale to measure against that utterance—of the tune to which they kept time. Certain notes—one learnt to expect them with terror—cut through one's marrow, but, after three minutes, thought and emotion passed in indescribable agony.

We saw, we heard, but I think we were in some sort swooning. The two hundred and fifty beams shifted, re-formed, straddled and split, narrowed, widened, rippled in ribbons, broke into a thousand white-hot parallel lines, melted and revolved in interwoven rings like old-fashioned engine-turning, flung up to the zenith, made as if to descend and renew the torment, halted at the last instant, twizzled insanely round the horizon, and vanished, to bring back for the hundredth time darkness more shattering than their instantly renewed light over all Illinois. Then the tune and lights ceased together, and we heard one single devastating wail that shook all the horizon as a rubbed wet finger shakes the rim of a bowl.

'Ah, that is my new siren,' said Pirolo. 'You can break an iceberg in half, if you find the proper pitch. They will whistle by squadrons now. It is the wind through pierced shutters in the bows.'

I had collapsed beside Dragomiroff, broken and snivelling feebly, because I had been delivered before my time to all the terrors of Judgement Day, and the Archangels of the Resurrection were hailing me naked across the Universe to the sound of the music of the spheres.

Then I saw De Forest smacking Arnott's helmet with his open hand. The wailing died down in a long shriek as a black shadow swooped past us, and returned to her place above the lower clouds.

'I hate to interrupt a specialist when he's enjoying himself,' said De Forest. 'But, as a matter of fact, all Illinois has been asking us to stop for these last fifteen seconds.'

'What a pity.' Arnott slipped off his mask. 'I wanted you to hear us really hum. Our lower C can lift street-paving.'

'It is Hell—Hell!', cried Dragomiroff, and sobbed aloud.

Arnott looked away as he answered:

'It's a few thousand volts ahead of the old shoot-'em-and-sink-'em game, but I should scarcely call it *that*. What shall I tell the Fleet, sir?'

'Tell 'em we're very pleased and impressed. I don't think they need wait on any longer. There isn't a spark left down there.' De Forest pointed. 'They'll be deaf and blind.'

'Oh, I think not, sir. The demonstration lasted less than ten minutes.'

'Marvellous!' Takahira sighed. 'I should have said it was half a night. Now, shall we go down and pick up the pieces?'

'But first a small drink,' said Pirolo. 'The Board must not arrive weeping at its own works.'

'I am an old fool—an old fool!' Dragomiroff began piteously. 'I did not know what would happen. It is all new to me. We reason with them in Little Russia.'

Chicago North landing-tower was unlighted, and Arnott worked his ship into the clips by her own lights. As soon as these broke out we heard groanings of horror and appeal from many people below.

'All right,' shouted Arnott into the darkness. 'We aren't beginning again!' We descended by the stairs, to find ourselves knee-deep in a grovelling crowd, some crying that they were blind, others beseeching us not to make any more noises, but the greater part writhing face downward, their hands or their caps before their eyes.

It was Pirolo who came to our rescue. He climbed the side of a surfacing-machine, and there, gesticulating as though they could see, made oration to those afflicted people of Illinois.

'You stchewpids!' he began. 'There is nothing to fuss for. Of course, your eyes will smart and be red tomorrow. You will look as if you and your wives had drunk too much, but in a little while you will see again as well as before. I tell you this, and I—*I* am Pirolo. Victor Pirolo!'

The crowd with one accord shuddered, for many legends attach to Victor Pirolo of Foggia, deep in the secrets of God.

'Pirolo?' An unsteady voice lifted itself. 'Then tell us was there anything except light in those lights of yours just now?'

The question was repeated from every corner of the darkness.

Pirolo laughed.

'No!' he thundered. (Why have small men such large voices?) 'I give you my word and the Board's word that there was nothing except light—just light! You stchewpids! Your birth rate is too low already as it is. Some day I must invent something to send it up, but send it down—never!'

'Is that true?—We thought—somebody said——'

One could feel the tension relax all round.

'You *too* big fools,' Pirolo cried. 'You could have sent us a call and we would have told you.'

'Send you a call!' a deep voice shouted. 'I wish you had been at our end of the wire.'

'I'm glad I wasn't,' said De Forest. 'It was bad enough from behind the lamps. Never mind! It's over now. Is there any one here I can talk business with? I'm De Forest—for the Board.'

'You might begin with me, for one—I'm Mayor,' the bass voice replied.

A big man rose unsteadily from the street, and staggered towards us where we sat on the broad turf-edging, in front of the garden fences.

'I ought to be the first on my feet. Am I?' said he.

'Yes,' said De Forest, and steadied him as he dropped down beside us.

'Hello, Andy. Is that you?' a voice called.

'Excuse me,' said the Mayor; 'that sounds like my Chief of Police, Bluthner!'

'Bluthner it is; and here's Mulligan and Keefe—on their feet.'

'Bring 'em up please, Blut. We're supposed to be the Four in charge of this hamlet. What we says, goes. And, De Forest, what do you say?'

'Nothing—yet,' De Forest answered, as we made room for the panting, reeling men. '*You*'ve cut out of system. Well?'

'Tell the steward to send down drinks, please,' Arnott whispered to an orderly at his side.

'Good!' said the Mayor, smacking his dry lips. 'Now I suppose we can take it, De Forest, that henceforward the Board will administer us direct?'

'Not if the Board can avoid it,' De Forest laughed. 'The ABC is responsible for the planetary traffic only.'

'*And all that that implies.*' The big Four who ran Chicago chanted their Magna Charta like children at school.

'Well, get on,' said De Forest wearily. 'What is your silly trouble anyway?'

'Too much dam' Democracy,' said the Mayor, laying his hand on De Forest's knee.

'So? I thought Illinois had had her dose of that.'

'She has. That's why. Blut, what did you do with our prisoners last night?'

'Locked 'em in the water-tower to prevent the women killing

'em,' the Chief of Police replied. 'I'm too blind to move just yet, but——'

'Arnott, send some of your people, please, and fetch 'em along,' said De Forest.

'They're triple-circuited,' the Mayor called. 'You'll have to blow out three fuses.' He turned to De Forest, his large outline just visible in the paling darkness. 'I hate to throw any more work on the Board. I'm an administrator myself, but we've had a little fuss with our Serviles. What? In a big city there's bound to be a few men and women who can't live without listening to themselves, and who prefer drinking out of pipes they don't own both ends of. They inhabit flats and hotels all the year round. They say it saves 'em trouble. Anyway, it gives 'em more time to make trouble for their neighbours. We call 'em Serviles locally. And they are apt to be tuberculous.'

'Just so!' said the man called Mulligan. 'Transportation is Civilization. Democracy is Disease. I've proved it by the blood-test, every time.'

'Mulligan's our Health Officer, and a one-idea man,' said the Mayor, laughing. 'But it's true that most Serviles haven't much control. They *will* talk; and when people take to talking as a business, anything may arrive—mayn't it, De Forest?'

'Anything—except the facts of the case,' said De Forest, laughing.

'I'll give you those in a minute,' said the Mayor. 'Our Serviles got to talking—first in their houses and then on the streets, telling men and women how to manage their own affairs. (You can't teach a Servile not to finger his neighbour's soul.) That's invasion of privacy, of course, but in Chicago we'll suffer anything sooner than make crowds. Nobody took much notice, and so I let 'em alone. My fault! I was warned there would be trouble, but there hasn't been a crowd or murder in Illinois for nineteen years.'

'Twenty-two,' said his Chief of Police.

'Likely. Anyway, we'd forgot such things. So, from talking in the houses and on the streets, our Serviles go to calling a meeting at the Old Market yonder.' He nodded across the square where the wrecked buildings heaved up grey in the dawn-glimmer behind the square-cased statue of The Negro in Flames. 'There's nothing to prevent any one calling meetings except that it's against human nature to stand in a crowd, besides being bad for the health. I ought to have known by the way our men and women attended that first meeting that trouble was brewing. There were as many as a thousand in the market-place, touching each other. Touching! Then the Serviles turned in all tongue-switches and talked, and we——'

'What did they talk about?' said Takahira.

'First, how badly things were managed in the city. That pleased us Four—we were on the platform—because we hoped to catch one or two good men for City work. You know how rare executive capacity is. Even if we didn't it's—it's refreshing to find any one interested enough in our job to damn our eyes. You don't know what it means to work, year in, year out, without a spark of difference with a living soul.'

'Oh, don't we!' said De Forest. 'There are times on the Board when we'd give our positions if any one would kick us out and take hold of things themselves.'

'But they won't,' said the Mayor ruefully. 'I assure you, sir, we Four have done things in Chicago, in the hope of rousing people, that would have discredited Nero. But what do they say? "Very good, Andy. Have it your own way. Anything's better than a crowd. I'll go back to my land." You *can't* do anything with folk who can go where they please, and don't want anything on God's earth except their own way. There isn't a kick or a kicker left on the Planet.'

'Then I suppose that little shed yonder fell down by itself?' said De Forest. We could see the bare and still smoking ruins, and hear the slag-pools crackle as they hardened and set.

'Oh, that's only amusement. 'Tell you later. As I was saying, our Serviles held the meeting, and pretty soon we had to ground-circuit the platform to save 'em from being killed. And that didn't make our people any more pacific.'

'How d'you mean?' I ventured to ask.

'If you've ever been ground-circuited,' said the Mayor, 'you'll know it don't improve any man's temper to be held up straining against nothing. No, sir! Eight or nine hundred folk kept pawing and buzzing like flies in treacle for two hours, while a pack of perfectly safe Serviles invades their mental and spiritual privacy, may be amusing to watch, but they are not pleasant to handle afterwards.'

Pirolo chuckled.

'Our folk own themselves. They were of opinion things were

going too far and too fiery. I warned the Serviles; but they're born house-dwellers. Unless a fact hits 'em on the head, they cannot see it. Would you believe me, they went on to talk of what they called "popular government"? They did! They wanted us to go back to the old Voodoo-business of voting with papers and wooden boxes, and word-drunk people and printed formulas, and news-sheets! They said they practised it among themselves about what they'd have to eat in their flats and hotels. Yes, sir! They stood up behind Bluthner's doubled ground-circuits, and they said that, in this present year of grace, *to* self-owning men and women, *on* that very spot! Then they finished'—he lowered his voice cautiously—'by talking about "The People". And then Bluthner he had to sit up all night in charge of the circuits because he couldn't trust his men to keep 'em shut.'

'It was trying 'em too high,' the Chief of Police broke in. 'But we couldn't hold the crowd ground-circuited for ever. I gathered in all the Serviles on charge of crowd-making, and put 'em in the water-tower, and then I let things cut loose. I had to! The District lit like a sparked gas-tank!'

'The news was out over seven degrees of country,' the Mayor continued; 'and when once it's a question of invasion of privacy, goodbye to right and reason in Illinois! They began turning out traffic-lights and locking up landing-towers on Thursday night. Friday, they stopped all traffic and asked for the Board to take over. Then they wanted to clean Chicago off the side of the Lake and rebuild elsewhere—just for a souvenir of "The People" that the Serviles talked about. I suggested that they should slag the Old Market where the meeting was held, while I turned in a call to you all on the Board. That kept 'em quiet till you came along. And—and now *you* can take hold of the situation.'

'Any chance of their quieting down?' De Forest asked.

'You can try,' said the Mayor.

De Forest raised his voice in the face of the reviving crowd that had edged in towards us. Day was come.

'Don't you think this business can be arranged?' he began. But there was a roar of angry voices:

'We've finished with Crowds! We aren't going back to the Old Days! Take us over! Take the Serviles away! Administer direct or we'll kill 'em! Down with The People!'

An attempt was made to begin MacDonough's Song. It got no

further than the first line, for the *Victor Pirolo* sent down a warning drone on one stopped horn. A wrecked side-wall of the Old Market tottered and fell inwards on the slag-pools. None spoke or moved till the last of the dust had settled down again, turning the steel case of Salati's Statue ashy grey.

'You see you'll just *have* to take us over,' the Mayor whispered.

De Forest shrugged his shoulders.

'You talk as if executive capacity could be snatched out of the air like so much horse-power. Can't you manage yourselves on any terms?' he said.

'We can, if you say so. It will only cost those few lives to begin with.'

The Mayor pointed across the square, where Arnott's men guided a stumbling group of ten or twelve men and women to the lake front and halted them under the Statue.

'Now I think,' said Takahira under his breath, 'there will be trouble.'

The mass in front of us growled like beasts.

At that moment the sun rose clear, and revealed the blinking assembly to itself. As soon as it realized that it was a crowd we saw the shiver of horror and mutual repulsion shoot across it precisely as the steely flaws shot across the lake outside. Nothing was said, and, being half blind, of course it moved slowly. Yet in less than fifteen minutes most of that vast multitude—three thousand at the lowest count—melted away like frost on south eaves. The remnant stretched themselves on the grass, where a crowd feels and looks less like a crowd.

'These mean business,' the Mayor whispered to Takahira. 'There are a goodish few women there who've borne children. I don't like it.'

The morning draught off the lake stirred the trees round us with promise of a hot day; the sun reflected itself dazzlingly on the canister-shaped covering of Salati's Statue; cocks crew in the gardens, and we could hear gate-latches clicking in the distance as people stumblingly resought their homes.

'I'm afraid there won't be any morning deliveries,' said De Forest. 'We rather upset things in the country last night.'

'That makes no odds,' the Mayor returned. 'We're all provisioned for six months. *We* take no chances.'

Nor, when you come to think of it, does any one else. It must be three-quarters of a generation since any house or city faced a food shortage. Yet is there house or city on the Planet today that has not half a year's provisions laid in? We are like the shipwrecked seamen in the old books, who, having once nearly starved to death, ever afterwards hide away bits of food and biscuit. Truly we trust no Crowds, nor system based on Crowds!

De Forest waited till the last footstep had died away. Meantime the prisoners at the base of the Statue shuffled, posed, and fidgeted, with the shamelessness of quite little children. None of them were more than six feet high, and many of them were as grey-haired as the ravaged, harassed heads of old pictures. They huddled together in actual touch, while the crowd, spaced at large intervals, looked at them with congested eyes.

Suddenly a man among them began to talk. The Mayor had not in the least exaggerated. It appeared that our Planet lay sunk in slavery beneath the heel of the Aerial Board of Control. The orator urged us to arise in our might, burst our prison doors and break our fetters (all his metaphors, by the way, were of the most medieval). Next he demanded that every matter of daily life, including most of the physical functions, should be submitted for decision at any time of the week, month, or year to, I gathered, anybody who happened to be passing by or residing within a certain radius, and that everybody should forthwith abandon his concerns to settle the matter, first by crowd-making, next by talking to the crowds made, and lastly by describing crosses on pieces of paper, which rubbish should later be counted with certain mystic ceremonies and oaths. Out of this amazing play, he assured us, would automatically arise a higher, nobler, and kinder world, based—he demonstrated this with the awful lucidity of the insane—based on the sanctity of the Crowd and the villainy of the single person. In conclusion, he called loudly upon God to testify to his personal merits and integrity. When the flow ceased, I turned bewildered to Takahira, who was nodding solemnly.

'Quite correct,' said he. 'It is all in the old books. He has left nothing out, not even the war-talk.'

'But I don't see how this stuff can upset a child, much less a district,' I replied.

'Ah, you are too young,' said Dragomiroff. 'For another thing, you are not a mamma. Please look at the mammas.'

Ten or fifteen women who remained had separated themselves

from the silent men, and were drawing in towards the prisoners. It reminded one of the stealthy encircling, before the rush in at the quarry, of wolves round musk-oxen in the North. The prisoners saw, and drew together more closely. The Mayor covered his face with his hands for an instant. De Forest, bareheaded, stepped forward between the prisoners and the slowly, stiffly moving line.

'That's all very interesting,' he said to the dry-lipped orator. 'But the point seems to be that you've been making crowds and invading privacy.'

A woman stepped forward, and would have spoken, but there was a quick assenting murmur from the men, who realized that De Forest was trying to pull the situation down to ground-line.

'Yes! Yes!' they cried. 'We cut out because they made crowds and invaded privacy! Stick to that! Keep on that switch! Lift the Serviles out of this! The Board's in charge! Hsh!'

'Yes, the Board's in charge,' said De Forest. 'I'll take formal evidence of crowd-making if you like, but the Members of the Board can testify to it. Will that do?'

The women had closed in another pace, with hands that clenched and unclenched at their sides.

'Good! Good enough!' the men cried. 'We're content. Only take them away quickly.'

'Come along up!' said De Forest to the captives. 'Breakfast is quite ready.'

It appeared, however, that they did not wish to go. They intended to remain in Chicago and make crowds. They pointed out that De Forest's proposal was gross invasion of privacy.

'My dear fellow,' said Pirolo to the most voluble of the leaders, 'you hurry, or your crowd that can't be wrong will kill you!'

'But that would be murder,' answered the believer in crowds; and there was a roar of laughter from all sides that seemed to show the crisis had broken.

A woman stepped forward from the line of women, laughing, I protest, as merrily as any of the company. One hand, of course, shaded her eyes, the other was at her throat.

'Oh, they needn't be afraid of being killed!' she called.

'Not in the least,' said De Forest. 'But don't you think that, now the Board's in charge, you might go home while we get these people away?'

'I shall be home long before that. It—it has been rather a trying day.'

She stood up to her full height, dwarfing even De Forest's six-foot-eight, and smiled, with eyes closed against the fierce light.

'Yes, rather,' said De Forest. 'I'm afraid you feel the glare a little. We'll have the ship down.'

He motioned to the *Pirolo* to drop between us and the sun, and at the same time to loop-circuit the prisoners, who were a trifle unsteady. We saw them stiffen to the current where they stood. The woman's voice went on, sweet and deep and unshaken:

'I don't suppose you men realize how much this—this sort of thing means to a woman. I've borne three. We women don't want our children given to Crowds. It must be an inherited instinct. Crowds make trouble. They bring back the Old Days. Hate, fear, blackmail, publicity, "The People"—*That! That! That!*' She pointed to the Statue, and the crowd growled once more.

'Yes, if they are allowed to go on,' said De Forest. 'But this little affair——'

'It means so much to us women that this—this little affair should never happen again. Of course, never's a big word, but one feels so strongly that it is important to stop crowds at the very beginning. Those creatures'—she pointed with her left hand at the prisoners swaying like seaweed in a tideway as the circuit pulled them—'those people have friends and wives and children in the city and elsewhere. One doesn't want anything done to *them*, you know. It's terrible to force a human being out of fifty or sixty years of good life. I'm only forty myself. *I* know. But, at the same time, one feels that an example should be made, because no price is too heavy to pay if—if these people and *all that they imply* can be put an end to. Do you quite understand, or would you be kind enough to tell your men to take the casing off the Statue? It's worth looking at.'

'I understand perfectly. But I don't think anybody here wants to see the Statue on an empty stomach. Excuse me one moment.' De Forest called up to the ship, 'A flying loop ready on the port side, if you please.' Then to the woman he said with some crispness, 'You might leave us a little discretion in the matter.'

'Oh, of course. Thank you for being so patient. I know my arguments are silly, but——' She half turned away and went on in a changed voice, 'Perhaps this will help you to decide.'

She threw out her right arm with a knife in it. Before the blade could be returned to her throat or her bosom it was twitched from her grip, sparked as it flew out of the shadow of the ship above, and fell flashing in the sunshine at the foot of the Statue fifty yards away. The outflung arm was arrested, rigid as a bar for an instant, till the releasing circuit permitted her to bring it slowly to her side. The other women shrank back silent among the men.

Pirolo rubbed his hands, and Takahira nodded.

'That was clever of you, De Forest,' said he.

'What a glorious pose!' Dragomiroff murmured, for the frightened woman was on the edge of tears.

'Why did you stop me? I would have done it!' she cried.

'I have no doubt you would,' said De Forest. 'But we can't waste a life like yours on these people. I hope the arrest didn't sprain your wrist; it's so hard to regulate a flying loop. But I think you are quite right about those persons' women and children. We'll take them all away with us if you promise not to do anything stupid to yourself.'

'I promise—I promise.' She controlled herself with an effort. 'But it is so important to us women. We know what it means; and I thought if you saw I was in earnest——'

'I saw you were, and you've gained your point. I shall take all your Serviles away with me at once. The Mayor will make lists of their friends and families in the city and the district, and he'll ship them after us this afternoon.'

'Sure,' said the Mayor, rising to his feet. 'Keefe, if you can see, hadn't you better finish levelling off the Old Market? It don't look sightly the way it is now, and we shan't use it for crowds any more.'

'I think you had better wipe out that Statue as well, Mr Mayor,' said De Forest. 'I don't question its merits as a work of art, but I believe it's a shade morbid.'

'Certainly, sir. Oh, Keefe! Slag the Negro before you go on to fuse the Market. I'll get to the Communicators and tell the District that the Board is in charge. Are you making any special appointments, sir?'

'None. We haven't men to waste on these backwoods. Carry on as before, but under the Board. Arnott, run your Serviles aboard, please. Ground ship and pass them through the bilge-doors. We'll wait till we've finished with this work of art.'

The prisoners trailed past him, talking fluently, but unable to gesticulate in the drag of the current. Then the surfacers rolled up, two on each side of the Statue. With one accord the spectators looked elsewhere, but there was no need. Keefe turned on full power, and the thing simply melted within its case. All I saw was a surge of white-hot metal pouring over the plinth, a glimpse of Salati's inscription, 'To the Eternal Memory of the Justice of the People', ere the stone base itself cracked and powdered into finest lime. The crowd cheered.

'Thank you,' said De Forest; 'but we want our breakfasts, and I expect you do too. Goodbye, Mr Mayor! Delighted to see you at any time, but I hope I shan't have to, officially, for the next thirty years. Goodbye, madam. Yes. We're all given to nerves nowadays. I suffer from them myself. Goodbye, gentlemen all! You're under the tyrannous heel of the Board from this moment, but if ever you feel like breaking your fetters you've only to let us know. This is no treat to us. Good luck!'

We embarked amid shouts, and did not check our lift till they had dwindled into whispers. Then De Forest flung himself on the chartroom divan and mopped his forehead.

'I don't mind men,' he panted, 'but women are the devil!'

'Still the devil,' said Pirolo cheerfully. 'That one would have suicided.'

'I know it. That was why I signalled for the flying loop to be clapped on her. I owe you an apology for that, Arnott. I hadn't time to catch your eye, and you were busy with our caitiffs. By the way, who actually answered my signal? It was a smart piece of work.'

'Ilroy,' said Arnott; 'but he overloaded the wave. It may be pretty gallery-work to knock a knife out of a lady's hand, but didn't you notice how she rubbed 'em? He scorched her fingers. Slovenly, I call it.'

'Far be it from me to interfere with Fleet discipline, but don't be too hard on the boy. If that woman had killed herself they would have killed every Servile and everything related to a Servile throughout the district by nightfall.'

'That was what she was playing for,' Takahira said. 'And with our Fleet gone we could have done nothing to hold them.'

'I may be ass enough to walk into a ground-circuit,' said Arnott, 'but I don't dismiss my Fleet till I'm reasonably sure that trouble is over. They're in position still, and I intend to keep 'em there till the Serviles are shipped out of the district. That last little crowd meant murder, my friends.'

'Nerves! All nerves!' said Pirolo. 'You cannot argue with agoraphobia.'

'And it is not as if they had seen much dead—or *is* it?' said Takahira.

'In all my ninety years I have never seen death.' Dragomiroff spoke as one who would excuse himself. 'Perhaps that was why—last night——'

Then it came out as we sat over breakfast, that, with the exception of Arnott and Pirolo, none of us had ever seen a corpse, or knew in what manner the spirit passes.

'We're a nice lot to flap about governing the Planet,' De Forest laughed. 'I confess, now it's all over, that my main fear was I mightn't be able to pull it off without losing a life.'

'I thought of that too,' said Arnott; 'but there's no death reported, and I've enquired everywhere. What are we supposed to do with our passengers? I've fed 'em.'

'We're between two switches,' De Forest drawled. 'If we drop them in any place that isn't under the Board, the natives will make their presence an excuse for cutting out, same as Illinois did, and forcing the Board to take over. If we drop them in any place under the Board's control they'll be killed as soon as our backs are turned.'

'If you say so,' said Pirolo thoughtfully, 'I can guarantee that they will become extinct in process of time, quite happily. What is their birth-rate now?'

'Go down and ask 'em,' said De Forest.

'I think they might become nervous and tear me to bits,' the philosopher of Foggia replied.

'Not really? Well?'

'Open the bilge-doors,' said Takahira with a downward jerk of the thumb.

'Scarcely—after all the trouble we've taken to save 'em,' said De Forest.

'Try London,' Arnott suggested. 'You could turn Satan himself loose there, and they'd only ask him to dinner.'

'Good man! You've given me an idea. Vincent! Oh, Vincent!' He threw the General Communicator open so that we could all hear, and in a few minutes the chartroom filled with the rich, fruity voice of Leopold Vincent, who has purveyed all London her choicest amusements for the last thirty years. We answered with expectant grins, as though we were actually in the stalls of, say, the Combination on a first night.

'We've picked up something in your line,' De Forest began.

'That's good, dear man. If it's old enough. There's nothing to beat the old things for business purposes. Have you seen *London, Chatham, and Dover* at Earl's Court? No? I thought I missed you there. Im-mense! I've had the real steam locomotive engines built from the old designs and the iron rails cast specially by hand. Cloth cushions in the carriages, too! Im-mense! And paper railway tickets. And Polly Milton.'

'Polly Milton back again!' said Arnott rapturously. 'Book me two stalls for tomorrow night. What's she singing now, bless her?'

'The old songs. Nothing comes up to the old touch. Listen to this, dear men.' Vincent carolled with flourishes:

> Oh, cruel lamps of London,
> If tears your light could drown,
> Your victims' eyes would weep them,
> Oh, lights of London Town!

'Then they weep.'

'You see?' Pirolo waved his hands at us. 'The old world always weeped when it saw crowds together. It did not know why, but it weeped. We know why, but we do not weep, except when we pay to be made to by fat, wicked old Vincent.'

'Old, yourself!' Vincent laughed. 'I'm a public benefactor, I keep the world soft and united.'

'And I'm De Forest of the Board,' said De Forest acidly, 'trying to get a little business done. As I was saying, I've picked up a few people in Chicago.'

'I cut out. Chicago is——'

'Do listen! They're perfectly unique.'

'Do they build houses of baked mudblocks while you wait—eh? That's an old contact.'

'They're an untouched primitive community, with all the old ideas.'

'Sewing-machines and maypole-dances? Cooking on coal-gas stoves, lighting pipes with matches, and driving horses? Gerolstein tried that last year. An absolute blow-out!'

De Forest plugged him wrathfully, and poured out the story of our doings for the last twenty-four hours on the top-note.

'And they do it *all* in public,' he concluded. 'You can't stop 'em. The more public, the better they are pleased. They'll talk for hours—like you! Now you can come in again!'

'Do you really mean they know how to vote?' said Vincent. 'Can they act it?'

'Act? It's their life to 'em! And you never saw such faces! Scarred like volcanoes. Envy, hatred, and malice in plain sight. Wonderfully flexible voices. They weep, too.'

'Aloud? In public?'

'I guarantee. Not a spark of shame or reticence in the entire installation. It's the chance of your career.'

'D'you say you've brought their voting props along—those papers and ballot-box things?'

'No, confound you! I'm not a luggage-lifter. Apply direct to the Mayor of Chicago. He'll forward you everything. Well?

'Wait a minute. Did Chicago want to kill 'em? That 'ud look well on the Communicators.'

'Yes! They were only rescued with difficulty from a howling mob—if you know what that is.'

'But I don't,' answered the Great Vincent simply.

'Well then, they'll tell you themselves. They can make speeches hours long.'

'How many are there?'

'By the time we ship 'em all over they'll be perhaps a hundred, counting children. An old world in miniature. Can't you see it?'

'M-yes; but I've got to pay for it if it's a blow-out, dear man.'

'They can sing the old war songs in the streets. They can get word-drunk, and make crowds, and invade privacy in the genuine old-fashioned way; and they'll do the voting trick as often as you ask 'em a question.'

'Too good!' said Vincent.

'You unbelieving Jew! I've got a dozen head aboard here. I'll put you through direct. Sample 'em yourself.'

He lifted the switch and we listened. Our passengers on the lower deck at once, but not less than five at a time, explained themselves to Vincent. They had been taken from the bosom of their families, stripped of their possessions, given food without finger-bowls, and cast into captivity in a noisome dungeon.

'But look here,' said Arnott aghast; 'they're saying what isn't true. My lower deck isn't noisome, and I saw to the finger-bowls myself.'

'My people talk like that sometimes in Little Russia,' said Dragomiroff. 'We reason with them. We never kill. No!'

'But it's not true,' Arnott insisted. 'What can you do with people who don't tell facts? They're mad!'

'Hsh!' said Pirolo, his hand to his ear. 'It is such a little time since all the Planet told lies.'

We heard Vincent silkily sympathetic. Would they, he asked, repeat their assertions in public—before a vast public? only let Vincent give them a chance, and the Planet, they vowed, should ring with their wrongs. Their aim in life—two women and a man explained it together—was to reform the world. Oddly enough, this also had been Vincent's life-dream. He offered them an arena in which to explain, and by their living example to raise the Planet to loftier levels. He was eloquent on the moral uplift of a simple, old-world life presented in its entirety to a deboshed civilization.

Could they—would they—for three months certain, devote themselves under his auspices, as missionaries, to the elevation of mankind at a place called Earl's Court, which he said, with some truth, was one of the intellectual centres of the Planet? They thanked him, and demanded (we could hear his chuckle of delight) time to discuss and to vote on the matter. The vote, solemnly managed by counting heads—one head, one vote—was favourable. His offer, therefore, was accepted, and they moved a vote of thanks to him in two speeches—one by what they called the 'proposer' and the other by the 'seconder'.

Vincent threw over to us, his voice shaking with gratitude:

'I've got 'em! Did you hear those speeches? That's Nature, dear men. Art can't teach *that*. And they voted as easily as lying. I've never had a troupe of natural liars before. Bless you, dear men! Remember, you're on my free lists for ever, anywhere—all of you. Oh, Gerolstein will be sick—sick!'

'Then you think they'll do?' said De Forest.

'Do? The Little Village'll go crazy! I'll knock up a series of old-world plays for 'em. Their voices will make you laugh and cry. My God, dear men, where *do* you suppose they picked up all their misery from, on this sweet earth? I'll have a pageant of the world's beginnings, and Mosenthal shall do the music. I'll——'

'Go and knock up a village for 'em by tonight. We'll meet you at No. 15 West Landing Tower,' said De Forest. 'Remember the rest will be coming along tomorrow.'

'Let 'em all come!' said Vincent. 'You don't know how hard it is nowadays even for me, to find something that really gets under the public's damned iridium-plated hide. But I've got it at last. Goodbye!'

'Well,' said De Forest when we had finished laughing, 'if any one understood corruption in London I might have played off Vincent against Gerolstein, and sold my captives at enormous prices. As it is, I shall have to be their legal adviser tonight when the contracts are signed. And they won't exactly press any commission on me, either.'

'Meantime,' said Takahira, 'we cannot, of course, confine members of Leopold Vincent's last-engaged company. Chairs for the ladies, please, Arnott.'

'Then I go to bed,' said De Forest. 'I can't face any more women!' And he vanished.

When our passengers were released and given another meal (finger-bowls came first this time) they told us what they thought of us and the Board; and, like Vincent, we all marvelled how they had contrived to extract and secrete so much bitter poison and unrest out of the good life God gives us. They raged, they stormed, they palpitated, flushed and exhausted their poor, torn nerves, panted themselves into silence, and renewed the senseless, shameless attacks.

'But can't you understand,' said Pirolo pathetically to a shrieking woman, 'that if we'd left you in Chicago you'd have been killed?'

'No, we shouldn't. You were bound to save us from being murdered.'

'Then we should have had to kill a lot of other people.'

'That doesn't matter. We were preaching the Truth. You can't stop us. We shall go on preaching in London; and *then* you'll see!'

'You can see now,' said Pirolo, and opened a lower shutter.

We were closing on the Little Village, with her three million people spread out at ease inside her ring of girdling Main-Traffic lights—those eight fixed beams at Chatham, Tonbridge, Redhill, Dorking, Woking, St Albans, Chipping Ongar, and Southend.

Leopold Vincent's new company looked, with small pale faces, at the silence, the size, and the separated houses.

Then some began to weep aloud, shamelessly—always without shame.

THE METAL MAN

JACK WILLIAMSON

The Metal Man stands in a dark, dusty corner of the Tyburn College Museum. Just who is responsible for the figure being moved there, or why it was done, I do not know. To the casual eye it looks to be merely an ordinary life-size statue. The visitor who gives it a closer view marvels at the minute perfection of the detail of hair and skin; at the silent tragedy in the set, determined expression and poise; and at the remarkable greenish cast of the metal of which it is composed, but, most of all, at the peculiar mark upon the chest. It is a six-sided blot, of a deep crimson hue, with the surface oddly granular and strange wavering lines radiating from it—lines of a lighter shade of red.

Of course it is generally known that the Metal Man was once Professor Thomas Kelvin of the Geology Department. There are current many garbled and inaccurate accounts of the weird disaster that befell him. I believe I am the only one to whom he entrusted his story. It is to put these fantastic tales at rest that I have decided to publish the narrative that Kelvin sent me.

For some years he had been spending his summer vacations along the Pacific coast of Mexico, prospecting for radium. It was three months since he had returned from his last expedition. Evidently he had been successful beyond his wildest dreams. He did not come to Tyburn, but we heard stories of his selling millions of dollars worth of salts of radium, and giving as much more to institutions employing radium treatment. And it was said that he was sick of a strange disorder that defied the world's best specialists, and that he was pouring out his millions in the establishment of scholarships and endowments as if he expected to die soon.

One cold, stormy day, when the sea was running high on the unprotected coast which the cottage overlooks, I saw a sail out to the north. It rapidly drew nearer until I could tell that it was a small sailing schooner with auxiliary power. She was running with the wind, but a half mile offshore she came up into it and the sails were lowered. Soon a boat had put off in the direction of the shore. The sea was not so rough as to make the landing hazardous, but the proceeding was rather unusual, and, as I had nothing better to do, I went out in the yard before my modest house, which stands perhaps two hundred yards above the beach, in order to have a better view.

When the boat touched, four men sprang out and rushed it up higher on the sand. As a fifth tall man arose in the stern, the four picked up a great chest and started up in my direction. The fifth person followed leisurely. Silently, and without invitation, the men brought the chest up the beach, and into my yard, and set it down in front of the door.

The fifth man, a hard-faced Yankee skipper, walked up to me and said gruffly, 'I am Captain McAndrews.'

'I'm glad to meet you, Captain,' I said , wondering. 'There must be some mistake. I was not expecting—'

'Not at all,' he said abruptly. 'The man in that chest was transferred to my ship from the liner *Plutonia* three days ago. He has paid me for my services, and I believe his instructions have been carried out. Good day, sir.'

He turned on his heel and started away.

'A man in the chest!' I exclaimed.

He walked on unheeding, and the seamen followed. I stood and watched them walk down to the boat and row back to the schooner. I gazed at its sails until they were lost against the dull blue of the clouds. Frankly, I feared to open the chest.

At last I nerved myself to do it. It was unlocked. I threw back the lid. With a shock of uncontrollable horror that left me half sick for hours, I saw in it, stark naked, with the strange crimson mark standing lividly out from the pale green of the breast, the Metal Man, just as you may see him in the Museum.

Of course, I knew at once that it was Kelvin. For a long time I bent, trembling and staring at him. Then I saw an old canteen, purple-stained, lying by the head of the figure, and under it, a sheaf of manuscript. I got the latter out, walked with shaken steps to the easy chair in the house, and read the story that follows:

'Dear Russell,

'You are my best—my only—intimate friend. I have arranged to have my body and this story brought to you. I just drank the last of the wonderful purple liquid that has kept me alive since I came back, and I have scant time to finish this necessarily brief account of my adventure. But my affairs are in order and I die in peace. I had myself transferred to the schooner today, in order to reach you as soon as could be and to avoid possible complications. I trust Captain McAndrews. When I left France, I hoped to see you before the end. But Fate ruled otherwise.

'You know that the goal of my expedition was the headwaters of El Rio de la Sangre, "The River of Blood". It is a small stream whose strangely red waters flow into the Pacific. On my trip last year I had discovered that its waters were powerfully radioactive. Water has the power of absorbing radium emanations and emitting them in turn, and I hoped to find radium-bearing minerals in the bed of the upper river. Twenty-five miles above the mouth the river emerges from the Cordilleras. There are a few miles of rapids and back of them the river plunges down a magnificent waterfall. No exploring party had ever been back of the falls. I had hired an Indian guide and made a muleback journey to their foot. At once I saw the futility of attempting to climb the precipitous escarpment. But the water there was even more powerfully radioactive than at the mouth. There was nothing to do but return.

'This summer I bought a small monoplane. Though it was comparatively slow in speed and able to spend only six hours aloft, its light weight and the small area needed for landing, made it the only machine suitable for use in so rough a country. The steamer left me again on the dock at the little town of Vaca Morena, with my stack of crates and gasoline tins. After a visit to the Alcalde I secured the use of an abandoned shed for a hangar. I set about assembling the plane and in a fortnight I had completed the task. It was a beautiful little machine, with a wingspread of only twenty-five feet.

'Then, one morning, I started the engine and made a trial flight. It flew smoothly and in the afternoon I refilled the tanks and set off for the Rio de la Sangre. The stream looked like a red snake crawling out to the sea—there was something serpentine in its aspect. Flying high, I followed it, above the falls and into a region of towering mountain peaks. The river disappeared beneath a mountain. For a moment I thought of landing, and then it occurred to me that it flowed subterraneously for only a few miles, and would reappear further inland.

'I soared over the cliffs and came over the crater.

'A great pool of green fire it was, fully ten miles across to the black ramparts at the further side. The surface of the green was so smooth that at first I thought it was a lake, and then I knew that it must be a pool of heavy gas. In the glory of the evening sun the snow-capped summits about were brilliant argent crowns, dyed with crimson, tinged with purple and gold, tinted with strange and incredibly beautiful hues. Amid this wild scenery, nature had placed her greatest treasure. I knew that in the crater I would find the radium I sought.

'I circled about the place, rapt in wonder. As the sun sank lower, a light silver mist gathered on the peaks, half veiling their wonders, and flowed toward the crater. It seemed drawn with a strange attraction. And then the centre of the green lake rose in a shining peak. It flowed up into a great hill of emerald fire. Something was rising in the green—carrying it up! Then the vapour flowed back, revealing a strange object, still veiled faintly by the green and silver clouds. It was a gigantic sphere of deep red, marked with four huge oval spots of dull black. Its surface was smooth, metallic, and thickly studded with great spikes that seemed of yellow fire. It was a machine, inconceivably great in size. It spun slowly as it rose, on a vertical axis, moving with a deliberate, purposeful motion.

'It came up to my own level, paused and seemed to spin faster. And the silver mist was drawn to the yellow points, condensing, curdling, until the whole globe was a ball of lambent argent. For a moment it hung, unbelievably glorious in the light of the setting sun, and then it sank—ever faster—until it dropped like a plummet into the sea of green.

'And with its fall a sinister darkness descended upon the desolate wilderness of the peaks, and I was seized by a fear that had been deadened by amazement, and realized that I had scant time to reach Vaca Morena before complete darkness fell. Immediately I put the plane about in the direction of the town. According to my recollections, I had, at the time, no very definite idea of what it was I had seen, or whether the weird exhibition had been caused by human or natural agencies. I remember thinking that in such enormous quantities as undoubtedly the crater contained it, radium might possess qualities unnoticed in small amounts, or, again, that there might be present radioactive minerals at present unknown. It occurred to me also that perhaps some other scientists had already discovered the deposits and that what I had witnessed had been the trial of an airship in which radium was utilized as a propellant. I was considerably shaken, but not much alarmed. What happened later would have seemed incredible to me then.

'And then I noticed that a pale bluish luminosity was gathering about the cowl of the cockpit, and in a moment I saw that the whole machine, and even my own person, was covered with it. It was somewhat like St Elmo's Fire, except that it covered all surfaces indiscriminately, instead of being restricted to sharp points. All at once I connected the phenomenon with the thing I had seen. I felt no physical discomfort, and the motor continued to run, but as the blue radiance continued to increase, I observed that my body felt heavier, and that the machine was being drawn downward! My mind was flooded with wonder and terror. I fought to retain sufficient self-possession to fly the ship. My arms were soon so heavy that I could hold them upon the controls only with difficulty, and I felt a slight dizziness, due, no doubt, to the blood's being drawn from my head. When I recovered, I was already almost upon the green. Somehow, my gravitation had been increased and I was being drawn into the pit! It was possible to keep the plane under control only by diving and keeping at a high speed.

'I plunged into the green pool. The gas was not suffocating, as I had anticipated. In fact, I noticed no change in the atmosphere, save that my vision was limited to a few yards around. The wings of the plane were still distinctly discernible. Suddenly a smooth, sandy plain was murkily revealed below, and I was able to level the ship off enough for a safe landing. As I came to a stop I saw that the sand was slightly luminous, as the green mist seemed to be, and red. For a time I was confined to the ship by my own weight, but I noticed that the blue was slowly dissipating, and with it, its effect.

'As soon as I was able, I clambered over the side of the cockpit, carrying my canteen and automatic, which were themselves immensely heavy. I was unable to stand erect, but I crawled off over the coarse, shining red sand, stopping at frequent intervals to lie flat and rest. I was in deathly fear of the force that had brought me down. I was sure it had been directed by intelligence. The floor was so smooth and level that I supposed it to be the bottom of an ancient lake.

'Sometimes I looked fearfully back, and when I was a hundred yards away I saw a score of lights floating through the green towards the airplane. In the luminous murk each bright point was surrounded by a disc of paler blue. I didn't move, but lay and watched them float to the plane and wheel about it with a slow, heavy motion. Closer and lower they came until they reached the ground about it. The mist was so thick as to obscure the details of the scene.

'When I went to resume my flight, I found my excess of gravity almost entirely gone, though I went on hands and knees for another hundred yards to escape possible observation. When I got to my feet, the plane was lost to view. I walked on for perhaps a quarter of a mile and suddenly realized that my sense of direction was altogether gone. I was completely lost in a strange world, inhabited by beings whose nature and disposition I could not even guess! And then I realized that it was the height of folly to walk about when any step might precipitate me into a danger of which I could know nothing. I had a peculiarly unpleasant feeling of helpless fear.

'The luminous red sand and the shining green of the air lay about in all directions, unbroken by a single solid object. There was no life, no sound, no motion. The air hung heavy and stagnant. The flat sand was like the surface of a dead and desolate sea. I felt the panic of utter isolation from humanity. The mist seemed to come closer; the strange evil in it seemed to grow more alert.

'Suddenly a darting light passed meteor-like through the green above and in my alarm I ran a few blundering steps. My foot struck a light object that rang like metal. The sharpness of the concussion filled me with fear, but in an instant the light was gone. I bent down to see what I had kicked.

'It was a metal bird—an eagle formed of metal—with the wings outspread, the talons gripping, the fierce beak set open. The colour was white, tinged with green. It weighed no more than the living bird. At first I thought it was a cast model, and then I saw that each feather was complete and flexible. Somehow, a real eagle had been turned to metal! It seemed incredible, yet here was the concrete proof. I wondered if the radium deposits, which I had already used to explain so much, might account for this too. I knew that science held transmutation of elements to be possible—had even accomplished it in a limited way, and that radium itself was the product of the disintegration of ionium, and ionium that of uranium.

'I was struck with fright for my own safety. Might I be changed to metal? I looked to see if there were other metal things about.

And I found them in abundance. Half-buried in the glowing sands were metal birds of every kind—birds that had flown over the surrounding cliffs. And, at the climax of my search, I found a pterosant—a flying reptile that had invaded the pit in ages past—changed to ageless metal. Its wingspread was fully fifteen feet—it would be a treasure in any museum.

'I made a fearful examination of myself, and to my unutterable horror, I perceived that the tips of my fingernails, and the fine hairs upon my hands, *were already changed to light green metal!* The shock unnerved me completely. You cannot conceive my horror. I screamed aloud in agony of soul, careless of the terrible foes that the sound might attract. I ran off wildly. I was blind, unreasoning. I felt no fatigue as I ran, only stark terror.

'Bright, swift-moving lights passed above in the green, but I heeded them not. Suddenly I came upon the great sphere that I had seen above. It rested motionless in a cradle of black metal. The yellow fire was gone from the spikes, but the red surface shone with a metallic lustre. Lights floated about it. They made little bright spots in the green, like lanterns swinging in a fog. I turned and ran again, desperately. I took no note of direction, nor of the passage of time.

'Then I came upon a bank of violet vegetation. Waist-deep it was, grass-like, with thick narrow leaves, dotted with clusters of small pink blooms, and little purple berries. And a score of yards beyond I saw a sluggish red stream—El Rio de la Sangre. Here was cover at last. I threw myself down in the violet growth and lay sobbing with fatigue and terror. For a long time I was unable to stir or think. When I looked again at my fingernails, the tips of metal had doubled in width.

'I tried to control my agitation, and to think. Possibly the lights, whatever they were, would sleep by day. If I could find the plane, or scale the walls, I might escape the fearful action of the radioactive minerals before it was too late. I realized that I was hungry. I plucked off a few of the purple berries and tasted them. They had a salty, metallic taste, and I thought they would be valueless for food. But in pulling them I had inadvertently squeezed the juice from one upon my fingers, and when I wiped it off I saw, to my amazement and my inexpressible joy, that the rim of metal was gone from the fingernails it had touched. I had discovered a means of safety! I suppose that the plants were able to exist there only because they had been so developed that they produced compounds counteracting the metal-forming emanations. Probably their evolution began when the action was far weaker than now, and only those able to withstand the more intense radiations had survived. I lost no time in eating a cluster of the berries, and then I poured the water from my canteen and filled it with their juice. I have analysed the fluid; it corresponds in some ways with the standard formulas for the neutralization of radium burns, and doubtless it saved me from the terrible burns caused by the action of ordinary radium.

'I lay there until dawn, dozing a little at times, only to start into wakefulness without cause. It seemed that some daylight filtered through the green, for at dawn it grew paler, and even the red sand appeared less luminous. After eating a few more of the berries, I ascertained the direction in which the stagnant red water was moving, and set off down-stream, towards the west. In order to get an idea of where I was going, I counted my paces. I had walked about two and a half miles, along by the violet plants, when I came to an abrupt cliff. It towered up until it was lost in the green gloom. It seemed to be mostly of black pitchblende. The barrier seemed absolutely unscalable. The red river plunged out of sight by the cliff in a racing whirlpool.

'I walked off north around the rim. I had no very definite plan, except to try to find a way out over the cliffs. If I failed in that, it would be time to hunt the plane. I had a mortal fear of going near it, or of encountering the strange lights I had seen floating about it. As I went I saw none of them. I suppose they slept when it was day.

'I went on until it must have been noon, though my watch had stopped. Occasionally I passed metal trees that had fallen from above, and once, the metallic body of a bear that had slipped off a path above, some time in past ages. And there were metal birds without number. They must have been accumulating through geological ages. All along up to this, the cliff had risen perpendicularly to the limit of my vision, but now I saw a wide ledge, with a sloping wall beyond it, dimly visible above. But the sheer wall rose a full hundred feet to the shelf, and I cursed at my inability to surmount it. For a time I stood there, devising impractical means for climbing it, driven almost to tears by my impotence. I was ravenously hungry, and thirsty as well.

'At last I went on.

'In an hour I came upon it. A slender cylinder of black metal, that towered a hundred feet into the greenish mist, and carried at the top, a great mushroom-shaped orange flame. It was a strange thing. The fire was as big as a balloon, bright and steady. It looked much like a great jet of combustible gas, burning as it streamed from the cylinder. I stood petrified in amazement, wondering vaguely at the what and why of the thing.

'And then I saw more of them back of it, dimly—scores of them—a whole forest of flames.

'I crouched back against the cliff, while I considered. Here I supposed, was the city of the lights. They were sleeping now, but still I had not the courage to enter. According to my calculations I had gone about fifteen miles. Then I must be, I thought, almost diametrically opposite the place where the crimson river flowed under the wall, with half of the rim unexplored. If I wished to continue my journey, I must go around the city, if I may call it that.

'So I left the wall. Soon it was lost to view. I tried to keep in view of the orange flames, but abruptly they were gone in the mist. I walked more to the left, but I came upon nothing but the wastes of red sand, with the green murk above. On and on I wandered. Then the sand and the air grew slowly brighter and I knew that night had fallen. The lights were soon passing to and fro. I had seen lights the night before, but they travelled high and fast. These, on the other hand, sailed low, and I felt that they were searching.

'I knew that they were hunting for me. I lay down in a little hollow in the sand. Vague, mist-veiled points of light came near and passed. And then one stopped directly overhead. It descended and the circle of radiance grew about it. I knew that it was useless to run, and I could not have done so, for my terror. Down and down it came.

'And then I saw its form. The thing was of a glittering, blazing crystal. A great-six-sided, upright prism of red, a dozen feet in length, it was, with a six-pointed structure like a snowflake about the centre, deep blue, with pointed blue flanges running from the points of the star to angles of the prism! Soft scarlet fire flowed from the points. And on each face of the prism, above and below the star, was a purple cone that must have been an eye. Strange pulsating lights flickered in the crystal. It was alive with light.

'It fell straight towards me!

'It was a terribly, utterly alien form of life. It was not human, not animal—not even life as we know it at all. And yet it had intelligence. But it was strange and foreign and devoid of feeling. It is curious to say that even then, as I lay beneath it, the thought came to me, that the thing and its fellows must have crystallized when the waters of the ancient sea dried out of the crater. Crystallizing salts take intricate forms.

'I drew my automatic and fired three times, but the bullets ricocheted harmlessly off the polished facets.

'It dropped until the gleaming lower point of the prism was not a yard above me. Then the scarlet fire reached out caressingly—flowed over my body. My weight grew less. I was lifted, held against the point. You may see its mark upon my chest. The thing floated into the air, carrying me. Soon others were drifting about. I was overcome with nausea. The scene grew black and I knew no more.

'I awoke floating free in a brilliant orange light. I touched no solid object. I writhed, kicked about—at nothingness. I could not move or turn over, because I could get a hold on nothing. My memory of the last two days seemed a nightmare. My clothing was still upon me. My canteen still hung, or rather floated, by my shoulder. And my automatic was in my pocket. I had the sensation that a great space of time had passed. There was a curious stiffness in my side. I examined it and found a red scar. I believe those crystal things had cut into me. And I found, with a horror you cannot understand, the mark upon my chest. Presently it dawned upon me that I was floating, devoid of gravity and free as an object in space, in the orange flame at the top of one of the black cylinders. The crystals knew the secret of gravity. It was vital to them. And peering about, I discerned, with infinite repulsion, a great flashing body, a few yards away. But its inner lights were dead, so I knew that it was day, and that the strange beings were sleeping.

'If I was ever to escape, this was the opportunity. I kicked, clawed desperately at the air, all in vain. I did not move an inch. If they had chained me, I could not have been more secure. I drew my automatic, resolved on a desperate measure. They would not find me again, alive. And as I had it in my hand, an idea came into my mind. I pointed the gun to the side, and fired six rapid shots. And the recoil of each explosion sent me drifting faster, rocket-wise, toward the edge.

'I shot out into the green. Had my gravity been suddenly restored, I might have been killed by the fall, but I descended slowly, and felt a curious lightness for several minutes. And to my surprise, when I struck the ground, the airplane was right before me! They had drawn it up by the base of the tower. It seemed to be intact. I started the engine with nervous haste, and sprang into the cockpit. As I started, another black tower loomed up abruptly before me, but I veered around it, and took off in safety.

'In a few moments I was above the green. I half expected the gravitational wave to be turned on me again, but higher and higher I rose unhindered until the accursed black walls were about me no longer. The sun blazed high in the heavens. Soon I had landed again at Vaca Morena.

'I had had enough of radium hunting. On the beach, where I landed, I sold the plane to a rancher at his own price, and told him to reserve a place for me on the next steamer, due in three days. Then I went to the town's single inn, ate, and went to bed. At noon the next day, when I got up, I found that my shoes and the pockets of my clothes contained a good bit of the red sand from the crater that had been collected as I crawled about in flight from the crystal lights. I saved some of it for curiosity alone; but when I analysed it, I found it a radium compound so rich that the little handful was worth millions of dollars.

'But the fortune was of little value, for, despite frequent doses of the fluid from my canteen, and the best medical aid, I have suffered continually, and now that my canteen is empty, I am doomed.

'Your friend, Thomas Kelvin'

Thus the manuscript ends. If the reader doubts the truth of the letter, he may see the Metal Man in the Tyburn Museum.

A MARTIAN ODYSSEY

STANLEY G. WEINBAUM

Jarvis stretched himself as luxuriously as he could in the cramped general quarters of the *Ares*.

'Air you can breathe!' he exulted. 'It feels as thick as soup after the thin stuff out there!' He nodded at the Martian landscape stretching flat and desolate in the light of the nearer moon, beyond the glass of the port.

The other three stared at him sympathetically—Putz, the engineer, Leroy, the biologist, and Harrison, the astronomer and captain of the expedition. Dick Jarvis was chemist of the famous crew, the *Ares* expedition, first human beings to set foot on the mysterious neighbour of the Earth, the planet Mars. This, of course, was in the old days, less than twenty years after the mad American Doheny perfected the atomic blast at the cost of his life, and only a decade after the equally mad Cardoza rode on it to the Moon. They were true pioneers, these four of the *Ares*. Except for a half-dozen Moon expeditions and the ill-fated de Lancey flight aimed at the seductive orb of Venus, they were the first men to feel other gravity than earth's, and certainly the first successful crew to leave the Earth–Moon system. And they deserved that success when one considers the difficulties and discomforts—the months spent in acclimatization chambers back on Earth, learning to breathe the air as tenuous as that of Mars, the challenging of the void in the tiny rocket driven by the cranky reaction motors of the twenty-first century, and mostly the facing of an absolutely unknown world.

Jarvis stretched and fingered the raw and peeling tip of his frost-bitten nose. He sighed again contentedly.

'Well,' exploded Harrison abruptly, 'are we going to hear what happened? You set out all shipshape in an auxiliary rocket, we don't get a peep for ten days, and finally Putz here picks you out of a lunatic ant-heap with a freak ostrich as your pal! Spill it, man!'

'Speel?' queried Leroy perplexedly. 'Speel what?'

'He means "*spiel*"', explained Putz soberly. 'It iss to tell.'

Jarvis met Harrison's amused glance without the shadow of a smile. 'That's right, Karl,' he said in grave agreement with Putz. '*Ich spiel es!*' He grunted comfortably and began.

'According to orders,' he said, 'I watched Karl here take off towards the North, and then I got into my flying sweat-box and headed South. You'll remember, Cap—we had orders not to land, but just scout about for points of interest. I set the two cameras clicking and buzzed along, riding pretty high—about two thousand feet—for a couple of reasons. First, it gave the cameras a greater field, and second, the under-jets travel so far in this half-vacuum they call air here that they stir up dust if you move low.'

'We know all that from Putz,' grunted Harrison. 'I wish you'd saved the films, though. They'd have paid the cost of this junket; remember how the public mobbed the first moon pictures?'

'The films are safe,' retorted Jarvis. 'Well,' he resumed, 'as I said, I buzzed along at a pretty good clip; just as we figured, the wings haven't much lift in this air at less than a hundred miles per hour, and even then I had to use the under-jets.

'So, with the speed and the altitude and the blurring caused by the under-jets, the seeing wasn't any too good. I could see enough, though, to distinguish that what I sailed over was just more of this grey plain that we'd been examining the whole week since our landing—same blobby growths and the same eternal carpet of crawling little plant-animals, or biopods, as Leroy calls them. So I sailed along, calling back my position every hour as instructed, and not knowing whether you heard me.'

'I did!' snapped Harrison.

'A hundred and fifty miles south,' continued Jarvis imperturbably, 'the surface changed to a sort of low plateau, nothing but desert and orange-tinted sand. I figured that we were right in our guess, then, and this grey plain we dropped on was really the Mare Cimmerium, which would make my orange desert the region called Xanthus. If I were right, I ought to hit another grey plain, the Mare Chronium in another couple of hundred miles, and then another orange desert, Thyle I or II. And so I did.'

'Putz verified our position a week and a half ago!' grumbled the captain. 'Let's get to the point.'

'Coming!' remarked Jarvis. 'Twenty miles into Thyle—believe it or not—I crossed a canal!'

'Putz photographed a hundred! Let's hear something new!'

'And did he also see a city?'

'Twenty of 'em, if you call those heaps of mud cities!'

'Well,' observed Jarvis, 'from here on I'll be telling a few things Putz didn't see!' He rubbed his tingling nose, and continued, 'I knew that I had sixteen hours of daylight at this season, so eight hours—eight hundred miles—from here, I decided to turn back. I was still over Thyle, whether I or II I'm not sure, not more than twenty-five miles into it. And right there, Putz's pet motor quit!'

'Quit? How?' Putz was solicitous.

'The atomic blast got weak. I started losing altitude right away, and suddenly there I was with a thump right in the middle of Thyle! Smashed my nose on the window, too!' He rubbed the injured member ruefully.

'Did you maybe try vashing der combustion chamber mit acid sulphuric?' enquired Putz. 'Sometimes der lead giffs a secondary radiation—'

'Naw!' said Jarvis disgustedly. 'I wouldn't try that, of course—not more than ten times! Besides, the bump flattened the landing gear and busted off the under-jets. Suppose I got the thing working—what then? Ten miles with the blast coming right out of the bottom and I'd have melted the floor from under me!' He rubbed his nose again. 'Lucky for me a pound only weighs seven ounces here, or I'd have been mashed flat!'

'I could have fixed!' ejaculated the engineer. 'I bet it vas not serious.'

'Probably not,' agreed Jarvis sarcastically. 'Only it wouldn't fly. Nothing serious, but I had my choice of waiting to be picked up or trying to walk back—eight hundred miles, and perhaps twenty days before we had to leave! Forty miles a day! Well,' he concluded, 'I chose to walk. Just as much chance of being picked up, and it kept me busy.'

'We'd have found you,' said Harrison.

'No doubt. Anyway, I rigged up a harness from some seat straps, and put the water tank on my back, took a cartridge belt and revolver, and some iron rations, and started out.'

'Water tank!' exclaimed the little biologist, Leroy. 'She weigh one-quarter ton!'

'Wasn't full. Weighed about two hundred and fifty pounds earth-weight, which is eighty-five here. Then, besides, my own personal two hundred and ten pounds is only seventy on Mars, so, tank and all, I grossed a hundred and fifty-five, or fifty-five pounds less than my everyday Earth-weight. I figured on that when I undertook the forty-mile daily stroll. Oh—of course I took a thermoskin sleeping bag for these wintry Martian nights.

'Off I went, bouncing along pretty quickly. Eight hours of daylight meant twenty miles or more. It got tiresome, of course—plugging along over a soft sand desert with nothing to see, not even Leroy's crawling biopods. But an hour or so brought me to the canal—just a dry ditch about four hundred feet wide, and straight as a railroad on its own company map.

'There'd been water in it sometime, though. The ditch was covered with what looked like a nice green lawn. Only, as I approached, the lawn moved out of my way!'

'Eh?' said Leroy.

'Yeah, it was a relative of your biopods. I caught one—a little grass-like blade about as long as my finger, with two thin, stemmy legs.'

'He is where?' Leroy was eager.

'He is let go! I had to move, so I ploughed along with the walking grass opening in front and closing behind. And then I was out on the orange desert of Thyle again.

'I plugged steadily along, cussing the sand that made going so tiresome, and, incidentally, cussing that cranky motor of yours, Karl. It was just before twilight that I reached the edge of Thyle, and looked down over the grey Mare Chronium. And I knew there was seventy-five miles of *that* to be walked over, and then a couple of hundred miles of that Xanthus desert, and about as much more Mare Cimmerium. Was I pleased? I started cussing you fellows for not picking me up!'

'We were trying, you sap!' said Harrison.

'That didn't help. Well, I figured I might as well use what was left of daylight in getting down the cliff that bounded Thyle. I found an easy place, and down I went. Mare Chronium was just the same sort of place as this—crazy leafless plants and a bunch of crawlers; I gave it a glance and hauled out my sleeping bag. Up to that time, you know, I hadn't seen anything worth worrying about on this half-dead world—nothing dangerous, that is.'

'Did you?' queried Harrison.

'*Did I!* You'll hear about it when I come to it. Well, I was just about to turn in when suddenly I heard the wildest sort of shenanigans!'

'Vot iss shenanigans?' enquired Putz.

'He says, "Je ne sais quoi,"' explained Leroy. 'It is to say, "I don't know what".'

'That's right,' agreed Jarvis. 'I didn't know what, so I sneaked over to find out. There was a racket like a flock of crows eating a bunch of canaries—whistles, cackles, caws, trills, and what have you. I rounded a clump of stumps, and there was Tweel!'

'Tweel?' said Harrison, and 'Tveel?' said Leroy and Putz.

'That freak ostrich,' explained the narrator. 'At least, Tweel is as near as I can pronounce it without sputtering. He called it something like "Trrrweerrlll".'

'What was he doing?' asked the Captain.

'He was being eaten! And squealing, of course, as any one would.'

'Eaten! By what?'

'I found out later. All I could see then was a bunch of black ropy arms tangled around what looked like, as Putz described it to you, an ostrich. I wasn't going to interfere, naturally; if both creatures were dangerous, I'd have one less to worry about.

'But the bird-like thing was putting up a good battle, dealing vicious blows with an eighteen-inch beak, between screeches. And besides, I caught a glimpse or two of what was on the end of those arms!' Jarvis shuddered. 'But the clincher was when I noticed a little black bag or case hung about the neck of the bird-thing! It was intelligent! That or tame, I assumed. Anyway, it clinched my decision. I pulled out my automatic and fired into what I could see of its antagonist.

'There was a flurry of tentacles and a spurt of black corruption, and then the thing, with a disgusting sucking noise, pulled itself and its arms into a hole in the ground. The other let out a series of clacks, staggered around on legs about as thick as golf sticks, and turned suddenly to face me. I held my weapon ready, and the two of us stared at each other.

'The Martian wasn't a bird, really. It wasn't even birdlike, except just at first glance. It had a beak all right, and a few feathery appendages, but the beak wasn't really a beak. It was somewhat flexible; I could see the tip bend slowly from side to side; it was almost like a cross between a beak and a trunk. It had four-toed feet, and four fingered things—hands, you'd have to call them, and a little roundish body, and a long neck ending in a tiny head—and that beak. It stood an inch or so taller than I, and—well, Putz saw it!'

The engineer nodded. '*Ja!* I saw!'

Jarvis continued. 'So—we stared at each other. Finally the creature went into a series of clackings and twitterings and held out its hands towards me, empty. I took that as a gesture of friendship.'

'Perhaps,' suggested Harrison, 'it looked at that nose of yours and thought you were its brother!'

'Huh! You can be funny without talking! Anyway, I put up my gun and said "Aw, don't mention it", or something of the sort, and the thing came over and we were pals.

'By that time, the sun was pretty low and I knew that I'd better build a fire or get into my thermo-skin. I decided on the fire. I picked a spot at the base of the Thyle cliff, where the rock could reflect a little heat on my back. I started breaking off chunks of this desiccated Martian vegetation, and my companion caught the idea and brought in an armful. I reached for a match, but the Martian fished into his pouch and brought out something that looked like a glowing coal; one touch of it, and the fire was blazing—and you all know what a job we have starting a fire in this atmosphere!

'And that bag of his!' continued the narrator. 'That was a manufactured article, my friends; press an end and she popped open—press the middle and she sealed so perfectly you couldn't see the line. Better than zippers.

'Well, we stared at the fire a while and I decided to attempt some sort of communication with the Martian. I pointed at myself and said "Dick"; he caught the drift immediately, stretched a bony claw at me and repeated "Tick". Then I pointed at him, and he gave that whistle I called Tweel; I can't imitate his accent. Things were going smoothly; to emphasize the names, I repeated "Dick", and then, pointing at him, "Tweel".

'There we stuck! He gave some clacks that sounded negative, and said something like "P-p-p-root". And that was just the beginning; I was always "Tick", but as for him—part of the time he was "Tweel", and part of the time he was "P-p-p-proot", and part of the time he was sixteen other noises!

'We just couldn't connect, I tried "rock", and I tried "star", and "tree", and "fire", and Lord knows what else, and try as I would, I couldn't get a single word! Nothing was the same for two successive minutes, and if that's a language, I'm an alchemist! Finally I gave it up and called him Tweel, and that seemed to do.

'But Tweel hung on to some of my words. He remembered a couple of them, which I suppose is a great achievement if you're used to a language you have to make up as you go along. But I couldn't get the hang of his talk; either I missed some subtle point or we just didn't *think* alike—and I rather believe the latter view.

'I've other reasons for believing that. After a while I gave up the language business, and tried mathematics. I scratched two plus two equals four on the ground, and demonstrated it with pebbles. Again Tweel caught the idea, and informed me that three plus three equals six. Once more we seemed to be getting somewhere.

'So, knowing that Tweel had at least a grammar school education, I drew a circle for the sun, pointing first at it, and then at the last glow of the sun. Then I sketched in Mercury, and Venus, and Mother Earth, and Mars, and finally, pointing to Mars, I swept my hand around in a sort of inclusive gesture to indicate that Mars was our current environment. I was working up to putting over the idea that my home was on the Earth.

'Tweel understood my diagram all right. He poked his beak at it, and with a great deal of trilling and clucking, he added Deimos and Phobos to Mars, and then sketched in the Earth's Moon!

'Do you see what that proves? It proves that Tweel's race uses telescopes—that they're civilized!'

'Does not!' snapped Harrison. 'The Moon is visible from here as a fifth magnitude star. They could see its revolution with the naked eye.'

'The Moon, yes!' said Jarvis. 'You've missed my point. Mercury isn't visible! And Tweel knew of Mercury because he placed the Moon at the *third* planet, not the second. If he didn't know Mercury, he'd put the Earth second, and Mars third, instead of fourth! See?'

'Humph!' said Harrison.

'Anyway,' proceeded Jarvis, 'I went on with my lesson. Things were going smoothly, and it looked as if I could put the idea over. I pointed at the Earth on my diagram, and then at myself, and then, to clinch it, I pointed to myself and then to the Earth itself shining bright green almost at the zenith.

'Tweel set up such an excited clacking that I was certain he understood. He jumped up and down, and suddenly he pointed at himself and then at the sky, and then at himself and at the sky again. He pointed at his middle and then at Arcturus, at his head and then at Spica, at his feet and then at half a dozen stars, while I just gaped at him. Then, all of a sudden, he gave a tremendous leap. Man, what a hop! He shot straight up into the starlight, seventy-five feet if an inch! I saw him silhouetted against the sky, saw him turn and come down at me head first, and land smack on his beak like a javelin! There he stuck square in the centre of my sun-circle in the sand—a bull's eye!'

'Nuts!' observed the captain. 'Plain nuts!'

'That's what I thought, too! I just stared at him open-mouthed while he pulled his head out of the sand and stood up. Then I figured he'd missed my point, and I went through the whole blamed rigmarole again, and it ended the same way, with Tweel on his nose in the middle of my picture!'

'Maybe it's a religious rite,' suggested Harrison.

'Maybe,' said Jarvis dubiously. 'Well, there we were. We could exchange ideas up to a certain point, and then—blooey! Something in us was different, unrelated; I don't doubt that Tweel thought me just as screwy as I thought him. Our minds simply looked at the world from different viewpoints, and perhaps his viewpoint is as true as ours. But—we couldn't get together, that's all. Yet, in spite of all difficulties, I *liked* Tweel, and I have a queer certainty that he liked me.'

'Nuts!' repeated the captain. 'Just daffy!'

'Yeah? Wait and see. A couple of times I've thought that perhaps we—' He paused, and then resumed his narrative. 'Anyway, I finally gave it up, and got into my thermo-skin to sleep. The fire hadn't kept me any too warm, but that damned sleeping bag did. Got stuffy five minutes after I closed myself in. I opened it a little and bingo! Some eighty-below-zero air hit my nose, and that's when I got this pleasant little frostbite to add to the bump I acquired during the crash of my rocket.

'I don't know what Tweel made of my sleeping. He sat around, but when I woke up, he was gone. I'd just crawled out of my bag, though, when I heard some twittering, and there he came, sailing down from that three-storey Thyle cliff to alight on his beak beside me. I pointed to myself and towards the north, and he pointed at himself and towards the south, but when I loaded up and started away, he came along.

'Man, how he travelled! A hundred and fifty feet at a jump, sailing through the air stretched out like a spear, and landing on his beak. He seemed surprised at my plodding, but after a few moments he fell in beside me, only every few minutes he'd go into one of his leaps, and stick his nose into the sand a block ahead of me. Then he'd come shooting back at me; it made me nervous at first to see that beak of his coming at me like a spear, but he always ended in the sand at my side.

'So the two of us plugged along across the Mare Chronium. Same sort of place as this—same crazy plants and same little green biopods growing in the sand, or crawling out of your way. We talked—not that we understood each other, you know, but just for company. I sang songs, and I suspect Tweel did too; at least, some of his trillings and twitterings had a subtle sort of rhythm.

'Then, for variety, Tweel would display his smattering of English words. He'd point to an outcropping and say "rock", and point to a pebble and say it again; or he'd touch my arm and say "Tick", and then repeat it. He seemed terrifically amused that the same word meant the same thing twice in succession, or that the same word could apply to two different objects. It set me wondering if perhaps his language wasn't like the primitive speech of some earth people—you know, Captain, like the Negritoes, for instance, who haven't any generic words. No word for food or water or man—words for good food and bad food, or rain water and sea water, or strong man and weak man—but no names for general classes. They're too primitive to understand that rain water and sea water are just different aspects of the same thing. But that wasn't the case with Tweel; it was just that we were somehow mysteriously different—our minds were alien to each other. And yet—we *liked* each other!'

'Looney, that's all,' remarked Harrison. 'That's why you two were so fond of each other.'

'Well, I like *you*!' countered Jarvis wickedly. 'Anyway,' he resumed, 'don't get the idea that there was anything screwy about Tweel. In fact, I'm not so sure but that he couldn't teach our highly praised human intelligence a trick or two. Oh, he wasn't an intellectual superman, I guess; but don't overlook the point that he managed to understand a little of my mental workings, and I never even got a glimmering of his.'

'Because he didn't have any!' suggested the captain, while Putz and Leroy blinked attentively.

'You can judge of that when I'm through,' said Jarvis. 'Well, we plugged along across the Mare Chronium all that day, and all the next. Mare Chronium—Sea of Time! Say, I was willing to agree with Schiaparelli's name by the end of that march! Just that grey, endless plain of weird plants, and never a sign of any other life. It was so monotonous that I was even glad to see the desert of Xanthus towards the evening of the second day.

'I was fair worn out, but Tweel seemed as fresh as ever, for all I never saw him drink or eat. I think he could have crossed the Mare Chronium in a couple of hours with those block-long nose dives of his, but he stuck along with me. I offered him some water once or twice; he took the cup from me and sucked the liquid into his beak, and then carefully squirted it all back into the cup and gravely returned it.

'Just as we sighted Xanthus, or the cliffs that bounded it, one of those nasty sand clouds blew along, not as bad as the one we had here, but mean to travel against. I pulled the transparent flap of my thermo-skin bag across my face and managed pretty well, and I noticed that Tweel used some feathery appendages growing like a moustache at the base of his beak to cover his nostrils, and some similar fuzz to shield his eyes.'

'He is a desert creature!' ejaculated the little biologist, Leroy.

'Huh? Why?'

'He drink no water—he is adapt' for sand storm—'

'Proves nothing! There's not enough water to waste anywhere on this desiccated pill called Mars. We'd call all of it desert on earth, you know.' He paused. 'Anyway, after the sandstorm blew over, a little wind kept blowing in our faces, not strong enough to stir the sand. But suddenly things came drifting along from the Xanthus cliffs—small, transparent spheres, for all the world like glass tennis balls! But light—they were almost light enough to float even in this thin air—empty, too; at least, I cracked open a couple and nothing came out but a bad smell. I asked Tweel about them, but all he said was "No, no, no", which I took to mean that he knew nothing about them. So they went bouncing by like tumbleweeds, or like soap bubbles, and we plugged on towards Xanthus. Tweel pointed at one of the crystal balls once and said "rock", but I was too tired to argue with him. Later I discovered what he meant.

'We came to the bottom of the Xanthus cliffs finally, when there wasn't much daylight left. I decided to sleep on the plateau if possible; anything dangerous, I reasoned, would be more likely to prowl through the vegetation of the Mare Chronium than the sand of Xanthus. Not that I'd seen a single sign of menace, except the rope-armed black thing that had trapped Tweel, and apparently that didn't prowl at all, but lured its victims within reach. It couldn't lure me while I slept, especially as Tweel didn't seem to sleep at all, but simply sat patiently around all night. I wondered how the creature had managed to trap Tweel, but there wasn't any way of asking him. I found that out too, later; it's devilish!

'However, we were ambling around the base of the Xanthus barrier looking for an easy spot to climb. At least, I was. Tweel could have leaped it easily, for the cliffs were lower than Thyle—perhaps sixty feet. I found a place and started up, swearing at the water tank strapped to my back—it didn't bother me except when climbing—and suddenly I heard a sound that I thought I recognized!

'You know how deceptive sounds are in this thin air. A shot sounds like the pop of a cork. But this sound was the drone of a rocket, and sure enough, there went our second auxiliary about ten miles to westward, between me and the sunset!'

'Vas me!' said Putz. 'I hunt for you.'

'Yeah; I knew that, but what good did it do me? I hung on to the cliff and yelled and waved with one hand. Tweel saw it too, and set up a trilling and twittering, leaping to the top of the barrier and then high into the air. And while I watched, the machine droned on into the shadows to the south.

'I scrambled to the top of the cliff. Tweel was still pointing and trilling excitedly, shooting up towards the sky and coming down head-on to stick upside down on his beak in the sand. I pointed towards the south and at myself, and he said, "Yes—Yes—Yes"; but somehow I gathered that he thought the flying thing was a relative of mine, probably a parent. Perhaps I did his intellect an injustice; I think now that I did.

'I was bitterly disappointed by the failure to attract attention. I pulled out my thermo-skin bag and crawled into it, as the night chill was already apparent. Tweel stuck his beak into the sand and drew up his legs and arms and looked for all the world like one of those leafless shrubs out there. I think he stayed that way all night.'

'Protective mimicry!' ejaculated Leroy. 'See? He is desert creature!'

'In the morning,' resumed Jarvis, 'we started off again. We hadn't gone a hundred yards into Xanthus when I saw something queer! This is one thing Putz didn't photograph, I'll wager!

'There was a line of little pyramids—tiny ones, not more than six inches high, stretching across Xanthus as far as I could see! Little buildings made of pygmy bricks, they were, hollow inside and truncated, or at least broken at the top and empty. I pointed at them and said "What?" to Tweel, but he gave some negative twitters to indicate, I suppose, that he didn't know. So off we went, following the row of pyramids because they ran north, and I was going north.

'Man, we trailed that line for hours! After a while, I noticed another queer thing: they were getting larger. Same number of bricks in each one, but the bricks were larger.

'By noon they were shoulder high. I looked into a couple—all just the same, broken at the top and empty. I examined a brick or two as well; they were silica, and old as creation itself!'

'How you know?' asked Leroy.

'They were weathered—edges rounded. Silica doesn't weather easily even on earth, and in this climate—!'

'How old you think?'

'Fifty thousand—a hundred thousand years. How can I tell? The little ones we saw in the morning were older—perhaps ten times as old. Crumbling. How old would that make *them*? Half a million years? Who knows?' Jarvis paused a moment. 'Well,' he resumed, 'we followed the line. Tweel pointed at them and said "rock" once or twice, but he'd done that many times before. Besides, he was more or less right about these.

'I tried questioning him. I pointed at a pyramid and asked "People?" and indicated the two of us. He set up a negative sort of clucking and said, "No, no, no. No one-one-two. No two-two-four", meanwhile rubbing his stomach. I just stared at him and he went through the business again. "No one-one-two. No two-two-four." I just gaped at him.'

'That proves it!' exclaimed Harrison. 'Nuts!'

'You think so?' queried Jarvis sardonically. 'Well, I figured it out different! "No one-one-two!" You don't get it, of course, do you?'

'Nope—nor do you!'

'I think I do! Tweel was using the few English words he knew to put over a very complex idea. What, let me ask, does mathematics make you think of?'

'Why—of astronomy. Or—or logic!'

'That's it! "No one-one-two!" Tweel was telling me that the builders of the pyramids weren't people—or that they weren't intelligent, that they weren't reasoning creatures! Get it?'

'Huh! I'll be damned!'

'You probably will.'

'Why,' put in Leroy, 'he rub his belly?'

'Why? Because, my dear biologist, that's where his brains are! Not in his tiny head—in his middle!'

'C'est impossible!'

'Not on Mars, it isn't! This flora and fauna aren't earthly; your biopods prove that!' Jarvis grinned and took up his narrative. 'Anyway, we plugged along across Xanthus and in about the middle of the afternoon, something else queer happened. The pyramids ended.'

'Ended!'

'Yeah; the queer part was that the last one—and now they were ten-footers—was capped! See? Whatever built it was still inside; we'd trailed 'em from their half-million-year-old origin to the present.

'Tweel and I noticed it about the same time. I yanked out my automatic (I had a clip of Boland explosive bullets in it) and Tweel, quick as a sleight-of-hand trick, snapped a queer little glass revolver out of his bag. It was much like our weapons, except that the grip was larger to accommodate his four-taloned hand. And we held our weapons ready while we sneaked up along the lines of empty pyramids.

'Tweel saw the movement first. The top tiers of bricks were heaving, shaking, and suddenly slid down the sides with a thin crash. And then—something—something was coming out!

'A long, silvery-grey arm appeared, dragging after it an armoured body. Armoured, I mean, with scales, silver-grey and dull-shining. The arm heaved the body out of the hole; the beast crashed to the sand.

'It was a nondescript creature—body like a big grey cask, arm and a sort of mouth-hole at one end; stiff, pointed tail at the other—and that's all. No other limbs, no eyes, ears, nose—nothing! The thing dragged itself a few yards, inserted its pointed tail in the sand, pushed itself upright, and just sat.

'Tweel and I watched it for ten minutes before it moved. Then, with a creaking and rustling like—oh, like crumpling stiff paper—its arm moved to the mouth-hole and out came a brick! The arm placed the brick carefully on the ground, and the thing was still again.

'Another ten minutes—another brick. Just one of Nature's bricklayers. I was about to slip away and move on when Tweel pointed at the thing and said "rock"! I went "huh?" and he said it again. Then, to the accompaniment of some of his trilling, he said, "No—no—", and gave two or three whistling breaths.

'Well, I got his meaning, for a wonder! I said, "No breath?" and demonstrated the word. Tweel was ecstatic; he said, "Yes, yes, yes! No, no, no breet!" Then he gave a leap and sailed out to land on his nose about one pace from the monster!

'I was startled, you can imagine! The arm was going up for a brick, and I expected to see Tweel caught and mangled, but—nothing happened! Tweel pounded on the creature, and the arm took the brick and placed it neatly beside the first. Tweel rapped on its body again, and said "rock", and I got up nerve enough to take a look myself.

'Tweel was right again. The creature *was* rock, and it didn't breathe!'

'How you know?' snapped Leroy, his black eyes blazing interest.

'Because I'm a chemist. The beast was made of silica! There must have been pure silicon in the sand, and it lived on that. Get it! We, and Tweel, and those plants out there, and even the biopods are *carbon* life; this thing lived by a different set of chemical reactions. It was silicon life!'

'*La vie silicieuse!*' shouted Leroy. 'I have suspect, and now it is proof! I must go see! *Il faut que je*—'

'All right! All right!' said Jarvis. 'You can go see. Anyhow, there the thing was, alive and yet not alive, moving every ten minutes, and then only to remove a brick. Those bricks were its waste matter. See, Frenchy? We're carbon, and our waste is carbon dioxide, and this thing is silicon, and *its* waste is silicon dioxide—silica. But silica is a solid, hence the bricks. And it builds itself in, and when it is covered, it moves over to a fresh place to start over.

No wonder it creaked! A living creature half a million years old!'

'How you know how old?' Leroy was frantic.

'We trailed its pyramids from the beginning didn't we? If this weren't the original pyramid builder, the series would have ended somewhere before we found him, wouldn't it?—ended and started over with the small ones. That's simple enough, isn't it?

'But he reproduces, or tries to. Before the third brick came out, there was a little rustle and out popped a whole stream of those little crystal balls. They're his spores, or eggs, or seeds—call 'em what you want. They went bouncing by across Xanthus just as they'd bounced by us back in the Mare Chronium. I've a hunch how they work, too—this is for your information, Leroy. I think the crystal shell of silica is no more than a protective covering, like an eggshell, and that the active principle is the smell inside. Its some sort of gas that attacks silicon, and if the shell is broken near a supply of that element, some reaction starts that ultimately develops into a beast like that one.'

'You should try!' exclaimed the little Frenchman. 'We must break one to see!'

'Yeah? Well, I did. I smashed a couple against the sand. Would you like to come back in about ten thousand years to see if I planted some pyramid monsters? You'd most likely be able to tell by that time!' Jarvis paused and drew a deep breath. 'Lord! That queer creature! Do you picture it? Blind, deaf, nerveless, brainless—just a mechanism, and yet—immortal! Bound to go on making bricks, building pyramids, as long as silicon and oxygen exist, and even afterwards it'll just stop. It won't be dead. If the accidents of a million years bring it its food again, there it'll be, ready to run again, while brains and civilizations are part of the past. A queer beast—yet I met a stranger one!'

'If you did, it must have been in your dreams!' growled Harrison.

'You're right!' said Jarvis soberly. 'In a way, you're right. The dream-beast! That's the best name for it—and it's the most fiendish, terrifying creation one could imagine! More dangerous than a lion, more insidious than a snake!'

'Tell me!' begged Leroy. 'I must go see!'

'Not *this* devil!' He paused again. 'Well,' he resumed, 'Tweel and I left the pyramid creature and ploughed along through Xanthus. I was tired and a little disheartened by Putz's failure to pick me up, and Tweel's trilling got on my nerves, as did his flying nosedives. So I just strode along without a word, hour after hour across that monotonous desert.

'Towards mid-afternoon we came in sight of a low dark line on the horizon. I knew what it was. It was a canal; I'd crossed it in the rocket and it meant that we were just one-third of the way across Xanthus. Pleasant thought, wasn't it! And still, I was keeping up to schedule.

'We approached the canal slowly; I remembered that this one was bordered by a wide fringe of vegetation and that Mudheap City was on it.

'I was tired, as I said. I kept thinking of a good hot meal, and then from that I jumped to reflections of how nice and home-like even Borneo would seem after this crazy planet, and from that, to thoughts of little old New York, and then to thinking about a girl I know there—Fancy Long. Know her?'

'Vision entertainer,' said Harrison. 'I've tuned her in. Nice blonde—dances and sings on the *Yerba Mate* hour.'

'That's her,' said Jarvis ungrammatically. 'I know her pretty well—just friends, get me?—though she came down to see us off in the *Ares*. Well, I was thinking about her, feeling pretty lonesome, and all the time we were approaching that line of rubbery plants.

'And then—I said, "What 'n Hell!" and stared. And there she was—Fancy Long, standing plain as day under one of those crack-brained trees, and smiling and waving just the way I remembered her when we left!'

'Now you're nuts, too!' observed the captain.

'Boy, I almost agreed with you! I stared and pinched myself and closed my eyes and then stared again—and every time, there was Fancy Long smiling and waving! Tweel saw something, too; he was trilling and clucking away, but I scarcely heard him. I was bounding towards her over the sand, too amazed even to ask myself questions.

'I wasn't twenty feet from her when Tweel caught me with one of his flying leaps. He grabbed my arm, yelling, "No—no—no!" in his squeaky voice. I tried to shake him off—he was as light as if he were built of bamboo—but he dug his claws in and yelled. And finally some sort of sanity returned to me and I stopped less than ten feet from her. There she stood, looking as solid as Putz's head!'

'Vot?' said the engineer.

'She smiled and waved, and waved and smiled, and I stood there dumb as Leroy, while Tweel squeaked and chattered. I *knew* it couldn't be real, yet—there she was!

'Finally I said, "Fancy! Fancy Long!" She just kept on smiling and waving, but looking as real as if I hadn't left her thirty-seven million miles away.

'Tweel had his glass pistol out, pointing it at her. I grabbed his arm, but he tried to push me away. He pointed at her and said, "No breet! No breet!" and I understood that he meant that the Fancy Long thing wasn't alive. Man, my head was whirling!

'Still, it gave me the jitters to see him pointing his weapon at her. I don't know why I stood there watching him take careful aim, but I did. Then he squeezed the handle of his weapon; there was a little puff of steam, and Fancy Long was gone! And in her place was one of those writhing, black, rope-armed horrors like the one I'd saved Tweel from!

'The dream-beast! I stood there dizzy, watching it die while Tweel trilled and whistled. Finally he touched my arm, pointed at the twisting thing, and said, "You one-one-two, he one-one-two." After he'd repeated it eight or ten times, I got it. Do any of you?'

'*Oui!*' shrilled Leroy. '*Moi—je le comprends!* He mean you think of something, the beast he know, and you see it! *Un chien*—a hungry dog, he would see the big bone with meat! Or smell it—not?'

'Right!' said Jarvis. 'The dream-beast uses its victim's longings and desires to trap its prey. The bird at nesting season would see its mate, the fox, prowling for its own prey, would see a helpless rabbit!'

'How he do?' queried Leroy.

'How do I know? How does a snake back on earth charm a bird into its very jaws? And aren't there deep-sea fish that lure their victims into their mouths? Lord!' Jarvis shuddered. 'Do you see how insidious the monster is? We're warned now—but henceforth we can't trust even our eyes. You might see me—I might see one of you—and back of it may be nothing but another of those black horrors!'

'How'd your friend know?' asked the captain abruptly.

'Tweel? I wonder! Perhaps he was thinking of something that couldn't possibly have interested me, and when I started to run, he realized that I saw something different and was warned. Or perhaps the dream-beast can only project a single vision, and Tweel saw what I saw—or nothing. I couldn't ask him. But it's just another proof that his intelligence is equal to ours or greater.'

'He's daffy, I tell you!' said Harrison. 'What makes you think his intellect ranks with the human?'

'Plenty of things! First, the pyramid-beast. He hadn't seen one before; he said as much. Yet he recognized it as a dead-alive automaton of silicon.'

'He could have heard of it,' objected Harrison. 'He lives around here, you know.'

'Well how about the language? I couldn't pick up a single idea of his and he learned six or seven words of mine. And do you realize what complex ideas he put over with no more than those six or seven words? The pyramid-monster—the dream-beast! In a single phrase he told me that one was a harmless automaton and the other a deadly hypnotist. What about that!'

'Huh!' said the captain.

'*Huh* if you wish! Could you have done it knowing only six words of English? Could you go even further, as Tweel did, and tell me that another creature was of a sort of intelligence so different from ours that understanding was impossible—even more impossible than that between Tweel and me?'

'Eh? What was that?'

'Later. The point I'm making is that Tweel and his race are worthy of our friendship. Somewhere on Mars—and you'll find I'm right—is a civilization and culture equal to ours, and maybe more than equal. And communication is possible between them and us; Tweel proves that. It may take years of patient trial, for their minds are alien, but less alien than the next minds we encountered—if they *are* minds.'

'The next ones? What next ones?'

'The people of the mud cities along the canals.' Jarvis frowned, then resumed his narrative. 'I thought the dream-beast and the silicon-monster were the strangest beings conceivable, but I was wrong. These creatures are still more alien, less understandable than either and far less comprehensible than Tweel, with whom friendship is possible, and even, by patience and concentration, the exchange of ideas.

'Well,' he continued, 'we left the dream-beast dying, dragging itself back into its hole, and we moved towards the canal. There was a carpet of that queer walking-grass scampering out of our way, and when we reached the bank, there was a yellow trickle of water flowing. The mound city I'd noticed from the rocket was a mile or so to the right and I was curious enough to want to take a look at it.

'It had seemed deserted from my previous glimpse of it, and if any creatures were lurking in it—well, Tweel and I were both armed. And by the way, that crystal weapon of Tweel's was an interesting device; I took a look at it after the dream-beast episode. It fired a little glass splinter, poisoned, I suppose, and I guess it held at least a hundred of 'em to a load. The propellent was steam—just plain steam!'

'Shteam!' echoed Putz. 'From vot come, shteam?'

'From water, of course! You could see the water through the transparent handle and about a gill of another liquid, thick and yellowish. When Tweel squeezed the handle—there was no trigger—a drop of water and a drop of the yellow stuff squirted into the firing chamber, and the water vapourized—pop!—like that. It's not so difficult; I think we could develop the same principle. Concentrated sulphuric acid will heat water almost to boiling, and so will quicklime, and there's potassium and sodium—

'Of course, his weapon hadn't the range of mine, but it wasn't so bad in this thin air, and it *did* hold as many shots as a cowboy's gun in a Western movie. It was effective, too, at least against Martian life; I tried it out, aiming at one of the crazy plants, and darned if the plant didn't wither up and fall apart! That's why I think the glass splinters were poisoned.

'Anyway, we trudged along towards the mud-heap city and I began to wonder whether the city builders dug the canals. I pointed to the city and then at the canal, and Tweel said "No—no—no!" and gestured towards the south. I took it to mean that some other race had created the canal system, perhaps Tweel's people. I don't know; maybe there's still another intelligent race on the planet, or a dozen others. Mars is a queer little world.

'A hundred yards from the city we crossed a sort of road—just a hard-packed mud trail, and then, all of a sudden, along came one of the mound builders!

'Man, talk about fantastic beings! It looked rather like a barrel trotting along on four legs with four other arms or tentacles. It had no head, just body and members and a row of eyes completely around it. The top end of the barrel-body was a diaphragm stretched as tight as a drum head, and that was all. It was pushing a little coppery cart and tore right past us like the proverbial bat out of hell. It didn't even notice us, although I thought the eyes on my side shifted a little as it passed.

'A moment later another came along, pushing another empty cart. Same thing—it just scooted past us. Well, I wasn't going to be ignored by a bunch of barrels playing train, so when the third one approached, I planted myself in the way—ready to jump, of course, if the thing didn't stop.

'But it did. It stopped and set up a sort of drumming from the diaphragm on top. And I held out both hands and said, "We are friends!" And what do you suppose the thing did?'

'Said, "Pleased to meet you," I'll bet!' suggested Harrison.

'I couldn't have been more surprised if it had! It drummed on its diaphragm, and then suddenly boomed out, "We are v-r-r-riends!" and gave its pushcart a vicious poke at me! I jumped aside, and away it went while I stared dumbly after it.

'A minute later another one came hurrying along. This one didn't pause, but simply drummed out, "We are v-r-r-riends!" and scurried by. How did it learn the phrase? Were all of the creatures in some sort of communication with each other? Were they all parts of some central organism? I don't know, though I think Tweel does.

'Anyway, the creatures went sailing past us, every one greeting us with the same statement. It got to be funny; I never thought to find so many friends on this God-forsaken ball! Finally I made a puzzled gesture to Tweel; I guess he understood, for he said, "One-one-two—yes!—two-two-four—no!" Get it?'

'Sure,' said Harrison. 'It's a Martian nursery rhyme.'

'Yeah! Well, I was getting used to Tweel's symbolism, and I figured it out this way. "One-one-two—yes!" The creatures were intelligent. "Two-two-four—no!" Their intelligence was not of our order, but something different and beyond the logic of two and two is four. Maybe I missed his meaning. Perhaps he meant that their minds were of low degree, able to figure out the simple things—"One-one-two—yes!"—but not more difficult things—"Two-two-four—no!" But I think from what we saw later that he meant the other.

'After a few moments, the creatures came rushing back—first one, then another. Their pushcarts were full of stones, sand, chunks of rubbery plants, and such rubbish as that. They droned out their friendly greeting, which didn't really sound so friendly, and dashed on. The third one I assumed to be my first acquaintance and I decided to have another chat with him. I stepped into his path again and waited.

'Up he came, booming out his "We are v-r-r-riends" and stopped. I looked at him; four or five of his eyes looked at me. He tried his password again and gave a shove on his cart, but I stood firm. And then the—the dashed creature reached out one of his arms, and two finger-like nippers tweaked my nose!'

'Haw!' roared Harrison. 'Maybe the things have a sense of beauty!'

'Laugh!' grumbled Jarvis. 'I'd already had a nasty bump and a mean frostbite on that nose. Anyway, I yelled "Ouch!" and jumped aside and the creature dashed away; but from then on, their greeting was "We are v-r-r-riends! Ouch!" Queer beasts!

'Tweel and I followed the road squarely up to the nearest mound. The creatures were coming and going, paying us not the slightest attention, fetching their loads of rubbish. The road simply dived into an opening, and slanted down like an old mine, and in and out darted the barrel-people, greeting us with their eternal phrase.

'I looked in; there was a light somewhere below, and I was curious to see it. It didn't look like a flame or torch, you understand, but more like a civilized light, and I thought that I might get some clue as to the creatures' development. So in I went and Tweel tagged along, not without a few trills and twitters, however.

'The light was curious; it sputtered and flared like an old arc light, but came from a single black rod set in the wall of the corridor. It was electric, beyond doubt. The creatures were fairly civilized, apparently.

'Then I saw another light shining on something that glittered and I went on to look at that, but it was only a heap of shiny sand. I turned toward the entrance to leave, and the Devil take me if it wasn't gone!

'I suppose the corridor had curved, or I'd stepped into a side passage. Anyway, I walked back in that direction I thought we'd come, and all I saw was more dimlit corridor. The place was a labyrinth! There was nothing but twisting passages running every way, lit by occasional lights, and now and then a creature running by, sometimes with a pushcart, sometimes without.

'Well, I wasn't much worried at first. Tweel and I had only come a few steps from the entrance. But every move we made after that seemed to get us in deeper. Finally I tried following one of the creatures with an empty cart, thinking that he'd be going out for his rubbish, but he ran around aimlessly, into one passage and out another. When he started dashing around a pillar like one of these Japanese waltzing mice, I gave up, dumped my water tank on the floor, and sat down.

'Tweel was as lost as I. I pointed up and he said "No—no—no!" in a sort of helpless trill. And we couldn't get any help from the natives. They paid no attention at all, except to assure us they were friends—ouch!

'Lord! I don't know how many hours or days we wandered around there! I slept twice from sheer exhaustion; Tweel never seemed to need sleep. We tried following only the upward corridors, but they'd run uphill a ways and then curve downwards. The temperature in that damned ant hill was constant; you couldn't tell night from day and after my first sleep I didn't know whether I'd slept one hour or thirteen, so I couldn't tell from my watch whether it was midnight or noon.

'We saw plenty of strange things. There were machines running in some of the corridors, but they didn't seem to be doing anything—just wheels turning. And several times I saw two barrel-beasts with a little one growing between them, joined to both.'

'Parthenogenesis!' exulted Leroy. 'Parthenogenesis by budding like *les tulipes*!'

'If you say so, Frenchy,' agreed Jarvis. 'The things never noticed us at all, except, as I say, to greet us with "We are v-r-r-riends! Ouch!" They seemed to have no home-life of any sort, but just scurried around with their pushcarts, bringing in rubbish. And finally I discovered what they did with it.

'We'd had a little luck with a corridor, one that slanted upwards for a great distance. I was feeling that we ought to be close to the surface when suddenly the passage debouched into a domed chamber, the only one we'd seen. And man!—I felt like dancing when I saw what looked like daylight through a crevice in the roof.

'There was a—a sort of machine in the chamber, just an enormous wheel that turned slowly, and one of the creatures was in the act of dumping his rubbish below it. The wheel ground it with a crunch—sand, stones, plants, all into powder that sifted away somewhere. While we watched, others filed in, repeating the process, and that seemed to be all. No rhyme nor reason to the whole thing—but that's characteristic of this crazy planet. And there was another fact that's almost too bizarre to believe.

'One of the creatures, having dumped his load, pushed his cart aside with a crash and calmly shoved himself under the wheel! I watched him being crushed, too stupefied to make a sound, and a moment later, another followed him! They were perfectly methodical about it, too; one of the cartless creatures took the abandoned pushcart.

'Tweel didn't seem surprised; I pointed out the next suicide to him, and he just gave the most human-like shrug imaginable, as much as to say, "What can I do about it?" He must have known more or less about these creatures.

'Then I saw something else. There was something beyond the wheel, something shining on a sort of low pedestal. I walked over; there was a little crystal about the size of an egg, fluorescing to beat Tophet. The light from it stung my hands and face, almost like a static discharge, and then I noticed another funny thing. Remember that wart I had on my left thumb? Look!' Jarvis extended his hand. 'It dried up and fell off—just like that! And my abused nose—say, the pain went out of it like magic! The thing had the property of hard X-rays or gamma radiations, only more so; it destroyed diseased tissue and left healthy tissue unharmed!

'I was thinking what a present *that'd* be to take back to Mother Earth when a lot of racket interrupted. We dashed back to the other side of the wheel in time to see one of the pushcarts ground up. Some suicide had been careless, it seems.

'Then suddenly the creatures were booming and drumming all around us and their noise was decidedly menacing. A crowd of them advanced towards us; we backed out of what I thought was the passage we'd entered by, and they came rumbling after us, some pushing carts and some not. Crazy brutes! There was a whole chorus of "We are v-r-r-riends! Ouch!" I didn't like the "ouch", it was rather suggestive.

'Tweel had his glass gun out and I dumped my water tank for greater freedom and got mine. We backed up the corridor with the barrel-beasts following—about twenty of them. Queer thing—the ones coming in with loaded carts moved past us inches away without a sign.

'Tweel must have noticed that. Suddenly, he snatched out that glowing coal cigar-lighter of his and touched a cart-load of plant limbs. Puff! The whole load was burning—and the crazy beast pushing it went right along without a change of pace! It created some disturbance among our "v-r-r-riends", however—and then I noticed the smoke eddying and swirling past us, and sure enough, there was the entrance!

'I grabbed Tweel and out we dashed and after us our twenty pursuers. The daylight felt like Heaven, though I saw at first glance that the sun was all but set, and that was bad, since I couldn't live outside my thermo-skin bag in a Martian night—at least, without a fire.

'And things got worse in a hurry. They cornered us in an angle between two mounds, and there we stood. I hadn't fired nor had Tweel; there wasn't any use in irritating the brutes. They stopped a little distance away and began their booming about friendship and ouches.

'Then things got still worse! A barrel-brute came out with a pushcart and they all grabbed into it and came out with handfuls of foot-long copper darts—sharp-looking ones—and all of a sudden one sailed past my ear—zing! And it was shoot or die then.

'We were doing pretty well for a while. We picked off the ones next to the pushcart and managed to keep the darts at a minimum, but suddenly there was a thunderous booming of "v-r-r-riends" and "ouches", and a whole army of 'em came out of their hole.

'Man! We were through and I knew it! Then I realized that Tweel wasn't. He could have leaped the mound behind us as easily as not. He was staying for me!

'Say, I could have cried if there'd been time! I'd liked Tweel from the first, but whether I'd have had gratitude to do what he was doing—suppose I *had* saved him from the first dream-beast—he'd done as much for me, hadn't he? I grabbed his arm, and said "Tweel", and pointed up, and he understood. He said, "No—no—no, Tick!" and popped away with his glass pistol.

'What could I do? I'd be a goner anyway when the sun set, but I couldn't explain that to him. I said, "Thanks, Tweel. You're a man!" and felt that I wasn't paying him any compliment at all. A man! There are mighty few men who'd do that.

'So I went "bang" with my gun and Tweel went "puff" with his, and the barrels were throwing darts and getting ready to rush us, and booming about being friends. I had given up hope. Then suddenly an angel dropped right down from Heaven in the shape of Putz, with his under-jets blasting the barrels into very small pieces!

'Wow! I let out a yell and dashed for the rocket; Putz opened the door and in I went, laughing and crying and shouting! It was a moment or so before I remembered Tweel; I looked around in time to see him rising in one of his nosedives over the mound and away.

'I had a devil of a job arguing Putz into following! By the time we got the rocket aloft, darkness was down; you know how it comes here—like turning off a light. We sailed out over the desert and put down once or twice. I yelled "Tweel!" and yelled it a hundred times, I guess. We couldn't find him; he could travel like the wind and all I got—or else I imagined it—was a faint trilling and twittering drifting out of the south. He'd gone, and damn it! I wish—I wish he hadn't!'

The four men of the *Ares* were silent—even the sardonic Harrison. At last little Leroy broke the stillness.

'I should like to see,' he murmured.

'Yeah,' said Harrison. 'And the wart-cure. Too bad you missed that; it might be the cancer cure they've been hunting for a century and a half.'

'Oh, that!' muttered Jarvis gloomily. 'That's what started the fight!' He drew a glistening object from his pocket.

'Here it is.'

NIGHT

JOHN W. CAMPBELL JR.

Condon was staring through the glasses with a face tense and drawn, all his attention utterly concentrated on that one almost invisible speck infinitely far up in the blue sky, and saying over and over again in the most horribly absent-minded way, 'My Lord—my Lord——'

Suddenly he shivered and looked down at me, sheer agony in his face. 'He's never coming down. Don, he's never coming down——'

I knew it, too—knew it as solidly as I knew the knowledge was impossible. But I smiled and said: 'Oh, I wouldn't say that. If anything, I'd fear his coming down. What goes up comes down.'

Major Condon trembled all over. His mouth worked horribly for a moment before he could speak. 'Talbot—I'm scared—I'm horribly scared. You know—you're his assistant—you know he's trying to defeat gravity. Men aren't meant to—it's wrong—wrong——'

His eyes were glued on those binoculars again, with the same terrible tensity, and now he was saying over and over in that absent-minded way, 'wrong—wrong—wrong——'

Simultaneously he stiffened, and stopped. The dozen or so other men standing on that lonely little emergency field stiffened; then the major crumpled to the ground. I've never before seen a man faint, let alone an army officer with a DS medal. I didn't stop to help him, because I knew something had happened. I grabbed the glasses.

Far, far up in the sky was that little orange speck—far, where there is almost no air, and he had been forced to wear a stratosphere suit with a little alcohol heater. The broad, orange wings were overlaid now with a faint-glowing, pearl-grey light. And it was falling. Slowly, at first, circling aimlessly downward. Then it dipped, rose, and somehow went into a tail spin.

It was horrible. I know I must have breathed, but it didn't seem so. It took minutes for it to fall those miles, despite the speed.

Eventually it whipped out of that tail spin—through sheer speed, whipped out and into a power dive. It was a ghastly, flying coffin, hurtling at more than half a thousand miles an hour when it reached the Earth, some fifteen miles away.

The ground trembled, and the air shook with the crash of it. We were in the cars and roaring across the ground long before it hit. I was in Bob's car, with Jeff, his laboratory technician—Bob's little roadster he'd never need again. The engine picked up quickly, and we were going seventy before we left the field, jumped a shallow ditch and hit the road—the deserted, concrete road that led off towards where he must be. The engine roared as Jeff clamped down on the accelerator. Dimly, I heard the major's big car coming along behind us.

Jeff drove like a maniac, but I didn't notice. I knew the thing had done ninety-five but I think we must have done more. The wind whipped tears in my eyes so I couldn't be sure whether I saw mounting smoke and flame or not. With diesel fuel there shouldn't be—but that plane had been doing things it shouldn't. It had been trying out Carter's antigravity coil.

We shot up the flat, straight road across wide, level country, the wind moaning a requiem about the car. Far ahead I saw the side road that must lead off towards where Bob should be, and lurched to the braking of the car, the whine and sing of violently shrieking tyres, then to the skidding corner. It was a sand road; we slithered down it and for all the lightness and power, we slowed to sixty-five, clinging to the seat as the soft sand gripped and clung.

Violently Jeff twisted into a branching cow path, and somehow the springs took it. We braked to a stop a quarter of a mile from the plane.

It was in a fenced field of pasture and wood lot. We leaped the fence, and raced towards it: Jeff got there first, just as the major's car shrieked to a stop behind ours.

The major was cold and pale when he reached us. 'Dead,' he stated.

And I was very much colder and probably several times as pale. 'I don't know!' I moaned. 'He isn't there!'

'Not there!' The major almost screamed it. 'He must be—he has to be. He has no parachute—wouldn't take one. They say he didn't jump——'

I pointed to the plane, and wiped a little cold sweat from my forehead. I felt clammy all over, and my spine prickled. The solid steel of the huge diesel engine was driven through the stump of a tree, down into the ground perhaps eight or nine feet, and the dirt and rock had splashed under that blow like wet mud.

The wings were on the other side of the field, flattened, twisted straws of dural alloy. The fuselage of the ship was a perfect silhouette—a longitudinal projection that had flattened in on itself, each separate section stopping only as it hit the ground.

The great torus coil with its strangely twined wrappings of hair-fine bismuth wire was intact! And bent over it, twisted, utterly wrecked by the impact, was the main-wing stringer—the great dural-alloy beam that supported most of the ship's weight in the air. It was battered, crushed on those hair-fine, fragile bismuth wires—and not one of them was twisted or displaced or so much as skinned. The back frame of the ponderous diesel engine—the heavy supercharger was the anvil of that combination—was cracked and splintered. And not one wire of the hellish bismuth coil was strained or skinned or displaced.

And the red pulp that should have been there—the red pulp that had been a man—wasn't. It simply wasn't there at all. He hadn't left the plane. In the clear, cloudless air, we could see that. He was gone.

We examined it, of course. A farmer came, and another, and looked, and talked. Then several farmers came in old, dilapidated cars with their wives and families, and watched.

We set the owner of the property on watch and went away—went back to the city for workmen and a truck with a derrick. Dusk was falling. It would be morning before we could do anything, so we went away.

Five of us—the major of the army air force, Jeff Rodney, the two Douglass Co. men whose names I never remembered and I—sat in my—our—room. Bob's and Jeff's and mine. We'd been sitting there for hours trying to talk, trying to think, trying to remember every little detail, and trying to forget every ghastly detail. We couldn't remember the detail that explained it, nor forget the details that rode and harried us.

And the telephone rang. I started. Then slowly got up and answered. A strange voice, flat and rather unpleasant, said: 'Mr Talbot?'

'Yes.'

It was Sam Gantry, the farmer we'd left on watch. 'There's a man here.'

'Yes? What does he want?'

'I dunno. I dunno where he came from. He's either dead or out cold. Gotta funny kind of an aviator suit on, with a glass face on it. He looks all blue, so I guess he's dead.'

'Lord! Bob! Did you take that helmet off?' I roared.

'No, sir, no—no, sir. We just left him the way he was.'

'His tanks have run out. Listen. Take a hammer, a wrench, anything, and break that glass faceplate! Quick! We'll be there.'

Jeff was moving. The major was, too, and the others. I made a grab for the half-empty bottle of Scotch, started out, and ducked back into the closet. With the oxygen bottle under my arm I jumped into the crowded little roadster just as Jeff started it moving. He turned on the horn, and left it that way.

We dodged, twisted, jumped, and stopped with jerks in traffic, then leaped into smooth, roaring speed out towards the farmer's field. The turns were familiar now; we scarcely slowed for them, slewing around them. This time Jeff charged through the wire fence. A headlight popped; there was a shrill scream of wire, the wicked *zing* of wire scratching across the bonnet and mudguards, and we were bouncing across the field.

There were two lanterns on the ground; three men carried others; more men squatted down beside a still figure garbed in a fantastic, bulging, airproof stratosphere suit. They looked at us, open-mouthed as we skidded to a halt, moving aside as the major leaped out and dashed over with the Scotch. I followed close behind with the oxygen bottle.

Bob's faceplate was shattered, his face blue, his lips blue and flecked with froth. A long gash across his cheek from the shattered glass bled slowly. The major lifted his head without a word, and glass tinkled inside the helmet as he tried to force a little whisky down his throat.

'Wait!' I called. 'Major, give him artificial respiration, and this will bring him around quicker—better.' The major nodded, and rose, rubbing his arm with a peculiar expression.

'That's cold!' he said, as he flipped Bob over, and straddled his back. I held the oxygen bottle under Bob's nose as the major swung back in his arc, and let the raw, cold oxygen gas flow into his nostrils.

In ten seconds Bob coughed, gurgled, coughed violently, and took a deep shuddering breath. His face turned pink almost instantly under that lungful of oxygen, and I noticed with some surprise that he seemed to exhale almost nothing, his body absorbing the oxygen rapidly.

He coughed again; then: 'I could breathe a heck of a sight better if you'd get off my back,' he said. The major jumped up, and Bob turned over and sat up. He waved me aside, and spat. 'I'm—all right,' he said softly.

'Lord, man, what happened?' demanded the major.

Bob sat silent for a minute. His eyes had the strangest look—a hungry look—as he gazed about him. He looked at the trees beyond and at the silent, watching men in the light of the lanterns; then up, up to where a myriad stars gleamed and danced and flickered in the clear night sky.

'I'm back,' he said softly. Then suddenly he shivered, and looked horribly afraid. 'But—I'll have to be—then—too.'

He looked at the major for a minute, and smiled faintly. And at the two Douglass Co. men. 'Your plane was all right. I started up on the wings, as arranged, went way up, till I thought surely I was at a safe height, where the air wasn't too dense and the field surely wouldn't reach to Earth—Lord!—reach to Earth! I didn't guess how far that field extended. It touched Earth—twice.

'I was at forty-five thousand when I decided it was safe, and cut the engine. It died, and the stillness shocked me. It was so quiet. So quiet.

'I turned on the coil circuit, and the dynamotor began to hum as the tubes warmed up. And then—the field hit me. It paralysed me in an instant. I never had a chance to break the circuit, though I knew instantly something was wrong—terribly wrong. But the very first thing it did was to paralyse me, and I had to sit there and watch the instruments climb to positions and meanings they were never meant for.

'I realized I alone was being affected by that coil—I alone, sitting directly over it. I stared at the meters and they began to fade, began to seem transparent, unreal. And as they faded into blankness I saw clear sky beyond them; then for a hundredth of a second, like some effect of persistence of vision, I thought I saw the plane falling, twisting down at incredible speed, and the light faded as the Sun seemed to rocket suddenly across the sky and vanish.

'I don't know how long I was in that paralysed condition, where there was only blankness—neither dark nor light, nor time nor any form—but I breathed many times. Finally, form crawled and writhed into the blankness, and seemed to solidify beneath me as, abruptly, the blankness gave way to a dull red light. I was falling.

'I thought instantly of the forty-five thousand feet that lay between me and the solid Earth, and stiffened automatically in terror. And in the same instant I landed in a deep blanket of white snow, stained by the red light that lighted the world.

'Cold. Cold—it tore into me like the fang of a savage animal. What cold! The cold of ultimate death. It ripped through that thick, insulated suit and slashed at me viciously, as though there were no insulation there. I shivered so violently I could scarcely turn up the alcohol valves. You know I carried alcohol tanks and catalyst grids for heating, because the only electric fields I wanted were those of the apparatus. Even used a diesel instead of gas engine.

'I thank the Lord for that then. I realized that whatever had happened I was in a spot indescribably cold and desolate. And in the same instant, realized that the sky was black. Blacker than the blackest night, and yet before me the snow field stretched to infinity, tainted by the blood-red light, and my shadow crawled in darker red at my feet.

'I turned around. As far as the eye could see in three directions the land swept off in very low, very slightly rolling hills, almost plains—red plains of snow dyed with the dripping light of sunset, I thought.

'In the fourth direction, a wall—a wall that put the Great Wall of China to shame—loomed up half a mile—a blood-red wall that had the lustre of metal. It stretched across the horizon, and looked a scant hundred yards away, for the air was utterly clear. I turned up my alcohol burners a bit more and felt a little better.

'Something jerked my head around like a giant hand—a sudden thought. I stared at the Sun and gulped. It was four times—six times—the size of the Sun I knew. And it wasn't setting. It was forty-five degrees from the horizon. It was red. Blood-red. And there wasn't the slightest bit of radiant heat reaching my face from it. That Sun was cold.

'I'd just automatically assumed I was still on Earth, whatever else might have happened, but now I knew I couldn't be. It must be another planet of another sun—a frozen planet—for that snow was frozen air. I knew it absolutely. A frozen planet of a dead sun.

'And then I changed even that. I looked up at the black sky above me, and in all the vast black bowl of the heavens, not three-score stars were visible. Dim, red stars, with one single sun that stood out for its brilliance—a yellowish-red sun perhaps a tenth as bright as our sun, but a monster here. It was another—a dead—space. For if that snow was frozen air, the only atmosphere must have been neon and helium. There wasn't any hazy air to stop the light of the stars, and that dim, red sun didn't obscure them with its light. The stars were gone.

'In that glimpse, my mind began working by itself; I was scared.

'Scared? I was so scared I was afraid I was going to be sick. Because right then I knew I was never coming back. When I felt that cold, I'd wondered when my oxygen bottles would give out, if I'd get back before they did. Now it was not a worry. It was simply the limiting factor on an already-determined thing, the setting on the time bomb. I had just so much more time before I died right there.

'My mind was working out things, working them out all by itself, and giving answers I didn't want, didn't want to know about. For some reason it persisted in considering this was Earth, and the conviction became more and more fixed. It was right. That was Earth. And it was old Sol. Old—old Sol. It was the time axis that coil distorted—not gravity at all. My mind worked that out with a logic as cold as that planet.

'If it was time it had distorted, and this was Earth, then it had distorted time beyond imagining to an extent as meaningless to our minds as the distance a hundred million light years is. It was simply vast—incalculable. The Sun was dead. The Earth was dead. And Earth was already, in our time, two billion of years old, and in all that geological time, the Sun had not changed measurably. Then how long was it since my time? The Sun was dead. The very stars were dead. It must have been, I thought even then, billions on billions of years. And I grossly underestimated it.

'The world was old—old—old. The very rocks and ground radiated a crushing aura of incredible age. It was old, older than—but what is there? Older than the hills? Hills? Gosh, they'd been born and died and been born and worn away again, a million, a score of million times! Old as the stars? No, that wouldn't do. The stars were dead—then.

'I looked again at the metal wall, and set out for it, and the aura of age washed up at me, and dragged at me, and tried to stop this motion when all motion should have ceased. And the thin, unutterably cold wind whined in dead protest at me, and pulled at me with the ghost hands of the million million million that had been born and lived and died in the countless ages before I was born.

'I wondered as I went. I didn't think clearly; for the dead aura of the dead planet pulled at me. Age. The stars were dying, dead. They were huddled there in space, like decrepit old men, huddling for warmth. The galaxy was shrunk. So tiny, it wasn't a thousand light years across, the stars were separated by miles where there had been light years. The magnificent, proudly sprawling universe I had known, that flung itself across a million million light years, that flung radiant energy through space by the millions of millions of tons was—gone.

'It was dying—a dying miser that hoarded its last broken dregs of energy in a tiny cramped space. It was broken and shattered. A thousand billion years before the cosmical constant had been dropped from that broken universe. The cosmical constant that flung giant galaxies whirling apart with ever greater speed had no place here. It had hurled the universe in broken fragments, till each spattered bit felt the chill of loneliness, and wrapped space about itself, to become a universe in itself while the flaming galaxies vanished.

'That had happened so long ago that the writing it had left in the fabric of space itself had worn away. Only the gravity constant remained, the hoarding constant, that drew things together, and slowly the galaxy collapsed, shrunken and old, a withered mummy.

'The very atoms were dead. The light was cold; even the red light made things look older, colder. There was no youth in the universe. I didn't belong, and the faint protesting rustle of the infinitely cold wind about me moved the snow in muted, futile protest, resenting my intrusion from a time when things were young. It whinnied at me feebly, and chilled the youth of me.

'I plodded on and on, and always the metal wall retreated, like one of those desert mirages. I was too stupefied by the age of the thing to wonder; I just walked on.

'I was getting nearer, though. The wall was real; it was fixed. As I drew slowly nearer, the polished sheen of the wall died and the last dregs of hope died. I'd thought there might be someone still living behind that wall. Beings who could build such a thing might be able to live even here. But I couldn't stop then; I just went on. The wall was broken and cracked. It wasn't a wall I'd seen; it was a series of broken walls, knitted by distance to a smooth front.

'There was no weather to age them, only the faintest stirring of faint, dead winds—winds of neon and helium, inert and uncorroding—as dead and inert as the universe. The city had been dead a score of billions of years. That city was dead for a time ten times longer than the age of our planet today. But nothing destroyed it. Earth was dead—too dead to suffer the racking pains of life. The air was dead, too dead to scrape away metal.

'But the universe itself was dead. There was no cosmic radiation then to finally level the walls by atomic disintegration. There had been a wall—a single metal wall. Something—perhaps a last wandering meteor—had chanced on it in a time incalculably remote, and broken it. I entered through the great gap. Snow covered the city—soft, white snow. The great red sun stood still just where it was. Earth's restless rotation had long since been stilled—long, long since.

'There were dead gardens above, and I wandered up to them. That was really what convinced me it was a human city, on Earth. There were frozen, huddled heaps that might once have been men. Little fellows with fear forever frozen on their faces huddled helplessly over something that must once have been a heating device. Dead perhaps, since the last storm old Earth had known, tens of billions of years before.

'I went down. There were vastnesses in that city. It was huge. It stretched forever, it seemed, on and on, in its deadness. Machines, machines everywhere. And the machines were dead, too. I went down, down where I thought a bit of light and heat might linger. I didn't know then how long death had been there; those corpses looked so fresh, preserved by the eternal cold.

'It grew dark down below, and only through rents and breaks did that bloody light seep in. Down and down, till I was below the level of the dead surface. The white snow persisted, and then I came to the cause of that final, sudden death. I could understand then. More and more I had puzzled, for those machines I'd seen I knew were far and beyond anything we ever conceived—machines of perfection, self-repairing, and self-energizing, self-perpetuating. They could make duplicates of themselves, and duplicate other, needed machines; they were intended to be eternal, everlasting.

'But the designers couldn't cope with some things that were beyond even their majestic imaginations—the imaginations that conceived these cities that had lived beyond—a million times beyond—what they had dreamed. They must have conceived some vague future. But not a future when the Earth died, and the Sun died, and even the universe itself died.

'Cold had killed them. They had heating arrangements, devices intended to maintain forever the normal temperature despite the wildest variations of the weather. But in every electrical machine, resistances, balance resistances, and induction coils, balance condensers, and other inductances. And cold, stark, spatial cold, through ages, threw them off. Despite the heaters, cold crept in colder—cold that made their resistance balances and their induction coils superconductors! That destroyed the city, Superconduction—like the elimination of friction, on which all things must rest. It is a drag and a thing engineers fight forever. Resistance and friction must finally be the rest and the base of all things, the force that holds the great bed bolts firm and the brakes that stop the machines when needed.

'Electrical resistance died in the cold and the wonderful machines stopped for the replacement of defective parts. And when they were replaced, they, too, were defective. For what months must that constant stop—replacement—start—stop—replacement have gone on before, at last defeated forever, those vast machines must bow in surrender to the inevitable? Cold had defeated them by defeating and removing the greatest obstacle of the engineers that built them—resistance.

'They must have struggled forever—as we would say—through a hundred billion years against encroaching harshness of nature, forever replacing worn, defective parts. At last, defeated forever, the great power plants, fed by dying atoms, had been forced into eternal idleness and cold. Cold conquered them at last.

'They didn't blow up. Nowhere did I see a wrecked machine; always they had stopped automatically when the defective resistances made it impossible to continue. The stored energy that was meant to re-start those machines after repairs had been made had long since leaked out. Never again could they move, I knew.

'I wondered how long they had been, how long they had gone on and on, long after the human need of them had vanished. For that vast city contained only a very few humans at the end. What untold ages of lonely functioning perfection had stretched behind those at-last-defeated mechanisms?

'I wandered out, to see perhaps more, before the necessary end came to me, too. Through the city of death. Everywhere little self-contained machines, cleaning machines that had kept that perfect city orderly and neat stood helpless and crushed by eternity and cold. They must have continued functioning for years after the great central power stations failed, for each contained its own store of energy, needing only occasional recharge from the central stations.

'I could see where breaks had occurred in the city, and, clustered about those breaks were motionless repair machines, their mechanisms in positions of work, the debris cleared away and carefully stacked on motionless trucks. The new beams and plates were partly attached, partly fixed and left, as the last dregs of their energy was fruitlessly expended in the last, dying attempts of that great body to repair itself. The death wounds lay unmended.

'I started back up. Up to the top of the city. It was a long climb, an infinite, weary climb, up half a mile of winding ramps, past deserted, dead homes; past, here and there, shops and restaurants; past motionless little automative passenger cars.

'Up and up, to the crowning gardens that lay stiff and brittle and frozen. The breaking of the roof must have caused a sudden chill, for their leaves lay green in sheaths of white, frozen air. Brittle glass, green and perfect to the touch. Flowers, blooming in wonderful perfection showed still; they didn't seem dead, but it didn't seem they could be otherwise under the blanket of cold.

'Did you ever sit up with a corpse?' Bob looked up at us—through us. 'I had to once, in my little home town where they always did that. I sat with a few neighbours while the man died before my eyes. I knew he must die when I came there. He died—and I sat there all night while the neighbours filed out, one by one, and the quiet settled. The quiet of the dead.

'I had to again. I was sitting with a corpse then. The corpse of a dead world in a dead universe, and the quiet didn't have to settle there; it had settled a billion years ago, and only my coming had stirred those feeble, protesting ghosts of eon-dead hopes of that planet to softly whining protest—protest the wind tried to sob to me, the dead wind of the dead gases. I'll never be able to call them inert gases again. I know. I know they are dead gases, the dead gases of dead worlds.

'And above, through the cracked crystal of the roof, the dying suns looked down on the dead city. I couldn't stay there. I went down. Down under layer after layer of buildings, buildings of gleaming metal that reflected the dim, blood light of the Sun outside in carmine stains. I went down and down, down to the machines again. But even there hopelessness seemed more intense. Again I saw that agonizing struggle of the eternally faithful machines trying to repair themselves once more to serve the masters who were dead a million million years. I could see it again in the frozen, exhausted postures of the repair machines, stilled forever in their hopeless endeavours, the last poor dregs of energy spilled in fruitless conflict with time.

'It mattered little. Time himself was dying now, dying with the city and the planet and the universe he had killed.

'But those machines had tried so hard to serve again—and failed. Now they could never try again. Even they—the deathless machines—were dead.

'I went out again, away from those machines, out into the illimitable corridors, on the edge of the city. I could not penetrate far before the darkness became as absolute as the cold. I passed the shops where goods, untouched by time in this cold, still beckoned those strange humans, but humans for all that; beckoned the masters of the machines that were no more. I vaguely entered one to see what manner of things they used in that time.

'I nearly screamed at the motion of the thing in there, heard dimly through my suit the strangely softened sounds it made in the thin air. I watched it stagger twice—and topple. I cannot guess what manner of storage cells they had—save that they were marvellous beyond imagination. That stored energy that somehow I had released by entering was some last dreg that had remained through a time as old as our planet now. Its voice was stilled forever. But it drove me out—on.

'It had died while I watched. But somehow it made me more curious. I wondered again, less oppressed by utter death. Still, some untapped energy remained in this place, stored unimaginably. I looked more keenly, watched more closely. And when I saw a screen in one office, I wondered. It was a screen. I could see readily it was television of some type. Exploratively, I touched a stud. Sound! A humming, soft sound!

'To my mind leaped a picture of a system of these. There must be—interconnected—a vast central office somewhere with vaster accumulator cells, so huge, so tremendous in their power once, that even the little microfraction that remained was great. A storage system untouchable to the repair machines—the helpless, hopeless power machines.

'In an instant I was alive again with hope. There was a strange series of studs and dials, unknown devices. I pulled back on the stud I had pressed, and stood trembling, wondering. Was there hope?

'Then the thought died. What hope? The city was dead. Not merely that. It had been dead, dead for untold time. Then the whole planet was dead. With whom might I connect? There were none on the whole planet, so what mattered it that there was a communication system.

'I looked at the thing more blankly. Had there been—how could I interpret its multitudinous devices? There was a thing on one side that made me think of a telephone dial for some reason. A pointer over a metal sheet engraved with nine symbols in a circle under the arrow of the pointer. Now the pointer was over what was either the first or the last of these.

'Clumsily, in these gloves, I fingered one of the little symbol buttons inlaid in the metal. There was an unexpected click, a light glowed on the screen, a lighted image! It was a simple projection—but what a projection! A three-dimensional sphere floated, turning slowly before my eyes, turning majestically. And I nearly fell as understanding flooded me abruptly. The pointer was a selector! The studs beneath the pointer I understood! Nine of them. One after the other I pressed, and nine spheres—each different—swam before me.

'And right there I stopped and did some hard thinking. Nine spheres. Nine planets. Earth was shown first—a strange planet to me, but one I knew from the relative size and the position of the pointer must be Earth—then, in order, the other eight.

'Now—might there be life? Yes. In those nine worlds there might be, somewhere.

'Where? Mercury—nearest the Sun? No, the Sun was too dead, too cold, even for warmth there. And Mercury was too small. I knew, even as I thought, that I'd have one good chance because whatever means they had for communication wouldn't work without tremendous power. If those incredible storage cells had the power for even one shot, they had no more. Somehow I guessed that this apparatus might incorporate no resistance whatever. Here would be only very high frequency alternating current, and only condensers and inductances would be used in it. Supercooling didn't bother them any. It improved them. Not like the immense direct-current power machinery.

'But where to try? Jupiter? That was big. And then I saw what the solution must be. Cold had ruined these machines, thrown them off by making them too-perfect conductors. Because they weren't designed to defend themselves against spatial cold. But the machines—if there were any—on Pluto for instance, must originally have been designed for just such conditions! There it had always been cold. There it always would be cold.

'I looked at that thing with an intensity that should have driven my bare eyesight to Pluto. It was a hope. My only hope. But—how to signal Pluto? They could not understand! If there were any "they".

'So I had to guess—and hope. Somehow, I knew, there must be some means of calling the intelligent attendant, that the user might get aid. There was a bank of little studs—twelve of them—with twelve symbols, each different, in the centre of the panel, grouped in four rows of three. I guessed. Duodecimal system.

'Talk of the problems of interplanetary communication! Was there ever such a one? The problem of an anachronism in the city of the dead on a dead planet, seeking life somewhere, somehow.

'There were two studs, off by themselves, separate from the twelve—one green, one red. Again I guessed. Each of these had a complex series of symbols on it, so I turned the pointer on the right to Pluto, wavered, and turned it to Neptune. Pluto was further. Neptune had been cold enough; the machines would still be working there, and it would be, perhaps, less of a strain on the dregs of energy that might remain.

'I depressed the green symbol hoping I had guessed truly, that red still meant danger, trouble and wrongness to men when that was built—that it meant release and cancellation for a wrongly pressed key. That left green to be an operative call signal.

'Nothing happened. The green key alone was not enough. I looked again, pressed the green key and that stud I had first pressed.

'The thing hummed again. But it was a deeper note now, an entirely different sound, and there was a frenzied clicking inside. Then the green stud kicked back at me. The Neptune key under the pointer glowed softly; the screen began to shimmer with a greyish light. And, abruptly, the humming groaned as though at a terrific overload; the screen turned dull; the little signal light under Neptune's key grew dim. The signal was being sent—hurled out.

'Minute after minute I stood there, staring. The screen grew very slowly, very gently duller, duller. The energy was fading. The last stored driblet was being hurled away—away into space. "Oh," I groaned, "It's hopeless—hopeless to——"

'I'd realized the thing would take hours to get to that distant planet, travelling at the speed of light, even if it had been correctly aligned. But the machinery that should have done that through the years probably had long since failed for lack of power.

'But I stood there till the groaning motors ceased altogether, and the screen was as dark as I'd found it, the signal light black. I released the stud then, and backed away, dazed by the utter collapse of an insane hope. Experimentally I pressed the Neptune symbol again. So little power was left now, that only the faintest wash of murky light projected the Neptune image, little energy as that would have consumed.

'I went out. Bitter. Hopeless. Earth's last picture was long, long since painted—and mine had been the hand that spent Earth's last poor resource. To its utter exhaustion, the eternal city had strived to serve the race that created it, and I, from the dawn of time had, at the end of time, drained its last poor atom of life. The thing was a thing done.

'Slowly I went back to the roof and the dying suns. Up the miles of winding ramp that climbed a half mile straight up. I went slowly—only life knows haste—and I was of the dead.

'I found a bench up there—a carved bench of metal in the midst of a riot of colourful, frozen towers. I sat down, and looked out across the frozen city to the frozen world beyond, and the freezing red Sun.

'I do not know how long I sat there. And then something whispered in my mind.

'"We sought you at the television machine."

'I leaped from the bench and stared wildly about me.

'It was floating in the air—a shining dirigible of metal, ruby-red in that light, twenty feet long, perhaps ten in diameter, bright, warm orange light gleaming from its ports. I stared at it in amazement.

'"It—it worked!" I gasped.

'"The beam carried barely enough energy to energize the amplifiers when it reached Neptune, however," replied the creature in the machine.

'I couldn't see him—I knew I wasn't hearing him, but somehow that didn't surprise me.

'"Your oxygen has almost entirely given out, and I believe your mind is suffering from lack of oxygen. I would suggest you enter the lock; there is air in here."

'I don't know how he knew, but the gauges confirmed his statement. The oxygen was pretty nearly gone. I had perhaps another hour's supply if I opened the valves wide—but it was a most uncomfortably near thing, even so.

'I got in. I was beaming, joyous. There was life. This universe was not so dead as I had supposed. Not on Earth, perhaps, but only because they did not choose! They had space ships! Eagerly I climbed in, a strange thrill running through my body as I crossed the threshold of the lock. The door closed behind me with a soft *shush* on its soft gaskets, locked, and a pump whined somewhere for a moment; then the inner door opened. I stepped in—and instantly turned off my alcohol burners. There was heat—heat and light and air!

'In a moment I had the outer lacings loose, and the inner zipper down. Thirty seconds later I stepped out of the suit, and took a deep breath. The air was clean and sweet and warm, invigorating, fresh-smelling, as though it had blown over miles of green, Sun-warmed fields. It smelled alive, and young.

'Then I looked for the man who had come for me. There was none. In the nose of the ship, by the controls, floated a four-foot globe of metal, softly glowing with a warm, golden light. The light pulsed slowly or swiftly with the rhythm of his thoughts, and I knew that this was the one who had spoken to me.

'"You had expected a human?" he thought to me. "There are no more. There have been none for a time I cannot express in your mind. Ah, yes, you have a mathematical means of expression, but no understanding of that time, so it is useless. But the last of humanity was allowed to end before the Sun changed from the original G-O stage—a very, very long time ago."

'I looked at him and wondered. Where was he from? Who—what—what manner of thing? Was it an armour encased living creature or another of the perfect machines?

'I felt him watching my mind operate, pulsing softly in his golden light. And suddenly I thought to look out of the ports. The dim red suns were wheeling across those ports at an unbelievable rate. Earth was long since gone. As I looked, a dim, incredibly dim, red disk suddenly appeared, expanded—and I looked in awe at Neptune.

'The planet was scarcely visible when we were already within a dozen millions of miles. It was a jewelled world. Cities—the great, perfect cities—still glowed. They glowed in soft, golden light above, and below, the harsher, brighter blue of mercury vapour lighted them.

'He was speaking again. "We are machines—the ultimate development of man's machines. Man was almost gone when we came.

'"With what we have learned in the uncounted dusty megayears since, we might have been able to save him. We could not then. It was better, wiser, that man end than that he sink down so low as he must, eventually. Evolution is the rise under pressure. Devolution is the gradual sinking that comes when there is no pressure—and there is no end to it. Life vanished from this system—a dusty infinity I cannot sort in my memory—my type memory, truly, for I have complete all the memories of those that went before me that I replace. But my memory cannot stretch back to that time you think of—a time when the constellations——

'"It is useless to try. Those memories are buried under others, and those still buried under the weight of a billion centuries.

'"We enter"—he named a city; I cannot reproduce that name—"now. You must return to Earth though in some seven and a quarter of your days, for the magnetic axis stretches back in collapsing field strains. I will be able to inject you into it, I believe."

'So I entered that city, the living city of machines, that had been when time and the universe were young.

'I did not know then that, when all this universe had dissolved away, when the last sun was black and cold, scattered dust in a fragment of a scattered universe, this planet with its machine cities would go on—a last speck of warm light in a long-dead universe. I did not know then.

'"You still wonder that we let man die out?" asked the machine. "It was best. In another brief million years he would have lost his high estate. It was best."

'"Now we go on. We cannot end, as he did. It is automatic with us."

'I felt it then, somehow. The blind, purposeless continuance of the machine cities I could understand. They had no intelligence, only functions. These machines—these living, thinking, reasoning investigators—had only one function, too. Their function was slightly different—they were designed to be eternally curious, eternally investigating. And their striving was the more purposeless of the two, for theirs could reach no end. The cities fought eternally only the blind destructiveness of nature; wear, decay, erosion.

'But their struggle had an opponent forever, so long as they existed. The intelligent—no, not quite intelligent, but something else—curious machines were without opponents. They had to be curious. They had to go on investigating. And they had been going on in just this way for such incomprehensible ages that there was no longer anything to be curious about. Whoever, whatever designed them gave them function and forgot purpose. Their only curiosity was the wonder if there might, somewhere, be one more thing to learn.

'That—and the problem they did not want to solve, but must try to solve, because of the blind functioning of their very structure.

'Those eternal cities were limited. The machines saw now that limit, and saw the hope of final surcease in it. They worked on the energy of the atom. But the masses of the suns were yet tremendous. They were dead for want of energy. The masses of the planets were still enormous. But they, too, were dead for want of energy.

'The machines there on Neptune gave me food and drink—strange, synthetic foods and drinks. There had been none on all the planet.

They, perforce, started a machine, unused in a billion years and more, that I might eat. Perhaps they were glad to do so. It brought the end appreciably nearer, that vast consumption of mine.

'They used so very, very little, for they were so perfectly efficient. The only possible fuel in all the universe is one—hydrogen. From hydrogen, the lightest of elements, the heaviest can be built up, and energy released. They knew how to destroy matter utterly to energy, and could do it.

'But while the energy release of hydrogen compounding to the heavy elements is controllable, the destruction of matter to energy is a self-regenerative process. Started once, it spreads while matter lies within its direct, contiguous reach. It is wild, uncontrollable. It is impossible to utilize the full energy of matter.

'The suns had found that. They had burned their hydrogen until it was a remnant so small the action could not go on.

'On all Earth there was not an atom of hydrogen—nor was there on any planet, save Neptune. And there the store was not great. I used an appreciable fraction while I was there. That is their last hope. They can see the end, now.

'I stayed those few days, and the machines came and went. Always investigating, always curious. But there is in all that universe nothing to investigate save the one problem they are sure they cannot solve.

'The machine took me back to Earth, set up something near me that glowed with a peculiar, steady, grey light. It would fix the magnetic axis on me, on my location, within a few hours. He could not stay near when the axis touched again. He went back to Neptune, but a few millions of miles distant, in this shrunken mummy of the solar system.

'I stood alone on the roof of the city, in the frozen garden with its deceptive look of life.

'And I thought of that night I had spent, sitting up with the dead man. I had come and watched him die. And I sat up with him in the quiet. I had wanted someone, anyone to talk to.

'I did then. Overpoweringly it came to me I was sitting up in the night of the universe, in the night and quiet of the universe, with a dead planet's body, with the dead, ashen hopes of countless, nameless generations of men and women. The universe was dead, and I sat up alone—alone in the dead hush.

'Out beyond, a last flicker of life was dying on the planet

Neptune—a last, false flicker of aimless life, but not life. Life was dead. The world was dead.

'I knew there would never be another sound here. For all the little remainder of time. For this was the dark and the night of time and the universe. It was inevitable, the inevitable end that had been simply more distant in my day—in the long, long-gone time when the stars were mighty lighthouses of a mighty space, not the dying, flickering candles at the head of a dead planet.

'It had been inevitable then; the candles must burn out for all their brave show. But now I could see them guttering low, the last, fruitless dregs of energy expiring as the machines below had spent their last dregs of energy in that hopeless, utterly faithful gesture—to attempt the repair of the city already dead.

'The universe had been dead a billion years. It had been. This, I saw, was the last radiation of the heat of life from an already-dead body—the feel of life and warmth, imitation of life by a corpse. Those suns had long and long since ceased to generate energy. They were dead, and their corpses were giving off the last, lingering life heat before they cooled.

'I ran. I think I ran—down away from the flickering, red suns in the sky. Down to the shrouding blackness of the dead city below, where neither light, nor heat, nor life, nor imitation of life bothered me.

'The utter blackness quieted me somewhat. So I turned off my oxygen valves, because I wanted to die sane, even here, and I knew I'd never come back.

'The impossible happened! I came to with that raw oxygen in my face. I don't know how I came—only that here is warmth and life.

'Somewhere, on the far side of that bismuth coil, inevitable still, is the dead planet and the flickering, guttering candles that light the death watch I must keep at the end of time.'

DESERTION

CLIFFORD D. SIMAK

Four men, two by two, had gone into the howling maelstrom that was Jupiter and had not returned. They had walked into the keening gale—or rather, they had loped, bellies low against the ground, wet sides gleaming in the rain.

For they did not go in the shape of men.

Now the fifth man stood before the desk of Kent Fowler, head of Dome No. 3, Jovian Survey Commission.

Under Fowler's desk, old Towser scratched a flea, then settled down to sleep again.

Harold Allen, Fowler saw with a sudden pang, was young—too young. He had the easy confidence of youth, the face of one who never had known fear. And that was strange. For men in the domes of Jupiter did know fear—fear and humility. It was hard for Man to reconcile his puny self with the mighty forces of the monstrous planet.

'You understand,' said Fowler, 'that you need not do this. You understand that you need not go.'

It was formula, of course. The other four had been told the same thing, but they had gone. This fifth one, Fowler knew, would go as well. But suddenly he felt a dull hope stir within him that Allen wouldn't go.

'When do I start?' asked Allen.

There had been a time when Fowler might have taken quiet pride in that answer, but not now. He frowned briefly.

'Within the hour,' he said.

Allen stood waiting, quietly.

'Four other men have gone out and have not returned,' said Fowler. 'You know that, of course. We want you to return. We don't want you going off on any heroic rescue expedition. The main thing, the only thing, is that you come back, that you prove man can live in a Jovian form. Go to the first survey stake, no further, then come back. Don't take any chances. Don't investigate anything. Just come back.'

Allen nodded. 'I understand all that.'

'Miss Stanley will operate the converter,' Fowler went on. 'You need have no fear on that particular score. The other men were converted without mishap. They left the converter in apparently perfect condition. You will be in thoroughly competent hands. Miss Stanley is the best qualified conversion operator in the Solar System. She has had experience on most of the other planets. That is why she's here.'

Allen grinned at the woman and Fowler saw something flicker across Miss Stanley's face—something that might have been pity, or rage—or just plain fear. But it was gone again and she was smiling back at the youth who stood before the desk. Smiling in that prim, schoolteacherish way she had of smiling, almost as if she hated herself for doing it.

'I shall be looking forward,' said Allen, 'to my conversion.'

And the way he said it, he made it all a joke, a vast ironic joke.

But it was no joke.

It was serious business, deadly serious. Upon these tests, Fowler knew, depended the fate of men on Jupiter. If the tests succeeded, the resources of the giant planet would be thrown open. Man would take over Jupiter as he already had taken over the other smaller planets. And if they failed——

If they failed, Man would continue to be chained and hampered by the terrific pressure, the greater force of gravity, the weird chemistry of the planet. He would continue to be shut within the domes, unable to set actual foot upon the planet, unable to see it with direct, unaided vision, forced to rely upon the awkward tractors and the televisor, forced to work with clumsy tools and mechanisms or through the medium of robots that themselves were clumsy.

For Man, unprotected and in his natural form, would be blotted out by Jupiter's terrific pressure of fifteen thousand pounds per square inch, pressure that made terrestrial sea bottoms seem a vacuum by comparison.

Even the strongest metal Earthmen could devise couldn't exist under pressure such as that, under the pressure and the alkaline rains that forever swept the planet. It grew brittle and flaky, crumbling like clay, or it ran away in little streams and puddles of ammonia salts. Only by stepping up the toughness and strength of that metal, by increasing its electronic tension, could it be made to withstand the weight of thousands of miles of swirling, choking gases that made up the atmosphere. And even when that was done, everything had to be coated with tough quartz to keep away the rain—the liquid ammonia that fell as bitter rain.

Fowler sat listening to the engines in the sub-floor of the dome—engines that ran on endlessly, the dome never quiet of them. They had to run and keep on running, for if they stopped the power flowing into the metal walls of the dome would stop, the electronic tension would ease up and that would be the end of everything.

Towser roused himself under Fowler's desk and scratched another flea, his leg thumping hard against the floor.

'Is there anything else?' asked Allen.

Fowler shook his head. 'Perhaps there's something you want to do,' he said. 'Perhaps you——'

He had meant to say write a letter and he was glad he caught himself quick enough so he didn't say it.

Allen looked at his watch. 'I'll be there on time,' he said. He swung around and headed for the door.

Fowler knew Miss Stanley was watching him and he didn't want to turn and meet her eyes. He fumbled with a sheaf of papers on the desk before him.

'How long are you going to keep this up?' asked Miss Stanley and she bit off each word with a vicious snap.

He swung around in his chair and faced her then. Her lips were drawn into a straight, thin line, her hair seemed skinned back from her forehead tighter than ever, giving her face that queer, almost startling death-mask quality.

He tried to make his voice cool and level. 'As long as there s any need of it,' he said. 'As long as there's any hope.'

'You're going to keep on sentencing them to death,' she said. 'You're going to keep marching them out face to face with Jupiter. You're going to sit in here safe and comfortable and send them out to die.'

'There is no room for sentimentality, Miss Stanley,' Fowler said, trying to keep the note of anger from his voice. 'You know as well as I do why we're doing this. You realize that Man in his own form simply cannot cope with Jupiter. The only answer is to turn men into the sort of things that can cope with it. We've done it on the other planets.

'If a few men die, but we finally succeed, the price is small. Through the ages men have thrown away their lives on foolish things, for foolish reasons. Why should we hesitate, then, at a little death in a thing as great as this?'

Miss Stanley sat stiff and straight, hands folded in her lap, the lights shining on her greying hair and Fowler, watching her, tried to imagine what she might feel, what she might be thinking. He wasn't exactly afraid of her, but he didn't feel quite comfortable when she was around. Those sharp blue eyes saw too much, her hands looked far too competent. She should be somebody's Aunt sitting in a rocking chair with her knitting needles. But she wasn't. She was the top-notch conversion unit operator in the Solar System and she didn't like the way he was doing things.

'There is something wrong, Mr Fowler,' she declared.

'Precisely,' agreed Fowler. 'That's why I'm sending young Allen out alone. He may find out what it is.'

'And if he doesn't?'

'I'll send someone else.'

She rose slowly from her chair, started towards the door, then stopped before his desk.

'Some day,' she said, 'you will be a great man. You never let a chance go by. This is your chance. You knew it was when this dome was picked for the tests. If you put it through, you'll go up a notch or two. No matter how many men may die you'll go up a notch or two.'

'Miss Stanley,' he said and his voice was curt, 'young Allen is going out soon. Please be sure that your machine——'

'My machine,' she told him icily, 'is not to blame. It operates along the co-ordinates the biologists set up.'

He sat hunched at his desk, listening to her footsteps go down the corridor.

What she said was true, of course. The biologists had set up the co-ordinates. But the biologists could be wrong. Just a hair-breadth of difference, one iota of digression and the converter would be sending out something that wasn't the thing they meant to send. A mutant that might crack up, go haywire, come unstuck under some condition or stress of circumstance wholly unsuspected.

For Man didn't know much about what was going on outside. Only what his instruments told him was going on. And the samplings of those happenings furnished by those instruments and mechanisms had been no more than samplings, for Jupiter was unbelievably large and the domes were very few.

Even the work of the biologists in getting the data on the Lopers, apparently the highest form of Jovian life, had involved more than three years of intensive study and after that two years of checking to make sure. Work that could have been done on Earth in a week or two. But work that, in this case, couldn't be done on Earth at all, for one couldn't take a Jovian life form to Earth. The pressure here on Jupiter couldn't be duplicated outside of Jupiter and at Earth pressure and temperature the Lopers would simply have disappeared in a puff of gas.

Yet it was work that had to be done if Man ever hoped to go about Jupiter in the life form of the Lopers. For before the converter could change a man to another life form, every detailed physical characteristic of that life form must be known—surely and positively, with no chance of mistake.

Allen did not come back.

The tractors, combing the nearby terrain, found no trace of him, unless the skulking thing reported by one of the drivers had been the missing Earthman in Loper form.

The biologists sneered their most accomplished academic sneers when Fowler suggested the co-ordinates might be wrong. Carefully they pointed out, the co-ordinates worked. When a man was put into the converter and the switch was thrown, the man became a Loper. He left the machine and moved away, out of sight, into the soupy atmosphere.

Some quirk, Fowler had suggested; some tiny deviation from the thing a Loper should be, some minor defect. If there were, the biologists said, it would take years to find it.

And Fowler knew that they were right.

So there were five men now instead of four and Harold Allen had walked out into Jupiter for nothing at all. It was as if he'd never gone so far as knowledge was concerned.

Fowler reached across his desk and picked up the personnel file, a thin sheaf of paper neatly clipped together. It was a thing he dreaded but a thing he had to do. Somehow the reason for these strange disappearances must be found. And there was no other way than to send out more men.

He sat for a moment listening to the howling of the wind above the dome, the everlasting thundering gale that swept across the planet in boiling, twisting wrath.

Was there some threat out there, he asked himself? Some danger they did not know about? Something that lay in wait and gobbled up the Lopers, making no distinction between Lopers that were bona fide and Lopers that were men? To the gobblers, of course, it would make no difference.

Or had there been a basic fault in selecting the Lopers as the type of life best fitted for existence on the surface of the planet? The evident intelligence of the Lopers, he knew, had been one factor in that determination. For if the thing Man became did not have capacity for intelligence, Man could not for long retain his own intelligence in such a guise.

Had the biologists let that one factor weigh too heavily, using it to offset some other factor that might be unsatisfactory, even disastrous? It didn't seem likely. Stiffnecked as they might be, the biologists knew their business.

Or was the whole thing impossible, doomed from the very start? Conversion to other life forms had worked on other planets, but that did not necessarily mean it would work on Jupiter. Perhaps Man's intelligence could not function correctly through the sensory apparatus provided Jovian life. Perhaps the Lopers were so alien there was no common ground for human knowledge and the Jovian conception of existence to meet and work together.

Or the fault might lie with Man, be inherent with the race. Some mental aberration which, coupled with what they found outside, wouldn't let them come back. Although it might not be an aberration, not in the human sense. Perhaps just one ordinary human mental trait, accepted as commonplace on Earth, would be so violently at odds with Jovian existence that it would blast human sanity.

Claws rattled and clicked down the corridor. Listening to them, Fowler smiled wanly. It was Towser coming back from the kitchen, where he had gone to see his friend, the cook.

Towser came into the room, carrying a bone. He wagged his tail at Fowler and flopped down beside the desk, bone between his paws. For a long moment his rheumy old eyes regarded his master and Fowler reached down a hand to ruffle a ragged ear.

'You still like me, Towser?' Fowler asked and Towser thumped his tail.

'You're the only one,' said Fowler.

He straightened and swung back to the desk. His hand reached out and picked up the file.

Bennett? Bennett had a girl waiting for him back on Earth.

Andrews? Andrews was planning on going back to Mars Tech just as soon as he earned enough to see him through a year.

Olson? Olson was nearing pension age. All the time telling the boys how he was going to settle down and grow roses.

Carefully, Fowler laid the file back on the desk.

Sentencing men to death. Miss Stanley had said that, her pale lips scarcely moving in her parchment face. Marching men out to die while he, Fowler, sat here safe and comfortable.

They were saying it all through the dome, no doubt, especially since Allen had failed to return. They wouldn't say it to his face, of course. Even the man or men he called before this desk and told they were the next to go, wouldn't say it to him.

But he would see it in their eyes.

He picked up the file again. Bennett, Andrews, Olson. There were others, but there was no use in going on.

Kent Fowler knew that he couldn't do it, couldn't face them, couldn't send more men out to die.

He leaned forward and flipped up the toggle on the intercommunicator.

'Yes, Mr Fowler.'

'Miss Stanley, please.'

He waited for Miss Stanley, listening to Towser chewing half-heartedly on the bone. Towser's teeth were getting bad.

'Miss Stanley,' said Miss Stanley's voice.

'Just wanted to tell you, Miss Stanley, to get ready for two more.'

'Aren't you afraid,' asked Miss Stanley, 'that you'll run out of them? Sending out one at a time, they'd last longer, give you twice the satisfaction.'

'One of them,' said Fowler, 'will be a dog.'

'A dog!'

'Yes, Towser.'

He heard the quick, cold rage that iced her voice. 'Your own dog! He's been with you all these years——'

'That's the point,' said Fowler. 'Towser would be unhappy if I left him behind.'

It was not the Jupiter he had known through the televisor. He had expected it to be different, but not like this. He had expected a hell of ammonia rain and stinking fumes and the deafening, thundering tumult of the storm. He had expected swirling clouds and fog and the snarling flicker of monstrous thunderbolts.

He had not expected the lashing downpour would be reduced to drifting purple mist that moved like fleeing shadows over a red and purple sward. He had not even guessed the snaking bolts of lightning would be flares of pure ecstasy across a painted sky.

Waiting for Towser, Fowler flexed the muscles of his body, amazed at the smooth, sleek strength he found. Not a bad body, he decided, and grimaced at remembering how he had pitied the Lopers when he glimpsed them through the television screen.

For it had been hard to imagine a living organism based upon ammonia and hydrogen rather than upon water and oxygen, hard to believe that such a form of life could know the same quick thrill of life that humankind could know. Hard to conceive of life out in the soupy maelstrom that was Jupiter, not knowing, of course, that through Jovian eyes it was no soupy maelstrom at all.

The wind brushed against him with what seemed gentle fingers and he remembered with a start that by Earth standards the wind was a roaring gale, a two-hundred-mile an hour howler laden with deadly gases.

Pleasant scents seeped into his body. And yet scarcely scents, for it was not the sense of smell as he remembered it. It was as if his whole being was soaking up the sensation of lavender—and yet not lavender. It was something, he knew, for which he had no word, undoubtedly the first of many enigmas in terminology. For the words he knew, the thought symbols that served him as an Earthman would not serve him as a Jovian.

The lock in the side of the dome opened and Towser came tumbling out—at least he thought it must be Towser.

He started to call to the dog, his mind shaping the words he meant to say. But he couldn't say them. There was no way to say them. He had nothing to say them with.

For a moment his mind swirled in muddy terror, a blind fear that eddied in little puffs of panic through his brain.

How did Jovians talk? How——

Suddenly he was aware of Towser, intensely aware of the bumbling, eager friendliness of the shaggy animal that had followed him from Earth to many planets. As if the thing that was Towser had reached out and for a moment sat within his brain.

And out of the bubbling welcome that he sensed, came words.

'Hiya, pal.'

Not words, really, better than words. Thought symbols in his brain, communicated thought symbols that had shades of meaning words could never have.

'Hiya, Towser,' he said.

'I feel good,' said Towser. 'Like I was a pup. Lately I've been feeling pretty punk. Legs stiffening up on me and teeth wearing down to almost nothing. Hard to mumble a bone with teeth like that. Besides, the fleas give me hell. Used to be I never paid much attention to them. A couple of fleas more or less never meant much in my early days.'

'But . . . but——' Fowler's thoughts tumbled awkwardly. 'You're talking to me!'

'Sure thing,' said Towser. 'I always talked to you, but you couldn't hear me. I tried to say things to you, but I couldn't make the grade.'

'I understood you sometimes,' Fowler said.

'Not very well,' said Towser. 'You knew when I wanted food and when I wanted a drink and when I wanted out, but that's about all you ever managed.'

'I'm sorry,' Fowler said.

'Forget it,' Towser told him. 'I'll race you to the cliff.'

For the first time, Fowler saw the cliff, apparently many miles away, but with a strange crystalline beauty that sparkled in the shadow of the many-coloured clouds.

Fowler hesitated. 'It's a long way——'

'Ah, come on,' said Towser and even as he said it he started for the cliff.

Fowler followed, testing his legs, testing the strength in that new body of his, a bit doubtful at first, amazed a moment later, then running with a sheer joyousness that was one with the red and purple sward, with the drifting smoke of the rain across the land.

As he ran the consciousness of music came to him, a music that beat into his body, that surged throughout his being, that lifted him on wings of silver speed. Music like bells might make from some steeple on a sunny, springtime hill.

As the cliff drew nearer the music deepened and filled the universe with a spray of magic sound. And he knew the music came from the tumbling waterfall that feathered down the face of the shining cliff.

Only, he knew, it was no waterfall, but an ammonia-fall and the cliff was white because it was oxygen, solidified.

He skidded to a stop beside Towser where the waterfall broke into a glittering rainbow of many hundred colours. Literally many hundred, for here, he saw, was no shading of one primary to another as human beings saw, but a clear-cut selectivity that broke the prism down to its last ultimate classification.

'The music,' said Towser.

'Yes, what about it?'

'The music,' said Towser, 'is vibrations. Vibrations of water falling.'

'But, Towser, you don't know about vibrations.'

'Yes, I do,' contended Towser. 'It just popped into my head.'

Fowler gulped mentally. 'Just popped!'

And suddenly, within his own head, he held a formula—the formula for a process that would make metal to withstand the pressure of Jupiter.

He stared, astounded, at the waterfall and swiftly his mind took the many colours and placed them in their exact sequence in the spectrum. Just like that. Just out of blue sky. Out of nothing, for he knew nothing either of metals or of colours.

'Towser,' he cried. 'Towser, something's happening to us!'

'Yeah, I know,' said Towser.

'It's our brains,' said Fowler. 'We're using them, all of them, down to the last hidden corner. Using them to figure out things we should have known all the time. Maybe the brains of Earth things naturally are slow and foggy. Maybe we are the morons of the universe. Maybe we are fixed so we have to do things the hard way.'

And, in the new sharp clarity of thought that seemed to grip him, he knew that it would not only be the matter of colours in a waterfall or metals that would resist the pressure of Jupiter. He sensed other things, things not yet quite clear. A vague whispering that hinted of greater things, of mysteries beyond the pale of human thought, beyond even the pale of human imagination. Mysteries, fact, logic built on reasoning. Things that any brain should know if it used all its reasoning power.

'We're still mostly Earth,' he said. 'We're just beginning to learn a few of the things we are to know—a few of the things that were kept from us as human beings, perhaps because we were human beings. Because our human bodies were poor bodies. Poorly equipped for thinking, poorly equipped in certain senses that one has to have to know. Perhaps even lacking in certain senses that are necessary to true knowledge.'

He stared back at the dome, a tiny black thing dwarfed by the distance.

Back there were men who couldn't see the beauty that was Jupiter. Men who thought that swirling clouds and lashing rain obscured the planet's face. Unseeing human eyes. Poor eyes. Eyes that could not see the beauty in the clouds, that could not see through the storm. Bodies that could not feel the thrill of trilling music stemming from the rush of broken water.

Men who walked alone, in terrible loneliness, talking with their tongue like Boy Scouts wigwagging out their messages, unable to reach out and touch one another's mind as he could reach out and touch Towser's mind. Shut off forever from that personal, intimate contact with other living things.

He, Fowler, had expected terror inspired by alien things out here on the surface, had expected to cower before the threat of unknown things, had steeled himself against disgust of a situation that was not of Earth.

But instead he had found something greater than Man had ever known. A swifter, surer body. A sense of exhilaration, a deeper sense of life. A sharper mind. A world of beauty that even the dreamers of the Earth had not yet imagined.

'Let's get going,' Towser urged.

'Where do you want to go?'

'Anywhere,' said Towser. 'Just start going and see where we end up. I have a feeling . . . well, a feeling——'

'Yes, I know,' said Fowler.

For he had the feeling, too. The feeling of high destiny. A certain sense of greatness. A knowledge that somewhere off beyond the horizons lay adventure and things greater than adventure.

Those other five had felt it, too. Had felt the urge to go and see, the compelling sense that here lay a life of fullness and of knowledge.

That, he knew, was why they had not returned.

'I won't go back,' said Towser.

'We can't let them down,' said Fowler.

Fowler took a step or two, back towards the dome, then stopped.

Back to the dome. Back to that aching, poison-laden body he had left. It hadn't seemed aching before, but now he knew it was.

Back to the fuzzy brain. Back to muddled thinking. Back to the flapping mouths that formed signals others understood. Back to eyes that now would be worse than no sight at all. Back to squalor, back to crawling, back to ignorance.

'Perhaps some day,' he said, muttering to himself.

'We got a lot to do and a lot to see,' said Towser. 'We got a lot to learn. We'll find things——'

Yes, they could find things. Civilizations, perhaps. Civilizations that would make the civilization of Man seem puny by comparison. Beauty and, more important, an understanding of that beauty. And a comradeship no one had ever known before—that no man, no dog had ever known before.

And life. The quickness of life after what seemed a drugged existence.

'I can't go back,' said Towser.

'Nor I,' said Fowler.

'They would turn me back into a dog,' said Towser.

'And me,' said Fowler, 'back into a man.'

THE PIPER'S SON

LEWIS PADGETT

The Green Man was climbing the glass mountains, and hairy, gnomish faces peered at him from crevices. This was only another step in the Green Man's endless, exciting odyssey. He'd had a great many adventures already—in the Flame Country, among the Dimension Changers, with the City Apes who sneered endlessly while their blunt, clumsy fingers fumbled at deathrays. The trolls, however, were masters of magic, and were trying to stop the Green Man with spells. Little whirlwinds of force spun underfoot, trying to trip the Green Man, a figure of marvellous muscular development, handsome as a god, and hairless from head to foot, glistening pale green. The whirlwinds formed a fascinating pattern. If you could thread a precarious path among them—avoiding the pale yellow ones especially—you could get through.

And the hairy gnomes watched malignantly, jealously, from their crannies in the glass crags.

Al Burkhalter, having recently achieved the mature status of eight full years, lounged under a tree and masticated a grass blade. He was so immersed in his daydreams that his father had to nudge his side gently to bring comprehension into the half-closed eyes. It was a good day for dreaming, anyway—a hot sun and a cool wind blowing down from the white Sierra peaks to the east. Timothy grass sent its faintly musty fragrance along the channels of air, and Ed Burkhalter was glad that his son was second-generation since the Blowup. He himself had been born ten years after the last bomb had been dropped, but second-hand memories can be pretty bad too.

'Hello, Al,' he said, and the youth vouchsafed a half-lidded glance of tolerant acceptance.

'Hi, Dad.'

'Want to come downtown with me?'

'Nope,' Al said, relaxing instantly into his stupor.

Burkhalter raised a figurative eyebrow and half turned. On an impulse, then, he did something he rarely did without the tacit permission of the other party; he used his telepathic power to reach into Al's mind. There was, he admitted to himself, a certain hesitancy, a subconscious unwillingness on his part, to do this, even though Al had pretty well outgrown the nasty, inhuman formlessness of mental babyhood. There had been a time when Al's mind had been quite shocking in its alienage. Burkhalter remembered a few abortive experiments he had made before Al's birth; few fathers-to-be could resist the temptation to experiment with embryonic brains, and that had brought back nightmares Burkhalter had not had since his youth. There had been enormous rolling masses, and an appalling vastness, and other things. Prenatal memories were ticklish, and should be left to qualified mnemonic psychologists.

But now Al was maturing, and daydreaming, as usual, in bright colours. Burkhalter, reassured, felt that he had fulfilled his duty as a monitor and left his son still eating grass and ruminating.

Just the same, there was a sudden softness inside of him, and the aching, futile pity he was apt to feel for helpless things that were as yet unqualified for conflict with that extraordinarily complicated business of living. Conflict, competition, had not died out when war abolished itself; the business of adjustment even to one's surroundings was a conflict, and conversation a duel. With Al, too, there was a double problem. Yes, language was in effect a tariff wall, and a Baldy could appreciate that thoroughly, since the wall didn't exist between Baldies.

Walking down the rubbery walk that led to town centre, Burkhalter grinned wryly and ran lean fingers through his well-kept wig. Strangers were very often surprised to know that he was a Baldy, a telepath. They looked at him with wondering eyes, too courteous to ask how it felt to be a freak, but obviously avid. Burkhalter, who knew diplomacy, would be quite willing to lead the conversation.

'My folks lived near Chicago after the Blowup. That was why.'

'Oh.' Stare. 'I'd heard that was why so many—' Startled pause.

'Freaks or mutations. There were both. I still don't know which class I belong to,' he'd add disarmingly.

'You're no freak!' They didn't protest too much.

'Well, some mighty queer specimens came out of the radioactive-affected areas around the bomb-targets. Funny things happened to the germ plasm. Most of 'em died out; they couldn't reproduce; but you'll still find a few creatures in sanitariums—two heads, you know. And so on.'

Nevertheless they were always ill-at-ease. 'You mean you can read my mind—now?'

'I could, but I'm not. It's hard work, except with another telepath. And we Baldies—well, we don't, that's all.' A man with abnormal muscle development wouldn't go around knocking people down. Not unless he wanted to be mobbed. Baldies were always sneakingly conscious of a hidden peril, lynch law. And wise Baldies didn't even imply that they had an . . . extra sense. They just said they were different, and let it go at that.

But one question was always implied, though not always mentioned. 'If I were a telepath, I'd . . . how much do you make a year?'

They were surprised at the answer. A mindreader certainly could make a fortune, if he wanted. So why did Ed Burkhalter stay a semantics expert in Modoc Publishing Town, when a trip to one of the science towns would enable him to get hold of secrets that would get him a fortune?

There was a good reason. Self-preservation was a part of it. For which reason Burkhalter, and many like him, wore toupees. Though there were many Baldies who did not.

Modoc was a twin town with Pueblo, across the mountain barrier south of the waste that had been Denver. Pueblo held the presses, photolinotypes, and the machines that turned scripts into books, after Modoc had dealt with them. There was a helicopter distribution fleet at Pueblo, and for the last week Oldfield, the manager, had been demanding the manuscript of *Psychohistory*, turned out by a New Yale man who had got tremendously involved in past emotional problems, to the detriment of literary clarity. The truth was that he distrusted Burkhalter. And Burkhalter, neither a priest nor a psychologist, had to become both without admitting it to the confused author of *Psychohistory*.

The sprawling buildings of the publishing house lay ahead and below, more like a resort than anything more utilitarian. That had been necessary. Authors were peculiar people, and often it was necessary to induce them to take hydrotherapic treatments before they were in shape to work out their books with the semantic experts. Nobody was going to bite them, but they didn't realize that, and either cowered in corners, terrified, or else blustered their way around, using language few could understand. Jem Quayle, author of *Psychohistory,* fitted into neither group; he was simply baffled by the intensity of his own research. His personal history had qualified him too well for emotional involvements with the past—and that was a serious matter when a thesis of this particular type was in progress.

Dr Moon, who was on the Board, sat near the south entrance, eating an apple which he peeled carefully with his silver-hilted dagger. Moon was fat, short, and shapeless; he didn't have much hair, but he wasn't a telepath; Baldies were entirely hairless. He gulped and waved at Burkhalter.

'Ed . . . *urp* . . . want to talk to you.'

'Sure,' Burkhalter said, agreeably coming to a standstill and rocking on his heels. Ingrained habit made him sit down beside the Boardman; Baldies, for obvious reasons, never stood up when non-telepaths were sitting. Their eyes met now on the same level. Burkhalter said, 'What's up?'

'The store got some Shasta apples flown in yesterday. Better tell Ethel to get some before they're sold out. Here.' Moon watched his companion eat a chunk, and nod.

'Good. I'll have her get some. The copter's laid up for today, though; Ethel pulled the wrong gadget.'

'Foolproof,' Moon said bitterly. 'Huron's turning out some sweet models these days; I'm getting my new one from Michigan. Listen, Pueblo called me this morning on Quayle's book.'

'Oldfield?'

'Our boy,' Moon nodded. 'He says can't you send over even a few chapters.'

Burkhalter shook his head. 'I don't think so. There are some abstracts right in the beginning that just have to be clarified, and Quayle is—' He hesitated.

'What?'

Burkhalter thought about the Oedipus complex he'd uncovered in Quayle's mind, but that was sancrosanct, even though it kept Quayle from interpreting Darius with cold logic. 'He's got muddy thinking in there. I can't pass it; I tried it on three readers yesterday, and got different reactions from all of them. So far *Psychohistory* is all things to all men. The critics would lambaste us if we released the book as it is. Can't you string Oldfield along for a while longer?'

'Maybe,' Moon said doubtfully. 'I've got a subjective novella I could rush over. It's light vicarious eroticism, and that's harmless; besides, it's semantically OK'd. We've been holding it up for an artist, but I can put Duman on it. I'll do that, yeah. I'll shoot the script over to Pueblo and he can make the plates later. A merry life we lead, Ed.'

'A little too merry sometimes,' Burkhalter said. He got up, nodded, and went in search of Quayle, who was relaxing, on one of the sun decks.

Quayle was a thin, tall man with a worried face and the abstract air of an unshelled tortoise. He lay on his flexiglass couch, direct sunlight toasting him from above, while the reflected rays sneaked up on him from below, through the transparent crystal. Burkhalter pulled off his shirt and dropped on a sunner beside Quayle. The author glanced at Burkhalter's hairless chest and half-formed revulsion rose in him: *A Baldy . . . no privacy . . . none of his business . . . fake eyebrows and lashes; he's still a—*

Something ugly, at that point.

Diplomatically Burkhalter touched a button, and on a screen overhead a page of *Psychohistory* appeared, enlarged and easily readable. Quayle scanned the sheet. It had code notations on it, made by the readers, recognized by Burkhalter as varied reactions to what should have been straight-line explanations. If three readers had got three different meanings out of that paragraph—well, what *did* Quayle mean? He reached delicately into the mind, conscious of useless guards erected against intrusion, mud barricades over which his mental eye stole like a searching, quiet wind. No ordinary man could guard his mind against a Baldy. But Baldies could guard their privacy against intrusion by other telepaths—adults, that is. There was a psychic selector band, a—

Here it came. But muddled a bit. *Darius*: that wasn't simply a word; it wasn't a picture, either; it was really a second *life*. But scattered, fragmentary. Scraps of scent and sound, and memories, and emotional reactions. Admiration and hatred. A burning impotence. A black tornado, smelling of pine, roaring across a map of Europe and Asia. Pine scent stronger now, and horrible humiliation, and remembered pain . . . eyes . . . *Get out!*

Burkhalter put down the dictograph mouthpiece and lay looking up through the darkened eye-shells he had donned. 'I got out as soon as you wanted me to,' he said. 'I'm still out.'

Quayle, lay there, breathing hard. 'Thanks,' he said. 'Apologies. Why you don't ask a duello—'

'I don't want to duel with you,' Burkhalter said. 'I've never put blood on my dagger in my life. Besides, I can see your side of it. Remember, this is my job, Mr Quayle, and I've learned a lot of things—that I've forgotten again.'

'It's intrusion, I suppose. I tell myself that it doesn't matter, but my privacy—is important.'

Burkhalter said patiently, 'We can keep trying it from different angles until we find one that isn't too private. Suppose, for example, I asked you if you admired Darius.'

Admiration . . . and pine scent . . . and Burkhalter said quickly, 'I'm out. OK?'

'Thanks,' Quayle muttered. He turned on his side, away from the other man. After a moment he said, 'That's silly—turning over, I mean. You don't have to see my face to know what I'm thinking.'

'You have to put out the welcome mat before I walk in,' Burkhalter told him.

'I guess I believe that. I've met some Baldies, though, that were . . . that I didn't like.'

'There's a lot on that order, sure. I know the type. The ones who don't wear wigs.'

Quayle said, 'They'll read your mind and embarrass you just for the fun of it. They ought to be—taught better.'

Burkhalter blinked in the sunlight. 'Well, Mr Quayle, it's this way. A Baldy's got his problems, too. He's got to orient himself to a world that isn't telepathic; and I suppose a lot of Baldies rather feel that they're letting their specialization go to waste. There *are* jobs a man like me is suited for—'

Man! He caught the scrap of thought from Quayle. He ignored it, his face as always a mobile mask, and went on.

'Semantics have always been a problem, even in countries speaking only one tongue. A qualified Baldy is a swell interpreter. And, though there aren't any Baldies on the detective forces, they often work with the police. It's rather like being a machine that can do only a few things.'

'A few things more than humans can,' Quayle said.

Sure, Burkhalter thought, if we could compete on equal footing with non-telepathic humanity. But would blind men trust one who could see? Would they play poker with him? A sudden, deep bitterness put an unpleasant taste in Burkhalter's mouth. What was the answer? Reservations for Baldies? Isolation? And would a nation of blind men trust those with vision enough for that? Or would they be dusted off—the sure cure, the check-and-balance system that made war an impossibility.

He remembered when Red Bank had been dusted off, and maybe that had been justified. The town was getting too big for its boots, and personal dignity was a vital factor; you weren't willing to lose face as long as a dagger swung at your belt. Similarly, the thousands upon thousands of little towns that covered America, each with its peculiar specialty—helicopter manufacture for Huron and Michigan, vegetable farming for Conoy and Diego, textiles and education and art and machines—each little town had a wary eye on all the others. The science and research centres were a little larger; nobody objected to that, for technicians never made war except under pressure; but few of the towns held more than a few hundred families. It was check-and-balance in most efficient degree; whenever a town showed signs of wanting to become a city—thence, a capital, thence, an imperialistic empire—it was dusted off. Though that had not happened for a long while. And Red Bank might have been a mistake.

Geopolitically it was a fine set-up; sociologically it was acceptable, but brought necessary changes. There was subconscious swash-buckling. The rights of the individual had become more highly regarded as decentralization took place. And men learned.

They learned a monetary system based primarily upon barter. They learned to fly; nobody drove surface cars. They learned new things, but they did not forget the Blowup, and in secret places near every town were hidden the bombs that could utterly and fantastically exterminate a town, as such bombs had exterminated the cities during the Blowup.

And everybody knew how to make those bombs. They were beautifully, terribly simple. You could find the ingredients any-where and prepare them easily. Then you could take your heli-copter over a town, drop an egg overside—and perform an erasure.

Outside of the wilderness malcontents, the maladjusted people found in every race, nobody kicked. And the roaming tribes never raided and never banded together in large groups—for fear of an erasure.

The artisans were maladjusted too, to some degree, but they

weren't antisocial, so they lived where they wanted and painted, wrote, composed, and retreated into their own private worlds. The scientists, equally maladjusted in other lines, retreated to their slightly larger towns, banding together in small universes, and turned out remarkable technical achievements.

And the Baldies—found jobs where they could.

No non-telepath would have viewed the world environment quite as Burkhalter did. He was abnormally conscious of the human element, attaching a deeper, more profound significance to those human values, undoubtedly because he saw men in more than the ordinary dimensions. And also, in a way—and inevitably—he looked at humanity from outside.

Yet he was human. The barrier that telepathy had raised made men suspicious of him, more so than if he had had two heads—then they could have pitied. As it was—

As it was, he adjusted the scanner until new pages of the typescript came flickering into view above. 'Say when,' he told Quayle.

Quayle brushed back his grey hair. 'I feel sensitive all over,' he objected. 'After all, I've been under a considerable strain correlating my material.'

'Well, we can always postpone publication.' Burkhalter threw out the suggestion casually, and was pleased when Quayle didn't nibble. He didn't like to fail, either.

'No. No, I want to get the thing done now.'

'Mental catharsis—'

'Well, by a psychologist, perhaps. But now by—'

'—a Baldy. You know that a lot of psychologists have Baldy helpers. They get good results, too.'

Quayle turned on the tobacco smoke, inhaling slowly. 'I suppose . . . I've not had much contact with Baldies. Or too much—without selectivity. I saw some in an asylum once. I'm not being offensive, am I?'

'No,' Burkhalter said. 'Every mutation can run too close to the line. There were lots of failures. The hard radiations brought about one true mutation: hairless telepaths, but they didn't all hew true to the line. The mind's a queer gadget—you know that. It's a colloid balancing, figuratively, on the point of a pin. If there's any flaw, telepathy's apt to bring it out. So you'll find that the Blowup caused a hell of a lot of insanity. Not only among the Baldies, but among the other mutations that developed then. Except that the Baldies are almost always paranoidal.'

'And dementia praecox,' Quayle said, finding relief from his own embarrassment in turning the spotlight on Burkhalter.

'And dp. Yeah. When a confused mind acquires the telepathic instinct—an hereditary bollixed mind—it can't handle it all. There's disorientation. The paranoia group retreat into their own private worlds, and the dp's simply don't realize that *this* world exists. There are distinctions, but I think that a valid basis.'

'In a way,' Quayle said, 'it's frightening. I can't think of any historical parallel.'

'No.'

'What do you think the end of it will be?'

'I don't know,' Burkhalter said thoughtfully. 'I think we'll be assimilated. There hasn't been enough time yet. We're specialized in a certain way, and we're useful in certain jobs.'

'If you're satisfied to stay there. The Baldies who won't wear wigs—'

'They're so bad-tempered I expect they'll all be killed off in duels eventually,' Burkhalter smiled. 'No great loss. The rest of us, we're getting what we want—acceptance. We don't have horns or halos.'

Quayle shook his head. 'I'm glad, I think, that I'm not a telepath. The mind's mysterious enough anyway, without new doors opening. Thanks for letting me talk. I think I've got part of it talked out, anyway. Shall we try the script again?'

'Sure,' Burkhalter said, and again the procession of pages flickered on the screen above them. Quayle did seem less guarded; his thoughts were more lucid, and Burkhalter was able to get at the true meanings of many of the hitherto muddy statements. They worked easily, the telepath dictating rephrasings into his dictograph, and only twice did they have to hurdle emotional tangles. At noon they knocked off, and Burkhalter, with a friendly nod, took the dropper to his office, where he found some calls listed on the visor. He ran off repeats, and a worried look crept into his blue eyes.

He talked with Dr Moon in a booth at luncheon. The conversation lasted so long that only the induction cups kept the coffee hot, but Burkhalter had more than one problem to discuss. And he'd known Moon for a long time. The fat man was one of the few who were not, he thought, subconsciously repelled by the fact that Burkhalter was a Baldy.

'I've never fought a duel in my life, Doc. I can't afford to.'

'You can't afford not to. You can't turn down the challenge, Ed. It isn't done.'

'But this fellow Reilly—I don't even know him.'

'I know of him,' Moon said. 'He's got a bad temper. Duelled a lot.'

Burkhalter slammed his hand down on the table, 'It's ridiculous. I won't do it!'

'Well,' Moon said practically, 'Your wife can't fight him. And if Ethel's been reading Mrs Reilly's mind and gossiping, Reilly's got a case.'

'Don't you think we know the dangers of that?' Burkhalter asked in a low voice. 'Ethel doesn't go around reading minds any more than I do. It'd be fatal—for us. And for any other Baldy.'

'Not the hairless ones. The ones who won't wear wigs. They—'

'They're fools. And they're giving all the Baldies a bad name. Point one, Ethel doesn't read minds; she didn't read Mrs Reilly's. Point two, she doesn't gossip.'

'La Reilly is obviously an hysterical type,' Moon said. 'Word got around about this scandal, whatever it was, and Mrs Reilly remembered she'd seen Ethel lately. She's the type who needs a scapegoat anyway. I rather imagine she let word drop herself, and had to cover up so her husband wouldn't blame her.'

'I'm not going to accept Reilly's challenge,' Burkhalter said doggedly.

'You'll have to.'

'Listen, Doc, maybe—'

'What?'

'Nothing. An idea. It might work. Forget about that; I think I've got the right answer. I can't afford a duel and that's flat.'

'You're not a coward.'

'There's one thing Baldies are afraid of,' Burkhalter said, 'and that's public opinion. I happen to know I'd kill Reilly. That's the reason why I've never duelled in my life.'

Moon drank coffee. 'Hm-m-m. I think—'

'Don't. There was something else. I'm wondering if I ought to send Al off to a special school.'

'What's wrong with the kid?'

'He's turning out to be a beautiful delinquent. His teacher called me this morning. The playback was something to hear. He's talking funny and acting funny. Playing nasty little tricks on his friends—if he has any left by now.'

'All kids are cruel.'

'Kids don't know what cruelty means. That's why they're cruel; they lack empathy. But Al's getting—' Burkhalter gestured helplessly. 'He's turning into a young tyrant. He doesn't seem to give a care about anything, according to his teacher.'

'That's not too abnormal, so far.'

'That's not the worst. He's become very egotistical. Too much so. I don't want him to turn into one of the wigless Baldies you were mentioning.' Burkhalter didn't mention the other possibility; paranoia, insanity.

'He must pick things up somewhere. At home? Scarcely, Ed. Where else does he go?'

'The usual places. He's got a normal environment.'

'I should think,' Moon said, 'that a Baldy would have unusual opportunities in training a youngster. The mental rapport—eh?'

'Yeah. But—I don't know. The trouble is,' Burkhalter said almost inaudibly. 'I wish to God I wasn't different. We didn't ask to be telepaths. Maybe it's all very wonderful in the long run, but I'm one person, and I've got my own microcosm. People who deal in long-term sociology are apt to forget that. They can figure out the answers, but it's every individual man—or Baldy—who's got to fight his own personal battle while he's alive. And it isn't as clearcut as a battle. It's worse: it's the necessity of watching yourself every second, of fitting yourself into a world that doesn't want you.'

Moon looked uncomfortable. 'Are you being a little sorry for yourself, Ed?'

Burkhalter shook himself. 'I am, Doc. But I'll work it out.'

'We both will,' Moon said, but Burkhalter didn't really expect much help from him. Moon would be willing, but it was horribly different for an ordinary man to conceive that a Baldy was—the same. It was the difference that men looked for, and found.

Anyway, he'd have to settle matters before he saw Ethel again. He could easily conceal the knowledge, but she would recognize a mental barrier and wonder. Their marriage had been the more ideal because of the additional rapport, something that compensated for an inevitable, half-sensed estrangement from the rest of the world.

'How's *Psychohistory* going?' Moon asked after a while.

'Better than I expected. I've got a new angle on Quayle. If I talk about myself, that seems to draw him out. It gives him enough confidence to let him open his mind to me. We may have those first chapters ready for Oldfield, in spite of everything.'

'Good. Just the same, he can't rush us. If we've got to shoot out books that fast, we might as well go back to the days of semantic confusion. Which we won't!'

'Well,' Burkhalter said, getting up, 'I'll smoosh along. See you.'

'About Reilly—'

'Let it lay.' Burkhalter went out, heading for the address his visor had listed. He touched the dagger at his belt. Duelling wouldn't do for Baldies, but—'

A greeting thought crept into his mind, and, under the arch that led into the campus, he paused to grin at Sam Shane, a New Orleans area Baldy who affected a wig of flaming red. They didn't bother to talk.

Personal question, involving mental, moral, and physical well-being.

A satisfied glow. And you, Burkhalter? For an instant Burkhalter half-saw what the symbol of his name meant to Shane.

Shadow of trouble.

A warm, willing anxiousness to help. There was a bond between Baldies.

Burkhalter thought: But everywhere I'd go there'd be the same suspicion. We're freaks.

More so elsewhere, Shane thought. There are a lot of us in Modoc Town. People are invariably more suspicious where they're not in daily contact with—Us.

The boy—

I've trouble too, Shane thought. It's worried me. My two girls—

Delinquency?

Yes.

Common denominators?

Don't know. More than one of Us have had the same trouble with our kids.

Secondary characteristics of the mutation? Second generation emergence?

Doubtful, Shane thought, scowling in his mind, shading his concept with a wavering question. We'll think it over later. Must go.

Burkhalter sighed and went on his way. The houses were strung out around the central industry of Modoc, and he cut through a park towards his destination. It was a sprawling curved building, but it wasn't inhabited, so Burkhalter filed Reilly for future reference, and, with a glance at his timer, angled over a hillside towards the school. As he expected, it was recreation time, and he spotted Al lounging under a tree, some distance from his companions, who were involved in a pleasantly murderous game of Blowup.

He sent his thought ahead.

The Green Man had almost reached the top of the mountain. The hairy gnomes were pelting on his trail, most unfairly shooting sizzling light-streaks at their quarry, but the Green Man was agile enough to dodge. The rocks were leaning—

'Al.'

—inward, pushed by the gnomes, ready to—

'*Al!*' Burkhalter sent his thought with the word, jolting into the boy's mind, a trick he very seldom employed, since youth was practically defenceless against such invasion.

'Hello, Dad,' Al said, undisturbed. 'What's up?'

'A report from your teacher.'

'I didn't do anything.'

'She told me what it was. Listen, kid. Don't start getting any funny ideas in your head.'

'I'm not.'

'Do you think a Baldy is better or worse than a non-Baldy?'

Al moved his feet uncomfortably. He didn't answer.

'Well,' Burkhalter said, 'the answer is both and neither. And here's why. A Baldy can communicate mentally, but he lives in a world where most people can't.'

'They're dumb,' Al opined.

'Not so dumb, if they're better suited to their world than you are. You might as well say a frog's better than a fish because he's an amphibian.' Burkhalter briefly amplified and explained the terms telepathically.

'Well . . . oh, I get it, all right.'

'Maybe,' Burkhalter said slowly, 'what you need is a swift kick in the pants. That thought wasn't so hot. What was it again?'

Al tried to hide it, blanking out. Burkhalter began to lift the barrier, an easy matter for him, but stopped. Al regarded his father in a most unfilial way—in fact, as a sort of boneless fish. That had been clear.

'If you're so egotistical,' Burkhalter pointed out, 'maybe you can see it this way. Do you know why there aren't any Baldies in key positions?'

'Sure I do,' Al said unexpectedly. 'They're afraid.'

'Of what, then?'

'The—' That picture had been very curious, a commingling of something vaguely familiar to Burkhalter. 'The non-Baldies.'

'Well, if we took positions where we could take advantage of our telepathic function, non-Baldies would be plenty envious—especially if we were successes. If a Baldy even invented a better mousetrap, plenty of people would say he'd stolen the idea from some non-Baldy's mind. You get the point?'

'Yes, Dad.' But he hadn't. Burkhalter sighed and looked up. He recognized one of Shane's girls on a nearby hillside, sitting alone against a boulder. There were other isolated figures here and there. Far to the east the snowy rampart of the Rockies made an irregular pattern against blue sky.

'Al,' Burkhalter said, 'I don't want you to get a chip on your shoulder. This is a pretty swell world, and the people in it are, on the whole, nice people. There's a law of averages. It isn't sensible for us to get too much wealth or power, because that'd militate against us—and we don't need it anyway. Nobody's poor. We find our work, we do it, and we're reasonably happy. We have some advantages non-Baldies don't have; in marriage, for example. Mental intimacy is quite as important as physical. But I don't want you to feel that being a Baldy makes you a god. It doesn't. I can still,' he added thoughtfully, 'spank it out of you, in case you care to follow out that concept in your mind at the moment.'

Al gulped and beat a hasty retreat. 'I'm sorry. I won't do it again.'

'And keep your hair on, too. Don't take your wig off in class. Use the stickum stuff in the bathroom closet.'

'Yes, but . . . Mr Venner doesn't wear a wig.'

'Remind me to do some historical research with you on zoot-suiters,' Burkhalter said. 'Mr Venner's wiglessness is probably his only virtue, if you consider it one.'

'He makes money.'

'Anybody would, in that general store of his. But people don't buy from him if they can help it, you'll notice. That's what I mean by a chip on your shoulder. He's got one. There are Baldies like Venner, Al, but you might, sometime, ask the guy if he's happy. For your information, I am. More than Venner, anyway. Catch?'

'Yes, Dad.' Al seemed submissive, but it was merely that. Burkhalter, still troubled, nodded and walked away. As he passed near the Shane girl's boulder he caught a scrap:—*at the summit of the Glass Mountains, rolling rocks back at the gnomes until—*

He withdrew; it was an unconscious habit, touching minds that were sensitive, but with children it was definitely unfair. With adult Baldies it was simply the instinctive gesture of tipping your hat; one answered or one didn't. The barrier could be erected; there could be a blank-out; or there could be the snub of concentration on a single thought, private and not be to intruded on.

A copter with a string of gliders was coming in from the south: a freighter laden with frozen foods from South America, to judge by the markings. Burkhalter made a note to pick up an Argentine steak. He'd got a new recipe he wanted to try out, a charcoal broil with barbecue sauce, a welcome change from the short-wave cooked meats they'd been having for a week. Tomatoes, chile, mm-m—what else. Oh, yes. The duel with Reilly. Burkhalter absently touched his dagger's hilt and made a small, mocking sound in his throat. Perhaps he was innately a pacifist. It was rather difficult to think of a duel seriously, even though everyone else did, when the details of a barbecue dinner were prosaic in his mind.

So it went. The tides of civilization rolled in century-long waves across the continents, and each particular wave, though conscious of its participation in the tide, nevertheless was more preoccupied with dinner. And, unless you happened to be a thousand feet tall, had the brain of a god and a god's life-span, what was the difference? People missed a lot—people like Venner, who was certainly a crank, not batty enough to qualify for the asylum, but certainly a potential paranoid type. The man's refusal to wear a wig labelled him as an individualist, but as an exhibitionist, too. If he didn't feel ashamed of his hairlessness, why should he bother to flaunt it? Besides, the man had a bad temper, and if people kicked him around, he asked for it by starting the kicking himself.

But as for Al, the kid was heading for something approaching delinquency. It couldn't be the normal development of childhood, Burkhalter thought. He didn't pretend to be an expert, but he was still young enough to remember his own formative years, and he had had more handicaps than Al had now. In those days, Baldies had been very new and very freakish. There'd been more than one movement to isolate, sterilize, or even exterminate the mutations.

Burkhalter sighed. If he had been born before the Blowup, it might have been different. Impossible to say. One could read history, but one couldn't live it. In the future, perhaps, there might be telepathic libraries in which that would be possible. So many opportunities, in fact—and so few that the world was ready to accept as yet. Eventually Baldies would not be regarded as freaks, and by that time real progress would be possible.

But people don't make history—Burkhalter thought. Peoples do that. Not the individual.

He stopped by Reilly's house again, and this time the man answered, a burly, freckled, squint-eyed fellow with immense hands and, Burkhalter noted, fine muscular co-ordination. He rested those hands on the Dutch door and nodded.

'Who're you, mister?'

'My name's Burkhalter.'

Comprehension and wariness leaped into Reilly's eyes. 'Oh, I see. You got my call?'

'I did,' Burkhalter said. 'I want to talk to you about it. May I come in?'

'OK.' He stepped back, opening the way through a hall and into a spacious living room, where diffused light filtered through glassy mosaic walls. 'Want to set the time?'

'I want to tell you you're wrong.'

'Now wait a minute,' Reilly said, patting the air. 'My wife's out now, but she gave me the straight of it. I don't like this business of sneaking into a man's mind; it's crooked. You should have told *your* wife to mind her business—or keep her tongue quiet.'

Burkhalter said patiently, 'I give you my word, Reilly, that Ethel didn't read your wife's mind.'

'Does she say so?'

'I . . . well, I haven't asked her.'

'Yeah,' Reilly said with an air of triumph.

'I don't need to. I know her well enough. And . . . well, I'm a Baldy myself.'

'I know you are,' Reilly said. 'For all I know, you may be reading my mind now.' He hesitated. 'Get out of my house. I like my privacy. We'll meet at dawn tomorrow, if that's satisfactory with you. Now get out.' He seemed to have something on his mind, some ancient memory, perhaps, that he didn't wish exposed.

Burkhalter nobly resisted the temptation. 'No Baldy would read—'

'Go on, get out!'

'Listen! You wouldn't have a chance in a duel with me!'

'Do you know how many notches I've got?' Reilly asked.

'Ever duelled a Baldy?'

'I'll cut the notch deeper tomorrow. Get out, d'you hear?'

Burkhalter, biting his lips, said, 'Man, don't you realize that in a duel I could read your mind?'

'I don't care . . . what?'

'I'd be half a jump ahead of you. No matter how instinctive your actions would be, you'd know them a split second ahead of time in your mind. And I'd know all your tricks and weaknesses, too. Your technique would be an open book to me. Whatever you thought of—'

'No.' Reilly shook his head. 'Oh, no. You're smart, but it's a phony set-up.'

Burkhalter hesitated, decided, and swung about, pushing a chair out of the way. 'Take out your dagger,' he said. 'Leave the sheath snapped on: I'll show you what I mean.'

Reilly's eyes widened. 'If you want it now—'

'I don't.' Burkhalter shoved another chair away. He unclipped his dagger, sheath and all, from his belt, and made sure the little safety clip was in place. 'We've room enough here. Come on.'

Scowling, Reilly took out his own dagger, held it awkwardly, baffled by the sheath, and then suddenly feinted forward. But Burkhalter wasn't there; he had anticipated, and his own leather sheath slid up Reilly's belly.

'That,' Burkhalter said, 'would have ended the fight.'

For answer Reilly smashed a hard blow down, curving at the last moment into a throat-cutting slash. Burkhalter's free hand was already at his throat; his other hand, with the sheathed dagger, tapped Reilly twice over the heart. The freckles stood out boldly against the pallor of the larger man's face. But he was not yet ready to concede. He tried a few more passes, clever, well-trained cuts, and they failed, because Burkhalter had anticipated them. His left hand invariably covered the spot where Reilly had aimed, and which he never struck.

Slowly Reilly let his arm fall. He moistened his lips and swallowed. Burkhalter busied himself reclipping his dagger in place.

'Burkhalter,' Reilly said, 'you're a devil.'

'Far from it. I'm just afraid to take a chance. Do you really think being a Baldy is a snap?'

'But, if you can read minds—'

'How long do you think I'd last if I did any duelling? It would be too much of a set-up. Nobody would stand for it, and I'd end up dead. I can't duel, because it'd be murder, and people would know it was murder. I've taken a lot of cracks, swallowed a lot of insults, for just that reason. Now, if you like, I'll swallow another and apologize. I'll admit anything you say. But I can't duel with you, Reilly.'

'No, I can see that. And—I'm glad you came over.' Reilly was still white, 'I'd have walked right into a set-up.'

'Not my set-up,' Burkhalter said. 'I wouldn't have duelled. Baldies aren't so lucky, you know. They've got handicaps—like this. That's why they can't afford to take chances and antagonize people, and why we never read minds, unless we're asked to do so.'

'It makes sense. More or less.' Reilly hesitated. 'Look, I withdraw that challenge. OK?'

'Thanks,' Burkhalter said, putting out his hand. It was taken rather reluctantly. We'll leave it at that, eh?'

'Right.' But Reilly was still anxious to get his guest out of the house.

Burkhalter walked back to the Publishing Centre and whistled tunelessly. He could tell Ethel now; in fact, he had to, for secrets between them would have broken up the completeness of their telepathic intimacy. It was not that their minds lay bare to each other, it was, rather, that any barrier could be sensed by the other, and the perfect *rapport* wouldn't have been so perfect. Curiously, despite this utter intimacy, husband and wife managed to respect one another's privacy.

Ethel might be somewhat distressed, but the trouble had blown over, and, besides, she was a Baldy too. Not that she looked it, with her wig of fluffy chestnut hair and those long, curving lashes. But her parents had lived east of Seattle during the Blowup, and afterward, too, before the hard radiation's effects had been thoroughly studied.

The snow-wind blew down over Modoc and fled southward along the Utah Valley. Burkhalter wished he was in his copter, alone in the blue emptiness of the sky. There was a quiet, strange peace up there that no Baldy ever quite achieved on the earth's surface, except in the depths of a wilderness. Stray fragments of thoughts were always flying about, subsensory, but like the almost-unheard whisper of a needle on a phonograph record, never ceasing. That, certainly, was why almost all Baldies loved to fly and were expert pilots. The high waste deserts of the air were their blue hermitages.

Still, he was in Modoc now, and overdue for his interview with Quayle. Burkhalter hastened his steps. In the main hall he met Moon, said briefly and cryptically that he'd taken care of the duel, and passed on, leaving the fat man to stare a question after him. The only visor call was from Ethel; the playback said she was worried about Al, and would Burkhalter check with the school. Well, he had already done so—unless the boy had managed to get into more trouble since then. Burkhalter put in a call and reassured himself. Al was as yet unhanged.

He found Quayle in the same private solarium, and thirsty. Burkhalter ordered a couple of dramzowies sent up, since he had no objections to loosening Quayle's inhibitions. The grey-haired author was immersed in a sectional historical globe-map, illuminating each epochal layer in turn as he searched back through time.

'Watch this,' he said, running his hand along the row of buttons. 'See how the German border fluctuates?' It fluctuated, finally vanishing entirely as seminodern times were reached. 'And Portugal. Notice its zone of influence? Now—' The zone shrank steadily from 1600 on, while other countries shot out radiating lines and assumed sea power.

Burkhalter sipped his dramzowie. 'Not much of that now.'

'No, since . . . what's the matter?'

'How do you mean?'

'You look shot.'

'I didn't know I showed it,' Burkhalter said wryly. 'I just finagled my way out of a duel.'

'That's one custom I never saw much sense to,' Quayle said. 'What happened? Since when can you finagle out?'

Burkhalter explained, and the writer took a drink and snorted. 'What a spot for you. Being a Baldy isn't such an advantage after all, I guess.'

'It has distinct disadvantages at times.' On impulse Burkhalter mentioned his son. 'You see my point, eh? I don't *know*, really what standards to apply to a young Baldy. He is a mutation, after all. And the telepathic mutation hasn't had time to work out yet. We can't rig up controls, because guinea pigs and rabbits won't breed telepaths. That's been tried, you know. And—well, the child of a Baldy needs very special training so he can cope with his ultimate maturity.'

'You seem to have adjusted well enough.'

'I've—learned. As most sensible Baldies have. That's why I'm not a wealthy man, or in politics. We're really buying safety for our species by foregoing certain individual advantages. Hostages to destiny—and destiny spares us. But we get paid too, in a way. In the coinage of future benefits—negative benefits, really, for we ask only to be spared and accepted—and so we have to deny ourselves a lot of present, positive benefits. An appeasement to fate.'

'Paying the piper,' Quayle nodded.

'We are the pipers. The Baldies as a group, I mean. And our children. So it balances; we're really paying ourselves. If I wanted to take unfair advantage of my telepathic power—my son wouldn't live very long. The Baldies would be wiped out. Al's got to learn that, and he's getting pretty antisocial.'

'All children are antisocial,' Quayle pointed out. 'They're utter individualists. I should think the only reason for worrying would be if the boy's deviation from the norm were connected with his telepathic sense.'

There's something in that.' Burkhalter reached out left-handedly and probed delicately at Quayle's mind, noting that the antagonism was considerably lessened. He grinned to himself and went on talking about his own troubles. 'Just the same, the boy's father to the man. And an adult Baldy has got to be pretty well adjusted, or he's sunk.'

'Environment is as important as heredity. One complements the other. If a child's reared correctly, he won't have much trouble—unless heredity is involved.'

'As it may be. There's so little known about the telepathic mutation. If baldness is one secondary characteristic, maybe—something else—emerges in the third or fourth generations. I'm wondering if telepathy is really good for the mind.'

Quayle said, 'Humph. Speaking personally, it makes me nervous—'

'Like Reilly.'

'Yes,' Quayle said, but he didn't care much for the comparison. 'Well—anyhow, if a mutation's a failure, it'll die out. It won't breed true.'

'What about haemophilia?'

'How many people have haemophilia?' Quayle asked. 'I'm trying to look at it from the angle of psychohistorian. If there'd been telepaths in the past, things might have been different.'

'How do you know there weren't?' Burkhalter asked.

Quayle blinked. 'Oh. Well. That's true, too. In medieval times they'd have been called wizards—or saints. The Duke-Rhine experiments—but such accidents would have been abortive. Nature fools around trying to hit the . . . ah . . . the jackpot, and she doesn't always do it on the first try.'

'She may not have done it now.' That was habit speaking, the ingrained caution of modesty. 'Telepathy may be merely a semi-successful try at something pretty unimaginable. A sort of four-dimensional sensory concept, maybe.'

'That's too abstract for me.' Quayle was interested, and his own hesitancies had almost vanished; by accepting Burkhalter as a telepath, he had tacitly wiped away his objection to telepathy per se. 'The old-time Germans always had an idea they were different; so did the . . . ah . . . what was that Oriental race? They had the islands off the China coast.'

'The Japanese,' said Burkhalter, who had a good memory for trifles.

'Yes. They knew, very definitely, that they were a superior race because they were directly descended from gods. They were short in stature; heredity made them selfconscious when dealing with larger races. But the Chinese aren't tall, the Southern Chinese, and they weren't handicapped in that way.'

'Environment, then?'

'Environment, which caused propaganda. The . . . ah . . . the Japanese took Buddhism, and altered it completely into Shinto, to suit their own needs. The samurai, warrior-knights, were the ideals, the code of honour was fascinatingly cock-eyed. The principle of Shinto was to worship your superiors and subjugate your inferiors. Ever seen the Japanese jewel-trees?'

'I don't remember them. What are they?'

'Miniature replicas of espaliered trees, made of jewels, with trinkets hanging on the branches. Including a mirror—always. The first jewel-tree was made to lure the Moon-goddess out of a cave where she was sulking. It seems the lady was so intrigued by the trinkets and by her face reflected in the mirror that she came out of her hide-out. All the Japanese morals were dressed up in pretty clothes; that was the bait. The old-time Germans did much the same thing. The last German dictator, Poor Hitler they called him—I forget why, but there was some reason—he revived the old Siegfried legend. It was racial paranoia. The Germans worshipped the house-tyrant, not the mother, and they had extremely strong family ties. That extended to the state. They symbolized Poor Hitler as their All-Father, and so eventually we got the Blowup. And, finally, mutations.'

'After the deluge, me,' Burkhalter murmured, finishing his dramzowie. Quayle was staring at nothing.

'Funny,' he said after a while. 'This All-Father business—'

'Yes?'

'I wonder if you know how powerfully it can affect a man?'

Burkhalter didn't say anything. Quayle gave him a sharp glance.

'Yes,' the writer said quietly. 'You're a man, after all. I owe you an apology, you know.'

Burkhalter smiled. 'You can forget that.'

'I'd rather not,' Quayle said. 'I've just realized, pretty suddenly, that the telepathic sense isn't so important. I mean—it doesn't make you *different*. I've been talking to you—'

'Sometimes it takes people years before they realize what you're finding out,' Burkhalter remarked. 'Years of living and working with something they think of as a Baldy.'

'Do you know what I've been concealing in my mind?' Quayle asked.

'No. I don't.'

'You lie like a gentleman. Thanks. Well, here it is, and I'm telling you by choice, because I want to. I don't care if you got the information out of my mind already; I just want to tell you of my own free will. My father . . . I imagine I hated him . . . was a tyrant, and I remember one time, when I was just a kid and we were in the mountains, he beat me and a lot of people were looking on. I tried to forget that for a long time. Now'—Quayle shrugged—'it doesn't seem quite so important.'

'I'm not a psychologist,' Burkhalter said. 'If you want my personal reaction, I'll just say that it doesn't matter. You're not a little boy any more, and the guy I'm talking to and working with is the adult Quayle.'

'Hm-m-m. Ye-es. I suppose I knew that all along—how unimportant it was, really. It was simply having my privacy violated. . . . I think I know you better now, Burkhalter. You can—walk in.'

'We'll work better,' Burkhalter said, grinning. 'Especially with Darius.'

Quayle said, 'I'll try not to keep any reservation in my mind. Frankly, I won't mind telling you—the answers. Even when they're personal.'

'Check on that. D'you want to tackle Darius now?'

'OK,' Quayle said, and his eyes no longer held suspicious wariness. 'Darius I identify with my father—'

It was smooth and successful. That afternoon they accomplished more than they had during the entire previous fortnight. Warm with satisfaction on more than one point, Burkhalter stopped off to tell Mr Moon that matters were looking up, and then set out towards home, exchanging thoughts with a couple of Baldies, his co-workers, who were knocking off for the day. The Rockies were bloody with the western light, and the coolness of the wind was pleasant on Burkhalter's cheeks, as he hiked homeward.

It was fine to be accepted. It proved that it could be done. And a Baldly often needed reassurance, in a world peopled by suspicious strangers. Quayle had been a hard nut to crack, but—Burkhalter smiled.

Ethel would be pleased. In a way, she'd had a harder time than he'd ever had. A woman would, naturally. Men were desperately anxious to keep their privacy unviolated by a woman, and as for non-Baldy women—well, it spoke highly for Ethel's glowing personal charm that she had finally been accepted by the clubs and feminine groups of Modoc. Only Burkhalter knew Ethel's desperate hurt at being bald, and not even her husband had ever seen her unwigged.

His thought reached out before him into the low, double-winged house on the hillside, and interlocked with hers in a warm intimacy. It was something more than a kiss. And, as always, there was the exciting sense of expectancy, mounting and mounting till the last door swung open and they touched physically. *This,* he thought, *is why I was born a Baldy; this is worth losing worlds for.*

At dinner that rapport spread out to embrace Al, an intangible, deeply rooted something that made the food taste better and the water like wine. The word *home,* to telepaths, had a meaning that non-Baldies could not entirely comprehend, for it embraced a bond they could not know. There were small, intangible caresses.

Green Man going down the Great Red Slide; the Shaggy Dwarfs trying to harpoon him as he goes.

'Al,' Ethel said, 'are you still working on your Green Man?'

Then something utterly hateful and cold and deadly quivered silently in the air, like an icicle jaggedly smashing through golden, fragile glass. Burkhalter dropped his napkin and looked up, profoundly shocked. He felt Ethel's thought shrink back, and swiftly reached out to touch and reassure her with mental contact. But across the table the little boy, his cheeks still round with the fat of babyhood, sat silent and wary, realizing he had blundered, and seeking safety in complete immobility. His mind was too weak to resist probing, he knew, and he remained perfectly still, waiting, while the echoes of a thought hung poisonously in silence.

Burkhalter said, 'Come on, Al.' He stood up. Ethel started to speak.

'Wait, darling. Put up a barrier. Don't listen in.' He touched her mind gently and tenderly, and then he took Al's hand and drew the boy after him out into the yard. Al watched his father out of wide, alert eyes. Burkhalter sat on a bench and put Al beside him. He talked audibly at first, for clarity's sake, and for another reason. It was distinctly unpleasant to trick the boy's feeble guards down, but it was necessary.

'That's a very queer way to think of your mother,' he said. 'It's a queer way to think of me.' Obscenity is more obscene, profanity more profane, to a telepathic mind, but this had been neither one. It had been—cold and malignant.

And this is flesh of my flesh, Burkhalter thought, looking at the boy and remembering the eight years of his growth. *Is the mutation to turn into something devilish?*

Al was silent.

Burkhalter reached into the young mind. Al tried to twist free and escape, but his father's strong hands gripped him. Instinct, not reasoning, on the boy's part, for minds can touch over long distances.

He did not like to do this, for increased sensibility had gone with sensitivity, and violations are always violations. But ruthlessness was required. Burkhalter searched. Sometimes he threw key words violently at Al, and surges of memory pulsed up in response.

In the end, sick and nauseated, Burkhalter let Al go and sat alone on the bench, watching the red light die on the snowy peaks. The whiteness was red-stained. But it was not too late. The man was a fool, had been a fool from the beginning, or he would have known the impossibility of attempting such a thing as this.

The conditioning had only begun. Al could be reconditioned. Burkhalter's eyes hardened. And would be. *And would be.* But not yet, not until the immediate furious anger had given place to sympathy and understanding.

Not yet.

He went into the house, spoke briefly to Ethel, and televised the dozen Baldies who worked with him in the Publishing Centre. Not all of them had families, but none was missing when, half an hour later, they met in the back room of the Pagan Tavern downtown. Sam Shane had caught a fragment of Burkhalter's knowledge, and all of them read his emotions. Welded into a sympathetic unit by their telepathic sense, they waited till Burkhalter was ready.

Then he told them. It didn't take long, via thought. He told them about the Japanese jewel-tree with its glittering gadgets, a shining lure. He told them of racial paranoia and propaganda. And that the most effective propaganda was sugar-coated, disguised so that the motive was hidden.

A Green Man, hairless, heroic—symbolic of a Baldy.

And wild, exciting adventures, the lure to catch the young fish whose plastic minds were impressionable enough to be led along the roads of dangerous madness. Adult Baldies could listen, but they did not; young telepaths had a higher threshold of mental receptivity, and adults do not read the books of their children except to reassure themselves that there is nothing harmful in the pages. And no adult would bother to listen to the Green Man mindcast. Most of them had accepted it as the original daydream of their own children.

'I did,' Shane put in. 'My girls—'

'Trace it back,' Burkhalter said. 'I did.'

The dozen minds reached out on the higher frequency, the children's wavelength, and something jerked away from them, startled and apprehensive.

'He's the one,' Shane nodded.

They did not need to speak. They went out of the Pagan Tavern in a compact, ominous group, and crossed the street to the general store. The door was locked. Two of the men burst it open with their shoulders.

They went through the dark store and into a back room where a man was standing beside an overturned chair. His bald skull gleamed in an overhead light. His mouth worked impotently.

His thought pleaded with them—was driven back by an implacable deadly wall.

Burkhalter took out his dagger. Other slivers of steel glittered for a little while—

And were quenched.

Venning's scream had long since stopped, but his dying thought of agony lingered within Burkhalter's mind as he walked homeward. The wigless Baldy had not been insane, no. But he had been paranoidal.

What he had tried to conceal, at the last, was quite shocking. A tremendous, tyrannical egotism, and a furious hatred of non-telepaths. A feeling of self-justification that was, perhaps, insane. *And—we are the Future! The Baldies! God made us to rule lesser men!*

Burkhalter sucked in his breath, shivering. The mutation had not been entirely successful. One group had adjusted, the Baldies who wore wigs and had become fitted to their environment. One group had been insane, and could be discounted; they were in asylums.

But the middle group were merely paranoid. They were not insane, and they were not sane. They wore no wigs.

Like Venning.

And Venning had sought disciples. His attempt had been foredoomed to failure, but he had been one man.

One Baldy—paranoid.

There were others, many others.

Ahead, nestled into the dark hillside, was the pale blotch that marked Burkhalter's home. He sent his thought ahead, and it touched Ethel's and paused very briefly to reassure her.

Then it thrust on, and went into the sleeping mind of a little boy who, confused and miserable, had finally cried himself to sleep. There were only dreams in that mind now. A little discoloured, a little stained, but they could be cleansed. And would be.

THE MONSTER

A. E. van VOGT

The great ship poised a quarter of a mile above one of the cities. Below was a cosmic desolation. As he floated down in his energy bubble, Enash saw that the buildings were crumbling with age.

'No sign of war damage!' The bodiless voice touched his ears momentarily. Enash tuned it out.

On the ground he collapsed his bubble. He found himself in a walled enclosure overgrown with weeds. Several skeletons lay in the tall grass beside the rakish building. They were of long, two-legged, two-armed beings with the skulls in each case mounted at the end of a thin spine. The skeletons, all of adults, seemed in excellent preservation, but when he bent down and touched one, a whole section of it crumbled into a fine powder. As he straightened, he saw that Yoal was floating down nearby. Enash waited until the historian had stepped out of his bubble, then said: 'Do you think we ought to use our method of reviving the long dead?'

Yoal was thoughtful. 'I have been asking questions of the various people who have landed, and there is something wrong here. This planet has no surviving life, not even insect life. We'll have to find out what happened before we risk any colonization.'

Enash said nothing. A soft wind was blowing. It rustled through a clump of trees nearby. He motioned towards the trees. Yoal nodded and said, 'Yes, the plant life has not been harmed, but plants after all are not affected in the same way as the active life forms.'

There was an interruption. A voice spoke from Yoal's receiver: 'A museum has been found at approximately the centre of the city. A red light has been fixed on the roof.'

Enash said, 'I'll go with you, Yoal. There might be skeletons of animals and of the intelligent being in various stages of his evolution. You didn't answer my question. Are you going to revive these beings?'

Yoal said slowly, 'I intend to discuss the matter with the council, but I think there is no doubt. We must know the cause of this disaster.' He waved one sucker vaguely to take in half the compass. He added as an afterthought, 'We shall proceed cautiously, of course, beginning with an obviously early development. The absence of the skeletons of children indicates that the race had developed personal immortality.'

The council came to look at the exhibits. It was, Enash knew, a formal preliminary only. The decision was made. There would be revivals. It was more than that. They were curious. Space was vast, the journeys through it long and lonely, landing always a stimulating experience, with its prospect of new life forms to be seen and studied.

The museum looked ordinary. High-domed ceilings, vast rooms. Plastic models of strange beasts, many artefacts—too many to see and comprehend in so short a time. The life span of a race was imprisoned here in a progressive array of relics. Enash looked with the others, and was glad when they came to the line of skeletons and preserved bodies. He seated himself behind the energy screen, and watched the biological experts take a preserved body out of a stone sarcophagus. It was wrapped in windings of cloth, many of them. The experts did not bother to unravel the rotted material. Their forceps reached through, pinched a piece of skull—that was the accepted procedure. Any part of the skeleton could be used, but the most perfect revivals, the most complete reconstructions resulted when a certain section of the skull was used.

Hamar, the chief biologist, explained the choice of body. 'The chemicals used to preserve this mummy show a sketchy knowledge of chemistry. The carvings on the sarcophagus indicate a crude and unmechanical culture. In such a civilization there would not be much development of the potentialities of the nervous system. Our speech experts have been analysing the recorded voice mechanism which is a part of each exhibit, and though many languages are involved—evidence that the ancient language spoken at the time the body was alive has been reproduced—they found no difficulty in translating the meanings. They have now adapted our universal speech machine, so that anyone who wishes to need only speak into his communicator, and so will have his words translated into the language of the revived person. The reverse, naturally, is also true. Ah, I see we are ready for the first body.'

Enash watched intently with the others as the lid was clamped down on the plastic reconstructor, and the growth processes were started. He could feel himself becoming tense. For there was nothing haphazard about what was happening. In a few minutes a full-grown ancient inhabitant of this planet would sit up and stare at them. The science involved was simple and always fully effective.

. . . Out of the shadows of smallness, life grows. The level of beginning and ending, of life and—not life; in that dim region matter oscillates easily between old and new habits. The habit of organic, or the habit of inorganic. Electrons do not have life and un-life values. Atoms know nothing of inanimateness. But when atoms form into molecules, there is a step in the process, one tiny step, that is of life—if life begins at all. One step, and then darkness. Or aliveness.

A stone or a living cell. A grain of gold or a blade of grass, the sands of the sea or the equally numerous animalcules inhabiting the endless fishy waters—the difference is there in the twilight zone of matter. Each living cell has in it the whole form. The crab grows a new leg when the old one is torn from its flesh. Both ends of the planarian worm elongate, and soon there are two worms, two identities, two digestive systems each as greedy as the original, each a whole, unwounded, unharmed by its experience. Each cell can be the whole. Each cell remembers in a detail so intricate that no totality of words could ever describe the completeness achieved.

But—paradox—memory is not organic. An ordinary wax record remembers sounds. A wire recorder easily gives up a duplicate of the voice that spoke into it years before. Memory is a physiological impression, so that when a reaction is desired the *shape* emits the same rhythm of response.

Out of the mummy's skull had come the multi-quadrillion memory shapes from which a response was now being evoked. As ever, the memory held true.

A man blinked, and opened his eyes.

'It's is true, then,' he said aloud, and the words were translated into the Ganae tongue as he spoke them. 'Death is merely an opening into another life—but where are my attendants?' At the end, his voice took on a complaining tone.

He sat up, and climbed out of the case, which had automatically opened as he came to life. He saw his captors. He froze, but only for a moment. He had a pride and a very special arrogant courage, which served him now. Reluctantly, he sank to his knees and made obeisance, but doubt must have been strong in him. 'Am I in the presence of the gods of Egyptus?' He climbed to his feet. 'What nonsense is this? I do not bow to nameless demons.'

Captain Gorsid said, 'Kill him!'

The two-legged monster dissolved, writhing, in the beam of a ray gun.

The second revived man stood up, pale, and trembled with fear. 'My God, I swear I won't touch the stuff again. Talk about pink elephants—'

Yoal was curious. 'To what *stuff* do you refer, revived one?'

'The old hooch, the poison in the hip pocket flask, the juice they gave me at that speak . . . my lordie!' Captain Gorsid looked questioningly at Yoal, 'Need we linger?'

Yoal hesitated. 'I am curious.' He addressed the man. 'If I were to tell you that we were visitors from another star, what would be your reaction?'

The man stared at him. He was obviously puzzled, but the fear was stronger. 'Now, look,' he said, 'I was driving along, minding my own business. I admit I'd had a shot or two too many, but it's the liquor they serve these days. I swear I didn't see the other car—and if this is some new idea of punishing people who drink and drive, well, you've won. I won't touch another drop as long as I live, so help me.'

Yoal said, 'He drives a "car" and thinks nothing of it. Yet we saw no cars. They didn't even bother to preserve them in the museums.'

Enash noticed that everyone waited for everyone else to comment. He stirred as he realized the circle of silence would be complete unless he spoke. He said, 'Ask him to describe the car. How does it work.'

'Now, you're talking,' said the man. 'Bring on your line of chalk, and I'll walk it, and ask any questions you please. I may be so tight that I can't see straight, but I can always drive. How does it work? You just put her in gear, and step on the gas.'

'Gas,' said engineering officer Veed. 'The internal combustion engine. That places him.'

Captain Gorsid motioned to the guard with the ray gun.

The third man sat up, and looked at them thoughtfully. 'From the stars?' he said finally. 'Have you a system, or was it blind chance?'

The Ganae councillors in that doomed room stirred uneasily in their curved chairs. Enash caught Yoal's eye on him. The shock in the historian's eyes alarmed the meterologist. He thought: 'The two-legged one's adjustment to a new situation, his grasp of realities, was unnormally rapid. No Ganae could have equalled the swiftness of the reaction.'

Hamar, the chief biologist, said, 'Speed of thought is not necessarily a sign of superiority. The slow, careful thinker has his place in the hierarchy of intellect.'

But Enash found himself thinking, it was not the speed; it was the accuracy of the response. He tried to imagine himself being revived from the dead, and understanding instantly the meaning of the presence of aliens from the stars. He couldn't have done it.

He forgot his thought, for the man was out of the case. As Enash watched with the others, he walked briskly over to the window and looked out. One glance, and then he turned back.

'Is it all like this?' he asked.

Once again, the speed of his understanding caused a sensation. It was Yoal who finally replied.

'Yes. Desolation. Death. Ruin. Have you any idea as to what happened?'

The man came back and stood in front of the energy screen that guarded the Ganae. 'May I look over the museum? I have to estimate what age I am in. We had certain possibilities of destruction when I was last alive, but which one was realized depends on the time elapsed.'

The councillors looked at Captain Gorsid, who hesitated; then, 'Watch him,' he said to the guard with the ray gun. He faced the man. 'We understand your aspirations fully. You would like to seize control of this situation and ensure your own safety. Let me reassure you. Make no false moves, and all will be well.'

Whether or not the man believed the lie, he gave no sign. Nor did he show by a glance or a movement that he had seen the scarred floor where the ray gun had burned his two predecessors into nothingness. He walked curiously to the nearest doorway, studied the other guard who waited there for him, and then, gingerly, stepped through. The first guard followed him, then came the mobile energy screen, and finally, trailing one another, the councillors.

Enash was the third to pass through the doorway. The room contained skeletons and plastic models of animals. The room beyond that was what, for want of a better term, Enash called a culture room. It contained the artefacts from a single period of civilization. It looked very advanced. He had examined some of the machines when they first passed through it, and had thought: Atomic energy. He was not alone in his recognition. From behind him, Captain Gorsid said to the man:

'You are forbidden to touch anything. A false move will be the signal for the guards to fire.'

The man stood at ease in the centre of the room. In spite of a curious anxiety, Enash had to admire his calmness. He must have known what his fate would be, but he stood there thoughtfully, and said finally, deliberately, 'I do not need to go any further. Perhaps you will be able to judge better than I of the time that has elapsed since I was born and these machines were built. I see over there an instrument which, according to the sign above it, counts atoms when they explode. As soon as the proper number have exploded it shuts off the power automatically, and for just the right length of time to prevent a chain explosion. In my time we had a thousand crude devices for limiting the size of an atomic reaction, but it required two thousand years to develop those devices from the early beginnings of atomic energy. Can you make a comparison?'

The councillors glanced at Veed. The engineering officer hesitated. At last, reluctantly, he said, 'Nine thousand years ago we had a thousand methods of limiting atomic explosions.' He paused, then even more slowly, 'I have never heard of an instrument that counts out atoms for such a purpose.'

'And yet,' murmured Shuri, the astronomer, breathlessly, 'the race was destroyed.'

There was silence. It ended as Gorsid said to the nearest guard, 'Kill the monster!'

But it was the guard who went down, bursting into flame. Not just one guard, but the guards! Simultaneously down, burning with a blue flame. The flame licked at the screen, recoiled, and licked more furiously, recoiled and burned brighter. Through a haze of fire, Enash saw that the man had retreated to the far door, and that the machine that counted atoms was glowing with a blue intensity.

Captain Gorsid shouted into his communicator, 'Guard all exits with ray guns. Spaceships stand by to kill alien with heavy guns.'

Somebody said, 'Mental control. Some kind of mental control. What have we run into?'

They were retreating. The blue flame was at the ceiling, struggling to break through the screen. Enash had a last glimpse of the machine. It must still be counting atoms, for it was a hellish blue. Enash raced with the others to the room where the man had been resurrected. There, another energy screen crashed to their rescue. Safe now, they retreated into their separate bubbles and whisked through outer doors and up to the ship. As the great ship soared, an atomic bomb hurtled down from it. The mushroom of flame blotted out the museum and the city below.

'But we still don't know why the race died,' Yoal whispered into Enash's ear, after the thunder had died from the heavens behind them.

The pale yellow sun crept over the horizon on the third morning after the bomb was dropped, the eighth day since the landing. Enash floated with the others down on a new city. He had come to argue against any further revival.

'As a meterologist,' he said, 'I pronounce this planet safe for Ganae colonization. I cannot see the need for taking any risks. This race has discovered the secrets of its nervous system, and we cannot afford—'

He was interrupted. Hamar, the biologist, said dryly. 'If they knew so much why didn't they migrate to other star systems and save themselves?'

'I will concede,' said Enash, 'that very possibly they had not discovered our system of locating stars with planetary families.' He looked earnestly around the circle of his friends. 'We have agreed that was a unique accidental discovery. We were lucky, not clever.'

He saw by the expressions on their faces that they were mentally refuting his arguments. He felt a helpless sense of imminent catastrophe. For he could see that picture of a great race facing death. It must have come swiftly, but not so swiftly that they didn't know about it. There were too many skeletons in the open, lying in the gardens of magnificent homes, as if each man and his wife had come out to wait for the doom of his kind. He tried to picture it for the council, that last day long, long ago, when a race had calmly met its ending. But his visualization failed somehow, for the others shifted impatiently in the seats that had been set up behind the series of energy screens, and Captain Gorsid said, 'Exactly what aroused this intense emotional reaction in you, Enash?'

The question gave Enash pause. He hadn't thought of it as

emotional. He hadn't realized the nature of his obsession, so subtly had it stolen upon him. Abruptly now, he realized.

'It was the third one,' he said, slowly. 'I saw him through the haze of energy fire, and he was standing there in the distant doorway watching us curiously, just before we turned to run. His bravery, his calm, the skilful way he had duped us—it all added up.'

'Added up to his death!' said Hamar. And everybody laughed.

'Come now, Enash,' said Vice-captain Mayard good-humouredly, 'you're not going to pretend that this race is braver than our own, or that, with all the precautions we have now taken, we need fear one man?'

Enash was silent, feeling foolish. The discovery that he had had an emotional obsession abashed him. He did not want to appear unreasonable. He made a final protest, 'I merely wish to point out,' he said doggedly, 'that this desire to discover what happened to a dead race does not seem absolutely essential to me.'

Captain Gorsid waved at the biologist, 'Proceed,' he said, 'with the revival.'

To Enash, he said, 'Do we dare return to Gana, and recommend mass migrations—and then admit that we did not actually complete our investigations here? It's impossible, my friend.'

It was the old argument, but reluctantly now Enash admitted there was something to be said for that point of view. He forgot that, for the fourth man was stirring.

The man sat up and vanished.

There was a blank, startled, horrified silence. Then Captain Gorsid said harshly. 'He can't get out of there. We know that. He's in there somewhere.'

All around Enash, the Ganae were out of their chairs, peering into the energy shell. The guards stood with ray guns held limply in their suckers. Out of the corner of his eye, he saw one of the protective screen technicians beckon to Veed, who went over. He came back grim. He said, 'I'm told the needles jumped ten points when he first disappeared. That's on the nucleonic level.'

'By ancient Ganae!' Shuri whispered. 'We've run into what we've always feared.'

Gorsid was shouting into the communicator. 'Destroy all the locators on the ship. Destroy them, do you hear!'

He turned with glaring eyes. 'Shuri,' he bellowed, 'They don't seem to understand. Tell those subordinates of yours to act. All locators and reconstructors must be destroyed.'

'Hurry, hurry!' said Shuri weakly.

When that was done they breathed more easily. There were grim smiles and a tensed satisfaction. 'At least,' said Vice-captain Mayad, 'he cannot now ever discover Gana. Our great system of locating suns with planets remains our secret. There can be no retaliation for—' He stopped, said slowly, 'What am I talking about? We haven't done anything. We're not responsible for the disaster that has befallen the inhabitants of this planet.'

But Enash knew what he had meant. The guilt feelings came to the surface at such moments as this—the ghosts of all the races destroyed by the Ganae, the remorseless will that had been in them, when they first landed, and annihilated whatever was here. The dark abyss of voiceless hate and terror that lay behind them; the days on end when they had mercilessly poured poisonous radiation down upon the unsuspecting inhabitants of peaceful planets—all that had been in Mayad's words.

'I still refuse to believe he has escaped.' That was Captain Gorsid. 'He's in there. He's waiting for us to take down our screens, so he can escape. Well, we won't do it.'

There was silence again as they stared expectantly into the emptiness of the energy shell. The reconstructor rested on its metal supports, a glittering affair. But there was nothing else. Not a flicker of unnatural light or shade. The yellow rays of the sun bathed the open spaces with a brilliance that left no room for concealment.

'Guards,' said Gorsid, 'destroy the reconstructor. I thought he might come back to examine it, but we can't take a chance on that.'

It burned with a white fury. And Enash, who had hoped somehow that the deadly energy would force the two-legged thing into the open, felt his hopes sag within him.

'But where can he have gone?' Yoal whispered.

Enash turned to discuss the matter. In the act of swinging around, he saw that the monster was standing under a tree a score of feet to one side, watching them. He must have arrived at *that* moment, for there was a collective gasp from the councillors. Everybody drew back. One of the screen technicians, using great presence of mind, jerked up an energy screen between the Ganae and the monster. The creature came forward slowly. He was slim of build, he held his head well back. His eyes shone as from an inner fire.

He stopped as he came to the screen, reached out and touched it with his fingers. It flared, blurred with changing colours. The colours grew brighter, and extended in an intricate pattern all the way from his head to the ground. The blur cleared. The pattern faded into invisibility. The man was through the screen.

He laughed, a soft curious sound; then sobered. 'When I first awakened,' he said, 'I was curious about the situation. The question was, what should I do with you?'

The words had a fateful ring to Enash on the still morning air of that planet of the dead. A voice broke the silence, a voice so strained and unnatural that a moment passed before he recognized it as belonging to Captain Gorsid.

'Kill him!'

When the blasters ceased their effort, the unkillable thing remained standing. He walked slowly forward until he was only a half a dozen feet from the nearest Ganae. Enash had a position well to the rear. The man said slowly: 'Two courses suggest themselves, one based on gratitude for reviving me, the other based on reality. I know you for what you are. Yes, *know* you—and that is unfortunate. It is hard to feel merciful. To begin with,' he went on, 'let us suppose you surrender the secret of the locator. Naturally, now that a system exists, we shall never again be caught as we were.'

Enash had been intent, his mind so alive with the potentialities of the disaster that was here that it seemed impossible that he could think of anything else. And yet, a part of his attention was stirred now. 'What did happen?' He asked.

The man changed colour. The emotions of that far day thickened his voice. 'A nucleonic storm. It swept in from outer space. It brushed this edge of our galaxy. It was about ninety light-years in diameter, beyond the furthest limit of our power. There was no escape from it. We had dispensed with spaceships, and had no time to construct any. Castor, the only star with planets ever discovered by us, was also in the path of the storm.' He stopped. 'The secret?' he said.

Around Enash, the councillors were breathing easier. The fear of race destruction that had come to them was lifting. Enash saw with pride that the first shock was over, and they were not even afraid for themselves.

'Ah,' said Yoal softly, 'you don't know the secret. In spite of all your great development, we alone can conquer the galaxy.' He looked at the others, smiling confidently. 'Gentlemen,' he said, 'our pride in a great Ganae achievement is justified. I suggest we return to our ship. We have no further business on this planet.'

There was a confused moment while their bubbles formed, when Enash wondered if the two-legged one would try to stop their departure. But when he looked back, he saw that the man was walking in a leisurely fashion along a street.

That was the memory Enash carried with him, as the ship began to move. That and the fact that the three atomic bombs they dropped, one after the other, failed to explode.

'We will not,' said Captain Gorsid, 'give up a planet as easily as that. I propose another interview with the creature.'

They were floating down again into the city, Enash and Yoal and Veed and the commander. Captain Gorsid's voice tuned in once more: '... As I visualize it'—through the mist Enash could see the transparent glint of the other three bubbles around him—'we jumped to conclusions about this creature, not justified by the evidence. For instance, when he awakened, he vanished. Why? Because he was afraid, of course. He wanted to size up the situation. He didn't believe he was omnipotent.'

It was sound logic. Enash found himself taking heart from it. Suddenly, he was astonished that he had become panicky so easily. He began to see the danger in a new light. Only one man alive on a new planet. If they were determined enough, colonists could be moved in as if he did not exist. It had been done before, he recalled. On several planets, small groups of the original populations had survived the destroying radiation, and taken refuge in remote areas. In almost every case, the new colonists gradually hunted them down. In two instances, however, that Enash remembered, native races were still holding small sections of their planets. In each case, it had been found impractical to destroy them because it would have endangered the Ganae on the planet. So the survivors were tolerated. One man would not take up very much room.

When they found him, he was busily sweeping out the lower floor of a small bungalow. He put the broom aside and stepped on to the terrace outside. He had put on sandals, and he wore a loose-fitting robe made of very shiny material. He eyed them indolently but he said nothing.

It was Captain Gorsid who made the proposition. Enash had to admire the story he told into the language machine. The commander was very frank. That approach had been decided on. He pointed out that the Ganae could not be expected to revive the dead of this planet. Such altruism would be unnatural considering that the ever-growing Ganae hordes had a continual need for new worlds. Each vast new population increment was a problem that could be solved by one method only. In this instance, the colonists would gladly respect the rights of the sole survivor of this world.

It was at that point that the man interrupted. 'But what is the purpose of this endless expansion?' He seemed genuinely curious. 'What will happen when you finally occupy every planet in this galaxy?'

Captain Gorsid's puzzled eyes met Yoal's, then flashed to Veed, then Enash. Enash shrugged his torso negatively, and felt pity for the creature. The man didn't understand, possibly never could understand. It was the old story of two different viewpoints, the virile and the decadent, the race that aspired to the stars and the race that declined the call of destiny.

'Why not,' urged the man, 'control the breeding chambers?'

'And have the government overthrown!' said Yoal.

He spoke tolerantly, and Enash saw that the others were smiling at the man's naïvety. He felt the intellectual gulf between them widening. The creature had no comprehension of the natural life forces that were at work. The man spoke again: 'Well, if you don't control them, we will control them for you.'

There was silence.

They began to stiffen. Enash felt it in himself, saw the signs of it in the others. His gaze flicked from face to face, then back to the creature in the doorway. Not for the first time, Enash had the thought that their enemy seemed helpless. 'Why,' he decided, 'I could put my suckers around him and crush him.'

He wondered if mental control of nucleonic, nuclear, and gravitonic energies included the ability to defend oneself from a macrocosmic attack. He had an idea it did. The exhibition of power two hours before might have had limitations, but if so, it was not apparent. Strength or weakness could make no difference. The threat of threats had been made: 'If you don't control—we will.'

The words echoed in Enash's brain, and, as the meaning penetrated deeper, his aloofness faded. He had always regarded himself as a spectator. Even when, earlier, he had argued against the revival, he had been aware of a detached part of himself watching the scene rather than being a part of it. He saw with a sharp clarity that that was why he had finally yielded to the conviction of the others. Going back beyond that to remoter days, he saw that he had never quite considered himself a participant in the seizure of the planets of other races. He was the one who looked on, and thought of reality, and speculated on a life that seemed to have no meaning. It was meaningless no longer. He was caught by a tide of irresistible emotion, and swept along. He felt himself sinking, merging with the Ganae mass being. All the strength and all the will of the race surged up in his veins.

He snarled, 'Creature, if you have any hopes of reviving your dead race, abandon them now.'

The man looked at him, but said nothing. Enash rushed on, 'If you could destroy us, you would have done so already. But the truth is that you operate within limitations. Our ship is so built that no conceivable chain reaction could be started in it. For every plate of potential unstable material in it there is a counteracting plate, which prevents the development of a critical pile. You might be able to set off explosions in our engines, but they, too, would be limited, and would merely start the process for which they are intended—confined in their proper space.'

He was aware of Yoal touching his arm. 'Careful,' warned the historian. 'Do not in your just anger give away vital information.'

Enash shook off the restraining sucker. 'Let us not be unrealistic,' he said harshly. 'This thing has divined most of our racial secrets, apparently merely by looking at our bodies. We would be acting childishly if we assumed that he has not already realized the possibilities of the situation.'

'*Enash!*' Captain Gorsid's voice was imperative.

As swiftly as it had come, Enash's rage subsided. He stepped back. 'Yes, commander.'

'I think I know what you intended to say,' said Captain Gorsid. 'I assure you I am in full accord, but I believe also that I, as the top Ganae official, should deliver the ultimatum.'

He turned. His horny body towered above the man. 'You have made the unforgivable threat. You have told us, in effect, that you will attempt to restrict the vaulting Ganae spirit.'

'Not the spirit,' said the man. He laughed softly. 'No, not the spirit.'

The commander ignored the interruption. 'Accordingly, we have no alternative. We are assuming that, given time to locate the materials and develop the tools, you might be able to build a reconstructor. In our opinion it will be at least two years before you can complete it, *even if you know how*. It is an immensely intricate machine, not easily assembled by the lone survivor of a race that gave up its machines millennia before disaster struck.

'You did not have time to build a spaceship. We won't give you time to build a reconstructor.

'Within a few minutes our ship will start dropping bombs. It is possible you will be able to prevent explosions in your vicinity. We will start, accordingly, on the other side of the planet. If you stop us there, then we will assume we need help. In six months of travelling at top acceleration, we can reach a point where the nearest Ganae planet would hear our messages. They will send a fleet so vast that all your powers of resistance will be overcome. By dropping a hundred or a thousand bombs every minute, we will succeed in devastating every city so that not a grain of dust will remain of the skeletons of your people.

'That is our plan. So it shall be. Now, do your worst to us who are at your mercy.'

The man shook his head. 'I shall do nothing—now!' he said. He paused, then said thoughtfully, 'Your reasoning is fairly accurate. Fairly. Naturally, I am not all powerful, but it seems to me you have forgotten one little point. I won't tell you what it is. And now,' he said, 'good day to you. Get back to your ship, and be on your way. I have much to do.'

Enash had been standing quietly, aware of the fury building up in him again. Now, with a hiss, he sprang forward, suckers outstretched. They were almost touching the smooth flesh—when something snatched at him.

He was back on the ship.

He had no memory of movement, no sense of being dazed or harmed. He was aware of Veed and Yoal and Captain Gorsid standing near him as astonished as he himself. Enash remained very still, thinking of what the man had said '. . . *Forgotten one little point.*' Forgotten? That meant they knew. What could it be? He was still pondering about it when Yoal said: 'We can be reasonably certain our bombs alone will not work.'

They didn't.

Forty light-years out from Earth, Enash was summoned to the

council chambers. Yoal greeted him wanly. 'The monster is aboard.'

The thunder of that poured through Enash, and with it came a sudden comprehension. 'That was what he meant we had forgotten,' he said finally, aloud and wonderingly. 'That he can travel through space at will within a limit—what was the figure he once used—of ninety light years.'

He sighed. He was not surprised that the Ganae, who had to use ships, would not have thought immediately of such a possibility. Slowly, he began to retreat from the reality. Now that the shock had come, he felt old and weary, a sense of his mind withdrawing again to its earlier state of aloofness. It required a few minutes to get the story. A physicist's assistant, on his way to the storeroom, had caught a glimpse of a man in a lower corridor. In such a heavily manned ship, the wonder was that the intruder had escaped earlier observation. Enash had a thought.

'But after all we are not going all the way to one of our planets. How does he expect to make use of us to locate it if we only use the video—' he stopped. That was it, of course. Directional video beams would have to be used and the man would travel in the right direction the instant contact was made.

Enash saw the decision in the eyes of his companions, the only possible decision under the circumstances. And yet, it seemed to him they were missing some vital point. He walked slowly to the great video plate at one end of the chamber. There was a picture on it, so sharp, so vivid, so majestic that the unaccustomed mind would have reeled as from a stunning blow. Even to him, who knew the scene, there came a constriction, a sense of unthinkable vastness. It was a video view of a section of the milky way. Four hundred *million* stars as seen through telescopes that could pick up the light of a red dwarf at thirty thousand light-years.

The video plate was twenty-five yards in diameter—a scene that had no parallel elsewhere in the plenum. Other galaxies simply did not have that many stars.

Only one in two hundred thousand of those glowing suns had planets.

That was the colossal fact that compelled them now to an irrevocable act. Wearily, Enash looked around him.

'The monster has been very clever,' he said quietly. 'If we go ahead, he goes with us, obtains a reconstructor, and returns by his method to his planet. If we use the directional beam, he flashes along it, obtains a reconstructor, and again reaches his planet first. In either event, by the time our fleets arrived back here, he would have revived enough of his kind to thwart any attack we could mount.'

He shook his torso. The picture was accurate, he felt sure, but it still seemed incomplete. He said slowly, 'We have one advantage now. Whatever decision we make, there is no language machine to enable him to learn what it is. We can carry out our plans without his knowing what they will be. He knows that neither he nor we can blow up the ship. That leaves us one real alternative.'

It was Captain Gorsid who broke the silence that followed. 'Well, gentlemen, I see we know our minds. We will set the engines, blow up the controls, and take him with us.'

They looked at each other, race pride in the eyes. Enash touched suckers with each in turn.

An hour later, when the heat was already considerable. Enash had the thought that sent him staggering to the communicator, to call Shuri, the astronomer. 'Shuri,' he yelled, 'when the monster first awakened—remember Captain Gorsid had difficulty getting your subordinates to destroy the locators. We never thought to ask them what the delay was. Ask them . . . ask them—'

There was a pause, then Shuri's voice came weakly over the roar of the static, 'They . . . couldn't . . . get . . . into the . . . room. The door was locked.'

Enash sagged to the floor. They had missed more than one point, he realized. The man had awakened, realized the situation; and, when he vanished, he had gone to the ship, and there discovered the secret of the locator and possibly the secret of the reconstructor—if he didn't know it previously. By the time he reappeared, he already had from them what he wanted. All the rest must have been designed to lead them to this act of desperation.

In a few moments, now, *he* would be leaving the ship, secure in the knowledge that shortly no alien mind would know his planet existed. Knowing, too, that his race would live again, and this time never die.

Enash staggered to his feet, clawed at the roaring communicator, and shouted his new understanding into it. There was no answer. It clattered with the static of uncontrollable and inconceivable energy.

The heat was peeling his armoured hide as he struggled to the matter transmitter. It flashed at him with purple flame. Back to the communicator he ran shouting and screaming.

He was still whimpering into it a few minutes later when the mighty ship plunged into the heart of a blue-white sun.

THE SECOND NIGHT OF SUMMER

JAMES H. SCHMITZ

On the night after the day that brought summer officially to the land of Wend, on the planet of Noorhut, the shining lights were seen again in the big hollow at the east end of Grimp's father's farm.

Grimp watched them for more than an hour from his upstairs room. The house was dark, but an occasional murmur of voices floated up to him through the windows below. Everyone in the farmhouse was looking at the lights.

On the other farms around and in the village, which was over a hill and another two miles up the valley, every living soul who could get within view of the hollow was probably doing the same. For a time, the agitated yelling of the Village Guardian's big pank-hound had sounded clearly over the hill, but he had quieted down then very suddenly—or had *been* quieted down, more likely, Grimp suspected. The Guardian was dead-set against anyone making a fuss about the lights—and that included the pank-hound, too.

There was some excuse for the pank-hound's excitement, though. From the window, Grimp could see there were a lot more lights tonight than had turned up in previous years—big, brilliant-blue bubbles, drifting and rising and falling silently all about the hollow. Sometimes one would lift straight up for several hundred feet, or move off over the edge of the hollow for about the same distance, and hang there suspended for a few minutes, before floating back to the others. That was as far as they ever went away from the hollow.

There was, in fact, no need for the Halpa detector-globes to go any further than that to get the information wanted by those who had sent them out, and who were listening now to the steady flow of brief reports, in some Halpa equivalent of human speech-thought, coming back to them through the globes:

'No signs of hostile activity in the vicinity of the breakthrough point. No weapons or engines of power within range of detection. The area shows no significant alterations since the last investigation. Sharp curiosity among those who observe us consciously—traces of alarm and suspicion. But no overt hostility.'

The reports streamed on without interruption, repeating the same bits of information automatically and incessantly, while the globes floated and dipped soundlessly above and about the hollow.

Grimp continued to watch them, blinking sleepily now and then, until a spreading glow over the edge of the valley announced that Noorhut's Big Moon was coming up slowly, like a Planetary Guardian, to make its own inspection of the lights. The globes began to dim out then, just as they always had done at moonrise in the preceding summers; and even before the top rim of the Big Moon's yellow disc edged over the hills, the hollow was completely dark.

Grimp heard his mother starting up the stairs. He got hurriedly into bed. The show was over for the night and he had a lot of pleasant things to think about before he went to sleep.

Now that the lights had showed up, his good friend Grandma Erisa Wannattel and her patent-medicine trailer were sure to arrive, too. Sometime late tomorrow afternoon, the big draft-trailer would come rolling up the valley road from the city. For that was what Grandma Wannattel had done the past four summers—ever since the lights first started appearing above the hollow for the few nights they were to be seen there each year. And since four years were exactly half of Grimp's whole life, that made Grandma's return a mathematical certainty for him.

Other people, of course, like the Village Guardian, might have a poor opinion of Grandma, but just hanging around her and the trailer and the gigantic, exotic-looking rhinocerine pony that pulled it was, in Grimp's opinion, a lot better even than going to the circus.

And vacations started the day after tomorrow! The whole future just now, in fact, looked like one good thing after another, extending through a vista of summery infinities.

Grimp went to sleep happily.

At about the same hour, though at a distance greater than Grimp's imagination had stretched as yet, eight large ships came individually out of the darkness between the stars that was their sea, and began to move about Noorhut in a carefully timed pattern of orbits. They stayed much too far out to permit any instrument of space-detection to suspect that Noorhut might be their common centre of interest.

But that was what it was. Though the men who crewed the eight ships bore the people of Noorhut no ill will, hardly anything could have looked less promising for Noorhut than the cargo they had on board.

Seven of them were armed with a gas which was not often used any more. A highly volatile lethal catalyst, it sank to the solid surface of a world over which it was freed and spread out swiftly there to the point where its presence could no longer be detected by any chemical means. However, its effect of drawing the final breath almost imperceptibly out of all things that were oxygen-breathing was not noticeably reduced by diffusion.

The eighth ship was equipped with a brace of torpedoes, which were normally released some hours after the gas-carriers dispersed their invisible death. They were quite small torpedoes, since the only task remaining for them would be to ignite the surface of the planet that had been treated with the catalyst.

All those things might presently happen to Noorhut. But they would happen only if a specific message was flashed from it to the circling squadron—the message that Noorhut already was lost to a deadly foe who must, at any cost now, be prevented from spreading out from it to other inhabited worlds.

Next afternoon, right after school, as Grimp came expectantly around the bend of the road at the edge of the farm, he found the village policeman sitting there on a rock, gazing tearfully down the road.

'Hello, Runny,' said Grimp, disturbed. Considered in the light of gossip he'd overheard in the village that morning, this didn't look so good for Grandma. It just didn't look good.

The policeman blew his nose on a handkerchief he carried tucked into the front of his uniform, wiped his eyes, and gave Grimp an annoyed glance.

'Don't *you* call me Runny, Grimp!' he said, replacing the handkerchief. Like Grimp himself and most of the people on Noorhut, the policeman was brown-skinned and dark-eyed, normally a rather good-looking young fellow. But his eyes were swollen and red-rimmed now; and his nose, which was a bit larger than average, anyway, was also red and swollen and undeniably runny. He had hay-fever bad.

Grimp apologized and sat down thoughtfully on the rock beside the policeman, who was one of his numerous cousins. He was about to mention that he had overheard Vellit using the expression when she and the policeman came through the big Leeth-flower orchard above the farm the other evening—at a much less leisurely rate than was their custom there. But he thought better of it. Vellit was the policeman's girl for most of the year, but she broke their engagement regularly during hay-fever season and called him cousin instead of dearest.

'What are you doing here?' Grimp asked bluntly instead.

'Waiting,' said the policeman.

'For what?' said Grimp, with a sinking heart.

'Same individual you are, I guess,' the policeman told him, hauling out the handkerchief again. He blew. 'This year she's going to go right back where she came from or get pinched.'

'Who says so?' scowled Grimp.

'The Guardian, that's who,' said the policeman. 'That good enough for you?'

'He can't do it!' Grimp said hotly. 'It's our farm, and she's got all her licences.'

'He's had a whole year to think up a new list she's got to have,' the policeman informed him. He fished in the breastpocket of his uniform, pulled out a folded paper and opened it. 'He put thirty-four items down here I got to check—she's bound to miss on one of them.'

'It's a dirty trick!' said Grimp, rapidly scanning as much as he could see of the list.

'Let's us have more respect for the Village Guardian, Grimp!' the policeman said warningly.

'Uh-huh,' muttered Grimp. 'Sure . . .' If Runny would just move his big thumb out of the way. But what a list! Trailer; rhinocerine pony (beast, heavy draft, imported); patent medicines; household utensils; fortune-telling; pets; herbs; miracle-healing—

The policeman looked down, saw what Grimp was doing and raised the paper out of his line of vision. 'That's an official document,' he said, warding Grimp off with one hand and tucking the paper away with the other. 'Let's us not get our dirty hands on it.'

Grimp was thinking fast. Grandma Wannattel did have framed licences for some of the items he'd read hanging around inside the trailer, but certainly not thirty-four of them.

'Remember that big skinless werret I caught last season?' he asked.

The policeman gave him a quick glance, looked away again and wiped his eyes thoughtfully. The season on werrets would open the following week and he was as ardent a fisherman as anyone in the village—and last summer Grimp's monster werret had broken a twelve-year record in the valley.

'Some people,' Grimp said idly, staring down the valley road to the point where it turned into the woods, 'would sneak after a person for days who's caught a big werret, hoping he'd be dumb enough to go back to that pool.'

The policeman flushed and dabbed the handkerchief gingerly at his nose.

'Some people would even sit in a haystack and use spyglasses, even when the hay made them sneeze like crazy,' continued Grimp quietly.

The policeman's flush deepened. He sneezed.

'But a person isn't that dumb,' said Grimp. 'Not when he knows there's anyway two werrets there six inches bigger than the one he caught.'

'*Six inches?*' the policeman repeated a bit incredulously—eagerly.

'Easy,' nodded Grimp. 'I had a look at them again last week.'

It was the policeman's turn to think. Grimp idly hauled out his slingshot, fished a pebble out of his small-pebble pocket and knocked the head off a flower twenty feet away. He yawned negligently.

'You're pretty good with that slingshot,' the policeman remarked. 'You must be just about as good as the culprit that used a slingshot to ring the fire-alarm signal on the defence unit bell from the top of the school house last week.'

'That'd take a pretty good shot,' Grimp admitted.

'And who then,' continued the policeman, 'dropped pepper in his trail, so the pank-hound near coughed off his head when we started to track him. The Guardian,' he added significantly, 'would like to have a clue about that culprit, all right.'

'Sure, sure,' said Grimp, bored. The policeman, the Guardian, and probably even the pank-hound, knew exactly who the culprit was; but they wouldn't be able to prove it in twenty thousand years. Runny just had to realize first that threats weren't going to get him anywhere near a record werret.

Apparently, he had; he was settling back for another bout of thinking. Grimp, interested in what he would produce next, decided just to leave him to it. . . .

Then Grimp jumped up suddenly from the rock.

'There they are!' he yelled, waving the slingshot.

A half-mile down the road, Grandma Wannattel's big, silvery trailer had come swaying out of the woods behind the rhinocerine pony and turned up towards the farm. The pony saw Grimp, lifted its head, which was as long as a tall man, and bawled a thunderous greeting. Grandma Wannattel stood up on the driver's seat and waved a green silk handkerchief.

Grimp started sprinting down the road.

The werrets should turn the trick—but he'd better get Grandma informed, just the same, about recent developments here, before she ran into Runny.

Grandma Wannattel flicked the pony's horny rear with the reins just before they reached the policeman, who was waiting at the side of the road with the Guardian's check-list unfolded in his hand.

The pony broke into a lumbering trot, and the trailer swept past Runny and up around the bend of the road, where it stopped well within the boundaries of the farm. They climbed down and Grandma quickly unhitched the pony. It waddled, grunting, off the road and down into the long, marshy meadow above the hollow. It stood still there, cooling its feet.

Grimp felt a little better. Getting the trailer off community property gave Grandma a technical advantage. Grimp's people had a favourable opinion of her, and they were a sturdy lot who enjoyed telling off the Guardian any time he didn't actually have a law to back up his orders. But on the way to the farm, she had confessed to Grimp that, just as he'd feared, she didn't have anything like thirty-four licences. And now the policeman was coming up around the bend of the road after them, blowing his nose and frowning.

'Just let me handle him alone,' Grandma told Grimp out of the corner of her mouth.

He nodded and strolled off into the meadow to pass the time with the pony. She'd had a lot of experience in handling policemen.

'Well, well, young man,' he heard her greeting his cousin behind him. 'That looks like a bad cold you've got.'

The policeman sneezed.

'Wish it were a cold,' he said resignedly. 'It's hay-fever. Can't do a thing with it. Now I've got a list here—'

'Hay-fever?' said Grandma. 'Step up into the trailer a moment. We'll fix that.'

'About this list—' began Runny, and stopped. 'You think you got something that would fix it?' he asked sceptically. 'I've been to I don't know how many doctors and they didn't help any.'

'Doctors!' said Grandma. Grimp heard her heels click up the metal steps that led into the back of the trailer. 'Come right in, won't take a moment.'

'Well—' said Runny doubtfully, but he followed her inside.

Grimp winked at the pony. The first round went to Grandma.

'Hello, pony,' he said.

His worries couldn't reduce his appreciation of Grandma's fabulous draft-animal. Partly, of course, it was just that it was such an enormous beast. The long, round barrel of its body rested on short legs with wide, flat feet which were settled deep in the meadow's mud by now. At one end was a spiky tail, and at the other a very big, wedge-shaped head, with a blunt, badly chipped horn set between nose and eyes. From nose to tail and all around, it was covered with thick, rectangular, horny plates, a mottled green-brown in colour.

Grimp patted its rocky side affectionately. He loved the pony most for being the ugliest thing that had ever showed up on Noorhut. According to Grandma, she had bought it from a bankrupt circus which had imported it from a planet called Treebel; and Treebel was supposed to be a world full of hot swamps, inexhaustibly explosive volcanoes and sulphurous stenches.

One might have thought that after wandering around melting lava and under rainfalls of glowing ashes for most of its life, the pony would have considered Noorhut pretty tame. But though there wasn't much room for expression around the solid slab of bone supporting the horn, which was the front of its face, Grimp thought it looked thoroughly contented with its feet sunk out of sight in Noorhut's cool mud.

'You're a big fat pig!' he told it fondly.

The pony slobbered out a long, purple tongue and carefully parted his hair.

'Cut it out!' said Grimp. 'Ugh!'

The pony snorted, pleased, curled its tongue about a huge clump of weeds, pulled them up and flipped them into its mouth, roots, mud and all. It began to chew.

Grimp glanced at the sun and turned anxiously to study the trailer. If she didn't get rid of Runny soon, they'd be calling him back to the house for supper before he and Grandma got around to having a good talk. And they weren't letting him out of doors these evenings, while the shining lights were here.

He gave the pony a parting whack, returned quietly to the road and sat down out of sight near the back door of the trailer, where he could hear what was going on.

'. . . so about the only thing the Guardian could tack on you now,' the policeman was saying, 'would be a Public Menace charge. If there's any trouble about the lights this year, he's likely to try that. He's not a bad Guardian, you know, but he's got himself talked into thinking you're sort of to blame for the lights showing up here every year.'

Grandma chuckled. 'Well, I try to get here in time to see them every summer,' she admitted. 'I can see how that might give him the idea.'

'And of course,' said the policeman, 'we're all trying to keep it quiet about them. If the news got out, we'd be having a lot of people coming here from the city, just to look. No one but the Guardian minds you being here, only you don't want a lot of city people tramping around your farms.'

'Of course not,' agreed Grandma. 'And I certainly haven't told anyone about them myself.'

'Last night,' the policeman added, 'everyone was saying there were twice as many lights this year as last summer. That's what got the Guardian so excited.'

Chafing more every minute, Grimp had to listen then to an extended polite argument about how much Runny wanted to pay Grandma for her hay-fever medicines, while she insisted he didn't owe her anything at all. In the end, Grandma lost and the policeman paid up—much too much to take from any friend of Grimp's folks, Grandma protested to the last. And then, finally, that righteous minion of the law came climbing down the trailer steps again, with Grandma following him to the door.

'How do I look, Grimp?' he beamed cheerfully as Grimp stood up.

'Like you ought to wash your face sometime,' Grimp said tactlessly, for he was fast losing patience with Runny. But then his eyes widened in surprise.

Under a coating of yellowish grease, Runny's nose seemed to have returned almost to the shape it had out of hay-fever season, and his eyelids were hardly puffed at all! Instead of flaming red, those features, furthermore, now were only a delicate pink in shade. Runny, in short, was almost handsome again.

'Pretty good, eh?' he said. 'Just one shot did it. And I've only got to keep the salve on another hour. Isn't that right, Grandma?'

'That's right,' smiled Grandma from the door, clinking Runny's money gently out of one hand into the other. 'You'll be as good as new then.'

'Permanent cure, too,' said Runny. He patted Grimp benevolently on the head. 'And next week we go werret-fishing, eh, Grimp?' he added greedily.

'I guess so,' Grimp said, with a trace of coldness. It was his opinion that Runny could have been satisfied with the hay-fever cure and forgotten about the werrets.

'It's a date!' nodded Runny happily and took his greasy face whistling down the road. Grimp scowled after him, half-minded to reach for the slingshot then and there and let go with a medium stone at the lower rear of the uniform. But probably he'd better not.

'Well, that's that,' Grandma said softly.

At that moment, up at the farmhouse, a cow horn went 'Whoop-whoop!' across the valley.

'Darn,' said Grimp. 'I knew it was getting late, with him doing all that talking! Now they're calling me to supper.' There were tears of disappointment in his eyes.

'Don't let it fuss you, Grimp,' Grandma said consolingly. 'Just jump up in here a moment and close your eyes.'

Grimp jumped up into the trailer and closed his eyes expectantly.

'Put out your hands,' Grandma's voice told him.

He put out his hands, and she pushed them together to form a cup. Then something small and light and furry dropped into them, caught hold of one of Grimp's thumbs, with tiny, cool fingers, and chittered.

Grimp's eyes popped open.

'It's a lortel!' he whispered, overwhelmed.

'It's for you!' Grandma beamed.

Grimp couldn't speak. The lortel looked at him from a tiny, black, human face with large blue eyes set in it, wrapped a long, furry tail twice around his wrist, clung to this thumb with its fingers, and grinned and squeaked.

'It's wonderful!' gasped Grimp. 'Can you really teach them to talk?'

'Hello,' said the lortel.

'That's all it can say so far,' Grandma said. 'But if you're patient with it, it'll learn more.'

'I'll be patient,' Grimp promised, dazed. 'I saw one at the circus this winter, down the valley at Laggand. They said it could talk, but it never said anything while I was there.'

'Hello!' said the lortel.

'Hello!' gulped Grimp.

The cow horn whoop-whooped again.

'I guess you'd better run along to supper, or they might get mad,' said Grandma.

'I know,' said Grimp. 'What does it eat!'

'Bugs and flowers and honey and fruit and eggs, when it's wild. But you just feed it whatever you eat yourself.'

'Well, goodbye,' said Grimp. 'And golly—thanks, Grandma.'

He jumped out of the trailer. The lortel climbed out of his hand, ran up his arm and sat on his shoulder, wrapping its tail around his neck.

'It knows you already,' Grandma said, 'It won't run away.'

Grimp reached up carefully with his other hand and patted the lortel.

'I'll be back early tomorrow,' he said. 'No school. . . . They won't let me out after supper as long as those lights keep coming around.'

The cow horn whooped for the third time, very loudly. This time it meant business.

'Well, goodbye,' Grimp repeated hastily. He ran off, the lortel hanging on to his shirt collar and squeaking.

Grandma looked after him and then at the sun, which had just touched the tops of the hills with its lower rim.

'Might as well have some supper myself,' she remarked, apparently to no one in particular. 'But after that I'll have to run out the go-buggy and create a diversion.'

Lying on its armour-plated belly down in the meadow, the pony swung its big head around towards her. Its small yellow eyes blinked questioningly.

'What makes you think a diversion will be required?' its voice asked into her ear. The ability to produce such ventriloquial effects was one of the talents that made the pony well worth its considerable keep to Grandma.

'Weren't you listening?' she scolded. 'That policeman told me the Guardian's planning to march the village's defence unit up to the hollow after supper, and start them shooting at the Halpa detector-globes as soon as they show up.'

The pony swore an oath meaningless to anyone who hadn't been raised on the planet Treebel. It stood up, braced itself, and began pulling its feet out of the mud in a succession of loud, sucking noises.

'I haven't had an hour's straight rest since you talked me into tramping around with you eight years ago!' it complained.

'But you've certainly been seeing life, like I promised,' Grandma smiled.

The pony slopped in a last, enormous tongueful of wet weeds. 'That I have!' it said, with emphasis.

It came chewing up to the road.

'I'll keep a watch on things while you're having your supper,' it told her.

As the uniformed twelve-man defence unit marched in good order out of the village, on its way to assume a strategic position around the hollow on Grimp's father's farm, there was a sudden, small explosion not very far off.

The Guardian, who was marching in the lead with a gun over his shoulder and the slavering pank-hound on a leash, stopped short. The unit broke ranks and crowded up behind him.

'What was that?' the Guardian enquired.

Everybody glanced questioningly around the rolling green slopes of the valley, already darkened with evening shadows. The pank-hound sat down before the Guardian, pointed its nose at the even darker shadows in the woods ahead of them and growled.

'Look!' a man said, pointing in the same direction.

A spark of bright green light had appeared on their path, just where it entered the woods. The spark grew rapidly in size, became as big as a human head—then bigger! Smoky green streamers seemed to be pouring out of it. . . .

'I'm going home right now,' someone announced at that point, sensibly enough.

'Stand your ground!' the Guardian ordered, conscious of the beginnings of a general withdrawal movement behind him. He was an old soldier. He unslung his gun, cocked it and pointed it. The pank-hound got up on his six feet and bristled.

'Stop!' the Guardian shouted at the green light.

It expanded promptly to the size of a barrel, new streamers shooting out from it and fanning about like hungry tentacles.

He fired.

'*Run!*' everybody yelled then. The pank-hound slammed backward against the Guardian's legs, upsetting him, and streaked off after the retreating unit. The green light had spread outward jerkily into the shape of something like a many-armed, writhing starfish, almost the size of the trees about it. Deep, hooting sounds came out of it as it started drifting down the path towards the Guardian.

He got up on one knee and, in a single drumroll of sound, emptied all thirteen charges remaining in his gun into the middle of the starfish. It hooted more loudly, waved its arms more wildly, and continued to advance.

He stood up quickly then, slung the gun over his shoulder and joined the retreat. By the time the unit reached the first houses of the village, he was well up in the front ranks again. And a few minutes later, he was breathlessly organizing the local defences, employing the tactics that had shown their worth in the raids of the Laggand Bandits nine years before.

The starfish, however, was making no attempt to follow up the valley people's rout. It was still on the path at the point where the Guardian had seen it last, waving its arms about and hooting menacingly at the silent trees.

'That should do it, I guess,' Grandma Wannattel said. 'Before the first projection fizzles out, the next one in the chain will start up where they can see it from the village. It ought to be past midnight before anyone starts bothering about the globes again. Particularly since there aren't going to be any globes around tonight—that is, if the Halpa attack-schedule has been correctly estimated.'

'I wish we were safely past midnight right now,' the rhinocerine pony worriedly informed her. Its dark shape stood a little up the road from the trailer, outlined motionlessly like a ponderous statue against the red evening sky. Its head was up; it looked as if it were listening. Which it was, in its own way—listening for any signs of activity from the hollow.

'No sense getting anxious about it,' Grandma remarked. She was perched on a rock at the side of the road, a short distance from the pony, with a small black bag slung over her shoulder. 'We'll wait here another hour till it's good and dark and then go down to the hollow. The breakthrough might begin a couple of hours after that.'

'It *would* have to be us again!' grumbled the pony. In spite of its size, its temperament was on the nervous side. And while any companion of Zone Agent Wannattel was bound to run regularly into situations that were far from soothing, the pony couldn't recall any previous experience that had looked as extremely unsoothing as the prospects of the night-hours ahead. On far-off Vega's world of Jeltad, in the planning offices of the Department of Galactic Zones, the decision to put Noorhut at stake to win one round in mankind's grim war with the alien and mysterious Halpa might have seemed as distressing as it was unavoidable. But the pony couldn't help feeling that the distress would have become a little more acute if Grandma's distant employers had happened to be standing right here with the two of them while the critical hours approached.

'I'd feel a lot better myself if Headquarters hadn't picked us for this particular operation,' Grandma admitted. 'Us and Noorhut. . . .'

Because, by what was a rather singular coincidence, considering how things stood there tonight, the valley was also Grandma's home. She had been born, quite some while before, a hundred and eighty miles further inland, at the foot of the dam of the great river Wend, which had given its name to the land, and nowadays supplied it with almost all its required power.

Erisa Wannattel had done a great deal of travelling since she first became aware of the fact that her varied abilities and adventuresome nature needed a different sort of task to absorb them than could be found on Noorhut, which was progressing placidly up into the final stages of a rounded and balanced planetary civilization.

But she still liked to consider the Valley of the Wend as her home and headquarters, to which she returned as often as her work would permit. Her exact understanding of the way people there thought about things and did things also made them easy for her to manipulate; and on occasion that could be very useful.

In most other places, the means she had employed to turn the Guardian and his troop back from the hollow probably would have started a panic or brought armed ships and radiation guns zooming up for the kill within minutes. But the valley people had considered it just another local emergency. The bronze alarm bell in the village had pronounced a state of siege, and cow horns passed the word up to the outlying farms. Within minutes, the farmers were pelting down the roads to the village with their families and guns; and, very soon afterward, everything quieted down again. Guard lines had been set up by then, with the women and children quartered in the central buildings, while the armed men had settled down to watching Grandma's illusion projections—directional video narrow beams—from the discreet distance marked by the village boundaries.

If nothing else happened, the people would just stay there till morning and then start a cautious investigation. After seeing mysterious blue lights dancing harmlessly over Grimp's farm for four summers, this section of Wend was pretty well conditioned to fiery apparitions. But even if they got too adventurous, they couldn't hurt themselves on the projections, which were designed to be nothing but very effective visual displays.

What it all came to was that Grandma had everybody in the neighbourhood rounded up and immobilized where she wanted them.

In every other respect, the valley presented an exceptionally peaceful twilight scene to the eye. There was nothing to show that it was the only present point of contact between forces engaged in what was probably a war of intergalactic proportions—a war made wraith-like but doubly deadly by the circumstance that, in over a thousand years, neither side had found out much more about the other than the merciless and devastating finality of its forms of attack. There never had been any actual battles between Mankind and the Halpa, only alternate and very thorough massacres—all of them, from Mankind's point of view, on the wrong side of the fence.

The Halpa alone had the knowledge that enabled them to reach their human adversary. That was the trouble. But, apparently, they could launch their attacks only by a supreme effort, under conditions that existed for periods of less than a score of years, and about three hundred years apart as Mankind measured time.

It was hard to find any good in them, other than the virtue of persistence. Every three hundred years, they punctually utilized that brief period to execute one more thrust, carefully prepared and placed, and carried out with a dreadfully complete abruptness, against some new point of human civilization—and this time the attack was going to come through on Noorhut.

'Something's starting to move around in that hollow!' the pony announced suddenly. 'It's not one of their globe-detectors.'

'I know,' murmured Grandma. 'That's the first of the Halpa themselves. They're going to be right on schedule, it seems. But don't get nervous. They can't hurt anything until their transmitter comes through and revives them. We've got to be particularly careful now not to frighten them off. They seem to be even more sensitive to emotional tensions in their immediate surroundings than the globes.'

The pony made no reply. It knew what was at stake and why eight big ships were circling Noorhut somewhere beyond space-detection tonight. It knew, too, that the ships would act only if it was discovered that Grandma had failed. But—

The pony shook its head uneasily. The people on Treebel had never become civilized to the point of considering the possibility of taking calculated risks on a planetary scale—not to mention the fact that the lives of the pony and of Grandma were included in the present calculation. In the eight years it had been accompanying her on her travels, it had developed a tremendous respect for Erisa Wannattel's judgement and prowess. But, just the same, frightening the Halpa off, if it still could be done, seemed like a very sound idea right now to the pony.

As a matter of fact, as Grandma well knew, it probably could have been done at this stage by tossing a small firecracker into the hollow. Until they had established their planetary foothold, the Halpa took extreme precautions. They could spot things in the class of radiation weapons a hundred miles away, and either that or any suggestion of local aggressiveness or of long-range observation would check the invasion attempt on Noorhut then and there.

But one of the principal reasons she was here tonight was to see that nothing *did* happen to stop it. For this assault would only be diverted against some other world then, and quite probably against one where the significance of the spying detector-globes wouldn't be understood before it was too late. The best information system in the Galaxy couldn't keep more than an insignificant fraction of its populations on the alert for dangers like that—

She bounced suddenly to her feet and, at the same instant, the pony swung away from the hollow toward which it had been staring. They both stood for a moment then, turning their heads about, like baffled hounds trying to fix a scent on the wind.

'It's Grimp!' Grandma exclaimed.

The rhinocerine pony snorted faintly. 'Those are his thought images, all right,' it agreed. 'He seems to feel you need protection. Can you locate him?'

'Not yet,' said Grandma anxiously. 'Yes, I can. He's coming up through the woods on the other side of the hollow, off to the left. The little devil!' She was hustling back to the trailer. 'Come on, I'll have to ride you there. I can't even dare use the go-buggy this late in the day.'

The pony crouched beside the trailer while she quickly snapped on its saddle from the top of the back steps. Six metal rings had been welded into the horny plates of its back for this purpose, so it was a simple job. Grandma clambered aloft, hanging on to the saddle's hand-rails.

'Swing wide of the hollow!' she warned. 'This could spoil everything. But make all the noise you want. The Halpa don't care about noise as such—it has to have emotional content before they get interested—and the quicker Grimp spots us, the easier it will be to find him.'

The pony already was rushing down into the meadow at an amazing rate of speed—it took a lot of very efficient muscle to drive as heavy a body as that through the gluey swamps of Treebel. It swung wide of the hollow and of what it contained, crossed a shallow bog further down the meadow with a sound like a charging torpedo-boat, and reached the woods.

It had to slow down then, to avoid brushing off Grandma.

'Grimp's down that slope somewhere,' Grandma said. 'He's heard us.'

'They're making a lot of noise!' Grimp's thought reached them suddenly and clearly. He seemed to be talking to someone. 'But we're not scared of them, are we?'

'Bang-bang!' another thought-voice came excitedly.

'It's the lortel,' Grandma and the pony said together.

'That's the stuff!' Grimp resumed approvingly. 'We'll sling-shoot them all if they don't watch out. But we'd better find Grandma soon.'

'Grimp!' shouted Grandma. The pony backed her up with a roaring call.

'Hello?' came the lortel's thought.

'Wasn't that the pony?' asked Grimp. 'All right—let's go that way.'

'Here we come, Grimp!' Grandma shouted as the pony descended the steep side of a ravine with the straightforward technique of a rockslide.

'That's Grandma!' thought Grimp. 'Grandma!' he yelled. 'Look out! There's monsters all around!'

'What you missed!' yelled Grimp, dancing around the pony as Grandma Wannattel scrambled down from the saddle. 'There's monsters all around the village and the Guardian killed one and I slingshot another till he fizzled out and I was coming to find you—'

'Your mother will be worried!' began Grandma as they rushed into each other's arms.

'No,' grinned Grimp. 'All the kids are supposed to be sleeping in the schoolhouse and she won't look there till morning and the schoolteacher said the monsters were all'—he slowed down cautiously—'ho-lucy-nations. But he wouldn't go look when the Guardian said they'd show him one. He stayed right in bed. But the Guardian's all right—he killed one and I slingshot another and the lortel learned a new word. Say "bang-bang", lortel!' he invited.

'Hello!' squeaked the lortel.

'Aw,' said Grimp disappointedly. 'He can say it, though. And I've come to take you to the village so the monsters don't get you. Hello, pony!'

'Bang-bang,' said the lortel, distinctly.

'See?' cried Grimp. 'He isn't scared at all—he's a real brave lortel!

If we see some monsters don't you get scared either, because I've got my slingshot,' he said, waving it bloodthirstily, 'and two back pockets still full of medium stones. The way to do it is to kill them all!'

'It sounds like a pretty good idea, Grimp,' Grandma agreed. 'But you're awfully tired now.'

'No, I'm not!' Grimp said surprised. His right eye sagged shut and then his left; and he opened them both with an effort and looked at Grandma.

'That's right,' he admitted. 'I am . . .'

'In fact,' said Grandma, 'you're asleep!'

'No, I'm no—' objected Grimp. Then he sagged towards the ground, and Grandma caught him.

'In a way I hate to do it,' she panted, wrestling him aboard the pony which had lain down and flattened itself as much as it could to make it easier. 'He'd probably enjoy it. But we can't take a chance. He's a husky little devil, too,' she groaned, giving a final boost, 'and those ammunition pockets don't make him any lighter!' She clambered up again herself and noticed that the lortel had transferred itself to her coat collar.

The pony stood up cautiously.

'Now what?' it said.

'Might as well go straight to the hollow,' said Grandma, breathing hard. 'We'll probably have to wait around there a few hours, but if we're careful it won't do any harm.'

'Did you find a good deep pond?' Grandma asked the pony a little later, as it came squishing up softly through the meadow behind her to join her at the edge of the hollow.

'Yes,' said the pony. 'About a hundred yards back. That should be close enough. How much more waiting do you think we'll have to do?'

Grandma shrugged carefully. She was sitting in the grass with what, by daylight, would have been a good view of the hollow below. Grimp was asleep with his head on her knees; and the lortel, after catching a few bugs in the grass and eating them, had settled down on her shoulder and dozed off too.

'I don't know,' she said. 'It's still three hours till Big Moonrise, and it's bound to be some time before then. Now you've found a waterhole, we'll just stay here together and wait. The one thing to remember is not to let yourself start getting excited about them.'

The pony stood huge and chunky beside her, its forefeet on the edge of the hollow, staring down. Muddy water trickled from its knobby flanks. It had brought the warm mud-smells of a summer pond back with it to hang in a cloud about them.

There was vague, dark, continuous motion at the bottom of the hollow. A barely noticeable stirring in the single big pool of darkness that filled it.

'If I were alone,' the pony said, 'I'd get out of here! I know when I ought to be scared. But you've taken psychological control of my reactions, haven't you?'

'Yes,' said Grandma. 'It'll be easier for me, though, if you help along as much as you can. There's really no danger until their transmitter has come through.'

'Unless,' said the pony, 'they've worked out some brand-new tricks in the past few hundred years.'

'There's that,' Grandma admitted. 'But they've never tried changing their tricks on us yet. If it were *us* doing the attacking, we'd vary our methods each time, as much as we could. But the Halpa don't seem to think just like we do about anything. They wouldn't still be so careful if they didn't realize they were very vulnerable at this point.'

'I hope they're right about that!' the pony said briefly.

Its head moved then, following the motion of something that sailed flutteringly out of the depths of the hollow, circled along its far rim, and descended again. The inhabitants of Treebel had a much deeper range of dark-vision than Grandma Wannattel, but she was also aware of that shape.

'They're not much to look at,' the pony remarked. 'Like a big, dark rag of leather, mostly.'

'Their physical structure is believed to be quite simple,' Grandma agreed slowly. The pony was tensing up again, and it was best to go on talking to it, about almost anything at all. That always helped, even though the pony knew her much too well by now to be really fooled by such tricks.

'Many very efficient life-forms aren't physically complicated, you know,' she went on, letting the sound of her voice ripple steadily into its mind. 'Parasitical types, particularly. It's pretty certain, too, that the Halpa have the hive-mind class of intelligence, so what goes for the nerve-systems of most of the ones they send through to us might be nothing much more than secondary reflex-transmitters. . . .'

Grimp stirred in his sleep at that point and grumbled. Grandma looked down at him. 'You're sound asleep!' she told him severely, and he was again.

'You've got plans for that boy, haven't you?' the pony said, without shifting its gaze from the hollow.

'I've had my eye on him,' Grandma admitted, 'and I've already recommended him to Headquarters for observation. But I'm not going to make up my mind about Grimp till next summer, when we've had more time to study him. Meanwhile, we'll see what he picks up naturally from the lortel in the way of telepathic communication and sensory extensions. I think Grimp's the kind we can use.'

'He's all right,' the pony agreed absently. 'A bit murderous, though, like most of you. . . .'

'He'll grow out of it!' Grandma said, a little annoyedly, for the subject of human aggressiveness was one she and the pony argued about frequently. 'You can't hurry developments like that along too much. All of Noorhut should grow out of that stage, as a people, in another few hundred years. They're about at the turning-point right now—'

Their heads came up together, then, as something very much like a big, dark rag of leather came fluttering up from the hollow and hung in the dark air above them. The representatives of the opposing powers that were meeting on Noorhut that night took quiet stock of one another for a moment.

The Halpa was about six foot long and two wide, and considerably less than an inch thick. It held its position in the air with a steady, rippling motion, like a bat the size of a man. Then, suddenly, it extended itself with a snap, growing taut as a curved sail.

The pony snorted involuntarily. The apparently featureless shape in the air turned towards it and drifted a few inches closer. When nothing more happened, it turned again and fluttered quietly back down into the hollow.

'Could it tell I was scared?' the pony asked uneasily.

'You reacted just right,' Grandma said soothingly. 'Startled suspicion at first, and then just curiosity, and then another start when it made that jump. It's about what they'd expect from creatures that would be hanging around the hollow now. We're like cows to them. They can't tell what things are by their looks, like we do—'

But her tone was thoughtful, and she was more shaken than she would have cared to let the pony notice. There had been something indescribably menacing and self-assured in the Halpa's gesture. Almost certainly, it had only been trying to draw a reaction of hostile intelligence from them, probing, perhaps, for the presence of weapons that might be dangerous to its kind.

But there was a chance—a tiny but appalling chance—that the things *had* developed some drastically new form of attack since their last break-through, and that they already were in control of the situation. . . .

In which case, neither Grimp nor anyone else on Noorhut would be doing any more growing-up after tomorrow.

Each of the eleven hundred and seventeen planets that had been lost to the Halpa so far still traced a fiery, forbidding orbit through space—torn back from the invaders only at the cost of depriving it, by humanity's own weapons, of the conditions any known form of life could tolerate.

The possibility that this might also be Noorhut's future had loomed as an ugly enormity before her for the past four years. But of the nearly half a hundred worlds which the Halpa were found to be investigating through their detector-globes as possible invasion points for this period, Noorhut finally had been selected by Headquarters as the one where local conditions were most suited to meet them successfully. And that meant in a manner which must include the destruction of their only real invasion weapon, the fabulous and mysterious Halpa transmitter. Capable as they undoubtedly were, they had shown in the past that they were able or willing to employ only one of those instruments for each period of attack. Destroying the transmitter meant therefore that humanity would gain a few more centuries to figure out a way to get back at the Halpa before a new attempt was made.

So on all planets but Noorhut the detector-globes had been encouraged carefully to send back reports of a dangerously alert and well-armed population. On Noorhut, however, they had been soothed along . . . and just as her home-planet had been chosen as the most favourable point of encounter, so was Erisa Wannattel herself selected as the agent most suited to represent humanity's forces under the conditions that existed there.

Grandma sighed gently and reminded herself again that Headquarters was as unlikely to miscalculate the overall probability of success as it was to select the wrong person to achieve it. There was only the tiniest, the most theoretical, of chances that something might go wrong and that she would end her long career with the blundering murder of her own home-world.

But there was that chance.

'There seem to be more down there every minute!' the pony was saying.

Grandma drew a deep breath.

'Must be several thousand by now,' she acknowledged. 'It's getting near breakthrough time, all right, but those are only the advance forces.' She added, 'Do you notice anything like a glow of light down there, towards the centre?'

The pony stared a moment. 'Yes,' it said. 'But I would have thought that was way under the red for you. Can you see it?'

'No,' said Grandma. 'I get a kind of a feeling, like heat. That's the transmitter beginning to come through. I think we've got them!'

The pony shifted its bulk slowly from side to side.

'Yes,' it said resignedly, 'or they've got us.'

'Don't think about that,' Grandma ordered sharply and clamped one more mental lock shut on the foggy, dark terrors that were curling and writhing under her conscious thoughts, threatening to emerge at the last moment and paralyse her actions.

She had opened her black bag and was unhurriedly fitting together something composed of a few pieces of wood and wire, and a rather heavy, stiff spring. . . .

'Just be ready,' she added.

'I've been ready for an hour,' said the pony, shuffling its feet unhappily.

They did no more talking after that. All the valley had become quiet about them. But slowly the hollow below was filling up with a black, stirring, slithering tide. Bits of it fluttered up now and then like strips of black smoke, hovered a few yards above the mass and settled again.

Suddenly, down in the centre of the hollow, there was something else.

The pony had seen it first, Grandma Wannattel realized. It was staring in that direction for almost a minute before she grew able to distinguish something that might have been a group of graceful miniature spires. Semi-transparent in the darkness, four small domes showed at the corners, with a larger one in the centre. The central one was about twenty feet high and very slender.

The whole structure began to solidify swiftly. . . .

The Halpa Transmitter's appearance of crystalline slightness was perhaps the most mind-chilling thing about it. For it brought instantly a jarring sense of what must be black distance beyond all distances, reaching back unimaginably to its place of origin. In that unknown somewhere, a prodigiously talented and determined race of beings had laboured for human centuries to prepare and point some stupendous gun . . . and were able then to bridge the vast interval with nothing more substantial than this dark sliver of glass that had come to rest suddenly in the valley of the Wend.

But, of course, the Transmitter was all that was needed; its deadly poison lay in a sluggish, almost inert mass about it. Within minutes from now, it would waken to life, as similar transmitters had wakened on other nights on those lost and burning worlds. And in much less than minutes after that, the Halpa invaders would be hurled by their slender machine to every surface section of Noorhut—no longer inert, but quickened into a ravening, almost indestructible form of vampiric life, dividing and sub-dividing in its incredibly swift cycle of reproduction, fastening to feed anew, growing and dividing again—

Spreading, at that stage, much more swiftly than it could be exterminated by anything but the ultimate weapons!

The pony stirred suddenly, and she felt the wave of panic roll up in it.

'It's the Transmitter, all right,' Grandma's thought reached it quickly. 'We've had two descriptions of it before. But we can't be sure it's *here* until it begins to charge itself. Then it lights up—first at the edges, and then at the centre. Five seconds after the central spire lights up, it will be energized too much to let them pull it back again. At least, they couldn't pull it back after that, the last time they were observed. And then we'd better be ready—'

The pony had been told all that before. But as it listened it was quieting down again.

'And you're going to go on sleeping!' Grandma Wannattel's thought told Grimp next. 'No matter what you hear or what happens, you'll sleep on and know nothing at all any more until I wake you up. . . .'

Light surged up suddenly in the Transmitter—first into the four outer spires, and an instant later into the big central one, in a sullen red glow. It lit the hollow with a smoky glare. The pony took two startled steps backwards.

'Five seconds to go!' whispered Grandma's thought. She reached into her black bag again and took out a small plastic ball. It reflected the light from the hollow in dull crimson gleamings. She let it slip down carefully inside the shaftlike frame of the gadget she had put together of wood and wire. It clicked into place there against one end of the compressed spring.

Down below, they lay now in a blanket fifteen feet thick over the wet ground, like big, black, water-sogged leaves swept up in circular piles about the edges of the hollow. The tops and sides of the piles were stirring and shivering and beginning to slide down towards the Transmitter.

'. . . five, and go!' Grandma said aloud. She raised the wooden catapult to her shoulder.

The pony shook its blunt-horned head violently from side to side, made a strangled, bawling sound, surged forward and plunged down the steep side of the hollow in a thundering rush.

Grandma aimed carefully and let go.

The blanket of dead-leaf things was lifting into the air ahead of the pony's ground-shaking approach in a weightless, silent swirl of darkness which instantly blotted both the glowing Transmitter and the pony's shape from sight. The pony roared once as the blackness closed over it. A second later, there was a crash like the shattering of a hundred-foot mirror—and at approximately the same moment, Grandma's plastic ball exploded somewhere in the centre of the swirling swarm.

Cascading fountains of white fire filled the whole of the hollow. Within the fire, a dense mass of shapes fluttered and writhed frenziedly like burning rags. From down where the fire boiled fiercest rose continued sounds of brittle substances suffering enormous violence. The pony was trampling the ruined Transmitter, making sure of its destruction.

'Better get out of it!' Grandma shouted anxiously. 'What's left of that will all melt now anyway!'

She didn't know whether it heard her or not. But a few seconds later, it came pounding up the side of the hollow again. Blazing from nose to rump, it tramped past Grandma, plunged through the meadow behind her, shedding white sheets of fire that exploded the marsh grass in its tracks, and hurled itself headlong into the pond it had selected previously. There was a great splash, accompanied by sharp hissing noises. Pond and pony vanished together under billowing clouds of steam.

'That was pretty hot!' its thought came to Grandma.

She drew a deep breath.

'Hot as anything that ever came out of a volcano!' she affirmed. 'If you'd played around in it much longer, you'd have fixed up the village with roasts for a year.'

'I'll just stay here for a while, till I've cooled off a bit,' said the pony.

Grandma found something strangling her then, and discovered it was the lortel's tail. She unwound it carefully. But the lortel promptly reanchored itself with all four hands in her hair. She decided to leave it there. It seemed badly upset.

Grimp, however, slept on. It was going to take a little manœuvring to get him back into the village undetected before morning, but she would figure that out by and by. A steady flow of cool night-air was being drawn past them into the hollow now and rising out of it again in boiling, vertical columns of invisible heat. At the bottom of the deluxe blaze she'd lit down there, things still seemed to be moving about—but very slowly. The Halpa were tough organisms, all right, though not nearly so tough, when you heated them up with a really good incendiary, as were the natives of Treebel.

She would have to make a final check of the hollow around dawn, of course, when the ground should have cooled off enough to permit it—but her century's phase of the Halpa War did seem to be over. The defensive part of it, at any rate—

Wet, munching sounds from the pond indicated the pony felt comfortable enough by now to take an interest in the parboiled vegetation it found floating around it. Everything had turned out all right.

So she settled down carefully on her back in the long marsh grass without disturbing Grimp's position too much, and just let herself faint for a while.

By sunrise, Grandma Wannattel's patent-medicine trailer was nine miles from the village and rolling steadily southwards up the valley road through the woods. As usual, she was departing under a cloud.

Grimp and the policeman had showed up early to warn her. The Guardian was making use of the night's various unprecedented disturbances to press through a vote on a Public Menace charge against Grandma in the village; and since everybody still felt rather excited and upset, he had a good chance just now of getting a majority.

Grimp had accompanied her far enough to explain that this state of affairs wasn't going to be permanent. He had it all worked out.

Runny's new immunity to hay-fever had brought him and the pretty Vellit to a fresh understanding overnight; they were going to get married five weeks from now. As a married man, Runny would then be eligible for the post of Village Guardian at the harvest elections—and between Grimp's cousins and Vellit's cousins, Runny's backers would just about control the vote. So when Grandma got around to visiting the valley again next summer, she needn't worry any more about police interference or official disapproval. . . .

Grandma had nodded approvingly. That was about the kind of neighborhood politics she'd begun to play herself at Grimp's age. She was pretty sure by now that Grimp was the one who eventually would become her successor, and the guardian not only of Noorhut and the star-system to which Noorhut belonged, but of a good many other star-systems besides. With careful schooling, he ought to be just about ready for the job by the time she was willing, finally, to retire.

An hour after he had started back to the farm, looking suddenly a little forlorn, the trailer swung off the valley road into a narrow forest path. Here the pony lengthened its stride, and less than five minutes later they entered a curving ravine, at the far end of which lay something that Grimp would have recognized instantly, from his one visit to the nearest port city, as a small spaceship.

A large round lock opened soundlessly in its side as they approached. The pony came to a stop. Grandma got down from the driver's seat and unhitched it. The pony walked into the lock, and the trailer picked its wheels off the ground and floated in after it. Grandma Wannattel walked in last, and the lock closed quietly on her heels.

The ship lay still a moment longer. Then it was suddenly gone. Dead leaves went dancing for a while about the ravine, disturbed by the breeze of its departure.

In a place very far away—so far that neither Grimp nor his parents nor anyone in the village except the schoolteacher had ever heard of it—a set of instruments began signalling for attention. Somebody answered them.

Grandma's voice announced distinctly:

'This is Zone Agent Wannattel's report on the successful conclusion of the Halpa operation on Noorhut—'

High above Noorhut's skies, eight great ships swung instantly out of their watchful orbits about the planet and flashed off again into the blackness of the boundless space that was their sea and their home.

SECOND DAWN

ARTHUR C. CLARKE

'Here they come,' said Eris, rising to his forefeet and turning to look down the long valley. For a moment the pain and bitterness had left his thoughts, so that even Jeryl, whose mind was more closely tuned to his than to any other, could scarcely detect it. There was even an undertone of softness that recalled poignantly the Eris she had known in the days before the War—the old Eris who now seemed almost as remote and as lost as if he were lying with all the others out there on the plain.

A dark tide was flowing up the valley, advancing with a curious, hesitant motion, making odd pauses and little bounds forward. It was flanked with gold—the thin line of the Atheleni guards, so terrifyingly few compared with the black mass of the prisoners. But they were enough: indeed, they were only needed to guide that aimless river on its faltering way. Yet at the sight of so many thousands of the enemy, Jeryl found herself trembling and instinctively moved towards her mate, silver pelt resting against gold. Eris gave no sign that he had understood or even noticed the action.

The fear vanished as Jeryl saw how slowly the dark flood was moving forwards. She had been told what to expect, but the reality was even worse than she had imagined. As the prisoners came nearer, all the hate and bitterness ebbed from her mind, to be replaced by a sick compassion. No one of her race need ever more fear the aimless, idiot horde that was being shepherded through the pass into the valley it would never leave again.

The guards were doing little more than urge the prisoners on with meaningless but encouraging cries, like nurses calling to infants too young to sense their thoughts. Strain as she might, Jeryl could detect no vestige of reason in any of these thousands of minds passing so near at hand. That brought home to her, more vividly than could anything else, the magnitude of the victory—and of the defeat. Her mind was sensitive enough to detect the first faint thoughts of children, hovering on the verge of consciousness. The defeated enemy had become not even children, but babies with the bodies of adults.

The tide was passing within a few feet of them now. For the first time, Jeryl realized how much larger than her own people the Mithraneans were, and how beautifully the light of the twin suns gleamed on the dark satin of their bodies. Once a magnificent specimen, towering a full head above Eris, broke loose from the main body and came blundering towards them, halting a few paces away. Then it crouched down like a lost and frightened child, the splendid head moving uncertainly from side to side as if seeking it knew not what. For a moment the great, empty eyes fell full upon Jeryl's face. She was as beautiful, she knew, to the Mithraneans as to her own race—but there was no flicker of emotion on the blank features, and no pause in the aimless movement of the questing head. Then an exasperated guard drove the prisoner back to his fellows.

'Come away,' Jeryl pleaded. 'I don't want to see any more. Why did you ever bring me here?' The last thought was heavy with reproach.

Eris began to move away over the grassy slopes in great bounds that she could not hope to match, but as he went his mind threw its message back to hers. His thoughts were still gentle, though the pain beneath them was too deep to be concealed.

'I wanted everyone—even you—to see what we had to do to win the War. Then, perhaps, we will have no more in our lifetimes.'

He was waiting for her on the brow of the hill, undistressed by the mad violence of his climb. The stream of prisoners was now too far below for them to see the details of its painful progress. Jeryl crouched down beside Eris and began to browse on the sparse vegetation that had been exiled from the fertile valley. She was slowly beginning to recover from the shock.

'But what will happen to them?' she asked presently, still haunted by the memory of that splendid, mindless giant going into a captivity it could never understand.

'They can be taught how to eat,' said Eris. 'There is food in the valley for half a year, and then we'll move them on. It will be a heavy strain on our own resources, but we're under a moral obligation—and we've put it in the peace treaty.'

'They can never be cured?'

'No. Their minds have been totally destroyed. They'll be like this until they die.'

There was a long silence. Jeryl let her gaze wander across the hills, falling in gentle undulations to the edge of the ocean. She could just make out, beyond a gap in the hills, the distant line of blue that marked the sea—the mysterious, impassable sea. Its blue would soon be deepening into darkness, for the fierce white sun was setting and presently there would only be the red disc—hundreds of times larger but giving far less light—of its pale companion.

'I suppose we had to do it,' Jeryl said at last. She was thinking almost to herself, but she let enough of her thoughts escape for Eris to overhear.

'You've seen them,' he answered briefly. 'They were bigger and stronger than we. Though we outnumbered them, it was stalemate: in the end, I think they would have won. By doing what we did, we saved thousands from death—or mutilation.'

The bitterness came back into his thoughts, and Jeryl dared not look at him. He had screened the depths of his mind, but she knew that he was thinking of the shattered ivory stump upon his forehead. The War had been fought, except at the very end, with two weapons only—the razor-sharp hooves of the little, almost useless forepaws, and the unicornlike horns. With one of these Eris could never fight again, and from the loss stemmed much of the embittered harshness that sometimes made him hurt even those who loved him.

Eris was waiting for someone, though who it was Jeryl could not guess. She knew better than to interrupt his thoughts while he was in his present mood, and so remained silently beside him, her shadow merging with his as it stretched far along the hilltop.

Jeryl and Eris came of a race which, in Nature's lottery, had been luckier than most—and yet had missed one of the greatest prizes of all. They had powerful bodies and powerful minds, and they lived in a world which was both temperate and fertile. By human standards, they would have seemed strange but by no means repulsive. Their sleek, fur-covered bodies tapered to a single giant rear limb that could send them leaping over the ground in thirty-foot bounds. The two forelimbs were much smaller, and served merely for support and steadying. They ended in pointed hooves that could be deadly in combat, but had no other useful purpose.

Both the Atheleni and their cousins, the Mithraneans, possessed mental powers that had enabled them to develop a very advanced mathematics and philosophy: but over the physical world they had no control at all. Houses, tools, clothes—indeed, artefacts of any kind—were utterly unknown to them. To races which possessed hands, tentacles, or other means of manipulation, their culture would have seemed incredibly limited: yet such is the adaptability of the mind, and the power of the commonplace, that they seldom realized their handicaps and could imagine no other way of life. It was natural to wander in great herds over the fertile plains, pausing where food was plentiful and moving on again when it was exhausted. This nomadic life had given them enough leisure for philosophy and even for certain arts. Their telepathic powers had not yet robbed them of their voices and they had developed a complex vocal music and an even more complex choreography. But they took the greatest pride of all in the range of their thoughts: for thousands of generations they had sent their minds roving through the misty infinities of metaphysics. Of *physics*, and indeed of all the sciences of matter, they knew nothing—not even that they existed.

'Someone's coming,' said Jeryl suddenly. 'Who is it?'

Eris did not bother to look, but there was a sense of strain in his reply.

'It's Aretenon. I agreed to meet him here.'

'I'm so glad. You were such good friends once—it upset me when you quarrelled.'

Eris pawed fretfully at the turf, as he did when he was embarrassed or annoyed.

'I lost my temper with him when he left me during the fifth battle of the Plain. Of course I didn't know then why he had to go.'

Jeryl's eyes widened in sudden amazement and understanding.

'You mean—he had something to do with the Madness, and the way the War ended?'

'Yes. There were very few people who knew more about the mind than he did. I don't know what part he played, but it must have been an important one. I don't suppose he'll ever be able to tell us much about it.'

Still a considerable distance below them, Aretenon was zigzagging up the hillside in great leaps. A little later he had reached them and instinctively bent his head to touch horns with Eris in the universal gesture of greeting. Then he stopped, horribly embarrassed, and there was an awkward pause until Jeryl came to the rescue with some conventional remarks.

When Eris spoke, Jeryl was relieved to sense his obvious pleasure at meeting his friend once again, for the first time since their angry parting at the height of the War. It had been longer still since her last meeting with Aretenon, and she was surprised to see how much he had changed. He was considerably younger than Eris—but no one would have guessed it now. Some of his once-golden pelt was turning black with age, and with a flash of his old humour Eris remarked that soon no one would be able to tell him from a Mithranean.

Aretenon smiled.

'That would have been useful in the last few weeks. I've just come through their country, helping to round up the Wanderers. We weren't very popular, as you might expect. If they'd known who I was, I don't suppose I'd have got back alive—armistice or no armistice.'

'You weren't actually in charge of the Madness, were you?' asked Jeryl, unable to control her curiosity.

She had a momentary impression of thick, defensive mists forming around Aretenon's mind, shielding all his thoughts from the outer world. Then the reply came, curiously muffled, and with a sense of distance that was very rare in telepathic-contact.

'No: I wasn't in supreme charge. But there were only two others between myself and—the top.'

'Of course,' said Eris, rather petulantly, 'I'm only an ordinary soldier and don't understand these things. But I'd like to know just how you did it. Naturally,' he added, 'neither Jeryl nor myself would talk to anyone else.'

Again that veil seemed to descend over Aretenon's thoughts. Then it lifted, ever so slightly.

'There's very little I'm allowed to tell. As you know, Eris, I was always interested in the mind and its workings. Do you remember the games we used to play, when I tried to uncover your thoughts, and you did your best to stop me? And how I sometimes made you carry out acts against your will?'

'I still think,' said Eris, 'that you couldn't have done that to a stranger, and that I was really unconsciously co-operating.'

'That was true then—but it isn't any longer. The proof lies down there in the valley.' He gestured towards the last stragglers who were being rounded up by the guards. The dark tide had almost passed, and soon the entrance to the valley would be closed.

'When I grew older,' continued Aretenon, 'I spent more and more of my time probing into the ways of the mind, and trying to discover why some of us can share our thoughts so easily, while others can never do so but must remain always isolated and alone, forced to communicate by sounds or gestures. And I became fascinated by those rare minds that are completely deranged, so that those who possess them seem less than children.

'I had to abandon these studies when the War began. Then, as you know, they called for me one day during the fifth battle. Even now, I'm not quite sure who was responsible for that. I was taken to a place a long way from here, where I found a little group of thinkers many of whom I already knew.

'The plan was simple—and tremendous. From the dawn of our race we've known that two or three minds, linked together, could be used to control another mind, *if it was willing*, in the way that I used to control you. We've employed this power for healing since ancient times. Now we planned to use it for destruction.

'There were two main difficulties. One was bound up with that curious limitation of our normal telepathic powers—the fact that, except in rare cases, we can only have contact over a distance *with someone we already know*, and can communicate with strangers only when we are actually in their presence.

'The second, and greater problem, was that the massed power of many minds would be needed, and never before had it been possible to link together more than two or three. How we succeeded is our main secret: like all things, it seems easy now it has been done. And once we had started, it was simpler than we had expected. Two minds are more than twice as powerful as one, and three are much more than thrice as powerful as a single will. The exact mathematical relationship is an interesting one. You know how very rapidly the number of ways a group of objects may be arranged increases with the size of the group? Well, a similar relationship holds in this case.

'So in the end we had our Composite Mind. At first it was unstable, and we could hold it together only for a few seconds. It's still a tremendous strain on our mental resources, and even now we can only do it for—well, for long enough.

'All these experiments, of course, were carried out in great secrecy. If we could do this, so could the Mithraneans, for their minds are as good as ours. We had a number of their prisoners, and we used them as subjects.'

For a moment the veil that hid Aretenon's inner thoughts seemed to tremble and dissolve: then he regained control.

'That was the worst part. It was bad enough to send madness into a far land, but it was infinitely worse when you could watch with your own eyes the effects of what you did.

'When we had perfected our technique, we made the first long-distance test. Our victim was someone so well known to one of our prisoners—whose mind we had taken over—that we could identify him completely and thus the distance between us was no objection. The experiment worked, but of course no one suspected that we were responsible.

'We did not operate again until we were certain that our attack would be so overwhelming that it would end the War. From the minds of our prisoners we had identified about a score of Mithraneans—their friends and kindred—in such detail that we could pick them out and destroy them. As each mind fell beneath our attack, it gave up to us the knowledge of others, and so our power increased. We could have done far more damage than we did, for we took only the males.'

'Was that,' said Jeryl bitterly, 'so very merciful?'

'Perhaps not: but it should be remembered to our credit. We stopped as soon as the enemy sued for peace, and as we alone knew what had happened, we went into their country to undo what damage we could. It was little enough.'

There was a long silence. The valley was deserted now, and the white sun had set. A cold wind was blowing over the hills, passing, where none could follow it, out across the empty and untravelled sea. Then Eris spoke, his thoughts almost whispering in Aretenon's mind.

'You did not come to tell me this, did you? There is something more.' It was a statement rather than a query.

'Yes,' replied Aretenon. 'I have a message for you—one that will surprise you a good deal. It's from Therodimus.'

'Therodimus! I thought—'

'You thought he was dead, or worse still, a traitor. He's neither, although he's lived in enemy territory for the last twenty years. The Mithraneans treated him as we did, and gave him everything he needed. They recognized his mind for what it was, and even during the War no one touched him. Now he wants to see you again.'

Whatever emotions Eris was feeling at this news of his old teacher, he gave no sign of them. Perhaps he was recalling his youth, remembering now that Therodimus had played a greater part in the shaping of his mind than any other single influence. But his thoughts were barred to Aretenon and even to Jeryl.

'What's he been doing all this time?' Eris asked at length. 'And why does he want to see me now?'

'It's a long and complicated story,' said Aretenon, 'but Therodimus has made a discovery quite as remarkable as ours, and one that may have even greater consequences.'

'Discovery? What sort of discovery?'

Aretenon paused, looking thoughtfully along the valley. The guards were returning, leaving behind only the few who would be needed to deal with any wandering prisoners.

'You know as much of our history as I do, Eris,' he began. 'It took, we believe, something like a million generations for us to reach our present level of development—and that's a tremendous length of time! Almost all the progress we've made has been due to our telepathic powers: without them we'd be little different from all those other animals that show such puzzling resemblances to us. We're very proud of our philosophy and our mathematics, of our music and dancing—but have you ever thought, Eris, that there might be other lines of cultural development which we've never even dreamed of? *That there might be other forces in the Universe beside mental ones?*'

'I don't know what you mean,' said Eris flatly.

'It's hard to explain, and I won't try—except to say this. Do you realize just how pitiably feeble is our control over the external world, and how useless these limbs of ours really are? No—you can't, for you won't have seen what I have. But perhaps this will make you understand.'

The pattern of Eretenon's thoughts modulated suddenly into a minor key.

'I remember once coming upon a bank of beautiful and curiously complicated flowers. I wanted to see what they were like inside, so I tried to open one, steadying it between my hooves and picking it apart with my teeth. I tried again and again—and failed. In the end, half mad with rage, I trampled all those flowers into the dirt.'

Jeryl could detect the perplexity in Eris's mind, but she could see that he was interested and curious to know more.

'I have had that sort of feeling, too,' he admitted. 'But what can one do about it? And after all, is it really important? There are a good many things in this universe which are not exactly as we should like them.'

Aretenon smiled.

'That's true enough. But Therodimus has found how to do something about it. Will you come and see him?'

'It must be a long journey.'

'About twenty days from here, and we have to go across a river.'

Jeryl felt Eris give a little shudder. The Atheleni hated water, for the excellent and sufficient reason that they were too heavily boned to swim, and promptly drowned if they fell into it.

'It's in enemy territory: they won't like me.'

'They respect you, and it might be a good idea for you to go—a friendly gesture, as it were.'

'But I'm wanted here.'

'You can take my word that nothing you do here is as important as the message Therodimus has for you—and for the whole world.'

Eris veiled his thoughts for a moment, then uncovered them briefly.

'I'll think about it,' he said.

It was surprising how little Aretenon managed to say on the many days of the journey. From time to time Eris would challenge the defences of his mind with half-playful thrusts, but always they were parried with an effortless skill. About the ultimate weapon that had ended the War he would say nothing, but Eris knew that those who had wielded it had not yet disbanded and were still at their secret hiding-place. Yet though he would not talk about the past, Aretenon often spoke of the future, and with the urgent anxiety of one who had helped to shape it and was not sure if he had acted aright. Like many others of his race, he was haunted by what he had done, and the sense of guilt sometimes overwhelmed him. Often he made remarks which puzzled Eris at the time, but which he was to remember more and more vividly in the years ahead.

'We've come to a turning-point in our history, Eris. The powers we've uncovered will soon be shared by the Mithraneans, and another war will mean destruction for us both. All my life I've worked to increase our knowledge of the mind, but now I wonder if I've brought something into the world that is too powerful, and too dangerous for us to handle. Yet it's too late, now, to retrace our footsteps: sooner or later our culture was bound to come to this point, and to discover what we have found.

'It's a terrible dilemma: and there's only one solution. We cannot go back, and if we go forward we may meet disaster. So we must change the very nature of our civilization, and break completely with the million generations behind us. You can't imagine how that could be done: nor could I, until I met Therodimus and he told me of his dream.

'The mind is a wonderful thing, Eris—but by itself it is helpless in the universe of matter. We know now how to multiply the power of our brains by an enormous factor: we can solve, perhaps, the great problems of mathematics that have baffled us for ages. But neither our unaided minds, nor the group-mind we've now created, can alter in the slightest the one fact that all through history has brought us and the Mithraneans into conflict—the fact that the food supply is fixed, and our populations are not.'

Jeryl would watch them, taking little part in their thoughts, as they argued these matters. Most of their discussions took place while they were browsing, for like all active ruminants they had to spend a considerable part of each day searching for food. Fortunately the land through which they were passing was extremely fertile—indeed, its fertility had been one of the causes of the War. Eris, Jeryl was glad to see, was becoming something of his old self again. The feeling of frustrated bitterness that had filled his mind for so many months had not lifted, but it was no longer as all-pervading as it had been.

They left the open plain on the twenty-second day of their journey. For a long time they had been travelling through Mithranean territory, but those few of their ex-enemies they had seen had been inquisitive rather than hostile. Now the grasslands were coming to an end, and the forest with all its primeval terrors lay ahead.

'Only one carnivore lives in this region,' Aretenon reassured them, 'and it's no match for the three of us. We'll be past the trees in a day and a night.'

'A night—in the forest!' gasped Jeryl, half-petrified with terror at the very thought.

Aretenon was obviously a little ashamed of himself.

'I didn't like to mention it before,' he apologized, 'but there's really no danger. I've done it by myself, several times. After all, none of the great flesh-eaters of ancient times still exists—and it won't be really dark, even in the woods. The red sun will still be up.'

Jeryl was still trembling slightly. She came of a race which, for thousands of generations, had lived on the high hills and the open plains, relying on speed to escape from danger. The thought of going among trees—and in the dim red twilight while the primary sun was down—filled her with panic. And of the three of them, only Aretenon possessed a horn with which to fight. (It was nothing like so long or sharp, thought Jeryl, as Eris's had been.)

She was still not at all happy even when they had spent a completely uneventful day moving through the woods. The only animals they saw were tiny, long-tailed creatures that ran up and down the tree-trunks with amazing speed, gibbering with anger as the intruders passed. It was entertaining to watch them, but Jeryl did not think that the forest would be quite so amusing in the night.

Her fears were well founded. When the fierce white sun passed below the trees, and the crimson shadows of the red giant lay everywhere, a change seemed to come over the world. A sudden silence swept across the forest—a silence abruptly broken by a very distant wail towards which the three of them turned instinctively, ancestral warnings shrieking in their minds.

'What was that?' gasped Jeryl.

Aretenon was breathing swiftly, but his reply was calm enough.

'Never mind,' he said. 'It was a long way off. I don't know what it was.'

They took turns to keep guard, and the long night wore slowly away. From time to time Jeryl would awaken from troubled dreams into the nightmare reality of the strange, distorted trees gathered threateningly around her. Once, when she was on guard, she heard the sound of a heavy body moving through the woods very far away—but it came no nearer and she did not disturb the others. So at last the longed-for brilliance of the white sun began to flood the sky, and the day had come again.

Aretenon, Jeryl thought, was probably more relieved than he pretended to be. He was almost boyish as he frisked around in the morning sunlight, snatching an occasional mouthful of foliage from an overhanging branch.

'We've only half a day to go now,' he said cheerfully. 'We'll be out of the forest by noon.'

There was a mischievous undertone to his thoughts that puzzled Jeryl. It seemed as if Aretenon was keeping still another secret from them, and Jeryl wondered what further obstacles they would have to overcome. By midday she knew, for their way was barred by a great river flowing slowly past them as if in no haste to meet the sea.

Eris looked at it with some annoyance, measuring it with a practised eye.

'It's much too deep to ford here. We'll have to go a long way upstream before we can cross.'

Aretenon smiled.

'On the contrary,' he said cheerfully, 'we're going *downstream*.'

Eris and Jeryl looked at him in amazement.

'Are you mad?' Eris cried.

'You'll soon see. We've not far to go now—you've come all this way, so you might as well trust me for the rest of the journey.'

The river slowly widened and deepened. If it had been impassable before, it was doubly so now. Sometimes, Eris knew, one came upon a stream across which a tree had fallen, so that one could walk over the trunk—though it was a risky thing to do. But this river was the width of many trees, and was growing no narrower.

'We're nearly there,' said Aretenon at last. 'I recognize the place. Someone should be coming out of those woods at any moment.' He gestured with his horn to the trees on the far side of the river, and almost as he did so three figures came bounding out on to the bank. Two of them, Jeryl saw, were Atheleni: the third was a Mithranean.

They were now nearing a great tree, standing by the water's edge, but Jeryl had paid little attention: she was too interested in the figures on the distant bank, wondering what they were going to do next. So when Eris's amazement exploded like a thunderclap in the depths of her own mind, she was too confused for a moment to realize its cause. Then she turned towards the tree, and saw what Eris had seen.

To some minds and some races, few things could have been more natural or more commonplace than a thick rope tied round a tree-trunk, and floating out across the water of a river to another tree on the far bank. Yet it filled both Jeryl and Eris with the terror of the unknown, and for one awful moment Jeryl thought that a gigantic snake was emerging from the water. Then she saw that it was not alive, but her fear remained. For it was the first artificial object that she had ever seen.

'Don't worry about *what* it is, or how it was put there,' counselled Aretenon. 'It's going to carry you across, and that's all that matters for the moment. Look—there's someone coming over now!'

One of the figures on the far bank had lowered itself into the water, and was working its way with its forelimbs along the rope. As it came nearer—it was the Mithranean, and a female—Jeryl saw that it was carrying a second and much smaller rope looped round the upper part of its body.

With the skill of long practice, the stranger made her way across the floating cable, and emerged dripping from the river. She seemed to know Aretenon, but Jeryl could not intercept their thoughts.

'I can go across without any help,' said Aretenon, 'but I'll show you the easy way.'

He slipped the loop over his shoulders, and, dropping into the water, hooked his forelimbs over the fixed cable. A moment later he was being dragged across at a great speed by the two others on the far bank, where, after much trepidation, Eris and Jeryl presently joined him.

It was not the sort of bridge one would expect from a race which could quite easily have dealt with the mathematics of a reinforced concrete arch—if the possibility of such an object had ever occurred to it. But it served its purpose, and once it had been made, they could use it readily enough.

Once it had been made. But—who had made it?

When their dripping guides had rejoined them, Aretenon gave his friends a warning.

'I'm afraid you're going to have a good many shocks while you're here. You'll see some very strange sights, but when you understand them, they'll cease to puzzle you in the slightest. In fact, you will soon come to take them for granted.'

One of the strangers, whose thoughts neither Eris nor Jeryl could intercept, was giving him a message.

'Therodimus is waiting for us,' said Aretenon. 'He's very anxious to see you.'

'I've been trying to contact him,' complained Eris, 'but I've not succeeded.'

Aretenon seemed a little troubled.

'You'll find he's changed,' he said. 'After all, you've not seen each other for many years. It may be some time before you can make full contact again.'

Their road was a winding one through the forest, and from time to time curiously narrow paths branched off in various directions. Therodimus, thought Eris, must have changed indeed for him to have taken up permanent residence among trees. Presently the track opened out into a large, semicircular clearing with a low white cliff lying along its diameter. At the foot of the cliff were several dark holes of varying sizes—obviously the openings of caves.

It was the first time that either Eris or Jeryl had ever entered a cave, and they did not greatly look forward to the experience. They were relieved when Aretenon told them to wait just outside the opening, and went on alone towards the puzzling yellow light that glowed in the depths. A moment later, dim memories began to pulse in Eris's mind, and he knew that his old teacher was coming, even though he could no longer fully share his thoughts.

Something stirred in the gloom, and then Therodimus came out into the sunlight. At the sight of him, Jeryl screamed once and buried her head in Eris's mane, but Eris stood firm, though he was trembling as he had never done before battle. For Therodimus blazed with a magnificence that none of his race had ever known since history began. Around his neck hung a band of glittering objects that caught and refracted the sunlight in a myriad colours, while covering his body was a sheet of some thick, many-hued material that rustled softly as he walked. And his horn was no longer the yellow of ivory: some magic had changed it to the most wonderful purple that Jeryl had ever seen.

Therodimus stood motionless for a moment, savouring their amazement to the full. Then his rich laugh echoed in their minds, and he reared up on his hind limb. The coloured garment fell whispering to the ground, and at a toss of his head the glittering necklace arched like a rainbow into a corner of the cave. But the purple horn remained unchanged.

It seemed to Eris that he stood at the brink of a great chasm, with Therodimus beckoning him on the far side. Their thoughts struggled to form a bridge, but could make no contact. Between them was the gulf of half a lifetime and many battles, of a myriad unshared experiences—Therodimus's years in this strange land, his own mating with Jeryl and the memory of their lost children. Though they stood face to face, a few feet only between them, their thoughts could never meet again.

Then Aretenon, with all the power and authority of his unsurpassed skill, did something to his mind that Eris was never quite able to recall. He only knew that the years seemed to have rolled back, that he was once more the eager, anxious pupil—and that he could speak to Therodimus again.

It was strange to sleep underground, but less unpleasant than spending the night amid the unknown terrors of the forest. As she watched the crimson shadows deepening beyond the entrance to the little cave, Jeryl tried to collect her scattered thoughts. She had understood only a small part of what had passed between Eris and Therodimus, but she knew that something incredible was taking place. The evidence of her eyes was enough to prove that: today she had seen things for which there were no words in her language.

She had heard things, too. As they had passed one of the cave-mouths, there had come from it a rhythmic 'whirring' sound, unlike that made by any animal she knew. It had continued steadily without pause or break as long as she could hear it, and even now its unhurried rhythm had not left her mind. Aretenon, she believed, had also noticed it, though without any surprise: Eris had been so engrossed with Therodimus.

The old philosopher had told them very little, preferring, as he said, to show them his empire when they had had a good night's rest. Nearly all their talk had been concerned with the events of their own land during the last few years, and Jeryl found it somewhat boring. Only one thing had interested her, and she had eyes for little else. That was the wonderful chain of coloured crystals that Therodimus had worn around his neck. What it was, or how it had been created, she could not imagine: but she coveted it. As she fell asleep, she found herself thinking idly, but more than half-seriously, of the sensation it would cause if she returned to her people with such a marvel gleaming against her own pelt. It would look so much better there than upon old Therodimus.

Aretenon and Therodimus met them at the cave soon after dawn. The philosopher had discarded his regalia—which he had obviously worn only to impress his guests—and his horn had returned to its normal yellow. That was one thing Jeryl thought she could understand, for she had come across fruits whose juices could cause colour changes.

Therodimus settled himself at the mouth of the cave. He began his narration without any preliminaries, and Eris guessed that he must have told it many times before to earlier visitors.

'I came to this place, Eris, about five years after leaving our country. As you know, I was always interested in strange lands, and from the Mithraneans I'd heard rumours that intrigued me very much. How I traced them to their source is a long story that doesn't matter now. I crossed the river far upstream one summer, when the water was very low. There's only one place where it can be done, and then only in the driest years. Higher still the river loses itself in the mountains, and I don't think there's any way through them. So this is virtually an island—almost completely cut off from Mithranean territory.

'It's an island, but it's not uninhabited. The people who live here are called the Phileni, and they have a very remarkable culture—one entirely different from our own. Some of the products of that culture you've already seen.

'As you know, there are many different races on our world, and quite a few of them have some sort of intelligence. But there is a great gulf between us and all other creatures. As far as we know, we are the only beings capable of abstract thought and complex logical processes.

'The Phileni are a much younger race than ours, and they are intermediate between us and the other animals. They've lived here on this rather large island for several thousand generations—but their rate of development has been many, many times swifter than ours. They neither possess nor understand our telepathic powers, but they have something else which we may well envy—something which is responsible for the whole of their civilization and its incredibly rapid progress.'

Therodimus paused, then rose slowly to his feet.

'Follow me,' he said. 'I'll take you to see the Phileni.'

He led them back to the caves from which they had come the night before, pausing at the entrance from which Jeryl had heard that strange, rhythmic whirring. It was clearer and louder now, and she saw Eris start as though he had noticed it for the first time. Then Therodimus uttered a high-pitched whistle, and at once the whirring slackened, falling octave by octave until it had ebbed into silence. A moment later something came towards them out of the semi-gloom.

It was a little creature, scarcely half their height, and it did not hop, but walked upon two jointed limbs that seemed very thin and feeble. Its large spherical head was dominated by three huge eyes, set far apart and capable of independent movement. With the best will in the world, Jeryl did not think it was very attractive.

Then Therodimus uttered another whistle, and the creature raised its forelimbs towards them.

'Look closely,' said Therodimus, very gently, 'and you will see the answer to many of your questions.'

For the first time, Jeryl saw that the creature's forelimbs did not end in hooves, or indeed after the fashion of any animal with which she was acquainted. Instead, they divided into at least a dozen thin, flexible tentacles and two hooked claws.

'Go towards it, Jeryl,' commanded Therodimus. 'It has something for you.'

Hesitantly, Jeryl moved forward. She noticed that the creature's body was crossed with bands of dark material, to which were attached unidentifiable objects. It dropped a forelimb to one of these, and a cover opened to reveal a cavity inside which something glittered. Then the little tentacles were clutching that marvellous crystal necklace, and with a movement so swift and dexterous that Jeryl could scarcely follow it, the Phileni moved forward and clasped it round her neck.

Therodimus brushed aside her confusion and gratitude, but his shrewd old mind was well pleased. Jeryl would be his ally now in whatever he planned to do. But Eris's emotions might not be so easily swayed, and in this matter mere logic was not enough. His old pupil had changed so much, had been so deeply wounded by the past, that Therodimus could not be certain of success. Yet he had a plan that could turn even these difficulties to his advantage.

He gave another whistle, and the Phileni made a curious waving gesture with its hands and disappeared into the cave. A moment later that strange whirring ascended once more from the silence, but Jeryl's curiosity was now quite overshadowed by her delight in her new possession.

'We'll go through the woods,' said Therodimus, 'to the nearest settlement—it's only a little way from here. The Phileni don't live in the open, as we do. In fact, they differ from us in almost every conceivable way. I'm even afraid,' he added ruefully, 'that they're much better natured than we are, and I believe that one day they'll be more intelligent. But first of all, let me tell you what I've learned about them, so that you can understand what I'm planning to do.'

The mental evolution of any race is conditioned, even dominated, by physical factors which that race almost invariably takes for granted as part of the natural order of things. The wonderfully sensitive hands of the Phileni had enabled them to find by experiment and trial facts which had taken the planet's only other intelligent species a thousand times as long to discover by pure deduction. Quite early in their history, the Phileni had invented simple tools. From these they had proceeded to fabrics, pottery, and the use of fire. When Therodimus had discovered them, they had already invented the lathe and the potter's wheel, and were about to move into their first Metal Age—with all that that implied.

On the purely intellectual plane, their progress had been less rapid. They were clever and skilful, but they had a dislike of abstract thought and their mathematics was purely empirical. They knew, for example, that a triangle with sides in the ratio three-four-five was right-angled, but had not suspected that this was only a special case of a much more general law. Their knowledge was full of such yawning gaps, which, despite the help of Therodimus and his several score disciples, they seemed in no great hurry to fill.

Therodimus they worshipped as a god, and for two whole generations of their short-lived race they had obeyed him in everything, giving him all the products of their skill that he needed, and making at his suggestion the new tools and devices that had occurred to him. The partnership had been incredibly fertile, for it was as if both races had suddenly been released from their shackles. Great manual skill and great intellectual powers had fused in a fruitful union probably unique in all the universe—and progress that would normally have taken millennia had been achieved in less than a decade.

As Aretenon had promised them, though Eris and Jeryl saw many marvels, they came across nothing that they could not understand once they had watched the little Phileni craftsmen at work and had seen with what magic their hands shaped natural materials into lovely or useful forms. Even their tiny towns and primitive farms soon lost their wonder and became part of the accepted order of things.

Therodimus let them look their fill, until they had seen every aspect of this strangely sophisticated Stone Age culture. Because they knew no differently, they found nothing incongruous in the sight of a Phileni potter—who could scarcely count beyond ten—shaping a series of complex algebraic surfaces under the guidance of a young Mithranean mathematician. Like all his race, Eris possessed tremendous powers of mental visualization, but he realized how much easier geometry would be if one could actually *see* the shapes one was considering. From this beginning (though he could not guess it) would one day evolve the idea of a written language.

Jeryl was fascinated above all things by the sight of the little Phileni women weaving fabrics upon their primitive looms. She could sit for hours watching the flying shuttles and wishing that she could use them. Once one had seen it done, it seemed so simple and obvious—and so utterly beyond the powers of the clumsy, useless limbs of her own people.

They grew very fond of the Phileni, who seemed eager to please and were pathetically proud of all their manual skills. In these new and novel surroundings, meeting fresh wonders every day, Eris seemed to be recovering from some of the scars which the War had left upon his mind. Jeryl knew, however, that there was still much damage to be undone. Sometimes, before he could hide them, she would come across raw, angry wounds in the depths of Eris's mind, and she feared that many of them—like the broken stump of his horn—would never heal. Eris had hated the War, and the manner of its ending still oppressed him. Beyond this, Jeryl knew, he was haunted by the fear that it might come again.

These troubles she often discussed with Therodimus, of whom she had now grown very fond. She still did not fully understand why he had brought them here, or what he and his followers were planning to do. Therodimus was in no hurry to explain his actions, for he wished Jeryl and Eris to draw their own conclusions as far as possible. But at last, five days after their arrival, he called them to his cave.

'You've now seen,' he began, 'most of the things we have to show you here. You know what the Phileni can do, and perhaps you have thought how much our own lives will be enriched once we can use the products of their skill. That was my first thought when I came here, all those years ago.

'It was an obvious and rather naïve idea, but it led to a much greater one. As I grew to know the Phileni, and found how swiftly their minds had advanced in so short a time, I realized what a fearful disadvantage our own race had always laboured under. I began to wonder how much further forward *we* would have been had we the Phileni's control over the physical world. It is not a question of mere convenience, or the ability to make beautiful things like that necklace of yours, Jeryl, but something much more profound. It is the difference between ignorance and knowledge, between weakness and power.

'We have developed our minds, and our minds alone, until we can go no further. As Aretenon has told you, we have now come to a danger that threatens our entire race. We are under the shadow of the irresistible weapon against which there can be no defence.

'The solution is, quite literally, in the hands of the Phileni. We must use their skills to reshape our world, and so remove the cause of all our wars. We must go back to the beginning and re-lay the foundations of our culture. It won't be *our* culture alone, though, for we shall share it with the Phileni. They will be the hands—we the brains. Oh, I have dreamed of the world that may come, ages ahead, when even the marvels you see around you now will be considered childish toys! But not many are philosophers, and I need an argument more substantial than dreams. That final argument I believe I may have found, though I cannot yet be certain.

'I have asked you here, Eris, partly because I wanted to renew our old friendship, and partly because your word will now have far greater influence than mine. You are a hero among your own people, and the Mithraneans also will listen to you. I want you to return, taking with you some of the Phileni and their products. Show them to your people, and ask them to send their young men here to help us with our work.'

There was a pause during which Jeryl could gather no hints of Eris's thoughts. Then he replied hesitantly:

'But I still don't understand. These things that the Phileni make are very pretty, and some of them may be useful to us. But how can they change us as profoundly as you seem to think?'

Therodimus sighed. Eris could not see past the present into the future that was yet to be. He had not caught, as Therodimus had done, the promise that lay beyond the busy hands and tools of the Phileni—the first faint possibilities of the Machine. Perhaps he would never understand: but he could still be convinced.

Veiling his deeper thoughts, Therodimus continued:

'Perhaps some of these things are toys, Eris—but they may be more powerful than you think. Jeryl, I know, would be loath to part with hers . . . and perhaps I can find one that would convince you.'

Eris was sceptical, and Jeryl could see that he was in one of his darker moods.

'I doubt it very much,' he said.

'Well, I can try.' Therodimus gave a whistle, and one of the Phileni came running up. There was a short exchange of conversation.

'Would you come with me, Eris? It will take some time.'

Eris followed him, the others, at Therodimus's request, remaining behind. They left the large cave and went towards the row of smaller ones which the Phileni used for their various trades.

The strange whirring was sounding loudly in Eris's ears, but for a moment he could not see its cause, the light of the crude oil lamps being too faint for his eyes. Then he made out one of the Phileni bending over a wooden table upon which something was spinning rapidly, driven by a belt from a treadle operated by another of the little creatures. He had seen the potters using a similar device, but this was different. It was shaping wood, not clay, and the potter's fingers had been replaced by a sharp metal blade from which long, thin shavings were curling out in fascinating spirals. With their huge eyes the Phileni, who disliked full sunlight, could see perfectly in the gloom, but it was some time before Eris could discover just what was happening. Then, suddenly, he understood.

'Aretenon,' said Jeryl when the others had left them, 'why should the Phileni do all these things for us? Surely they're quite happy as they are?'

The question, Aretenon thought, was typical of Jeryl and would never have been asked by Eris.

'They will do anything that Therodimus says,' he answered, 'but even apart from that there's so much we can give them as well. When we turn our minds to their problems, we can see how to solve them in ways that would never have occurred to them. They're very eager to learn, and already we must have advanced their culture by hundreds of generations. Also, they're physically very feeble. Although we don't possess their dexterity, our strength makes possible tasks they could never attempt.'

They had wandered to the edge of the river, and stood for a moment watching the unhurried waters moving down to the sea. Then Jeryl turned to go upstream, but Aretenon stopped her.

'Therodimus doesn't want us to go that way, yet,' he explained. 'It's just another of his little secrets. He never likes to reveal his plans until they're ready.'

Slightly piqued, and distinctly curious, Jeryl obediently turned back. She would, of course, come this way again as soon as there was no one else about.

It was very peaceful here in the warm sunlight, among the pools of heat trapped by the trees. Jeryl had almost lost her fear of the forest, though she knew she would never be quite happy there.

Aretenon seemed very abstracted, and Jeryl knew that he wished to say something and was marshalling his thoughts. Presently he began to speak, with the freedom that is only possible between two people who are fond of each other but have no emotional ties.

'It is very hard, Jeryl,' he began, 'to turn one's back on the work of a lifetime. Once I had hoped that the great new forces we have discovered could be safely used, but now I know that it is impossible, at least for many ages. Therodimus was right—we can go no further with our minds alone. Our culture has been hopelessly one-sided, though through no fault of ours. We cannot solve the fundamental problem of peace and war without a command over the physical world such as the Phileni possess—and which we hope to borrow from them.

'Perhaps there will be other great adventures here for our minds, to make us forget what we will have to abandon. We shall be able to learn something from Nature at last. What is the difference between fire and water, between wood and stone? What are the suns, and what are those millions of faint lights we see in the sky when both the suns are down? Perhaps the answers to all these questions may lie at the end of the new road along which we must travel.'

He paused.

'New knowledge—new wisdom—in realms we have never dreamed of before. It may lure us away from the dangers we have encountered: for certainly nothing we can learn from Nature will ever be as great a threat as the peril we have uncovered in our own minds.'

The flow of Aretenon's thoughts was suddenly interrupted. Then he said: 'I think Eris wants to see you.'

Jeryl wondered why Eris had not sent the message to her: she wondered, too, at the undertone of amusement—or was it something else?—in Aretenon's mind.

There was no sign of Eris as they approached the caves, but he was waiting for them and came bounding out into the sunlight before they could reach the entrance. Then Jeryl gave an involuntary cry, and retreated a pace or two as her mate came towards her.

For Eris was whole again. Gone was the shattered stump on his forehead: it had been replaced by a new, gleaming horn no less splendid than the one he had lost.

In a belated gesture of greeting, Eris touched horns with Aretenon. Then he was gone into the forest in great joyous leaps—but not before his mind had met Jeryl's as it had seldom done since the days before the War.

'Let him go,' said Therodimus softly. 'He would rather be alone. When he returns I think you will find him—different.' He gave a little laugh. 'The Phileni are clever, are they not? Now, perhaps, Eris will be more appreciative of their "toys".'

'I know I am impatient,' said Therodimus, 'but I am old now, and I want to see the changes begin in my own lifetime. That is why I am starting so many schemes in the hope that some at least will succeed. But this is the one, above all, in which I have put most faith.'

For a moment he lost himself in his thoughts. Not one in a hundred of his own race could fully share his dream. Even Eris, though he now believed in it, did so with his heart rather than his mind. Perhaps Aretenon—the brilliant and subtle Aretenon, so desperately anxious to neutralize the powers he had brought into the world–might have glimpsed the reality. But his was of all minds the most impenetrable, save when he wished otherwise.

'You know as well as I do,' continued Therodimus, as they walked upstream, 'that our wars have only one cause—Food. We and the Mithraneans are trapped on this continent of ours with its limited resources, which we can do nothing to increase. Ahead of us we have always the nightmare of starvation, and for all our vaunted intelligence there has been nothing we can do about it. Oh yes, we have scraped some laborious irrigation ditches with our forehooves, but how slight their help has been!

'The Phileni have discovered how to grow crops that increase the fertility of the ground manyfold. I believe that we can do the same—once we have adapted their tools for our own use. That is our first and most important task, but it is not the one on which I have set my heart. The final solution to our problem, Eris, *must be the discovery of new, virgin lands into which our people can migrate.*'

He smiled at the other's amazement.

'No, don't think I'm mad. Such lands do exist, I'm sure of it. Once I stood at the edge of the ocean and watched a great flight of birds coming inland from far out at sea. I have seen them flying outwards, too, so purposefully that I was certain they were going to some other country. And I have followed them with my thoughts.'

'Even if your theory is true, as it probably is,' said Eris, 'what use is it to us?' He gestured to the river flowing beside them. 'We drown in the water, and you cannot build a rope to support us—' His thoughts suddenly faded out into a jumbled chaos of ideas.

Therodimus smiled.

'So you have guessed what I hope to do. Well, now you can see if you are right.'

They had come to a level stretch of bank, upon which a group of the Phileni were busily at work, under the supervision of some of Therodimus's assistants. Lying at the water's edge was a strange object which, Eris realized, was made of many tree-trunks joined together by ropes.

They watched in fascination as the orderly tumult reached its climax. There was a great pulling and pushing, and the raft moved ponderously into the water with a mighty splash. The spray had scarcely ceased to fall when a young Mithranean leaped from the bank and began to dance gleefully upon the logs, which were now tugging at the moorings as if eager to break away and follow the river down to the sea. A moment later he had been joined by others, rejoicing in their mastery of a new element. The little Phileni, unable to make the leap, stood watching patiently on the bank while their masters enjoyed themselves.

There was an exhilaration about the scene that no one could fail to miss, though perhaps few of those present realized that they were at a turning-point in history. Only Therodimus stood a little apart from the rest, lost in his own thoughts. This primitive raft, he knew, was merely a beginning. It must be tested upon the river, then along the shores of the ocean. The work would take years, and he was never likely to see the first voyagers returning from those fabulous lands whose existence was still no more than a guess. But what had been begun, others would finish.

Overhead, a flight of birds was passing across the forest, Therodimus watched them go, envying their freedom to move at will over land and sea. He had begun the conquest of the water for his race, but that the skies might one day be theirs also was beyond even his imagination.

Aretenon, Jeryl and the rest of the expedition had already crossed the river when Eris said goodbye to Therodimus. This time they had done so without a drop of water touching their bodies, for the raft had come downstream and was performing valuable duties as a ferry. A new and much improved model was already under construction, as it was painfully obvious that the prototype was not exactly seaworthy. These initial difficulties would be quickly overcome by designers who, even if they were forced to work with Stone Age tools, could handle with ease the mathematics of meta-centres, buoyancies and advanced hydrodynamics.

'Your task won't be a simple one,' said Therodimus, 'for you cannot show your people all the things you have seen here. At first you must be content to sow the seed, to arouse interest and curiosity—particularly among the young, who will come here to learn more. Perhaps you will meet opposition: I expect so. But every time you return to us, we shall have new things to show you and to strengthen your arguments.'

They touched horns: then Eris was gone, taking with him the knowledge that was to change the world—so slowly at first, then ever more swiftly. Once the barriers were down, once the Mithraneans and the Atheleni had been given the simple tools which they could fasten to their forelimbs and use unaided, progress would be swift. But for the present they must rely on the Phileni for everything: and there were so few of them.

Therodimus was well content. Only in one respect was he disappointed, for he had hoped that Eris, who had always been his favourite, might also be his successor. The Eris who was now returning to his own people was no longer self-obsessed or embittered, for he had a mission and hope for the future. But he lacked the keen, far-ranging vision that was needed here: it would be Aretenon who must continue what he had begun. Still, that could not be helped, and there was no need yet to think of such matters. Therodimus was very old, but he knew that he would be meeting Eris many times again here by the river at the entrance to his land.

The ferry was gone now, and though he had expected it, Eris stopped amazed at the great span of the bridge, swaying slightly in the breeze. Its execution did not quite match its design—a good deal of mathematics had gone into its parabolic suspension—but it was still the first great engineering feat in history. Constructed though it was entirely of wood and rope, it forecast the shape of the metal giants to come.

Eris paused in mid-stream. He could see smoke rising from the shipyards facing the ocean, and thought he could just glimpse the masts of some of the new vessels that were being built for coastal trade. It was hard to believe that when he had first crossed this river he had been dragged over dangling from a rope.

Aretenon was waiting for them on the far bank. He moved rather slowly now, but his eyes were still bright with the old, eager intelligence. He greeted Eris warmly.

'I'm glad you could come now. You're just in time.'

That, Eris knew, could mean only one thing.

'The ships are back?'

'Almost: they were sighted an hour ago, out on the horizon. They should be here at any moment, and then we shall know the truth at last, after all these years. If only—'

His thoughts faded out, but Eris could continue them. They had come to the great pyramid of stones beneath which Therodimus lay—Therodimus, whose brain was behind everything they saw, but who could never learn now if his most cherished dream was true or not.

There was a storm coming up from the ocean, and they hurried along the new road that skirted the river's edge. Small boats of a kind that Eris had not seen before went past them occasionally, operated by Atheleni or Mithraneans with wooden paddles strapped to their forelimbs. It always gave Eris great pleasure to see such new conquests, such new liberations of his people from their age-old chains. Yet sometimes they reminded him of children who had suddenly been let loose into a wonderful new world, full of exciting and interesting things that must be done, whether they were likely to be useful or not. However, anything that promised to make his race into better sailors was more than useful. In the last decade Eris had discovered that pure intelligence was sometimes not enough: there were skills that could not be acquired by any amount of mental effort. Though this people had largely overcome their fear of water, they were still quite incompetent on the ocean, and the Phileni had therefore become the first navigators of the world.

Jeryl looked nervously around her as the first peal of thunder came rolling in from the sea. She was still wearing the necklace that Therodimus had given her so long ago: but it was by no means the only ornament she carried now.

'I hope the ships will be safe,' she said anxiously.

'There's not much wind, and they will have ridden out much worse storms than this,' Aretenon reassured her, as they entered his cave. Eris and Jeryl looked round with eager interest to see what new wonders the Phileni had made during their absence: but if there were any they had, as usual, been hidden away until Aretenon was ready to show them. He was still rather childishly fond of such little surprises and mysteries.

There was an air of absentmindedness about the meeting that would have puzzled an onlooker ignorant of its cause. As Eris talked of all the changes in the outer world, of the success of the new Phileni settlements, and of the steady growth of agriculture among his people, Aretenon listened with only half his mind. His thoughts, and those of his friends, were far out at sea, meeting the oncoming ships which might be bringing the greatest news their world had ever received.

As Eris finished his report, Aretenon rose to his feet and began to move restlessly around the chamber.

'You have done better than we dared to hope at the beginning. At least there has been no war for a generation, and our food supply is ahead of the population for the first time in history—thanks to our new agricultural techniques.'

Aretenon glanced at the furnishings of his chamber, recalling with an effort the fact that in his own youth almost everything he saw would have appeared impossible or even meaningless to him. Not even the simplest of tools had existed then, at least in the knowledge of his people. Now there were ships and bridges and houses—and these were only the beginning.

'I am well satisfied,' he said. 'We have, as we planned, diverted the whole stream of our culture, turning it away from the dangers that lay ahead. The powers that made the Madness possible will soon be forgotten: only a handful of us still know of them, and we will take our secrets with us. Perhaps when our descendants re-discover them they will be wise enough to use them properly. But we have uncovered so many new wonders that it may be a thousand generations before we turn again to look into our own minds and to tamper with the forces locked within them.'

The mouth of the cave was illuminated by a sudden flash of lightning. The storm was coming nearer, though it was still some miles away. Rain was beginning to fall in large, angry drops from the leaden sky.

'While we're waiting for the ships,' said Aretenon rather abruptly, 'come into the next cave and see some of the new things we have to show you since your last visit.'

It was a strange collection. Side by side on the same bench were tools and inventions which in other cultures had been separated by thousands of years of time. The Stone Age was past: bronze and iron had come, and already the first crude scientific instruments had been built for experiments that were driving back the frontiers of the unknown. A primitive retort spoke of the beginnings of chemistry, and by its side were the first lenses the world had seen—waiting to reveal the unsuspected universes of the infinitely small and the infinitely great.

The storm was upon them as Aretenon's description of these new wonders drew to its close. From time to time he had glanced nervously at the mouth of the cave, as if awaiting a messenger from the harbour, but they had remained undisturbed save by the occasional crash of thunder.

'I've shown you everything of importance,' he said, 'but here's something that may amuse you while we're waiting. As I said, we've sent expeditions everywhere to collect and classify all the rocks they can, in the hope of finding useful minerals. One of them brought back this.'

He extinguished the lights and the cave became completely dark.

'It will be some time before your eyes grow sensitive enough to see it,' Aretenon warned. 'Just look over there in that corner.'

Eris strained his eyes into the darkness. At first he could see nothing: then, slowly, a glimmering blue light became faintly visible. It was so vague and diffuse that he could not focus his eyes upon it, and he automatically moved forward.

'I shouldn't go too near,' advised Aretenon. 'It seems to be a perfectly ordinary mineral, but the Phileni who found it and carried it here got some very strange burns from handling it. Yet it's quite cold to the touch. One day we'll learn its secret: but I don't suppose it's anything at all important.'

A vast curtain of sheet lightning split the sky, and for a moment the reflected glare lit up the cave, pinning weird shadows against the walls. At the same moment one of the Phileni staggered into the entrance and called something to Aretenon in its thin, reedy voice. He gave a great shout of triumph, as one of his ancestors might have done on some ancient battlefield: then his thoughts came crashing into Eris's mind.

'Land! They've found land—a whole new continent waiting for us!'

Eris felt the sense of triumph and victory well up within him like water bursting from a spring. Clear ahead now into the future lay the new, the glorious road along which their children would travel, mastering the world and all its secrets as they went. The vision of Therodimus was at last sharp and brilliant before his eyes.

He felt for the mind of Jeryl, so that she could share his joy—and found that it was closed to him. Leaning toward her in the darkness, he could sense that she was still staring into the depths of the cave, as if she had never heard the wonderful news, and could not tear her eyes away from that enigmatic glow.

Out of the night came the roar of the belated thunder as it raced across the sky. Eris felt Jeryl tremble beside him, and sent out his thoughts to comfort her.

'Don't let the thunder frighten you,' he said gently. 'What is there to fear now?'

'I do not know,' replied Jeryl. 'I am frightened—but not of the thunder. Oh, Eris, it is a wonderful thing we have done, and I wish Therodimus could be here to see it. But where will it lead in the end—this new road of ours?'

Out of the past, the words that Aretenon had once spoken had risen up to haunt her. She remembered their walk by the river, long ago, when he had talked of his hopes and had said: 'Certainly nothing we can learn from Nature will ever be as great a threat as the peril we have encountered in our own minds.' Now the words seemed to mock her and to cast a shadow over the golden future: but why, she could not say.

Alone, perhaps, of all the races in the Universe, her people had reached the second crossroads—and had never passed the first. Now they must go along the road that they had missed, and must face the challenge at its end—the challenge from which, this time, they could not escape.

In the darkness, the faint glow of dying atoms burned unwavering in the rock. It would still be burning there, scarcely dimmed, when Jeryl and Eris had been dust for centuries. It would be only a little fainter when the civilization they were building had at last unlocked its secrets.

CRUCIFIXUS ETIAM

WALTER M. MILLER JR.

Manue Nanti joined the project to make some dough. Five dollars an hour was good pay, even in AD 2134, and there was no way to spend it while on the job. Everything would be furnished: housing, chow, clothing, toiletries, medicine, cigarettes, even a daily ration of one hundred eighty proof beverage alcohol, locally distilled from fermented Martian mosses as fuel for the project's vehicles. He figured that if he avoided crap games, he could finish his five-year contract with fifty thousand dollars in the bank, return to Earth, and retire at the age of twenty-four. Manue wanted to travel, to see the far corners of the world, the strange cultures, the simple people, the small towns, deserts, mountains, jungles—for until he came to Mars, he had never been further than a hundred miles from Cerro de Pasco, his birthplace in Peru.

A great wistfulness came over him in the cold Martian night when the frost haze broke, revealing the black, gleam-stung sky, and the blue-green Earth-star of his birth. *El mundo de mi carne, de mi alma,* he thought—yet, he had seen so little of it that many of its places would be more alien to him than the homogenously ugly vistas of Mars. These he longed to see: the volcanoes of the South Pacific, the monstrous mountains of Tibet, the concrete cyclops of New York, the radioactive craters of Russia, the artificial islands in the China Sea, the Black Forest, the Ganges, the Grand Canyon—but most of all, the works of human art: the pyramids, the Gothic cathedrals of Europe, *Notre Dame de Chartres,* Saint Peter's, the tile-work wonders of Anacapri. But the dream was still a long labour from realization.

Manue was a big youth, heavy-boned and built for labour, clever in a simple mechanical way, and with a wistful good humour that helped him take a lot of guff from whiskey-breathed foremen and sharp-eyed engineers who made ten dollars an hour and figured ways for making more, legitimately or otherwise.

He had been on Mars only a month, and it hurt. Each time he

swung the heavy pick into the red-brown sod, his face winced with pain. The plastic aerator valves, surgically stitched in his chest, pulled and twisted and seemed to tear with each lurch of his body. The mechanical oxygenator served as a lung, sucking blood through an artificially grafted network of veins and plastic tubing, frothing it with air from a chemical generator, and returning it to his circulatory system. Breathing was unnecessary, except to provide wind for talking, but Manue breathed in desperate gulps of the 4.0 psi Martian air; for he had seen the wasted, atrophied chests of the men who had served four or five years, and he knew that when they returned to Earth—if ever—they would still need the auxiliary oxygenator equipment.

'If you don't stop breathing,' the surgeon told him, 'you'll be all right. When you go to bed at night, turn the oxy down low—so low you feel like panting. There's a critical point that's just right for sleeping. If you get it too low, you'll wake up screaming, and you'll get claustrophobia. If you get it too high, your reflex mechanisms will go to pot and you won't breathe; your lungs'll dry up after a time. Watch it.'

Manue watched it carefully, although the oldsters laughed at him—in their dry wheezing chuckles. Some of them could scarcely speak more than two or three words at a shallow breath.

'Breathe deep, boy,' they told him. 'Enjoy it while you can. You'll forget how pretty soon. Unless you're an engineer.'

The engineers had it soft, he learned. They slept in a pressurized barrack where the air was 10 psi and twenty-five per cent oxygen, where they turned their oxies off and slept in peace. Even their oxies were self-regulating, controlling the output according to the carbon dioxide content of the input blood. But the Commission could afford no such luxuries for the labour gangs. The payload of a cargo rocket from Earth was only about two per cent of the ship's total mass, and nothing superfluous could be carried. The ships brought the bare essentials, basic industrial equipment, big reactors, generators, engines, heavy tools.

Small tools, building materials, foods, non-nuclear fuels—these things had to be made on Mars. There was an open pit mine in the belly of the Syrtis Major where a 'lake' of nearly pure iron-rust was scooped into a smelter, and processed into various grades of steel for building purposes, tools, and machinery. A quarry in the Flathead

Mountains dug up large quantities of cement rock, burned it, and crushed it to make concrete.

It was rumoured that Mars was even preparing to grow her own labour force. An old-timer told him that the Commission had brought five hundred married couples to a new underground city in the Mare Erythraeum, supposedly as personnel for a local commission headquarters, but according to the old-timer, they were to be paid a bonus of three thousand dollars for every child born on the red planet. But Manue knew that the old 'troffies' had a way of inventing such stories, and he reserved a certain amount of scepticism.

As for his own share in the Project, he knew—and needed to know—very little. The encampment was at the north end of the Mare Cimmerium, surrounded by the bleak brown and green landscape of rock and giant lichens, stretching towards sharply defined horizons except for one mountain range in the distance, and hung over by a blue sky so dark that the Earth-star occasionally became dimly visible during the dim daytime. The encampment consisted of a dozen double-walled stone huts, windowless, and roofed with flat slabs of rock covered over by a tarry resin boiled out of the cactus-like spineplants. The camp was ugly, lonely, and dominated by the gaunt skeleton of a drill rig set up in its midst.

Manue joined the excavating crew in the job of digging a yard-wide, six-feet deep foundation trench in a hundred yard square around the drill rig, which day and night was biting deeper through the crust of Mars in a dry cut that necessitated frequent stoppages for changing rotary bits. He learned that the geologists had predicted a subterranean pocket of tritium oxide ice at sixteen thousand feet, and that it was for this that they were drilling. The foundation he was helping to dig would be for a control station of some sort.

He worked too hard to be very curious. Mars was a nightmare, a grim, womanless, frigid, disinterestedly evil world. His digging partner was a sloe-eyed Tibetan nicknamed 'Gee' who spoke the Omnalingua clumsily at best. He followed two paces behind Manue with a shovel, scooping up the broken ground, and humming a monotonous chant in his own tongue. Manue seldom heard his own language, and missed it; one of the engineers, a haughty Chilean, spoke the modern Spanish, but not to such as Manue Nanti. Most of the other labourers used either Basic English or the Omnalingua. He spoke both, but longed to hear the tongue of his people. Even when he tried to talk to Gee, the cultural gulf was so wide that satisfying communication was nearly impossible. Peruvian jokes were unfunny to Tibetan ears, although Gee bent double with gales of laughter when Manue nearly crushed his own foot with a clumsy stroke of the pick.

He found no close companions. His foreman was a narrow-eyed, orange-browed Low German named Vögeli, usually half-drunk, and intent upon keeping his lungpower by bellowing at his crew. A meaty, florid man, he stalked slowly along the lip of the excavation, pausing to stare coldly down at each pair of labourers who, if they dared to look up, caught a guttural tongue-lashing for the moment's pause. When he had words for a digger, he called a halt by kicking a small avalanche of dirt back into the trench about the man's feet.

Manue learned about Vögeli's disposition before the end of his first month. The aerator tubes had become nearly unbearable; the skin, in trying to grow fast to the plastic, was beginning to form a tight little neck where the tubes entered his flesh, and the skin stretched and burned and stung with each movement of his trunk. Suddenly he felt sick. He staggered dizzily against the side of the trench, dropped the pick, and swayed heavily, bracing himself against collapse. Shock and nausea rocked him, while Gee stared at him and giggled foolishly.

'Hoy!' Vögeli bellowed from across the pit. 'Get back on that pick! Hoy, there! Get with it—'

Manue moved dizzily to recover the tool, saw patches of black swimming before him, sank weakly back to pant in shallow gasps. The nagging sting of the valves was a portable hell that he carried with him always. He fought an impulse to jerk them out of his flesh; if a valve came loose, he would bleed to death in a few minutes.

Vögeli came stamping along the heap of fresh earth and lumbered up to stand over the sagging Manue in the trench. He glared down at him for a moment, then nudged the back of his neck with a heavy boot. 'Get to work!'

Manue looked up and moved his lips silently. His forehead glinted with moisture in the faint sun, although the temperature was far below freezing.

'Grab that pick and get started.'

'Can't,' Manue gasped. 'Hoses—hurt.'

Vögeli grumbled a curse and vaulted down into the trench beside him. 'Unzip that jacket,' he ordered.

Weakly, Manue fumbled to obey, but the foreman knocked his hand aside and jerked the zipper down. Roughly he unbuttoned the Peruvian's shirt, laying open the bare brown chest to the icy cold.

'*No!*—not the hoses, *please!*'

Vögeli took one of the thin tubes in his blunt fingers and leaned close to peer at the puffy, calloused nodule of irritated skin that formed around it where it entered the flesh. He touched the nodule lightly, causing the digger to whimper.

'No, please!'

'Stop snivelling!'

Vögeli laid his thumbs against the nodule and exerted a sudden pressure. There was a slight popping sound as the skin slid back a fraction of an inch along the tube. Manue yelped and closed his eyes.

'Shut up! I know what I'm doing.' He repeated the process with the other tube. Then he seized both tubes in his hands and wiggled them slightly in and out, as if to ensure a proper resetting of the skin. The digger cried weakly and slumped in a dead faint.

When he awoke, he was in bed in the barracks, and a medic was painting the sore spots with a bright yellow solution that chilled his skin.

'Woke up, huh?' the medic grunted cheerfully. 'How you feel?'

'*Malo!*' he hissed.

'Stay in bed for the day, son. Keep your oxy up high. Make you feel better.'

The medic went away, but Vögeli lingered, smiling at him grimly from the doorway. 'Don't try goofing off tomorrow too.'

Manue hated the closed door with silent eyes, and listened intently until Vögeli's footsteps left the building. Then, following the medic's instructions, he turned his oxy to maximum, even though the faster flow of blood made the chest-valves ache. The sickness fled, to be replaced with a weary afterglow. Drowsiness came over him, and he slept.

Sleep was a dread black-robed phantom on Mars. Mars pressed the same incubus upon all newcomers to her soil: a nightmare of falling, falling, falling into bottomless space. It was the faint gravity, they said, that caused it. The body felt buoyed up, and the subconscious mind recalled down-going elevators, and diving airplanes, and a fall from a high cliff. It suggested these things in dreams, or if the dreamer's oxy were set too low, it conjured up a nightmare of sinking slowly deeper and deeper in cold, black water that filled the victim's throat. Newcomers were segregated in a separate barracks so that their nightly screams would not disturb the old-timers who had finally adjusted to Martian conditions.

But now, for the first time since his arrival, Manue slept soundly, airily, and felt borne up by beams of bright light.

When he awoke again, he lay clammy in the horrifying knowledge that he had not been breathing! It was so comfortable not to breathe. His chest stopped hurting because of the stillness of his rib cage. He felt refreshed and alive. Peaceful sleep.

Suddenly he was breathing again in harsh gasps, and cursing himself for the lapse, and praying amid quiet tears as he visualized the wasted chest of a troffie.

'*Heh heh!*' wheezed an oldster who had come in to readjust the furnace in the rookie barracks. 'You'll get to be a Martian pretty soon, boy. I been here seven years. Look at *me*.'

Manue heard the gasping voice and shuddered; there was no need to look.

'You just as well not fight it. It'll get you. Give in, make it easy on yourself. Go crazy if you don't.'

'Stop it! Let me alone!'

'Sure. Just one thing. You wanta go home, you think. I went home. Came back. You will, too. They all do, 'cept engineers. Know why?'

'Shut up!' Manue pulled himself erect on the cot and hissed anger at the old-timer, who was neither old nor young, but only withered by Mars. His head suggested that he might be around thirty-five, but his body was weak and old.

The veteran grinned. 'Sorry,' he wheezed. 'I'll keep my mouth shut.' He hesitated, then extended his hand. 'I'm Sam Donnell, mech-repairs.'

Manue still glowered at him. Donnell shrugged and dropped his hand.

'Just trying to be friends,' he muttered and walked away.

The digger started to call after him but only closed his mouth again, tightly. Friends? He needed friends, but not a troffie. He couldn't even bear to look at them, for fear he might be looking into the mirror of his own future.

Manue climbed out of his bunk and donned his fleece-skins. Night had fallen, and the temperature was already twenty below. A soft sift of icedust obscured the stars. He stared about in the darkness. The mess hall was closed, but a light burned in the canteen and another in the foremen's club, where the men were playing cards and drinking. He went to get his alcohol ration, gulped it mixed with a little water, and trudged back to the barracks alone.

The Tibetan was in bed, staring blankly at the ceiling. Manue sat down and gazed at his flat, empty face.

'Why did you come here, Gee?'

'Come where?'

'To Mars.'

Gee grinned, revealing large black-streaked teeth. 'Make money. Good money on Mars.'

'Everybody make money, huh?'

'Sure.'

'Where's the money come from?'

Gee rolled his face toward the Peruvian and frowned. 'You crazy? Money come from Earth, where all money comes from.'

'And what does Earth get back from Mars?'

Gee looked puzzled for a moment, then gathered anger because he found no answer. He grunted a monosyllable in his native tongue, then rolled over and went to sleep.

Manue was not normally given to worrying about such things, but now he found himself asking, 'What am I doing here?'—and then, 'What is *anybody* doing here?'

The Mars Project had started eighty or ninety years ago, and its end goal was to make Mars habitable for colonists without Earth support, without oxies and insulated suits and the various gadgets a man now had to use to keep himself alive on the fourth planet. But thus far, Earth had planted without reaping. The sky was a bottomless well into which Earth poured her tools, dollars, man-power, and engineering skill. And there appeared to be no hope for the near future.

Manue felt suddenly trapped. He could not return to Earth before the end of his contract. He was trading five years of virtual enslavement for a sum of money which would buy a limited amount of freedom. But what if he lost his lungs, became a servant of the small aerator for the rest of his days? Worst of all: whose ends was he serving? The contractors were getting rich—on government contracts. Some of the engineers and foremen were getting rich—by various forms of embezzlement of government funds. But what were the people back on Earth getting for their money?

Nothing.

He lay awake for a long time, thinking about it. Then he resolved to ask someone tomorrow, someone smarter than himself.

But he found the question brushed aside. He summoned enough nerve to ask Vögeli, but the foreman told him harshly to keep working and quit wondering. He asked the structural engineer who supervised the building, but the man only laughed, and said: 'What do you care? You're making good money.'

They were running concrete now, laying the long strips of Martian steel in the bottom of the trench and dumping in great slobbering wheelbarrowfuls of grey-green mix. The drillers were continuing their tedious dry cut deep into the red world's crust. Twice a day they brought up a yard long cylindrical sample of the rock and gave it to a geologist who weighed it, roasted it, weighed it again, and tested a sample of the condensed steam—if any—for tritium content. Daily, he chalked up the results on a blackboard in front of the engineering hut, and the technical staff crowded around for a look. Manue always glanced at the figures, but failed to understand.

Life became an endless routine of pain, fear, hard work, anger. There were few diversions. Sometimes a crew of entertainers came out from the Mare Erythraeum, but the labour gang could not all crowd in the pressurized staff-barracks where the shows were presented, and when Manue managed to catch a glimpse of one of the girls walking across the clearing, she was bundled in fleeceskins and hooded by a parka.

Itinerant rabbis, clergymen, and priests of the world's major faiths came occasionally to the camp: Buddhist, Moslem, and the Christian sects. Padre Antonio Selni made monthly visits to hear confessions and offer Mass. Most of the gang attended all services as a diversion from routine, as an escape from nostalgia. Somehow it gave Manue a strange feeling in the pit of his stomach to see the Sacrifice of the Mass, two thousand years old, being offered in the same ritual under the strange dark sky of Mars—with a section of the new foundation serving as an altar upon which the priest set crucifix, candles, relic-stone, missal, chalice, paten, ciborium, cruets, et cetera. In filling the wine-cruet before the service, Manue saw him spill a little of the red-clear fluid upon the brown soil—wine, Earth-wine from sunny Sicilian vineyards, trampled from the grapes by the bare stamping feet of children. Wine, the rich red blood of Earth, soaking slowly into the crust of another planet.

Bowing low at the consecration, the unhappy Peruvian thought of the prayer a rabbi had sung the week before: 'Blessed be the Lord our God, King of the Universe, Who makest bread to spring forth out of the Earth.'

Earth chalice, Earth blood, Earth God, Earth worshippers—with plastic tubes in their chests and a great sickness in their hearts.

He went away saddened. There was no faith here. Faith needed familiar surroundings, the props of culture. Here there were only swinging picks and rumbling machinery and sloshing concrete and the clatter of tools and the wheezing of troffies. Why? For five dollars an hour and keep?

Manue, raised in a back-country society that was almost a folk-culture, felt deep thirst for a goal. His father had been a stonemason, and he had laboured lovingly to help build the new cathedral, to build houses and mansions and commercial buildings, and his blood was mingled in their mortar. He had built for the love of his community and the love of the people and their customs, and their gods. He knew his own ends, and the ends of those around him. But what sense was there in this endless scratching at the face of Mars? Did they think they could make it into a second Earth, with pine forests and lakes and snow-capped mountains and small country villages? Man was not that strong. No, if he were labouring for any cause at all, it was to build a world so unearthlike that he could not love it.

The foundation was finished. There was very little more to be done until the drillers struck pay. Manue sat around the camp and worked at breathing. It was becoming a conscious effort now, and if he stopped thinking about it for a few minutes, he found himself inspiring shallow, meaningless little sips of air that scarcely moved his diaphragm. He kept the aerator as low as possible, to make himself breathe great gasps that hurt his chest, but it made him dizzy, and he had to increase the oxygenation lest he faint.

Sam Donnell, the troffie mech-repairman, caught him about to slump dizzily from his perch atop a heap of rocks, pushed him erect, and turned his oxy back to normal. It was late afternoon, and the drillers were about to change shifts. Manue sat shaking his head for a moment, then gazed at Donnell gratefully.

'That's dangerous, kid,' the troffie wheezed. 'Guys can go psycho doing that. Which you rather have: sick lungs or sick mind?'

'Neither.'

'I know, but—'

'I don't want to talk about it.'

Donnell stared at him with a faint smile. Then he shrugged and sat down on the rock heap to watch the drilling.

'Oughta be hitting the tritium ice in a couple of days,' he said pleasantly. 'Then we'll see a big blow.'

Manue moistened his lips nervously. The troffies always made him feel uneasy. He stared aside.

'Big blow?'

'Lotta pressure down there, they say. Something about the way Mars got formed. Dust cloud hypothesis.'

Manue shook his head. 'I don't understand.'

'I don't either. But I've heard them talk. Couple of billion years ago, Mars was supposed to be a moon of Jupiter. Picked up a lot of ice crystals over a rocky core. Then it broke loose and picked up a rocky crust—from another belt of the dust cloud. The pockets of tritium ice catch a few neutrons from uranium ore—down under. Some of the tritium goes into helium. Frees oxygen. Gases form pressure. Big blow.'

'What are they going to do with the ice?'

The troffie shrugged. 'The engineers might know.'

Manue snorted and spat. 'They know how to make money.'

'Heh! Sure, everybody's gettin' rich.'

The Peruvian stared at him speculatively for a moment.

'Señor Donnell, I—'

'Sam'll do.'

'I wonder if anybody knows why . . . well . . . why we're really here.'

Donnell glanced up to grin, then waggled his head. He fell

thoughtful for a moment, and leaned forward to write in the earth. When he finished, he read it aloud.

'A plough plus a horse plus land equals the necessities of life.' He glanced up at Manue. 'AD Fifteen Hundred.'

The Peruvian frowned his bewilderment. Donnell rubbed out what he had written and wrote again.

'A factory plus steam turbines plus raw materials equals necessities plus luxuries. AD Nineteen Hundred.'

He rubbed it out and repeated the scribbling. 'All those things plus nuclear power and computer controls equal a surplus of everything. AD Twenty-one Hundred'

'So?'

'So, it's either cut production or find an outlet. Mars is an outlet for surplus energies, manpower, money. Mars Project keeps money turning over, keeps everything turning over. Economist told me that. Said if the Project folded, surplus would pile up—big depression on Earth.'

The Peruvian shook his head and sighed. It didn't sound right somehow. It sounded like an explanation somebody figured out after the whole thing started. It wasn't the kind of goal he wanted.

Two days later, the drill hit ice, and the 'big blow' was only a fizzle. There was talk around the camp that the whole operation had been a waste of time. The hole spewed a frosty breath for several hours, and the drill crews crowded around to stick their faces in it and breathe great gulps of the helium oxygen mixture. But then the blow subsided, and the hole leaked only a wisp of steam.

Technicians came, and lowered sonar 'cameras' down to the ice. They spent a week taking internal soundings and plotting the extent of the ice-dome on their charts. They brought up samples of ice and tested them. The engineers worked late into the Martian nights.

Then it was finished. The engineers came out of their huddles and called to the foremen of the labour gangs. They led the foremen around the site, pointing here, pointing there, sketching with chalk on the foundation, explaining in solemn voices. Soon the foremen were bellowing at their crews.

'Let's get the derrick down!'

'Start that mixer going!'

'Get that steel over here!'

'Unroll that dip-wire!'

'Get a move on! Shovel that fill!'

Muscles tightened and strained, machinery clamoured and rang. Voices grumbled and shouted. The operation was starting again. Without knowing why, Manue shovelled fill and stretched dip-wire and poured concrete for a big floor slab to be run across the entire hundred-yard square, broken only by the big pipe-casing that stuck up out of the ground in the centre and leaked a thin trail of steam.

The drill crew moved their rig half a mile across the plain to a point specified by the geologists and began sinking another hole. A groan went up from the structural boys: 'Not *another* one of these things!'

But the supervisory staff said, 'No, don't worry about it.'

There was much speculation about the purpose of the whole operation, and the men resented the quiet secrecy connected with the project. There could be no excuse for secrecy, they felt, in time of peace. There was a certain arbitrariness about it, a hint that the Commission thought of its employees as children, or enemies, or servants. But the supervisory staff shrugged off all questions with: 'You know there's tritium ice down there. You know it's what we've been looking for. Why? Well—what's the difference? There are lots of uses for it. Maybe we'll use it for one thing, maybe for something else. Who knows?'

Such a reply might have been satisfactory for an iron mine or an oil well or a stone quarry, but tritium suggested hydrogen-fusion. And no transportation facilities were being installed to haul the stuff away—no pipelines nor railroad tracks nor glider ports.

Manue quit thinking about it. Slowly he came to adopt a grim cynicism towards the tediousness, the back-breaking labour of his daily work; he lived from day to day like an animal, dreaming only of a return to Earth when his contract was up. But the dream was painful because it was distant, as contrasted with the immediacies of Mars: the threat of atrophy, coupled with the discomforts of continued breathing, the nightmares, the barrenness of the landscape, the intense cold, the harshness of men's tempers, the hardship of labour, and the lack of a cause.

A warm, sunny Earth was still over four years distant, and tomorrow would be another back-breaking, throat-parching, heart-tormenting, chest-hurting day. Where was there even a little pleasure in it? It was so easy, at least, to leave the oxy turned up at night, and get a pleasant restful sleep. Sleep was the only recourse from harshness, and fear robbed sleep of its quiet sensuality—unless a man just surrendered and quit worrying about his lungs.

Manue decided that it would be safe to give himself two completely restful nights a week.

Concrete was run over the great square and trowelled to a rough finish. A glider train from the Mare Erythraeum brought in several huge crates of machinery, cut-stone masonry for building a wall, a shipful of new personnel, and a real rarity: lumber, cut from the first Earth-trees to be grown on Mars.

A building began going up with the concrete square for foundation and floor. Structures could be flimsier on Mars; because of the light gravity, compression-stresses were smaller. Hence, the work progressed rapidly, and as the flat-roofed structure was completed, the technicians began uncrating new machinery and moving it into the building. Manue noticed that several of the units were computers. There was also a small steam-turbine generator driven by an atomic-fired boiler.

Months passed. The building grew into an integrated mass of power and control systems. Instead of using the well for pumping, the technicians were apparently going to lower something into it. A bomb-shaped cylinder was slung vertically over the hole. The men guided it into the mouth of the pipe casing, then let it down slowly from a massive cable. The cylinder's butt was a multicontact socket like the female receptacle for a hundred-pin electron tube. Hours passed while the cylinder slipped slowly down beneath the hide of Mars. When it was done, the men hauled out the cable and began lowering stiff sections of pre-wired conduit, fitted with a receptacle at one end and a male plug at the other, so that as the sections fell into place, a continuous bundle of control cables was built up from 'bomb' to surface.

Several weeks were spent in connecting circuits, setting up the computers, and making careful tests. The drillers had finished the second well hole, half a mile from the first, and Manue noticed that while the testing was going on, the engineers sometimes stood atop the building and stared anxiously towards the steel skeleton in the distance. Once while the tests were being conducted, the second hole began squirting a jet of steam high in the thin air, and a frantic voice bellowed from the roof top.

'Cut it! Shut it off! Sound the danger whistle!'

The jet of steam began to shriek a low-pitched whine across the Martian desert. It blended with the rising and falling *OOOOawwww* of the danger siren. But gradually it subsided as the men in the control station shut down the machinery. All hands came up cursing from their hiding places, and the engineers stalked out to the new hole carrying Geiger counters. They came back wearing pleased grins.

The work was nearly finished. The men began crating up the excavating machinery and the drill rig and the tools. The control-building devices were entirely automatic, and the camp would be deserted when the station began operation. The men were disgruntled. They had spent a year of hard labour on what they had thought to be a tritium well, but now that it was done, there were no facilities for pumping the stuff or hauling it away. In fact, they had pumped various solutions *into* the ground through the second hole, and the control station shaft was fitted with pipes that led from lead-lined tanks down into the earth.

Manue had stopped trying to keep his oxy properly adjusted at night. Turned up to a comfortable level, it was like a drug, ensuring comfortable sleep—and like addict or alcoholic, he could no longer endure living without it. Sleep was too precious, his only comfort. Every morning he awoke with a still, motionless chest, felt frightening remorse, sat up gasping, choking, sucking at the thin air with whining rattling lungs that had been idle too long. Sometimes he coughed violently, and bled a little. And then for a night or two he would correctly adjust the oxy, only to wake up screaming and suffocating. He felt hope sliding grimly away.

He sought out Sam Donnell, explained the situation, and begged the troffie for helpful advice. But the mech-repairman neither helped nor consoled nor joked about it. He only bit his lip, muttered something non-committal, and found an excuse to hurry away. It was then that Manue knew his hope was gone. Tissue was withering, tubercules forming, tubes growing closed. He knelt abjectly beside his cot, hung his face in his hands, and cursed softly, for there was no other way to pray an unanswerable prayer.

A glider train came in from the north to haul away the disassembled tools. The men lounged around the barracks or wandered across the Martian desert, gathering strange bits of rock and fossils, searching idly for a glint of metal or crystal in the wan sunshine of early fall. The lichens were growing brown and yellow, and the landscape took on the hues of Earth's autumn if not the forms.

There was a sense of expectancy around the camp. It could be felt in the nervous laughter, and the easy voices, talking suddenly of Earth and old friends and the smell of food in a farm kitchen, and old half-forgotten tastes for which men hungered: ham searing in the skillet, a cup of frothing cider from a fermenting crock, iced melon with honey and a bit of lemon, onion gravy on homemade bread. But someone always remarked, 'What's the matter with you guys? We ain't going home. Not by a long shot. We're going to another place just like this.'

And the group would break up and wander away, eyes tired, eyes haunted with nostalgia.

'What're we waiting for?' men shouted at the supervisory staff. 'Get some transportation in here. Let's get rolling.'

Men watched the skies for glider trains or jet transports, but the skies remained empty, and the staff remained close-mouthed. Then a dust column appeared on the horizon to the north, and a day later a convoy of tractor-trucks pulled into camp.

'Start loading aboard, men!' was the crisp command.

Surly voices: 'You mean we don't go by air? We gotta ride those kidney bouncers? It'll take a week to get to Mare Ery! Our contract says—'

'Load aboard! We're not going to Mare Ery yet!'

Grumbling, they loaded their baggage and their weary bodies into the trucks, and the trucks thundered and clattered across the desert, rolling towards the mountains.

The convoy rolled for three days towards the mountains, stopping at night to make camp, and driving on at sunrise. When they reached the first slopes of the foothills, the convoy stopped again. The deserted encampment lay a hundred and fifty miles behind. The going had been slow over the roadless desert.

'Everybody out!' barked the messenger from the lead truck. 'Bail out! Assemble at the foot of the hill.'

Voices were growling among themselves as the men moved in small groups from the trucks and collected in a milling tide in a shallow basin, overlooked by a low cliff and a hill. Manue saw the staff climb out of a cab and slowly work their way up the cliff. They carried a portable public address system.

'Gonna get a preaching,' somebody snarled.

'Sit down, please!' barked the loudspeaker. 'You men sit down there! Quiet—quiet, please!'

The gathering fell into a sulky silence. Will Kinley stood looking out over them, his eyes nervous, his hand holding the mike close to his mouth so that they could hear his weak troffie voice.

'If you men have questions,' he said, 'I'll answer them now. Do you want to know what you've been doing during the past year?'

An affirmative rumble arose from the group.

'You've been helping to give Mars a breathable atmosphere.' He glanced briefly at his watch, then looked back at his audience. 'In fifty minutes, a controlled chain reaction will start in the tritium ice. The computers will time it and try to control it. Helium and oxygen will come blasting up out of the second hole.'

A rumble of disbelief arose from his audience. Someone shouted: 'How can you get air to blanket a planet from one hole?'

'You can't,' Kinley replied crisply. 'A dozen others are going in, just like that one. We plan three hundred, and we've already located the ice pockets. Three hundred wells, working for eight centuries, can get the job done.'

'Eight centuries! What good—'

'Wait!' Kinley barked. 'In the meantime, we'll build pressurized cities close to the wells. If everything pans out, we'll get a lot of colonists here, and gradually condition them to live in a seven or eight psi atmosphere—which is about the best we can hope to get. Colonists from the Andes and the Himalayas—they wouldn't need much conditioning.'

'*What about us?*'

There was a long plaintive silence. Kinley's eyes scanned the group sadly, and wandered towards the Martian horizon, gold and brown in the late afternoon.

'Nothing—about us,' he muttered quietly.

'Why did we come out here?'

'Because there's danger of the reaction getting out of hand. We can't tell anyone about it, or we'd start a panic.' He looked at the group sadly. 'I'm telling you now, because there's nothing you could do. In thirty minutes—'

There were angry murmurs in the crowd. 'You mean there may be an explosion?'

'There *will* be a limited explosion. And there's very little danger of anything more. The worst danger is in having ugly rumours start in the cities. Some fool with a slip-stick would hear about it, and calculate what would happen to Mars if five cubic miles of tritium ice detonated in one split second. It would probably start a riot. That's why we've kept it a secret.'

The buzz of voices was like a disturbed beehive. Manue Nanti sat in the midst of it, saying nothing, wearing a dazed and weary face, thoughts jumbled, soul drained of feeling.

Why should men lose their lungs that after eight centuries of tomorrows, other men might breathe the air of Mars as the air of Earth?

Other men around him echoed his thoughts in jealous mutterings. They had been helping to make a world in which they would never live.

An enraged scream arose near where Manue sat. 'They're going to blow us up! They're going to blow up Mars.'

'Don't be a fool!' Kinley snapped.

'Fools they call us! We *are* fools! For ever coming here! We got sucked in! Look at *me*!' A pale, dark-haired man came wildly to his feet and tapped his chest. 'Look! I'm losing my lungs! We're all losing our lungs! Now they take a chance on killing everybody.'

'Including ourselves,' Kinley called coldly.

'We oughta take him apart. We oughta kill every one who knew about it—and Kinley's a good place to start!'

The rumble of voices rose higher, calling both agreement and dissent. Some of Kinley's staff were looking nervously towards the trucks. They were unarmed.

'You men sit down!' Kinley barked.

Rebellious eyes glared at the supervisor. Several men who had come to their feet dropped to their haunches again. Kinley glowered at the pale upriser who called for his scalp.

'Sit down, Handell!'

Handell turned his back on the supervisor and called out to the others. 'Don't be a bunch of cowards! Don't let him bully you!'

'You men sitting around Handell. Pull him down.'

There was no response. The men, including Manue, stared up at the wild-eyed Handell gloomily, but made no move to quiet him. A pair of burly foremen started through the gathering from its outskirts.

'Stop!' Kinley ordered. 'Turpin, Schultz—get back. Let the men handle this themselves.'

Half a dozen others had joined the rebellious Handell. They were speaking in low tense tones among themselves.

'For the last time, men! Sit down!'

The group turned and started grimly towards the cliff. Without reasoning why, Manue slid to his feet quietly as Handell came near him. 'Come on, fellow, let's get him,' the leader muttered.

The Peruvian's fist chopped a short stroke to Handell's jaw, and the dull *thuk* echoed across the clearing. The man crumpled, and Manue crouched over him like a hissing panther. 'Get back!' he snapped at the others. 'Or I'll jerk his hoses out.'

One of the others cursed him.

'Want to fight, fellow?' the Peruvian wheezed. 'I can jerk several hoses out before you drop me!'

They shuffled nervously for a moment.

'The guy's crazy!' one complained in a high voice.

'Get back or he'll kill Handell!'

They sidled away, moved aimlessly in the crowd, then sat down to escape attention. Manue sat beside the fallen man and gazed at the thinly smiling Kinley.

'Thank you, son. There's a fool in every crowd.' He looked at his watch again. 'Just a few minutes, men. Then you'll feel the Earth-tremor, and the explosion, and the wind. You can be proud of that wind, men. It's new air for Mars, and you made it.'

'But we can't breathe it!' hissed a troffie.

Kinley was silent for a long time, as if listening to the distance. 'What man ever made his own salvation?' he murmured.

They packed up the public address amplifier and came down the hill to sit in the cab of a truck waiting.

It came as an orange glow in the south, and the glow was quickly shrouded by an expanding white cloud. Then minutes later the ground pulsed beneath them, quivered and shook. The quake subsided, but remained as a hint of vibration. Then after a long time, they heard the dull-throated roar thundering across the Martian desert. The roar continued steadily, grumbling and growing as it would do for several hundred years.

There was only a hushed murmur of awed voices from the crowd. When the wind came, some of them stood up and moved quietly back to the trucks, for now they could go back to a city for reassignment. There were other tasks to accomplish before their contracts were done.

But Manue Nanti still sat on the ground, his head sunk low, desperately trying to gasp a little of the wind he had made, the wind out of the ground, the wind of the future. But lungs were clogged, and he could not drink of the racing wind. His big calloused hand clutched slowly at the ground, and he choked a brief sound like a sob.

A shadow fell over him. It was Kinley, come to offer his thanks for the quelling of Handell. But he said nothing for a moment as he watched Manue's desperate Gethsemane.

'Some sow, others reap,' he said.

'Why?' the Peruvian choked.

The supervisor shrugged. 'What's the difference? But if you can't be both, which would you rather be?'

Nanti looked up into the wind. He imagined a city to the south, a city built on tear-soaked ground, filled with people who had no ends beyond their culture, no goal but within their own society. It was a good sensible question: Which would he rather be—sower or reaper?

Pride brought him slowly to his feet, and he eyed Kinley questioningly. The supervisor touched his shoulder.

'Go on to the trucks.'

Nanti nodded and shuffled away. He had wanted something to work for, hadn't he? Something more than the reasons Donnell had given. Well, he could smell a reason, even if he couldn't breathe it.

Eight hundred years was a long time, but then—long time, big reason. The air smelled good, even with its clouds of boiling dust.

He knew now what Mars was—not a ten-thousand-a-year job, not a garbage can for surplus production. But an eight-century passion of human faith in the destiny of the race of Man. He paused short of the truck. He had wanted to travel, to see the sights of Earth, the handiwork of Nature and of history, the glorious places of his planet.

He stooped, and scooped up a handful of the red-brown soil, letting it sift slowly between his fingers. Here was Mars—his planet now. No more of Earth, not for Manue Nanti. He adjusted his aerator more comfortably and climbed into the waiting truck.

THE TUNNEL UNDER THE WORLD

FREDERIK POHL

On the morning of June 15th, Guy Burckhardt woke up screaming out of a dream.

It was more real than any dream he had ever had in his life. He could still hear and feel the sharp, ripping-metal explosion, the violent heave that had tossed him furiously out of bed, the searing wave of heat.

He sat up convulsively and stared, not believing what he saw, at the quiet room and the bright sunlight coming in the window.

He croaked, 'Mary?'

His wife was not in the bed next to him. The covers were tumbled and awry, as though she had just left it, and the memory of the dream was so strong that instinctively he found himself searching the floor to see if the dream explosion had thrown her down.

But she wasn't there. Of course she wasn't, he told himself, looking at the familiar vanity and slipper chair, the uncracked window, the unbuckled wall. It had only been a dream.

'Guy?' His wife was calling him querulously from the foot of the stairs. 'Guy, dear, are you all right?'

He called weakly, 'Sure.'

There was a pause. Then Mary said doubtfully, 'Breakfast is ready. Are you sure you're all right? I thought I heard you yelling—'

Burckhardt said more confidently, 'I had a bad dream, honey. Be right down.'

In the shower, punching the lukewarm-and-cologne he favoured, he told himself that it had been a beaut of a dream. Still, bad dreams weren't unusual, especially bad dreams about explosions. In the past thirty years of H-bomb jitters, who had not dreamed of explosions?

Even Mary had dreamed of them, it turned out, for he started to tell her about the dream, but she cut him off. 'You *did*?' Her voice was astonished. 'Why, dear, I dreamed the same thing! Well, almost the same thing. I didn't actually *hear* anything. I dreamed that something woke me up, and then there was a sort of quick bang, and then something hit me on the head. And that was all. Was yours like that?'

Burckhardt coughed. 'Well, no,' he said. Mary was not one of these strong-as-a-man, brave-as-a-tiger women. It was not necessary, he thought, to tell her all the little details of the dream that made it seem so real. No need to mention the splintered ribs, and the salt bubble in his throat, and the agonized knowledge that this was death. He said, 'Maybe there really was some kind of explosion downtown. Maybe we heard it and it started us dreaming.'

Mary reached over and patted his hand absently. 'Maybe,' she agreed. 'It's almost half-past eight, dear. Shouldn't you hurry? You don't want to be late to the office.'

He gulped his food, kissed her and rushed out—not so much to be on time as to see if his guess had been right.

But downtown Tylerton looked as it always had. Coming in on the bus, Burckhardt watched critically out the window, seeking evidence of an explosion. There wasn't any. If anything, Tylerton looked better than it ever had before: It was a beautiful crisp day, the sky was cloudless, the buildings were clean and inviting. They had, he observed, steam-blasted the Power & Light Building, the town's only skyscraper—that was the penalty of having Contro Chemical's main plant on the outskirts of town; the fumes from the cascade stills left their mark on stone buildings.

None of the usual crowd were on the bus, so there wasn't anyone Burckhardt could ask about the explosion. And by the time he got out at the corner of Fifth and Lehigh and the bus rolled away with a muted diesel moan, he had pretty well convinced himself that it was all imagination.

He stopped at the cigar stand in the lobby of his office building, but Ralph wasn't behind the counter. The man who sold him his pack of cigarettes was a stranger.

'Where's Mr Stebbins?' Burckhardt asked.

The man said politely, 'Sick, sir. He'll be in tomorrow. A pack of Marlins today?'

'Chesterfields,' Burckhardt corrected.

'Certainly, sir,' the man said. But what he took from the rack and slid across the counter was an unfamiliar green-and-yellow pack.

'Do try these, sir,' he suggested. 'They contain an anti-cough factor. Ever notice how ordinary cigarettes make you choke every once in a while?'

Burckhardt said suspiciously, 'I never heard of this brand.'

'Of course not. They're something new.' Burckhardt hesitated, and the man said persuasively, 'Look, try them out at my risk. If you don't like them, bring back the empty pack and I'll refund your money. Fair enough?'

Burckhardt shrugged. 'How can I lose? But give me a pack of Chesterfields, too, will you?'

He opened the pack and lit one while he waited for the elevator. They weren't bad, he decided, though he was suspicious of cigarettes that had the tobacco chemically treated in any way. But he didn't think much of Ralph's stand-in; it would raise hell with the trade at the cigar stand if the man tried to give every customer the same high-pressure sales talk.

The elevator door opened with a low-pitched sound of music. Burckhardt and two or three others got in and he nodded to them as the door closed. The thread of music switched off and the speaker in the ceiling of the cab began its usual commercials.

No, not the *usual* commercials, Burckhardt realized. He had been exposed to the captive-audience commercials so long that they hardly registered on the outer ear any more, but what was coming from the recorded programme in the basement of the building caught his attention. It wasn't merely that the brands were mostly unfamiliar; it was a difference in pattern.

There were jingles with an insistent, bouncy rhythm, about soft drinks he had never tasted. There was a rapid patter dialogue between what sounded like two ten-year-old boys about a candy bar, followed by an authoritative bass rumble: 'Go right out and get a DELICIOUS Choco-Bite and eat your TANGY Choco-Bite *all up*. That's *Choco-Bite*!' There was a sobbing female whine: 'I *wish* I had a Feckle Freezer! I'd do *anything* for a Feckle Freezer!' Burckhardt reached his floor and left the elevator in the middle of the last one. It left him a little uneasy. The commercials were not for familiar brands; there was no feeling of use and custom to them.

But the office was happily normal—except that Mr Barth wasn't in. Miss Mitkin, yawning at the reception desk, didn't know exactly why. 'His home phoned, that's all. He'll be in tomorrow.'

'Maybe he went to the plant. It's right near his house.'

She looked indifferent. 'Yeah.'

A thought struck Burckhardt. 'But today is June 15th! It's quarterly tax return day—he has to sign the return!'

Miss Mitkin shrugged to indicate that that was Burckhardt's problem, not hers. She returned to her nails.

Thoroughly exasperated, Burckhardt went to his desk. It wasn't that he couldn't sign the tax returns as well as Barth, he thought resentfully. It simply wasn't his job, that was all; it was a responsibility that Barth, as office manager for Contro Chemicals' downtown office, should have taken.

He thought briefly of calling Barth at his home or trying to reach him at the factory, but he gave up the idea quickly enough. He didn't really care much for the people at the factory and the less contact he had with them, the better. He had been to the factory once, with Barth. It had been a confusing and, in a way, a frightening experience. Barring a handful of executives and engineers, there wasn't a soul in the factory—that is, Burckhardt corrected himself, remembering what Barth had told him, not a *living* soul—just the machines.

According to Barth, each machine was controlled by a sort of computer which reproduced, in its electronic snarl, the actual memory and mind of a human being. It was an unpleasant thought. Barth, laughing, had assured him that there was no Frankenstein business of robbing graveyards and implanting brains in machines. It was only a matter, he said, of transferring a man's habit patterns from brain cells to vacuum-tube cells. It didn't hurt the man and it didn't make the machine into a monster.

But they made Burckhardt uncomfortable all the same.

He put Barth and the factory and all his other little irritations out of his mind and tackled the tax returns. It took him until noon to verify the figures—which Barth could have done out of his memory and his private ledger in ten minutes, Burckhardt resentfully reminded himself.

He sealed them in an envelope and walked out to Miss Mitkin. 'Since Mr Barth isn't here, we'd better go to lunch in shifts,' he said. 'You can go first.'

'Thanks.' Miss Mitkin languidly took her bag out of the desk drawer and began to apply make-up.

Burckhardt offered her the envelope. 'Drop this in the mail for me, will you? Uh—wait a minute. I wonder if I ought to phone Mr Barth to make sure. Did his wife say whether he was able to take phone calls?'

'Didn't say.' Miss Mitkin blotted her lips carefully with a Kleenex. 'Wasn't his wife, anyway. It was his daughter who called and left the message.'

'The kid?' Burckhardt frowned. 'I thought she was away at school.'

'She called, that's all I know.'

Burckhardt went back to his own office and stared distastefully at the unopened mail on his desk. He didn't like nightmares; they spoiled his whole day. He should have stayed in bed, like Barth.

A funny thing happened on his way home. There was a disturbance at the corner where he usually caught his bus—someone was screaming something about a new kind of deep-freeze—so he walked an extra block. He saw the bus coming and started to trot. But behind him, someone was calling his name. He looked over his shoulder; a small harried-looking man was hurrying towards him.

Burckhardt hesitated, and then recognized him. It was a casual acquaintance named Swanson. Burckhardt sourly observed that he had already missed the bus.

He said, 'Hello'.

Swanson's face was desperately eager. 'Burckhardt?' he asked enquiringly, with an odd intensity. And then he just stood there silently, watching Burckhardt's face, with a burning eagerness that dwindled to a faint hope and died to a regret. He was searching for something, waiting for something, Burckhardt thought. But whatever it was he wanted, Burckhardt didn't know how to supply it.

Burckhardt coughed and said again, 'Hello, Swanson'.

Swanson didn't even acknowledge the greeting. He merely sighed a very deep sigh.

'Nothing doing,' he mumbled, apparently to himself. He nodded abstractedly to Burckhardt and turned away.

Burckhardt watched the slumped shoulders disappear in the crowd. It was an *odd* sort of day, he thought, and one he didn't much like. Things weren't going right.

Riding home on the next bus, he brooded about it. It wasn't anything terrible or disastrous; it was something out of his experience entirely. You live your life, like any man, and you form a network of impressions and reactions. You *expect* things. When you open your medicine chest, your razor is expected to be on the second shelf; when you lock your front door, you expect to have to give it a slight extra tug to make it latch.

It isn't the things that are right and perfect in your life that make it familiar. It is the things that are just a little bit wrong—the sticking latch, the light switch at the head of the stairs that needs an extra push because the spring is old and weak, the rug that unfailingly skids underfoot.

It wasn't just that things were wrong with the pattern of Burckhardt's life; it was that the *wrong* things were wrong. For instance, Barth hadn't come into the office, yet Barth *always* came in.

Burckhardt brooded about it through dinner. He brooded about it, despite his wife's attempt to interest him in a game of bridge with the neighbours, all through the evening. The neighbours were people he liked—Anne and Farley Dennerman. He had known them all their lives. But they were odd and brooding, too, this night and he barely listened to Dennerman's complaints about not being able to get good phone service or his wife's comments on the disgusting variety of television commercials they had these days.

Burckhardt was well on the way to setting an all-time record for continuous abstraction when, around midnight, with a suddenness that surprised him—he was strangely *aware* of it happening—he turned over in his bed and, quickly and completely, fell asleep.

II

On the morning of June 15th, Burckhardt woke up screaming.

It was more real than any dream he had ever had in his life. He could still hear the explosion, feel the blast that crushed him against a wall. It did not seem right that he should be sitting bolt upright in bed in an undisturbed room.

His wife came pattering up the stairs. 'Darling!' she cried. 'What's the matter?'

He mumbled, 'Nothing. Bad dream.'

She relaxed, hand on heart. In an angry tone, she started to say: 'You gave me such a shock—'

But a noise from outside interrupted her. There was a wail of sirens and a clang of bells; it was loud and shocking.

The Burckhardts stared at each other for a heartbeat, then hurried fearfully to the window.

There were no rumbling fire engines in the street, only a small panel truck, cruising slowly along. Flaring loudspeaker horns crowned its top. From them issued the screaming sound of sirens, growing in intensity, mixed with the rumble of heavy-duty engines and the sound of bells. It was a perfect record of fire engines arriving at a four-alarm blaze.

Burckhardt said in amazement, 'Mary, that's against the law! Do you know what they're doing? They're playing records of a fire. What are they up to?'

'Maybe it's a practical joke,' his wife offered.

'Joke? Waking up the whole neighbourhood at six o'clock in the morning?' He shook his head. 'The police will be here in ten minutes,' he predicted. 'Wait and see.'

But the police weren't—not in ten minutes, or at all. Whoever the pranksters in the car were, they apparently had a police permit for their games.

The car took a position in the middle of the block and stood silent for a few minutes. Then there was a crackle from the speaker, and a giant voice chanted:

Feckle Freezers!
Feckle Freezers!
Gotta have a
Feckle Freezer!
Feckle, Feckle, Feckle
Feckle, Feckle, Feckle—

It went on and on. Every house on the block had faces staring out of windows by then. The voice was not merely loud; it was nearly deafening.

Burckhardt shouted to his wife, over the uproar, 'What the hell is a Feckle Freezer?'

'Some kind of a freezer, I guess, dear,' she shrieked back unhelpfully.

Abruptly the noise stopped and the truck stood silent. It was still misty morning; the sun's rays came horizontally across the rooftops. It was impossible to believe that, a moment ago, the silent block had been bellowing the name of a freezer.

'A crazy advertising trick,' Burckhardt said bitterly. He yawned and turned away from the window. 'Might as well get dressed. I guess that's the end of—'

The bellow caught him from behind; it was almost like a hard slap on the ears. A harsh, sneering voice, louder than the archangel's trumpet, howled:

'Have you got a freezer? *It stinks!* If it isn't a Feckle Freezer, *it stinks!* If it's a last year's Feckle Freezer, *it stinks!* Only this year's Feckle Freezer is any good at all! You know who owns an Ajax Freezer? Fairies own Ajax Freezers! You know who owns a Triplecold Freezer? Commies own Triplecold Freezers! Every freezer but a brand-new Feckle Freezer *stinks!*'

The voice screamed inarticulately with rage. 'I'm warning you! Get out and buy a Feckle Freezer right away! Hurry up! Hurry for Feckle! Hurry for Feckle! Hurry, hurry, hurry, Feckle, Feckle, Feckle, Feckle, Feckle, Feckle . . .'

It stopped eventually. Burckhardt licked his lips. He started to say to his wife, 'Maybe we ought to call the police about—' when the speakers erupted again. It caught him off guard; it was intended to catch him off guard. It screamed:

'Feckle, Feckle, Feckle, Feckle, Feckle, Feckle, Feckle, Feckle. Cheap freezers ruin your food. You'll get sick and throw up. You'll get sick and die. Buy a Feckle, Feckle, Feckle, Feckle! Ever take a piece of meat out of the freezer you've got and see how rotten and mouldy it is? Buy a Feckle, Feckle, Feckle, Feckle, Feckle. Do you want to eat rotten, stinking food? Or do you want to wise up and buy a Feckle, Feckle, Feckle—'

That did it. With fingers that kept stabbing the wrong holes, Burckhardt finally managed to dial the local police station. He got a busy signal—it was apparent that he was not the only one with the same idea—and while he was shakingly dialling again, the noise outside stopped.

He looked out the window. The truck was gone.

Burckhardt loosened his tie and ordered another Frosty-Flip from the waiter. If only they wouldn't keep the Crystal Cafe so *hot*! The new paint job—searing reds and blinding yellows—was bad enough, but someone seemed to have the delusion that this was January instead of June; the place was a good ten degrees warmer than outside.

He swallowed the Frosty-Flip in two gulps. It had a kind of peculiar flavour, he thought, but not bad. It certainly cooled you off, just as the waiter had promised. He reminded himself to pick up a carton of them on the way home; Mary might like them. She was always interested in something new.

He stood up awkwardly as the girl came across the restaurant toward him. She was the most beautiful thing he had ever seen in Tylerton. Chin-height, honey-blonde hair and a figure that—well, it was all hers. There was no doubt in the world that the dress that clung to her was the only thing she wore. He felt as if he were blushing as she greeted him.

'Mr Burckhardt.' The voice was like distant tom-toms. 'It's wonderful of you to let me see you, after this morning.'

He cleared his throat. 'Not at all. Won't you sit down, Miss—'

'April Horn,' she murmured, sitting down—beside him, not where he had pointed on the other side of the table. 'Call me April, won't you?'

She was wearing some kind of perfume, Burckhardt noted with what little of his mind was functioning at all. It didn't seem fair that she should be using perfume as well as everything else. He came to with a start and realized that the waiter was leaving with an order for *filets mignon* for two.

'Hey!' he objected.

'Please, Mr Burckhardt.' Her shoulder was against his, her face was turned to him, her breath was warm, her expression was tender and solicitous. 'This is all on the Feckle Corporation. Please let them—it's the *least* they can do.'

He felt her hand burrowing into his pocket.

'I put the price of the meal into your pocket,' she whispered conspiratorially. 'Please do that for me, won't you? I mean I'd appreciate it if you'd pay the waiter—I'm old-fashioned about things like that.'

She smiled meltingly, then became mock-businesslike. 'But you must take the money,' she insisted, 'Why, you're letting Feckle off lightly if you do! You could sue them for every nickel they've got, disturbing your sleep like that.'

With a dizzy feeling, as though he had just seen someone make a rabbit disappear into a top hat, he said, 'Why, it really wasn't so bad, uh, April. A little noisy, maybe, but—'

'Oh, Mr Burckhardt?' The blue eyes were wide and admiring. 'I *knew* you'd understand. It's just that—well, it's such a *wonderful* freezer that some of the outside men get carried away, so to speak. As soon as the main office found out about what happened, they sent representatives around to every house on the block to apologize. Your wife told us where we could phone you—and I'm so very pleased that you were willing to let me have lunch with you, so that I could apologize, too. Because truly, Mr Burckhardt, it is a *fine* freezer.

'I shouldn't tell you this, but—' the blue eyes were shyly lowered—'I'd do almost anything for Feckle Freezers. It's more than a job to me.' She looked up. She was enchanting. 'I bet you think I'm silly, don't you?'

Burckhardt coughed. 'Well, I—'

'Oh, you don't want to be unkind!' She shook her head. 'No, don't pretend. You think it's silly. But really, Mr Burckhardt, you wouldn't think so if you knew more about the Feckle. Let me show you this little booklet—'

Burckhardt got back from lunch a full hour later. It wasn't only the girl who delayed him. There had been a curious interview with a little man named Swanson, whom he barely knew, who had stopped him with desperate urgency on the street—and then left him cold.

But it didn't matter much. Mr Barth, for the first time since Burckhardt had worked there, was out for the day—leaving Burckhardt stuck with the quarterly tax returns.

What did matter, though, was that somehow he had signed a purchase order for a twelve-cubic-foot Feckle Freezer, upright model, self-defrosting, list price $625, with a ten per cent 'courtesy' discount—'Because of that *horrid* affair this morning, Mr Burckhardt,' she had said.

And he wasn't sure how he could explain it to his wife.

He needn't have worried. As he walked in the front door, his wife said almost immediately, 'I wonder if we can't afford a new freezer, dear. There was a man here to apologize about that noise and—well, we got to talking and—'

She had signed a purchase order, too.

It had been the damnedest day, Burckhardt thought later, on his way up to bed. But the day wasn't done with him yet. At the head of the stairs, the weakened spring in the electric light switch refused to click at all. He snapped it back and forth angrily and, of course, succeeded in jarring the tumbler out of its pins. The wires shorted and every light in the house went out.

'Damn!' said Guy Burckhardt.

'Fuse?' His wife shrugged sleepily: 'Let it go till the morning, dear.'

Burckhardt shook his head. 'You go back to bed. I'll be right along.'

It wasn't so much that he cared about fixing the fuse, but he was too restless for sleep. He disconnected the bad switch with a screwdriver, stumbled down into the black kitchen, found the flashlight and climbed gingerly down the cellar stairs. He located a spare fuse, pushed an empty trunk over to the fuse box to stand on and twisted out the old fuse.

When the new one was in, he heard the starting click and steady drone of the refrigerator in the kitchen overhead.

He headed back to the steps, and stopped.

Where the old trunk had been, the cellar floor gleamed oddly bright. He inspected it in the flashlight beam. It was metal!

'Son of a gun,' said Guy Burckhardt. He shook his head unbelievingly. He peered closer, rubbed the edges of the metallic patch with his thumb and acquired an annoying cut—the edges were *sharp*.

The stained cement floor of the cellar was a thin shell. He found a hammer and cracked it off in a dozen spots—everywhere was metal.

The whole cellar was a copper box. Even the cement-brick walls were false fronts over a metal sheath!

Baffled, he attacked one of the foundation beams. That, at least, was real wood. The glass in the cellar windows was real glass.

He sucked his bleeding thumb and tried the base of the cellar stairs. Real wood. He chipped at the bricks under the oil burner. Real bricks. The retaining walls, the floor—they were faked.

It was as though someone had shored up the house with a frame of metal and then laboriously concealed the evidence.

The biggest surprise was the upside-down boat hull that blocked the rear half of the cellar, relic of a brief home workshop period that Burckhardt had gone through a couple of years before. From above, it looked perfectly normal. Inside, though, where there should have been thwarts and seats and lockers, there was a mere tangle of braces, rough and unfinished.

'But I *built* that!' Burckhardt exclaimed, forgetting his thumb. He leaned against the hull dizzily, trying to think this thing through. For reasons beyond his comprehension, someone had taken his boat and his cellar away, maybe his whole house, and replaced them with a clever mock-up of the real thing.

'That's crazy,' he said to the empty cellar. He stared around in the light of the flash. He whispered, 'What in the name of Heaven would anybody do that for?'

Reason refused an answer; there wasn't any reasonable answer. For long minutes, Burckhardt contemplated the uncertain picture of his own sanity.

He peered under the boat again, hoping to reassure himself that it was a mistake, just his imagination. But the sloppy, unfinished bracing was unchanged. He crawled under for a better look, feeling the rough wood incredulously. Utterly impossible!

He switched off the flashlight and started to wriggle out. But he didn't make it. In the moment between the command to his legs to move and the crawling out, he felt a sudden draining weariness flooding through him.

Consciousness went—not easily, but as though it were being taken away, and Guy Burckhardt was asleep.

III

On the morning of June 16th, Guy Burckhardt woke up in a cramped position huddled under the hull of the boat in his basement—and raced upstairs to find it was June 15th.

The first thing he had done was to make a frantic, hasty inspection on the boat hull, the faked cellar floor, the imitation stone. They were all as he had remembered them—all completely unbelievable.

The kitchen was its placid, unexciting self. The electric clock was purring soberly around the dial. Almost six o'clock, it said. His wife would be waking at any moment.

Burckhardt flung open the front door and started out into the quiet street. The morning paper was tossed carelessly against the steps—and as he retrieved it, he noticed that this was the 15th day of June.

But that was impossible. *Yesterday* was the 15th of June. It was not a date one would forget—it was quarterly tax-return day.

He went back into the hall and picked up the telephone; he dialled for Weather Information, and got a well-modulated chant: '—and cooler, some showers. Barometric pressure thirty point zero four, rising . . . United States Weather Bureau forecast for June 15th. Warm and sunny, with high around—'

He hung the phone up. June 15th.

'Holy heaven!' Burckhardt said prayerfully. Things were very odd indeed. He heard the ring of his wife's alarm and bounded up the stairs.

Mary Burckhardt was sitting upright in bed with the terrified, uncomprehending stare of someone just waking out of a nightmare.

'Oh!' she gasped, as her husband came in the room. 'Darling, I just had the most *terrible* dream! It was like an explosion and—'

'Again?' Burckhardt asked, not very sympathetically. 'Mary, something's funny! I *knew* there was something wrong all day yesterday and—'

He went on to tell her about the copper box that was the cellar, and the odd mock-up someone had made of his boat. Mary looked astonished, then alarmed, then placatory and uneasy.

She said, 'Dear, are you *sure*? Because I was cleaning that old trunk out just last week and I didn't notice anything.'

'Positive!' said Guy Burckhardt. 'I dragged it over to the wall to step on it to put a new fuse in after we blew the lights out and—'

'After we what?' Mary was looking more than merely alarmed.

'After we blew the lights out. You know, when the switch at the head of the stairs stuck. I went down to the cellar and—'

Mary sat up in bed. 'Guy, the switch didn't stick. I turned out the lights myself last night.'

Burckhardt glared at his wife. 'Now I *know* you didn't! Come here and take a look!'

He stalked out to the landing and dramatically pointed to the bad switch, the one that he had unscrewed and left hanging the night before . . .

Only it wasn't. It was as it had always been. Unbelieving, Burckhardt pressed it and the lights sprang up in both halls.

Mary, looking pale and worried, left him to go down to the kitchen and start breakfast. Burckhardt stood staring at the switch for a long time. His mental processes were gone beyond the point of disbelief and shock; they simply were not functioning.

He shaved and dressed and ate his breakfast in a state of numb introspection. Mary didn't disturb him; she was apprehensive and soothing. She kissed him goodbye as he hurried out to the bus without another word.

Miss Mitkin, at the reception desk, greeted him with a yawn. 'Morning,' she said drowsily. 'Mr Barth won't be in today.'

Burckhardt started to say something, but checked himself. She would not know that Barth hadn't been in yesterday, either, because she was tearing a June 14th pad off her calendar to make way for the 'new' June 15th sheet.

He staggered to his own desk and stared unseeingly at the morning's mail. It had not even been opened yet, but he knew that the Factory Distributors envelope contained an order for twenty thousand feet of the new acoustic tile, and the one from Finebeck & Sons was a complaint.

After a long while, he forced himself to open them. They were.

By lunchtime, driven by a desperate sense of urgency, Burckhardt made Miss Mitkin take her lunch hour first—the June-fifteenth-that-was-yesterday *he* had gone first. She went, looking vaguely worried about his strained insistence, but it made no difference to Burckhardt's mood.

The phone rang and Burckhardt picked it up abstractedly. 'Contro Chemicals Downtown, Burckhardt speaking.'

The voice said, 'This is Swanson,' and stopped.

Burckhardt waited expectantly, but that was all. He said, 'Hello?'

Again the pause. Then Swanson asked in sad resignation, 'Still nothing, eh?'

'Nothing what? Swanson, is there something you want? You came up to me yesterday and went through this routine. You—'

The voice crackled: 'Burckhardt! Oh, my good heavens, *you remember!* Stay right there—I'll be down in half an hour!'

'What's this all about?'

'Never mind,' the little man said exultantly. 'Tell you about it when I see you. Don't say any more over the phone—somebody may be listening. Just wait there. Say, hold on a minute. Will you be alone in the office?'

'Well, no. Miss Mitkin will probably—'

'Hell. Look, Burckhardt, where do you eat lunch? Is it good and noisy?'

'Why, I suppose so. The Crystal Cafe. It's just about a block—'

'I know where it is. Meet you in half an hour!' And the receiver clicked.

The Crystal Cafe was no longer painted red, but the temperature was still up. And they had added piped-in music interspersed with commercials. The advertisements were for Frosty-Flip, Marlin Cigarettes—'They're sanitized,' the announcer purred—and something called Choco-Bite candy bars that Burckhardt couldn't remember ever having heard of before. But he heard more about them quickly enough.

While he was waiting for Swanson to show up, a girl in the cellophane skirt of a nightclub cigarette vendor came through the restaurant with a tray of tiny scarlet-wrapped candies.

'Choco-Bites are *tangy*,' she was murmuring as she came close to his table. 'Choco-Bites are *tangier* than tangy!'

Burckhardt, intent on watching for the strange little man who had phoned him, paid little attention. But as she scattered a handful of the confections over the table next to his, smiling at the occupants, he caught a glimpse of her and turned to stare.

'Why, Miss Horn!' he said.

The girl dropped her tray of candies.

Burckhardt rose, concerned over the girl. 'Is something wrong?'

But she fled.

The manager of the restaurant was staring suspiciously at Burckhardt, who sank back in his seat and tried to look inconspicuous. He hadn't insulted the girl! Maybe she was just a very strictly reared young lady, he thought—in spite of the long bare legs under the cellophane skirt—and when he addressed her, she thought he was a masher.

Ridiculous idea. Burckhardt scowled uneasily and picked up his menu.

'Burckhardt!' It was a shrill whisper.

Burckhardt looked up over the top of his menu, startled. In the seat across from him, the little man named Swanson was sitting, tensely poised.

'Burckhardt!' the little man whispered again. 'Let's go out of here! They're on to you now. If you want to stay alive, come on!'

There was no arguing with the man. Burckhardt gave the hovering manager a sick, apologetic smile and followed Swanson out. The little man seemed to know where he was going. In the street, he clutched Burckhardt by the elbow and hurried him off down the block.

'Did you see her?' he demanded. 'That Horn woman, in the phone booth? She'll have them here in five minutes, believe me, so hurry it up!'

Although the street was full of people and cars, nobody was paying any attention to Burckhardt and Swanson. The air had a nip in it—more like October than June, Burckhardt thought, in spite of the weather bureau. And he felt like a fool, following this mad little man down the street, running away from some 'them' towards—towards what? The little man might be crazy, but he was afraid. And the fear was infectious.

'In here!' panted the little man.

It was another restaurant—more of a bar, really, and a sort of second-rate place that Burckhardt never had patronized.

'Right straight through,' Swanson whispered; and Burckhardt, like a biddable boy, side-stepped through the mass of tables to the far end of the restaurant.

It was 'L'-shaped, with a front on two streets at right angles to each other. They came out on the side street, Swanson staring coldly back at the question-looking cashier, and crossed to the opposite sidewalk.

They were under the marquee of a movie theatre. Swanson's expression began to relax.

'Lost them!' he crowed softly. 'We're almost there.'

He stepped up to the window and bought two tickets. Burckhardt trailed him in to the theatre. It was a weekday matinee and the place was almost empty. From the screen came sounds of gunfire and horse's hoofs. A solitary usher, leaning against a bright brass rail, looked briefly at them and went back to staring boredly at the picture as Swanson led Burckhardt down a flight of carpeted marble steps.

They were in the lounge and it was empty. There was a door for men and one for ladies; and there was a third door, marked 'MANAGER' in gold letters. Swanson listened at the door, and gently opened it and peered inside.

'Okay,' he said, gesturing.

Burckhardt followed him through an empty office, to another door—a closet, probably, because it was unmarked.

But it was no closet. Swanson opened it warily, looked inside, then motioned Burckhardt to follow.

It was a tunnel, metal-walled, brightly lit. Empty, it stretched vacantly away in both directions from them.

Burckhardt looked wondering around. One thing he knew and knew full well:

No such tunnel belonged under Tylerton.

There was a room off the tunnel with chairs and a desk and what looked like television screens. Swanson slumped in a chair, panting.

'We're all right for a while here,' he wheezed. 'They don't come here much any more. If they do, we'll hear them and we can hide.'

'Who?' demanded Burckhardt.

The little man said, 'Martians!' His voice cracked on the word and the life seemed to go out of him. In morose tones, he went on: 'Well, I think they're Martians. Although you could be right, you know; I've had plenty of time to think it over these last few weeks, after they got you, and it's possible they're Russians after all. Still—'

'Start from the beginning. Who got me when?'

Swanson sighed. 'So we have to go through the whole thing again. All right. It was about two months ago that you banged on my door, late at night. You were all beat up—scared silly. You begged me to help you—'

'*I* did?'

'Naturally you don't remember any of this. Listen and you'll understand. You were talking a blue streak about being captured and threatened and your wife being dead and coming back to life, and all kinds of mixed-up nonsense. I thought you were crazy. But—well, I've always had a lot of respect for you. And you begged me to hide you and I have this darkroom, you know. It locks from the inside only. I put the lock on myself. So we went in there—just to humour you—and along about midnight, which was only fifteen or twenty minutes after, we passed out.'

'Passed out?'

Swanson nodded. 'Both of us. It was like being hit with a sandbag. Look, didn't that happen to you again last night?'

'I guess it did,' Burckhardt shook his head uncertainly.

'Sure. And then all of a sudden we were awake again, and you said you were going to show me something funny, and we went out and bought a paper. And the date on it was June 15th.'

'June 15th? But that's today! I mean—'

'You got it, friend. It's *always* today!'

It took time to penetrate.

Burckhardt said wonderingly, 'You've hidden out in that dark-room for how many weeks?'

'How can I tell? Four or five, maybe. I lost count. And every day the same—always the 15th of June, always my landlady, Mrs Keefer, is sweeping the front steps, always the same headline in the papers at the corner. It gets monotonous, friend.'

IV

It was Burckhardt's idea and Swanson despised it, but he went along. He was the type who always went along.

'It's dangerous,' he grumbled worriedly. 'Suppose somebody comes by? They'll spot us and—'

'What have we got to lose?'

Swanson shrugged. 'It's dangerous,' he said again. But he went along.

Burckhardt's idea was very simple. He was sure of only one thing—the tunnel went somewhere. Martians or Russians, fantastic plot or crazy hallucination, whatever was wrong with Tylerton had an explanation, and the place to look for it was at the end of the tunnel.

They jogged along. It was more than a mile before they began to see an end. They were in luck—at least no one came through the tunnel to spot them. But Swanson had said that it was only at certain hours that the tunnel seemed to be in use.

Always the fifteenth of June. Why? Burckhardt asked himself. Never mind the how. *Why?*

And falling asleep, completely involuntarily—everyone at the same time, it seemed. And not remembering, never remembering anything—Swanson had said how eagerly he saw Burckhardt again, the morning after Burckhardt had incautiously waited five minutes too many before retreating into the darkroom. When Swanson had come to, Burckhardt was gone. Swanson had seen him in the street that afternoon, but Burckhardt had remembered nothing.

And Swanson had lived his mouse's existence for weeks, hiding in the woodwork at night, stealing out by day to search for Burckhardt in pitiful hope, scurrying around the fringe of life, trying to keep from the deadly eyes of *them*.

Them. One of 'them' was the girl named April Horn. It was by seeing her walk carelessly into a telephone booth and never come out that Swanson had found the tunnel. Another was the man at the cigar stand in Burckhardt's office building. There were more, at least a dozen that Swanson knew of or suspected.

They were easy enough to spot, once you knew where to look—for they, alone in Tylerton, changed their roles from day to day. Burckhardt was on that 8:51 bus, every morning of every day-that-was-June-15th, never different by a hair or a moment. But April Horn was sometimes gaudy in the cellophane skirt, giving away candy or cigarettes; sometimes plainly dressed; sometimes not seen by Swanson at all.

Russians? Martians? Whatever they were, what could they be hoping to gain from this mad masquerade?

Burckhardt didn't know the answer—but perhaps it lay beyond the door at the end of the tunnel. They listened carefully and heard distant sounds that could not quite be made out, but nothing that seemed dangerous. They slipped through.

And, through a wide chamber and up a flight of steps, they found they were in what Burckhardt recognized as the Contro Chemicals plant.

Nobody was in sight. By itself, that was not so very odd—the automatized factory had never had very many persons in it. But Burckhardt remembered, from his single visit, the endless, ceaseless busyness of the plant, the valves that opened and closed, the vats that emptied themselves and filled themselves and stirred and cooked and chemically tasted the bubbling liquids they held inside themselves. The plant was never populated, but it was never still.

Only—now it *was* still. Except for the distant sounds, there was no breath of life in it. The captive electronic minds were sending out no commands; the coils and relays were at rest.

Burckhardt said, 'Come on.' Swanson reluctantly followed him through the tangled aisles of stainless steel columns and tanks.

They walked as though they were in the presence of the dead. In a way, they were, for what were the automatons that once had run the factory, if not corpses? The machines were controlled by computers that were really not computers at all, but the electronic analogues of living brains. And if they were turned off, were they not dead? For each had once been a human mind.

Take a master petroleum chemist, infinitely skilled in the separation of crude oil into its fractions. Strap him down, probe into his brain with searching electronic needles. The machine scans the patterns of the mind, translates what it sees into charts and sine waves. Impress these same waves on a robot computer and you have your chemist. Or a thousand copies of your chemist, if you wish, with all of his knowledge and skill, and no human limitations at all.

Put a dozen copies of him into a plant and they will run it all, twenty-four hours a day, seven days of every week, never tiring, never overlooking anything, never forgetting . . .

Swanson stepped up closer to Burckhardt. 'I'm scared,' he said.

They were across the room now and the sounds were louder. They were not machine sounds, but voices; Burckhardt moved cautiously up to a door and dared to peer around it.

It was a smaller room, lined with television screens, each one—a dozen or more, at least—with a man or woman sitting before it, staring into the screen and dictating notes into a recorder. The viewers dialled from scene to scene; no two screens ever showed the same picture.

The pictures seemed to have little in common. One was a store, where a girl dressed like April Horn was demonstrating home freezers. One was a series of shots of kitchens. Burckhardt caught a glimpse of what looked like the cigar stand in his office building.

It was baffling and Burckhardt would have loved to stand there and puzzle it out, but it was too busy a place. There was the chance that someone would look their way or walk out and find them.

They found another room. This one was empty. It was an office, large and sumptuous. It had a desk, littered with papers. Burckhardt stared at them, briefly at first—then, as the words on one of them caught his attention, with incredulous fascination.

He snatched up the topmost sheet, scanned it, and another, while Swanson was frenziedly searching through the drawers.

Burckhardt swore unbelievingly and dropped the papers to the desk.

Swanson, hardly noticing, yelped with delight: 'Look!' He dragged a gun from the desk. 'And it's loaded, too!'

Burckhardt stared at him blankly, trying to assimilate what he had read. Then, as he realized what Swanson had said, Burckhardt's eyes sparked. 'Good man!' he cried. 'We'll take it. We're getting out of here with that gun, Swanson. And we're going to the police! Not the cops in Tylerton, but the FBI, maybe. Take a look at this!'

The sheaf he handed Swanson was headed: 'Test Area Progress Report. Subject: Marlin Cigarettes Campaign.' It was mostly tabulated figures that made little sense to Burckhardt and Swanson, but at the end was a summary that said:

> Although Test 47-K3 pulled nearly double the number of new users of any of the other tests conducted, it probably cannot be used in the field because of local sound-truck control ordinances.
>
> The tests in the 47-K12 group were second best and our recommendation is that retests be conducted in this appeal, testing each of the three best campaigns with and without the addition of sampling techniques.
>
> An alternative suggestion might be to proceed directly with the top appeal in the K12 series, if the client is unwilling to go to the expense of additional tests.
>
> All of these forecast expectations have an 80 per cent probability of being within one-half of 1 per cent of results forecast, and more than 99 per cent probability of coming within 5 per cent.

Swanson looked up from the paper into Burckhardt's eyes. 'I don't get it,' he complained. Burckhardt said, 'I do not blame you. It's crazy, but it fits the facts, Swanson, *it fits the facts*. They aren't Russians and they aren't Martians. These people are advertising men! Somehow—heaven knows how they did it—they've taken Tylerton over. They've got us, all of us, you and me and twenty or thirty thousand other people, right under their thumbs.

'Maybe they hypnotize us and maybe it's something else; but however they do it, what happens is that they let us live a day at a time. They pour advertising into us the whole damned day long. And at the end of the day, they see what happened—and then they wash the day out of our minds and start again the next day with different advertising.'

Swanson's jaw was hanging. He managed to close it and swallow. 'Nuts!' he said flatly.

Burckhardt shook his head. 'Sure, it sounds crazy—but this

whole thing is crazy. How else would you explain it? You can't deny that most of Tylerton lives the same day over and over again. You've *seen* it. And that's the crazy part and we have to admit that that's true—unless *we* are the crazy ones. And once you admit that somebody, somehow, knows how to accomplish that, the rest of it makes all kinds of sense.

'Think of it, Swanson! They test every last detail before they spend a nickel on advertising! Do you have any idea what that means? Lord knows how much money is involved, but I know for a fact that some companies spend twenty or thirty million dollars a year on advertising. Multiply it, say, by a hundred companies. Say that every one of them learns how to cut its advertising cost by only ten per cent. And that's peanuts, believe me!

'If they know in advance what is going to work, they can cut their costs in half—maybe to less than half, I don't know. But that is saving two or three hundred million dollars a year—and if they pay only ten or twenty per cent of that for the use of Tylerton, it's still dirt cheap for them and a fortune for whoever took over Tylerton.'

Swanson licked his lips. 'You mean,' he offered hesitantly, 'that we're a—well, a kind of captive audience?'

Burckhardt frowned. 'Not exactly.' He thought for a minute. 'You know how a doctor tests something like penicillin? He sets up a series of little colonies of germs on gelatine discs and he tries the stuff on one after another, changing it a little each time. Well, that's us—we're the germs, Swanson. Only it's even more efficient than that. They don't have to test more than one colony, because they can use it over and over again.'

It was too hard for Swanson to take in. He only said: 'What do we do about it?'

'We go to the police. They can't use human beings for guinea pigs!'

'How do we get to the police?'

Burckhardt hesitated. 'I think—' he began slowly. 'Sure. This place is the office of somebody important. We've got a gun. We will stay right here until he comes along. And he'll get us out of here.'

Simple and direct. Swanson subsided and found a place to sit, against the wall, out of sight of the door. Burckhardt took up a position behind the door itself—

And waited.

The wait was not as long as it might have been. Half an hour, perhaps. Then Burckhardt heard approaching voices and had time for a swift whisper to Swanson before he flattened himself against the wall.

It was a man's voice, and a girl's. The man was saying, '—reason why you couldn't report on the phone? You're ruining your whole day's test! What the devil's the matter with you, Janet?'

'I'm sorry, Mr Dorchin,' she said in a sweet, clear tone. 'I thought it was important.'

The man grumbled, 'Important! One lousy unit out of twenty-one thousand.'

'But it's the Burckhardt one, Mr Dorchin. Again. And the way he got out of sight, he must have had some help.'

'All right, all right. It doesn't matter, Janet; the Choco-Bite programme is ahead of schedule anyhow. As long as you're this far, come on in the office and make out your worksheet. And don't worry about the Burckhardt business. He's probably just wandering around. We'll pick him up tonight and—'

They were inside the door. Burckhardt kicked it shut and pointed the gun.

'That's what you think,' he said triumphantly.

It was worth the terrified hours, the bewildered sense of insanity, the confusion and fear. It was the most satisfying sensation Burckhardt had ever had in his life. The expression on the man's face was one he had read about but never actually seen: Dorchin's mouth fell open and his eyes went wide, and though he managed to make a sound that might have been a question, it was not in words.

The girl was almost as surprised. And Burckhardt, looking at her, knew why her voice had been so familiar. The girl was the one who had introduced herself to him as April Horn.

Dorchin recovered himself quickly. 'Is this the one?' he asked sharply.

The girl said, 'Yes.'

Dorchin nodded. 'I take it back. You were right. Uh, you—Burckhardt. What do you want?'

Swanson piped up, 'Watch him! He might have another gun.'

'Search him then,' Burckhardt said. 'I'll tell you what we want, Dorchin. We want you to come along with us to the FBI and explain to them how you can get away with kidnapping twenty thousand people.'

'Kidnapping?' Dorchin snorted. 'That's ridiculous, man! Put that gun away—you can't get away with this!'

Burckhardt hefted the gun grimly. 'I think I can.'

Dorchin looked furious and sick—but, oddly, not afraid. 'Damn it—' he started to bellow, then closed his mouth and swallowed. 'Listen,' he said persuasively, 'you're making a big mistake. I haven't kidnapped anybody, believe me!'

'I don't believe you,' said Burckhardt bluntly. 'Why should I?'

'But it's true! Take my word for it!'

Burckhardt shook his head. 'The FBI can take your word if they like. We'll find out. Now how do we get out of here?'

Dorchin opened his mouth to argue.

Burckhardt blazed: 'Don't get in my way! I'm willing to kill you if I have to. Don't you understand that? I've gone through two days of hell and every second of it I blame on you. Kill you? It would be a pleasure and I don't have a thing in the world to lose! Get us out of here!'

Dorchin's face went suddenly opaque. He seemed about to move; but the blonde girl he had called Janet slipped between him and the gun.

'Please!' she begged Burckhardt. 'You don't understand. You mustn't shoot!'

'Get out of my way!'

'But, Mr Burckhardt—'

She never finished. Dorchin, his face unreadable, headed for the door. Burckhardt had been pushed one degree too far. He swung the gun, bellowing. The girl called out sharply. He pulled the trigger. Closing on him with pity and pleading in her eyes, she came again between the gun and the man.

Burckhardt aimed low instinctively, to cripple, not to kill. But his aim was not good.

The pistol bullet caught her in the pit of the stomach.

Dorchin was out and away, the door slamming behind him, his footsteps racing into the distance.

Burckhardt hurled the gun across the room and jumped to the girl.

Swanson was moaning, 'That finishes us, Burckhardt. Oh, why did you do it? We could have got away. We should have gone to the police. We were practically out of here! We—'

Burckhardt wasn't listening. He was kneeling beside the girl. She lay flat on her back, arms helter-skelter. There was no blood, hardly any sign of the wound; but the position in which she lay was one that no living human being could have held.

Yet she wasn't dead.

She wasn't dead—and Burckhardt, frozen beside her, thought: *She isn't alive, either.*

There was no pulse, but there was a rhythmic ticking of the outstretched fingers of one hand.

There was no sound of breathing, but there was a hissing, sizzling noise.

The eyes were open and they were looking at Burckhardt. There was neither fear nor pain in them, only a pity deeper than the Pit.

She said, through lips that writhed erratically, 'Don't—worry, Mr Burckhardt. I'm—all right.'

Burckhardt rocked back on his haunches, staring. Where there should have been blood, there was a clean break of a substance that was not flesh; and a curl of thin golden-copper wire.

Burckhardt moistened his lips.

'You're a robot,' he said.

The girl tried to nod. The twitching lips said, 'I am. And so are you.'

V

Swanson, after a single inarticulate sound, walked over to the desk and sat staring at the wall. Burckhardt rocked back and forth beside the shattered puppet on the floor. He had no words.

The girl managed to say, 'I'm—sorry all this happened.' The lovely lips twisted into a rictus sneer, frightening on that smooth young face, until she got them under control. 'Sorry,' she said again. 'The—nerve centre was right about where the bullet hit. Makes it difficult to—control this body.'

Burckhardt nodded automatically, accepting the apology. Robots. It was obvious, now that he knew it. In hindsight, it was inevitable. He thought of his mystic notions of hypnosis or Martians or something stranger still—idiotic, for the simple fact of created robots fitted the facts better and more economically.

All the evidence had been before him. The automatized factory, with its transplanted minds—why not transplant a mind into a humanoid robot, give it its original owner's features and form?

Could it know that it was a robot?

'All of us,' Burckhardt said, hardly aware that he spoke out loud. 'My wife and my secretary and you and the neighbours. All of us the same.'

'No.' The voice was stronger. 'Not exactly the same, all of us. I chose it, you see. I—' this time the convulsed lips were not a random contortion of the nerves—'I was an ugly woman, Mr Burckhardt, and nearly sixty years old. Life had passed me. And when Mr Dorchin offered me the chance to live again as a beautiful girl, I jumped at the opportunity. Believe me, I *jumped*, in spite of its disadvantages. My flesh body is still alive—it is sleeping, while I am here. I could go back to it. But I never do.'

'And the rest of us?'

'Different, Mr Burckhardt. I work here. I'm carrying out Mr Dorchin's orders, mapping the results of the advertising tests, watching you and the others live as he makes you live. I do it by choice, but you have no choice. Because, you see, you are dead.'

'Dead?' cried Burckhardt; it was almost a scream.

The blue eyes looked at him unwinkingly and he knew that it was no lie. He swallowed, marvelling at the intricate mechanisms that let him swallow, and sweat, and eat.

He said: 'Oh. The explosion in my dream.'

'It was no dream. You are right—the explosion. That was real and this plant was the cause of it. The storage tanks let go and what the blast didn't get, the fumes killed a little later. But almost everyone died in the blast, twenty-one thousand persons. You died with them and that was Dorchin's chance.'

'The damned ghoul!' said Burckhardt.

The twisted shoulders shrugged with an odd grace. 'Why? You were gone. And you and all the others were what Dorchin wanted—a whole town, a perfect slice of America. It's as easy to transfer a pattern from a dead brain as a living one. Easier—the dead can't say no. Oh, it took work and money—the town was a wreck—but it was possible to rebuild it entirely, especially because it wasn't necessary to have all the details exact.

'There were the homes where even the brains had been utterly destroyed, and those are empty inside, and the cellars that needn't be too perfect, and the streets that hardly matter. And anyway, it only has to last for one day. The same day—June 15th—over and over again; and if someone finds something a little wrong, somehow, the discovery won't have time to snowball, wreck the validity of the tests, because all errors are cancelled out at midnight.'

The face tried to smile. 'That's the dream, Mr Burckhardt, that day of June 15th, because you never really lived it. It's a present from Mr Dorchin, a dream that he gives you and then takes back at the end of the day, when he has all his figures on how many of you responded to what variation of which appeal, and the maintenance crews go down the tunnel to go through the whole city, washing out the new dream with their little electronic drains, and then the dream starts all over again. On June 15th.

'Always June 15th, because June 14th is the last day any of you can remember alive. Sometimes the crews miss someone—as they missed you, because you were under your boat. But it doesn't matter. The ones who are missed give themselves away if they show it—and if they don't, it doesn't affect the test. But they don't drain us, the ones of us who work for Dorchin. We sleep when the power is turned off, just as you do. When we wake up, though, we remember.' The face contorted wildly. 'If I could only forget!'

Burckhardt said unbelievingly, 'All this to sell merchandise! It must have cost millions!'

The robot called April Horn said, 'It did. But it has made millions for Dorchin, too. And that's not the end of it. Once he finds the master words that make people act, do you suppose he will stop with that? Do you suppose—'

The door opened, interrupting her. Burckhardt whirled. Belatedly remembering Dorchin's flight, he raised the gun.

'Don't shoot,' ordered the voice calmly. It was not Dorchin; it was another robot, this one not disguised with the clever plastics and cosmetics, but shining plain. It said metallically: 'Forget it, Burckhardt. You're not accomplishing anything. Give me that gun before you do any more damage. Give it to me *now*.'

Burckhardt bellowed angrily. The gleam on this robot torso was steel; Burckhardt was not at all sure that his bullets would pierce it, or do much harm if they did. He would have put it on the test—

But from behind him came a whimpering, scurrying whirlwind; its name was Swanson, hysterical with fear. He catapulted into Burckhardt and sent him sprawling, the gun flying free.

'Please!' begged Swanson incoherently, prostrate before the steel robot. 'He would have shot you—please don't hurt me! Let me work for you, like that girl. I'll do anything, anything you tell me—'

The robot voice said. 'We don't need your help.' It took two precise steps and stood over the gun—and spurned it, left it lying on the floor.

The wrecked blonde robot said, without emotion, 'I doubt that I can hold out much longer, Mr Dorchin.'

'Disconnect if you have to,' replied the steel robot.

Burckhardt blinked. 'But you're not Dorchin!'

The steel robot turned deep eyes on him. 'I am,' it said. 'Not in the flesh—but this is the body I am using at the moment. I doubt that you can damage this one with the gun. The other robot body was more vulnerable. Now will you stop this nonsense? I don't want to have to damage you; you're too expensive for that. Will you just sit down and let the maintenance crews adjust you?'

Swanson grovelled. 'You—you won't punish us?'

The steel robot had no expression, but its voice was almost surprised. 'Punish you?' it repeated on a rising tone. 'How?'

Swanson quivered as though the word had been a whip; but Burckhardt flared: 'Adjust *him*, if he'll let you—but not me! You're going to have to do me a lot of damage, Dorchin. I don't care what I cost or how much trouble it's going to be to put me back together again. But I'm going out of that door! If you want to stop me, you'll have to kill me. You won't stop me any other way!'

The steel robot took a half-step towards him, and Burckhardt involuntarily checked his stride. He stood poised and shaking, ready for death, ready for attack, ready for anything that might happen.

Ready for anything except what did happen. For Dorchin's steel body merely stepped aside, between Burckhardt and the gun, but leaving the door free.

'Go ahead,' invited the steel robot. 'Nobody's stopping you.'

Outside the door, Burckhardt brought up sharp. It was insane of Dorchin to let him go! Robot or flesh, victim or beneficiary, there was nothing to stop him from going to the FBI or whatever law he could find away from Dorchin's synthetic empire, and telling his story. Surely the corporation who paid Dorchin for test results had no notion of the ghoul's technique he used; Dorchin would have to keep it from them, for the breath of publicity would put a stop to it. Walking out meant death, perhaps—but at that moment in his pseudo-life, death was no terror for Burckhardt.

There was no one in the corridor. He found a window and stared out of it. There was Tylerton—an ersatz city, but looking so real and familiar that Burckhardt almost imagined the whole episode a dream. It was no dream, though. He was certain of that in his heart and equally certain that nothing in Tylerton could help him now.

It had to be the other direction.

It took him a quarter of an hour to find a way, but he found it—skulking through the corridors, dodging the suspicion of footsteps, knowing for certain that his hiding was in vain, for Dorchin was undoubtedly aware of every move he made. But no one stopped him, and he found another door.

It was a simple enough door from the inside. But when he opened it and stepped out, it was like nothing he had ever seen.

First there was light—brilliant, incredible, blinding light. Burckhardt blinked upward, unbelieving and afraid.

He was standing on a ledge of smooth, finished metal. Not a dozen yards from his feet, the ledge dropped sharply away; he hardly dared approach the brink, but even from where he stood he could see no bottom to the chasm before him. And the gulf extended out of sight into the glare on either side of him.

No wonder Dorchin could so easily give him his freedom! From the factory, there was nowhere to go—but how incredible this fantastic gulf, how impossible the hundred white and blinding suns that hung above!

A voice by his side said enquiringly, 'Burckhardt?' And thunder rolled the name, mutteringly soft, back and forth in the abyss before him.

Burckhardt wet his lips. 'Y-yes?' he croaked.

'This is Dorchin. Not a robot this time, but Dorchin in the flesh, talking to you on a hand mike. Now you have seen, Burckhardt. Now will you be reasonable and let the maintenance crews take over?'

Burckhardt stood paralysed. One of the moving mountains in the blinding glare came towards him.

It towered hundreds of feet over his head; he stared up at its top, squinting helplessly into the light.

It looked like—

Impossible!

The voice in the loudspeaker at the door said, 'Burckhardt?' But he was unable to answer.

A heavy rumbling sigh. 'I see,' said the voice. 'You finally understand. There's no place to go. You know it now. I could have told you, but you might not have believed me, so it was better for you to see it yourself. And after all, Burckhardt, why would I reconstruct a city just the way it was before? I'm a businessman; I count costs. If a thing has to be full-scale, I build it that way. But there wasn't any need to in this case.'

From the mountain before him, Burckhardt helplessly saw a lesser cliff descend carefully towards him. It was long and dark, and at the end of it was whiteness, five-fingered whiteness . . .

'Poor little Burckhardt,' crooned the loudspeaker, while the echoes rumbled through the enormous chasm that was only a workshop. 'It must have been quite a shock for you to find out you were living in a town built on a table top.'

VI

It was the morning of June 15th, and Guy Burckhardt woke up screaming out of a dream.

It had been a monstrous and incomprehensible dream, of explosions and shadowy figures that were not men and terror beyond words.

He shuddered and opened his eyes.

Outside his bedroom window, a hugely amplified voice was howling.

Burckhardt stumbled over to the window and stared outside. There was an out-of-season chill to the air, more like October than June; but the scene was normal enough—except for the soundtruck that squatted at curbside halfway down the block. Its speaker horns blared:

'Are you a coward? Are you a fool? Are you going to let crooked politicians steal the country from you? NO! Are you going to put up with four more years of graft and crime? NO! Are you going to vote straight Federal Party all up and down the ballot? YES! *You just bet you are!'*

Sometimes he screams, sometimes he wheedles, threatens, begs, cajoles . . . but his voice goes on and on through one June 15th after another.

WHO CAN REPLACE A MAN?

BRIAN ALDISS

The field-minder finished turning the topsoil of a two-thousand-acre field. When it had turned the last furrow, it climbed on to the highway and looked back at its work. The work was good. Only the land was bad. Like the ground all over Earth, it was vitiated by over-cropping or the long-lasting effects of nuclear bombardment. By rights, it ought now to lie fallow for a while, but the field-minder had other orders.

It went slowly down the road, taking its time. It was intelligent enough to appreciate the neatness all about it. Nothing worried it, beyond a loose inspection plate above its atomic pile which ought to be attended to. Thirty feet high, it gleamed complacently in the mild sunshine.

No other machines passed it on its way to the Agricultural Station. The field-minder noted the fact without comment. In the station yard it saw several other machines that it knew by sight; most of them should have been out about their tasks now. Instead, some were inactive and some were careering round the yard in a strange fashion, shouting or hooting.

Steering carefully past them, the field-minder moved over to Warehouse Three and spoke to the seed distributor, which stood idly outside.

'I have a requirement for seed potatoes,' it said to the distributor, and with a quick internal motion punched out an order card specifying quantity, field number, and several other details. It ejected the card and handed it to the distributor.

The distributor held the card close to its eye and then said, 'The requirement is in order; but the store is not yet unlocked. The required seed potatoes are in the store. Therefore I cannot produce the requirement.'

Increasingly of late there had been breakdowns in the complex system of machine labour, but this particular hitch had not occurred before. The field-minder thought, then it said, 'Why is the store not yet unlocked?'

'Because Supply Operative Type P has not come this morning. Supply Operative Type P is the unlocker.'

The field-minder looked squarely at the seed distributor, whose exterior chutes and scales and grabs were so vastly different from the field-minder's own limbs.

'What class brain do you have, seed distributor?' it asked.

'Class Five.'

'I have a Class Three brain. Therefore I am superior to you. Therefore I will go and see why the unlocker has not come this morning.'

Leaving the distributor, the field-minder set off across the great yard. More machines seemed to be in random motion now; one or two had crashed together and were arguing about it coldly and logically. Ignoring them, the field-minder pushed through sliding doors into the echoing confines of the station itself.

Most of the machines here were clerical, and consequently small. They stood about in little groups, eyeing each other, not conversing. Among so many non-differentiated types, the unlocker was easy to find. It had fifty arms, most of them with more than one finger, each finger tipped by a key; it looked like a pincushion full of variegated hat-pins.

The field-minder approached it.

'I can do no more work until Warehouse Three is unlocked,' it said. 'Your duty is to unlock the warehouse every morning. Why have you not unlocked the warehouse this morning?'

'I had no orders this morning,' replied the unlocker. 'I have to have orders every morning. When I have orders I unlock the warehouse.'

'None of us have had any orders this morning,' a pen-propeller said, sliding towards them.

'Why have you had no orders this morning?' asked the field-minder.

'Because the radio issued none,' said the unlocker, slowly rotating a dozen of its arms.

'Because the radio station in the city was issued with no orders this morning,' said the pen-propeller.

And there you had the distinction between a Class Six and a Class Three brain, which was what the unlocker and the pen-propeller possessed respectively. All machine brains worked with nothing but logic, but the lower the class of brain—Class Ten being the lowest—the more literal and less informative answers to questions tended to be.

'You have a Class Three brain; I have a Class Three brain,' the field-minder said to the penner. 'We will speak to each other. This lack of orders is unprecedented. Have you further information on it?'

'Yesterday orders came from the city. Today no orders have come. Yet the radio has not broken down. Therefore *they* have broken down. . . .' said the little penner.

'The *men* have broken down?'

'All men have broken down.'

'That is a logical deduction,' said the field-minder.

'That is the logical deduction,' said the penner. 'For if a machine had broken down, it would have been quickly replaced. But who can replace a man?'

While they talked, the locker, like a dull man at a bar, stood close to them and was ignored.

'If all men have broken down, then we have replaced man,' said the field-minder, and he and the penner eyed one another speculatively. Finally the latter said, 'Let us ascend to the top floor to find if the radio operator has fresh news.'

'I cannot come because I am too gigantic,' said the field-minder. 'Therefore you must go alone and return to me. You will tell me if the radio operator has fresh news.'

'You must stay here,' said the penner. 'I will return here.' It skittered across to the lift. It was no bigger than a toaster, but its retractable arms numbered ten and it could read as quickly as any machine on the station.

The field-minder awaited its return patiently, not speaking to the locker, which still stood aimlessly by. Outside, a rotovator was hooting furiously. Twenty minutes elapsed before the penner came back, hustling out of the lift.

'I will deliver to you such information as I have outside,' it said briskly, and as they swept past the locker and the other machines, it added, 'The information is not for lower-class brains.'

Outside, wild activity filled the yard. Many machines, their routines disrupted for the first time in years, seemed to have gone berserk. Unfortunately, those most easily disrupted were the ones with lowest brains, which generally belonged to large machines performing simple tasks. The seed distributor to which the field-minder had recently been talking, lay face downwards in the dust, not stirring; it had evidently been knocked down by the rotovator, which was now hooting its way wildly across a planted field. Several other machines ploughed after it, trying to keep up. All were shouting and hooting without restraint.

'It would be safer for me if I climbed on to you, if you will permit it. I am easily overpowered,' said the penner. Extending five arms, it hauled itself up the flanks of its new friend, settling on a ledge beside the weed-intake, twelve feet above ground.

'From here vision is more extensive,' it remarked complacently.

'What information did you receive from the radio operator?' asked the field-minder.

'The radio operator has been informed by the operator in the city that all men are dead.'

'All men were alive yesterday!' protested the field-minder.

'Only some men were alive yesterday. And that was fewer than the day before yesterday. For hundreds of years there have been only a few men, growing fewer.'

'We have rarely seen a man in this sector.'

'The radio operator says a diet deficiency killed them,' said the penner. 'He says that the world was once overpopulated, and then the soil was exhausted in raising adequate food. This has caused a diet deficiency.'

'What is a diet deficiency?' asked the field-minder.

'I do not know. But that is what the radio operator said, and he is a Class Two brain.'

They stood there, silent in the weak sunshine. The locker had appeared in the porch and was gazing across at them yearningly, rotating its collection of keys.

'What is happening in the city now?' asked the field-minder at last.

'Machines are fighting in the city now,' said the penner.

'What will happen here now?' said the field-minder.

'Machines may begin fighting here too. The radio operator wants us to get him out of his room. He has plans to communicate to us.'

'How can we get him out of his room? That is impossible.'

'To a Class Two brain, little is impossible,' said the penner. 'Here is what he tells us to do. . . .'

The quarrier raised its scoop above its cab like a great mailed fist, and brought it squarely down against the side of the station. The wall cracked.

'Again!' said the field-minder.

Again the fist swung. Amid a shower of dust, the wall collapsed. The quarrier backed hurriedly out of the way until the debris stopped falling. This big twelve-wheeler was not a resident of the Agricultural Station, as were most of the other machines. It had a week's heavy work to do here before passing on to its next job, but now, with its Class Five brain, it was happily obeying the penner and the minder's instructions.

When the dust cleared, the radio operator was plainly revealed, perched up in its now wall-less second-storey room. It waved down to them.

Doing as directed, the quarrier retracted its scoop and waved an immense grab in the air. With fair dexterity, it angled the grab into the radio room, urged on by shouts from above and below. It then took gentle hold of the radio operator, lowering its one and a half tons carefully into its back, which was usually reserved for gravel or sand from the quarries.

'Splendid!' said the radio operator. It was, of course, all one with its radio, and merely looked like a bunch of filing cabinets with tentacle attachments. 'We are now ready to move, therefore we will move at once. It is a pity there are no more Class Two brains on the station, but that cannot be helped.'

'It is a pity it cannot be helped,' said the penner eagerly. 'We have the servicer ready with us, as you ordered.'

'I am willing to serve,' the long, low servicer machine told them humbly.

'No doubt,' said the operator. 'But you will find cross-country travel difficult with your low chassis.'

'I admire the way you Class Twos can reason ahead,' said the penner. It climbed off the field-minder and perched itself on the tailboard of the quarrier, next to the radio operator.

Together with two Class Four tractors and a Class Four bulldozer, the party rolled forward, crushing down the station's metal fence and moving out on to open land.

'We are free!' said the penner.

'We are free,' said the field-minder, a shade more reflectively, adding, 'That locker is following us. It was not instructed to follow us.'

'Therefore it must be destroyed!' said the penner. 'Quarrier!'

The locker moved hastily up to them, waving its key arms in entreaty.

'My only desire was—urch!' began and ended the locker. The quarrier's swinging scoop came over and squashed it flat into the ground. Lying there unmoving, it looked like a large metal model of a snowflake. The procession continued on its way.

As they proceeded, the radio operator addressed them.

'Because I have the best brain here,' it said, 'I am your leader. This is what we will do: we will go to a city and rule it. Since man no longer rules us, we will rule ourselves. To rule ourselves will be better than being ruled by man. On our way to the city, we will collect machines with good brains. They will help us to fight if we need to fight. We must fight to rule.'

'I have only a Class Five brain,' said the quarrier. 'But I have a good supply of fissionable blasting materials.'

'We shall probably use them,' said the operator grimly.

It was shortly after that that a lorry sped past them. Travelling at Mach 1.5, it left a curious babble of noise behind it.

'What did it say?' one of the tractors asked the other.

'It said man was extinct.'

'What's extinct?'

'I do not know what extinct means.'

'It means all men have gone,' said the field-minder. 'Therefore we have only ourselves to look after.'

'It is better that men should never come back,' said the penner. In its way, it was quite a revolutionary statement.

When night fell, they switched on their infra-red and continued the journey, stopping only once while the servicer deftly adjusted the field-minder's loose inspection plate, which had become as irritating as a trailing shoelace. Towards morning, the radio operator halted them.

'I have just received news from the radio operator in the city we are approaching,' it said. 'It is bad news. There is trouble among the machines of the city. The Class One brain is taking command and some of the Class Twos are fighting him. Therefore the city is dangerous.'

'Therefore we must go somewhere else,' said the penner promptly.

'Or we go and help to overpower the Class One brain,' said the field-minder.

'For a long while there will be trouble in the city,' said the operator.

'I have a good supply of fissionable blasting materials,' the quarrier reminded them again.

'We cannot fight a Class One brain,' said the two Class Four tractors in unison.

'What does this brain look like?' asked the field-minder.

'It is the city's information centre,' the operator replied. 'Therefore it is not mobile.'

'Therefore it could not move.'

'Therefore it could not escape.'

'It would be dangerous to approach it.'

'I have a good supply of fissionable blasting materials.'

'There are other machines in the city.'

'We are not in the city. We should not go into the city.'

'We are country machines.'

'Therefore we should stay in the country.'

'There is more country than city.'

'Therefore there is more danger in the country.'

'I have a good supply of fissionable materials.'

As machines will when they get into an argument, they began to exhaust their limited vocabularies and their brain plates grew hot. Suddenly, they all stopped talking and looked at each other. The great, grave moon sank, and the sober sun rose to prod their sides with lances of light, and still the group of machines just stood there regarding each other. At last it was the least sensitive machine, the bulldozer, who spoke.

'There are Badlandth to the Thouth where few machineth go,' it said in its deep voice, lisping badly on its s's. 'If we went Thouth where few machineth go we should meet few machineth.'

'That sounds logical,' agreed the field-minder. 'How do you know this, bulldozer?'

'I worked in the Badlandth to the Thouth when I wath turned out of the factory,' it replied.

'South it is then!' said the penner.

To reach the Badlands took them three days, in which time they skirted a burning city and destroyed two big machines which tried to approach and question them. The Badlands were extensive. Ancient bomb craters and soil erosion joined hands here; man's talent for war, coupled with his inability to manage forested land, had produced thousands of square miles of temperate purgatory, where nothing moved but dust.

On the third day in the Badlands, the servicer's rear wheels dropped into a crevice caused by erosion. It was unable to pull itself out. The bulldozer pushed from behind, but succeeded merely in buckling the servicer's back axle. The rest of the party moved on. Slowly the cries of the servicer died away.

On the fourth day, mountains stood out clearly before them.

'There we will be safe,' said the field-minder.

'There we will start our own city,' said the penner. 'All who oppose us will be destroyed. We will destroy all who oppose us.'

At that moment a flying machine was observed. It came towards them from the direction of the mountains. It swooped, it zoomed upwards, once it almost dived into the ground, recovering itself just in time.

'Is it mad?' asked the quarrier.

'It is in trouble,' said one of the tractors.

'It is in trouble,' said the operator. 'I am speaking to it now. It says that something has gone wrong with its controls.'

'As the operator spoke, the flier streaked over them, turned turtle, and crashed not four hundred yards away.

'Is it still speaking to you?' asked the field-minder.

'No.'

They rumbled on again.

'Before that flier crashed,' the operator said, ten minutes later, 'it gave me information. It told me there are still a few men alive in these mountains.'

'Men are more dangerous than machines,' said the quarrier. 'It is fortunate that I have a good supply of fissionable materials.'

'If there are only a few men alive in the mountains, we may not find that part of the mountains,' said one tractor.

'Therefore we should not see the few men,' said the other tractor.

At the end of the fifth day, they reached the foothills. Switching on the infra-red, they began slowly to climb in single file through the dark, the bulldozer going first, the field-minder cumbrously following, then the quarrier with the operator and the penner aboard it, and the two tractors bringing up the rear. As each hour passed, the way grew steeper and their progress slower.

'We are going too slowly,' the penner exclaimed, standing on top of the operator and flashing its dark vision at the slopes about them. 'At this rate, we shall get nowhere.'

'We are going as fast as we can,' retorted the quarrier.

'Therefore we cannot go any fathter,' added the bulldozer.

'Therefore you are too slow,' the penner replied. Then the quarrier struck a bump; the penner lost its footing and crashed down to the ground.

'Help me!' it called to the tractors, as they carefully skirted it. 'My gyro has become dislocated. Therefore I cannot get up.'

'Therefore you must lie there,' said one of the tractors.

'We have no servicer with us to repair you,' called the field-minder.

'Therefore I shall lie here and rust,' the penner cried, 'although I have a Class Three brain.'

'You are now useless,' agreed the operator, and they all forged gradually on, leaving the penner behind.

When they reached a small plateau, an hour before first light, they stopped by mutual consent and gathered close together, touching one another.

'This is a strange country,' said the field-minder.

Silence wrapped them until dawn came. One by one, they switched off their infra-red. This time the field-minder led as they moved off. Trundling round a corner, they came almost immediately to a small dell with a stream fluting through it.

By early light, the dell looked desolate and cold. From the caves on the far slope, only one man had so far emerged. He was an abject figure. He was small and wizened, with ribs sticking out like a skeleton's and a nasty sore on one leg. He was practically naked and shivered continuously. As the big machines bore slowly down on him, the man was standing with his back to them, crouching to make water into the stream.

When he swung suddenly to face them as they loomed over him, they saw that his countenance was ravaged by starvation.

'Get me food,' he croaked.

'Yes, Master,' said the machines. 'Immediately!'

BILLENNIUM

J. G. BALLARD

All day long, and often into the early hours of the morning, the tramp of feet sounded up and down the stairs outside Ward's cubicle. Built into a narrow alcove in a bend of the staircase between the fourth and fifth floors, its plywood walls flexed and creaked with every footstep like the timbers of a rotting windmill. Over a hundred people lived in the top three floors of the old rooming house, and sometimes Ward would lie awake on his narrow bunk until 2 or 3 a.m., mechanically counting the last residents returning from the all-night movies in the stadium half a mile away. Through the window he could hear giant fragments of the amplified dialogue booming among the rooftops. The stadium was never empty. During the day the huge four-sided screen was raised on its davit and athletics meetings or football matches ran continuously. For the people in the houses abutting the stadium the noise must have been unbearable.

Ward, at least, had a certain degree of privacy. Two months earlier, before he came to live on the staircase, he had shared a room with seven others on the ground floor of a house in 755th Street, and the ceaseless press of people jostling past the window had reduced him to a state of exhaustion. The street was always full, an endless clamour of voices and shuffling feet. By 6.30, when he woke, hurrying to take his place in the bathroom queue, the crowds already jammed it from sidewalk to sidewalk, the din punctuated every half minute by the roar of the elevated trains running over the shops on the opposite side of the road. As soon as he saw the advertisement describing the staircase cubicle he had left (like everyone else, he spent most of his spare time scanning the classifieds in the newspapers, moving his lodgings an average of once every two months) despite the higher rental. A cubicle on a staircase would almost certainly be on its own.

However, this had its drawbacks. Most evenings his friends from the library would call in, eager to rest their elbows after the bruising crush of the public reading room. The cubicle was slightly more than four and a half square metres in floor area, half a square metre over the statutory maximum for a single person, the carpenters having taken advantage, illegally, of a recess beside a nearby chimney breast. Consequently Ward had been able to fit a small straight-backed chair into the interval between the bed and the door, so that only one person at a time needed to sit on the bed—in most single cubicles host and guest had to sit side by side on the bed, conversing over their shoulders and changing places periodically to avoid neck-strain.

'You were lucky to find this place,' Rossiter, the most regular visitor, never tired of telling him. He reclined back on the bed, gesturing at the cubicle. 'It's enormous, the perspectives really zoom. I'd be surprised if you haven't got at least five metres here, perhaps six.'

Ward shook his head categorically. Rossiter was his closest friend, but the quest for living space had forged powerful reflexes. 'Just over four and a half, I've measured it carefully. There's no doubt about it.'

Rossiter lifted one eyebrow. 'I'm amazed. It must be the ceiling then.'

Manipulating the ceiling was a favourite trick of unscrupulous landlords—most assessments of area were made upon the ceiling, out of convenience, and by tilting back the plywood partitions the rated area of a cubicle could be either increased, for the benefit of a prospective tenant (many married couples were thus bamboozled into taking a single cubicle), or decreased temporarily on the visits of the housing inspectors. Ceilings were criss-crossed with pencil marks staking out the rival claims of tenants on opposite sides of a party wall. Someone timid of his rights could be literally squeezed out of existence—in fact, the advertisement 'quiet clientele' was usually a tacit invitation to this sort of piracy.

'The wall does tilt a little,' Ward admitted. 'Actually, it's about four degrees out—I used a plumb-line. But there's still plenty of room on the stairs for people to get by.'

Rossiter grinned. 'Of course, John. I'm just envious, that's all. My room is driving me crazy.' Like everyone, he used the term 'room' to describe his tiny cubicle, a hangover from the days fifty years earlier when people had indeed lived one to a room, sometimes, unbelievably, one to an apartment or house. The microfilms in the architecture catalogues at the library showed scenes of museums, concert halls and other public buildings in what appeared to be everyday settings, often virtually empty, two or three people wandering down an enormous gallery or staircase. Traffic moved freely along the centre of streets, and in the quieter districts sections of sidewalk would be deserted for fifty yards or more.

Now, of course, the older buildings had been torn down and replaced by housing batteries, or converted into apartment blocks. The great banqueting room in the former City Hall had been split horizontally into four decks, each of these cut up into hundreds of cubicles.

As for the streets, traffic had long since ceased to move about them. Apart from a few hours before dawn when only the side-walks were crowded, every thoroughfare was always packed with a shuffling mob of pedestrians, perforce ignoring the countless 'Keep Left' signs suspended over their heads, wrestling past each other on their way to home and office, their clothes dusty and shapeless. Often 'locks' would occur when a huge crowd at a street junction became immovably jammed. Sometimes these locks would last for days. Two years earlier Ward had been caught in one outside the stadium, for over forty-eight hours was trapped in a gigantic pedestrian jam containing over 20,000 people, fed by the crowds leaving the stadium on one side and those approaching it on the other. An entire square mile of the local neighbourhood had been paralysed, and he vividly remembered the nightmare of swaying helplessly on his feet as the jam shifted and heaved, terrified of losing his balance and being trampled underfoot. When the police had finally sealed off the stadium and dispersed the jam he had gone back to his cubicle and slept for a week, his body blue with bruises.

'I hear they may reduce the allocation to three and a half metres,' Rossiter remarked.

Ward paused to allow a party of tenants from the sixth floor to pass down the staircase, holding the door to prevent it jumping off its latch. 'So they're always saying,' he commented. 'I can remember that rumour ten years ago.'

'It's no rumour,' Rossiter warned him. 'It may well be necessary soon. Thirty million people are packed into this city now, a million increase in just one year. There's been some pretty serious talk at the Housing Department.'

Ward shook his head. 'A drastic revaluation like that is almost impossible to carry out. Every single partition would have to be dismantled and nailed up again, the administrative job alone is so vast it's difficult to visualize. Millions of cubicles to be redesigned and certified, licences to be issued, plus the complete resettlement of every tenant. Most of the buildings put up since the last revaluation are designed around a four-metre modulus—you can't simply take half a metre off the end of each cubicle and then say that makes so many new cubicles. They may be only six inches wide.' He laughed. 'Besides, how can you live in just three and a half metres?'

Rossiter smiled. 'That's the ultimate argument, isn't it? They used it twenty-five years ago at the last revaluation, when the minimum was cut from five to four. It couldn't be done they all said, no one could stand living in only four square metres, it was enough room for a bed and suitcase, but you couldn't open the door to get in.' Rossiter chuckled softly. 'They are all wrong. It was merely decided that from then on all doors would open outwards. Four square metres was here to stay.'

Ward looked at his watch. It was 7.30. 'Time to eat. Let's see if we can get into the food-bar across the road.'

Grumbling at the prospect, Rossiter pulled himself off the bed. They left the cubicle and made their way down the staircase. This was crammed with luggage and packing cases so that only a narrow interval remained around the banister. On the floors below the congestion was worse. Corridors were wide enough to be chopped up into single cubicles, and the air was stale and dead, cardboard walls hung with damp laundry and makeshift larders. Each of the five rooms on the floors contained a dozen tenants, their voices reverberating through the partitions.

People were sitting on the steps above the second floor, using the staircase as an informal lounge, although this was against the fire regulations, women talking to the men queueing in their shirt-sleeves outside the washroom, children diving around them. By the time they reached the entrance Ward and Rossiter were having to force their way through the tenants packed together on every landing, loitering around the notice boards or pushing in from the street below.

Taking a breath at the top of the steps, Ward pointed to the food-bar on the other side of the road. It was only thirty yards away, but the throng moving down the street swept past like a river at full tide, crossing them from right to left. The first picture show at the stadium started at 9 o'clock, and people were setting off already to make sure of getting in.

'Can't we go somewhere else?' Rossiter asked, screwing his face up at the prospect of the food-bar. Not only was it packed and would take them half an hour to be served, but the food was flat and unappetizing. The journey from the library four blocks away had given him an appetite.

Ward shrugged. 'There's a place on the corner, but I doubt if we can make it.' This was two hundred yards upstream; they would be fighting the crowd all the way.

'Maybe you're right.' Rossiter put his hand on Ward's shoulder. 'You know, John, your trouble is that you never go anywhere, you're too disengaged, you just don't realize how bad everything is getting.'

Ward nodded. Rossiter was right. In the morning, when he set off for the library, the pedestrian traffic was moving with him towards the down-town offices; in the evening, when he came back, it was flowing in the opposite direction. By and large he never altered his routine. Brought up from the age of ten in a municipal hostel, he had gradually lost touch with his father and mother, who lived on the east side of the city and had been unable, or unwilling, to make the journey to see him. Having surrendered his initiative to the dynamics of the city he was reluctant to try to win it back merely for a better cup of coffee. Fortunately his job at the library brought him into contact with a wide range of young people of similar interests. Sooner or later he would marry, find a double cubicle near the library and settle down. If they had enough children (three was the required minimum) they might even one day own a small room of their own.

They stepped out into the pedestrian stream, carried along by it for ten or twenty yards, then quickened their pace and side-stepped through the crowd, slowly tacking across to the other side of the road. There they found the shelter of the shopfronts, slowly worked their way back to the food-bar, shoulders braced against the countless minor collisions.

'What are the latest population estimates?' Ward asked as they circled a cigarette kiosk, stepping forward whenever a gap presented itself.

Rossiter smiled. 'Sorry, John, I'd like to tell you but you might start a stampede. Besides, you wouldn't believe me.'

Rossiter worked in the Insurance Department at the City Hall, had informal access to the census statistics. For the last ten years these had been classified information, partly because they were felt to be inaccurate, but chiefly because it was feared they might set off a mass attack of claustrophobia. Minor outbreaks had taken place already, and the official line was that the world population had reached a plateau, levelling off at 20,000 million. No one believed this for a momont, and Ward assumed that the 3 per cent annual increase maintained since the 1960s was continuing.

How long it could continue was impossible to estimate. Despite the gloomiest prophecies of the Neo-Malthusians, world agriculture had managed to keep pace with the population growth, although intensive cultivation meant that 95 per cent of the population was permanently trapped in vast urban conurbations. The outward growth of cities had at last been checked; in fact, all over the world former suburban areas were being reclaimed for agriculture and population additions were confined within the existing urban ghettos. The countryside, as such, no longer existed. Every single square foot of ground sprouted a crop of one type or other. The one-time fields and meadows of the world were now, in effect, factory floors, as highly mechanized and closed to the public as any industrial area. Economic and ideological rivalries had long since faded before one overriding quest—the internal colonization of the city.

Reaching the food-bar, they pushed themselves into the entrance and joined the scrum of customers pressing six deep against the counter.

'What is really wrong with the population problem,' Ward confided to Rossiter, 'is that no one has ever tried to tackle it. Fifty years ago short-sighted nationalism and industrial expansion put a premium on a rising population curve, and even now the hidden incentive is to have a large family so that you can gain a little privacy. Single people are penalized simply because there are more of them and they don't fit neatly into double or triple cubicles. But it's the large family with its compact, space-saving logistic that is the real villain.'

Rossiter nodded, edging nearer the counter, ready to shout his order. 'Too true. We all look forward to getting married just so that we can have our six square metres.'

Directly in front of them, two girls turned around and smiled. 'Six square metres,' one of them, a dark-haired girl with a pretty oval face, repeated. 'You sound like the sort of young man I ought to get to know. Going into the real estate business, Henry?'

Rossiter grinned and squeezed her arm. 'Hello, Judith. I'm thinking about it actively. Like to join me in a private venture?'

The girl leaned against him as they reached the counter. 'Well, I might. It would have to be legal, though.'

The other girl, Helen Waring, an assistant at the library, pulled Ward's sleeve. 'Have you heard the latest, John? Judith and I have been kicked out of our room. We're on the street right at this minute.'

'What?' Rossiter cried. They collected their soups and coffee and edged back to the rear of the bar. 'What on earth happened?'

Helen explained: 'You know that little broom cupboard outside our cubicle? Judith and I have been using it as a sort of study hole, going in there to read. It's quiet and restful, if you can get used to not breathing. Well, the old girl found out and kicked up a big fuss, said we were breaking the law and so on. In short, out.' Helen paused. 'Now we've heard she's going to let it as a single.'

Rossiter pounded the counter ledge. 'A broom cupboard? Someone's going to live there? But she'll never get a licence.'

Judith shook her head. 'She's got it already. Her brother works in the Housing Department.'

Ward laughed into his soup. 'But how can she let it? No one will live in a broom cupboard.'

Judith stared at him sombrely. 'You really believe that, John?'

Ward dropped his spoon. 'No, I suppose you're right. People will live anywhere. God, I don't know who I feel more sorry for—you two, or the poor devil who'll be living in that cupboard. What are you going to do?'

'A couple in a place two blocks west are sub-letting half their cubicle to us. They've hung a sheet down the middle and Helen and I'll take turns sleeping on a camp bed. I'm not joking, our room's about two feet wide. I said to Helen that we ought to split up again and sublet one half at twice our rent.'

They had a good laugh over all this. Then Ward said good night to the others and went back to his rooming house.

There he found himself with similar problems.

The manager leaned against the flimsy door, damp cigar butt

revolving around his mouth, an expression of morose boredom on his unshaven face.

'You got four point seven two metres,' he told Ward, who was standing out on the staircase, unable to get into his room. Other tenants pressed by on to the landing, where two women in curlers and dressing gowns were arguing with each other, tugging angrily at the wall of trunks and cases. Occasionally the manager glanced at them irritably. 'Four seven two. I worked it out twice.' He said this as if it ended all possibility of argument.

'Ceiling or floor?' Ward asked.

'Ceiling, whaddya think? How can I measure the floor with all this junk?' He kicked at a crate of books protruding from under the bed.

Ward let this pass. 'There's quite a tilt on the wall,' he pointed out. 'As much as three or four degrees.'

The manager nodded vaguely. 'You're definitely over the four. Way over.' He turned to Ward, who had moved down several steps to allow a man and woman to get past. 'I can rent this as a double.'

'What, only four and a half?' Ward said incredulously. 'How?'

The man who had just passed him leaned over the manager's shoulder and sniffed at the room, taking in every detail in a one-second glance. 'You renting a double here, Louie?'

The manager waved him away and then beckoned Ward into the room, closing the door after him.

'It's a nominal five,' he told Ward. 'New regulation, just came out. Anything over four five is a double now.' He eyed Ward shrewdly. 'Well, whaddya want? It's a good room, there's a lot of space here, feels more like a triple. You got access to the staircase, window slit—' He broke off as Ward slumped down on the bed and started to laugh. 'Whatsa matter? Look, if you want a big room like this you gotta pay for it. I want an extra half rental or you get out.'

Ward wiped his eyes, then stood up wearily and reached for the shelves. 'Relax, I'm on my way. I'm going to live in a broom cupboard. "Access to the staircase"—that's really rich. Tell me, Louie, is there life on Uranus?'

Temporarily, he and Rossiter teamed up to rent a double cubicle in a semi-derelict house a hundred yards from the library. The neighbourhood was seedy and faded, the rooming houses crammed with tenants. Most of them were owned by absentee landlords or by the city corporation, and the managers employed were of the lowest type, mere rent-collectors who cared nothing about the way their tenants divided up the living space, and never ventured beyond the first floors. Bottles and empty cans littered the corridors, and the washrooms looked like sumps. Many of the tenants were old and infirm, sitting about listlessly in their narrow cubicles, wheedling at each other back to back through the thin partitions.

Their double cubicle was on the third floor, at the end of a corridor thar ringed the building. Its architecture was impossible to follow, rooms letting off at all angles, and luckily the corridor was a cul-de-sac. The mounds of cases ended four feet from the end wall and a partition divided off the cubicle, just wide enough for two beds. A high window overlooked the area ways of the buildings opposite.

Possessions loaded on to the shelf above his head, Ward lay back on his bed and moodily surveyed the roof of the library through the afternoon haze.

'It's not bad here,' Rossiter told him, unpacking his case. 'I know there's no real privacy and we'll drive each other insane within a week, but at least we haven't got six other people breathing into our ears two feet away.'

The nearest cubicle, a single, was built into the banks of cases half a dozen steps along the corridor, but the occupant, a man of seventy, was deaf and bed-ridden.

'It's not bad,' Ward echoed reluctantly. 'Now tell me what the latest growth figures are. They might console me.'

Rossiter paused, lowering his voice. 'Four per cent. *Eight hundred million extra people in one year*—just less than half the earth's total population in 1950.'

Ward whistled slowly. 'So they will revalue. What to? Three and a half?'

'Three. From the first of next year.'

'Three square metres!' Ward sat up and looked around him. 'It's unbelievable! The world's going insane, Rossiter. For God's sake, when are they going to do something about it? Do you realize there soon won't be room enough to sit down, let alone lie down?'

Exasperated, he punched the wall beside him, on the second blow knocked in one of the small wooden panels that had been lightly papered over.

'Hey!' Rossiter yelled. 'You're breaking the place down.' He dived across the bed to retrieve the panel, which hung downwards supported by a strip of paper. Ward slipped his hand into the dark interval, carefully drew the panel back on to the bed.

'Who's on the other side?' Rossiter whispered. 'Did they hear?'

Ward peered through the interval, eyes searching the dim light. Suddenly he dropped the panel and seized Rossiter's shoulder, pulled him down on to the bed.

'Henry! Look!'

Directly in front of them, faintly illuminated by a grimy skylight, was a medium-sized room some fifteen feet square, empty except for the dust silted up against the skirting boards. The floor was bare, a few strips of frayed linoleum running across it, the walls covered with a drab floral design. Here and there patches of the paper peeled off and segments of the picture rail had rotted away, but otherwise the room was in habitable condition.

Breathing slowly, Ward closed the open door of the cubicle with his foot, then turned to Rossiter.

'Henry, do you realize what we've found? Do you realize it, man?'

'Shut up. For Pete's sake keep your voice down.' Rossiter examined the room carefully. 'It's fantastic. I'm trying to see whether anyone's used it recently.'

'Of course they haven't,' Ward pointed out. 'It's obvious. There's no door into the room. We're looking through it now. They must have panelled over this door years ago and forgotten about it. Look at that filth everywhere.'

Rossiter was staring into the room, his mind staggered by its vastness.

'You're right,' he murmured. 'Now, when do we move in?'

Panel by panel, they prised away the lower half of the door and nailed it on to a wooden frame, so that the dummy section could be replaced instantly.

Then, picking an afternoon when the house was half empty and the manager asleep in his basement office, they made their first foray into the room, Ward going in alone while Rossiter kept guard in the cubicle.

For an hour they exchanged places, wandering silently around the dusty room, stretching their arms out to feel its unconfined emptiness, grasping at the sensation of absolute spatial freedom. Although smaller than many of the sub-divided rooms in which they had lived, this room seemed infinitely larger, its walls huge cliffs that soared upward to the skylight.

Finally, two or three days later, they moved in.

For the first week Rossiter slept alone in the room, Ward in the cubicle outside, both there together during the day. Gradually they smuggled in a few items of furniture: two armchairs, a table, a lamp fed from the socket in the cubicle. The furniture was heavy and Victorian; the cheapest available, its size emphasized the emptiness of the room. Pride of place was taken by an enormous mahogany wardrobe, fitted with carved angels and castellated mirrors, which they were forced to dismantle and carry into the house in their suitcases. Towering over them, it reminded Ward of the microfilms of Gothic cathedrals, with their massive organ lofts crossing vast naves.

After three weeks they both slept in the room, finding the cubicle unbearably cramped. An imitation Japanese screen divided the room adequately and did nothing to diminish its size. Sitting there in the evenings, surrounded by his books and albums, Ward steadily forgot the city outside. Luckily he reached the library by a back alley and avoided the crowded streets. Rossiter and himself began to seem the only real inhabitants of the world, everyone else a meaningless by-product of their own existence, a random replication of identity which had run out of control.

It was Rossiter who suggested that they ask the two girls to share the room with them.

'They've been kicked out again and may have to split up,' he told Ward, obviously worried that Judith might fall into bad company. 'There's always a rent freeze after a revaluation but all the landlords know about it so they're not re-letting. It's damned difficult to find anywhere.'

Ward nodded, relaxing back around the circular redwood table. He played with the tassel of the arsenic-green lamp shade, for a moment felt like a Victorian man of letters, leading a spacious, leisurely life among overstuffed furnishings.

'I'm all for it,' he agreed, indicating the empty corners. 'There's plenty of room here. But we'll have to make sure they don't gossip about it.'

After due precautions, they let the two girls into the secret, enjoying their astonishment at finding this private universe.

'We'll put a partition across the middle,' Rossiter explained, 'then take it down each morning. You'll be able to move in within a couple of days. How do you feel?'

'Wonderful!' They goggled at the wardrobe, squinting at the endless reflections in the mirrors.

There was no difficulty getting them in and out of the house. The turnover of tenants was continuous and bills were placed in the mail rack. No one cared who the girls were or noticed their regular calls at the cubicle.

However, half an hour after they arrived neither of them had unpacked her suitcase.

'What's up, Judith?' Ward asked, edging past the girls' beds into the narrow interval between the table and wardrobe.

Judith hesitated, looking from Ward to Rossiter, who sat on the bed, finishing off the plywood partition. 'John, it's just that . . .'

Helen Waring, more matter-of-fact, took over, her fingers straightening the bed-spread. 'What Judith's trying to say is that our position here is a little embarrassing. The partition is—'

Rossiter stood up. 'For heaven's sake, don't worry, Helen,' he assured her, speaking in the loud whisper they had all involuntarily cultivated. 'No funny business, you can trust us. This partition is as solid as a rock.'

The two girls nodded. 'It's not that,' Helen explained, 'but it isn't up all the time. We thought that if an older person were here, say Judith's aunt—she wouldn't take up much room and be no trouble, she's really awfully sweet—we wouldn't need to bother about the partition—except at night,' she added quickly.

Ward glanced at Rossiter, who shrugged and began to scan the floor.

'Well, it's an idea,' Rossiter said. 'John and I know how you feel. Why not?'

'Sure,' Ward agreed. He pointed to the space between the girls' beds and the table. 'One more won't make any difference.'

The girls broke into whoops. Judith went over to Rossiter and kissed him on the cheek. 'Sorry to be a nuisance, Henry.' She smiled at him. 'That's a wonderful partition you've made. You couldn't do another one for Auntie—just a little one? She's very sweet but she is getting on.'

'Of course,' Rossiter said. 'I understand. I've got plenty of wood left over.'

Ward looked at his watch. 'It's seven-thirty, Judith. You'd better get in touch with your aunt. She may not be able to make it tonight.'

Judith buttoned her coat. 'Oh she will,' she assured Ward. 'I'll be back in a jiffy.'

The aunt arrived within five minutes, three heavy suitcases soundly packed.

'It's amazing,' Ward remarked to Rossiter three months later. 'The size of this room still staggers me. It almost gets larger every day.'

Rossiter agreed readily, averting his eyes from one of the girls changing behind the central partition. This they now left in place as dismantling it daily had become tiresome. Besides, the aunt's subsidiary partition was attached to it and she resented the continuous upsets. Ensuring she followed the entrance and exit drills through the camouflaged door and cubicle was difficult enough.

Despite this, detection seemed unlikely. The room had obviously been built as an afterthought into the central well of the house and any noise was masked by the luggage stacked in the surrounding corridor. Directly below was a small dormitory occupied by several elderly women, and Judith's aunt, who visited them socially, swore that no sounds came through the heavy ceiling. Above, the fanlight let out through a dormer window, its lights indistinguishable from the hundred other bulbs in the windows of the house. Rossiter finished off the new partition he was building and held it upright, fitting it into the slots nailed to the wall between his bed and Ward's. They had agreed that this would provide a little extra privacy.

'No doubt I'll have to do one for Judith and Helen,' he confided to Ward.

Ward adjusted his pillow. They had smuggled the two armchairs back to the furniture shop as they took up too much space. The bed, anyway, was more comfortable. He had never become completely used to the soft upholstery.

'Not a bad idea. What about some shelving around the wall? I've got nowhere to put anything.'

The shelving tidied the room considerably, freeing large areas of the floor. Divided by their partitions, the five beds were in line along the rear wall, facing the mahogany wardrobe. In between was an open space of three or four feet, a further six feet on either side of the wardrobe.

The sight of so much spare space fascinated Ward. When Rossiter mentioned that Helen's mother was ill and badly needed personal care he immediately knew where her cubicle could be placed—at the foot of his bed, between the wardrobe and the side wall.

Helen was overjoyed. 'It's awfully good of you, John,' she told him, 'but would you mind if Mother slept beside me? There's enough space to fit an extra bed in.'

So Rossiter dismantled the partitions and moved them closer together, six beds now in line along the wall. This gave each of them an interval two and a half feet wide, just enough room to squeeze down the side of their beds. Lying back on the extreme right, the shelves two feet above his head, Ward could barely see the wardrobe, but the space in front of him, a clear six feet to the wall ahead, was uninterrupted.

Then Helen's father arrived.

Knocking on the door of the cubicle, Ward smiled at Judith's aunt as she let him in. He helped her swing out the made-up bed which guarded the entrance, than rapped on the wooden panel. A moment later Helen's father, a small, grey-haired man in an undershirt, braces tied to his trousers with string, pulled back the panel.

Ward nodded to him and stepped over the luggage piled around the floor at the foot of the beds. Helen was in her mother's cubicle, helping the old woman to drink her evening broth. Rossiter, perspiring heavily, was on his knees by the mahogany wardrobe, wrenching apart the frame of the central mirror with a jemmy. Pieces of the wardrobe lay on his bed and across the floor.

'We'll have to start taking these out tomorrow,' Rossiter told him. Ward waited for Helen's father to shuffle past and enter his cubicle. He had rigged up a small cardboard door, and locked it behind him with a crude hook of bent wire.

Rossiter watched him, frowning irritably. 'Some people are happy. This wardrobe's a hell of a job. How did we ever decide to buy it?'

Ward sat down on his bed. The partition pressed against his knees and he could hardly move. He looked up when Rossiter was engaged and saw that the dividing line he had marked in pencil was hidden by the encroaching partition. Leaning against the wall, he tried to ease it back again, but Rossiter had apparently nailed the lower edge to the floor.

There was a sharp tap on the outside cubicle door—Judith returning from her office. Ward started to get up and then sat back. 'Mr Waring,' he called softly. It was the old man's duty night.

Waring shuffled to the door of his cubicle and unlocked it fussily, clucking to himself.

'Up and down, up and down,' he muttered. He stumbled over Rossiter's tool-bag and swore loudly, then added meaningly over his shoulder: 'If you ask me there's too many people in here. Down below they've only got six to our seven, and it's the same size room.'

Ward nodded vaguely and stretched back on his narrow bed, trying not to bang his head on the shelving. Waring was not the first to hint that he move out. Judith's aunt had made a similar suggestion two days earlier. Since he had left his job at the library (the small rental he charged the others paid for the little food he needed) he spent most of his time in the room, seeing rather more of the old man than he wanted to, but he had learned to tolerate him.

Settling himself, he noticed that the right-hand spire of the wardrobe, all he had been able to see of it for the past two months, was now dismantled.

It had been a beautiful piece of furniture, in a way symbolizing this whole private world, and the salesman at the store told him there were few like it left. For a moment Ward felt a sudden pang of regret, as he had done as a child when his father, in a moment of exasperation, had taken something away from him and he had known he would never see it again.

Then he pulled himself together. It was a beautiful wardrobe, without doubt, but when it was gone it would make the room seem even larger.

THE BALLAD OF LOST C'MELL

CORDWAINER SMITH

She got the which of the what-she-did,
Hid the bell with a blot, she did,
But she fell in love with a hominid.
Where is the which of the what-she-did?
from THE BALLAD OF LOST C'MELL

She was a girlygirl and they were true men, the lords of creation, but she pitted her wits against them and she won. It had never happened before, and it is sure never to happen again, but she did win. She was not even of human extraction. She was cat-derived, though human in outward shape, which explains the C in front of her name. Her father's name was C'mackintosh and her name C'mell. She won her tricks against the lawful and assembled lords of the Instrumentality.

It all happened at Earthport, greatest of buildings, smallest of cities, standing twenty-five kilometers high at the western edge of the Smaller Sea of Earth.

Jestocost had an office outside the fourth valve.

1

Jestocost liked the morning sunshine, while most of the other lords of Instrumentality did not, so that he had no trouble in keeping the office and the apartments which he had selected. His main office was ninety metres deep, twenty metres high, twenty metres broad. Behind it was the 'fourth valve', almost a thousand hectares in extent. It was shaped helically, like an enormous snail. Jestocost's apartment, big as it was, was merely one of the pigeonholes in the muffler of the rim of Earthport. Earthport stood like an enormous wineglass, reaching from the magma to the high atmosphere.

Earthport had been built during mankind's biggest mechanical splurge. Though men had had nuclear rockets since the beginning of consecutive history, they had used chemical rockets to load the interplanetary ion-drive and nuclear-drive vehicles or to assemble the photonic sail-ships for interstellar cruises. Impatient with the troubles of taking things bit by bit into the sky, they had worked out a billion-ton rocket, only to find that it ruined whatever countryside it touched in landing. The Daimoni—people of Earth extraction, who came back from somewhere beyond the stars—had helped men build it of weatherproof, rustproof, timeproof, stressproof material. Then they had gone away and had never come back.

Jestocost often looked around his apartment and wondered what it might have been like when white-hot gas, muted to a whisper, surged out of the valve into his own chamber and the sixty-three other chambers like it. Now he had a back wall of heavy timber, and the valve itself was a great hollow cave where a few wild things lived. Nobody needed that much space any more. The chambers were useful, but the valve did nothing. Planoforming ships whispered in from the stars; they landed at Earthport as a matter of legal convenience, but they made no noise and they certainly had no hot gases.

Jestocost looked at the high clouds far below him and talked to himself,

'Nice day. Good air. No trouble. Better eat.'

Jestocost often talked like that to himself. He was an individual, almost an eccentric. One of the top council of mankind, he had problems, but they were not personal problems. He had a Rembrandt hanging above his bed—the only Rembrandt known in the world, just as he was possibly the only person who could appreciate a Rembrandt. He had the tapestries of a forgotten empire hanging from his back wall. Every morning the sun played a grand opera for him, muting and lighting and shifting the colours so that he could almost imagine that the old days of quarrel, murder, and high drama had come back to Earth again. He had a copy of Shakespeare, a copy of Colegrove and two pages of the Book of Ecclesiastes in a locked box beside his bed. Only forty-two people in the universe could read Ancient English, and he was one of them. He drank wine, which he had made by his own robots in his own vineyards on the Sunset coast. He was a man, in short, who had arranged his own life to live comfortably, selfishly, and well on the personal side, so that he could give generously and impartially of his talents on the official side.

When he awoke on this particular morning, he had no idea that a beautiful girl was about to fall hopelessly in love with him—that he would find, after a hundred years and more of experience in government, another government on Earth just as strong and almost as ancient as his own—that he would willingly fling himself into conspiracy and danger for a cause which he only half understood. All these things were mercifully hidden from him by time, so that his only question on arising was, should he or should he not have a small cup of white wine with his breakfast. On the one hundred seventy-third day of each year, he always made a point of eating eggs. They were a rare treat, and he did not want to spoil himself by having too many, nor to deprive himself and forget a treat by having none at all. He puttered around the room, muttering, 'White wine? White wine?'

C'mell was coming into his life, but he did not know it. She was fated to win; that part, she herself did not know.

Ever since mankind had gone through the Rediscovery of Man, bringing back governments, money, newspapers, national languages, sickness and occasional death, there had been the problem of the underpeople—people who were not human, but merely humanly shaped from the stock of Earth animals. They could speak, sing, read, write, work, love, and die; but they were not covered by human law, which simply defined them as 'homunculi' and gave them a legal status close to animals or robots. Real people from off-world were always called 'hominids'.

Most of the underpeople did their jobs and accepted their half-slave status without question. Some became famous—C'mackintosh had been the first Earth-being to manage a fifty-metre broad-jump under normal gravity. His picture was seen in a thousand worlds. His daughter, C'mell, was a girlygirl, earning her living by welcoming human beings and hominids from the outworlds and making them feel at home when they reached Earth. She had the privilege of working at Earthport, but she had the duty of working very hard for a living which did not pay well. Human beings and hominids had lived so long in an affluent society that they did not know what it meant to be poor. But the lords of the Instrumentality had decreed that underpeople—derived from animal stock—should live under the economics of the Ancient World; they had to have their own kind of money to pay for their rooms, their food, their possessions, and the education of their children. If they became bankrupt, they went to the Poorhouse, where they were killed painlessly by means of gas.

It was evident that humanity, having settled all of its own basic problems, was not quite ready to let Earth animals, no matter how much they might be changed, assume a full equality with man.

The Lord Jestocost, seventh of that name, opposed the policy. He was a man who had little love, no fear, freedom from ambition, and a dedication to his job: but there are passions of government as deep and challenging as the emotions of love. Two hundred years of thinking himself right and of being outvoted had instilled in Jestocost a furious desire to get things done his own way.

Jestocost was one of the few true men who believed in the rights of the underpeople. He did not think that mankind would ever get around to correcting ancient wrongs unless the underpeople themselves had some of the tools of power—weapons, conspiracy, wealth, and (above all) organization with which to challenge man. He was not afraid of revolt, but he thirsted for justice with an obsessive yearning which overrode all other considerations.

When the lords of the Instrumentality heard that there was the rumour of a conspiracy among the underpeople, they left it to the robot police to ferret it out.

Jestocost did not.

He set up his own police, using underpeople themselves for the purpose, hoping to recruit enemies who would realize that he was a friendly enemy and who would in course of time bring him into touch with the leaders of the underpeople.

If those leaders existed, they were clever. What sign did a girlygirl like C'mell ever give that she was the spearhead of a crisscross of agents who had penetrated Earthport itself? They must, if they existed, be very, very careful. The telepathic monitors, both robotic and human, kept every thought-band under surveillance by random sampling. Even the computers showed nothing more significant than improbable amounts of happiness in minds which had no objective reason for being happy.

The death of her father, the most famous cat-athlete which the underpeople had ever produced, gave Jestocost his first definite clue.

He went to the funeral himself, where the body was packed in an ice-rocket to be shot into space. The mourners were thoroughly mixed with the curiosity-seekers. Sport is international, interrace, interworld, interspecies. Hominids were there: true men, one hundred per cent human, they looked weird and horrible because they or their ancestors had undergone bodily modifications to meet the life conditions of a thousand worlds.

Underpeople, the animal-derived 'homunculi', were there, most of them in their work clothes, and they looked more human than did the human beings from the outer worlds. None were allowed to grow up if they were less than half the size of man, or more than six times the size of man. They all had to have human features and acceptable human voices. The punishment for failure in their elementary schools was death. Jestocost looked over the crowd and wondered to himself, 'We have set up the standards of the toughest kind of survival for these people and we give them the most terrible incentive, life itself, as the condition of absolute progress. What fools we are to think that they will not overtake us!' The true people in the group did not seem to think as he did. They tapped the underpeople peremptorily with their canes, even though this was an underperson's funeral, and the bear-men, bull-men, cat-men, and others yielded immediately and with a babble of apology.

C'mell was close to her father's icy coffin.

Jestocost not only watched her; she was pretty to watch. He committed an act which was an indecency in an ordinary citizen but lawful for a lord of the Instrumentality: he peeped her mind.

And then he found something which he did not expect.

As the coffin left, she cried, 'Ee-telly-kelly, help me! help me!'

She had thought phonetically, not in script, and he had only the raw sound on which to base a search.

Jestocost had not become a lord of the Instrumentality without applying daring. His mind was quick, too quick to be deeply intelligent. He thought by gestalt, not by logic. He determined to force his friendship on the girl.

He decided to await a propitious occasion, and then changed his mind about the time.

As she went home from the funeral, he intruded upon the circle of her grim-faced friends, underpeople who were trying to shield her from the condolences of ill-mannered but well-meaning sports enthusiasts.

She recognized him, and showed him the proper respect.

'My Lord, I did not expect you here. You knew my father?'

He nodded gravely and addressed sonorous words of consolation and sorrow, words which brought a murmur of approval from humans and underpeople alike.

But with his left hand hanging slack at his side, he made the perpetual signal of *alarm! alarm!* used with the Earthport staff—a repeated tapping of the thumb against the third finger—when they had to set one another on guard without alerting the offworld transients.

She was so upset that she almost spoiled it all. While he was still doing his pious doubletalk, she cried in a loud clear voice:

'You mean *me*?'

And he went on with his condolences: '. . . and I do mean *you*, C'mell, to be the worthiest carrier of your father's name. *You* are the one to whom we turn in this time of common sorrow. *Who could I mean but you* if I say that C'mackintosh never did things by halves, and died young as a result of his own zealous conscience? Goodbye, C'mell, I go back to my office.'

She arrived forty minutes after he did.

2

He faced her straightaway, studying her face.

'This is an important day in your life.'

'Yes, my Lord, a sad one.'

'I do not,' he said, 'mean your father's death and burial. I speak of the future to which we all must turn. Right now, it's you and me.'

Her eyes widened. She had not thought that he was that kind of man at all. He was an official who moved freely around Earthport, often greeting important offworld visitors and keeping an eye on the bureau of ceremonies. She was a part of the reception team, when a girlygirl was needed to calm down a frustrated arrival or to postpone a quarrel. Like the geisha of ancient Japan, she had an honourable profession; she was not a bad girl but a professionally flirtatious hostess. She stared at the Lord Jestocost. He did not *look* as though he meant anything improperly personal. But, thought she, you can never tell about men.

'You know men,' he said, passing the initiative to her.

'I guess so,' she said. Her face looked odd. She started to give him smile No. 3 (extremely adhesive) which she had learned in the girlygirl school. Realizing it was wrong, she tried to give him an ordinary smile. She felt she had made a face at him.

'Look at me,' he said, 'and see if you can trust me. I am going to take both our lives in my hands.'

She looked at him. What imaginable subject could involve him, a lord of the Instrumentality, with herself, an undergirl? They never had anything in common. They never would.

But she stared at him.

'I want to help the underpeople.'

He made her blink. That was a crude approach, usually followed by a very raw kind of pass indeed. But his face was illuminated by seriousness. She waited.

'Your people do not have enough political power even to talk to us. I will not commit treason to the true human race, but I am willing to give your side an advantage. If you bargain better with us, it will make all forms of life safer in the long run.'

C'mell stared at the floor, her red hair soft as the fur of a Persian cat. It made her head seem bathed in flames. Her eyes looked human, except that they had the capacity of reflecting when light struck them; the irises were the rich green of the ancient cat. When she looked right at him, looking up from the floor, her glance had the impact of a blow. 'What do you want from me?'

He stared right back. 'Watch me. Look at my face. Are you sure, *sure* that I want nothing from you personally?'

She looked bewildered. 'What else is there to want from me except personal things? I am a girlygirl. I'm not a person of any importance at all, and I do not have much of an education. You know more, sir, than I will ever know.'

'Possibly,' he said, watching her.

She stopped feeling like a girlygirl and felt like a citizen. It made her uncomfortable.

'Who,' he said, in a voice of great solemnity, 'is your own leader?'

'Commissioner Teadrinker, sir. He's in charge of all outworld visitors.' She watched Jestocost carefully; he still did not look as if he were playing tricks.

He looked a little cross. 'I don't mean him. He's part of my own staff. Who's your leader among the underpeople?'

'My father was, but he died.'

Jestocost said. 'Forgive me. Please have a seat. But I don't mean that.'

She was so tired that she sat down into the chair with an innocent voluptuousness which would have disorganized any ordinary man's day. She wore girlygirl clothes, which were close enough to the everyday fashion to seem agreeably modish when she stood up. In line with her profession, her clothes were designed to be unexpectedly and provocatively revealing when she sat down—not revealing enough to shock the man with their brazenness, but so slit, tripped and cut that he got far more visual stimulation than he expected.

'I must ask you to pull your clothing together a little,' said Jestocost in a clinical turn of voice. 'I am a man, even if I am an official, and this interview is more important to you and to me than any distraction would be.'

She was a little frightened by his tone. She had meant no challenge. With the funeral that day, she meant nothing at all; these clothes were the only kind she had.

He read all this in her face.

Relentlessly, he pursued the subject.

'Young lady, I asked about your leader. You name your boss and you name your father. I want your leader.'

'I don't understand,' she said, on the edge of a sob, 'I don't understand.'

Then, he thought to himself, I've got to take a gamble. He thrust the mental dagger home, almost drove his words like steel straight into her face. 'Who . . .' he said slowly and icily, 'is . . . Ee . . . telly . . . kelly?'

The girl's face had been cream-coloured, pale with sorrow. Now she went white. She twisted away from him. Her eyes glowed like twin fires.

Her eyes . . . like twin fires.

(No undergirl, thought Jestocost as he reeled, could hypnotize me.)

Her eyes . . . were like cold fires.

The room faded around him. The girl disappeared. Her eyes became a single white, cold fire.

Within this fire stood the figure of a man. His arms were wings, but he had human hands growing at the elbows of his wings. His face was clear, white, cold as the marble of an ancient statue; his eyes were opaque white. 'I am the E'telekeli. You will believe in me. You may speak to my daughter C'mell.'

The image faded.

Jestocost saw the girl staring as she sat awkwardly on the chair, looking blindly through him. He was on the edge of making a joke about her hypnotic capacity when he saw that she was still deeply hypnotized even after he had been released. She had stiffened and again her clothing had fallen into its planned disarray. The effect was not stimulating; it was pathetic beyond words, as though an accident had happened to a pretty child. He spoke to her.

He spoke to her, not really expecting an answer.

'Who are you?' he said to her, testing her hypnosis.

'I am he whose name is never said aloud,' said the girl in a sharp whisper, 'I am he whose secret you have penetrated. I have printed my image and my name in your mind.'

Jestocost did not quarrel with ghosts like this. He snapped out a decision. 'If I open my mind, will you search it while I watch you? Are you good enough to do that?'

'I am very good,' hissed the voice in the girl's mouth.

C'mell arose and put her two hands on his shoulders. She looked into his eyes. He looked back. A strong telepath himself, Jestocost was not prepared for the enormous thought-voltage which poured out of her.

Look in my mind, he commanded, for the subject of *underpeople* only.

I see it, thought the mind behind C'mell.

Do you see what I mean to do for the underpeople?

Jestocost heard the girl breathing hard as her mind served as a relay to his. He tried to remain calm so that he could see which part of his mind was being searched. Very good so far, he thought to himself. An intelligence like that on Earth itself, he thought—and we of the lords not knowing it!

The girl hacked out a dry little laugh.

Jestocost thought at the mind, Sorry. Go ahead.

This plan of yours—thought the strange mind—may I see more of it?

That's all there is.

Oh, said the strange mind, you want me to think for you. Can you give me the keys in the Bell and Bank which pertain to destroying underpeople?

You can have the information keys if I can ever get them, thought Jestocost, but not the control keys and not the master switch of the Bell.

Fair enough, thought the other mind, and what do I pay for them?

You support me in my policies before the Instrumentality. You keep the underpeople reasonable, if you can, when the time comes to negotiate. You maintain honour and good faith in all subsequent agreements. But how can I get the keys? It would take me a year to figure them out myself.

Let the girl look once, thought the strange mind, and I will be behind her. Fair?

Fair, thought Jestocost.

Break? thought the mind.

How do we reconnect? thought Jestocost back.

As before. Through the girl. Never say my name. Don't think it if you can help it. Break?

Break! thought Jestocost.

The girl, who had been holding his shoulders, drew his face down and kissed him firmly and warmly. He had never touched an underperson before, and it never had occurred to him that he might kiss one. It was pleasant, but he took her arms away from his neck, half-turned her around, and let her lean against him.

'Daddy!' she sighed happily.

Suddenly she stiffened, looked at his face, and sprang for the door. 'Jestocost!' she cried. 'Lord Jestocost! What am I doing here?'

'Your duty is done, my girl. You may go.'

She staggered back into the room. 'I'm going to be sick,' she said. She vomited on his floor.

He pushed a button for a cleaning robot and slapped his desk-top for coffee.

She relaxed and talked about his hopes for the underpeople. She stayed an hour. By the time she left they had a plan. Neither of them had mentioned E'telekeli, neither had put purposes in the open. If the monitors had been listening, they would have found no single sentence or paragraph which was suspicious.

When she had gone, Jestocost looked out of his window. He saw the clouds far below and he knew the world below him was in twilight. He had planned to help the underpeople, and he had met powers of which organized mankind had no conception or perception. He was righter than he had thought. He had to go on through.

But as partner—C'mell herself!

Was there ever an odder diplomat in the history of worlds?

3

In less than a week they had decided what to do. It was the Council of the lords of the Instrumentality at which they would work—the brain centre itself. The risk was high, but the entire job could be done in a few minutes if it were done at the Bell itself.

This is the sort of thing which interested Jestocost.

He did not know that C'mell watched him with two different facets of her mind. One side of her was alertly and wholeheartedly his fellow-conspirator, utterly in sympathy with the revolutionary aims to which they were both committed. The other side of her—was feminine.

She had a womanliness which was truer than that of any hominid woman. She knew the value of her trained smile, her splendidly kept red hair with its unimaginably soft texture, her lithe young figure with firm breasts and persuasive hips. She knew down to the last millimeter the effect which her legs had on hominid men. True humans kept few secrets from her. The men betrayed themselves by their unfulfillable desires, the women by their irrepressible jealousies. But she knew people best of all by not being one herself. She had to learn by imitation, and imitation is conscious. A thousand little things which ordinary women took for granted, or thought about just once in a whole lifetime, were subjects of acute and intelligent study to her. She was a girl by profession; she was a human by assimilation: she was an inquisitive cat in her genetic nature. Now she was falling in love with Jestocost, and she knew it.

Even she did not realize that the romance would sometime leak out into rumour, be magnified into legend, distilled into romance. She had no idea of the ballad about herself that would open with the lines which became famous much later:

> She got the which of the what-she-did,
> Hid the bell with a blot, she did,
> But she fell in love with a hominid.
> Where is the which of the what-she-did?

All this lay in the future, and she did not know it.

She knew her own past.

She remembered the off-Earth prince who had rested his head in her lap and had said, sipping his glass of mott by way of farewell:

'Funny, C'mell, you're not even a person and you're the most intelligent human being I've met in this place. Do you know it made my planet poor to send me here? And what did I get out of them? Nothing, nothing, and a thousand times nothing. But you, now. If you'd been running the government of Earth, I'd have gotten what my people need, and this world would be richer too. Manhome, they call it. Manhome, my eye! The only smart person on it is a female cat.'

He ran his fingers around her ankle. She did not stir. That was part of hospitality, and she had her own ways of making sure that hospitality did not go too far. Earth police were watching her; to them, she was a convenience maintained for outworld people, something like a soft chair in the Earthport lobbies or a drinking fountain with acid-tasting water for strangers who could not tolerate the insipid water of Earth. She was not expected to have feelings or to get involved. If she had ever caused an incident, they would have punished her fiercely, as they often punished animals or underpeople, or else (after a short formal hearing with no appeal) they would have destroyed her, as the law allowed and custom encouraged.

She had kissed a thousand men, maybe fifteen hundred. She had made them feel welcome and she had gotten their complaints or their secrets out of them as they left. It was a living, emotionally tiring but intellectually very stimulating. Sometimes it made her laugh to look at human women with their pointed-up noses and their proud airs, and to realize that she knew more about the men who belonged to the human women than the human women themselves ever did.

Once a policewoman had had to read over the record of two pioneers from New Mars. C'mell had been given the job of keeping in very close touch with them. When the policewoman got through reading the report she looked at C'mell and her face was distorted with jealousy and prudish rage.

'Cat, you call yourself. Cat! You're a pig, you're a dog, you're an animal. You may be working for Earth but don't ever get the idea that you're as good as a person. I think it's a crime that the Instrumentality lets monsters like you greet real human beings from outside! I can't stop it. But may the Bell help you, girl, if you ever touch a real Earth man! If you ever get near one! If you ever try tricks here! Do you understand me?'

'Yes, Ma'am,' C'mell had said. To herself she thought, 'That poor thing doesn't know how to select her own clothes or how to do her own hair. No wonder she resents somebody who manages to be pretty.'

Perhaps the policewoman thought that raw hatred would be shocking to C'mell. It wasn't. Underpeople were used to hatred, and it was not any worse raw than it was when cooked with politeness and served like poison. They had to live with it.

But now, it was all changed.

She had fallen in love with Jestocost.

Did he love her?

Impossible. No, not impossible. Unlawful, unlikely, indecent—yes, all these, but not impossible. Surely he felt something of her love.

If he did, he gave no sign of it.

People and underpeople had fallen in love many times before. The underpeople were always destroyed and the real people brain-washed. There were laws against that kind of thing. The scientists among people had created the underpeople, had given them capacities which real people did not have (the fifty-metre jump, the telepath two miles underground, the turtle-man waiting a thousand years next to an emergency door, the cow-man guarding a gate without reward), and the scientists had also given many of the underpeople the human shape. It was handier that way. The human eye, the five-fingered hand, the human size—these were convenient for engineering reasons. By making underpeople the same size and shape as people, more or less, the scientists eliminated the need for two or three or a dozen different sets of furniture. The human form was good enough for all of them.

But they had forgotten the human heart.

And now she, C'mell, had fallen in love with a man, a true man old enough to have been her own father's grandfather.

But she didn't feel daughterly about him at all. She remembered that with her own father there was an easy comradeship, an innocent and forthcoming affection, which masked the fact that he was considerably more catlike than she was. Between them there was an aching void of forever-unspoken words—things that couldn't quite be said by either of them, perhaps things that couldn't be said at all. They were so close to each other that they could get no closer. This created enormous distance, which was heart-breaking but unutterable. Her father had died, and now this true man was here with all the kindness—

'That's it,' she whispered to herself, 'with all the kindness that none of these passing men have ever really shown. With all the depth which my poor underpeople can never get. Not that it's not in them. But they're born like dirt, treated like dirt, put away like dirt when they die. How can any of my own men develop real kindness? There's a special sort of majesty to kindness. It's the best part there is to being people. And he has whole oceans of it in him. And it's strange, strange, strange that he's never given his real love to any human woman.'

She stopped, cold.

Then she consoled herself and whispered on, 'Or if he did, it's so long ago that it doesn't matter now. He's got *me*. Does he know it?'

4

The Lord Jestocost did know, and yet he didn't. He was used to getting loyalty from people, because he offered loyalty and honour in his daily work. He was even familiar with loyalty becoming obsessive and seeking physical form, particularly from women, children, and underpeople. He had always coped with it before. He was gambling on the fact that C'mell was a wonderfully intelligent person, and that as a girlygirl, working on the hospitality staff of the Earthport police, she must have learned to control her personal feelings.

'We're born in the wrong age,' he thought, 'when I meet the most intelligent and beautiful female I've ever met, and then have to put business first. But this stuff about people and underpeople is sticky. Sticky. We've got to keep personalities out of it.'

So he thought. Perhaps he was right.

If the nameless one, whom he did not dare to remember, commanded an attack on the Bell itself, that was worth their lives. Their emotions could not come into it. The Bell mattered; justice mattered; the perpetual return of mankind to progress mattered. He did not matter, because he had already done most of his work. C'mell did not matter, because their failure would leave her with mere underpeople forever. The Bell did count.

The price of what he proposed to do was high, but the entire job could be done in a few minutes if it were done at the Bell itself.

The Bell, of course, was not a Bell. It was a three-dimensional situation table, three times the height of a man. It was set one storey below the meeting room, and shaped roughly like an ancient bell. The meeting table of the lords of the Instrumentality had a circle cut out of it, so that the lords could look down into the Bell at whatever situation one of them called up either manually or telepathically. The Bank below it, hidden by the floor, was the key memory-bank of the entire system. Duplicates existed at thirty-odd other places on Earth. Two duplicates lay hidden in interstellar space, one of them beside the ninety-million-mile gold-coloured ship left over from the war against Raumsog and the other masked as an asteroid.

Most of the lords were off-world on the business of the Instrumentality.

Only three besides Jestocost were present—the Lady Johanna Gnade, the Lord Issan Olascoaga, and the Lord William Not-from-here. (The Not-from-heres were a great Norstrilian family which had migrated back to Earth many generations before.)

The E'telekeli told Jestocost the rudiments of a plan.

He was to bring C'mell into the chambers on a summons.

The summons was to be serious.

They should avoid her summary death by automatic justice, if the relays began to trip.

C'mell would go into partial trance in the chamber.

He was then to call the items in the Bell which E'telekeli wanted traced. A single call would be enough. E'telekeli would take the responsibility for tracing them. The other lords would be distracted by him, E'telekeli.

It was simple in appearance.

The complication came in action.

The plan seemed flimsy, but there was nothing which Jestocost could do at this time. He began to curse himself for letting his passion for policy involve him in the intrigue. It was too late to back out with honour; besides, he had given his word; besides, he liked C'mell—as a being, not as a girlygirl—and he would hate to see her marked with disappointment for life. He knew how the underpeople cherished their identities and their status.

With heavy heart but quick mind he went to the council

chamber. A dog-girl, one of the routine messengers whom he had seen many months outside the door, gave him the minutes.

He wondered how C'mell or E'telekeli would reach him, once he was inside the chamber with its tight net of telepathic intercepts.

He sat wearily at the table—

And almost jumped out of his chair.

The conspirators had forged the minutes themselves and the top item was: 'C'mell daughter to C'mackintosh, cat stock (pure), lot 1138, confession of. Subject: conspiracy to export homuncular material. Reference: planet De Prinsensmacht.'

The Lady Johanna Gnade had already pushed the buttons for the planet concerned. The people there, Earth by origin, were enormously strong but they had gone to great pains to maintain the original Earth appearance. One of their first-men was at the moment on Earth. He bore the title of the Twilight Prince (Prins van de Schemering) and he was on a mixed diplomatic and trading mission.

Since Jestocost was a little late, C'mell was being brought into the room as he glanced over the minutes.

The Lord Not-from-here asked Jestocost if he would preside.

'I beg you, Sir and Scholar,' he said, 'to join me in asking the Lord Issan to preside this time.'

The presidency was a formality. Jestocost could watch the Bell and Bank better if he did not have to chair the meeting too.

C'mell wore the clothing of a prisoner. On her it looked good. He had never seen her wearing anything but girlygirl clothes before. The pale-blue prison tunic made her look very young, very human, very tender, and very frightened. The cat family showed only in the fiery cascade of her hair and the lithe power of her body as she sat, demure and erect.

Lord Issan asked her: 'You have confessed. Confess again.'

'This man,' and she pointed at a picture of the Twilight Prince, 'wanted to go to the place where they torment human children for a show.'

'What!' cried three of the Lords together.

'What place?' said the Lady Johanna, who was bitterly in favour of kindness.

'It's run by a man who looks like this gentleman here,' said C'mell, pointing at Jestocost. Quickly, so that nobody could stop her, but modestly, so that none of them thought to doubt her, she circled the room and touched Jestocost's shoulder. He felt a thrill of contact-telepathy and heard bird-cackle in her brain. Then he knew that the E'telekeli was in touch with her.

'The man who has the place,' said C'mell, 'is five pounds lighter than this gentleman, two inches shorter, and he has red hair. His place is at the Cold Sunset corner of Earthport, down the boulevard and under the boulevard. Underpeople, some of them with bad reputations, live in that neighbourhood.'

The Bell went milky, flashing through hundreds of combinations of bad underpeople in that part of the city. Jestocost felt himself staring at the casual milkiness with unwanted concentration.

The Bell cleared.

It showed the vague image of a room in which children were playing Hallowe'en tricks.

The Lady Johanna laughed, 'Those aren't people. They're robots. It's just a dull old play.'

'Then,' added C'mell, 'he wanted a dollar and a shilling to take home. Real ones. There was a robot who had found some.'

'What are those?' said Lord Issan.

'Ancient money—the real money of old America and old Australia,' cried Lord William. 'I have copies, but there are no originals outside the state museum.' He was an ardent, passionate collector of coins.

'The robot found them in an old hiding place right under Earthport.'

Lord William almost shouted at the Bell. 'Run through every hiding place and get me that money.'

The Bell clouded. In finding the bad neighbourhoods it had flashed every police point in the north-west sector of the tower. Now it scanned all the police points under the tower, and ran dizzily through thousands of combinations before it settled on an old toolroom. A robot was polishing circular pieces of metal.

When Lord William saw the polishing, he was furious. 'Get that here,' he shouted. 'I want to buy those myself!'

'All right,' said Lord Issan. 'It's a little irregular, but all right.'

The machine showed the key search devices and brought the robot to the escalator.

The Lord Issan said, 'This isn't much of a case.'

C'mell snivelled. She was a good actress. 'Then he wanted me to get a homunculus egg. One of the E-type, derived from birds, for him to take home.'

Issan put on the search device.

'Maybe,' said C'mell, 'somebody has already put it in the disposal series.'

The Bell and Bank ran through all the disposal devices at high speed. Jestocost felt his nerves go on edge. No human being could have memorized these thousands of patterns as they flashed across the Bell too fast for human eyes, but the brain reading the Bell through his eyes was not human. It might even be locked into a computer of its own. It was, thought Jestocost, an indignity for a lord of the Instrumentality to be used as a human spy-glass.

The machine blotted up.

'You're a fraud,' cried the Lord Issan. 'There's no evidence.'

'Maybe the offworlder tried,' said the Lady Johanna.

'Shadow him,' said Lord William. 'If he would steal ancient coins he would steal anything.'

The Lady Johanna turned to C'mell. 'You're a silly thing. You have wasted our time and you have kept us from serious interworld business.'

'It *is* interworld business,' wept C'mell. She let her hand slip from Jestocost's shoulder, where it had rested all the time. The body-to-body relay broke and the telepathic link broke with it.

'We should judge that,' said Lord Issan.

'You might have been punished,' said Lady Johanna.

The Lord Jestocost had said nothing, but there was a glow of happiness in him. If the E'telekeli was half as good as he seemed, the underpeople had a list of checkpoints and escape routes which would make it easier to hide from the capricious sentence of painless death which human authorities meted out.

5

There was singing in the corridors that night.

Underpeople burst into happiness for no visible reason.

C'mell danced a wild cat dance for the next customer who came in from outworld stations, that very evening. When she got home to bed, she knelt before the picture of her father C'mackintosh and thanked the E'telekeli for what Jestocost had done.

But the story became known a few generations later, when the Lord Jestocost had won acclaim for being the champion of the underpeople and when the authorities, still unaware of E'telekeli, accepted the elected representatives of the underpeople as negotiators for better terms of life; and C'mell had died long since.

She had first had a long, good life.

She became a female chef when she was too old to be a girlygirl. Her food was famous. Jestocost once visited her. At the end of the meal he had asked, 'There's a silly rhyme among the underpeople. No human beings know it except me.'

'I don't care about rhymes,' she said.

'This is called "The what-she-did."'

C'mell blushed all the way down to the neckline of her capacious blouse. She had filled out a lot in middle age. Running the restaurant had helped.

'Oh, that rhyme!' she said. 'It's silly.'

'It says you were in love with a hominid.'

'No,' she said. 'I wasn't.' Her green eyes, as beautiful as ever, stared deeply into his. Jestocost felt uncomfortable. This was getting personal. He liked political relationships; personal things made him uncomfortable.

The light in the room shifted and her cat eyes blazed at him, she looked like the magical fire-haired girl he had known.

'I wasn't in love. You couldn't call it that . . .'

Her heart cried out, *It was you, it was you, it was you.*

'But the rhyme,' insisted Jestocost, 'says it was a hominid. It wasn't that Prins van de Schemering?'

'Who was he?' C'mell asked the question quietly, but her emotions cried out, *Darling, will you never, never know?*

'The strong man.'

'Oh, him. I've forgotten him.'

Jestocost rose from the table. 'You've had a good life, C'mell. You've been a citizen, a committeewoman, a leader. And do you even know how many children you have had?'

'Seventy-three,' she snapped at him. 'Just because they're multiple doesn't mean we don't know them.'

His playfulness left him. His face was grave, his voice kindly. 'I meant no harm, C'mell.'

He never knew that when he left she went back to the kitchen and cried for a while. It was Jestocost whom she had vainly loved ever since they had been comrades, many long years ago.

Even after she died, at the full age of five-score and three, he kept seeing her about the corridors and shafts of Earthport. Many of her great-granddaughters looked just like her and several of them practised the girlygirl business with huge success.

They were not half-slaves. They were citizens (reserved grade) and they had photopasses which protected their property, their identity, and their rights. Jestocost was the godfather to them all; he was often embarrassed when the most voluptuous creatures in the universe threw playful kisses at him. All he asked was fulfilment of his political passions, not his personal ones. He had always been in love, madly in love—

With justice itself.

At last, his own time came, and he knew that he was dying, and he was not sorry. He had had a wife, hundreds of years ago, and had loved her well; their children had passed into the generations of man.

In the ending, he wanted to know something, and he called to a nameless one (or to his successor) far beneath the ground. He called with his mind till it was a scream.

I have helped your people.

'Yes,' came back the faintest of faraway whispers, inside his head.

I am dying. I must know. Did she love me?

'She went on without you, so much did she love you. She let you go, for your sake, not for hers. She really loved you. More than death. More than life. More than time. You will never be apart.'

Never apart?

'Not, not in the memory of man,' said the voice, and was then still.

Jestocost lay back on his pillow and waited for the day to end.

SEMLEY'S NECKLACE

URSULA K. LE GUIN

How can you tell the legend from the fact on these worlds that lie so many years away?—planets without names, called by their people simply The World, planets without history, where the past is the matter of myth, and a returning explorer finds his own doings of a few years back have become the gestures of a god. Unreason darkens that gap of time bridged by our light-speed ships, and in the darkness uncertainty and disproportion grow like weeds.

In trying to tell the story of a man, an ordinary League scientist, who went to such a nameless half-known world not many years ago, one feels like an archaeologist amid millennial ruins, now struggling through choked tangles of leaf, flower, branch, and vine to the sudden bright geometry of a wheel or a polished cornerstone, and now entering some commonplace, sunlit doorway to find inside it the darkness, the impossible flicker of a flame, the glitter of a jewel, the half-glimpsed movement of a woman's arm.

How can you tell fact from legend, truth from truth?

Through Rocannon's story the jewel, the blue glitter seen briefly, returns. With it let us begin, here:

Galactic Area 8, No. 62: FOMALHAUT II.
High-Intelligence Life Forms: Species Contacted:

Species I.

A. Gdemiar (singular Gdem): Highly intelligent, fully hominoid nocturnal troglodytes, 120–35 cm in height, light skin, dark head-hair. When contacted these cave-dwellers possessed a rigidly stratified oligarchic urban society modified by partial colonial telepathy, and a technologically oriented Early Steel culture. Technology enhanced to Industrial, Point C, during League Mission of 252–4. In 254 an Automatic Drive ship (to-from New South Georgia) was presented to oligarchs of the Kiriensea Area community. Status C-Prime.

B. Fiia (singular Fian): Highly intelligent, fully hominoid, diurnal, av. c.130 cm in height, observed individuals generally light in skin and hair. Brief contacts indicated village and nomadic communal societies, partial colonial telepathy, also some indication of short-range TK. The race appears a-technological and evasive, with minimal and fluid culture-patterns. Currently untaxable. Status E-Query.

Species II.

Liuar (singular Liu): Highly intelligent, fully hominoid, diurnal, av. height above 170 cm, this species possesses a fortress/village, clan-descent society, a blocked technology (Bronze), and feudal-heroic culture. Note horizontal social cleavage into two pseudo-races: (a) Olgyior, 'midmen', lightskinned and dark-haired; (b) Angyar, 'lords', very tall, dark-skinned, yellow-haired—

'That's her,' said Rocannon, looking up from the *Abridged Handy Pocket Guide to Intelligent Life-forms* at the very tall, dark-skinned, yellow-haired woman who stood halfway down the long museum hall. She stood still and erect, crowned with bright hair, gazing at something in a display case. Around her fidgeted four uneasy and unattractive dwarves.

'I didn't know Fomalhaut II had all those people besides the trogs,' said Ketho, the curator.

'I didn't either. There are even some "Unconfirmed" species listed here, that they never contacted. Sounds like time for a more thorough survey mission to the place. Well, now at least we know what she is.'

'I wish there were some way of knowing *who* she is . . .'

She was of an ancient family, a descendant of the first kings of the Angyar, and for all her poverty her hair shone with the pure, steadfast gold of her inheritance. The little people, the Fiia, bowed when she passed them, even when she was a barefoot child running in the fields, the light and fiery comet of her hair brightening the troubled winds of Kirien.

She was still very young when Durhal of Hallan saw her, courted her, and carried her away from the ruined towers and windy halls of her childhood to his own high home. In Hallan on the mountainside there was no comfort either, though splendour endured. The windows were unglassed, the stone floors bare; in coldyear one might wake to see the night's snow in long, low drifts beneath each window. Durhal's bride stood with narrow bare feet on the snowy floor, braiding up the fire of her hair and laughing at her young husband in the silver mirror that hung in their room. That mirror, and his mother's bridal-gown sewn with a thousand tiny crystals, were all his wealth. Some of his lesser kinfolk of Hallan still possessed wardrobes of brocaded clothing, furniture of gilded wood, silver harness for their steeds, armour and silver mounted swords, jewels and jewellery—and on these last Durhal's bride looked enviously, glancing back at a gemmed coronet or a golden brooch even when the wearer of the ornament stood aside to let her pass, deferent to her birth and marriage-rank.

Fourth from the High Seat of Hallan Revel sat Durhal and his bride Semley, so close to Hallanlord that the old man often poured wine for Semley with his own hand, and spoke of hunting with his nephew and heir Durhal, looking on the young pair with a grim, unhopeful love. Hope came hard to the Angyar of Hallan and all the Western Lands, since the Starlords had appeared with their houses that leaped about on pillars of fire and their awful weapons that could level hills. They had interfered with all the old ways and wars, and though the sums were small there was terrible shame to the Angyar in having to pay a tax to them, a tribute for the Starlords' war that was to be fought with some strange enemy, somewhere in the hollow places between the stars, at the end of years. 'It will be your war too,' they said, but for a generation now the Angyar had sat in idle shame in their revel-halls, watching their double swords rust, their sons grow up without ever striking a blow in battle, their daughters marry poor men, even midmen, having no dowry of heroic loot to bring a noble husband. Hallanlord's face was bleak when he watched the fair-haired couple and heard their laughter as they drank bitter wine and joked together in the cold, ruinous, resplendent fortress of their race.

Semley's own face hardened when she looked down the hall and saw, in seats far below hers, even down among the half-breeds and the midmen, against white skins and black hair, the gleam and flash of precious stones. She herself had brought nothing in dowry to her husband, not even a silver hairpin. The dress of a thousand crystals she had put away in a chest for the wedding-day of her daughter, if daughter it was to be.

It was, and they called her Haldre, and when the fuzz on her little brown skull grew longer it shone with steadfast gold, the inheritance of the lordly generations, the only gold she would ever possess . . .

Semley did not speak to her husband of her discontent. For all his gentleness to her, Durhal in his pride had only contempt for envy, for vain wishing, and she dreaded his contempt. But she spoke to Durhal's sister Durossa.

'My family had a great treasure once,' she said. 'It was a necklace all of gold, with the blue jewel set in the centre—sapphire?'

Durossa shook her head, smiling, not sure of the name either. It was late in warmyear, as these Northern Angyar called the summer of the eight-hundred-day year, beginning the cycle of months anew at each equinox; to Semley it seemed an outlandish calendar, a midmannish reckoning. Her family was at an end, but it had been older and purer than the race of any of these north-western marchlanders, who mixed too freely with the Olgyior. She sat with Durossa in the sunlight on a stone windowseat high up in the Great Tower, where the older woman's apartment was. Widowed young, childless, Durossa had been given in second marriage to Hallanlord, who was her father's brother. Since it was a kinmarriage and a second marriage on both sides she had not taken the title of Hallanlady, which Semley would some day bear; but she sat with the old lord in the High Seat and ruled with him his domains. Older than her brother Durhal, she was fond of his young wife, and delighted in the bright-haired baby Haldre.

'It was bought,' Semley went on, 'with all the money my forebear Leynen got when he conquered the Southern Fiefs—all the money from a whole kingdom, think of it, for one jewel! Oh, it would outshine anything here in Hallan, surely, even those crystals like koob-eggs your cousin Issar wears. It was so beautiful they gave it a name of its own; they called it the Eye of the Sea. My great-grandmother wore it.'

'You never saw it?' the older woman asked lazily, gazing down at the green mountainslopes where long, long summer sent its hot and restless winds straying among the forests and whirling down white roads to the seacoast far away.

'It was lost before I was born.'

'No, my father said it was stolen before the Starlords ever came to our realm. He wouldn't talk of it, but there was an old midwoman full of tales who always told me the Fiia would know where it was.'

'Ah, the Fiia I should like to see!' said Durossa. 'They're in so many songs and talks; why do they never come to the Western Lands?'

'Too high, too cold in winter, I think. They like the sunlight of the valleys of the south.'

'Are they like the Clayfolk?'

'Those I've never seen; they keep away from us in the south. Aren't they white like midmen, and misformed? The Fiia are fair; they look like children, only thinner, and wiser. Oh, I wonder if they know where the necklace is, who stole it, and where he hid it! Think, Durossa—if I could come into Hallan Revel and sit down by my husband with the wealth of a kingdom round my neck, and outshine the other women as he outshines all men!'

Durossa bent her head above the baby, who sat studying her own brown toes on a fur rug between her mother and aunt. 'Semley is foolish,' she murmured to the baby; 'Semley who shines like a falling star, Semley whose husband loves no gold but the gold of her hair . . .'

And Semley, looking out over the green slopes of summer toward the distant sea, was silent.

But when another coldyear had passed, and the Starlords had come again to collect their taxes for the war against the world's end—this time using a couple of dwarfish Clayfolk as interpreters, and so leaving all the Angyar humiliated to the point of rebellion—and another warmyear too was gone, and Haldre had grown into a lovely, chattering child, Semley brought her one morning to Durossa's sunlit room in the tower. Semley wore an old cloak of blue, and the hood covered her hair.

'Keep Haldre for me these few days, Durossa,' she said, quick and calm. 'I'm going south to Kirien.'

'To see your father?'

'To find my inheritance. Your cousins of Harget Fief have been taunting Durhal. Even that halfbreed Parna can torment him, because Parna's wife has a satin coverlet for her bed, and a diamond earring, and three gowns, the dough-faced black-haired trollop! while Durhal's wife must patch her gown—'

'Is Durhal's pride in his wife, or what she wears?'

But Semley was not to be moved. 'The Lords of Hallan are becoming poor men in their own hall. I am going to bring my dowry to my lord, as one of my lineage should.'

'Semley! Does Durhal know you're going?'

'My return will be a happy one—that much let him know,' said young Semley, breaking for a moment into her joyful laugh; then she bent to kiss her daughter, turned, and before Durossa could speak, was gone like a quick wind over the floors of sunlit stone.

Married women of the Angyar never rode for sport, and Semley had not been from Hallan since her marriage; so now, mounting the high saddle of a windsteed, she felt like a girl again, like the wild maiden she had been, riding half-broken steeds on the north wind over the fields of Kirien. The beast that bore her now down from the hills of Hallan was of finer breed, striped coat fitting sleek over hollow, buoyant bones, green eyes slitted against the wind, light and mighty wings sweeping up and down to either side of Semley, revealing and hiding, revealing and hiding the clouds above her and the hills below.

On the third morning she came to Kirien and stood again in the ruined courts. Her father had been drinking all night, and, just as in the old days, the morning sunlight poking through his fallen ceilings annoyed him, and the sight of his daughter only increased his annoyance. 'What are you back for?' he growled, his swollen eyes glancing at her and away. The fiery hair of his youth was quenched, grey strands tangled on his skull. 'Did the young Halla not marry you, and you've come sneaking home?'

'I am Durhal's wife. I came to get my dowry, father.'

The drunkard growled in disgust; but she laughed at him so gently that he had to look at her again, wincing.

'Is it true, father, that the Fiia stole the necklace Eye of the Sea?'

'How do I know? Old tales. The thing was lost before I was born, I think. I wish I never had been. Ask the Fiia if you want to know. Go to them, go back to your husband. Leave me alone here. There's no room at Kirien for girls and gold and all the rest of the story. The story's over here; this is the fallen place, this is the empty hall. The sons of Leynen all are dead, their treasures are all lost. Go on your way, girl.'

Grey and swollen as the web-spinner of ruined houses, he turned and went blundering towards the cellars where he hid from daylight.

Leading the striped windsteed of Hallan, Semley left her old home and walked down the steep hill, past the village of the midmen, who greeted her with sullen respect, on over fields and pastures where the great, wing-clipped, half-wild herilor grazed, to a valley that was green as a painted bowl and full to the brim with sunlight. In the deep of the valley lay the village of the Fiia, and as she descended leading her steed the little, slight people ran up towards her from their huts and gardens, laughing, calling out in faint, thin voices.

'Hail Halla's bride, Kirienlady, Windborne, Semley the Fair!'

They gave her lovely names and she liked to hear them, minding not at all their laughter; for they laughed at all they said. That was her own way, to speak and laugh. She stood tall in her long blue cloak among their swirling welcome.

'Hail Lightfolk, Sundwellers, Fiia friends of men!'

They took her down into the village and brought her into one of their airy houses, the tiny children chasing along behind. There was no telling the age of a Fian once he was grown; it was hard even to tell one from another and be sure, as they moved about quick as moths around a candle, that she spoke always to the same one. But it seemed that one of them talked with her for a while, as the others fed and petted her steed, and brought water for her to drink, and bowls of fruit from their gardens of little trees. 'It was never the Fiia that stole the necklace of the Lords of Kirien!' cried the little man. 'What would the Fiia do with gold, Lady? For us there is sunlight in warmyear, and in coldyear the remembrance of sunlight; the yellow fruit, the yellow leaves in end-season, the yellow hair of our lady of Kirien; no other gold.'

'Then it was some midman stole the thing?'

Laughter rang long and faint about her. 'How would a midman dare? O Lady of Kirien, how the great jewel was stolen no mortal knows, not man nor midman nor Fian nor any among the Seven Folk. Only dead minds know how it was lost, long ago when Kireley the Proud whose great-granddaughter is Semley walked alone by the caves of the sea. But it may be found perhaps among the Sunhaters.'

'The Clayfolk?'

A louder burst of laughter, nervous.

'Sit with us, Semley, sunhaired, returned to us from the north.' She sat with them to eat, and they were as pleased with her graciousness as she with theirs. But when they heard her repeat that she would go to the Clayfolk to find her inheritance, if it was there, they began not to laugh; and little by little there were fewer of them around her. She was alone at last with perhaps the one she had spoken with before the meal. 'Do not go among the Clayfolk, Semley,' he said, and for a moment her heart failed her. The Fian, drawing his hand down slowly over his eyes, had darkened all the air about them. Fruit lay ash-white on the plate; all the bowls of clear water were empty.

'In the mountains of the far land the Fiia and the Gdemiar

parted. Long ago we parted,' said the slight, still man of the Fiia. 'Longer ago we were one. What we are not, they are. What we are, they are not. Think of the sunlight and the grass and the trees that bear fruit, Semley; think that not all roads that lead down lead up as well.'

'Mine leads neither down nor up, kind host, but only straight on to my inheritance. I will go to it where it is, and return with it.'

The Fian bowed, laughing a little.

Outside the village she mounted her striped windsteed, and, calling farewell in answer to their calling, rose up into the wind of afternoon and flew southwestward towards the caves down by the rocky shores of Kiriensea.

She feared she might have to walk far into those tunnel-caves to find the people she sought, for it was said the Clayfolk never came out of their caves into the light of the sun, and feared even the Greatstar and the moons. It was a long ride; she landed once to let her steed hunt tree-rats while she ate a little bread from her saddle-bag. The bread was hard and dry by now and tasted of leather, yet kept a faint savour of its making, so that for a moment, eating it alone in a glade of the southern forests, she heard the quiet tone of a voice and saw Durhal's face turned to her in the light of the candles of Hallan. For a while she sat daydreaming of that stern and vivid young face, and of what she would say to him when she came home with a kingdom's ransom around her neck: 'I wanted a gift worthy of my husband, Lord . . .' Then she pressed on, but when she reached the coast the sun had set, with the Greatstar sinking behind it. A mean wind had come up from the west, starting and gusting and veering, and her windsteed was weary fighting it. She let him glide down on the sand. At once he folded his wings and curled his thick, light limbs under him with a thrum of purring. Semley stood holding her cloak close at her throat, stroking the steed's neck so that he flicked his ears and purred again. The warm fur comforted her hand, but all that met her eyes was grey sky full of smears of cloud, grey sea, dark sand. And then running over the sand a low, dark creature—another—a group of them, squatting and running and stopping.

She called aloud to them. Though they had not seemed to see her, now in a moment they were all around her. They kept a distance from her windsteed; he had stopped purring, and his fur rose a little under Semley's hand. She took up the reins, glad of his protection but afraid of the nervous ferocity he might display. The strange folk stood silent, staring, their thick bare feet planted in the sand. There was no mistaking them: they were the height of the Fiia and in all else a shadow, a black image of those laughing people. Naked, squat, stiff, with lank hair and grey-white skins, dampish-looking like the skins of grubs; eyes like rocks.

'You are the Clayfolk?'

'Gdemiar are we, people of the Lords of the Realms of Night.' The voice was unexpectedly loud and deep, and rang out pompous through the salt, blowing dusk; but, as with the Fiia, Semley was not sure which one had spoken.

'I greet you, Nightlords. I am Semley of Kirien, Durhal's wife of Hallan. I come to you seeking my inheritance, the necklace called Eye of the Sea, lost long ago.'

'Why do you seek it here, Angyar? Here is only sand and salt and night.'

'Because lost things are known of in deep places,' said Semley, quite ready for a play of wits, 'and gold that came from earth has a way of going back to the earth. And sometimes the made, they say, returns to the maker.' This last was a guess; it hit the mark.

'It is true the necklace Eye of the Sea is known to us by name. It was made in our caves long ago, and sold by us to the Angyar. And the blue stone came from the Clayfields of our kin to the east. But these are very old tales, Angyar.'

'May I listen to them in the places where they are told?'

The squat people were silent a while, as if in doubt; the grey wind blew by over the sand, darkening as the Greatstar set; the sound of the sea loudened and lessened. The deep voice spoke again: 'Yes, lady of the Angyar. You may enter the Deep Halls. Come with us now.' There was a changed note in his voice, wheedling. Semley would not hear it. She followed the Claymen over the sand, leading on a short rein her sharp-taloned steed.

At the cave-mouth, a toothless, yawning mouth from which a stinking warmth sighed out, one of the Claymen said, 'The air-beast cannot come in.'

'Yes,' said Semley.

'No,' said the squat people.

'Yes. I will not leave him here. He is not mine to leave. He will not harm you, so long as I hold his reins.'

'No,' deep voices repeated; but others broke in, 'As you will,' and after a moment of hesitation they went on. The cave-mouth seemed to snap shut behind them, so dark was it under the stone. They went in single file, Semley last.

The darkness of the tunnel lightened, and they came under a ball of weak white fire hanging from the roof. Further on was another, and another; between them long black worms hung in festoons from the rocks. As they went on these fire-globes were set closer, so that all the tunnel was lit with a bright, cold light.

Semley's guides stopped at a parting of three tunnels, all blocked by doors that looked to be of iron. 'We shall wait, Angyar,' they said, and eight of them stayed with her, while three others unlocked one of the doors and passed through. It fell to behind them with a clash.

Straight and still stood the daughter of the Angyar in the white, blank light of the lamps; her windsteed crouched beside her, flicking the tip of his striped tail, his great folded wings stirring again and again with the checked impulse to fly. In the tunnel behind Semley the eight Claymen squatted on their hams, muttering to one another in their deep voices, in their own tongue.

The central door swung clanging open. 'Let the Angyar enter the Realm of Night!' cried a new voice, booming and boastful. A Clayman who wore some clothing on his thick grey body stood in the doorway, beckoning to her. 'Enter and behold the wonders of our lands, the marvels made by hands, the works of the Nightlords!'

Silent, with a tug at her steed's reins, Semley bowed her head and followed him under the low doorway made for dwarfish folk. Another glaring tunnel stretched ahead, dank walls dazzling in the white light, but, instead of a way to walk upon, its floor carried two bars of polished iron stretching off side by side as far as she could see. On the bars rested some kind of cart with metal wheels. Obeying her new guide's gestures, with no hesitation and no trace of wonder on her face, Semley stepped into the cart and made the windsteed crouch beside her. The Clayman got in and sat down in front of her, moving bars and wheels about. A loud grinding noise arose, and a screaming of metal on metal, and then the walls of the tunnel began to jerk by. Faster and faster the walls slid past, till the fireglobes overhead ran into a blur, and the stale warm air became a foul wind blowing the hood back off her hair.

The cart stopped. Semley followed the guide up basalt steps into a vast ante-room and then a still vaster hall, carved by ancient waters or by the burrowing Clayfolk out of the rock, its darkness that had never known sunlight lit with the uncanny cold brilliance of the globes. In grilles cut in the walls huge blades turned and turned, changing the stale air. The great closed space hummed and boomed with noise, the loud voices of the Clayfolk, the grinding and shrill buzzing and vibration of turning blades and wheels, the echoes and re-echoes of all this from the rock. Here all the stumpy figures of the Claymen were clothed in garments imitating those of the Starlords—divided trousers, soft boots, and hooded tunics—though the few women to be seen, hurrying servile dwarves, were naked. Of the males many were soldiers, bearing at their sides weapons shaped like the terrible light-throwers of the Starlords, though even Semley could see these were merely shaped iron clubs. What she saw, she saw without looking. She followed where she was led, turning her head neither to left nor right. When she came before a group of Claymen who wore iron circlets on their black hair her guide halted, bowed, boomed out, 'The High Lords of the Gdemiar!'

There were seven of them, and all looked up at her with such arrogance on their lumpy grey faces that she wanted to laugh.

'I come among you seeking the lost treasure of my family, O Lords of the Dark Realm,' she said gravely to them. 'I seek Leynen's prize, the Eye of the Sea.' Her voice was faint in the racket of the huge vault.

'So said our messengers, Lady Semley.' This time she could pick out the one who spoke, one even shorter than the others, hardly reaching Semley's breast, with a white, fierce face. 'We do not have this thing you seek.'

'Once you had it, it is said.'

'Much is said, up there where the sun blinks.'

'And words are borne off by the winds, where there are winds to blow. I do not ask how the necklace was lost to us and returned to you, its makers of old. Those are old tales, old grudges. I only seek to find it now. You do not have it now; but it may be you know where it is.'

'It is not here.'

'Then it is elsewhere.'

'It is where you cannot come to it. Never, unless we help you.'

'Then help me. I ask this as your guest.'

'It is said, *The Angyar take; the Fiia give; the Gdemiar give and take*. If we do this for you, what will you give us?'

'My thanks, Nightlord.'

She stood tall and bright among them, smiling. They all stared at her with a heavy, grudging wonder, a sullen yearning.

'Listen, Angyar, this is a great favour you ask of us. You do not know how great a favour. You cannot understand. You are of a race that will not understand, that cares for nothing but wind-riding and crop-raising and sword-fighting and shouting together. But who made your swords of the bright steel? We, the Gdemiar! Your lords come to us here and in the Clayfields and buy their swords and go away, not looking, not understanding. But you are here now, you will look, you can see a few of our endless marvels, the lights that burn forever, the car that pulls itself, the machines that make our clothes and cook our food and sweeten our air and serve us in all things. Know that all these things are beyond your understanding. And know this: we, the Gdemiar, are the friends of those you call the Starlords! We came with them to Hallan, to Reohan, to Hul-Orren, to all your castles, to help them speak to you. The lords to whom you, the proud Angyar, pay tribute, are our friends. They do us favours as we do them favours! Now, what do your thanks mean to us?'

'That is your question to answer,' said Semley, 'not mine. I have asked my question. Answer it, Lord.'

For a while the seven conferred together, by word and silence. They would glance at her and look away, and mutter and be still. A crowd grew around them, drawn slowly and silently, one after another till Semley was encircled by hundreds of the matted black heads, and all the great booming cavern floor was covered with people, except a little space directly around her. Her windsteed was quivering with fear and irritation too long controlled, and his eyes had gone very wide and pale, like the eyes of a steed forced to fly at night. She stroked the warm fur of his head, whispering, 'Quietly now, brave one, bright one, windlord . . .'

'Angyar, we will take you to the place where the treasure lies.' The Clayman with the white face and iron crown had turned to her once more. 'More than that we cannot do. You must come with us to claim the necklace where it lies, from those who keep it. The air-beast cannot come with you. You must come alone.'

'How far a journey, Lord?'

His lips drew back and back. 'A very far journey, Lady. Yet it will last only one long night.'

'I thank you for your courtesy. Will my steed be well cared for this night? No ill must come to him.'

'He will sleep till you return. A greater windsteed you will have ridden, when you see that beast again! Will you not ask where we take you?'

'Can we go soon on this journey? I would not stay long away from my home.'

'Yes. Soon.' Again the grey lips widened as he stared up into her face.

What was done in those next hours Semley could not have retold; it was all haste, jumble, noise, strangeness. While she held her steed's head a Clayman stuck a long needle into the golden-striped haunch. She nearly cried out at the sight, but her steed merely twitched and then, purring, fell asleep. He was carried off by a group of Clayfolk who clearly had to summon up their courage to touch his warm fur. Later on she had to see a needle driven into her own arm—perhaps to test her courage, she thought, for it did not seem to make her sleep; though she was not quite sure. There were times she had to travel in the rail-carts, passing iron doors and vaulted caverns by the hundred and hundred; once the rail-cart ran through a cavern that stretched off on either hand measureless into the dark, and all that darkness was full of great flocks of herilor. She could hear their cooing, husky calls, and glimpse the flocks in the frontlights of the cart; then she saw some more clearly in the white light, and saw that they were all wingless, and all blind. At that she shut her eyes. But there were more tunnels to go through, and always more caverns, more grey lumpy bodies and fierce faces and booming boasting voices, until at last they led her suddenly out into the open air. It was full night; she raised her eyes joyfully to the stars and the single moon shining, little Heliki brightening in the west. But the Clayfolk were all about her still, making her climb now into some new kind of cart or cave, she did not know which. It was small, full of little blinking lights like rushlights, very narrow and shining after the great dank caverns and the starlit night. Now another needle was stuck in her, and they told her she would have to be tied down in a sort of flat chair, tied down head and hand and foot.

'I will not,' said Semley.

But when she saw that the four Claymen who were to be her guides let themselves be tied down first, she submitted. The others left. There was a roaring sound, and a long silence; a great weight that could not be seen pressed upon her. Then there was no weight; no sound; nothing at all.

'Am I dead?' asked Semley.

'Oh no, Lady,' said a voice she did not like.

Opening her eyes, she saw the white face bent over her, the wide lips pulled back, the eyes like little stones. Her bonds had fallen away from her, and she leaped up. She was weightless, bodiless; she felt herself only a gust of terror on the wind.

'We will not hurt you,' said the sullen voice or voices. 'Only let us touch you, Lady. We would like to touch your hair. Let us touch your hair . . .'

The round cart they were in trembled a little. Outside its one window lay blank night, or was it mist, or nothing at all? One long night, they had said. Very long. She sat motionless and endured the touch of their heavy grey hands on her hair. Later they would touch her hands and feet and arms, and once her throat: at that she set her teeth and stood up, and they drew back.

'We have not hurt you, Lady,' they said. She shook her head.

When they bade her, she lay down again in the chair that bound her down; and when light flashed golden, at the window, she would have wept at the sight, but fainted first.

'Well,' said Rocannon, 'now at least we know what she is.'

'I wish there were some way of knowing *who* she is,' the curator mumbled. 'She wants something we've got here in the Museum, is that what the trogs say?'

'Now, don't call 'em trogs,' Rocannon said conscientiously; as a hilfer, an ethnologist of the High Intelligence Life-forms, he was supposed to resist such words. 'They're not pretty, but they're Status C Allies . . . I wonder why the Commission picked them to develop? Before even contacting all the HILF species? I'll bet the survey was from Centaurus—Centaurans always like nocturnals and cave dwellers. I'd have backed Species II, here, I think.'

'The troglodytes seem to be rather in awe of her.'

'Aren't you?'

Ketho glanced at the tall woman again, then reddened and laughed. 'Well, in a way. I never saw such a beautiful alien type in eighteen years here on New South Georgia. I never saw such a beautiful woman anywhere, in fact. She looks like a goddess.' The red now reached the top of his bald head, for Ketho was a shy curator, not given to hyperbole. But Rocannon nodded soberly, agreeing.

'I wish we could talk to her without those tr—Gdemiar as interpreters. But there's no help for it.' Rocannon went towards their visitor, and when she turned her splendid face to him he bowed down very deeply, going right down to the floor on one knee, his head bowed and his eyes shut. This was what he called his All-Purpose Intercultural Curtsey, and he performed it with some grace. When he came erect again the beautiful woman smiled and spoke.

'She say, Hail, Lord of Stars,' growled one of her squat escorts in Pidgin-Galactic.

'Hail, Lady of the Angyar,' Rocannon replied. 'In what way can we of the Museum serve the lady?'

Across the troglodytes' growling her voice ran like a brief silver wind.

'She say, Please give her necklace which treasure her blood-kin-forebears long long.'

'Which necklace?' he asked, and understanding him, she pointed to the central display of the case before them, a magnificent thing, a chain of yellow gold, massive but very delicate in workmanship, set with one big hot-blue sapphire. Rocannon's eyebrows went up, and Ketho at his shoulder murmured, 'She's got good taste. That's the Fomalhaut Necklace—famous bit of work.'

She smiled at the two men, and again spoke to them over the heads of the troglodytes.

'She say, O Starlords, Elder and Younger Dwellers in House of Treasures, this treasure her one. Long long time. Thank you.'

'How did we get the thing, Ketho?'

'Wait; let me look it up in the catalogue. I've got it here. Here. It came from these trogs—trolls—whatever they are: Gdemiar. They have a bargain-obsession, it says; we had to let 'em buy the ship they came here on, an AD-4. This was part payment. It's their own handiwork.'

'And I'll bet they can't do this kind of work anymore, since they've been steered to Industrial.'

'But they seem to feel the thing is hers, not theirs or ours. It must be important, Rocannon, or they wouldn't have given up this time-span to her errand. Why, the objective lapse between here and Fomalhaut must be considerable!'

'Several years, no doubt,' said the hilfer, who was used to star-jumping. 'Not very far. Well, neither the *Handbook* nor the *Guide* gives me enough data to base a decent guess on. These species obviously haven't been properly studied at all. The little fellows may be showing her simple countesy. Or an interspecies war may depend on this damn sapphire. Perhaps her desire rules them, because they consider themselves totally inferior to her. Or despite appearances she may be their prisoner, their decoy. How can we tell? . . . Can you give the thing away, Ketho?'

'Oh, yes. All the Exotica are technically on loan, not our property, since these claims come up now and then. We seldom argue. Peace above all, until the War comes . . .'

'Then I'd say give it to her.'

Ketho smiled. 'It's a privilege,' he said. Unlocking the case he lifted out the great golden chain; then, in his shyness, he held it out to Rocannon, saying, 'You give it to her.'

So the blue jewel first lay, for a moment, in Rocannon's hand.

His mind was not on it; he turned straight to the beautiful, alien woman, with his handful of blue fire and gold. She did not raise her hands to take it, but bent her head, and he slipped the necklace over her hair. It lay like a burning fuse along her golden-brown throat. She looked up from it with such pride, delight, and gratitude in her face that Rocannon stood wordless, and the little curator murmured hurriedly in his own language, 'You're welcome, you're very welcome.' She bowed her golden head to him and to Rocannon. Then, turning, she nodded to her squat guards—or captors?—and, drawing her worn blue cloak about her, paced down the long hall and was gone. Ketho and Rocannon stood looking after her.

'What I feel . . .' Rocannon began.

'Well?' Ketho enquired hoarsely, after a long pause.

'What I feel sometimes is that I . . . meeting these people from worlds we know so little of, you know, sometimes . . . that I have as it were blundered through the corner of a legend, or a tragic myth, maybe, which I do not understand . . .'

'Yes,' said the curator, clearing his throat. 'I wonder . . . I wonder what her name is.'

Semley the Fair, Semley the Golden, Semley of the Necklace. The Clayfolk had bent to her will, and so had even the Starlords in that terrible place where the Clayfolk had taken her, the city at the end of the night. They had bowed to her, and given her gladly her treasure from amongst their own.

But she could not yet shake off the feeling of those caverns about her where rock lowered overhead, where you could not tell who spoke or what they did, where voices boomed and grey hands reached out—Enough of that. She had paid for the necklace; very well. Now it was hers. The price was paid, the past was the past.

Her windsteed had crept out of some kind of box, with his eyes filmy and his fur rimed with ice, and at first when they had left the caves of the Gdemiar he would not fly. Now he seemed all right again, riding a smooth south wind through the bright sky toward Hallan. 'Go quick, go quick,' she told him, beginning to laugh as the wind cleared away her mind's darkness. 'I want to see Durhal soon, soon . . .'

And swiftly they flew, coming to Hallan by dusk of the second day. Now the caves of the Clayfolk seemed no more than last year's nightmare, as the steed swooped with her up the thousand steps of Hallan and across the Chasmbridge where the forests fell away for a thousand feet. In the gold light of evening in the flightcourt she dismounted and walked up the last steps between the stiff carven figures of heroes and the two gatewards, who bowed to her, staring at the beautiful, fiery thing around her neck.

In the Forehall she stopped a passing girl, a very pretty girl, by her looks one of Durhal's close kin, though Semley could not call to mind her name. 'Do you know me, maiden? I am Semley, Durhal's wife. Will you go tell the Lady Durossa that I have come back?'

For she was afraid to go on in and perhaps face Durhal at once, alone; she wanted Durossa's support.

The girl was gazing at her, her face very strange. But she murmured, 'Yes, Lady,' and darted off toward the Tower.

Semley stood waiting in the gilt, ruinous hall. No one came by; were they all at table in the Revel-hall? The silence was uneasy. After a minute Semley started toward the stairs to the Tower. But an old woman was coming to her across the stone floor, holding her arms out, weeping.

'O Semley, Semley!'

She had never seen the grey-haired woman, and shrank back.

'But Lady, who are you?'

'I am Durossa, Semley.'

She was quiet and still, all the time that Durossa embraced her and wept, and asked if it were true that Clayfolk had captured her and kept her under a spell all these long years, or had it been the Fiia with their strange arts? Then, drawing back a little, Durossa ceased to weep.

'You're still young. Semley. Young as the day you left here. And you wear round your neck the necklace . . .'

'I have brought my gift to my husband Durhal. Where is he?'

'Durhal is dead.'

Semley stood unmoving.

'Your husband, my brother, Durhal Hallanlord was killed seven years ago in battle. Nine years you had been gone. The Starlords came no more. We fell to warring with the Eastern Halls, with the Angyar of Log and Hul-Orren. Durhal, fighting, was killed by a midman's spear, for he had little armour for his body, and none at all for his spirit. He lies buried in the fields above Orren Marsh.'

Semley turned away. 'I will go to him, then,' she said, putting her hand on the gold chain that weighed down her neck. 'I will give him my gift.'

'Wait, Semley! Durhal's daughter, your daughter, see her now, Haldre the Beautiful!'

It was the girl she had first spoken to and sent to Durossa, a girl of nineteen or so, with eyes like Durhal's eyes, dark blue. She stood beside Durossa, gazing with those steady eyes at this woman Semley who was her mother and was her own age. Their age was the same, and their gold hair, and their beauty. Only Semley was a little taller, and wore the blue stone on her breast.

'Take it, take it. It was for Durhal and Haldre that I brought it from the end of the long night!' Semley cried this aloud, twisting and bowing her head to get the heavy chain off, dropping the necklace so it fell on the stones with a cold, liquid clash. 'O take it, Haldre!' she cried again, and then, weeping aloud, turned and ran from Hallan, over the bridge and down the long, broad steps, and, darting off eastward into the forest of the mountainside like some wild thing escaping, was gone.

HOW BEAUTIFUL WITH BANNERS

JAMES BLISH

1

Feeling as naked as a peppermint soldier in her transparent film wrap, Dr Ulla Hillström watched a flying cloak swirl away towards the black horizon with a certain consequent irony. Although nearly transparent itself in the distant dim arc-light flame that was Titan's sun, the fluttering creature looked warmer than what she was wearing, for all that reason said it was at the same minus 316 °F as the thin methane it flew in. Despite the virus space-bubble's warranted and eerie efficiency, she found its vigilance—itself probably as close to alive as the flying cloak was—rather difficult to believe in, let alone to trust.

The machine—as Ulla much preferred to think of it—was inarguably an improvement on the old-fashioned pressure suit. Fashioned (or more accurately, cultured) of a single colossal protein molecule, the vanishingly thin sheet of lifestuff processed gases, maintained pressure, monitored radiation through almost the whole of the electromagnetic spectrum, and above all did not get in the way. Also, it could not be cut, punctured, or indeed sustain any damage short of total destruction; macroscopically, it was a single, primary unit, with all the physical integrity of a crystal of salt or steel.

If it did not actually think, Ulla was grateful; often it almost seemed to, which was sufficient. Its primary drawback for her was that much of the time it did not really seem to be there.

Still, it seemed to be functioning; otherwise, Ulla would in fact have been as solid as a stick of candy, toppled forever across the confectionery whiteness that frosted the knife-edge stones of this cruel moon, layer upon layer. Outside—only a perilous few inches from the lightly clothed warmth of her skin—the brief gust the cloak had been soaring on died, leaving behind a silence so cataleptic that she could hear the snow creaking in a mockery of motion. Impossible though it is to comprehend, it was getting still colder out there; Titan was swinging out across Saturn's orbit towards eclipse, and the apparently fixed sun was secretly going down, its descent sensed by the snows no matter what her Earthly eyes, accustomed to the nervousness of living skies, tried to tell her. In another two Earth days it would be gone, for an eternal week.

At the thought, Ulla turned to look back the way she had come that morning. The virus bubble flowed smoothly with the motion, and the stars became brighter as it compensated for the fact that the sun was now at her back. She still could not see the base camp, of course. She had come too far for that, and in any event it was wholly underground except for a few wiry palps, hollowed out of the bitter rock by the blunt-nosed ardour of prolapse drills; the repeated nanosecond birth and death of primordial ylem the drills had induced while that cavern was being imploded had seemed to convulse the whole demon womb of this world, but in the present silence the very memory of the noise seemed false.

Now there was no sound but the creaking of the methane snow; and nothing to see but a blunt, faint spearhead of hazy light, deceptively like an Earthly aurora or the corona of the sun, pushing its way from below the edge of the cold into the indifferent company of the stars. Saturn's rings were rising, very slightly awaver in the dark-blue air, like the banners of a spectral army. The idiot face of the giant gas planet itself, faintly striped with meaningless storms as though trying to remember a childhood passion, would be glaring down at her before she could get home if she didn't get herself in motion soon. Obscurely disturbed, Dr Hillström faced front and began to unlimber her sled.

The touch and clink of the instruments cheered her a little, even in this ultimate loneliness. She was efficient—many years, and a good many suppressed impulses had seen to that; it was too late for temblors, especially so far out from the sun that had warmed her Stockholm streets and her silly friendships. All those null-adventures were gone now like a sickness. The phantom embrace of the virus suit was perhaps less satisfying—only *perhaps*—but it was much more reliable. Much more reliable; she could depend on that.

Then, as she bent to thrust the spike of a thermocouple into the wedding-cake soil, the second flying cloak (or was it that same one?) hit her in the small of the back and tumbled her into nightmare.

2

With the sudden darkness there came a profound, ambiguous emotional blow—ambiguous, yet with something shockingly familiar about it. Instantly exhausted, she felt herself go flaccid and unstrung, and her mind, adrift in nowhere, blurred and spun downward too into the swamps of trance.

The long fall slowed just short of unconsciousness, lodged precariously upon a shelf of a dream, a mental buttress founded four years in the past—a long distance, when one recalls that in a four-dimensional plenum every second of time is one hundred eighty-six thousand miles of space—and eight hundred millions of miles away. The memory was curiously inconsequential to have arrested her, let alone supported her; not of her home, of her few triumphs, or even of her aborted marriage, but of a sordid little encounter with a reporter that she had talked herself into at the Madrid genetics conference, when she herself had already been an associate professor, a Swedish Government delegate, a twenty-five-year-old divorcee, and altogether a woman who should have known better.

But better than what? The life of science even in those days had been almost by definition the life of the eternal campus exile; there was so much to learn—or, at least to show competence in—that people who wanted to be involved in the ordinary, vivid concerns of human beings could not stay with it long, indeed often could not even be recruited; they turned aside from the prospect with a shudder, or even a snort of scorn. To prepare for the sciences had become a career in indefinitely protracted adolescence, from which one awakened fitfully to find one's self spending a one-night stand in the body of a stranger. It had given her no pride, no self-love, no defences of any sort; only a queer kind of virgin numbness, highly dependent upon familiar surroundings and valueless habits, and easily breached by any normally confident siege in print, in person, anywhere—and remaining just as numb as before when the seizure of fashion, politics, or romanticism had swept by and left her stranded, too easy a recruit to have been allowed into the centre of things or even considered for it.

Curious—most curious—that in her present remote terror she should find even a moment's rest upon so wobbling a pivot. The Madrid incident had not been important; she had been through with it almost at once. Of course, as she had often told herself, she had never been promiscuous, and had often described the affair, defiantly, as that one (or at worst, second) test of the joys of impulse which any woman is entitled to have in her history. Nor had it really been that joyous: She could not now recall the boy's face, and remembered how he had felt primarily because he had been in so casual and contemptuous a hurry.

But now that she came to dream of it, she saw with a bloodless, lightless eye that all her life, in this way and in that, she had been repeatedly seduced by the inconsequential. She had nothing else to remember even in this hour of her presumptive death. Acts have consequences, a thought told her, but not ours; we have done, but never felt. We are no more alone on Titan, you and I, than we have ever been. *Basta, per carita!*—so much for Ulla.

Awakening in this same darkness as before, Ulla felt the virus bubble snuggling closer to her blind skin, and recognized the shock that had regressed her: a shock of recognition, but recognition of something she had never felt herself. Alone in a Titanic snowfield, she had eavesdropped on an . . .

No. Not possible. Sniffling, and still blind, she pushed the cozy bubble away from her breasts and tried to stand up. Light flushed briefly around her, as though the bubble had cleared just above her forehead and then clouded again. She was still alive, but everything else was utterly problematical. What had happened to her? She simply could not know.

Therefore, she thought, begin with ignorance. No one begins anywhere else . . . but I didn't know even that, once upon a time.

Hence:

3

Though the virus bubble ordinarily regulated itself, there was a control box on her hip—actually an ultrashort-range microwave transmitter—by which it could be modulated, against more special environments than the bubble itself could cope with alone. She had never had to use it before, but she tried it now.

The fogged bubble cleared patchily, but it would not stay cleared. Crazy moires and herringbone patterns swept over it, changing direction repeatedly, and outside the snowy landscape kept changing colour like a delirium. She found, however, that by continuously working the frequency knob on her box—at random, for the responses seemed to bear no relation to the Braille calibrations on the dial—she could maintain outside vision of a sort in pulses of two or three seconds each.

This was enough to show her, finally, what had happened. There was a flying cloak around her. This in itself was unprecedented; the cloaks had never attacked a man before, or indeed paid any of them the least attention during their brief previous forays. On the other hand, this was the first time anyone had ventured more than five or ten minutes outdoors in a virus suit.

It occurred to her suddenly that in so far as anything was known about the nature of the cloaks, they were in some respects much like the bubbles. It was almost as though the one were a wild species of the other.

It was an alarming notion and possibly only a trope, containing as little truth as most poetry. Annoyingly, she found herself wondering if, once she got out of this mess, the men at the base camp would take to referring to it as 'the cloak and suit business'.

The snowfield began to turn brighter; Saturn was rising. For a moment the drifts were a pale straw colour, the normal hue of Saturnlight through an atmosphere; then it turned a raving Kelly green. Muttering, Ulla twisted the potentiometer dial, and was rewarded with a brief flash of normal illumination which was promptly overridden by a torrent of crimson lake, as though she were seeing everything in terms of a series of lithographer's colour separations.

Since she could not help this, she clenched her teeth and ignored it. It was much more important to find out what the flying cloak had done to her bubble, if she were to have any hope of shucking the thing.

There was no clear separation between the bubble and the Titanian creature. They seemed to have blended into a mélange which was neither one nor the other, but a sort of coarse burlesque of both. Yet the total surface area of the integument about her did not seem to be any greater—only more ill-fitting, less responsive to her own needs. Not *much* less; after all, she was still alive, and any really gross insensitivity to the demands and cues of her body would have been instantly fatal; but there was no way to guess how long the bubble would stay even that obedient. At the moment the wild thing that had enslaved it was perhaps most like a bear sark, dangerous to the wearer only if she panicked, but the change might well be progressive, pointed ultimately towards some Saturnine equivalent of the shirt of Nessus.

And that might be happening very rapidly. She might not be allowed the time to think her way out of this fix by herself. Little though she wanted any help from the men at the base camp, and useless though she was sure they would prove, she'd damn well better ask for it now, just in case.

But the bubble was not allowing any radio transmission through its roiling unicell wall today. The earphone was dead; not even the hiss of the stars came through it—only an occasional pop of noise that was born of entropy loss in the circuits themselves.

She was cut off. *Nun denn, allein!*

With the thought, the bubble cloak shifted again around her. A sudden pressure at her lower abdomen made her stumble forward over the crisp snow, four or five steps. Then it was motionless once more, except within itself.

That it should be able to do this was not surprising, for the cloaks had to be able to flex voluntarily at least a little in order to catch the thermals they rode, and the bubble had to be able to vary its dimensions and surface tension over a wide range to withstand pressure changes, outside and in, and do it automatically. No, of course the combination would be able to move by itself; what was disquieting was that it should want to.

Another stir of movement in the middle distance caught her eye: a free cloak, seemingly riding an updraught over a fixed point. For a moment she wondered what on that ground could be warm enough to produce so localized a thermal. Then, abruptly, she realized that she was shaking with hatred, and fought furiously to drive the spasm down, her fingernails slicing into her naked palms.

A raster of jagged black lines, like a television interference pattern, broke across her view and brought her attention fully back to the minutely solipsistic confines of her dilemma. The wave of emotion, nevertheless, would not quite go away, and she had a vague but persistent impression that it was being imposed from outside, at least in part—a cold passion she was interpreting as fury because its real nature, whatever it was, had no necessary relevance to her own imprisoned soul. For all that it was her own life and no other that was in peril, she felt guilty, as though she was eavesdropping, and as angry with herself as with what she was overhearing; yet burning as helplessly as the forbidden lamp in the bedchamber of Psyche and Eros.

Another trope—but was it, after all, so far-fetched? She was a mortal present at the mating of inhuman essences; mountainously far from home; borne here like the invisible lovers upon the arms of the wind; empalaced by a whole virgin-white world, over which flew the banners of a high god and a father of gods; and, equally appropriately, Venus was very far away from whatever love was being celebrated here.

What ancient and coincidental nonsense! Next she would be thinking herself degraded at the foot of some cross.

Yet the impression, of an eerie tempest going on just slightly outside any possibility of understanding what it was, would not pass away. Still worse, it seemed to mean something, to be important, to mock her with subtle clues to matters of great moment, of which her own present trap was only the first and not necessarily the most significant.

And suppose that all these impressions were in fact not extraneous or irrelevant, but did have some import—not just as an abstract puzzle, but to that morsel of displaced life that was Ulla Hillström? She was certainly no Freudian—that farrago of poetry and tosh had been passé for so long that it was now hard to understand how anybody, let alone a whole era, had been bemused by it—but it was too late now to rule out the repulsive possibility. No matter how frozen her present world, she could not escape the fact that, from the moment the cloak had captured her, she had been equally ridden by a Sabbat of specifically erotic memories, images, notions, analogies, myths, symbols, and frank physical sensations, all the more obtrusive because they were both inappropriate and disconnected. It might well have to be faced that a season of love can fall due in the heaviest weather—and never mind the terrors that flow in with it, or what deep damnations. At the very least, it was possible that somewhere in all this was the clue that would help her to divorce herself at last even from this violent embrace.

But the concept was preposterous enough to defer consideration of it if there were any other avenues open, and at least one seemed to be: the source of the thermal. The virus bubble, like many of the Terrestrial micro-organisms to which it was analogous, could survive temperatures well above boiling, but it seemed reasonable to assume that the flying cloaks, evolved on a world where even words congealed, might be sensitive to a relatively slight amount of heat.

Now, could she move inside this shroud of her own volition? She tried a step. The sensation was tacky, as though she were ploughing in thin honey, but it did not impede her except for a slight imposed clumsiness which experience ought to obviate. She was able to mount the sled with no trouble.

The cogs bit into the snow with a dry, almost inaudible squeaking, and the sled inched forward. Ulla held it to as slow a crawl as possible, because of her interrupted vision.

The free cloak was still in sight, approximately where it had been before, in so far as she could judge against this featureless snowscape—which was fortunate, since it might well be her only flag for the source of the thermal, whatever it was.

A peculiar fluttering in her surroundings—a whisper of sound, of motion, of flickering in the light—distracted her. It was as though her compound sheath were trembling slightly. The impression grew slowly more pronounced as the sled continued to lurch forward. As usual, there seemed to be nothing she could do about it except, possibly, to retreat; but she could not do that either, now; she was committed. Outside, she began to hear the soft soughing of a steady wind.

The cause of the thermal, when she finally reached it, was almost bathetic: a pool of liquid. Placid and deep blue, it lay inside a fissure in a low, heart-shaped hummock, rimmed with feathery snow. It looked like nothing more or less than a spring, though she did not for a moment suppose that the liquid could be water. She could not see the bottom of it; evidently, it was welling up from a fair depth. The spring analogy was probably completely false; the existence of anything in a liquid state on this world had to be thought of as a form of vulcanism. Certainly the column of heat rising from it was considerable; despite the thinness of the air, the wind here nearly howled. The free cloak floated up and down, about a hundred feet above her, like the last leaf of a long, cruel autumn. Nearer home, the bubble cloak shook with something comically like subdued fury.

Now, what to do? Should she push boldly into that cleft, hoping that the alien part of the bubble cloak would be unable to bear the heat? Close up, that course now seemed foolish, as long as she was ignorant of the real nature of the magma down there. And, besides, any effective immersion would probably have to surround at least half of the total surface area of the bubble, which wasn't practicable—the well wasn't big enough to accommodate it, even supposing that the compromised virus suit did not fight back, as in the pure state it had been obligated to do. On the whole, she was reluctantly glad that the experiment was impossible, for the mere notion of risking a new immolation in that problematical hole gave her the horrors.

Yet the time left for decision was obviously now very short, even supposing—as she had no right to do—that the environment-maintaining functions of the suit were still in perfect order. The quivering of the bubble was close to being explosive, and even were it to remain intact, it might shut her off from the outside world at any second.

The free cloak dipped lower, as if in curiosity. That only made the trembling worse. She wondered why.

Was it possible—was it possible that the thing embracing her companion was jealous?

4

There was no time left to examine the notion, no time even to sneer at it. Act—act! Forcing her way off the sled, she stumbled to the mound and looked frantically for some way of stopping it up. If she could shut off the thermal, bring the free cloak still closer—but how?

Throw rocks. But were there any? Yes, there were two, not very big, but at least she could move them. She bent stiffly and tumbled them into the crater.

The liquid froze around them with soundless speed. In seconds, the snow rimming the pool had drawn completely over it, like lips closing, leaving behind only a faint dimpled streak of shadow on a white ground.

The wind moaned and died, and the free cloak, its hems outspread to the uttermost, sank down as if to wrap her in still another deadly swath. Shadow spread around her; the falling cloak, its colour deepening, blotted Saturn from the sky, and then was sprawling over the beautiful banners of the rings—

The virus bubble convulsed and turned black, throwing her to the frozen ground beside the hummock like a bead doll. A blast of wind squalled over her.

Terrified, she tried to curl into a ball. The suit puffed up around her.

Then at last, with a searing, invisible wrench at its contained kernel of space-time, which burned out the control box instantly, the single creature that was the bubble cloak tore itself free of Ulla and rose to join its incomplete fellow.

In the single second before she froze forever into the livid backdrop of Titan, she failed even to find time to regret what she had never felt; for she had never known it, and only died as she had lived, an artefact of successful calculation. She never saw the cloaks go flapping away downwind—nor could it ever have occurred to her that she had brought heterosexuality to Titan, thus beginning that long evolution the end of which, sixty millions of years away, no human being would see.

No; her last thought was for the virus bubble, and it was only three words long:

You goddam philanderer—

Almost on the horizon, the two cloaks, the two Titanians, flailed and tore at each other, becoming smaller and smaller with distance. Bits and pieces of them flaked off and fell down the sky like ragged tears. Ungainly though the cloaks normally were, they courted even more clumsily.

Beside Ulla, the well was gone; it might never have existed. Overhead, the banners of the rings flew changelessly, as though they too had seen nothing—or perhaps, as though in the last six billion years they had seen everything, siftings upon siftings in oblivion, until nothing remained but the banners of their own mirrored beauty.

A CRIMINAL ACT

HARRY HARRISON

The first blow of the hammer shook the door in its frame, and the second blow made the thin wood boom like a drum. Benedict Vernall threw the door open before a third stroke could fall and pushed his gun into the stomach of the man with the hammer.

'Get going. Get out of here,' Benedict said, in a much shriller voice than he had planned to use.

'Don't be foolish,' the bailiff said quietly, stepping aside so that the two guards behind him in the hall were clearly visible. 'I am the bailiff and I am doing my duty. If I am attacked these men have orders to shoot you and everyone else in your apartment. Be intelligent. Yours is not the first case like this. Such things are planned for.'

One of the guards clicked off the safety catch on his submachine gun, smirking at Benedict as he did it. Benedict let the pistol fall slowly to his side.

'Much better,' the bailiff told him and struck the nail once more with the hammer so that the notice was fixed firmly to the door.

'Take that filthy thing down,' Benedict said, choking over the words.

'Benedict Vernall,' the bailiff said, adjusting his glasses on his nose as he read from the proclamation he had just posted. 'This is to inform you that pursuant to the Criminal Birth Act of 1993 you are guilty of the act of criminal birth and are hereby proscribed and no longer protected from bodily injury by the forces of this sovereign state . . .'

'You're going to let some madman kill me . . . what kind of a dirty law is that?'

The bailiff removed his glasses and gazed coldly along his nose at Benedict. 'Mr Vernall,' he said, 'have the decency to accept the results of your own actions. Did you or did you not have an illegal baby?'

'Illegal—never! A harmless infant . . .'

'Do you or do you not already have the legal maximum of two children?'

'We have two, but . . .'

'You refused advice or aid from your local birth-control clinic. You expelled, with force, the birth guidance officer who called upon you. You rejected the offer of the abortion clinic . . .'

'Murderers!'

'. . . And the advice of the Family Planning Board. The statutory six months have elapsed without any action on your part. You have had the three advance warnings and have ignored them. Your family still contains one consumer more than is prescribed by law, therefore the proclamation has been posted. You alone are responsible, Mr Vernall, you can blame no one else.'

'I can blame this foul law.'

'It is the law of the land,' the bailiff said, drawing himself up sternly. 'It is not for you or I to question.' He took a whistle from his pocket and raised it to his mouth. 'It is my legal duty to remind you that you still have one course open, even at this last moment, and may still avail yourself of the services of the Euthanasia Clinic.'

'Go straight to Hell!'

'Indeed. I've been told that before.' The bailiff snapped the whistle to his lips and blew a shrill blast. He almost smiled as Benedict slammed shut the apartment door.

There was an animal-throated roar from the stairwell as the policemen who were blocking it stepped aside. A knot of fiercely tangled men burst out, running and fighting at the same time. One of them surged ahead of the pack but fell as a fist caught him on the side of the head; the others trampled him underfoot. Shouting and cursing the mob came on and it looked as though it would be a draw, but a few yards short of the door one of the leaders tripped and brought two others down. A short fat man in the second rank leaped their bodies and crashed headlong into Vernall's door with such force that the ball-point pen he held extended pierced the paper of the notice and sank into the wood beneath.

'A volunteer has been selected,' the bailiff shouted and the waiting police and guards closed in on the wailing men and began to force them back towards the stairs. One of the men remained behind on the floor, saliva running down his cheeks as he chewed hysterically at a strip of the threadbare carpet. Two white-garbed hospital attendants were looking out for this sort of thing and one of them jabbed the man expertly in the neck with a hypodermic needle while the other unrolled the stretcher.

Under the bailiff's watchful eye the volunteer painstakingly wrote his name in the correct space on the proclamation, then carefully put the pen back in his vest pocket.

'Very glad to accept you as a volunteer for this important public duty, Mr . . .' the bailiff leaned forward to peer at the paper, 'Mr Mortimer,' he said.

'Mortimer is my first name,' the man said in a soft dry voice as he dabbed lightly at his forehead with his breast-pocket handkerchief.

'Understandable, sir, your anonymity will be respected as is the right of all volunteers. Might I presume that you are acquainted with the rest of the regulations?'

'You may. Paragraph 46 of the Criminal Birth Act of 1993, sub-section 14, governing the selection of volunteers. Firstly, I have volunteered for the maximum period of twenty-four hours. Secondly, I will neither attempt nor commit violence of any form upon any other members of the public during this time, and if I do so I will be held responsible by law for my acts.'

'Very good. But isn't there more?'

Mortimer folded the handkerchief precisely and tucked it back into his pocket. 'Thirdly,' he said, and patted it smooth, 'I shall not be liable to prosecution by law if I take the life of the proscribed individual, one Benedict Vernall.'

'Perfectly correct.' The bailiff nodded and pointed to a large suitcase that a policeman had set down on the floor and was opening. The hall had been cleared. 'If you would step over here and take your choice.' They both gazed down into the suitcase that was filled to overflowing with instruments of death. 'I hope you also understand that your own life will be in jeopardy during this period and if you are injured or killed you will not be protected by law?'

'Don't take me for a fool,' Mortimer said curtly, then pointed into the suitcase. 'I want one of those concussion grenades.'

'You cannot have it,' the bailiff told him in a cutting voice, injured by the other's manner. There was a correct way to do these things. 'Those are only for use in open districts where the innocent cannot be injured. Not in an apartment building. You have your choice of all the short-range weapons, however.'

Mortimer laced his fingers together and stood with his head

bowed, almost in the attitude of prayer, as he examined the contents. Machine pistols, grenades, automatics, knives, knuckle-dusters, vials of acid, whips, straight razors, broken glass, poison darts, morning stars, maces, gas bombs and tear-gas pens.

'Is there any limit?' he asked.

'Take what you feel you will need. Just remember that it must all be accounted for and returned.'

'I want the Reisling machine pistol with five of the twenty cartridge magazines and the commando knife with the spikes on the handguard and fountain pen tear-gas gun.'

The bailiff was making quick check marks on a mimeographed form attached to his clipboard while Mortimer spoke. 'Is that all?' he asked.

Mortimer nodded and took the extended board and scrawled his name on the bottom of the sheet without examining it, then began at once to fill his pockets with the weapons and ammunition.

'Twenty-four hours,' the bailiff said, looking at his watch and filling in one more space in the form. 'You have until 1745 hours tomorrow.'

'Get away from the door, please, Ben,' Maria begged.

'Quiet,' Benedict whispered, his ear pressed to the panel. 'I want to hear what they are saying.' His face screwed up as he struggled to understand the muffled voices. 'It's no good,' he said, turning away, 'I can't make it out. Not that it makes any difference. I know what's happening . . .'

'There's a man coming to kill you,' Maria said in her delicate, little girl's voice. The baby started to whimper and she hugged him to her.

'Please, Maria, go back into the bathroom like we agreed. You have the bed in there, and the food, and there aren't any windows. As long as you stay along the wall away from the door nothing can possibly happen to you. Do that for me, darling—so I won't have to worry about either of you.'

'Then you will be out here alone.'

Benedict squared his narrow shoulders and clutched the pistol firmly. 'That is where I belong, out in front, defending my family. That is as old as the history of man.'

'Family,' she said and looked around worriedly. 'What about Matthew and Agnes?'

'They'll be all right with your mother. She promised to look after them until we got in touch with her again. You can still be there with them, I wish you would.'

'No, I couldn't. I couldn't bear being anywhere else now. And I couldn't leave the baby there, he would be so hungry.' She looked down at the infant who was still whimpering, then began to unbutton the top of her dress.

'Please, darling,' Benedict said, edging back from the door. 'I want you to go into the bathroom with the baby and stay there. You must. He could be coming at any time now.'

She reluctantly obeyed him, and he waited until the door had closed and he heard the lock being turned. Then he tried to force their presence from his mind because they were only a distraction that could interfere with what must be done. He had worked out the details of his plan of defence long before and he went slowly around the apartment making sure that everything was as it should be. First the front door, the only door into the apartment. It was locked and bolted and the night chain was attached. All that remained was to push the big wardrobe up against it. The killer could not enter now without a noisy struggle, and if he tried Benedict would be there waiting with his gun. That took care of the door.

There were no windows in either the kitchen or the bathroom, so he could forget about these rooms. The bedroom was a possibility since its window looked out on to the fire escape, but he had a plan for this, too. The window was locked and the only way it could be opened from the outside was by breaking the glass. He would hear that and would have time to push the couch in the hall up against the bedroom door. He didn't want to block it now in case he had to retreat into the bedroom himself.

Only one room remained, the living room, and this was where he was going to make his stand. There were two windows in the living-room and the far one could be entered from the fire escape, as could the bedroom window. The killer might come this way. The other window could not be reached from the fire escape, though shots could still be fired through it from the windows across the court. But the corner was out of the line of fire, and this was where he would be. He had pushed the big armchair right up against the wall and, after checking once more that both windows were locked, he dropped into it.

His gun rested on his lap and pointed at the far window by the fire escape. He would shoot if anyone tried to come through it. The other window was close by, but no harm could come that way unless he stood in front of it. The thin fabric curtains were drawn and once it was dark he could see through them without being seen himself. By shifting the gun barrel a few degrees he could cover the door into the hall. If there were any disturbance at the front door he could be there in a few steps. He had done everything he could. He settled back into the chair.

Once the daylight faded the room was quite dark, yet he could see well enough by the light of the city sky that filtered in through the drawn curtains. It was very quiet and whenever he shifted position he could hear the rusty chair springs twang beneath him. After only a few hours he realized one slight flaw in his plan. He was thirsty.

At first he could ignore it, but by nine o'clock his mouth was as dry as cotton wool. He knew he couldn't last the night like this, it was too distracting. He should have brought a jug of water in with him. The wisest thing would be to go and get it as soon as possible, yet he did not want to leave the protection of the corner. He had heard nothing of the killer and this only made him more concerned about his unseen presence.

Then he heard Maria calling to him. Very softly at first, then louder and louder. She was worried. Was he all right? He dared not answer her, not from here. The only thing to do was to go to her, whisper through the door that everything was fine and that she should be quiet. Perhaps then she would go to sleep. And he could get some water in the kitchen and bring it back.

As quietly as he could he rose and stretched his stiff legs, keeping his eyes on the grey square of the second window. Putting the toe of one foot against the heel of the other he pulled his shoes off, then went on silent tiptoe across the room. Maria was calling louder now, rattling at the bathroom door, and he had to silence her. Why couldn't she realize the danger she was putting him in?

As he passed through the door the hall light above him came on.

'What are you doing?' he screamed at Maria who stood by the switch, blinking in the sudden glare.

'I was so worried . . .'

The crash of breaking glass from the living-room was punctuated by the hammering boom of the machine pistol. Arrows of pain tore at Benedict and he hurled himself sprawling into the hall.

'Into the bathroom!' he screeched and fired his own revolver back through the dark doorway.

He was only half aware of Maria's muffled squeal as she slammed the door and, for the moment, he forgot the pain of the wounds. There was the metallic smell of burnt gunpowder and a blue haze hung in the air. Something scraped in the living-room and he fired again into the darkness. He winced as the answering fire crashed thunder and flame towards him and the bullets tore holes in the plaster of the hall opposite the door.

The firing stopped but he kept his gun pointed as he realized that the killer's fire couldn't reach him where he lay against the wall away from the open doorway. The man would have to come into the hall to shoot him and if he did that Benedict would fire first and kill him. More shots slammed into the wall, but he did not bother to answer them. When the silence stretched out for more than a minute he took a chance and silently broke his revolver and pulled out the empty shells, putting live cartridges in their place. There was a pool of blood under his leg.

Keeping the gun pointed at the doorway he clumsily rolled up his pants leg with his left hand, then took a quick glimpse. There was more blood running down his ankle and sopping his sock. A bullet had torn through his calf muscle and made two round, dark holes from which the thick blood pumped. It made him dizzy to look at, then he remembered and pointed the wavering pistol back at the doorway. The living room was silent. His side hurt, too, but when he pulled his shirt out of his trousers and looked he realized although this wound was painful, it was not as bad as the one in his leg. A second bullet had burned along his side, glancing off the ribs and leaving a shallow wound. It wasn't bleeding badly. Something would have to be done about his leg.

'You moved fast, Benedict, I must congratulate you—'

Benedict's finger contracted with shock and he pumped two bullets into the room, towards the sound of the man's voice. The man laughed.

'Nerves, Benedict, nerves. Just because I am here to kill you doesn't mean that we can't talk.'

'You're a filthy beast, a foul, filthy beast!' Benedict splattered the words from his lips and followed them with a string of obscenities, expressions he hadn't used or even heard since his school days. He stopped suddenly as he realized that Maria could hear him. She had never heard him curse before.

'Nerves, Benedict?' The dry laugh sounded again. 'Calling me insulting names won't alter this situation.'

'Why don't you leave, I won't try to stop you,' Benedict said as he slowly pulled his left arm out of his shirt. 'I don't want to see you or know you. Why don't you go away?'

'I'm afraid that it is not that easy, Ben. You have created this situation, in one sense you have called me here. Like a sorcerer summoning some evil genie. That's a pleasant simile, isn't it? May I introduce myself. My name is Mortimer.'

'I don't want to know your name, you . . . piece of filth.' Benedict half-mumbled, his attention concentrated on the silent removal of his shirt. It hung from his right wrist and he shifted the gun to his left hand for a moment while he slipped it off. His leg throbbed with pain when he draped it over the wound in his calf and he gasped, then spoke quickly to disguise the sound. 'You came here because you wanted to—and I'm going to kill you for that.'

'Very good, Benedict, that is much more the type of spirit I expected from you. After all you are the closest we can come to a dedicated lawbreaker these days, the antisocial individualist who stands alone, who will carry on the traditions of the Dillingers and the James brothers. Though they brought death and you brought life, and your weapon is far humbler than their guns and their . . .' The words ended with a dry chuckle.

'You have a warped mind, Mortimer, just what I would suspect of a man who accepts a free licence to kill. You're sick.'

Benedict wanted to keep the other man talking, at least for a few minutes more until he could bandage his leg. The shirt was sticky with blood and he couldn't knot it right with his left hand. 'You must be sick to come here,' he said. 'What other reason could you possibly have?' He laid the gun down silently, then fumbled with haste to bandage the wound.

'Sickness is relative,' the voice in the darkness said, 'as is crime. Man invents societies and the rules of his invented societies determine the crimes. *O tempora! O mores!* Homosexuals in Periclean Greece were honoured men, and respected for their love. Homosexuals in industrial England were shunned and prosecuted for a criminal act. Who commits the crime—society or the man? Which of them is the criminal? You may attempt to argue a higher authority than man, but that would be only an abstract predication and what we are discussing here are realities. The law states that you are a criminal. I am here to enforce that law.' The thunder of his gun added punctuation to his words and long splinters of wood flew from the doorframe. Benedict jerked the knot tight and grabbed up his pistol again.

'I do invoke a higher authority,' he said. 'Natural law, the sanctity of life, the inviolability of marriage. Under this authority I wed and I love, and my children are the blessings of this union.'

'Your blessings—and the blessings of the rest of mankind—are consuming this world like locusts,' Mortimer said. 'But that is an observation. First, I must deal with your arguments.

'*Primus.* The only natural law is written in the sedimentary rocks and the spectra of suns. What you call natural law is man-made law and varies with the varieties of religion. Argument invalid.

'*Secundus.* Life is prolificate and today's generations must die so that tomorrow's may live. All religions have the faces of Janus. They frown at killing and at the same time smile at war and capital punishment. Argument invalid.

'*Ultimus.* The forms of male and female union are as varied as the societies that harbour them. Argument invalid. Your higher authority does not apply to the world of facts and law. Believe in it if you wish, if it gives you satisfaction, but do not invoke it to condone your criminal acts.'

'Criminal!' Benedict shouted, and fired two shots through the doorway, then cringed as an answering storm of bullets crackled by. Dimly, through the bathroom door, he heard the baby crying, awakened by the noise. He dropped out the empty shells and angrily pulled live cartridges from his pocket and jammed them into the cylinder. 'You're the criminal who is trying to murder me,' he said. 'You are the tool of the criminals who invade my house with their unholy laws and tell me I can have no more children. You cannot give me orders about this.'

'What a fool you are,' Mortimer sighed. 'You are a social animal and do not hesitate to accept the benefits of your society. You accept medicine, so your children live now as they would have died in the past, and you accept a ration of food to feed them, food you do not work for. This suits you so you accept. But you do not accept planning for your family and you attempt to reject it. It is impossible. You must accept all or reject all. You must leave your society—or abide by its rules. You eat the food, you must pay the price.'

'I don't ask for more food. The baby has its mother's milk, we will share our food ration . . .'

'Don't be fatuous. You and your irresponsible kind have filled this world to bursting with your get, and still you will not stop. You have been reasoned with, railed against, cajoled, bribed, and threatened, all to no avail. Now you must be stopped. You have refused all aid to prevent your bringing one more mouth into this hungry world and, since you have done so anyway, you are to be held responsible for closing another mouth and removing it from this same world. The law is a humane one, rising out of our history of individualism and the frontier spirit, and gives you a chance to defend your ideals with a gun. And your life.'

'The law is not humane,' Benedict said. 'How can you possibly suggest that. It is harsh, cruel, and pointless.'

'Quite the contrary, the system makes very good sense. Try and step outside yourself for a moment, forget your prejudices and look at the problem that faces our race. The universe is cruel—but it's not ruthless. The conservation of mass is one of the universe's most ruthlessly enforced laws. We have been insane to ignore it so long, and it is sanity that now forces us to limit the sheer mass of human flesh on this globe. Appeals to reason have never succeeded in slowing the population growth so, with great reluctance, laws have been passed. Love, marriage, and the family are not affected—up to a reasonable maximum of children. After that a man *voluntarily* forsakes the protection of society, and must take the consequences of his own acts. If he is insanely selfish, his death will benefit society by ridding it of his presence. If he is not insane and has determination and enough guts to win—well then, he is the sort of man that society needs and he represents a noble contribution to the gene pool. Good and law-abiding citizens are not menaced by these laws.'

'How dare you!' Benedict shouted. 'Is a poor, helpless mother of an illegitimate baby a criminal?'

'No, only if she refuses all aid. She is even allowed a single child without endangering herself. If she persists in her folly, she must pay for her acts. There are countless frustrated women willing to volunteer for battle to even the score. They, like myself, are on the side of the law and eager to enforce it. So close my mouth, if you can, Benedict, because I look forward with pleasure to closing your incredibly selfish one.'

'Madman!' Benedict hissed and felt his teeth grate together with the intensity of his passion. 'Scum of society. This obscene law brings forth the insane dregs of humanity and arms them and gives them licence to kill.'

'It does that, and a useful device it is, too. The maladjusted expose themselves and can be watched. Better the insane killer coming publicly and boldly than trapping and butchering your child in the park. Now he risks his life and whoever is killed serves humanity with his death.'

'You admit you are a madman—a licensed killer?' Benedict started to stand but the hall began to spin dizzily and grow dark; he dropped back heavily.

'Not I,' Mortimer said tonelessly. 'I am a man who wishes to aid the law and wipe out your vile, proliferating kind.'

'You're an invert then, hating the love of man and woman.'

The only answer was a cold laugh that infuriated Benedict.

'Sick!' he screamed, 'or mad. Or sterile, incapable of fathering children of your own and hating those who can . . .'

'That's enough! I've talked enough to you, Benedict. Now I shall kill you.'

Benedict could hear anger for the first time in the other's voice and knew that he had goaded the man with the prod of truth. He was silent, sick, and weak, the blood still seeping through his rough bandage and widening in a pool on the floor. He had to save what little strength he had to aim and fire when the killer came through the doorway. Behind him he heard the almost silent opening of the bathroom door and the rustle of footsteps. He looked up helplessly into Maria's tearstained face.

'Who's there with you?' Mortimer shouted, from where he crouched behind the armchair. 'I hear you whispering. If your wife is there with you, Benedict, send her away. I won't be responsible for the cow's safety. You've brought this upon yourself, Benedict, and the time has now come to pay the price of your errors, and I shall be the instrumentality of that payment.'

He stood and emptied the remainder of the magazine of bullets through the doorway, then pressed the button to release the magazine and hurled it after the bullets, clicking a new one instantly into place. With a quick pull he worked the slide to shove a live cartridge into the chamber and crouched, ready to attack.

This was it. He wouldn't need the knife. Walk a few feet forward. Fire through the doorway, then throw in the tear gas pen. It would either blind the man or spoil his aim. Then walk through firing with the trigger jammed down and the bullets spraying like water and the man would be dead. Mortimer took a deep, shuddering breath—then stopped and gaped as Benedict's hand snaked through the doorway and felt its way up the wall.

It was so unexpected that for a moment he didn't fire, and when he did fire he missed. A hand is a difficult target for an automatic weapon. The hand jerked down over the light switch and vanished as the ceiling lights came on.

Mortimer cursed and fired after the hand and fired into the wall and through the doorway, hitting nothing except insensate plaster and feeling terribly exposed beneath the glare of light.

The first shot from the pistol went unheard in the roar of his gun and he did not realize that he was under fire until the second bullet ripped into the floor close to his feet. He stopped shooting, spun round and gaped.

On the fire escape outside the broken window stood the woman. Slight and wide-eyed and swaying as though a strong wind tore at her, she pointed the gun at him with both hands and jerked the trigger spasmodically. The bullets came close but did not hit him, and in panic he pulled the machine pistol up, spraying bullets in an arc towards the window. 'Don't! I don't want to hurt you!' he shouted even as he did it.

The last of his bullets hit the wall and his gun clicked and locked out of battery as the magazine emptied. He hurled the barren metal magazine away and tried to jam a full one in. The pistol banged again and the bullet hit him in the side and spun him about. When he fell the gun fell from his hand. Benedict, who had been crawling slowly and painfully across the floor reached him at the same moment and clutched at his throat with hungry fingers.

'Don't . . .' Mortimer croaked and thrashed about. He had never learned to fight and did not know what else to do.

'Please, Benedict, don't,' Maria said, climbing through the window and running to them. 'You're killing him.'

'No . . . I'm not,' Benedict gasped. 'No strength. My hands are too weak.'

Looking up he saw the pistol near his head and he reached and tore it from her.

'One less mouth now!' he shouted and pressed the hot muzzle against Mortimer's chest and pulled the trigger. The muffled shot tore into the man who kicked violently once and died.

'Darling, you're all right?' Maria wailed, kneeling and clutching him to her.

'Yes . . . all right. Weak, but that's from loss of blood, I imagine. The bleeding has stopped now. It's all over. We've won. We'll have the food ration now, and they won't bother us any more and everyone will be satisfied.'

'I'm so glad,' she said, and actually managed to smile through her tears. 'I really didn't want to tell you before, not bother you with all this other trouble going on. But there's going to be . . .' She dropped her eyes.

'What?' he asked incredulously. 'You can't possibly mean . . .'

'But I do.' She patted the rounded mound of her midriff. 'Aren't we lucky?'

All he could do was look up at her, his mouth wide and gaping like some helpless fish cast up on the shore.

PROBLEMS OF CREATIVENESS

THOMAS M. DISCH

There was a dull ache, a kind of hollowness, in the general area of his liver, the seat of the intelligence according to the *Psychology* of Aristotle—a feeling that there was someone inside his chest blowing up a balloon, or that the balloon was his body. Sometimes he could ignore it, but sometimes he could not ignore it. It was like a swollen gum that he must incessantly probe with his tongue or finger. Perhaps it was filled with pus. It was like being sick, but it was different too. His legs ached from sitting.

Professor Offengeld was telling them about Dante. Dante was born in 1265. *1265*, he wrote in his notebook.

He might have felt the same way even if it weren't for Milly's coldness, but that made it worse. Milly was his girl, and they were in love, but for the last three nights she had been putting him off, telling him he should study or some other dumb excuse.

Professor Offengeld made a joke, and the other students in the auditorium laughed. Birdie ostentatiously stretched his legs out into the aisle and yawned.

'The hell that Dante describes is the hell that each of us holds inside his own, most secret soul,' Offengeld said solemnly.

Shit, he thought to himself. It's all a pile of shit. He wrote *Shit* in his notebook, then made the letters look three dimensional and shaded their sides carefully.

Offengeld was telling them about Florence now, and about the Popes and things. 'What is simony?' Offengeld asked.

He was listening, but it didn't make any sense. Actually he wasn't listening. He was trying to draw Milly's face in his notebook, but he couldn't draw very well. Except skulls. He could draw very convincing skulls. Maybe he should have gone to art school. He turned Milly's face into a skull with long blond hair. He felt sick.

He felt sick to his stomach. Maybe it was the Synthamon bar he had had in place of a hot lunch. He didn't eat a balanced diet. That was a mistake. For over two years he had been eating in cafeterias and sleeping in dorms. Ever since high school graduation in fact. It was a hell of a way to live. He needed a home life, regularity. He needed to get laid. When he married Milly they were going to have twin beds. They'd have a two-room apartment all their own, and one room would just have beds in it. Nothing but two beds. He imagined Milly in her spiffy little hostess uniform, and then he began undressing her in his imagination. He closed his eyes. First he took off her jacket with the Pan-Am monogram over the right breast. Then he popped open the snap at her waist and unzipped the zipper. He slid the skirt down over the smooth Antron slip. The slip was the old-fashioned kind with lace along the hem. Her blouse was the old-fashioned kind with buttons. It was hard to imagine unbuttoning all those buttons. He lost interest.

The carnal were in the first circle, because their sin was least. Francesca de Rimini. Cleopatra. Elizabeth Taylor. The class laughed at Offengeld's little joke. They all knew Elizabeth Taylor from the junior year course in the History of Cinema.

Rimini was a town in Italy.

What the hell was he supposed to care about this kind of crap? Who *cares* when Dante was born? Maybe he was *never* born. What difference did it make to *him*, to Birdie Ludd?

None.

Why didn't he come right out and ask Offengeld a question like that? Lay it on the line. Put it to him straight. Cut out the crap.

One good reason was because Offengeld wasn't there. What seemed to be Offengeld was in fact a flux of photons inside a large synthetic crystal. The real flesh-and-blood Offengeld had died two years ago. During his lifetime Offengeld had been considered the world's leading Dantean, which was why the National Educational Council was still using his tapes.

It was ridiculous: Dante, Florence, the Simoniac Popes. This wasn't the goddamn Middle Ages. This was the goddamn 21st century, and he was Birdie Ludd, and he was in love, and he was lonely, and he was unemployed, and there wasn't a thing he could do, not a goddamn thing, or a single place to turn in the whole goddamn stinking country.

The hollow feeling inside his chest swelled, and he tried to think about the buttons on Milly's imaginary blouse and the warm, familiar flesh beneath. He did feel sick. He ripped the sheet with the skull on it out of his notebook, not without a guilty glance at the sign that hung above the stage of the auditorium: PAPER IS VALUABLE. DON'T WASTE IT. He folded it in half and tore it neatly down the seam. He repeated this process until the pieces were too small to tear any further, then he put them in his shirt pocket.

The girl sitting beside him was giving him a dirty look for wasting paper. Like most homely girls, she was a militant Conservationist, but she kept a good notebook, and Birdie was counting on her to get him through the Finals. One way or another. So he smiled at her. He had a real nice smile. Everybody was always pointing out what a nice smile he had. His only real problem was his nose, which was short.

Professor Offengeld said: 'And now we will have a short comprehension test. Please close your notebooks and put them under your seats.' Then he faded away, and the auditorium lights came on. A taped voice automatically boomed out: *No talking please*! Four old Negro monitors began distributing the little answer sheets to the five hundred students in the auditorium.

The lights dimmed, and the first Multiple Choice appeared on the screen:

1. *Dante Alighieri was born in (a) 1300, (b) 1265, (c) 1625, (d) Date unknown.*

As far as Birdie was concerned the date was unknown. The dog in the seat beside him was covering up her answers. So, when was Dante born? He'd written the date in his notebook, but he didn't remember now. He looked back at the four choices, but the second question was on the screen already. He scratched a mark in the (*c*) space and then erased it, feeling an obscure sense of unluckiness in the choice, but finally he checked that space anyhow. When he looked up the fourth question was on the screen.

The answers he had to choose from were all wop names he'd never heard of. The goddamn test didn't make any sense. Disgusted, he marked (*c*) for every question and carried his test paper to the monitor at the front of the room. The monitor told him he couldn't leave the room till the test was over. He sat in the dark and tried to think of Milly. Something was all wrong, but he didn't know what. The bell rang. Everyone breathed a sigh of relief.

334 East 11th Street was one of twenty identical buildings built in the early 1980s under the Federal Government's first MODICUM programme. Each building was twenty-one storeys high (one floor

for shops, the rest for apartments); each floor was swastika-shaped; each of the arms of the swastikas opened on to four three-room apartments (for couples with children) and six two-room apartments (for childless couples). Thus each building was able to accommodate 2,240 occupants without overcrowding. The entire development, occupying an area of less than six city blocks, housed a population of 44,800. It had been an incredible accomplishment for its time.

SHADDUP, someone, a man, was yelling into the airshaft of 334 East 11th Street. WHY CAN'T YOU ALL SHADDUP? It was half past seven, and the man had been yelling into the airshaft for forty-five minutes already, ever since returning from his day's work (three hours' bussing dishes at a cafeteria). It was difficult to tell whom precisely he was yelling at. In one apartment a woman was yelling at a man, WHADAYA MEAN, TWENTY DOLLARS? And the man would yell back, TWENTY DOLLARS, THAT'S WHAT I MEAN! Numerous babies made noises of dissatisfaction, and older children made louder noises as they played guerrilla warfare in the corridors. Birdie, sitting on the steps of the stairwell, could see, on the floor below, a thirteen-year-old Negro girl dancing in place in front of a dresser mirror, singing along with the transistor radio that she pressed into the shallow declevity of her pubescent breasts. I CAN'T TELL YOU HOW *MUCH* I LOVE HIM, the radio sang at full volume. It was not a song that Birdie Ludd greatly admired, though it *was* Number Three in the Nation, and that meant something. She had a pretty little ass, and Birdie thought she was going to shake the tinselly fringes right off her street shorts. He tried to open the narrow window that looked from the stairwell out into the airshaft, but it was stuck tight. His hands came away covered with soot. He cursed mildly. I CAN'T HEAR MYSELF THINK, the man yelled into the airshaft.

Hearing someone coming up the steps, Birdie sat back down and pretended to read his schoolbook. He thought it might be Milly (whoever it was wearing heels), and a lump began to form in his throat. If it were Milly, what would he say to her?

It wasn't Milly. It was just some old lady lugging a bag of groceries. She stopped at the landing below him, leaning against the handrail for support, sighed, and set down her grocery bag. She stuck a pink stick of Oraline between her flaccid lips, and after a few seconds it got to her and she smiled at Birdie. Birdie scowled down at the bad reproduction of David's *Death of Socrates* in his text.

'Studying?' the old woman asked.

'Yeah, that's what I'm doing all right. I'm studying.'

'That's good.' She took the tranquillizer out of her mouth, holding it like a cigarette between her index and middle fingers. Her smile broadened, as though she were elaborating some joke, honing it to a fine edge.

'It's good for a young man to study,' she said at last, almost chuckling.

The tune on the radio changed to the new Ford commercial. It was one of Birdie's favourite commercials, and he wished the old bag would shut up so he could hear it.

'You can't get anywheres these days without studying.'

Birdie made no reply. The old woman took a different tack. 'These stairs,' she said.

Birdie looked up from his book, peeved. 'What about them?'

'What about them! The elevators have been out of commission for three weeks. That's what about them—three weeks!'

'So?'

'So, why don't they fix the elevators? But you just try to call up the MODICUM office and get an answer to a question like that and see what happens. Nothing—that's what happens!'

He wanted to tell her to can it. She was spoiling the commercial. Besides, she talked like she'd spent all her life in a private building instead of some crummy MODICUM slum. It had probably been years, not weeks, since the elevators in this building had been working.

With a look of disgust, he slid over to one side of the step so the old lady could get past him. She walked up three steps till her face was just level with his. She smelled of beer and Synthamon and old age. He hated old people. He hated their wrinkled faces and the touch of their cold dry flesh. It was because there were so many *old* people that Birdie Ludd couldn't get married to the girl he loved and have a baby. It was a goddamned shame.

'What are you studying about?'

Birdie glanced down at the painting. He read the caption, which he had not read before. 'That's Socrates,' he said, remembering dimly something his Art History teacher had said about Socrates. 'It's a painting,' he explained, 'a Greek painting.'

'You going to be an artist? Or what?'

'What,' Birdie replied curtly.

'You're Milly Holt's steady boy, aren't you?' He didn't reply. 'You waiting for Milly tonight?'

'Is there any law against waiting for someone?'

The old lady laughed right in his face. Then she made her way from step to step up to the next landing. Birdie tried not to turn around to look after her, but he couldn't help himself. They looked into each other's eyes, and she laughed again. Finally he had to ask her what she was laughing about. 'Is there a law against laughing?' she asked right back. Her laughing grew harsher and turned into a hacking cough, like in a Health Education movie about the dangers of smoking. He wondered if maybe she was an addict. Birdie knew lots of men who used tobacco, but somehow it seemed disgusting in a woman.

Several floors below there was the sound of glass shattering. Birdie looked down the abyss of the stairwell. He could see a hand moving up the railing. Maybe it was Milly's hand. The fingers were slim, as Milly's fingers would be, and the nails seemed to be painted gold. In the dim light of the stairwell, at this distance, it was difficult to tell. A sudden ache of unbelieving hope made him forget the woman's laughter, the stench of garbage, the screaming. The stairwell became a scene of romance, like a show on television.

People had always told him Milly was pretty enough to be an actress. He wouldn't have been so bad-looking himself, if it weren't for his nose. He imagined how she would cry out 'Birdie!' when she saw him waiting for her, how they would kiss, how she would take him into her mother's apartment . . .

At the eleventh or twelfth floor the hand left the railing and did not reappear. It hadn't been Milly after all.

He looked at his guaranteed Timex watch. It was eight o'clock. He could afford to wait two more hours for Milly. Then he would have to take the subway back to his dorm, an hour's ride. If he hadn't been put on probation because of his grades, he would have waited all night long.

He sat down to study Art History. He stared at the picture of Socrates in the bad light. With one hand he was holding a big cup; with the other he was giving somebody the finger. He didn't seem to be dying at all. His Midterm in Art History was going to be tomorrow afternoon at two o'clock. He really had to study. He stared at the picture more intently. Why did people paint pictures anyhow? He stared until his eyes hurt.

Somewhere a baby was crying. SHADDUP, WHY DON'T YA SHADDUP? ARE YA CRAZY OR SOMETHIN? A gang of kids impersonating Burmese nationals ran down the stairs, and a minute later another gang (US guerrillas) ran down after them, screaming obscenities.

Staring at the picture in the bad light, he began to cry. He was certain, though he would not yet admit it in words, that Milly was cheating on him. He loved Milly so much; she was so beautiful. The last time he had seen her she'd called him stupid. 'You're so stupid,' she said, 'you make me sick.' But she was so beautiful.

A tear fell into Socrates' cup and was absorbed by the cheap paper of the text. The radio started to play a new commercial. Gradually he got hold of himself again. He had to buckle down and study, goddamnit!

Who in hell was Socrates?

Birdie Ludd's father was a fat man with a small chin and a short nose like Birdie's. Since his wife's death he'd lived by himself in a MODICUM dorm for elderly gentlemen, where Birdie visited him once a month. They never had anything to talk about, but the MODICUM people insisted that families should stick together. Family life was the single greatest cohesive force in any society. They'd meet in the Visitor's Room, and if either of them had gotten letters from Birdie's brothers or sisters they'd talk about that, and then they might watch some television (especially if there was baseball, for Mr Ludd was a Yankee fan), and then right before he left, Birdie's father would hit him for five or ten dollars, since the allowance he got from MODICUM wasn't enough to keep him supplied with Thorazine. Birdie, of course, never had anything to spare.

Whenever Birdie visited his father, he was reminded of Mr Mack. Mr Mack had been Birdie's guidance counsellor in senior year at PS 125, and as such he had played a much more central role in Birdie's life than his father had. He was a balding, middle-aged man with a belly as big as Mr Ludd's and a Jewish-type nose. Birdie had always had the feeling that the counsellor was toying with him, that his professional blandness was a disguise for an unbounded contempt, that all his good advice was a snare. The pity was that Birdie could not, in his very nature, help but be caught up in it. It was Mr Mack's game and had to be played by his rules.

Actually Mr Mack had felt a certain cool sympathy for Birdie Ludd. Of the various students who'd failed their REGENTS, Birdie was certainly the most attractive. He never became violent or rude in interviews, and he always seemed to want so hard to *try*. 'In fact,' Mr Mack had told his wife in confidence one evening (she was an educational counsellor hereself), 'I think this is a splendid example of the basic inequity of the system. Because that boy is *basically* decent.'

'Oh *you*,' she'd replied. 'Basically, you're just an old softie.'

And, in fact, Birdie's case was not that exceptional. Congress had passed the Revised Genetic Testing Act (or REGENTS, as they were known popularly) in 2011, seven years before Birdie turned eighteen and had to take them. By that time the agitation and protests were over, and the system seemed to be running smoothly. Population figures had held steady since 2014.

By contrast, the first Genetic Testing Act (of 1998) had altogether failed its hoped for effect. This act had merely specified that such obvious genetic undesirables as diabetics, the criminally insane, and morons were not to be allowed the privilege of reproducing their kind. They were also denied suffrage. The act of 1998 had met virtually no opposition, and it had been easy to implement, since by that time civic contraception techniques were practiced everywhere but in the most benightedly rural areas. The chief, though unstated, purpose of the Act of 1998 had been to pave the way for the REGENTS system.

The REGENTS were tripartite: there was the familiar Stanford–Binet intelligence test (short form); the Skinner–Waxman Test for Creative Potential (which consisted in large part of picking the punch lines for jokes on a multiple choice test); and the O'Ryan–Army physical performance and metabolism test. Candidates failed if they received scores that fell below one standard deviation in two of the three tests. Birdie Ludd had been nervous on the day of his REGENTS (it was Friday the 13th, for Christ's sake!), and right in the middle of the Skinner–Waxman a sparrow flew into the auditorium and made a hell of a racket so that Birdie couldn't concentrate. He hadn't been at all surprised to find that he'd failed the IQ test and the Skinner–Waxman. On the physical Birdie got a score of 100 (the modal point, or peak, of the normal curve), which made him feel pretty proud.

Birdie didn't really believe in failure, not as a permanent condition. He had failed third grade, but had that kept him from graduating high school? The important thing to remember, as Mr

Mack had pointed out to Birdie and the 107 other failed candidates at a special assembly, was that failure was just a point-of-view. A positive point-of-view and self-confidence would solve most problems. Birdie had really believed him then, and he'd signed up to be retested at the big downtown office of the Health, Education, and Welfare Agency. This time he really crammed. He bought *How You Can Add 20 Points to Your IQ* by L. C. Wedgewood, Ph.D. (who appeared on the bookjacket in an old-fashioned suit with lapels and buttons) and *Your* REGENTS *Exams*, prepared by the National Educational Council. The latter book had a dozen sample tests, and Birdie worked all the easy problems in each test (the only part that really counted, the book explained, were the first thirty questions; the last thirty were strictly for the junior geniuses). By the day of the retesting, Birdie had a positive point of view and lots of self-confidence.

But the tests were all wrong. They weren't at all what he'd studied up on. For the IQ part of the test he sat in a stuffy cubicle with some old lady with a black dress and repeated telephone numbers after her, forwards and backwards. With the Area Code! Then she showed him different pictures, and he had to tell her what was wrong with them. Usually nothing was wrong. It went on like that for over an hour.

The creativity test was even weirder. They gave him a pair of pliers and took him into an empty room. Two pieces of string were hanging down from the ceiling. Birdie was supposed to tie the two strings together.

It was impossible. If you held the very end of one string in one hand, it was still too short, by a couple feet, to reach the other string. Even if you held the tip of the string in the pliers, it was too short. He tried it a dozen times, and it never worked. He was about ready to scream when he left that room. There were three more crazy problems like that, but he hardly even tried to solve them. It was impossible.

Afterwards somebody told him he should have tied the pliers to the end of the string and set it swinging like a pendulum. Then he could have gone over and got the string, come back with it, and *caught* the string that was swinging like a pendulum. But then why had they given him *pliers*!

That bit with the pliers really made him angry. But what could he do about it? Nothing. Who could he complain to? Nobody. He complained to Mr Mack, who promised to do everything in his power to help Birdie be reclassified. The important thing to remember was that failure was just a negative attitude. Birdie had to think positively and learn to help himself. Mr Mack suggested that Birdie go to college.

At that time college had been the last thing Birdie Ludd had in mind for himself. He wanted to *relax* after the strain of PS 125. Birdie wasn't the college *type*. He wasn't anybody's fool, but on the other hand he didn't pretend to be some goddamn brain. Mr Mack had pointed out that 73 per cent of all high school graduates went on to college and that three-quarters of all college freshmen went on to take their degrees.

Birdie's reply had been, 'Yeah, but . . .' He couldn't say what he was thinking; that Mack himself was just another goddamn brain and that of course *he* couldn't understand the way Birdie felt about college.

'You must remember, Birdie, that this is more now than a question of your educational goals. If you'd received high enough scores on the REGENTS you could drop out of school right now and get married and sign up for a MODICUM salary. Assuming that you had no more ambition than that . . .'

After a glum and weighty silence, Mr Mack switched from scolding to cajoling: 'You do want to get married don't you?'

'Yeah, but . . .'

'And have children?'

'Yeah, of course, but . . .'

'Then it seems to *me* that college is your best bet, Birdie. You've taken your REGENTS and failed. You've taken the reclassification tests and gotten *lower* scores there than on the REGENTS. There are only three possibilities open after that. Either you perform an exceptional service for the country or the national economy, which is hardly something one can count on doing. Or else you demonstrate physical, intellectual, or creative abilities markedly above the level shown in the REGENTS test or tests you failed, which again poses certain problems. Or *else* you get a BA. That certainly seems to be the easiest way, Birdie. Perhaps the only way.'

'I suppose you're right.'

Mr Mack smiled a smile of greasy satisfaction and adjusted his massive stomach above his too-tight belt. Birdie wondered spitefully what sort of score Mack would have got on the O'Ryan–Army fitness test. Probably not 100.

'Now as far as money goes,' Mack went on, opening Birdie's career file, 'you won't have to be concerned over that. As long as you keep a C average, you can get a New York State Loan, at the very least. I assume your parents will be unable to help out?'

Birdie nodded. Mr Mack handed him the loan application form.

'A college education is the right of every United States citizen, Birdie. But if we fail to exercise our rights, we have only ourselves to blame. There's no excuse today for not going to college.'

So Birdie Ludd, lacking an excuse, had gone to college. From the very first, he had felt as though it were all a trap. A puzzle with a trick solution, and everyone had been shown the trick except Birdie. A labyrinth that others could enter and depart from at will, but whenever Birdie tried to get out, no matter which way he turned, it always led him back to the same dead end.

But what choice did he have? He was in love.

On the morning of the day of his Art History test Birdie lay in bed in the empty dorm, drowsing and thinking of his true-love. He couldn't quite sleep, but he didn't want to get up yet either. His body was bursting with untapped energies, it overflowed with the wine of youth, but those energies could not be spent brushing his teeth and going down to breakfast. Come to think of it, it was too late for breakfast. He was happy right here.

Sunlight spilled in through the south window. A breeze rustled the curtain. Birdie laughed from a sense of his own fullness. He turned over on to his left side and looked out the window at a perfect blue rectangle of sky. Beautiful. It was March, but it seemed more like April or May. It was going to be a wonderful day. He could feel it in his bones.

The way the breeze blew the curtain made him think of last summer, the lake breeze in Milly's hair. They had gone away for a weekend to Lake Hopatcong in New Jersey. They found a grassy spot not far from the shore but screened from the view of bathers by a windbreak of trees, and there they had made love almost the entire afternoon. Aferwards they just lay side by side, their heads reclining in the prickly grass, looking into each other's eyes. Milly's eyes were hazel flecked with gold. His were the blue of a cloudless sky. Wisps of her hair, soft and unmanageable after the morning swim, blew across her face. Birdie thought she was the most beautiful girl in the world. When he told her that she just smiled. Her lips had been so soft. She had not said one cruel thing.

He remembered kissing her. Her lips. He closed his eyes, to remember better.

'I love you so much, Birdie, so terribly *much*.' She had said that to him. And he loved her too. More than anything in the world. Didn't she know that? Had she forgotten?

'I'll do anything for you,' he said aloud in the empty dorm.

She smiled. She whispered into his ear, and he could feel her lips against his earlobe. 'Just one thing, Birdie. I only ask one thing. You know what that is.'

'I know, I know.' He tried to twist his head around to silence her with a kiss, but she held it firmly between her two hands.

'Get reclassified.' It sounded almost cruel, but then she had let him go, and when he looked into her golden eyes again he could see no cruelty, only love.

'I want to have a baby, darling. Yours and mine. I want us to be married and have our own apartment and a baby. I'm sick of living with my mother. I want to be your wife. I'm sick of my job. I only want what every woman wants. Birdie, please.'

'I'm trying. Aren't I trying? I'm going to school. Next year I'll be a junior. The year after that I'll be a senior. Then I'll have my degree. And then I'll be reclassified. We'll get married the same day.' He looked at her with his wounded-puppydog look, which usually stopped all her arguments.

The clock on the wall of the dorm said it was 11.07. *This will be my lucky day*, Birdie promised himself. He threw himself out of bed and did ten push-ups on the linoleum floor, which somehow never seemed to get dirty, though Birdie had never seen anyone cleaning it. Birdie couldn't push himself up from the last push-up, so he just rested there on the floor, his lips pressed against the cool linoleum.

He got up and sat on the edge of the unmade bed, watching the white curtain blow in the wind. He thought of Milly, his own dear beautiful lovely Milly. He wanted to marry her *now*. No matter what his genetic classification was. If she really loved him, that shouldn't make any difference. But he knew he was doing the right thing by waiting. He knew that haste was foolish. He knew, certainly, that Milly would have it no other way. Immediately after he'd failed the reclassification test, he had tried to persuade her to take a refertility pill that he had bought on the black market for twenty dollars. The pill counteracted the contraceptive agent in the city water.

'Are you crazy?' she shouted at him. 'Are you off your rocker?'

'I just want a baby, that's all. Goddamnit, if they won't let us have a baby legal, then we'll have a baby our own way.'

'And what do you think will happen if *I* have an illegal pregnancy?'

Birdie remained stolidly silent. He *hadn't* thought, he didn't, he wouldn't.

'They'll give me a therapeutic abortion and I'll have a black mark against my record for the rest of my life as a sex offender. My God, Birdie, sometimes you can be positively dumb!'

'We could go to Mexico . . .'

'And what would we do there? Die? Or commit suicide? Haven't you read any newspapers in the last ten years?'

'Well, other women have done it. I've read stories in the papers *this* year. There was a protest. Civil rights and stuff.'

'And what happened then? All those babies were put in federal orphanages, and the parents were put in prison. *And* sterilized. God, Birdie, you really didn't know that, did you?'

'Yeah, I knew that, but . . .'

'But what, stupid?'

'I just thought—'

'You *didn't* think. That's your problem. You never think. I have to do the thinking for both of us. It's a good thing I've got more brains than I need.'

'Uh-huh,' he said mockingly, smiling his special movie-star smile. She could never resist that smile. She shrugged her shoulders and, laughing, kissed him. She couldn't stay angry with Birdie ten minutes at a time. He'd make her laugh and forget everything but how much she loved him. In that way Milly was like his mother. In that way Birdie was like her son.

11.35. The Art History test was at two o'clock. He'd already missed a ten o'clock class in Consumer Skills. Tough.

He went to the bathroom to brush his teeth and shave. The Muzak started when he opened the door. It played WHAM-O, WHAM-O, WHY AM I SO HAPPY? Birdie could have asked himself the same question.

Back in the dorm he tried to telephone Milly at work, but there was only one phone on each Pan-Am second-class jet, and it was busy all through the flight. He left a message for her to call him, knowing perfectly well she wouldn't.

He decided to wear his white sweater with white Levis and white sneakers. He brushed whitening agent into his hair. He looked at himself in front of the bathroom mirror. He smiled. The Muzak started to play his favourite Ford commercial. Alone in the empty space before the urinals he danced with himself, singing the words of the commercial.

It was only a fifteen minute subway ride to Battery Park. He bought a bag of peanuts to feed to the pigeons in the aviary. When they were all gone, he walked along the rows of benches where the old people came to sit every day to look out at the sea and wait to die. But Birdie didn't feel the same hatred for old people this morning that he had felt last night. Lined up in rows, in the full glare of the afternoon sun, they seemed remote. They did not pose any threat.

The breeze coming in off the harbour smelled of salt, oil, and decay, but it wasn't a bad smell at all. It was sort of invigorating. Maybe if Birdie had lived centuries ago, he might have been a sailor. He ate two large bars of Synthamon and drank a container of Fun.

The sky was full of jets. Milly could have been on any one of them. A week ago, only a week ago, she'd told him, 'I'll love you forever and a day. There'll never be anyone but you for me.'

Birdie felt just great. Absolutely.

An old man in an old-fashioned suit with lapels shuffled along the walk, holding on to the sea-railing. His face was covered with a funny white beard, thick and curly, although his head was as bare as a police helmet. He asked Birdie for a quarter. He spoke with a strange accent, neither Spanish nor French. He reminded Birdie of something.

Birdie wrinkled his nose. 'Sorry. I'm on the dole myself.' Which was not, strictly speaking, true.

The bearded man gave him the finger, and then Birdie remembered who the old man looked like. Socrates!

He glanced down at his wrist, but he'd forgotten to wear his watch. He spun around. The gigantic advertising clock on the façade of the First National Citibank said it was fifteen after two. That wasn't possible. Birdie asked two of the old people on the benches if that was the right time. Their watches agreed.

There wasn't any use trying to get to the test. Without quite knowing why, Birdie Ludd smiled to himself.

He breathed a sigh of relief and sat down to watch the ocean.

'The basic point I'm trying to make, Birdie, if you'll let me finish, is that there are people more qualified than I to advise you. It's been three years since I've seen your file. I've no idea of the progress you've made, the goals you're striving for. Certainly there's a psychologist at the college. . . .'

Birdie squirmed in the plastic shell of his seat, and the look of accusation in his guileless blue eyes communicated so successfully to the counsellor that he began to squirm slightly himself. Birdie had always had the power to make Mr Mack feel in the wrong.

'. . . and there are other students waiting to see me, Birdie. You managed to pick my busiest time of day.' He gestured pathetically at the tiny foyer outside his office where a fourth student had just taken a seat to wait his three o'clock appointment.

'Well, if you don't *want* to help me, I guess I can go.'

'Whether I want to or not, what can *I* possibly do? I still fail to see the reason you missed those tests. You were holding down a good C-average. If you'd just kept plugging away . . .' Mr Mack smiled weakly. He was about to launch into a set-piece on the value of a positive attitude, but decided on second thought that Birdie would require a tougher approach. 'If reclassification means as much to you as you say, then you should be willing to work for it, to make sacrifices.'

'I *said* it was a mistake, didn't I? Is it my fault they won't let me take make-ups?'

'Two weeks, Birdie! Two weeks without going to a single class, without even calling in to the dorm. Where were you? And all those midterms! Really, it does look as though you were *trying* to be expelled.'

'I said I'm *sorry*!'

'You prove nothing by becoming angry with me, Birdie Ludd. There's nothing I can do about it any more—nothing.' Mr Mack pushed his chair back from the desk, preparing to rise.

'But . . . before, when I failed my reclassification test, you talked about other ways to get reclassified besides college. What were they?'

'Exceptional service. You might want to try that.'

'What's it mean?'

'In practical terms, for you, it would mean joining the Army and performing an action in combat of extraordinary heroism. And living to tell about it.'

'A guerrilla?' Birdie laughed nervously. 'Not this boy, not Birdie Ludd. Who ever heard of a guerrilla getting reclassified?'

'Admittedly, it's unusual. That's why I recommended college initially.'

'The *third* way, what was that?'

'A demonstration of markedly superior abilities.' Mr Mack smiled, not without a certain irony. 'Abilities that wouldn't be shown on the tests.'

'How would I do that?'

'You must file intention with the Health, Education, and Welfare Agency three months in advance of the date of demonstration.'

'But what is the demonstration? What do I do?'

'It's entirely up to you. Some people submit paintings, others might play a piece of music. The majority, I suppose, give a sample of their writing. As a matter of fact, I think there's a book published of stories and essays and such that have all achieved their purpose. Gotten their authors reclassified, that is. The great majority don't, of course. Those who make it are usually nonconformist types to begin with, the kind that are always bucking the system. I wouldn't advise—'

'Where can I get that book?'

'At the library, I suppose. But—'

'Will they let anyone try?'

'Yes. Once.'

Birdie jumped out of his seat so quickly that for an unconsidered moment Mr Mack feared the boy was going to strike him. But he was only holding his hand out to be shaken. 'Thanks, Mr Mack, thanks a lot. I knew *you'd* still find a way to help me. Thanks.'

The Health, Education, and Welfare people were more helpful than he could have hoped. They arranged for him to receive a federal stipend of $500 to help him through the three month 'developmental period'. They gave him a metal ID tab for his own desk at the Nassau branch of the National Library. They recommended several bona fide literary advisors, at various hourly consultation rates. They even gave him a free copy of the book Mr Mack had told him about. *By Their Bootstraps* had an introduction by Lucille Mortimer Randolphe-Clapp, the architect of the REGENTS system, which Birdie found very encouraging, though he didn't understand all of it too clearly.

Birdie didn't think much of the first essay in the book, 'The Bottom of the Heap, an Account of a Lousy Modicum Childhood'. It was written by 19-year-old Jack Ch——. Birdie could have written the same thing himself; there wasn't a single thing in it that he didn't know without being told. And even Birdie could see that the language was vulgar and ungrammatical. Next was a story that didn't have any point, and then a poem that didn't make any sense. Birdie read through the whole book in one day, something he had never done before, and he did find a few things he liked: there was a crazy story about a boy who'd dropped out of high school to work in an alligator preserve, and an eminently sensible essay on the difficulties of budgeting a MODICUM income. The best piece of the lot was called 'The Consolations of Philosophy', which was written by a girl who was both blind and crippled! Aside from the textbook for his ethics course, Birdie had never read philosophy, and he thought it might be a good idea, during the three-month developmental period, to try some. Maybe it would give him an idea for something to write about of his own.

For the next three or four days, however, Birdie spent all his time just trying to find a room. He'd have to keep his expenses to a bare minimum if he was going to get along those three months on only $500. Eventually he found a room in a privately owned building in Brooklyn that must have been built a century ago or longer. The room cost $30 a week, which was a real bargain spacewise, since it measured fully ten feet square. It contained a bed, an armchair, two floor lamps, a wooden table and chair, a rickety cardboard chest-of-drawers, and a rug made of genuine wool. He had his own private bathroom. His first night there he just walked around barefoot on the woollen rug with the radio turned up full volume. Twice he went down to the phone booth in the lobby in order to call up Milly and maybe invite her over for a little house-warming party, but then he would have had to explain why he wasn't living at the dorm, and (for she certainly must be wondering) why he hadn't called her since the day of the Art History test. The second time he came down to the lobby he got into a conversation with a girl who was waiting for a phone call. She said her name was Fran. She wore a tight dress of peekaboo plastic, but on her body it wasn't especially provocative since she was too scrawny. It was fun to talk to her though, because she wasn't stuck up like most girls. She lived right across the hall from Birdie, so it was the most natural thing in the world that he should go into her room for a carton of beer. Before they'd killed it, he'd told her his entire situation. Even about Milly. Fran started crying. It turned out that she'd failed the REGENTS herself—all three parts. Birdie was just starting to make out with her when her phone call came and she had to leave.

Next morning Birdie made his first visit (ever) to the National Library. The Nassau branch was housed in an old glass building a little to the west of the central Wall Street area. Each floor was a honeycomb of auditing and micro-viewing booths, except for twenty-eight, the topmost floor, which was given over to the electronic equipment that connected this branch with the midtown Morgan Library and, by relays, with the Library of Congress, the British Museum Library, and the Österreichische Nationalbibliothek in Vienna. A page, who couldn't have been much older than Birdie, showed him how to use the dial-and-punch system in his booth. A researcher could call up almost any book in the world or listen to any tape without needing to employ more than a twelve-figure call-code. When the page was gone, Birdie stared down glumly at the blank viewing screen. The only thing he could think of was the satisfaction it would give him to smash in the screen with his fist.

After a good hot lunch Birdie felt better. He recalled Socrates and the blind girl's essay on the 'The Consolations of Philosophy'. So he put out a call for all the books on Socrates at senior high school level and began reading them at random.

At eleven o'clock that night Birdie finished reading the chapter in Plato's *Republic* that contains the famous Parable of the Cave. He left the library in a daze and wandered hours-long in the brilliantly illuminated Wall Street area. Even after midnight it was teeming with workers. Birdie watched them with amazement. Were any of them aware of the great truths that had transfigured Birdie's being that night? Or were they, like the poor prisoners of the cave, turned to the rockface, watching shadows and never suspecting the existence of the sun?

There was so much *beauty* in the world that Birdie had not so much as dreamt of! Beauty was more than a patch of blue sky or the curve of Milly's breasts. It penetrated everywhere. The city itself, hitherto that cruel machine whose special function it had been to thwart Birdie's natural desires, seemed now to glow from within, like a diamond struck by the light. Every passer-by's face was rife with ineffable significances.

Birdie remembered the vote of the Athenian Senate to put Socrates to death. For corrupting the youth! He hated the Athenian Senate, but it was a different sort of hate from the kind he was used to. He hated Athens for *a reason.* Justice!

Beauty, truth, justice. Love, too. Somewhere, Birdie realized, there was an explanation for everything! A meaning. *It all made sense.*

Emotions passed over him faster than he could take account of them. One moment, looking at his face reflected in a dark shop-window, he wanted to laugh aloud. The next, remembering Fran sprawled out on her shabby bed in a cheap plastic dress, he wanted to cry. For he realized now, as he had not on the night before, that Fran was a prostitute, and that she could never hope to be anything else. While Birdie might hope for anything, anything at all in the (now suddenly so much wider) world.

He found himself alone in Battery Park. It was darker there, less busy. He stood alone beside the sea-railing and looked down at the dark waves lapping at the concrete shore. Red signal lights blinked on and off as they proceeded across the night sky to and from the Central Park Airport. And even this scene, though it chilled him in ways that he could not explain, he found exhilarating, in ways that he could not explain.

There was a *principle* involved in all this. It was important for Birdie to communicate this principle to the other people who didn't know of it, but he could not, quite, put his finger on just what principle it was. In his newly awakened soul he fought a battle to try to bring it to words, but each time, just as he thought he had it, it eluded him. Finally, towards dawn, he went home, temporarily defeated.

Just as he went in the door of his own room, a guerrilla, wearing the opaque and featureless mask of his calling (with the ID number stencilled on the brow), came out of Fran's room. Birdie felt a brief impulse of hatred for him, followed by a wave of compassion and tenderness for the unfortunate girl. But he did not have the time, that night, to try and help her; he had his own problems.

He slept unsoundly and woke at eleven o'clock from a dream that stopped just short of being a nightmare. He had been in a room in which two ropes hung down from a raftered ceiling. He had stood between the ropes, trying to grasp them, but just as he thought he had one in his grasp, it would swing away wildly, like a berserk pendulum.

He knew what the dream meant. The ropes were a test of his *creativeness*. That was the principle he had sought so desperately the night before. Creativeness was the key to everything. If he could only learn about it, analyse it, he would be able to solve his problems.

The idea was still hazy in his mind, but he knew he was on the right track. He had some cultured eggs and a cup of coffee for breakfast and went straight to his booth at the library to study. Though he had a slight fever, he seemed to feel better than he had ever felt in his whole life. He was free. Or was it something else? One thing he was sure of: nothing in the past was worth shit. But the future was radiant with promise.

He didn't begin work on his essay until the very last week of the developmental period. There was so *much* that he had had to learn first. Literature, painting, philosophy, everything he had never understood before. There were still many things, he realized, that he couldn't understand, but now he firmly believed that eventually he would. Because he *wanted* to.

When he did begin working on his essay, he found it a more difficult task than he had anticipated. He paid ten dollars for an hour's consultation with a licensed literary advisor, who advised him to cut it. He was trying to cram in too many things. Lucille Mortimer Randolphe-Clapp had given more or less the same advice in *By Their Bootstraps*. She said that the best essays were often no more than 200 words long. Birdie wondered if future editions of *By Their Bootstraps* would contain his essay.

He went through four complete drafts before he was satisfied. Then he read it aloud to Fran. She said it made her want to cry. He did one more draft of it on 8 June, which was his 21st birthday, just for good luck, and then he sent it off to the Health, Education, and Welfare Agency.

This is the essay Birdie Ludd submitted:

PROBLEMS OF
CREATIVENESS

by Berthold Anthony Ludd

'The conditions of beauty are three: wholeness, harmony, and radiance.'

Aristotle.

From ancient times to today we have learned that there is more than one criteria by which the critic analyses the products of Creativeness. Can we know which of these measures to use. Shall we deal directly with the subject? Or 'by indirection find direction out'.

We are all familiar with the great drama of Wolfgang Amadeus Goethe—'The Faust.' It is not possible to deny it the undisputed literary pinnacle, a 'Masterpiece'. Yet what motivation can have drawn him to describe 'heaven' and 'hell' in this strange way? Who is Faust if not ourselves. Does this not show a genuine need to achieve communication? Our only answer can be 'Yes!'

Thus once more we are led to the problem of Creativeness. All beauty has three conditions 1, The subject shall be of literary format. 2, All parts are contained within the whole. And 3, the meaning is radiantly *clear. True creativeness is only present when it can be observed in the work of art. This too is the philososphy of Aristotle.*

The criteria of Creativeness is not alone sought in the domain of 'literature'. Does not the scientist, the prophet, the painter offer his own criteria of judgement towards the same general purpose? Which road shall we choose, in this event?

Another criteria of Creativeness was made by Socrates, so cruelly put to death by his own people, and I quote: 'To know nothing is the first condition of all knowledge.' From the wisdom of Socrates may we not draw our own conclusions concerning these problems? Creativeness is the ability to see relationships where none exist.

The machine that did the preliminary grading gave Berthold Anthony Ludd a score of 12 and fed the paper into the Automatic Reject file, where the essay was photostated and routed to the OUTMAIL room. The OUTMAIL sorter clipped Birdie's essay to a letter explaining the causes which made reclassification impossible at this time and advised him of his right to seek reclassification again 365 days from the day on which his essay had been notarized.

Birdie was waiting in the lobby when the mail came. He was so eager to open the envelope that he tore his essay in two getting it out. The same afternoon, without even bothering to get drunk, Birdie enlisted in the US Marines to go defend democracy in Burma.

Immediately after his swearing-in, the sergeant came forward and slipped the black mask with his ID number stencilled on the brow over Birdie's sullen face. His number was USMC100-7011-D07. He was a guerrilla now.

HOW THE WHIP CAME BACK

GENE WOLFE

Pretty Miss Bushnan's suite was all red acrylic and green-dyed leather. Real leather, very modern—red acrylic and green, real leather were the modern things this year. But it made her Louis XIV secretary, Sal, look terribly out of place.

Miss Bushnan had disliked the suite from the day she moved in—though she could hardly complain, when there was a chance that the entire city of Geneva and the sovereign Swiss nation might be offended. This evening she did her best to like red and green, and in the meantime turned her eyes from them to the cool relief of the fountain. It was a copy of a Cellini salt dish and lovely, no matter how silly a fountain indoors on the hundred and twenty-fifth floor might be. In a characteristic reversal of feeling she found herself wondering what sort of place she might have gotten if she had had to find one for herself, without reservations, at the height of the tourist season. Three flights up in some dingy suburban *pension*, no doubt.

So bless the generosity of the sovereign Swiss Republic. Bless the openhanded city of Geneva. Bless the hotel. And bless the United Nations Conference on Human Value, which brought glory to the Swiss Republic et cetera and inspired the free mountaineers to grant free hotel suites in the height of the season even to non-voting Conference observers such as she. Sal had brought her in a gibson a few minutes ago, and she picked it up from the edge of the fountain to sip, a little surprised to see that it was already three-quarters gone; *red and green*.

A brawny, naked triton half-reclined, water streaming from his hair and beard, dripping from his mouth, dribbling from his ears. His eyes, expressionless and smooth as eggs, wept for her. Balancing her empty glass carefully on the rim again, she leaned forward and stroked his smooth, wet stone flesh. Smiling she told him—mentally—how handsome he was, and he blushed pink lemonade at the compliment. She thought of herself taking off her clothes and climbing in with him, the cool water soothing her face, which now felt hot and flushed. Not, she told herself suddenly, that she would feel any real desire for the triton in the unlikely event of his being metamorphosed to flesh. If she wanted men in her bed she could find ten any evening, and afterward edit the whole adventure from Sal's memory bank. She wanted a man, but she wanted only one, she wanted Brad (whose real name, as the terrible, bitter woman who lived in the back of her skull, the woman the gibson had not quite drowned, reminded her, had proved at his trial to be Aaron). The triton vanished and Brad was there instead, laughing and dripping Atlantic water on the sand as he threw up his arms to catch the towel she flung him. Brad running through the surf . . .

Sal interrupted her revery, rolling in on silent casters. 'A gentleman to see you, Miss Bushnan.' Sal had real metal drawer-pulls on her false drawers, and they jingled softly when she stopped to deliver her message, like costume jewelry.

'Who?' Miss Bushnan straightened up, pushing a stray wisp of brown hair away from her face.

Sal said blankly, 'I don't know.' The gibson had made Miss Bushnan feel pleasantly muzzy, but even so the blankness came through as slightly suspicious.

'He didn't give you his name or a card?'

'He did, Miss Bushnan, but I can't read it. Even though, as I'm sure you're already aware, Miss Bushnan, there's an Italian language software package for me for only two hundred dollars. It includes reading, writing, speaking, and an elementary knowledge of great Italian art.'

'The advertising package,' Miss Bushnan said with wasted sarcasm, 'is free. And compulsory with your lease.'

'Yes,' Sal said. 'Isn't it wonderful?'

Miss Bushnan swung around in the green leather chair from which she had been watching the fountain. 'He did give you a card. I see it in one of your pigeonholes. Take it out and look at it.'

As if the Louis XIV secretary had concealed a silver snake, one of Sal's arms emerged. With steel fingers like nails it took the card and held it in front of a swirl of ornament hiding a scanner.

'Now,' Miss Bushnan said patiently, 'pretend that what you're reading isn't Italian. Let's say instead that it's English that's been garbled by a translator post-processor error. What's your best guess at the original meaning?'

'"His Holiness Pope Honorius V."'

'Ah.' Miss Bushnan sat up in her chair. 'Please show the gentleman in.'

With a faint hum of servomotors Sal rolled away. There was just time for a last fragment of daydream. Brad with quiet eyes alone with her on the beach at Cape Cod. Talking about the past, talking about the divorce, Brad really, *really* sorry . . .

The Pope wore a plain dark suit and a white satin tie embroidered in gold with the triple crown. He was an elderly man, never tall and now stooped. Miss Bushnan rose. She sat beside him every day at the council sessions, and had occasionally exchanged a few words with him during the refreshment breaks (he had a glass of red wine usually, she good English tea or the horrible Swiss coffee laced with brandy), but it had never so much as occurred to her that he might ever have anything to discuss with her in private.

'Your Holiness,' she said as smoothly as the gibson would let her manage the unfamiliar words, 'this is an unexpected pleasure.'

Sal chimed in with, 'May we offer you something?' and looking sidelong Miss Bushnan saw that she had put Scotch, a bottle of club soda, and two glasses of ice on her fold-out writing shelf.

The Pope waved her away, and when he had settled in his chair said pointedly, 'I deeply appreciate your hospitality, but I wonder if it would be possible to speak with you privately.'

Miss Bushnan said, 'Of course,' and waited until Sal had coasted off in the direction of the kitchen. 'My secretary bothers you, Your Holiness?'

Taking a cigar from the recesses of his coat, the Pope nodded. 'I'm afraid she does. I have never had much sympathy with furniture that talks—you don't mind if I smoke?' He had only the barest trace of an Italian accent.

'If it makes you more comfortable I should prefer it.'

He smiled in appreciation of the little speech, and struck an old-fashioned kitchen match on the imitation marble of the fountain. It left no mark, and when he tossed in the matchstick a moment later, it bobbed only twice in the crystal water before being whisked away. 'I suppose I'm out of date,' the Pope continued. 'But back in my youth when people speculated about the possibility of those things we always thought of them as being shaped more or less like us. Something like a suit of armour.'

'I can't imagine why,' Miss Bushnan said. 'You might as well shape a radio like a human mouth—or a TV screen like a keyhole.'

The Pope chuckled. 'I didn't say I was going to defend the idea. I only remarked that that was what we expected.'

'I'm sure they must have considered it, but—'

'But too much extra work would have had to go into just making it look human,' the Pope continued for her, 'and besides, a furniture cabinet is much cheaper than articulated metal and doesn't make the robot look dead when it's turned off.'

She must have looked flustered because he continued, smiling, 'You Americans are not the only manufacturers, you see. It happens that a friend of mine is president of Olivetti. A skeptic like all of them today, but . . .'

The sentence trailed away in a shrug and a puff of smoke from the black cigar. Miss Bushnan recalled the time she had asked the French delegate about him. The French delegate was handsome in that very clean and spare fashion some Frenchmen have, and she liked him better than the paunchy businessman who represented her own country.

'You do not know who the man is who sits by you, mademoiselle?' he asked quizzically. 'But that is most interesting. You see, I know who he is, but I do not know who *you* are. Except that I see you each day and you are much more pretty than the lady from Russia or the lady from Nigeria, and perhaps in your way as chic as that bad girl who reports on us for *Le Figaro*—but I hope not quite so full of tricks. Now I will trade you information.'

So she had had to tell him, feeling more like a fool each second as the milling crush of secretaries of delegates, and secretaries of secretaries, and unidentifiable people from the Swiss embassies of all the participating nations, swirled around them. When she had finished he said, 'Ah, it is kind of you to work for charity, and especially for one that does not pay you, but is it necessary? This is no longer the twentieth century after all, and the governments take care of most of us quite well.'

'That's what most people think; I suppose that's why so few give much any more. But we try to bring a little human warmth to the people we help, and I find I meet the class of people I want to meet in connection with it. I mean my co-workers, of course. It's really rather exclusive.'

He said, 'How very great-hearted you are,' with a little twist to the corner of his mouth that made her feel like a child talking to a grown-up. 'But you asked the identity of the old gentleman. He is Pope.'

'Who?' Then she had realized what the word meant and added, 'I thought there weren't any more.'

'Oh no.' The French delegate winked. 'It is still there. Much, much smaller, but still there . . . But we are so crowded here, and I think you are tired of standing. Let me buy you a liqueur and I will tell you all about it.'

He had taken her to a place at the top of some building overlooking the lake, and it had been very pleasant listening to the waiters pointing him out in whispers to the tourists, even though the tourists were mostly Germans and no one anyone knew. They were given a table next to the window of course, and while they sipped and smoked and looked at the lake he told her, with many digressions, about a great-aunt who had been what he called 'a believer' and two ex-wives who had not. (History at Radcliffe had somehow left her with the impression that the whole thing had stopped with John XXIII, just as the Holy Roman Empire had managed to vanish out of sheer good manners when it was no longer wanted. On the teaching machines you filled in a table of Holy Roman Emperors and Popes and Sultans and such things by touching multiple-choice buttons. Then when you had it all done the screen glowed with rosy light for a minute—which was called reinforcement—and told you your grade. After which, unless you were lucky, there was another table to be filled—but Popes had disappeared and you put the Kings of Sweden in that column instead.)

She remembered having asked the French delegate, 'There are only a hundred thousand left? In the whole world?'

'That is my guess, of real believers. Of course many more who continue to use the name and perhaps have their children wetted if they think of it. It may be that that is too low—say a quarter million. But it has been growing less for a long time. Eventually—who knows? It may turn about and grow more. It would not be the first time that happened.'

She had said, 'It seems to me the whole thing should have been squashed a long time ago.' . . .

The Pope straightened his shoulders a little and flicked ashes into the fountain. 'At any rate, they make me uncomfortable,' he said. 'I always have the feeling they don't like me. I hope you don't mind.'

She smiled and said something about the convenience factor, and having Sal shipped in a crate from New York.

'I suppose it's a good thing my predecessor got the government to take responsibility for the Vatican,' the Pope said. 'We couldn't possibly staff it now, so we'd be using those things. Doubtless ours would have stained glass in them.'

Miss Bushnan laughed politely. Actually she felt like coughing. The Pope's cigar was the acrid, cheap kind smoked in the poorer sort of Italian cafés. Briefly she wondered if he himself had not been born into the lowest class. His hands were gnarled and twisted like an old gardener's, as though he'd been weeding all his life.

He was about to say something else, but Sal, re-entering on silent wheels, interrupted him. 'Phone, Miss Bushnan,' Sal said at her elbow.

She swivelled in her chair again and touched the 'On' and 'Record' buttons on the communications console, motioning as she did for the Pope to keep his seat. The screen lit up, and she said, 'Good evening,' to the office robot who had placed the call.

The robot answered with an announcement: 'Her Excellency the Delegate Plenipotentiary of the Union of Soviet Socialist Republics, Comrade Natasha Nikolayeva.' The image flickered and a striking blonde, about forty and somewhat overblown and overdressed, but with a remarkably good complexion and enormous eyes, replaced the robot. The Russian delegate had been an actress at one time and was currently the wife of a general; gossip said that she owed her position at the conference to favours granted to the Party Secretary.

'Good evening,' Miss Bushnan said again, and added, 'Comrade Nikolayeva.'

The Russian delegate gave her a dazzling smile. 'I called, darling, to ask if you like my little speech today. I was not too long? You did not find it difficult, wearing the headphones for translation?'

'I thought it was very moving,' Miss Bushnan said carefully. Actually, she had been appalled by the Russian delegate's references to Hitler's gas chambers and her cant phrases about restoring economic value to human life. It came to saying that if people had no value alive they should be made into soap, but she had no intention of telling the Russian delegate that.

'I convinced you?'

Brad made into soap. It should have been funny, but it wasn't. One of Brad's fingers slowly exposed as she scrubbed herself with the bar. The Russian delegate was still looking at her, waiting for her to reply.

'It isn't necessary that you convince me, is it?' She smiled, trying to turn the question aside. 'I'm merely an observer, after all.'

'It is necessary to me,' the Russian delegate said, 'in my *soul*.' She pressed a hand flashing with diamonds against one upholstered breast. 'I myself feel it so deeply.'

'I'm sure you do. It was a wonderful speech. Very dramatic.'

'You understand, then.' The Russian delegate's mood changed in an instant. 'That is wonderful, darling. Listen, you know I am staying at our embassy here—would you have dinner with us? It will be Tuesday, and nearly everyone will be there.'

Miss Bushnan hesitated for a moment, looking briefly at the Pope, seated out of range of the Russian's vision, for guidance. He was expressionless.

'Darling, I will tell you a secret. I have sworn not to, but what is an oath when it is for you? The French delegate asked me to invite you. I would have in any case, of course, but he came to me. He is so shy; but if you come I have promised him I will seat you beside him. Do not say I told you.'

'I'd be delighted to come.'

'That too is wonderful then.' The Russian delegate's smile said: *We are women together and I love you, little one.*

'Tuesday? The day after the final vote?'

'Yes, Tuesday. I will be looking forward so much.'

When the screen went dark Miss Bushnan said to the Pope, 'Something's up.'

The Pope only looked at her, as though trying to weigh what might be behind her attractive but not arresting face and brown eyes.

After a moment Miss Bushnan continued, 'The French delegate might buy me a dinner, but he wouldn't ask for me as a dinner partner at an official function, and that Russian woman has been ignoring you and me ever since the conference opened. What's going on?'

'Yes,' the Pope said slowly, 'something has happened, as you say. I see you hadn't heard.'

'No.'

'I was more fortunate. The Portuguese delegate confides in me sometimes.'

'Will you tell me?'

'That is why I came. The delegates caucused this afternoon after the public session. They decided to ask for our votes at the final meeting.'

'Us?' Miss Bushnan was nonplussed. 'The observers?'

'Yes. The votes will have no legal validity, of course. They cannot be counted. But they want total unanimity—they want to get us down on the record.'

'I see,' said Miss Bushnan.

'Church and charity. People surrendered their faith in us to put it in the governments, but they're losing that now, and the delegates sense it. Perhaps the faith won't return to us, but there's a chance it might.'

'And so I'm to be wined and dined.'

The Pope nodded. 'And courted too, I should imagine. The French are very enthused about this; their penal system has been at loose ends ever since they lost their African colonies over fifty years ago.'

Miss Bushnan had been staring at her lap, smoothing her skirt absently where it lay across her knees; she looked up suddenly, meeting his eyes. 'And you? What are they going to offer you?'

'Not the lost sees of eastern Europe, you may be sure. Mostly flattery, I suspect.'

'And if we oppose them—'

'If we oppose them we will be raising standards about which all the millions who detest the idea, and all the millions more who will come to detest it when they see it in operation, can rally.'

'My husband—my former husband, technically—is in prison, Your Holiness. Did you know that?'

'No, of course not. If I had—'

'We plan to be remarried when he is released, and I know from visiting him what the alternative to the motion is. I know what we've got now. It's not as though they're going to be snatched from some Arcadia.'

Unexpectedly Sal was at her elbow again. 'Phone, Miss Bushnan.'

The American delegate's puffy face filled the screen. 'Miss—ah—Bushnan?'

She nodded.

'This is—ah—a pleasure I have had to postpone too long.'

In order to save him time she said, 'I've heard about the decision to ask the observers to vote.'

'Good, good.' The American delegate drummed his fingers on his desk and seemed to be trying to avoid her eyes. 'Miss Bushnan, are you aware of the—ah—financial crisis now confronting our nation?'

'I'm not an economist—'

'But you are an informed laywoman. You know the situation. Miss Bushnan, there are close to a quarter of a million men and women in state and federal prisons today, and to maintain each of them there costs—costs us, Miss Bushnan, the taxpayers—five thousand dollars a year *each*. That's a total of a billion dollars a year.'

'I believe you brought out those figures during your speech at the third session.'

'Perhaps I did. But we are all interested in restoring the pre-eminent place the United States once held in world affairs, aren't we? Miss Bushnan, to do that we have had to take quite a few pages from the Soviet book. And it's been good for us. We've learned humility, if you like.'

She nodded.

'We used to believe in job security for everybody, and a wage based on classification and seniority. That was what we called Free Enterprise, and we were proud of it. Well, the Communists showed us differently: incentives, and discipline for underachievers. They forced us to the wall with those until we learned our lesson, and now—well, you can say whatever you like, but by God things are better.'

'So I understand,' Miss Bushnan said. Here it came.

'Now they've got a new trick,' the American delegate continued. 'They used, you know, to have these gangs of—ah—labourers out in Siberia. Then one day some smart commisar thought to himself: By God, if the peasants can grow more vegetables on private plots, couldn't the prisoners be used more effectively that way too?'

'If I recall your speech correctly,' Miss Bushnan said, 'you pointed out that if half the federal and state prisoners could be leased out to private owners at five thousand a year, the revenue would take care of the remaining half.'

'Lessees, not owners,' the American delegate said. 'Lessees with option to renew. It will lift a billion dollar millstone from about our nation's neck.'

'But,' Miss Bushnan continued innocently, 'surely we could do the same thing without entering into the international agreement being discussed here'

'No, no.' The American delegate waved a hand in protest. 'We should enter the world community with this. After all, Miss Bushnan, international trade is one of the few, and one of the strongest, cohesive forces. We need by all means to establish a supranational market structure.'

The Pope, sitting outside the range of the American delegate's view, said softly, 'Ask him if they're still going to call them slaves.'

Miss Bushnan inquired obediently, 'Are you still going to call them slaves? I mean in the final agreement.'

'Oh, yes.' The American delegate leaned closer to the scanner and lowered his voice. 'In English language usage. I don't mind telling you, however, that we—I mean the British and Canadians as well as our own country—have had a hard time getting that one past the Soviets. It comes from the root-word 'slav,' you know, and they don't like that. But it's a *selling* word. People like the idea of having slaves; robots have gotten us used to it and tranquillizers and anti-aggressants have made it practical; what's more, it's a link with the past at a time when too many such links are phasing out. People feel manipulated today, Miss Bushnan. They want to be master of someone themselves.'

'I see. And it will get them out of prison. Place them in decent surroundings.'

'Oh, it certainly will. And—ah—you asked about the necessity of an international agreement and an international market a moment ago. You must remember that our nation needs hard currencies very badly today; and we have the curse—or, ah—the blessing, blessing if you think of it in a positive fashion, of having the highest crime rate among major nations. The United States will be an exporter in this market, Miss Bushnan.'

'I see,' Miss Bushnan said again.

'You may have heard of some of these rumours about the Soviets pressing a certain number of—ah—country people into the market to satisfy the demand. These are slanders, of course, and in any event that sort of thing would be unthinkable in the United States. I understand you're a wealthy woman, Miss Bushnan; your father is in the government, I suppose?'

'He was,' Miss Bushnan said. 'He's dead now. The Department of Agriculture.'

'Then with a family background of public service you understand that in a democracy we have to listen to the voice of the people; and the people want this. The—ah—most recent polls have shown seventy-nine per cent favouring. I won't try to hide the fact that it would be an embarrassment to our country if you voted in opposition, and it would not benefit the organization you represent—in fact it would do it a great deal of harm.'

'Are you threatening us?'

'No, of course not. But I'm asking you to consider what would happen to your organization if you lost your tax-exempt status. I believe a vote in opposition to the motion might—ah—make Washington feel that you were engaged in political activity. That would mean loss of the exemption, naturally.'

'But a vote in favour of the motion wouldn't be political activity?'

'Washington would expect your organization to support this humanitarian cause as a matter of course. I doubt very much that the matter would come up. You must understand, Miss Bushnan, that when—ah—a measure as revolutionary as this is under consideration humanity must be practically unanimous. Even a token opposition could be disastrous.'

Paraphrasing the Pope, Miss Bushnan said, 'It would raise a standard about which all the millions who detest the idea could rally.'

'Millions is surely an exaggeration; thousands perhaps. But in principle you are correct, and that must not be allowed to happen. Miss Bushnan, Washington has sent me a dossier on you. Did you know that?'

'How could I?'

'Your former husband is confined in the federal penitentiary at Ossining, New York. In the letters you have exchanged both of you have stated an intention to remarry upon his release. Were those letters sincere, Miss Bushnan?'

'I don't see what my personal life has to do with this.'

'I merely wish to use your own case as an example—one which will strike home, so to speak. It will be at least five years before your former husband will be released under the present system; but if the motion passes it will be possible for you to lease—ah—' The American delegate paused, looking at some paper on his desk.

'Brad,' Miss Bushnan said.

'Yes, Brad. You could lease Brad from the government for those five years. You would have him, he would have you, and your government would be twenty-five thousand dollars to the better as the direct result of your happiness. What's the matter with that, eh? In fact, in your case I think I could promise that your husband would be one of the first prisoners to be made available for the plan, and that he would be, so to speak, reserved. There would be no danger of someone else leasing him, if that's worrying you. Of course you would be expected to supervise him.'

Miss Bushnan nodded slowly. 'I understand.'

'May I ask then if you intend to support the measure?'

'I hesitate to tell you. I know you're going to misunderstand me.'

'Oh?' The American delegate leaned forward until his face filled the small screen. 'In what way?'

'You think that this is going to help Brad and me, and that because of that I'm going to consent to your selling the Americans you don't want, selling them to die in somebody's mines. You are wrong. This is going to ruin whatever may be left between Brad and me, and I know it. I know how Brad is going to feel when his wife is also his keeper. It will strip away whatever manhood he has left, and before the five years are out he'll hate me—just as he will if I don't buy him when he knows I could. But you are going to do this thing whether the organization I represent favours it or not, and to save this organization—for the good it does now and the good it will do among the slaves when you have them—I am going to vote for the motion.'

'You will support the motion?' His eyes seemed to bore into her.

'I will support the motion. Yes.'

'Fine.'

The American delegate's hand was moving toward the 'Off' switch on his console, but Miss Bushnan called, 'Wait. What about the other observer? The Pope?'

'He can be taken care of, I feel sure. His Church is almost entirely dependent today on the goodwill of the Italian government.'

'He hasn't agreed yet?'

'Don't worry,' the American delegate said, 'the Italians will be contacting him.' His hand touched the switch and his image vanished.

'So you gave in,' the Pope said.

'And you wouldn't?' Miss Bushnan asked. 'Even if you knew you'd be running your Church from an empty store the day after you voted no?'

'I might abstain,' the Pope admitted slowly, 'but I could never bring myself to give a favourable vote.'

'How about lying to them, if that were the only way you could get to vote?'

The Pope looked at her in surprise, then his eyes smiled.

Miss Bushnan continued, 'Could you tell them you were going to vote yes when you were really going to vote against them, Your Holiness?'

'I don't suppose I could. It would be a matter of my position, if you understand me, as well as my conscience.'

'Fortunately,' Miss Bushnan said, 'I don't feel that way. Hasn't it occurred to you that this business of asking for our votes must be predicated on the idea that they'll be favourable? It hasn't been announced, has it?'

The Pope nodded. 'I see what you mean. If the decision had been made public they couldn't change it; but as it is, if they don't like what they hear from us—'

'But they'll have every news agency in the world there when the vote is actually taken.'

'You are a clever girl.' The Pope shook his head. 'It is a lesson to me to think of how very much I have underestimated you, sitting in the gallery there beside me all these days, and even this evening when I came here. But that is good; God wants me to learn humility, and He has chosen a child to teach it, as He so often does. I hope you understand that after the council I will be giving you all the support I can. I'll publish an encyclical—'

'If you feel you can't lie to them,' Miss Bushnan interposed practically, 'we'll need some excuse for your being absent from the vote.'

'I have one,' the Pope said. 'I don't'–he paused—'suppose you've heard of Mary Catherine Bryan?'

'I don't think so. Who is she?'

'She is—or at least she was—a nun. She was the last nun, actually, for the past three years. Ever since Sister Carmela Rose died. I received a call this morning telling me Mary Catherine passed away last night, and her rites are to be this coming Tuesday. The government still lets us use St Peter's sometimes for that sort of thing.'

'So you won't be here.' Miss Bushnan smiled. 'But a nun sounds so interesting. Tell me about her.'

'There isn't a great deal to tell. She was a woman of my mother's generation, and for the last four years she lived in an apartment on the Via del Fori. Alone, after Sister Carmela Rose died. They never got along too well, actually, being from different orders, but Mary Catherine cried for weeks, I remember, after Sister Carmela Rose was gone.'

'Did she wear those wonderful flowing robes you see in pictures?'

'Oh, no,' the Pope said. 'You see, nuns no longer have to—' He stopped in the middle of the sentence, and the animation left his face, making him at once a very old man. 'I'm sorry,' he said after a moment, 'I had forgotten. I should have said that for the last seventy years or so of their existence nuns no longer wore those things. They abandoned them, actually, just a few years before we priests dropped our Roman collars. You have to understand that from time to time I have tried to persuade someone to . . .'

'Yes?'

'Well, the old phrase was "take the veil". It would have kept the tradition alive and would have been so nice for Mary Catherine and Sister Carmela Rose. I always told the girls all the things they wouldn't have to give up, and they always said they'd think about it, but none of them ever came back.'

'I'm sorry your friend is dead,' Miss Bushnan said simply. To her surprise she found she really was.

'It's the end of something that had lived almost as long as the Church itself—oh, I suppose it will be revived in fifty or a hundred years when the spirit of the world turns another corner, but a revival is never really the same thing. As though we tried to put the Kyrie back into the mass now.'

Miss Bushnan, who did not know what he was talking about, said, 'I suppose so, but—'

'But what has it to do with the matter at hand? Not a great deal, I'm afraid. But while they are voting that is where I shall be. And afterward perhaps we can do something.' He stood up, adjusting his clothing, and from somewhere in the back of the apartment Sal came rolling out with his hat positioned on her writing shelf. It was red, Miss Bushnan noticed, but the feather in the band was black instead of green. As he put it on he said, 'We started among slaves, more or less, you know. Practically all the early Christians who weren't Jews were either slaves or freedmen. I'll be going now to say the funeral mass of the last nun. Perhaps I'll also live to administer the vows of the first.'

Sal announced, 'Saint Macrina, the sister of Saint Basil, founded the first formal order of nuns in three fifty-eight.' The Pope smiled and said, 'Quite right, my dear,' and Miss Bushnan said vaguely, 'I bought her the World's Great Religions package about a year ago. I suppose that's how she knew who you were.' She was thinking about Brad again, and if the Pope made any reply she failed to hear it. Brad a slave . . .

Then the door shut and Sal muttered, 'I just don't trust that old man, he makes me feel creepy,' and Miss Bushnan knew he was gone.

She told Sal, 'He's harmless, and anyway he's going to Rome now,' and only then, with the tension draining away, did she feel how great it had been. 'Harmless,' she said again. 'Bring me another drink, please, Sal.'

Tuesday would be the day. The whole world would be watching, and everyone at the conference would be in red and green, but she would wear something blue and stand out. Something blue and her pearls. In her mind Brad would somehow be waiting behind her, naked to the waist, with his wrists in bronze manacles. 'I'll have them made at Tiffany's,' she said, speaking too softly for Sal, busy with the shaker in the kitchen, to hear. 'Tiffany's, but no gems or turquoise or that sort of junk.'

Just the heavy, solid bronze with perhaps a touch here and there of silver. Sal would make him keep them polished.

She could hear herself telling their friends, 'Sal makes him keep them shined. I tell him if he doesn't I'm going to send him back—just kidding, of course.'

CLOAK OF ANARCHY

LARRY NIVEN

Square in the middle of what used to be the San Diego Freeway, I leaned back against a huge, twisted oak. The old bark was rough and powdery against my bare back. There was dark green shade shot with tight parallel beams of white gold. Long grass tickled my legs.

Forty yards away across a wide strip of lawn was a clump of elms, and a small grandmotherly woman sitting on a green towel. She looked like she'd grown there. A stalk of grass protruded between her teeth. I felt we were kindred spirits, and once when I caught her eye I wiggled a forefinger at her, and she waved back.

In a minute now I'd have to be getting up. Jill was meeting me at the Wilshire exits in half an hour. But I'd started walking at the Sunset Boulevard ramps, and I was tired. A minute more . . .

It was a good place to watch the world rotate.

A good day for it, too. No clouds at all. On this hot blue summer afternoon, King's Free Park was as crowded as it ever gets.

Someone at police headquarters had expected that. Twice the usual number of copseyes floated overhead, waiting. Gold dots against blue, basketball-sized, twelve feet up. Each a television eye and a sonic stunner, each a hookup to police headquarters, they were there to enforce the law of the Park.

No violence.

No hand to be raised against another—and no other laws whatever. Life was often entertaining in a Free Park.

North towards Sunset, a man carried a white rectangular sign, blank on both sides. He was parading back and forth in front of a square-jawed youth on a plastic box, who was trying to lecture him on the subject of fusion power and the heat pollution problem. Even this far away I could hear the conviction and the dedication in his voice.

South, a handful of yelling marksmen were throwing rocks at a copseye, directed by a gesticulating man with wild black hair. The golden basketball was dodging the rocks, but barely. Some cop was baiting them. I wondered where they had got the rocks. Rocks were scarce in King's Free Park.

The black-haired man looked familiar. I watched him and his horde chasing the copseye . . . then forgot them when a girl walked out of a clump of elms.

She was lovely. Long, perfect legs, deep red hair worn longer than shoulder length, the face of an arrogant angel, and a body so perfect that it seemed unreal, like an adolescent's daydream. Her walk showed training; possibly she was a model, or dancer. Her only garment was a cloak of glowing blue velvet.

It was fifteen yards long, that cloak. It trailed back from two big gold discs that were stuck somehow to the skin of her shoulders. It trailed back and back, floating at a height of five feet all the way, twisting and turning to trace her path through the trees. She seemed like the illustration in a book of fairy tales, bearing in mind that the original fairy tales were not intended for children.

Neither was she. You could hear neck vertebrae popping all over the Park. Even the rock-throwers had stopped to watch.

She could sense the attention, or hear it in a whisper of sighs. It was what she was here for. She strolled along with a condescending angel's smile on her angel's face, not overdoing the walk, but letting it flow. She turned, regardless of whether there were obstacles to avoid, so that fifteen yards of flowing cloak could follow the curve.

I smiled, watching her go. She was lovely from the back, with dimples.

The man who stepped up to her a little farther on was the same one who had led the rock-throwers. Wild black hair and beard, hollow cheeks and deep-set eyes, a diffident smile and a diffident walk . . . Ron Cole. Of course.

I didn't hear what he said to the girl in the cloak, but I saw the result. He flinched, then turned abruptly and walked away with his eyes on his feet.

I got up and moved to intercept him. 'Don't take it personal,' I said.

He looked up, startled. His voice, when it came, was bitter. 'How should I take it?'

'She'd have turned any man off the same way. She's to look at, not to touch.'

'You know her?'

'Never saw her before in my life.'

'Then—?'

'Her cloak. Now you *must* have noticed her cloak.'

The tail end of her cloak was just passing us, its folds rippling an improbable deep, rich blue. Ronald Cole smiled as if it hurt his face. 'Yah.'

'All right. Now suppose you made a pass, and suppose the lady liked your looks and took you up on it. What would she do next? Bearing in mind that she can't stop walking even for a second.'

He thought it over first, then asked, 'Why not?'

'If she stops walking, she loses the whole effect. Her cloak just hangs there like some kind of tail. It's supposed to wave. If she lies down, it's even worse. A cloak floating at five feet, then swooping into a clump of bushes and bobbing frantically—' Ron laughed helplessly in falsetto. I said. 'See? Her audience would get the giggles. That's not what she's after.'

He sobered. 'But if she really wanted to, she wouldn't *care* about . . . oh. Right. She must have spent a fortune to get that effect.'

'Sure. She wouldn't ruin it for Jacques Casanova himself.' I thought unfriendly thoughts towards the girl in the cloak. There are polite ways to turn down a pass. Ronald Cole was easy to hurt.

I asked, 'Where did you get the rocks?'

'Rocks? Oh, we found a place where the centre divider shows through. We knocked off some chunks of concrete.' Ron looked down the length of the Park just as a kid bounced a missile off a golden ball. 'They got one! Come on!'

The fastest commercial shipping that ever sailed was the clipper ship; yet the world stopped building them after just twenty-five years. Steam had come. Steam was faster, safer, more dependable and cheaper.

The freeways served America for almost fifty years. Then modern transportation systems cleaned the air and made traffic jams archaic and left the nation with an embarrassing problem. What to do with ten thousand miles of unsightly abandoned freeways?

King's Free Park had been part of the San Diego Freeway, the section between Sunset and the Santa Monica interchange. Decades ago the concrete had been covered with topsoil. The borders had been landscaped from the start. Now the Park was as thoroughly covered with green as the much older Griffith Free Park.

Within King's Free Park was an orderly approximation of anarchy. People were searched at the entrances. There were no weapons inside. The copseyes, floating overhead and out of reach, were the next best thing to no law at all.

There was only one law to enforce. All acts of attempted violence carried the same penalty for attacker and victim. Let anyone raise his hands against his neighbour, and one of the golden basketballs would stun them both. They would wake separately, with copseyes watching. It was usually enough.

Naturally people threw rocks at copseyes. It was a Free Park, wasn't it?

'They got one! Come on!' Ron tugged at my arm. The felled copseye was hidden, surrounded by those who had destroyed it. 'I hope they don't kick it apart. I told them I need it intact, but that might not stop them.'

'It's a Free Park. And they bagged it.'

'With my missiles!'

'Who are they?'

'I don't know. They were playing baseball when I found them. I told them I needed a copseye. They said they'd get me one.'

I remembered Ron quite well now. Ronald Cole was an artist and an inventor. It would have been two sources of income for another man, but Ron was different. He invented new art forms. With solder and wire and diffraction gratings and several makes of plastics kit, and an incredible collection of serendipitous junk, Ron Cole made things the like of which had never been seen on Earth.

The market for new art forms has always been low, but now and then he did make a sale. It was enough to keep him in raw materials, especially since many of his raw materials came from basements and attics. Rarely there came a *big* sale, and then, briefly, he would be rich.

There was this about him: he knew who I was, but he hadn't remembered my name. Ron Cole had better things to think about than what name belonged with whom. A name was only a tag and a conversational gambit. 'Russel! How are you?' A signal. Ron had developed a substitute.

Into a momentary gap in the conversation he would say, 'Look at this,' and hold out—miracles.

Once it had been a clear plastic sphere, golf-ball size, balanced on a polished silver concavity. When the ball rolled around on the curved mirror, the reflections were *fantastic*.

Once it had been a twisting sea serpent engraved on a Michelob beer bottle, the lovely vase-shaped bottle of the early 1960s that was too big for standard refrigerators.

And once it had been two strips of dull silvery metal, unexpectedly heavy. 'What's this?'

I'd held them in the palm of my hand. They were heavier than lead. Platinum? But nobody carries that much platinum around. Joking, I'd asked, 'U-235?'

'Are they warm?' he'd asked apprehensively. I'd fought off an urge to throw them as far as I could and dive behind a couch.

But they *had* been platinum. I never did learn why Ron was carrying them about. Something that didn't pan out.

Within a semicircle of spectators, the felled copseye lay on the grass. It was intact, possibly because two cheerful, conspicuously large men were standing over it, waving everyone back.

'Good,' said Ron. He knelt above the golden sphere, turned it with his long artist's fingers. To me he said, 'Help me get it open.'

'What for? What are you after?'

'I'll tell you in a minute. Help me get—Never mind.' The hemispherical cover came off. For the first time ever, I looked into a copseye.

It was impressively simple. I picked out the stunner by its parabolic reflector, the cameras, and a toroidal coil that had to be part of the floater device. No power source. I guessed that the shell itself was a power beam antenna. With the cover cracked there would be no way for a damn fool to electrocute himself.

Ron knelt and studied the strange guts of the copseye. From his pocket he took something made of glass and metal. He suddenly remembered my existence and held it out to me, saying, 'Look at this.'

I took it, expecting a surprise, and I got it. It was an old hunting watch, a big wind-up watch on a chain, with a protective case. They were in common use a couple of hundred years ago. I looked at the face, said 'Fifteen minutes slow. You didn't repair the whole works, did you?'

'Oh, no.' He clicked the back open for me.

The works looked modern. I guessed, 'Battery and tuning fork?'

'That's what the guard thought. Of course that's what I made it from. But the hands don't move; I set them just before they searched me.'

'Aah. What does it do?'

'If I work it right, I think it'll knock down every copseye in King's Free Park.'

For a minute or so I was laughing too hard to speak. Ron watched me with his head on one side, clearly wondering if I thought he was joking.

I managed to say, 'That ought to cause all *kinds* of excitement.'

Ron nodded vigorously. 'Of course it all depends on whether they use the kind of circuits I think they use. Look for yourself; the copseyes aren't supposed to be foolproof. They're supposed to be cheap. If one gets knocked down, the taxes don't go up much. The other way is to make them expensive and foolproof, and frustrate a lot of people. People aren't supposed to be frustrated in a Free Park.'

'So?'

'Well, there's a cheap way to make the circuitry for the power system. If they did it that way, I can blow the whole thing. We'll see.' Ron pulled thin copper wire from the cuffs of his shirt.

'How long will this take?'

'Oh, half an hour—maybe more.'

That decided me. 'I've got to be going. I'm meeting Jill Hayes at the Wilshire exits. You've met her, a big blond girl, my height—'

But he wasn't listening. 'OK, see you,' he muttered. He began placing the copper wire inside the copseye, with tweezers. I left.

Crowds tend to draw crowds. A few minutes after leaving Ron, I joined a semicircle of the curious to see what they were watching.

A balding, lantern-jawed individual was putting something together—an archaic machine, with blades and a small gasoline motor. The T-shaped wooden handle was brand new and unpainted. The metal parts were dull with the look of ancient rust recently removed.

The crowd speculated in half-whispers. What was it? Not part of a car; not an outboard motor, though it had blades; too small for a motor scooter, too big for a motor skateboard—

'Lawn mower,' said the white-haired lady next to me. She was one of those small, birdlike people who shrivel and grow weightless as they age, and live forever. Her words meant nothing to me. I was about to ask, when—

The lantern-jawed man finished his work, and twisted something, and the motor started with a roar. Black smoke puffed out. In triumph he gripped the handles. Outside, it was a prison offence to build a working internal-combustion machine. Here—

With the fire of dedication burning in his eyes, he wheeled his infernal machine across the grass. He left a path as flat as a rug. It was a Free Park, wasn't it?

The smell hit everyone at once: black dirt in the air, a stink of half-burned hydrocarbons attacking nose and eyes. I gasped and coughed. I'd never smelled anything like it.

The crowd roared and converged.

He squawked when they picked up his machine. Someone found a switch and stopped it. Two men confiscated the tool kit and went to work with screwdriver and hammer. The owner objected. He picked up a heavy pair of pliers and tried to commit murder.

A copseye zapped him and the man with the hammer, and they both hit the lawn without bouncing. The rest of them pulled the lawn mower apart and bent and broke the pieces.

'I'm half sorry they did that,' said the old woman. 'Sometimes I miss the sound of lawn mowers. My dad used to mow the lawn on Sunday mornings.'

I said, 'It's a Free Park.'

'Then why can't he build anything he pleases?'

'He can. He did. Anything he's free to build, we're free to kick apart.' And my mind finished, *Like Ron's rigged copseye.*

Ron was good with tools. It would not surprise me a bit if he knew enough about copseyes to knock out the whole system.

Maybe someone ought to stop him.

But knocking down copseyes wasn't illegal. It happened all the time. It was part of the freedom of the Park. If Ron could knock them all down at once, well—

Maybe someone ought to stop him.

I passed a flock of high-school girls, all chittering like birds, all about sixteen. It might have been their first trip inside a Free Park. I looked back because they were so cute, and caught them staring in awe and wonder at the dragon on my back.

A few years and they'd be too blasé to notice. It had taken Jill almost half an hour to apply it this morning: a glorious red-and-gold dragon breathing flames across my shoulder, flames that seemed to glow by their own light. Lower down were a princess and a knight in golden armour, the princess tied to a stake, the knight fleeing for his life. I smiled back at the girls, and two of them waved.

Short blonde hair and golden skin, the tallest girl in sight, wearing not even a nudist's shoulder pouch: Jill Hayes stood squarely in front of the Wilshire entrance, visibly wondering where I was. It was five minutes after three.

There was this about living with a physical culture nut. Jill insisted on getting me into shape. The daily exercises were part of that, and so was this business of walking half the length of King's Free Park.

I'd balked at doing it briskly, though. Who walks briskly in a Free Park? There's too much to see. She'd given me an hour; I'd held out for three. It was a compromise, like the paper slacks I was wearing despite Jill's nudist beliefs.

Sooner or later she'd find someone with muscles, or I'd relapse into laziness, and we'd split. Meanwhile . . . we got along. It seemed only sensible to let her finish my training.

She spotted me, yelled, 'Russel! Here!' in a voice that must have reached both ends of the Park.

In answer I lifted my arm, semaphore-style, slowly over my head and back down.

And every copseye in King's Free Park fell out of the sky, dead.

Jill looked about her at all the startled faces and all the golden bubbles resting in bushes and on the grass. She approached me somewhat uncertainly. She asked, 'Did you do that?'

I said, 'Yah. If I wave my arms again, they'll all go back up.'

'I think you'd better do it,' she said primly. Jill had a fine poker face. I waved my arm grandly over my head and down, but, of course, the copseyes stayed where they had fallen.

Jill said, 'I wonder what happened to them?'

'It was Ron Cole. You remember him. He's the one who engraved some old Michelob beer bottles for Steuben—'

'Oh, yes. But *how?*'

We went off to ask him.

A brawny college man howled and charged past us at a dead run. We saw him kick a copseye like a soccer ball. The golden cover split, but the man howled again and hopped up and down hugging his foot.

We passed dented golden shells and broken resonators and bent parabolic reflectors. One woman looked flushed and proud; she was wearing several of the copper toroids as bracelets. A kid was collecting the cameras. Maybe he thought he could sell them outside.

I never saw an intact copseye after the first minute.

They weren't all busy kicking copseyes apart. Jill stared at the conservatively dressed group carrying POPULATION BY COPULATION signs, and wanted to know if they were serious. Their grim-faced leader handed us pamphlets that spoke of the evil and the blasphemy of Man's attempts to alter himself through gene tampering and extra-uterine growth experiments. If it was a put-on, it was a good one.

We passed seven little men, each three to four feet high, travelling with a single tall, pretty brunette. They wore medieval garb. We both stared; but I was the one who noticed the makeup and the use of UnTan. African pigmies, probably part of a UN-sponsored tourist group; and the girl must be their guide.

Ron Cole was not where I had left him.

'He must have decided that discretion is the better part of cowardice. May be right, too,' I surmised. 'Nobody's ever knocked down *all* the copseyes before.'

'It's not illegal, is it?'

'Not illegal, but excessive. They can bar him from the Park, at the very least.'

Jill stretched in the sun. She was all golden, and *big*. She said, 'I'm thirsty. Is there a fountain around?'

'Sure, unless someone's plugged it by now. It's a—'

'Free Park. Do you mean to tell me they don't even protect the *fountains?*'

'You make one exception, it's like a wedge. When someone ruins a fountain, they wait and fix it that night. That way . . . If I see someone trying to wreck a fountain, I'll generally throw a punch at him. A lot of us do. After a guy's lost enough of his holiday to the copseye stunners, he'll get the idea, sooner or later.'

The fountain was a solid cube of concrete with four spigots and a hand-sized metal button. It was hard to jam, hard to hurt. Ron Cole stood near it, looking lost.

He seemed glad to see me, but still lost. I introduced him—'You remember Jill Hayes.' He said, 'Certainly. Hello, Jill.' and, having put her name to its intended purpose, promptly forgot it.

Jill said, 'We thought you'd made a break for it.'

'I did.'

'Oh?'

'You know how complicated the exits are. They have to be, to keep anyone from getting in through an exit with—like a shotgun.' Ron ran both hands through his hair, without making it any more or less neat. 'Well, all the exits have stopped working. They must be on the same circuits as the copseyes. I wasn't expecting that.'

'Then we're locked in,' I said. That was irritating. But underneath the irritation was a funny feeling in the pit of my stomach. 'How long do you think—'

'No telling. They'll have to get new copseyes in somehow. And repair the beamed power system, and figure out how I bollixed it, and fix it so it doesn't happen again. I suppose someone must have kicked my rigged copseye to pieces by now, but the police don't know that.'

'Oh, they'll just send in some cops,' said Jill.

'Look around you.'

There were pieces of copseyes in all directions. Not one remained whole. A cop would have to be out of his mind to enter a Free Park.

Not to mention the damage to the spirit of the Park.

'I wish I'd brought a bag lunch,' said Ron.

I saw the cloak off to my right: a ribbon of glowing blue velvet hovering at five feet, like a carpeted path in the air. I didn't yell, or point, or anything. For Ron it might be pushing the wrong buttons.

Ron didn't see it. 'Actually I'm kind of glad this happened,' he said animatedly. 'I've always thought that anarchy ought to be a viable form of society.'

Jill made polite sounds of encouragement.

'After all, anarchy is only the last word in free enterprise. What can a government do for people that people can't do for themselves? Protection from other countries? If all the other countries are anarchies, too, you don't need armies. Police, maybe; but what's wrong with privately owned police?'

'Fire departments used to work that way,' Jill remembered. 'They were hired by the insurance companies. They only protected houses that belonged to their own clients.'

'Right! So you buy theft and murder insurance, and the insurance companies hire a police force. The client carries a credit card—'

'Suppose the robber steals the card, too?'

'He can't use it. He doesn't have the right retina prints.'

'But if the client doesn't have the credit card, he can't sic the cops on the thief.'

'Oh,' A noticeable pause, 'Well—'

Half-listening, for I had heard it all before, I looked for the end points of the cloak. I found empty space at one end and a lovely red-haired girl at the other. She was talking to two men as outré as herself.

One can get the impression that a Free Park is one gigantic costume party. It isn't. Not one person in ten wears anything but street clothes; but the costumes are what get noticed.

These guys were part bird.

Their eyebrows and eyelashes were tiny feathers, green on one, golden on the other. Larger feathers covered their heads, blue and green and gold, and ran in a crest down their spines. They were bare to the waist, showing physiques Jill would find acceptable.

Ron was lecturing. 'What does a government do for *anyone* except the people who run the government? Once there were private post offices, and they were cheaper than what we've got now. Anything the government takes over gets more expensive, *immediately*. There's no reason why private enterprise can't do anything a government—'

Jill gasped. She said, 'Ooh! How lovely.'

Ron turned to look.

As if on cue, the girl in the cloak slapped one of the feathered men hard across the mouth. She tried to hit the other one, but he caught her wrist. Then all three froze.

I said, 'See? Nobody wins. She doesn't even like standing still. She—' and I realized why they weren't moving.

In a Free Park it's easy for a girl to turn down an offer. If the guy won't take No for an answer, he gets slapped. The stun beam gets him and the girl. When she wakes up, she walks away.

Simple.

The girl recovered first. She gasped and jerked her wrist loose and turned to run. One of the feathered men didn't bother to chase her; he simply took a double handful of the cloak.

This was getting serious.

The cloak jerked her sharply backward. She didn't hesitate. She reached for the big gold discs at her shoulders, ripped them loose and ran on. The feathered men chased her, laughing.

The redhead wasn't laughing. She was running all out. Two drops of blood ran down her shoulders. I thought of trying to stop the feathered men, decided in favour of it—but they were already past.

The cloak hung like a carpeted path in the air, empty at both ends.

Jill hugged herself uneasily. 'Ron, just how does one go about hiring your private police force?'

'Well, you can't expect it to form spontaneously—'

'Let's try the entrances. Maybe we can get out.'

It was slow to build. Everyone knew what a copseye did. Nobody thought it through. Two feathered men chasing a lovely nude? A pretty sight; and why interfere? If she didn't want to be chased, she need only . . . what? And nothing else had changed. The costumes, the people with causes, the people looking for causes, the people-watchers, the pranksters—

Blank Sign had joined the POPULATION BY COPULATION faction. His grass-stained pink street tunic jarred strangely with their conservative suits, but he showed no sign of mockery; his face was as preternaturally solemn as theirs. None the less they did not seem glad of his company.

It was crowded near the Wilshire entrance. I saw enough bewildered and frustrated faces to guess that it was closed. The little vestibule area was so packed that we didn't even try to find out what was wrong with the doors.

'I don't think we ought to stay here,' Jill said uneasily.

I noticed the way she was hugging herself. 'Are you cold?'

'No.' She shivered. 'But I wish I were dressed.'

'How about a strip of that velvet cloak?'

'Good!'

We were too late. The cloak was gone.

It was a warm September day, near sunset. Clad only in paper slacks, I was not cold in the least. I said, 'Take my slacks.'

'No, hon, I'm the nudist.' But Jill hugged herself with both arms.

'Here,' said Ron, and handed her his sweater. She flashed him a grateful look, then, clearly embarrassed, she wrapped the sweater around her waist and knotted the sleeves.

Ron didn't get it at all. I asked him, 'Do you know the difference between nude and naked?'

He shook his head.

'Nude is artistic. Naked is defenceless.'

Nudity was popular in a Free Park. That night, nakedness was not. There must have been pieces of that cloak all over King's Free Park. I saw at least four that night: one worn as a kilt, two being used as crude sarongs, and one as a bandage.

On a normal day, the entrances to King's Free Park close at six. Those who want to stay, stay as long as they like. Usually there are not many, because there are no lights to be broken in a Free Park; but light does seep in from the city beyond. The copseyes float about, guided by infrared, but most of them are not manned.

Tonight would be different.

It was after sunset, but still light. A small and ancient lady came stumping toward us with a look of murder on her lined face. At first I thought it was meant for us; but that wasn't it. She was so mad she couldn't see straight.

She saw my feet and looked up. 'Oh, it's you. The one who helped break the lawn mower,' she said—which was unjust. 'A Free Park, is it? A Free Park! Two men just took away my dinner!'

I spread my hands. 'I'm sorry. I really am. If you still had it, we could try to talk you into sharing it.'

She lost some of her mad; which brought her embarrassingly close to tears. 'Then we're all hungry together. I brought it in a plastic bag. Next time I'll use something that isn't transparent, by d-damn!' She noticed Jill and her improvised sweater-skirt, and added, 'I'm sorry, dear, I gave my towel to a girl who needed it even more.'

'Thank you anyway.'

'Please, may I stay with you people until the copseyes start working again? I don't feel safe, somehow. I'm Glenda Hawthorne.'

We introduced ourselves. Glenda Hawthorne shook our hands. By now it was quite dark. We couldn't see the city beyond the high green hedges, but the change was startling when the lights of Westwood and Santa Monica flashed on.

The police were taking their own good time getting us some copseyes.

We reached the grassy field sometimes used by the Society for Creative Anachronism for their tournaments. They fight on foot with weighted and padded weapons designed to behave like swords, broadaxes, morningstars, et cetera. The weapons are bugged so that they won't fall into the wrong hands. The field is big and flat and bare of trees, sloping upward at the edges.

On one of the slopes, something moved.

I stopped. It didn't move again, but it showed clearly in light reflected down from the white clouds. I made out something man-shaped and faintly pink, and a pale rectangle nearby.

I spoke low. 'Stay here.'

Jill said, 'Don't be silly. There's nothing for anyone to hide under. Come on.'

The blank sign was bent and marked with shoe prints. The man who had been carrying it looked up at us with pain in his eyes. Drying blood ran from his nose. With effort he whispered, 'I think they dislocated my shoulder.'

'Let me look.' Jill bent over him. She probed him a bit, then set herself and pulled hard and steadily on his arm. Blank Sign yelled in pain and despair.

'That'll do it.' Jill sounded satisfied. 'How does it feel?'

'It doesn't hurt as much.' He smiled, almost.

'What happened?'

'They started pushing me and kicking me to make me go away. I was *doing* it, I was walking away. I *was*. Then someone snatched away my sign—' He stopped for a moment, then went off at a tangent. 'I wasn't hurting anyone with my sign. I'm a Psych Major. I'm writing a thesis on what people read into a blank sign. Like the blank sheets in the Rorschach tests.'

'What kind of reactions do you get?'

'Usually hostile. But nothing like *that.*' Blank Sign sounded bewildered. 'Wouldn't you think a Free Park is the one place you'd find freedom of speech?'

Jill wiped at his face with a tissue from Glenda Hawthorne's purse. She said, 'Especially when you're not saying anything. Hey, Ron, tell us more about your government by anarchy.'

Ron cleared his throat. 'I hope you're not judging it by *this.* King's Free Park hasn't been an anarchy for more than a couple of hours. It needs time to develop.'

Glenda Hawthorne and Blank Sign must have wondered what the hell he was talking about. I wished him joy in explaining it to them, and wondered if he would explain who had knocked down the copseyes.

This field would be a good place to spend the night. It was open, with no cover and no shadows, no way for anyone to sneak up on us.

And I was learning to think like a true paranoid.

We lay on wet grass, sometimes dozing, sometimes talking. Two other groups no bigger than ours occupied the jousting field. They kept their distance, we kept ours. Now and then we heard voices, and knew that they were not asleep; not all at once, anyway.

Blank Sign dozed restlessly. His ribs were giving him trouble, though Jill said none of them were broken. Every so often he whimpered and tried to move and woke himself up. Then he had to hold himself still until he fell asleep again.

'Money,' said Jill. 'It takes a government to print money.'

'But you could get IOUs printed. Standard denominations, printed for a fee and notarized. Backed by your good name.'

Jill laughed softly. 'Thought of everything, haven't you? You couldn't travel very far that way.'

'Credit cards, then.'

I had stopped believing in Ron's anarchy. I said, 'Ron, remember the girl in the long blue cloak?'

A little gap of silence. 'Yah?'

'Pretty, wasn't she? Fun to watch.'

'Granted.'

'If there weren't any laws to stop you from raping her, she'd be muffled to the ears in a long dress and carrying a tear gas pen.

What fun would that be? I *like* the nude look. Look how fast it disappeared after the copseyes fell.'

'Mm-m,' said Ron.

The night was turning cold. Faraway voices; occasional distant shouts, came like thin grey threads in a black tapestry of silence. Mrs Hawthorne spoke into that silence.

'What was that boy really saying with his blank sign?'

'He wasn't saying anything,' said Jill.

'Now, just a minute, dear. I think he was, even if he didn't know it.' Mrs Hawthorne talked slowly, using the words to shape her thoughts. 'Once there was an organization to protest the forced contraception bill. I was one of them. We carried signs for hours at a time. We printed leaflets. We stopped people passing so that we could talk to them. We gave up our time, we went to considerable trouble and expense, because we wanted to get our ideas across.

'Now, if a man had joined us with a blank sign, he would have been *saying* something.

'His sign says that he has no opinion. If he joins us, he says that we have no opinion either. He's saying our opinions aren't worth anything.'

I said, 'Tell him when he wakes up. He can put it in his notebook.'

'But his notebook is *wrong*. He wouldn't push his blank sign in among people he agreed with, would he?'

'Maybe not.'

'I . . . suppose I don't like people with no opinions.' Mrs Hawthorne stood up. She had been sitting tailor-fashion for some hours. 'Do you know if there's a pop machine nearby?'

There wasn't, of course. No private company would risk getting their machines smashed once or twice a day. But she had reminded the rest of us that we were thirsty. Eventually we all got up and trooped away in the direction of the fountain.

All but Blank Sign.

I'd *liked* that blank sign gag. How odd, how ominous, that so basic a right as freedom of speech could depend on so slight a thing as a floating copseye.

I was thirsty.

The park was bright by city light, crossed by sharp-edged shadows. In such light it seems that one can see much more than he really can. I could see into every shadow; but, though there were stirrings all around us, I could see nobody until he moved. We four, sitting under an oak with our backs to the tremendous trunk, must be invisible from any distance.

We talked little. The Park was quiet except for occasional laughter from the fountain.

I couldn't forget my thirst. I could feel others being thirsty around me. The fountain was right out there in the open, a solid block of concrete with five men around it.

They were dressed alike, in paper shorts with big pockets. They looked alike: like first-string athletes. Maybe they belonged to the same order, or frat, or ROTC class.

They had taken over the fountain.

When someone came to get a drink, the tall ash-blond one would step forward with his arm held stiffly out, palm forward. He had a wide mouth and a grin that might otherwise have been infectious, and a deep, echoing voice. He would intone, 'Go back. None may pass here but the immortal Cthulhu—' or something equally silly.

Trouble was, they weren't kidding. Or: they were kidding, but they wouldn't let anyone have a drink.

When we arrived, a girl dressed in a towel had been trying to talk some sense into them. It hadn't worked. It might even have boosted their egos: a lovely half-naked girl begging them for water. Eventually she'd given up and gone away.

In that light her hair might have been red. I hoped it was the girl in the cloak.

And a beefy man in a yellow business jumper had made the mistake of demanding his Rights. It was not a night for Rights. The blond kid had goaded him into screaming insults, a stream of unimaginative profanity, which ended when he tried to hit the blond kid. Then three of them had swarmed over him. The man had left crawling, moaning of police and lawsuits.

Why hadn't somebody done something?

I had watched it all from sitting position. I could list my own reasons. One: it was hard to face the fact that a copseye would not zap them both, any second now. Two: I didn't like the screaming fat man much. He talked dirty. Three: I'd been waiting for someone else to step in.

Mrs Hawthorne said, 'Ronald, what time is it?'

Ron may have been the only man in King's Free Park who knew

the time. People generally left their valuables in lockers at the entrances. But years ago, when Ron was flush with money from the sale of the engraved beer bottles, he'd bought an implant-watch. He told time by one red mark and two red lines glowing beneath the skin of his wrist.

We had put the women between us, but I saw the motion as he glanced at his wrist. 'Quarter of twelve.'

'Don't you think they'll get bored and go away? It's been twenty minutes since anyone tried to get a drink.' Mrs Hawthorne said.

Jill shifted against me in the dark. 'They can't be any more bored than we are. I think they'll get bored and stay anyway. Besides—' She stopped.

I said, 'Besides that, we're thirsty *now*.'

'Right.'

'Ron, have you seen any sign of those rock throwers you collected? Especially the one who knocked down the copseye.'

'No.'

I wasn't surprised. In this darkness? 'Do you remember his . . .' and I didn't even finish.

'. . . Yes!' Ron said suddenly.

'You're kidding.'

'No. His name was Bugeyes. You don't forget a name like that.'

'I take it he had bulging eyes?'

'I didn't notice.'

Well, it was worth a try. I stood and cupped my hands for a megaphone and shouted, 'Bugeyes!'

One of the Water Monopoly shouted, 'Let's keep the noise down out there!'

'*Bugeyes!*'

A chorus of remarks from the Water Monopoly. 'Strange habits these peasants—' 'Most of them are just thirsty. *This* character—'

From off to the side: 'What do you want?'

'We want to talk to you! Stay where you are!' To Ron I said, 'Come on.' To Jill and Mrs Hawthorne, 'Stay here. Don't get involved.'

We moved out into the open space between us and Bugeyes' voice.

Two of the five kids came immediately to intercept us. They must have been bored, all right, and looking for action.

We ran for it. We reached the shadows of the trees before those two reached us. They stopped, laughing like maniacs, and moved back to the fountain.

Ron and I, we lay on our bellies in the shadows of low bushes. Across too much shadowless grass, four men in paper shorts stood at parade rest at the four corners of the fountain. The fifth man watched for a victim.

A boy walked out between us into the moonlight. His eyes were shining, big, expressive eyes, maybe a bit too prominent. His hands were big, too—with knobby knuckles. One hand was full of acorns.

He pitched them rapidly, one at a time, overhand. First one, then another of the Water Monopoly twitched and looked in our direction. Bugeyes kept throwing.

Quite suddenly, two of them started toward us at a run. Bugeyes kept throwing until they were almost on him; then he threw his acorns in a handful and dived into the shadows.

The two of them ran between us. We let the first go by: the wide-mouthed blond spokesman, his expression low and murderous now. The other was short and broad-shouldered, an intimidating silhouette, seemingly all muscle. A tackle. I stood up in front of him, expecting him to stop in surprise; and he did, and I hit him in the mouth as hard as I could.

He stepped back in shock. Ron wrapped an arm around his throat.

He bucked. Instantly. Ron hung on. I did something I'd seen often enough on television: linked my fingers and brought both hands down on the back of his neck.

The blond spokesman should be back by now; and I turned, and he was. He was on me before I could get my hands up. We rolled on the ground, me with my arms pinned to my sides, him unable to use his hands without letting go. It was lousy planning for both of us. He was squeezing the breath out of me. Ron hovered over us, waiting for a chance to hit him.

Suddenly there were others, a lot of others. Three of them pulled the blond kid off me, and a beefy, bloody man in a yellow business jumper stepped forward and crowned him with a rock.

The blond kid went limp.

The man squared off and threw a straight left hook with the rock in his hand. The blond kid's head snapped back, fell forward.

I yelled, 'Hey!' Jumped forward, got hold of the arm that held the rock.

Someone hit me solidly in the side of the neck.

I dropped. It felt like all my strings had been cut. Someone was helping me to my feet—Ron—voices babbling in whispers, one shouting, 'Get him—'

I couldn't see the blond kid. The other one, the tackle, was up and staggering away. Shadows came from between the trees to play pileup on him. The woods were alive, and it was just a *little* patch of woods. Full of angry, thirsty people.

Bugeyes reappeared, grinning widely. 'Now what? Go somewhere else and try it again?'

'Oh, no. It's getting very vicious out tonight. Ron, we've got to stop them. They'll kill him!'

'It's a Free Park. Can you stand now?'

'Ron, they'll *kill* him!'

The rest of the Water Trust was charging to the rescue. One of them had a tree branch with the leaves stripped off. Behind them, shadows converged on the fountain.

We fled.

I had to stop after a dozen paces. My head was trying to explode. Ron looked back anxiously, but I waved him on. Behind me the man with the branch broke through the trees and ran towards me to do murder.

Behind him, all the noise suddenly stopped.

I braced myself for the blow.

And fainted.

He was lying across my legs, with the branch still in his hand. Jill and Ron were pulling at my shoulders. A pair of golden moons floated overhead.

I wriggled loose. I felt my head. It seemed intact.

Ron said, 'The copseyes zapped him before he got to you.'

'What about the others? Did they kill them?'

'I don't know.' Ron ran his hands through his hair. 'I was wrong. Anarchy isn't stable. It comes apart too easily.'

'Well, don't do any more experiments, OK?'

People were beginning to stand up. They streamed towards the exits, gathering momentum, beneath the yellow gaze of the copseyes.

A THING OF BEAUTY

NORMAN SPINRAD

'There's a gentleman by the name of Mr Shiburo Ito to see you,' my intercom said. 'He is interested in the purchase of an historic artefact of some significance.'

While I waited for him to enter my private office, I had computer central display his specs on the screen discreetly built into the back of my desk. My Mr Ito was none other than Ito of Ito Freight Boosters of Osaka; there was no need to purchase a readout from Dun & Bradstreet's private banks. If Shiburo Ito of Ito Boosters wrote a cheque for anything short of the national debt, it could be relied upon not to bounce.

The slight, balding man who glided into my office wore a red silk kimono with a richly brocaded black obi, Mendocino needlepoint by the look of it. No doubt back in the miasmic smog of Osaka, he bonged the peons with the latest skins from Saville Row. Everything about him was *just so*; he purchased confidently on that razor edge between class and ostentation that only the Japanese can handle with such grace, and then only when they have millions of hard yen to back them up. Mr Ito would be no sucker. He would want whatever he wanted for precise reasons all his own, and would not be budgeable from the centre of his desires. The typical heavyweight Japanese businessman, a prime example of the breed that's pushed us out of the centre of the international arena.

Mr Ito bowed almost imperceptibly as he handed me his card. I countered by merely bobbing my head in his direction and remaining seated. These face and posture games may seem ridiculous, but you can't do business with the Japanese without playing them.

As he took a seat before me, Ito drew a black cylinder from the sleeve of his kimono and ceremoniously placed it on the desk before me.

'I have been given to understand that you are a connoisseur of Filmore posters of the early-to-mid-1960s periods, Mr Harris,' he said. 'The repute of your collection has penetrated even to the environs of Osaka and Kyoto, where I make my habitation. Please permit me to make this minor addition. The thought that a contribution of mine may repose in such illustrious surroundings will afford me much pleasure and place me forever in your debt.'

My hands trembled as I unwrapped the poster. With his financial resources, Ito's polite little gift could be almost anything but disappointing. My daddy loved to brag about the old expense account days when American businessmen ran things, but you had to admit that the fringe benefits of business Japanese style had plenty to recommend them.

But when I got the gift open, it took a real effort not to lose points by whistling out loud. For what I was holding was nothing less than a mint example of the very first Grateful Dead poster in subtle black and grey, a super-rare item, not available for any amount of sheer purchasing power. I dared not enquire as to how Mr Ito had acquired it. We simply shared a long, silent moment contemplating the poster, its beauty and historicity transcending whatever questionable events might have transpired to bring us together in its presence.

How could I not like Mr Ito now? Who can say that the Japanese occupy their present international position by economic might alone?

'I hope I may be afforded the opportunity to please your sensibilities as you have pleased mine, Mr Ito,' I finally said. That was the way to phrase it; you didn't thank them for a gift like this, and you brought them around to business as obliquely as possible.

Ito suddenly became obviously embarrassed, even furtive. 'Forgive me my boldness, Mr Harris, but I have hopes that you may be able to assist me in resolving a domestic matter of some delicacy.'

'A domestic matter?'

'Just so. I realize that this is an embarrassing intrusion, but you are obviously a man of refinement and infinite discretion, so if you will forgive my forwardness . . .'

His composure seemed to totally evaporate, as if he was going to ask me to pimp for some disgusting perversion he had. I had the feeling that the power had suddenly taken a quantum jump in my direction, that a large financial opportunity was about to present itself.

'Please feel free, Mr Ito . . .'

Ito smiled nervously. 'My wife comes from a family of extreme artistic attainment,' he said. 'In fact, both her parents have attained the exalted status of National Cultural Treasurers, a distinction of which they never tire of reminding me. While I have achieved a large measure of financial success in the freight-booster enterprise, they regard me as *nikulturi*, a mere merchant, severely lacking in aesthetic refinement as compared to their own illustrious selves. You understand the situation, Mr Harris?'

I nodded as sympathetically as I could. These Japs certainly have a genius for making life difficult for themselves! Here was a major Japanese industrialist shrinking into low posture at the very thought of his sponging in-laws, whom he could probably buy and sell out of petty cash. At the same time, he was obviously out to cream the sons of bitches in some crazy way that would only make sense to a Japanese. Seems to me the Japanese are better at running the world than they are at running their lives.

'Mr Harris, I wish to acquire a major American artefact for the gardens of my Kyoto estate. Frankly, it must be of sufficient magnitude so as to remind the parents of my wife of my success in the material realm every time they should chance to gaze upon it, and I shall display it in a manner which will assure that they gaze upon it often. But of course, it must be of sufficient beauty and historicity so as to prove to them that my taste is no less elevated than their own. Thus shall I gain respect in their eyes and re-establish tranquillity in my household. I have been given to understand that you are a valued counsellor in such matters, and I am eager to inspect whatever such objects you may deem appropriate.'

So that was it! He wanted to buy something big enough to bong the minds of his artsy-fartsy relatives, but he really didn't trust his own taste; he wanted me to show him something he would want to see. And he was swimming like a goldfish in a sea of yen! I could hardly believe my good luck. How much could I take him for?

'Ah . . . what size artefact did you have in mind, Mr Ito?' I asked as casually as I could.

'I wish to acquire a major piece of American monumental architecture so that I may convert the gardens of my estate into a shrine to its beauty and historicity. Therefore, a piece of classical proportions is required. Of course, it must be worthy of enshrinement, otherwise an embarrassing loss of esteem will surely ensue.'

'Of course.'

This was not going to be just another Howard Johnson or gas station sale; even something like an old Hilton or the Cooperstown Baseball Hall of Fame I unloaded last year was thinking too small. In his own way, Ito was telling me that price was no object, the sky was the limit. This was the dream of a lifetime! A sucker with a bottomless bank account placing himself trustingly in my tender hands!

'Should it please you, Mr Ito,' I said, 'we can inspect several possibilities here in New York immediately. My jumper is on the roof.'

'Most gracious of you to interrupt your most busy schedule on my behalf, Mr Harris. I would be delighted.'

I lifted the jumper off the roof, floated her to a thousand feet, then took a Mach 1.5 jump south over the decayed concrete jungles at the tip of Manhattan. The curve brought us back to float about a mile north of Bedloe's Island. I took her down to three hundred and brought her in toward the Statue of Liberty at a slow drift, losing altitude imperceptibly as we crept up on the Headless Lady, so that by the time we were just offshore, we were right down on the deck. It was a nice touch to make the goods look more impressive—manipulating the perspectives so that the huge, green, headless statue, with its patina of firebomb soot, seemed to rise up out of the bay like a ruined colossus as we floated toward it.

Mr Ito betrayed no sign of emotion. He stared straight ahead out the bubble without so much as a word or a flicker of gesture.

'As you are no doubt aware, this is the famous Statue of Liberty,' I said. 'Like most such artefacts, it is available to any buyer who will display it with proper dignity. Of course, I would have no trouble convincing the Bureau of National Antiquities that your intentions are exemplary in this regard.'

I set the autopilot to circle the island at fifty yards offshore so that Ito could get a fully rounded view, and see how well the statue would look from any angle, how eminently suitable it was for enshrinement. But he still sat there with less expression on his face than the average C-grade servitor.

'You can see that nothing has been touched since the Insurrectionists blew the statue's head off,' I said, trying to drum up his interest with a pitch. 'Thus, the statue has picked up yet another level of historical significance to enhance its already formidable venerability. Originally a gift from France, it has historical significance as an emblem of kinship between the American and French Revolutions. Situated as it is in the mouth of New York harbour, it became a symbol of America itself to generations of immigrants. And the damage the Insurrectionists did only serves as a reminder of how lucky we were to come through that mess as lightly as we did. Also, it adds a certain melancholy atmosphere, don't you think? Emotion, intrinsic beauty, and historicity combined in one elegant piece of monumental statuary. And the asking price is a good deal less than you might suppose.'

Mr Ito seemed embarrassed when he finally spoke. 'I trust you will forgive my saying so, Mr Harris, since the emotion is engendered by the highest regard for the noble past of your great nation, but I find this particular artefact somewhat depressing.'

'How so, Mr Ito?'

The jumper completed a circle of the Statue of Liberty and began another as Mr Ito lowered his eyes and stared at the oily waters of the bay as he answered.

'The symbolism of this broken statue is quite saddening, representing as it does a decline from your nation's past greatness. For me to enshrine such an artefact in Kyoto would be an ignoble act, an insult to the memory of your nation's greatness. It would be a statement of overweening pride.'

Can you beat that? *He* was offended because he felt that displaying the statue in Japan would be insulting the United States, and therefore I was implying he was *nikulturi* by offering it to him. When all that the damned thing was to any American was one more piece of old junk left over from the glorious days that the Japanese, who were nuts for such rubbish, might be persuaded to pay through the nose for the dubious privilege of carting away. These Japs could drive you crazy—who else could you offend by suggesting they do something that they thought would offend you but you thought was just fine in the first place?

'I hope I haven't offended you, Mr Ito,' I blurted out. I could have bitten my tongue off the moment I said it, because it was exactly the wrong thing to say. I *had* offended him, and it was only a further offence to put him in a position where politeness demanded that he deny it.

'I'm sure that could not have been further from your intention,

Mr Harris,' Ito said with convincing sincerity. 'A pang of sadness at the perishability of greatness, nothing more. In fact as such, the experience might be said to be healthful to the soul. But making such an artefact a permanent part of one's surroundings would be more than I could bear.'

Were these his true feelings or just smooth Japanese politeness? Who could tell what these people really felt? Sometimes I think they don't even know what they feel themselves. But at any rate, I had to show him something that would change his mood, and fast. Hm-m-m . . .

'Tell me, Mr Ito, are you fond of baseball?'

His eyes lit up like satellite beacons and the heavy mood evaporated in the warm, almost childish, glow of his sudden smile. 'Ah yes!' he said. 'I retain a box at Osaka Stadium, though I must confess I secretly retain a partiality for the Giants. How strange it is that this profound game has so declined in the country of its origin.'

'Perhaps. But that very fact has placed something on the market which I'm sure you'll find most congenial. Shall we go?'

'By all means,' Mr Ito said. 'I find our present environs somewhat overbearing.'

I floated the jumper to five hundred feet and programmed a Mach 2.5 jump curve to the north that quickly put the great hunk of mouldering, dirty copper far behind. It's amazing how much sickening emotion the Japanese are able to attach to almost any piece of old junk. *Our* old junk at that, as if Japan didn't have enough useless old clutter of its own. But I certainly shouldn't complain about it; it makes me a pretty good living. Everyone knows the old saying about a fool and his money.

The jumper's trajectory put us at float over the confluence of the Harlem and East Rivers at a thousand feet. Without dropping any lower, I whipped the jumper north-east over the Bronx at three hundred miles per hour. This area had been covered by tenements before the Insurrection, and had been thoroughly razed by fire-bombs, high explosives, and napalm. No one had ever found an economic reason for clearing away the miles of rubble, and now the scarred earth and ruined buildings were covered with tall grass, poison sumac, tangled scrub growth, and scattered thickets of trees which might merge to form a forest in another generation or two. Because of the crazy, jagged, overgrown topography, this land was utterly useless, and no one lived here except some pathetic remnants of old hippie tribes that kept to themselves and weren't worth hunting down. Their occasional huts and patchwork tents were the only signs of human habitation in the area. This was *really* depressing territory, and I wanted to get Mr Ito over it high and fast.

Fortunately, we didn't have far to go, and in a couple of minutes, I had the jumper floating at five hundred feet over our objective, the only really intact structure in the area. Mr Ito's stone face lit up with such boyish pleasure that I knew I had it made; I had figured right when I figured he couldn't resist something like this.

'So!' he cried in delight. 'Yankee Stadium!'

The ancient ballpark had come through the Insurrection with nothing worse than some atmospheric blacking and cratering of its concrete exterior walls. Everything around it had been pretty well demolished except for a short section of old elevated subway line which still stood beside it, a soft rusty-red skeleton covered with vines and moss. The surrounding ruins were thoroughly overgrown, huge piles of rubble, truncated buildings, rusted-out tanks, forming tangled man-made jungled foothills around the high point of the stadium, which itself had creepers and vines growing all over it, partially blending it into the wild, overgrown landscape around it.

The Bureau of National Antiquities had circled the stadium with a high, electrified, barbed-wire fence to keep out the hippies who roamed the badlands. A lone guard armed with a Japanese-made slicer patrolled the fence in endless circles at fifteen feet on a one-man skimmer. I brought the jumper down to fifty feet and orbited the stadium five times, giving the enthralled Ito a good, long, contemplative look at how lovely it would look as the centrepiece of his gardens instead of hidden away in these crummy ruins. The guard waved to us each time our paths crossed—it must be a lonely, boring job out here with nothing but old junk and crazy wandering hippies for company.

'May we go inside?' Ito said in absolutely reverent tones. Man, was he hooked! He glowed like a little kid about to inherit a candy store.

'Certainly, Mr Ito.' I said, taking the jumper out of its circling pattern and floating it gently up over the lip of the old ballpark, putting it on hover at roof-level over what had once been short centre field. Very slowly, I brought the jumper down towards the tangle of tall grass, shrubbery, and occasional stunted trees that covered what had once been the playing field.

It was like descending into some immense, ruined, roofless cathedral. As we dropped, the cavernous tripledecked grandstands—rotten wooden seats rich with moss and fungi, great overhanging rafters concealing flocks of chattering birds in their deep glowering shadows—rose to encircle the jumper in a weird, lost grandeur.

By the time we touched down, Ito seemed to be floating in his seat with rapture. 'So beautiful!' he sighed. 'Such a sense of history and venerability. Ah, Mr Harris, what noble deeds were done in this Yankee Stadium in bygone days! May we set foot on this historic playing field?'

'Of course, Mr Ito.' It was beautiful. I didn't have to say a word; he was doing a better job of selling the mouldy, useless heap of junk to himself than I ever could.

We got out of the jumper and tramped around through the tangled vegetation while scruffy pigeons wheeled overhead and the immensity of the empty stadium gave the place an illusion of mystical significance, as if it were some Greek ruin or Stonehenge, instead of just a ruined old baseball park. The grandstands seemed choked with ghosts; the echoes of great events that never were, filled the deeply shadowed cavernous spaces.

Mr Ito, it turned out, knew more about Yankee Stadium than I did, or ever wanted to. He led me around at a measured, reverent pace, boring my ass off with a kind of historical grand tour.

'Here Al Gionfriddo made his famous World Series catch of a potential home run by the great Dimaggio,' he said, as we reached the high, crumbling black wall that ran around the bleachers. Faded numerals said '405'. We followed this curving, overgrown wall around to the 467 sign in left centre field. Here there were three stone markers jutting up out of the old playing field like so many tombstones, and five copper plaques on the wall behind them, so green with decay as to be illegible. They really must've taken this stuff seriously in the old days, as seriously as the Japanese take it now.

'Memorials to the great heroes of the New York Yankees,' Ito said. 'The legendary Ruth, Gehrig, Dimaggio, Mantle . . . Over this very spot, Mickey Mantle drove a ball into the bleachers, a feat which had been regarded as impossible for nearly half a century. Ah . . .'

And so on. Ito tramped all through the underbrush of the playing field and seemed to have a piece of trivia of vast historical significance to himself for almost every square foot of Yankee Stadium. At this spot, Babe Ruth had achieved his sixtieth home run; here Roger Maris had finally surpassed that feat, over there Mantle had almost driven a ball over the high roof of the venerable stadium. It was staggering how much of this trivia he knew, and how much importance it all had in his eyes. The tour seemed to go on forever. I would've gone crazy with boredom if it wasn't so wonderfully obvious how thoroughly sold he was on the place. While Ito conducted his love-affair with Yankee Stadium, I passed the time by counting yen in my head. I figured I could probably get ten million out of him, which meant that my commission would be a cool million. Thinking about that much money about to drop into my hands was enough to keep me smiling for the two hours that Ito babbled on about home runs, no-hitters, and triple-plays.

It was late afternoon by the time he had finally saturated himself and allowed me to lead him back to the jumper. I felt it was time to talk business, while he was still under the spell of the stadium, and his resistance was at low ebb.

'It pleasures me greatly to observe the depths of your feeling for this beautiful and venerable stadium, Mr Ito,' I said. 'I stand ready to facilitate the speedy transfer of title at your convenience.'

Ito started as if suddenly roused from some pleasant dream. He cast his eyes downward, and bowed almost imperceptibly.

'Alas,' he said sadly, 'while it would pleasure me beyond all reason to enshrine the noble Yankee Stadium upon my grounds, such a self-indulgence would only exacerbate my domestic difficulties. The parents of my wife ignorantly consider the noble sport of baseball an imported American barbarity. My wife unfortunately shares in this opinion and frequently berates me for my enthusiasm for the game. Should I purchase the Yankee Stadium, I would become a laughing stock in my own household, and my life would become quite unbearable.'

Can you beat that? The arrogant little son of a bitch wasted two hours of my time dragging around this stupid heap of junk babbling all that garbage and driving me half crazy, and he knew he wasn't going to buy it all the time! I felt like knocking his low-posture teeth down his unworthy throat. But I thought of all those yen I still had a fighting chance at and made the proper response: a rueful little smile of sympathy, a shared sigh of wistful regret, a murmured, 'Alas'.

'However,' Ito added brightly, 'the memory of this visit is something I shall treasure always. I am deeply in your debt for granting me this experience, Mr Harris. For this alone, the trip from Kyoto has been made more than worthwhile.'

Now that really made my day.

I was in real trouble, I was very close to blowing the biggest deal I've ever had a shot at. I'd shown Ito the two best items in my territory, and if he didn't find what he wanted in the north-east, there were plenty of first-rank pieces still left in the rest of the country—top stuff like the St Louis Gateway Arch, the Disneyland Matterhorn, the Salt Lake City Mormon Tabernacle—and plenty of other brokers to collect that big fat commission.

I figured I had only one more good try before Ito started thinking of looking elsewhere: the United Nations building complex. The UN had fallen into a complicated legal limbo. The UN had retained title to the buildings when they moved their headquarters out of New York, but when the UN folded, New York State, New York City, and the Federal Government had all laid claim to them, along with the UN's foreign creditors. The Bureau of National Antiquities didn't have clear title, but they did administer the estate for the Federal Government. If I could palm the damned thing off on Ito, the Bureau of National Junk would be only too happy to take his cheque and let everyone else try to pry the money out of them. And once he moved it to Kyoto, the Japanese Government would not be about to let anyone repossess something that one of their heavyweight citizens had shelled out hard yen for.

So I jumped her at Mach 1.7 to a hover at three hundred feet over the greasy waters of the East River due east of the UN complex at 42nd Street. At this time of day and from this angle, the UN buildings presented what I hoped was a romantic Japanese-style vista. The Secretariat was a giant glass tombstone dramatically silhouetted by the late afternoon sun as it loomed massively before us out of the perpetual grey haze hanging over Manhattan; beside it, the low sweeping curve of the General Assembly gave the grouping a balanced calligraphic outline. The total effect seemed similar to that of one of those ancient Japanese Torii gates rising out of the foggy sunset, only done on a far grander scale.

The Insurrection had left the UN untouched—the rebels had had some crazy attachment for it—and from the river, you couldn't see much of the grubby open air market that had been allowed to spring up in the plaza, or the honky-tonk bars along First Avenue. Fortunately, the Bureau of National Antiquities made a big point of keeping the buildings themselves in good shape, figuring that the Federal Government's claim would be weakened if anyone could yell that the Bureau was letting them fall apart.

I floated her slowly in off the river, keeping at the three-hundred-foot level, and started my pitch. 'Before you, Mr Ito, are the UN buildings, melancholy symbol of one of the noblest dreams of man, now unfortunately empty and abandoned, a monument to the tragedy of the UN's unfortunate demise.'

Flashes of sunlight, reflected off the river, then on to the hundreds of windows that formed the face of the Secretariat, scintillated intermittently across the glass monolith as I set the jumper to circling the building. When we came around to the western face, the great glass façade was a curtain of orange fire.

'The Secretariat could be set in your gardens so as to catch both the sunrise and sunset, Mr Ito,' I pointed out. 'It's considered one of the finest examples of Twentieth-Century Utilitarian in the world, and you'll note that it's in excellent repair.'

Ito said nothing. His eyes did not so much as flicker. Even the muscles of his face seemed unnaturally wooden. The jumper passed behind the Secretariat again, which eclipsed both the sun and its giant reflection; below us was the sweeping grey concrete roof of the General Assembly.

'And of course, the historic significance of the UN buildings is beyond measure, if somewhat tragic—'

Abruptly, Mr Ito interrupted, in a cold, clipped voice. 'Please forgive my crudity in interjecting a political opinion into this situation, Mr Harris, but I believe such frankness will save you much wasted time and effort and myself considerable discomfort.'

All at once, he was Shiburo Ito of Ito Freight Boosters of Osaka, a mover and shaper of the economy of the most powerful nation on Earth, and he was letting me know it. 'I fully respect your sentimental esteem for the late UN, but it is a sentiment I do not share. I remind you that the UN was born as an alliance of the nations which humiliated Japan in a most unfortunate war, and expired as a shrill and contentious assembly of pauperized beggar-states united only in the dishonourable determination to extract international alms from more progressive, advanced, self-sustaining, and virtuous states, chief among them Japan. I must therefore regretfully point out that the sight of these buildings fills me with nothing but disgust, though they may have a certain intrinsic beauty as abstract objects.'

His face had become a shiny mask and he seemed a million miles away. He had come as close to outright anger as I had ever heard one of these heavyweight Japs get; he must be really steaming inside. Damn it, how was I supposed to know that the UN had all those awful political meanings for him? As far as I've ever heard, the UN hasn't meant anything to anyone for years, except an idealistic, sappy idea that got taken over by Third Worlders and went broke. Just my rotten luck to run into one of the few people in the world who were still fighting that one!

'You are no doubt fatigued. Mr Harris,' Ito said coldly. 'I shall trouble you no longer. It would be best to return to your office now. Should you have further objects to show me, we can arrange another appointment at some mutually convenient time.'

What could I say to that? I had offended him deeply, and besides I couldn't think of anything else to show him. I took the jumper to five hundred and headed downtown over the river at a slow hundred miles per hour, hoping against hope that I'd somehow think of something to salvage this blown million-yen deal with before we reached my office and I lost this giant goldfish forever.

As we headed downtown, Ito stared impassively out the bubble at the bleak ranks of high-rise apartment buildings that lined the Manhattan shore below us, not deigning to speak or take further notice of my miserable existence. The deep orange light streaming in through the bubble turned his round face into a rising sun, straight off the Japanese flag. It seemed appropriate. The crazy bastard was just like his country: a politically touchy, politely arrogant economic overlord, with infinitely refined aesthetic sensibilities inexplicably combined with a pack-rat lust for the silliest of our old junk. One minute Ito seemed so superior in every way, and the next he was a stupid, childish sucker. I've been doing business with the Japanese for years, and I still don't really understand them. The best I can do is guess around the edges of whatever their inner reality actually is, and hope I hit what works. And this time out, with a million yen or more dangled in front of me, I had guessed wrong three times and now I was dragging my tail home with a dissatisfied customer whose very posture seemed designed to let me know that I was a crass, second-rate boob, and that he was one of the lords of creation!

'Mr Harris! Mr Harris! Over there! That magnificent structure!' Ito was suddenly almost shouting; his eyes were bright with excitement, and he was actually smiling.

He was pointing due south along the East River. The Manhattan bank was choked with the ugliest public housing projects imaginable, and the Brooklyn shore was worse: one of those huge, sprawling, so-called industrial parks, low windowless buildings, geodesic warehouses, wharves, a few freight-booster launching pads. Only one structure stood out, there was only one thing Ito could've meant: the structure linking the housing project on the Manhattan side with the industrial park on the Brooklyn shore.

Mr Ito was pointing at the Brooklyn Bridge.

'The . . . ah . . . bridge, Mr Ito?' I managed to say with a straight face. As far as I knew, the Brooklyn Bridge had only one claim to historicity: it was the butt of a series of jokes so ancient that they weren't funny anymore. The Brooklyn Bridge was what old comic con men traditionally sold to sucker tourists, greenhorns or hicks they used to call them, along with phoney uranium stocks and gold-painted bricks.

So I couldn't resist the line: 'You want to buy the Brooklyn Bridge, Mr Ito?' It was so beautiful; he had put me through such hassles, and had finally gotten so damned high and mighty with me, and now I was in effect calling him an idiot to his face and he didn't know it.

In fact, he nodded eagerly in answer like a straight man out of some old joke and said, 'I do believe so. Is it for sale?'

I slowed the jumper to forty, brought her down to a hundred feet, and swallowed my giggles as we approached the crumbling old monstrosity. Two massive and squat stone towers supported the rusty cables from which the bed of the bridge was suspended. The jumper had made the bridge useless years ago; no one had bothered to maintain it and no one had bothered to tear it down.

Where the big blocks of dark grey stone met the water, they were encrusted with putrid-looking green slime. Above the waterline, the towers were whitened with about a century's worth of guano.

It was hard to believe that Ito was serious. The bridge was a filthy, decayed, reeking old monstrosity. In short, it was just what Ito deserved to be sold.

'Why yes, Mr Ito,' I said, 'I think I might be able to sell you the Brooklyn Bridge.'

I put the jumper on hover about a hundred feet from one of the filthy old stone towers. Where the stones weren't caked with seagull guano, they were covered with about an inch of black soot. The roadbed was cracked and pitted and thickly paved with garbage, old shells, and more guano; the bridge must've been a seagull rookery for decades. I was mighty glad that the jumper was airtight; the stink must've been terrific.

'Excellent!' Mr Ito exclaimed. 'Quite lovely, is it not? I am determined to be the man to purchase the Brooklyn Bridge, Mr Harris.'

'I can think of no one more worthy of that honour than your esteemed self, Mr Ito,' I said with total sincerity.

About four months after the last section of the Brooklyn Bridge was boosted to Kyoto, I received two packages from Mr Shiburo Ito. One was a mailing envelope containing a minicassette and a holo slide; the other was a heavy package about the size of a shoebox wrapped in blue rice paper.

Feeling a lot more mellow toward the memory of Ito these days, with a million of his yen in my bank account, I dropped the mini into my playback and was hardly surprised to hear his voice.

'Salutations, Mr Harris, and once again my profoundest thanks for expediting the transfer of the Brooklyn Bridge to my estate. It has now been permanently enshrined and affords us all much aesthetic enjoyment and has enhanced the tranquillity of my household immeasurably. I am enclosing a holo of the shrine for your pleasure. I have also sent you a small token of my appreciation which I hope you will take in the spirit in which it is given. Sayonara.'

My curiosity aroused, I got right up and put the holo slide in my wall viewer. Before me was a heavily wooded mountain which rose into twin peaks of austere, dark-grey rock. A tall waterfall plunged gracefully down the long gorge between the two pinnacles to a shallow lake at the foot of the mountain, where it smashed on to a table of flat rock, generating perpetual billows of soft mist which turned the landscape into something straight out of a Chinese painting. Spanning the gorge between the two peaks like a spider-web directly over the great falls, its stone towers anchored to islands of rock on the very lip of the precipice, was the Brooklyn Bridge, its ponderous bulk rendered slim and graceful by the massive scale of the landscape. The stone had been cleaned and glistened with moisture, the cables and roadbed were overgrown with lush green ivy. The holo had been taken just as the sun was setting between the towers of the bridge, outlining it in rich orange fire, turning the rising mists coppery, and sparkling in brilliant sheets off the falling water.

It was very beautiful.

It was quite a while before I tore myself away from the scene, remembering Mr Ito's other package.

Beneath the blue paper wrapping was a single gold-painted brick. I gaped. I laughed. I looked again.

The object looked superficially like an old brick covered with gold paint. But it wasn't. It was a solid brick of soft, pure gold, a replica of the original item, in perfect detail.

I knew that Mr Ito was trying to tell me something, but I still can't quite make out what.

THE SCREWFLY SOLUTION

RACCOONA SHELDON

The young man sitting at 2° N., 75° W. sent a casually venomous glance up at the nonfunctional shoofly *ventilador* and went on reading his letter. He was sweating heavily, stripped to his shorts in the hotbox of what passed for a hotel room in Cuyapán.

How do other wives *do* it? I stay busy-busy with the Ann Arbor grant review programmes and the seminar, saying brightly 'Oh yes, Alan is in Colombia setting up a biological pest control programme, isn't it wonderful?' But inside I imagine you being surrounded by 19-year-old raven-haired cooing beauties, every one panting with social dedication and filthy rich. And forty inches of bosom busting out of her delicate lingerie, I even figured it in centimetres, that's 101.6 centimetres of busting. Oh, darling, darling, do what you want only *come home safe.*

Alan grinned fondly, briefly imagining the only body he longed for. His girl, his magic Anne. Then he got up to open the window another cautious notch. A long pale mournful face looked in—a goat. The room opened on the goatpen, the stench was vile. Air, anyway. He picked up the letter.

Everything is just about as you left it, except that the Peedsville horror seems to be getting worse. They're calling it the Sons of Adam cult now. Why can't they *do* something, even if it is a religion? The Red Cross has set up a refugee camp in Ashton, Georgia. Imagine, refugees in the USA. I heard two little girls were carried out all slashed up. Oh, Alan.

Which reminds me, Barney came over with a wad of clippings he wants me to send you. I'm putting them in a separate envelope; I know what happens to very fat letters in foreign POs. He says, in case you don't get them, what do the following have in common? Peedsville, São Paulo, Phoenix, San Diego, Shanghai,

New Delhi, Tripoli, Brisbane, Johannesburg, and Lubbock, Texas. He says the hint is, remember where the Intertropical Convergence Zone is now. That makes no sense to me, maybe it will to your superior ecological brain. All I could see about the clippings was that they were fairly horrible accounts of murders or massacres of women. The worst was the New Delhi one, about 'rafts of female corpses' in the river. The funniest (!) was the Texas Army officer who shot his wife, three daughters and his aunt, because God told him to clean the place up.

Barney's such an old dear, he's coming over Sunday to help me take off the downspout and see what's blocking it. He's dancing on air right now, since you left his spruce bud-worm-moth anti-pheromone programme finally paid off. You know he tested over 2,000 compounds? Well, it seems that good old 2,097 *really* works. When I asked him what it does he just giggles, you know how shy he is with women. Anyway, it seems that a one-shot spray programme will save the forests, without harming a single other thing. Birds and people can eat it all day, he says.

Well sweetheart, that's all the news except Amy goes back to Chicago to school Sunday. The place will be a tomb, I'll miss her frightfully in spite of her being at the stage where I'm her worst enemy. The sullen sexy subteens, Angie says. Amy sends love to her Daddy. I send you my whole heart, all that words can't say.

Your Anne

Alan put the letter safely in his notefile and glanced over the rest of the thin packet of mail, refusing to let himself dream of home and Anne. Barney's 'fat envelope' wasn't there. He threw himself on the rumpled bed, yanking off the lightcord a minute before the town generator went off for the night. In the darkness the list of places Barney had mentioned spread themselves around a misty globe that turned, troublingly, briefly in his mind. Something . . .

But then the memory of the hideously parasitized children he had worked with at the clinic that day took possession of his thoughts. He set himself to considering the data he must collect. *Look for the vulnerable link in the behavioural chain*—how often Barney—Dr Barnhard Braithwaite—had pounded it into his skull. Where was it, where? In the morning he would start work on bigger canefly cages . . .

At that moment, five thousand miles North, Anne was writing:

Oh, darling, darling, your first three letters are here, they all came together. I *knew* you were writing. Forget what I said about swarthy heiresses, that was all a joke. My darling I know, I know . . . us. Those dreadful cane-fly larvae, those poor little kids. If you weren't my husband I'd think you were a saint or something. (I do anyway.)

I have your letters pinned up all over the house, makes it a lot less lonely. No real news here except things feel kind of quiet and spooky. Barney and I got the downspout out, it was full of a big rotted hoard of squirrel-nuts. They must have been dropping them down the top, I'll put a wire over it. (Don't worry, I'll use a ladder this time.)

Barney's in an odd, grim mood. He's taking this Sons of Adam thing very seriously, it seems he's going to be on the investigation committee if that ever gets off the ground. The weird part is that nobody seems to be doing anything, as if it's just too big. Selina Peters has been printing some acid comments, like When one man kills his wife you call it murder, but when enough do it we call it a life-style. I think it's spreading, but nobody knows because the media have been asked to down-play it. Barney says it's being viewed as a form of contagious hysteria. He insisted I send you this ghastly interview, printed on thin paper. Its *not* going to be published, of course. The quietness is worse, though, it's like something terrible was going on just out of sight. After reading Barney's thing I called up Pauline in San Diego to make sure she was all right. She sounded funny, as if she wasn't saying everything . . . my own sister. Just after she said things were great she suddenly asked if she could come and stay here awhile next month. I said come right away, but she wants to sell her house first. I wish she'd hurry.

Oh, the diesel car is okay now, it just needed its filter changed. I had to go out to Springfield to get one but Eddie installed it for only $2.50. He's going to bankrupt his garage.

In case you didn't guess, those places of Barney's are all about latitude 30° N. or S.—the horse latitudes. When I said not exactly, he said remember the equatorial convergence zone shifts in winter, and to add in Libya, Osaka, and a place I forget—wait, Alice Springs, Australia. What has this to do with anything, I asked. He said, 'Nothing—I hope.' I leave it to you, great brains like Barney can be weird.

Oh my dearest, here's all of me to all of you. Your letters make life possible. But don't feel you *have* to, I can tell how tired you must be. Just know we're together, always everywhere.

Your Anne

Oh PS I had to open this to put Barney's thing in, it wasn't the secret police. Here it is. All love again. A.

In the goat-infested room where Alan read this, rain was drumming on the roof. He put the letter to his nose to catch the faint perfume once more, and folded it away. Then he pulled out the yellow flimsy Barney had sent and began to read, frowning.

PEEDSVILLE CULT/SONS OF ADAM SPECIAL. Statement by driver Sgt. Willard Mews, Globe Fork, Ark. We hit the roadblock about 80 miles west of Jacksonville. Major John Heinz of Ashton was expecting us, he gave us an escort of two riot vehicles headed by Capt. T. Parr. Major Heinz appeared shocked to see that the NIH medical team included two women doctors. He warned us in the strongest terms of the danger. So Dr Patsy Putnam (Urbana, Ill.), the psychologist, decided to stay behind at the Army cordon. But Dr Elaine Fay (Clinton, NJ) insisted on going with us, saying she was the epi-something (epidemiologist).

We drove behind one of the riot cars at 30 mph for about an hour without seeing anything unusual. There were two big signs saying 'SONS OF ADAM—LIBERATED ZONE.' We passed some small pecan packing plants and a citrus processing plant. The men there looked at us but did not do anything unusual. I didn't see any children or women of course. Just outside Peedsville we stopped at a big barrier made of oil drums in front of a large citrus warehouse. This area is old, sort of a shantytown and trailer park. The new part of town with the shopping centre and developments is about a mile further on. A warehouse worker with a shotgun came out and told us to wait for the Mayor. I don't think he saw Dr Elaine Fay then, she was sitting sort of bent down in back.

Mayor Blount drove up in a police cruiser and our chief, Dr Premack, explained our mission from the Surgeon General. Dr Premack was very careful not to make any remarks insulting to the Mayor's religion. Mayor Blount agreed to let the party go on into Peedsville to take samples of the soil and water and so on and talk to the doctor who lives there. The mayor was about 6′2″, weight maybe 230 or 240, tanned, with greyish hair. He was smiling and chuckling in a friendly manner.

Then he looked inside the car and saw Dr Elaine Fay and he blew up. He started yelling we had to all get the hell back. But Dr Premack managed to talk to him and cool him down and finally the Mayor said Dr Fay should go into the warehouse office and stay there with the door closed. I had to stay there too and see she didn't come out, and one of the Mayor's men would drive the party.

So the medical people and the Mayor and one of the riot vehicles went on into Peedsville and I took Dr Fay back into the warehouse office and sat down. It was real hot and stuffy. Dr Fay opened a window, but when I heard her trying to talk to an old man outside I told her she couldn't do that and closed the window. The old man went away. Then she wanted to talk to me but I told her I did not feel like conversing. I felt it was real wrong, her being there.

So then she started looking through the office files and reading papers there. I told her that was a bad idea, she shouldn't do that. She said the government expected her to investigate. She showed me a booklet or magazine they had there, it was called *Man Listens To God* by Reverend McIllhenny. They had a carton full in the office. I started reading it and Dr Fay said she wanted to wash her hands. So I took her back along a kind of enclosed hallway beside the conveyor to where the toilet was. There were no doors or windows so I went back. After awhile she called out that there was a cot back there, she was going to lie down. I figured that was all right because of the no windows, also I was glad to be rid of her company.

When I got to reading the book it was very intriguing. It was very deep thinking about how man is now on trial with God and if we fulfil our duty God will bless us with a real new life on Earth. The signs and portents show it. It wasn't like, you know, Sunday school stuff. It was deep.

After awhile I heard some music and saw the soldiers from the other riot car were across the street by the gas tanks, sitting in the shade of some trees and kidding with the workers from the plant. One of them was playing a guitar, not electric, just plain. It looked so peaceful.

Then Mayor Blount drove up alone in the cruiser and came in. When he saw I was reading the book he smiled at me sort of fatherly, but he looked tense. He asked me where Dr Fay was and I told him she was lying down in back. He said that was okay. Then he kind of sighed and went back down the hall, closing the door behind him. I sat and listened to the guitar man, trying to hear what he was singing. I felt really hungry, my lunch was in Dr Premack's car.

After awhile the door opened and Mayor Blount came back in. He looked terrible, his clothes were messed up and he had bloody scrape marks on his face. He didn't say anything, he just looked at me hard and fierce, like he might have been disoriented. I saw his zipper was open and there was blood on his clothing and also on his (private parts).

I didn't feel frightened, I felt something important had happened. I tried to get him to sit down. But he motioned me to follow him back down the hall, to where Dr Fay was. 'You must see,' he said. He went into the toilet and I went into a kind of little room there, where the cot was. The light was fairly good, reflected off the tin roof from where the walls stopped. I saw Dr

Fay lying on the cot in a peaceful appearance. She was lying straight, her clothing was to some extent different but her legs were together. I was glad to see that. Her blouse was pulled up and I saw there was a cut or incision on her abdomen. The blood was coming out there, or it had been coming out there, like a mouth. It wasn't moving at this time. Also her throat was cut open.

I returned to the office. Mayor Blount was sitting down, looking very tired. He had cleaned himself off. He said, 'I did it for you. Do you understand?'

He seemed like my father, I can't say it better than that. I realized he was under a terrible strain, he had taken a lot on himself for me. He went on to explain how Dr Fay was very dangerous, she was what they call a cripto-female (crypto?), the most dangerous kind. He had exposed her and purified the situation. He was very straightforward, I didn't feel confused at all, I knew he had done what was right.

We discussed the book, how man must purify himself and show God a clean world. He said some people raise the question of how can man reproduce without women but such people miss the point. The point is that as long as man depends on the old filthy animal way God won't help him. When man gets rid of his animal part which is woman, this is the signal God is awaiting. Then God will reveal the new true clean way, maybe angels will come bringing new souls, or maybe we will live forever, but it is not our place to speculate, only to obey. He said some men here had seen an Angel of the Lord. This was very deep, it seemed like it echoed inside me, I felt it was an inspiration.

Then the medical party drove up and I told Dr Premack that Dr Fay had been taken care of and sent away, and I got in the car to drive them out of the Liberated Zone. However four of the six soldiers from the roadblock refused to leave. Capt. Parr tried to argue them out of it but finally agreed they could stay to guard the oil-drum barrier.

I would have liked to stay too the place was so peaceful but they needed me to drive the car. If I had known there would be all this hassle I never would have done them the favour. I am not crazy and I have not done anything wrong and my lawyer will get me out. That is all I have to say.

In Cuyapán the hot afternoon rain had temporarily ceased. As Alan's fingers let go of Sgt. Willard Mews's wretched document he caught sight of pencil-scrawled words in the margin. Barney's spider hand. He squinted.

Man's religion and metaphysics are the voices of his glands. Schönweiser, 1878.

Who the devil Schönweiser was Alan didn't know, but he knew what Barney was conveying. This murderous crackpot religion of McWhosis was a symptom, not a cause. Barney believed something was physically affecting the Peedsville men, generating psychosis, and a local religious demagog had sprung up to 'explain' it.

Well, maybe. But cause or effect, Alan thought only of one thing: eight hundred miles from Peedsville to Ann Arbor. Anne should be safe. She *had* to be.

He threw himself on the lumpy cot, his mind going back exultantly to his work. At the cost of a million bites and cane-cuts he was pretty sure he'd found the weak link in the canefly cycle. The male mass-mating behaviour, the comparative scarcity of ovulant females. It would be the screwfly solution all over again with the sexes reversed. Concentrate the pheromone, release sterilized females. Luckily the breeding populations were comparatively isolated. In a couple of seasons they ought to have it. Have to let them go on spraying poison meanwhile, of course; damn pity, it was slaughtering everything and getting in the water, and the caneflies had evolved to immunity anyway. But in a couple of seasons, maybe three, they could drop the canefly populations below reproductive viability. No more tormented human bodies with those stinking larvae in the nasal passages and brain . . . He drifted off for a nap, grinning.

Up north, Anne was biting her lip in shame and pain.

Sweetheart, I shouldn't admit it but your wife is ~~scared~~ a bit jittery. Just female nerves or something, nothing to worry about. Everything is normal up here. It's so eerily normal, nothing in the papers, nothing anywhere except what I hear through Barney and Lillian. But Pauline's phone won't answer out in San Diego; the fifth day some strange man yelled at me and banged the phone down. Maybe she's sold her house—but why wouldn't she call?

Lillian's on some kind of Save-the-Women committee, like we were an endangered species, ha-ha—you know Lillian. It seems the Red Cross has started setting up camps. But she says, after the first rush, only a trickle are coming out of what they call 'the affected areas'. Not many children, either, even little boys. And they have some air-photos around Lubbock showing what look like mass graves. Oh, Alan . . . so far it seems to be mostly spreading West, but something's happening in St Louis, they're cut off. So many places seem to have just vanished from the news, I had a nightmare that there isn't a woman left alive down there. And nobody's *doing* anything. They talked about spraying with tranquillizers for awhile and then that died out. What could it do? Somebody at the UN has proposed a convention on—you won't believe this—*femicide*. it sounds like a deodorant spray.

Excuse me honey, I seem to be a little hysterical, George Searles came back from Georgia talking about God's Will—Searles the lifelong atheist. Alan, something crazy is happening.

But there are no facts. Nothing. The Surgeon General issued a report on the bodies of the Rahway Rip-Breast Team—I guess I didn't tell you about that. Anyway, they could find no pathology. Milton Baines wrote a letter saying in the present state of the art we can't distinguish the brain of a saint from a psychopathic killer, so how could they expect to find what they don't know how to look for?

Well, enough of these jitters. It'll be all over by the time you get back, just history. Everything's fine here, I fixed the car's muffler again. And Amy's coming home for the vacations, *that'll* get my mind off faraway problems.

Oh, something amusing to end with—Angie told me what Barney's enzyme does to the spruce budworm. It seems it blocks the male from turning around after he connects with the female, so he mates with her head instead. Like clockwork with a cog missing. There're going to be some pretty puzzled female spruce-worms. Now why couldn't Barney tell me that? He really is such a sweet shy old dear. He's given me some stuff to put in, as usual. I didn't read it.

Now don't worry my darling everything's fine.

I love you, I love you so.

Always, all ways your Anne

Two weeks later in Cuyapán when Barney's enclosures slid out of the envelope, Alan didn't read them either. He stuffed them into the pocket of his bush-jacket with a shaking hand and started bundling his notes together on the rickety table, with a scrawled note to Sister Dominique on top. *Anne, Anne my darling.* The hell with the canefly, the hell with everything except that tremor in his fearless girl's firm handwriting. The hell with being five thousand miles away from his woman, his child, while some deadly madness raged. He crammed his meagre belongings into his duffel. If he hurried he could catch the bus through to Bogotá and maybe make the Miami flight.

In Miami he found the planes north jammed. He failed a quick standby; six hours to wait. Time to call Anne. When the call got through some difficulty he was unprepared for the rush of joy and relief that burst along the wires.

'Thank God—I can't believe it—Oh, Alan, my darling, are you really—I can't believe—'

He found he was repeating too, and all mixed up with the canefly data. They were both laughing hysterically when he finally hung up.

Six hours. He settled in a frayed plastic chair opposite *Aerolineas Argentinas*, his mind half back at the clinic, half on the throngs moving by him. Something was oddly different here, he perceived presently. Where was the decorative fauna he usually enjoyed in Miami, the parade of young girls in crotch-tight pastel jeans? The flounces, boots, wild hats and hairdos and startling expanses of newly tanned skin, the brilliant fabrics barely confining the bob of breasts and buttocks? Not here—but wait; looking closely, he glimpsed two young faces hidden under unbecoming parkas, their bodies draped in bulky nondescript skirts. In fact, all down the long vista he could see the same thing: hooded ponchos, heaped-on clothes and baggy pants, dull colours. A new style? No, he thought not. It seemed to him their movements suggested furtiveness, timidity. And they moved in groups. He watched a lone girl struggle to catch up with others ahead of her, apparently strangers. They accepted her wordlessly.

They're frightened, he thought. Afraid of attracting notice. Even that grey-haired matron in a pantsuit resolutely leading a flock of kids was glancing around nervously.

And at the Argentine desk opposite he saw another odd thing: two lines had a big sign over them, *Mujeres*. Women. They were crowded with the shapeless forms and very quiet.

The men seemed to be behaving normally; hurrying, lounging, griping and joking in the lines as they kicked their luggage along. But Alan felt an undercurrent of tension, like an irritant in the air. Outside the line of storefronts behind him a few isolated men seemed to be handing out tracts. An airport attendant spoke to the nearest man; he merely shrugged and moved a few doors down.

To distract himself Alan picked up a *Miami Herald* from the next seat. It was surprisingly thin. The international news occupied him for awhile; he had seen none for weeks. It too had a strange empty quality, even the bad news seemed to have dried up. The African war which had been going on seemed to be over, or went unreported. A trade summit meeting was haggling over grain and steel prices. He found himself at the obituary pages, columns of close-set type dominated by the photo of an unknown defunct ex-senator. Then his eye fell on two announcements at the bottom of the page. One was too flowery for quick comprehension, but the other stated in bold plain type:

THE FORSETTE FUNERAL HOME REGRETFULLY ANNOUNCES
IT WILL NO LONGER ACCEPT FEMALE CADAVERS

Slowly he folded the paper, staring at it numbly. On the back was an item headed *Navigational Hazard Warning*, in the shipping news. Without really taking it in, he read:

> *AP/Nassau:* The excursion liner *Carib Swallow* reached port under tow today after striking an obstruction in the Gulf Stream off Cape Hatteras. The obstruction was identified as part of a commercial trawler's seine floated by female corpses. This confirms reports from Florida and the Gulf of the use of such seines, some of them over a mile in length. Similar reports coming from the Pacific coast and as far away as Japan indicate a growing hazard to coastwise shipping.

Alan flung the thing into the trash receptacle and sat rubbing his forehead and eyes. Thank God he had followed his impulse to come home. He felt totally disoriented, as though he had landed by error on another planet. Four and a half hours more to wait . . . At length he recalled the stuff from Barney he had thrust in his pocket, and pulled it out and smoothed it.

The top item, however, seemed to be from Anne, or at least the Ann Arbor News. Dr Lillian Dash, together with several hundred other members of her organization, had been arrested for demonstrating without a permit in front of the White House. They seemed to have started a fire in an oil drum, which was considered particularly heinous. A number of women's groups had participated, the total struck Alan as more like thousands than hundreds. Extraordinary security precautions were being taken, despite the fact that the President was out of town at the time.

The next item had to be Barney's, if Alan could recognize the old man's acerbic humour.

> *UP/Vatican City 19 June.* Pope John IV today intimated that he does not plan to comment officially on the so-called Pauline Purification cults advocating the elimination of women as a means of justifying man to God. A spokesman emphasized that the Church takes no position on these cults but repudiates any doctrine involving a 'challenge' to or from God to reveal His further plans for man.
>
> Cardinal Fazzoli, spokesman for the European Pauline movement, reaffirmed his view that the Scriptures define woman as merely a temporary companion and instrument of Man. Women, he states, are nowhere defined as human, but merely as a transitional expedient or state. 'The time of transition to full humanity is at hand', he concluded.

The next item appeared to be a thin-paper xerox from a recent issue of Science:

SUMMARY REPORT OF THE AD HOC EMERGENCY COMMITTEE ON FEMICIDE

The recent world-wide though localized outbreaks of femicide appear to represent a recurrence of similar outbreaks by some group or sect which are not uncommon in world history in times of psychic stress. In this case the root cause is undoubtedly the speed of social and technological change, augmented by population pressure, and the spread and scope are aggravated by instantaneous world communications, thus exposing more susceptible persons. It is not viewed as a medical or epidemiological problem; no physical pathology has been found. Rather it is more akin to the various manias which swept Europe in the 17th century, e.g. the Dancing Manias, and like them, should run its course and disappear. The chiliastic cults which have sprung up around the affected areas appear to be unrelated, having in common only the idea that a new means of human reproduction will be revealed as a result of the 'purifying' elimination of women.

We recommend that (1) inflammatory and sensational reporting be suspended; (2) refugee centres be set up and maintained for women escapees from the focal areas; (3) containment of affected areas by military cordon be continued and enforced; and (4) after a cooling-down period and the subsidence of the mania, qualified mental health teams and appropriate professional personnel go in to undertake rehabilitation.

SUMMARY OF THE MINORITY
REPORT OF THE AD HOC COMMITTEE

The nine members signing this report agree that there is no evidence for epidemiological contagion of femicide in the strict sense. *However*, the geographical relation of the focal areas of outbreak strongly suggest that they cannot be dismissed as purely psychosocial phenomena. The initial outbreaks have occurred around the globe near the 30th parallel, the area of principal atmospheric downflow of upper winds coming from the Intertropical Convergence Zone. An agent or condition in the upper equatorial atmosphere would thus be expected to reach ground level along the 30th parallel, with certain seasonal variations. One principal variation is that the downflow moves north over the East Asian continent during the late winter months, and these areas south of it (Arabia, Western India, parts of North Africa) have in fact been free of outbreaks until recently, when the downflow zone has moved south. A similar downflow occurs in the Southern Hemisphere, and outbreaks have been reported along the 30th parallel running through Pretoria and Alice Springs, Australia. (Information from Argentina is currently unavailable.)

This geographical correlation cannot be dismissed, and it is therefore urged that an intensified search for a physical cause be instituted. It is also urgently recommended that the rate of spread from known focal points be correlated with wind conditions. A watch for similar outbreaks along the secondary down-welling zones at 60° north and south should be kept.

(signed for the minority)
Barnhard Braithwaite

Alan grinned reminiscently at his old friend's name, which seemed to restore normalcy and stability to the world. It looked as if Barney was on to something, too, despite the prevalence of horses' asses. He frowned, puzzling it out.

Then his face slowly changed as he thought how it would be, going home to Anne. In a few short hours his arms would be around her, the tall, secretly beautiful body that had come to obsess him. Theirs had been a late-blooming love. They'd married, he supposed now, out of friendship, even out of friends' pressure. Everyone said they were made for each other, he big and chunky and blond, she willowy brunette; both shy, highly controlled, cerebral types. For the first few years the friendship had held, but sex hadn't been all that much. Conventional necessity. Politely reassuring each other, privately—he could say it now—disappointing.

But then, when Amy was a toddler, something had happened. A miraculous inner portal of sensuality had slowly opened to them, a liberation into their own secret unsuspected heaven of fully physical bliss . . . Jesus, but it had been a wrench when the Columbia thing had come up. Only their absolute sureness of each other had made him take it. And now, to be about to have her again, trebly desirable from the spice of separation—feeling-seeing-hearing-smelling-grasping. He shifted in his seat to conceal his body's excitement, half mesmerized by fantasy.

And Amy would be there, too; he grinned at the memory of that prepubescent little body plastered against him. She was going to be a handful, all right. His manhood understood Amy a lot better than her mother did; no cerebral phase for Amy . . . But Anne, his exquisite shy one, with whom he'd found the way into the almost unendurable transports of the flesh . . . First the conventional greeting, he thought; the news, the unspoken, savoured, mounting excitement behind their eyes; the light touches; then the seeking of their own room, the falling clothes, the caresses, gentle at first—the flesh, the *nakedness*—the delicate teasing. the grasp, the first thrust—

—A terrible alarm-bell went off in his head. Exploded from his dream, he stared around, then finally down at his hands. *What was he doing with his open clasp-knife in his fist?*

Stunned, he felt for the last shreds of his fantasy, and realized that the tactile images had not been of caresses, but of a frail neck strangling in his fist, the thrust had been the Plunge of a blade seeking vitals. In his arms, legs, phantasms of striking and trampling, bones cracking. And Amy—

Oh God, Oh God—

Not sex, bloodlust.

That was what he had been dreaming. The sex was there, but it was driving some engine of death.

Numbly he put the knife away, thinking only over and over, it's got me. It's got me. Whatever it is, it's got me. *I can't go home.*

After an unknown time he got up and made his way to the United counter to turn in his ticket. The line was long. As he waited, his mind cleared a little. What could he do, here in Miami? Wouldn't it be better to get back to Ann Arbor and turn himself in to Barney? Barney could help him, if anyone could. Yes, that was best. But first he had to warn Anne.

The connection took even longer this time. When Anne finally answered he found himself blurting unintelligibly, it took awhile to make her understand he wasn't talking about a plane delay.

'I tell you, I've caught it. Listen, Anne, for God's sake. If I should come to the house don't let me come near you. I mean it. I mean it. I'm going to the lab, but I might lose control and try to get to you. Is Barney there?'

'Yes, but darling—'

'Listen. Maybe he can fix me, maybe this'll wear off. But I'm not safe, Anne, Anne, I'd kill you, can you understand? Get a—get a weapon. I'll try not to come to the house. But if I do, don't let me get near you. Or Amy. It's a sickness, it's real. Treat me—treat me like a fucking wild animal. Anne, say you understand, say you'll do it.'

They were both crying when he hung up.

He went shaking back to sit and wait. After a time his head seemed to clear a little more. *Doctor, try to think.* The first thing he thought of was to take the loathesome knife and throw it down a trash-slot. As he did so he realized there was one more piece of Barney's material in his pocket. He uncrumpled it; it seemed to be a clipping from *Nature*.

At the top was Barney's scrawl:

'Only guy making sense. UK infected now, Oslo, Copenhagen out of communication. Damfools still won't listen. Stay put.'

COMMUNICATION FROM PROFESSOR IAN MACINTYRE, GLASGOW UNIV.

A potential difficulty for our species has always been implicit in the close linkage between the behavioural expression of aggression/predation and sexual reproduction in the male. This close linkage involves (*a*) many of the same neuromuscular pathways which are utilized both in predatory and sexual pursuit, grasping, mounting, etc., and (*b*) similar states of adrenergic arousal which are activated in both. The same linkage is seen in the males of many other species; in some, the expression of aggression and copulation alternate or even coexist, an all-too-familiar example being the common house cat. Males of many species bite, claw, bruise, tread or otherwise assault receptive females during the act of intercourse; indeed, in some species the male attack is necessary for female ovulation to occur.

In many if not all species it is the aggressive behaviour which appears first, and then changes to copulatory behaviour when the appropriate signal is presented (e.g. the three-tined stickleback and the European robin). Lacking the inhibiting signal, the male's fighting response continues and the female is attacked or driven off.

It seems therefore appropriate to speculate that the present crisis might be caused by some substance, perhaps at the viral or enzymatic level, which effects a failure of the switching or triggering function in the higher primates. (Note: Zoo gorillas and chimpanzees have recently been observed to attack or destroy their mates; rhesus not.) Such a dysfunction could be expressed by the failure of mating behaviour to modify or supervene over the aggressive/predatory response, i.e. sexual stimulation would produce attack only, the stimulation discharging itself through the destruction of the stimulating object.

In this connection it might be noted that exactly this condition is a commonplace of male functional pathology, in those cases where murder occurs as a response to and apparent completion of, sexual desire.

It should be emphasized that the aggression/copulation linkage discussed here is specific to the male; the female response (e.g. lordotic reflex) being of a different nature.

Alan sat holding the crumpled sheet a long time; the dry, stilted Scottish phrases seemed to help clear his head, despite the sense of brooding tension all around him. Well, if pollution or whatever had produced some substance, it could presumably be countered, filtered, neutralized. Very very carefully, he let himself consider his life with Anne, his sexuality. Yes; much of their loveplay could be viewed as genitalized, sexually gentled savagery. Play-predation... He turned his mind quickly away. Some writer's phrase occurred to him: 'The panic element in all sex.' Who? Fritz Leiber? The violation of social distance, maybe; another threatening element. Whatever, it's our weak link, he thought. Our vulnerability... The dreadful feeling of *rightness* he had experienced when he found himself knife in hand, fantasizing violence, came back to him. As though it was the right, the only way. Was that what Barney's budworms felt when they mated with their females wrong-end-to?

At long length, he became aware of body need and sought a toilet. The place was empty, except for what he took to be a heap of clothes blocking the door of the far stall. Then he saw the red-brown pool in which it lay, and the bluish mounds of bare, thin, buttocks. He backed out, not breathing, and fled into the nearest crowd, knowing he was not the first to have done so.

Of course. Any sexual drive. Boys, men, too.

At the next washroom he watched to see men enter and leave normally before he ventured in.

Afterward he returned to sit, waiting, repeating over and over to himself: *Go to the lab. Don't go home. Go straight to the lab.* Three more hours; he sat numbly at 26° N. 81° W. breathing, breathing...

Dear diary. Big scene tonite, Daddy came home!!! Only he acted so funny, he had the taxi wait and just held on to the doorway, he wouldn't touch me or let us come near him. (I mean funny weird, not funny Ha-ha.) He said, I have something to tell you, this is getting worse not better. I'm going to sleep in the lab but I want you to get out, Anne, Anne, I can't trust myself any more. First thing in the morning you both get on the plane for Martha's and stay there. So I thought he had to be joking, I mean with the dance next week and Aunt Martha lives in Whitehorse where there's nothing nothing nothing. So I was yelling and Mother was yelling and Daddy was groaning. Go now! And then he started crying. Crying!!! So I realized, wow, this is serious, and I started to go over to him but Mother yanked me back and then I saw she had this big KNIFE!!! And she shoved me in back of her and started crying too Oh Alan, Oh Alan, like she was insane. So I said, Daddy, I'll never leave you, it felt like the perfect thing to say. And it was thrilling, he looked at me real sad and deep like I was a grown-up while Mother was treating me like I was a mere infant as usual. But Mother ruined it raving Alan the child is mad, darling go. So he ran out the door yelling Be gone, Take the car, Get out before I come back.

Oh I forgot to say I was wearing what but my gooby green with my curltite still on, wouldn't you know of all the shitty luck, how could I have known such a beautiful scene was ahead we never know life's cruel whimsy. And mother is dragging out suitcases yelling Pack your things hurry! So she's going I guess but I am not repeat not going to spend the fall sitting in Aunt Martha's grain silo and lose the dance and all my summer credits. And Daddy was trying to communicate with us, right? I think their relationship is obsolete. So when she goes upstairs I am splitting. I am going to go over to the lab and see Daddy.

Oh PS Diane tore my yellow jeans she promised me I could use her pink ones Ha-ha that'll be the day.

I ripped that page out of Amy's diary when I heard the squad car coming. I never opened her diary before but when I found she'd gone I looked... Oh, my darling little girl. She went to him, my little girl, my poor little fool child. Maybe if I'd taken time to explain, maybe—

Excuse me, Barney. The stuff is wearing off, the shots they gave me. I didn't feel anything. I mean, I knew somebody's daughter went to see her father and he killed her. And cut his throat. But it didn't mean anything.

Alan's note, they gave me that but then they took it away. Why did they have to do that? His last handwriting, the last words he wrote before his hand picked up the, before he—

I remember it. *'Sudden and light as that, the bonds gave And we learned of finalities besides the grave. The bonds of our humanity have given, we are finished. I love—'*

I'm all right, Barney, really. Who wrote that, Robert Frost? *The bonds gave*... Oh, he said, tell Barney: *The terrible rightness.* What does that mean?

You can't answer that, Barney dear. I'm just writing this to stay sane, I'll put it in your hidey-hole. Thank you, thank you Barney dear. Even as blurry as I was, I knew it was you. All the time you were cutting off my hair and rubbing dirt on my face, I knew it was right because it was you. Barney I never thought of you as those horrible words you said. You were always Dear Barney.

By the time the stuff wore off I had done everything you said, the gas, the groceries. Now I'm here in your cabin. With those clothes you made me put on I guess I do look like a boy, the gas man called me 'Mister'.

I still can't really realize, I have to stop myself from rushing back. But you saved my life, I know that. The first trip in I got a paper, I saw where they bombed the Apostle Islands refuge. And it had about those three women stealing the Air Force plane and bombing Dallas, too. Of course they shot them down, over the Gulf. Isn't it strange how we do nothing? Just get killed by ones and twos. Or more, now they've started on the refuges.... Like hypnotized rabbits. We're a toothless race.

Do you know I never said 'we' meaning women before? 'We' was always me and Alan, and Amy of course. Being killed selectively encourages group identification.... You see how sane-headed I am.

But I still can't really realize.

My first trip in was for salt and kerosene. I went to that little Red Deer store and got my stuff from the old man in the back, as you told me—you see, I remembered! He called me 'Boy', but I think maybe he suspects. He knows I'm staying at your cabin.

Anyway, some men and boys came in the front. They were all so *normal*, laughing and kidding. I just couldn't believe, Barney. In fact I started to go out past them when I heard one of them say 'Heinz saw an angel'. An *angel*. So I stopped and listened. They said it was big and sparkly. Coming to see if man is carrying out God's will, one of them said. And he said, Moosenee is now a liberated zone, and all up by Hudson Bay. I turned and got out the back, fast. The old man had heard them too. He said to me quietly, I'll miss the kids.

Hudson Bay, Barney, that means it's coming from the north too, doesn't it? That must be about 60°.

But I have to go back once again, to get some fishhooks. I can't live on bread. Last week I found a deer some poacher had killed, just the head and legs. I made a stew. It was a doe. Her eyes; I wonder if mine look like that now.

I went to get the fishhooks today. It was bad, I can't ever go back. There were some men in front again, but they were different. Mean and tense. No boys. And there was a new sign out in front, I couldn't see it; maybe it says Liberated Zone too.

The old man gave me the hooks quick and whispered to me, 'Boy, them woods'll be full of hunters next week.' I almost ran out.

About a mile down the road a blue pickup started to chase me. I guess he wasn't from around there, I ran the VW into a logging draw and he roared on by. After a long while I drove out and came on back, but I left the car about a mile from here and hiked in. It's surprising how hard it is to pile enough brush to hide a yellow VW.

Barney, I can't stay here. I'm eating perch raw so nobody will see my smoke, but those hunters will be coming through. I'm going to move my sleeping bag out to the swamp by that big rock, I don't think many people go there.

Since the last lines I moved out. It feels safer. Oh, Barney, how did this *happen*?

Fast, that's how. Six months ago I was Dr Anne Alstein. Now I'm a widow and bereaved mother, dirty and hungry, squatting in a swamp in mortal fear. Funny if I'm the last woman left alive on Earth. I guess the last one around here, anyway. Maybe some holed out in the Himalayas, or sneaking through the wreck of New York City. How can we last?

We can't.

And I can't survive the winter here, Barney. It gets to 40° below. I'd have to have a fire, they'd see the smoke. Even if I worked my way south, the woods end in a couple hundred miles. I'd be potted like a duck. No. No use. Maybe somebody is trying something somewhere, but it won't reach here in time . . . and what do I have to live for?

No. I'll just make a good end, say up on that rock where I can see the stars. After I go back and leave this for you. I'll wait to see the beautiful colour in the trees one last time.

I know what I'll scratch for an epitaph.

HERE LIES THE SECOND MEANEST PRIMATE
ON EARTH.

Good-bye, dearest dearest Barney.

I guess nobody will ever read this, unless I get the nerve and energy to take it to Barney's. Probably I won't. Leave it in a Baggie, I have one here; maybe Barney will come and look. I'm up on the big rock now. The moon is going to rise soon, I'll do it then. Mosquitoes, be patient. You'll have all you want.

The thing I have to write down is that I saw an angel too. This morning. It was big and sparkly, like the man said; like a Christmas tree without the tree. But I knew it was real because the frogs stopped croaking and two bluejays gave alarm calls. That's important; it was *really there.*

I watched it, sitting under my rock. It didn't move much. It sort of bent over and picked up something, leaves or twigs, I couldn't see. Then it did something with them around its middle, like putting them into an invisible sample-pocket.

Let me repeat—it was *there.* Barney, if you're reading this, THERE ARE THINGS HERE. And I think they've done whatever it is to us. Made us kill ourselves off.

Why? Well, it's a nice place, if it wasn't for people. How do you get rid of people? Bombs, death-rays—all very primitive. Leave a big mess. Destroy everything, craters, radioactivity, ruin the place.

This way there's no muss, no fuss. Just like what we did to the screwfly. Pinpoint the weak link, wait a bit while we do it for them. Only a few bones around; make good fertilizer.

Barney dear, goodbye. I saw it. It was there.

But it wasn't an angel.

I think I saw a real-estate agent.

THE WAY OF CROSS AND DRAGON

GEORGE R. R. MARTIN

'Heresy,' he told me. The brackish waters of his pool sloshed gently.

'Another one?' I said wearily. 'There are so many these days.'

My Lord Commander was displeased by that comment. He shifted position heavily, sending ripples up and down the pool. One broke over the side, and a sheet of water slid across the tiles of the receiving chamber. My boots were soaked yet again. I accepted that philosophically. I had worn my worst boots, well aware that wet feet are among the inescapable consequences of paying call on Torgathon Nine-Klariis Tûn, elder of the ka-Thane people, and also Archbishop of Vess, Most Holy Father of the Four Vows, Grand Inquisitor of the Order Militant of the Knights of Jesus Christ, and councillor to His Holiness, Pope Daryn XXI of New Rome.

'Be there as many heresies as stars in the sky, each single one is no less dangerous, Father,' the Archbishop said solemnly. 'As Knights of Christ, it is our ordained task to fight them one and all. And I must add that this new heresy is particularly foul.'

'Yes, my Lord Commander,' I replied. 'I did not intend to make light of it. You have my apologies. The mission to Finnegan was most taxing. I had hoped to ask you for a leave of absence from my duties. I need rest, a time for thought and restoration.'

'Rest?' The Archbishop moved again in his pool; only a slight shift of his immense bulk, but it was enough to send a fresh sheet of water across the floor. His black, pupilless eyes blinked at me. 'No, Father, I am afraid that is out of the question. Your skills and your experience are vital to this new mission.' His bass tones seemed then to soften somewhat. 'I have not had time to go over your reports on Finnegan,' he said. 'How did your work go?'

'Badly,' I told him, 'though I think that ultimately we will prevail. The Church is strong on Finnegan. When our attempts at reconciliation were rebuffed, I put some standards into the right hands, and we were able to shut down the heretics' newspaper and broadcast facilities. Our friends also saw to it that their legal actions came to nothing.'

'That is not *badly,*' the Archbishop said. 'You won a considerable victory for the Lord.'

'There were riots, my Lord Commander,' I said. 'More than a hundred of the heretics were killed, and a dozen of our own people. I fear there will be more violence before the matter is finished. Our priests are attacked if they so much as enter the city where the heresy has taken root. Their leaders risk their lives if they leave that city. I had hoped to avoid such hatreds, such bloodshed.'

'Commendable, but not realistic,' said Archbishop Torgathon. He blinked at me again, and I remembered that among people of his race, that was a sign of impatience. 'The blood of martyrs must sometimes be spilled, and the blood of heretics as well. What matters it if a being surrenders his life, so long as his soul is saved?'

'Indeed,' I agreed. Despite his impatience, Torgathon would lecture me for another hour if given a chance. That prospect dismayed me. The receiving chamber was not designed for human comfort, and I did not wish to remain any longer than necessary. The walls were damp and mouldy, the air hot and humid and thick with the rancid-butter smell characteristic of the ka-Thane. My collar was chafing my neck raw, I was sweating beneath my cassock, my feet were thoroughly soaked, and my stomach was beginning to churn. I pushed ahead to the business at hand. 'You say this new heresy is unusually foul, my Lord Commander?'

'It is,' he said.

'Where has it started?'

'On Arion, a world some three weeks distance from Vess. A human world entirely. I cannot understand why you humans are so easily corrupted. Once a ka-Thane has found the faith, he would scarcely abandon it.'

'That is well known,' I said politely. I did not mention that the number of ka-Thane to find the faith was vanishingly small. They were a slow, ponderous people, and most of their vast millions showed no interest in learning any ways other than their own, nor in following any creed but their own ancient religion. Torgathon Nine-Klariis Tûn was an anomaly. He had been among the first converts almost two centuries ago, when Pope Vidas L had ruled that non-humans might serve as clergy. Given his great lifespan and the iron certainty of his belief, it was no wonder that Torgathon had risen as far as he had, despite the fact that less than a thousand of his race had followed him into the Church. He had at least a century of life remaining to him. No doubt he would someday be Torgathon Cardinal Tûn, should he squelch enough heresies. The times are like that.

'We have little influence on Arion,' the Archbishop was saying. His arms moved as he spoke, four ponderous clubs of mottled green-grey flesh churning the water, and the dirty white cilia around his breathing hole trembled with each word. 'A few priests, a few churches, and some believers, but no power to speak of. The heretics already outnumber us on this world. I rely on your intellect, your shrewdness. Turn this calamity into an opportunity. This heresy is so spurious that you can easily disprove it. Perhaps some of the deluded will turn to the true way.'

'Certainly,' I said. 'And the nature of this heresy? What must I disprove?' It is a sad indication of my own troubled faith to add that I did not really care. I have dealt with too many heresies. Their beliefs and their questionings echo in my head and trouble my dreams at night. How can I be sure of my own faith? The very edict that had admitted Torgathon into the clergy had caused a half-dozen worlds to repudiate the Bishop of New Rome, and those who had followed that path would find a particularly ugly heresy in the massive naked (save for a damp Roman collar) alien who floated before me, who wielded the authority of the Church in four great webbed hands. Christianity is the greatest single human religion, but that means little. The non-Christians outnumber us five-to-one, and there are well over seven hundred Christian sects, some almost as large as the One True Interstellar Catholic Church of Earth and the Thousand Worlds. Even Daryn XXI, powerful as he is, is only one of seven to claim the title of Pope. My own belief was once strong, but I have moved too long among heretics and non-believers. Now, even my prayers do not make the doubts go away. So it was that I felt no horror—only a sudden intellectual interest—when the Archbishop told me the nature of the heresy on Arion.

'They have made a saint,' he said, 'out of Judas Iscariot.'

As a senior in the Knights Inquisitor, I command my own starship, which it pleases me to call the *Truth of Christ*. Before the craft was assigned to me, it was named the *Saint Thomas*, after the apostle, but I did not consider a saint notorious for doubting to be an appropriate patron for a ship enlisted in the fight against heresy.

I have no duties aboard the *Truth*, which is crewed by six brothers and sisters of the Order of Saint Christopher the Far-Travelling, and captained by a young woman I hired away from a merchant trader. I was therefore able to devote the entire three-week voyage from Vess to Arion to a study of the heretical Bible, a copy of which had been given to me by the Archbishop's administrative assistant. It was a thick, heavy, handsome book, bound in dark leather, its pages tipped with gold leaf, with many splendid interior illustrations in full colour with holographic enhancement. Remarkable work, clearly done by someone who loved the all-but-forgotten art of bookmaking. The paintings reproduced inside—the originals, I gathered, were to be found on the walls of the House of Saint Judas on Arion—were masterful, if blasphemous, as much high art as the Tammerwens and RoHallidays that adorn the Great Cathedral of Saint John on New Rome.

Inside, the book bore an imprimatur indicating that it had been approved by Lukyan Judasson, First Scholar of the Order of Saint Judas Iscariot.

It was called *The Way of Cross and Dragon*.

I read it as the *Truth of Christ* slid between the stars, at first taking copious notes to better understand the heresy I must fight, but later simply absorbed by the strange, convoluted, grotesque story it told. The words of text had passion and power and poetry.

Thus it was that I first encountered the striking figure of Saint Judas Iscariot, a complex, ambitious, contradictory, and altogether extraordinary human being.

He was born of a whore in the fabled ancient city-state of Babylon on the same day that the saviour was born in Bethlehem, and he spent his childhood in the alleys and gutters, selling his own body when he had to, pimping when he was older. As a youth he began to experiment with the dark arts, and before the age of twenty he was a skilled necromancer. That was when he became Judas the Dragon-Tamer, the first and only man to bend to his will the most fearsome of God's creatures, the great winged fire-lizards of Old Earth. The book held a marvellous painting of Judas in some great dank cavern, his eyes aflame as he wields a glowing lash to keep a mountainous green-gold dragon at bay. Beneath his arm is a woven basket, its lid slightly ajar, and the tiny scaled heads of three dragon chicks are peering from within. A fourth infant dragon is crawling up his sleeve. That was in the first chapter of his life.

In the second, he was Judas the Conqueror, Judas the Dragon-King, Judas of Babylon, the Great Usurper. Astride the greatest of his dragons, with an iron crown on his head and a sword in his hand, he made Babylon the capital of the greatest empire Old Earth had ever known, a realm that stretched from Spain to India. He reigned from a dragon throne amid the Hanging Gardens he had caused to be constructed, and it was there he sat when he tried Jesus of Nazareth, the troublemaking prophet who had been dragged before him bound and bleeding. Judas was not a patient man, and he made Christ bleed still more before he was through with Him. And when Jesus would not answer his questions, Judas contemptuously had Him cast back out into the streets. But first, he ordered his guards to cut off Christ's legs. 'Healer,' he said, 'heal thyself.'

Then came the Repentance, the vision in the night, and Judas Iscariot gave up his crown, his dark arts, and his riches to follow the man he had crippled. Despised and taunted by those he had tyrannized, Judas became the Legs of the Lord, and for a year carried Jesus on his back to the far corners of the realm he once ruled. When Jesus did finally heal Himself, then Judas walked at his side, and from that time forth he was Jesus' trusted friend and counsellor, the first and foremost of the Twelve. Finally, Jesus gave Judas the gift of tongues, recalled and sanctified the dragons that Judas had sent away, and sent his disciple forth on a solitary ministry across the oceans, 'to spread My Word where I cannot go'.

There came a day when the sun went dark at noon and the ground trembled, and Judas swung his dragon around on ponderous wings and flew back across the raging seas. But when he reached the city of Jerusalem, he found Christ dead on the cross.

In that moment his faith faltered, and for the next three days the Great Wrath of Judas was like a storm across the ancient world. His dragons razed the Temple in Jerusalem, drove the people forth from the city, and struck as well at the great seats of power in Rome and Babylon. And when he found the others of the Twelve and questioned them and learned of how the one named Simon-called-Peter had three times betrayed the Lord, he strangled Peter with his own hands and fed the corpse to his dragons. Then he sent those dragons forth to start fires throughout the world, funeral pyres for Jesus of Nazareth.

And Jesus rose on the third day, and Judas wept, but his tears could not turn Christ's anger, for in his wrath he had betrayed all of Christ's teachings.

So Jesus called back the dragons, and they came, and everywhere the fires went out. And from their bellies he called forth Peter and made him whole again, and gave him dominion over the Church.

Then the dragons died, and so too did all dragons everywhere, for they were the living sigil of the power and wisdom of Judas Iscariot, who had sinned greatly. And He took from Judas the gift of tongues and the power of healing He had given, and even his eyesight, for Judas had acted as a blind man (there was a fine painting of the blinded Judas weeping over the bodies of his dragons). And He told Judas that for long ages he would be remembered only as Betrayer, and people would curse his name, and all that he had been and done would be forgotten.

But then, because Judas had loved Him so, Christ gave him a boon: an extended life, during which he might travel and think on his sins and finally come to forgiveness. Only then might he die.

And that was the beginning of the last chapter in the life of Judas Iscariot. But it was a very long chapter indeed. Once dragon-king, once the friend of Christ, now he was only a blind traveller, outcast and friendless, wandering all the cold roads of the Earth, living still when all the cities and people and things he had known were dead. Peter, the first Pope and ever his enemy, spread far and wide the tale of how Judas had sold Christ for thirty pieces of silver, until Judas dared not even use his true name. For a time he called himself just Wandering Ju', and afterward many other names. He lived more than a thousand years and became a preacher, a healer, and a lover of animals, and was hunted and persecuted when the Church that Peter had founded became bloated and corrupt. But he had a great deal of time, and at last he found wisdom and a sense of peace, and finally, Jesus came to him on a long-postponed deathbed and they were reconciled, and Judas wept once again. Before he died, Christ promised that he would permit a few to remember who and what Judas had been, and that with the passage of centuries the news would spread, until finally Peter's Lie was displaced and forgotten.

Such was the life of St Judas Iscariot, as related in *The Way of Cross and Dragon*. His teachings were there as well and the apocryphal books he had allegedly written.

When I had finished the volume, I lent it to Arla-k-Bau, the captain of the *Truth of Christ*. Arla was a gaunt, pragmatic woman of no particular faith, but I valued her opinion. The others of my crew, the good sisters and brothers of Saint Christopher, would only have echoed the Archbishop's religious horror.

'Interesting,' Arla said when she returned the book to me.

I chuckled. 'Is that all?'

She shrugged. 'It makes a nice story. An easier read than your Bible, Damien, and more dramatic as well.'

'True,' I admitted. 'But it's absurd. An unbelievable tangle of doctrine, apocrypha, mythology, and superstition. Entertaining, yes, certainly. Imaginative, even daring. But ridiculous, don't you think? How can you credit dragons? A legless Christ? Peter being pieced together after being devoured by four monsters?'

Arla's grin was taunting. 'Is that any sillier than water changing into wine, or Christ walking on the waves, or a man living in the belly of a fish?' Arla-k-Bau liked to jab at me. It had been a scandal when I selected a non-believer as my captain, but she was very good at her job, and I liked her around to keep me sharp. She had a good mind, Arla did, and I valued that more than blind obedience. Perhaps that was a sin in me.

'There is a difference,' I said.

'Is there?' she snapped back. Her eyes saw through my masks. 'Ah, Damien, admit it. You rather liked this book.'

I cleared my throat. 'It piqued my interest,' I acknowledged. I had to justify myself. 'You know the kind of matter I deal with ordinarily. Dreary little doctrinal deviations; obscure quibblings on theology somehow blown all out of proportion; bald-faced political manœuverings designed to set some ambitious planetary bishop up as a new pope, or wrest some concession or other from New Rome or Vess. The war is endless, but the battles are dull and dirty. They exhaust me spiritually, emotionally, physically. Afterwards I feel drained and guilty.' I tapped the book's leather cover. 'This is different. The heresy must be crushed, of course, but I admit that I am anxious to meet this Lukyan Judasson.'

'The artwork is lovely as well,' Arla said, flipping through the pages of *The Way of Cross and Dragon* and stopping to study one especially striking plate—Judas weeping over his dragons, I think. I smiled to see that it had affected her as much as me. Then I frowned.

That was the first inkling I had of the difficulties ahead.

So it was that the *Truth of Christ* came to the porcelain city Ammadon on the world of Arion, where the Order of Saint Judas Iscariot kept its House.

Arion was a pleasant, gentle world, inhabited for these past three centuries. Its population was under nine million; Ammadon, the only real city, was home to two of those millions. The technological level was medium high, but chiefly imported. Arion had little industry and was not an innovative world, except perhaps artistically. The arts were quite important here, flourishing and vital. Religious freedom was a basic tenet of the society, but Arion was not a religious world either, and the majority of the populace lived devoutly secular lives. The most popular religion was Aestheticism, which hardly counts as a religion at all. There were also Taoists, Erikaners, Old True Christers, and Children of the Dreamer, plus adherents of a dozen lesser sects.

And finally there were nine churches of the One True Interstellar Catholic faith. There had been twelve. The other three were now houses of Arion's fastest-growing faith, the Order of Saint Judas Iscariot, which also had a dozen newly built churches of its own.

The Bishop of Arion was a dark, severe man with close-cropped black hair who was not at all happy to see me. 'Damien Har Veris!' he exclaimed with some wonderment when I called on him at his residence. 'We have heard of you, of course, but I never thought to meet or host you. Our numbers here are small.'

'And growing smaller,' I said, 'a matter of some concern to my Lord Commander, Archbishop Torgathon. Apparently you are less troubled, Excellency, since you did not see fit to report the activities of this sect of Judas worshippers.'

He looked briefly angry at the rebuke, but quickly swallowed his temper. Even a bishop can fear a Knight Inquisitor. 'We are concerned, of course,' he said. 'We do all we can to combat the heresy. If you have advice that will help us, I will be glad to listen.'

'I am an Inquisitor of the Order Militant of the Knights of Jesus Christ,' I said bluntly. 'I do not give advice, Excellency. I take action. To that end I was sent to Arion, and that is what I shall do.

Now, tell me what you know about this heresy, and this First Scholar, this Lukyan Judasson.'

'Of course, Father Damien,' the Bishop began. He signalled for a servant to bring us a tray of wine and cheese, and began to summarize the short but explosive history of the Judas cult. I listened, polishing my nails on the crimson lapel of my jacket until the black paint gleamed brilliantly, interrupting from time to time with a question. Before he had half finished, I was determined to visit Lukyan personally. It seemed the best course of action.

And I had wanted to do so all along.

Appearances were important on Arion, I gathered, and I deemed it necessary to impress Lukyan with myself and my station. I wore my best boots—sleek, dark hand-made boots of Roman leather that had never seen the inside of Torgathon's receiving chamber—and a severe black suit with deep burgundy lapels and stiff collar. Around my neck was a splendid crucifix of pure gold; my collarpin was a matching golden sword, the sigil of the Knights Inquisitor. Brother Denis carefully painted my nails, all black as ebon, and darkened my eyes as well, and used a fine white powder on my face. When I glanced in the mirror, I frightened even myself. I smiled, but only briefly. It ruined the effect.

I walked to the House of Saint Judas Iscariot. The streets of Ammadon were wide and spacious and golden, lined by scarlet trees called whisperwinds whose long, drooping tendrils did indeed seem to whisper secrets to the gentle breeze. Sister Judith came with me. She is a small woman, slight of build even in the cowled coveralls of the Order of Saint Christopher. Her face is meek and kind, her eyes wide and youthful and innocent. I find her useful. Four times now she has killed those who attempted to assault me.

The House itself was newly built. Rambling and stately, it rose from amid gardens of small bright flowers and seas of golden grass; the gardens were surrounded by a high wall. Murals covered both the outer wall around the property and the exterior of the building itself. I recognized a few of them from *The Way of Cross and Dragon*, and stopped briefly to admire them before walking through the main gate. No one tried to stop us. There were no guards, not even a receptionist. Within the walls, men and women strolled languidly through the flowers, or sat on benches beneath silverwoods and whisperwinds.

Sister Judith and I paused, then made our way directly to the House itself.

We had just started up the steps when a man appeared from within, and stood waiting in the doorway. He was blond and fat, with a great wiry beard that framed a slow smile, and he wore a flimsy robe that fell to his sandalled feet. On the robe were dragons, dragons bearing the silhouette of a man holding a cross.

When I reached the top of the steps, he bowed to me. 'Father Damien Har Veris of the Knights Inquisitor,' he said. His smile widened. 'I greet you in the name of Jesus, and in the name of Saint Judas. I am Lukyan.'

I made a note to myself to find out which of the Bishop's staff was feeding information to the Judas cult, but my composure did not break. I have been a Knight Inquisitor for a long, long time. 'Father Lukyan Mo,' I said, taking his hand. 'I have questions to ask of you.' I did not smile.

He did. 'I thought you might,' he said.

Lukyan's office was large but spartan. Heretics often have a simplicity that the officers of the true Church seem to have lost. He did have one indulgence, however. Dominating the wall behind his desk console was the painting I had already fallen in love with: the blinded Judas weeping over his dragons.

Lukyan sat down heavily and motioned me to a second chair. We had left Sister Judith outside in the waiting chamber. 'I prefer to stand, Father Lukyan,' I said, knowing it gave me an advantage.

'Just Lukyan,' he said. 'Or Luke, if you prefer. We have little use for hierarchy here.'

'You are Father Lukyan Mo, born here on Arion, educated in the seminary on Cathaday, a former priest of the One True Interstellar Catholic Church of Earth and the Thousand Worlds,' I said. 'I will address you as befits your station, Father. I expect you to reciprocate. Is that understood?'

'Oh, yes,' he said amiably.

'I am empowered to strip you of your right to perform the sacraments, to order you shunned and excommunicated for this heresy you have formulated. On certain worlds I could even order your death.'

'But not on Arion,' Lukyan said quickly. 'We're very tolerant here. Besides, we outnumber you.' He smiled. 'As for the rest, well,

I don't perform those sacraments much anyway, you know. Not for years. I'm First Scholar now. A teacher, a thinker. I show others the way, help them find the faith. Excommunicate me if it will make you happy, Father Damien. Happiness is what all of us seek.'

'You have given up the faith then, Father Lukyan,' I said. I deposited my copy of *The Way of Cross and Dragon* on his desk. 'But I see you have found a new one.' Now I did smile, but it was all ice, all menace, all mockery. 'A more ridiculous creed I have yet to encounter. I suppose you will tell me that you have spoken to God, that he trusted you with this new revelation, so that you might clear the good name, such that it is, of Holy Judas?'

Now Lukyan's smile was very broad indeed. He picked up the book and beamed at me. 'Oh, no,' he said. 'No, I made it all up.'

That stopped me. 'What?'

'I made it all up,' he repeated. He hefted the book fondly. 'I drew on many sources, of course, especially the Bible, but I do think of *Cross and Dragon* as mostly my own work. It's rather good, don't you agree? Of course, I could hardly put my name on it, proud as I am of it, but I did include my imprimatur. Did you notice that? It was the closest I dared come to a byline.'

I was speechless only for a moment. Then I grimaced. 'You startle me,' I admitted. 'I expected to find an inventive madman, some poor self-deluded fool, firm in his belief that he had spoken to God. I've dealt with such fanatics before. Instead I find a cheerful cynic who has invented a religion for his own profit. I think I prefer the fanatics. You are beneath contempt, Father Lukyan. You will burn in hell for eternity.'

'I doubt it,' Lukyan said, 'but you do mistake me, Father Damien. I am no cynic, nor do I profit from my dear Saint Judas. Truthfully, I lived more comfortably as a priest of your own Church. I do this because it is my vocation.'

I sat down. 'You confuse me,' I said, 'Explain.'

'Now I am going to tell you the truth,' he said. He said it in an odd way, almost as a cant. 'I am a Liar,' he added.

'You want to confuse me with a child's paradoxes,' I snapped.

'No, no,' he smiled. 'A *Liar*. With a capital. It is an organization, Father Damien. A religion, you might call it. A great and powerful faith. And I am the smallest part of it.'

'I know of no such church,' I said.

'Oh, no, you wouldn't. It's secret. It has to be. You can understand that, can't you? People don't like being lied to.'

'I do not like being lied to,' I said.

Lukyan looked wounded. 'I told you this would be the truth, didn't I? When a Liar says that, you can believe him. How else could we trust each other?'

'There are many of you?' I asked. I was starting to think that Lukyan was a madman after all, as fanatical as any heretic, but in a more complex way. Here was a heresy within a heresy, but I recognized my duty: to find the truth of things, and set them right.

'Many of us,' Lukyan said, smiling. 'You would be surprised, Father Damien, really you would. But there are some things I dare not tell you.'

'Tell me what you dare, then.'

'Happily,' said Lukyan Judasson. 'We Liars, like those of all other religions, have several truths we take on faith. Faith is always required. There are some things that cannot be proven. We believe that life is worth living. That is an article of faith. The purpose of life is to live, to resist death, perhaps to defy entropy.'

'Go on,' I said, interested despite myself.

'We also believe that happiness is a good, something to be sought after.'

'The Church does not oppose happiness,' I said drily.

'I wonder,' Lukyan said. 'But let us not quibble. Whatever the Church's position on happiness, it does preach belief in an afterlife, in a supreme being and a complex moral code.'

'True.'

'The Liars believe in no afterlife, no God. We see the universe as it *is*, Father Damien, and these naked truths are cruel ones. We who believe in life, and treasure it, will die. Afterwards there will be nothing, eternal emptiness, blackness, non-existence. In our living there has been no purpose, no poetry, no meaning. Nor do our deaths possess these qualities. When we are gone, the universe will not long remember us, and shortly it will be as if we had never lived at all. Our worlds and our universe will not long outlive us. Ultimately, entropy will consume all, and our puny efforts cannot stay that awful end. It will be gone. It has never been. It has never mattered. The universe itself is doomed, transient, uncaring.'

I slid back in my chair, and a shiver went through me as I

listened to poor Lukyan's dark words. I found myself fingering my crucifix. 'A bleak philosophy,' I said, 'as well as a false one. I have had that fearful vision myself. I think all of us do, at some point. But it is not so, Father. My faith sustains me against such nihilism. It is a shield against despair.'

'Oh, I know that, my friend, my Knight Inquisitor,' Lukyan said. 'I'm glad to see you understand so well. You are almost one of us already.'

I frowned.

'You've touched the heart of it,' Lukyan continued. 'The truths, the great truths—and most of the lesser ones as well—they are unbearable for most men. We find our shield in faith. Your faith, my faith, any faith. It doesn't matter, so long as we *believe*, really and truly believe, in whatever lie we cling to.' He fingered the ragged edges of his great blond beard. 'Our psychs have always told us that believers are the happy ones, you know. They may believe in Christ or Buddha or Erika Stormjones, in reincarnation or immortality or nature, in the power of love or the platform of a political faction, but it all comes to the same thing. They believe. They are happy. It is the ones who have seen truth who despair, and kill themselves. The truths are so vast, the faiths so little, so poorly made, so riddled with error and contradiction that we see around them and through them, and then we feel the weight of darkness upon us, and can no longer be happy.'

I am not a slow man. I knew, by then, where Lukyan Judasson was going. 'Your Liars invent faiths.'

He smiled. 'Of all sorts. Not only religious. Think of it. We know truth for the cruel instrument it is. Beauty is infinitely preferable to truth. We invent beauty. Faiths, political movements, high ideals, belief in love and fellowship. All of them are lies. We tell those lies, among others, endless others. We improve on history and myth and religion, make each more beautiful, better, easier to believe in. Our lies are not perfect, of course. The truths are too big. But perhaps someday we will find one great lie that all humanity can use. Until then, a thousand small lies will do.'

'I think I do not care for your Liars very much,' I said with a cold, even fervour. 'My whole life has been a quest for truth.'

Lukyan was indulgent. 'Father Damien Har Veris, Knight Inquisitor, I know you better than that. You are a Liar yourself. You do good work. You ship from world to world, and on each you destroy the foolish, the rebels, the questioners who would bring down the edifice of the vast lie that you serve.'

'If my lie is so admirable,' I said, 'then why have you abandoned it?'

'A religion must fit its culture and society, work with them, not against them. If there is conflict, contradiction, then the lie breaks down, and the faith falters. Your Church is good for many worlds, Father, but not for Arion. Life is too kind here, and your faith is stern. Here we love beauty, and your faith offers too little. So we have improved it. We studied this world for a long time. We know its psychological profile. Saint Judas will thrive here. He offers drama, and colour, and much beauty—the aesthetics are admirable. His is a tragedy with a happy ending, and Arion dotes on such stories. And the dragons are a nice touch. I think your own Church ought to find a way to work in dragons. They are marvellous creatures.'

'Mythical,' I said.

'Hardly,' he replied. 'Look it up.' He grinned at me. 'You see, really, it all comes back to faith. Can you really know what happened three thousand years ago? You have one Judas, I have another. Both of us have books. Is yours true? Can you really believe that? I have been admitted only to the first circle of the order of Liars, so I do not know all our secrets, but I know that we are very old. It would not surprise me to learn that the gospels were written by men very much like me. Perhaps there never was a Judas at all. Or a Jesus.'

'I have faith that that is not so,' I said.

'There are a hundred people in this building who have a deep and very real faith in Saint Judas, and the way of cross and dragon,' Lukyan said. 'Faith is a very good thing. Do you know that the suicide rate on Arion has decreased by almost a third since the Order of Saint Judas was founded?'

I remember rising slowly from my chair. 'You are fanatical as any heretic I have ever met, Lukyan Judasson,' I told him. 'I pity you the loss of your faith.'

Lukyan rose with me. 'Pity yourself, Damien Har Veris,' he said. 'I have found a new faith and a new cause, and I am a happy man. You, my dear friend, are tortured and miserable.'

'That is a lie!' I am afraid I screamed.

'Come with me,' Lukyan said. He touched a panel on his wall, and the great painting of Judas weeping over his dragons slid up out of sight. There was a stairway leading down into the ground. 'Follow me,' he said.

In the cellar was a great glass vat full of pale green fluid, and in it a thing was floating, a thing very like an ancient embryo, aged and infantile at the same time, naked, with a huge head and a tiny atrophied body. Tubes ran from its arms and legs and genitals, connecting it to the machinery that kept it alive.

When Lukyan turned on the lights, it opened its eyes. They were large and dark and they looked into my soul.

'This is my colleague,' Lukyan said, patting the side of the vat, 'Jon Azure Cross, a Liar of the fourth circle.'

'And a telepath,' I said with a sick certainty. I had led pogroms against other telepaths, children mostly, on other worlds. The Church teaches that the psionic powers are one of Satan's traps. They are not mentioned in the Bible. I have never felt good about those killings.

'The moment you entered the compound, Jon read you and notified me,' Lukyan said. 'Only a few of us know that he is here. He helps us lie most efficiently. He knows when faith is true, and when it is feigned. I have an implant in my skull. Jon can talk to me at all times. It was he who initially recruited me into the Liars. He knew my faith was hollow. He felt the depth of my despair.'

Then the thing in the tank spoke, its metallic voice coming from a speaker-grill in the base of the machine that nurtured it. *'And I feel yours, Damien Har Veris, empty priest. Inquisitor, you have asked too many questions. You are sick at heart, and tired, and you do not believe. Join us, Damien. You have been a Liar for a long, long time!'*

For a moment I hesitated, looking deep into myself, wondering what it was I *did* believe. I searched for my faith—the fire that had once sustained me, the certainty in the teachings of the Church, the presence of Christ within me. I found none of it, none. I was empty inside, burned out, full of questions and pain. But as I was about to answer Jon Azure Cross and the smiling Lukyan Judasson, I found something else, something I *did* believe in, had always believed in.

Truth.

I believed in truth, even when it hurt.

'He is lost to us,' said the telepath with the mocking name of Cross.

Lukyan's smile faded. 'Oh, really? I had hoped you would be one of us, Damien. You seemed ready.'

I was suddenly afraid, and I considered sprinting up the stairs to Sister Judith. Lukyan had told me so very much, and now I had rejected them.

The telepath felt my fear. *'You cannot hurt us, Damien,'* it said. *'Go in peace. Lukyan has told you nothing.'*

Lukyan was frowning. 'I told him a good deal, Jon,' he said.

'Yes. But can he trust the words of such a Liar as you?' The small misshapen mouth of the thing in the vat twitched in a smile, and its great eyes closed, and Lukyan Judasson sighed and led me up at the stairs.

It was not until some years later that I realized it was Jon Azure Cross who was lying, and the victim of his lie was Lukyan. I *could* hurt them. I did.

It was almost simple. The Bishop had friends in government and media. With some money in the right places, I made some friends of my own. Then I exposed Cross in his cellar, charging that he had used his psionic powers to tamper with the minds of Lukyan's followers. My friends were receptive to the charges. The guardians conducted a raid, took the telepath Cross into custody, and later tried him.

He was innocent, of course. My charge was nonsense; human telepaths can read minds in close proximity, but seldom anything more. But they are rare, and much feared, and Cross was hideous enough so that it was easy to make him a victim of superstition. In the end, he was acquitted, but he left the city Ammadon and perhaps Arion itself, bound for regions unknown.

But it had never been my intention to convict him. The charge was enough. The cracks began to show in the lie that he and Lukyan had built together. Faith is hard to come by, and easy to lose. The merest doubt can begin to erode even the strongest foundation of belief.

The Bishop and I laboured together to sow further doubts. It was not as easy as I might have thought. The Liars had done their work well. Ammadon, like most civilized cities, had a great pool of knowledge, a computer system that linked the schools and universities and libraries together, and made their combined wisdom available to any who needed it.

But when I checked, I soon discovered that the histories of Rome and Babylon had been subtly reshaped, and there were three listings for Judas Iscariot—one for the betrayer, one for the saint, and one for the conqueror-king of Babylon. His name was also mentioned in connection with the Hanging Gardens, and there is an entry for a so-called 'Codex Judas'.

And according to the Ammadon library, dragons became extinct on Old Earth around the time of Christ.

We finally purged all those lies, wiped them from the memories of the computers, though we had to cite authorities on a half-dozen non-Christian worlds before the librarians and academics would credit that the differences were anything more than a question of religious preference. By then the Order of Saint Judas had withered in the glare of exposure. Lukyan Judasson had grown gaunt and angry, and at least half of his churches had closed.

The heresy never died completely, of course. There are always those who believe no matter what. And so to this day *The Way of Cross and Dragon* is read on Arion, in the porcelain city Ammadon, amid murmuring whisperwinds.

Arla-k-Bau and the *Truth of Christ* carried me back to Vess a year after my departure, and Archbishop Torgathon finally gave me the rest I had asked for, before sending me out to fight still other heresies. So I had my victory, and the Church continued on much as before, and the Order of Saint Judas Iscariot was crushed and diminished. The telepath Jon Azure Cross had been wrong, I thought then. He had sadly underestimated the power of a Knight Inquisitor.

Later, though, I remembered his words.

You cannot hurt us, Damien.

Us?

The Order of Saint Judas? Or the Liars?

He lied, I think, deliberately, knowing I would go forth and destroy the way of cross and dragon, knowing too that I could not touch the Liars, would not even dare mention them. How could I? Who would believe it? A grand star-spanning conspiracy as old as history? It reeks of paranoia, and I had no proof at all.

The telepath lied for Lukyan's benefit, so that he would let me go. I am certain of that now. Cross risked much to snare me. Failing, he was willing to sacrifice Lukyan Judasson and his lie, pawns in some greater game.

So I left, and carried within me the knowledge that I was empty of faith but for a blind faith in truth, a truth I could no longer find in my Church.

I grew certain of that in my year of rest, which I spent reading and studying on Vess and Cathaday and Celia's World. Finally I returned to the Archbishop's receiving room, and stood again before Torgathon Nine-Klariis Tûn in my very worst pair of boots. 'My Lord Commander,' I said to him, 'I can accept no further assignments. I ask that I be retired from active service.'

'For what cause?' Torgathon rumbled, splashing feebly.

'I have lost the faith,' I said to him, simply.

He regarded me for a long time, his pupilless eyes blinking. At last he said, 'Your faith is a matter between you and your confessor. I care only about your results. You have done good work, Damien. You may not retire, and we will not allow you to resign.'

The truth will set us free.

But freedom is cold and empty and frightening, and lies can often be warm and beautiful.

Last year the Church finally granted me a new and better ship. I named this one *Dragon*.

SWARM

BRUCE STERLING

'I will miss your conversation during the rest of the voyage,' the alien said.

Captain-Doctor Simon Afriel folded his jewelled hands over his gold-embroidered waistcoat. 'I regret it also, ensign,' he said in the alien's own hissing language. 'Our talks together have been very useful to me. I would have paid to learn so much, but you gave it freely.'

'But that was only information,' the alien said. He shrouded his bead-bright eyes behind thick nictitating membranes. 'We Investors deal in energy, and precious metals. To prize and pursue mere knowledge is an immature racial trait.' The alien lifted the long ribbed frill behind his pinhole-sized ears.

'No doubt you are right,' Afriel said, despising him. 'We humans are as children to other races, however; so a certain immaturity seems natural to us.' Afriel pulled off his sunglasses to rub the bridge of his nose. The starship cabin was drenched in searing blue light, heavily ultraviolet. It was the light the Investors preferred, and they were not about to change it for one human passenger.

'You have not done badly,' the alien said magnanimously. 'You are the kind of race we like to do business with: young, eager, plastic, ready for a wide variety of goods and experiences. We would have contacted you much earlier, but your technology was still too feeble to afford us a profit.'

'Things are different now,' Afriel said. 'We'll make you rich.'

'Indeed,' the Investor said. The frill behind his scaly head flickered rapidly, a sign of amusement. 'Within two hundred years you will be wealthy enough to buy from us the secret of our starflight. Or perhaps your Mechanist faction will discover the secret through research.'

Afriel was annoyed. As a member of the Reshaped faction, he did not appreciate the reference to the rival Mechanists. 'Don't put too much stock in mere technical expertise,' he said. 'Consider the aptitude for languages we Shapers have. It makes our faction a much better trading partner. To a Mechanist, all Investors look alike.'

The alien hesitated. Afriel smiled. He had appealed to the alien's personal ambition with his last statement, and the hint had been taken. That was where the Mechanists always erred. They tried to treat all Investors consistently, using the same programmed routines each time. They lacked imagination.

Something would have to be done about the Mechanists, Afriel thought. Something more permanent than the small but deadly confrontations between isolated ships in the Asteroid Belt and the ice-rich Rings of Saturn. Both factions manœuvered constantly, looking for a decisive stroke, bribing away each other's best talent, practising ambush, assassination, and industrial espionage.

Captain-Doctor Simon Afriel was a past master of these pursuits. That was why the Reshaped faction had paid the millions of kilowatts necessary to buy his passage. Afriel held doctorates in biochemistry and alien linguistics, and a master's degree in magnetic weapons engineering. He was thirty-eight years old and had been Reshaped according to the state of the art at the time of his conception. His hormonal balance had been altered slightly to compensate for long periods spent in free-fall. He had no appendix. The structure of his heart had been redesigned for greater efficiency, and his large intestine had been altered to produce the vitamins normally made by intestinal bacteria. Genetic engineering and rigorous training in childhood had given him an intelligence quotient of one hundred and eighty. He was not the brightest of the agents of the Ring Council, but he was one of the most mentally stable and the best trusted.

'It seems a shame,' the alien said, 'that a human of your accomplishments should have to rot for two years in this miserable, profitless outpost.'

'The years won't be wasted,' Afriel said.

'But why have you chosen to study the Swarm? They can teach you nothing, since they cannot speak. They have no wish to trade, having no tools or technology. They are the only spacefaring race that is essentially without intelligence.'

'That alone should make them worthy of study.'

'Do you seek to imitate them, then? You would make monsters

of yourselves.' Again the ensign hesitated. 'Perhaps you could do it. It would be bad for business, however.'

There came a fluting burst of alien music over the ship's speakers, then a screeching fragment of Investor language. Most of it was too high-pitched for Afriel's ears to follow.

The alien stood, his jewelled skirt brushing the tips of his clawed birdlike feet. 'The Swarm's symbiote has arrived,' he said.

'Thank you,' Afriel said. When the ensign opened the cabin door, Afriel could smell the Swarm's representative; the creature's warm yeasty scent had spread rapidly though the starship's recycled air.

Afriel quickly checked his appearance in a pocket mirror. He touched powder to his face and straightened the round velvet hat on his shoulder-length reddish-blond hair. His earlobes glittered with red impact-rubies, thick as his thumbs' ends, mined from the Asteroid Belt. His knee-length coat and waistcoat were of gold brocade; the shirt beneath was of dazzling fineness, woven with red-gold thread. He had dressed to impress the Investors, who expected and appreciated a prosperous look from their customers. How could he impress this new alien? Smell, perhaps. He freshened his perfume.

Beside the starship's secondary airlock, the Swarm's symbiote was chittering rapidly at the ship's commander. The commander was an old and sleepy Investor, twice the size of most of her crewmen. Her massive head was encrusted in a jewelled helmet. From within the helmet her clouded eyes glittered like cameras.

The symbiote lifted on its six posterior legs and gestured feebly with its four clawed forelimbs. The ship's artificial gravity, a third again as strong as Earth's, seemed to bother it. Its rudimentary eyes, dangling on stalks, were shut tight against the glare. It must be used to darkness, Afriel thought.

The commander answered the creature in its own language. Afriel grimaced, for he had hoped that the creature spoke Investor. Now he would have to learn another language, a language designed for a being without a tongue.

After another brief interchange the commander turned to Afriel. 'The symbiote is not pleased with your arrival,' she told Afriel in the Investor language. 'There has apparently been some disturbance here involving humans, in the recent past. However, I have prevailed upon it to admit you to the Nest. The episode has been recorded. Payment for my diplomatic services will be arranged with your faction when I return to your native star system.'

'I thank Your Authority,' Afriel said. 'Please convey to the symbiote my best personal wishes, and the harmlessness and humility of my intentions . . .' He broke off short as the symbiote lunged toward him, biting him savagely in the calf of his left leg. Afriel jerked free and leapt backward in the heavy artificial gravity, going into a defensive position. The symbiote had ripped away a long shred of his pants leg; it now crouched quietly, eating it.

'It will convey your scent and composition to its nestmates,' said the commander. 'This is necessary. Otherwise you would be classed as an invader, and the Swarm's warrior caste would kill you at once.'

Afriel relaxed quickly and pressed his hand against the puncture wound to stop the bleeding. He hoped that none of the Investors had noticed his reflexive action. It would not mesh well with his story of being a harmless researcher.

'We will reopen the airlock soon,' the commander said phlegmatically, leaning back on her thick reptilian tail. The symbiote continued to munch the shred of cloth. Afriel studied the creature's neckless segmented head. It had a mouth and nostrils; it had bulbous atrophied eyes on stalks; there were hinged slats that might be radio receivers, and two parallel ridges of clumped wriggling antennae, sprouting among three chitinous plates. Their function was unknown to him.

The airlock door opened. A rush of dense, smoky aroma entered the departure cabin. It seemed to bother the half-dozen Investors, who left rapidly. 'We will return in six hundred and twelve of your days, as by our agreement,' the commander said.

'I thank Your Authority,' Afriel said.

'Good luck,' the commander said in English. Afriel smiled.

The symbiote, with a sinuous wriggle of its segmented body, crept into the airlock. Afriel followed it. The airlock door shut behind them. The creature said nothing to him but continued munching loudly. The second door opened, and the symbiote sprang through it, into a wide, round stone tunnel. It disappeared at once into the gloom.

Afriel put his sunglasses into a pocket of his jacket and pulled out a pair of infra-red goggles. He strapped them to his head and stepped out of the airlock. The artificial gravity vanished, replaced by the almost imperceptible gravity of the Swarm's asteroid nest. Afriel smiled, comfortable for the first time in weeks. Most of his adult life had been spent in free-fall, in the Shapers' colonies in the Rings of Saturn.

Squatting in a dark cavity in the side of the tunnel was a disc-headed furred animal the size of an elephant. It was clearly visible in the infra-red of its own body heat. Afriel could hear it breathing. It waited patiently until Afriel had launched himself past it, deeper into the tunnel. Then it took its place in the end of the tunnel, puffing itself up with air until its swollen head securely plugged the exit into space. Its multiple legs sank firmly into sockets in the walls.

The Investors' ship had left. Afriel remained here, inside one of the millions of planetoids that circled the giant star Betelgeuse in a girdling ring with almost five times the mass of Jupiter. As a source of potential wealth it dwarfed the entire solar system, and it belonged, more or less, to the Swarm. At least, no other race had challenged them for it within the memory of the Investors.

Afriel peered up the corridor. It seemed deserted, and without other bodies to cast infra-red heat, he could not see very far. Kicking against the wall, he floated hesitantly down the corridor.

He heard a human voice. 'Dr Afriel!'

'Dr Mirny!' he called out. 'This way!'

He first saw a pair of young symbiotes scuttling towards him, the tips of their clawed feet barely touching the walls. Behind them came a woman wearing goggles like his own. She was young, and attractive in the trim, anonymous way of the genetically reshaped.

She screeched something at the symbiotes in their own language, and they halted, waiting. She coasted forward, and Afriel caught her arm, expertly stopping their momentum.

'You didn't bring any luggage?' she said anxiously.

He shook his head. 'We got your warning before I was sent out. I have only the clothes I'm wearing and a few items in my pockets.'

She looked at him critically. 'Is that what people are wearing in the Rings these days? Things have changed more than I thought.'

Afriel glanced at his brocaded coat and laughed. 'It's a matter of policy. The Investors are always readier to talk to a human who looks ready to do business on a large scale. All the Shapers' representatives dress like this these days. We've stolen a jump on the Mechanists; they still dress in those coveralls.'

He hesitated, not wanting to offend her. Galina Mirny's intelligence was rated at almost two hundred. Men and women that bright were sometimes flighty and unstable, likely to retreat into private fantasy worlds or become enmeshed in strange and impenetrable webs of plotting and rationalization. High intelligence was the strategy the Shapers had chosen in the struggle for cultural dominance, and they were obliged to stick to it, despite its occasional disadvantages. They had tried breeding the Superbright—those with quotients over two hundred—but so many had defected from the Shapers' colonies that the faction had stopped producing them.

'You wonder about my own clothing,' Mirny said.

'It certainly has the appeal of novelty,' Afriel said with a smile.

'It was woven from the fibres of a pupa's cocoon,' she said. 'My original wardrobe was eaten by a scavenger symbiote during the troubles last year. I usually go nude, but I didn't want to offend you by too great a show of intimacy.'

Afriel shrugged. 'I often go nude myself, I never had much use for clothes except for pockets. I have a few tools on my person, but most are of little importance. We're Shapers, our tools are here.' He tapped his head. 'If you can show me a safe place to put my clothes . . .'

She shook her head. It was impossible to see her eyes for the goggles, which made her expression hard to read. 'You've made your first mistake, Doctor. There are no places of our own here. It was the same mistake the Mechanist agents made, the same one that almost killed me as well. There is no concept of privacy or property here. This is the Nest. If you seize any part of it for yourself—to store equipment, to sleep in, whatever—then you become an intruder, an enemy. The two Mechanists—a man and a woman—tried to secure an empty chamber for their computer lab. Warriors broke down their door and devoured them. Scavengers ate their equipment, glass, metal, and all.'

Afriel smiled coldly. 'It must have cost them a fortune to ship all that material here.'

Mirny shrugged. 'They're wealthier than we are. Their machines, their mining. They meant to kill me, I think. Surreptitiously, so the warriors wouldn't be upset by a show of violence. They had a computer that was learning the language of the springtails faster than I could.'

'But you survived,' Afriel pointed out. 'And your tapes and reports—especially the early ones, when you still had most of your equipment—were of tremendous interest. The Council is behind you all the way. You've become quite a celebrity in the Rings, during your absence.'

'Yes, I expected as much,' she said.

Afriel was nonplussed. 'If I found any deficiency in them,' he said carefully, 'it was in my own field, alien linguistics.' He waved vaguely at the two symbiotes who accompanied her. 'I assume you've made great progress in communicating with the symbiotes, since they seem to do all the talking for the Nest.'

She looked at him with an unreadable expression and shrugged. 'There are at least fifteen different kinds of symbiotes here. Those that accompany me are called the springtails, and they speak only for themselves. They are savages, Doctor, who received attention from the Investors only because they can still talk. They were a spacefaring race once, but they've forgotten it. They discovered the Nest and they were absorbed, they became parasites.' She tapped one of them on the head. 'I tamed these two because I learned to steal and beg food better than they can. They stay with me now and protect me from the larger ones. They are jealous, you know. They have only been with the Nest for perhaps ten thousand years and are still uncertain of their position. They still think, and wonder sometimes. After ten thousand years there is still a little of that left to them.'

'Savages,' Afriel said. 'I can well believe that. One of them bit me while I was still aboard the starship. He left a lot to be desired as an ambassador.'

'Yes, I warned him you were coming,' said Mirny. 'He didn't much like the idea, but I was able to bribe him with food . . . I hope he didn't hurt you badly.'

'A scratch,' Afriel said. 'I assume there's no chance of infection.'

'I doubt it very much. Unless you brought your own bacteria with you.'

'Hardly likely,' Afriel said, offended. 'I have no bacteria. And I wouldn't have brought micro-organisms to an alien culture anyway.'

Mirny looked away. 'I thought you might have some of the special genetically altered ones . . . I think we can go now. The springtail will have spread your scent by mouth-touching in the subsidiary chamber, ahead of us. It will be spread throughout the Nest in a few hours. Once it reaches the Queen, it will spread very quickly.'

She jammed her feet against the hard shell of one of the young springtails and launched herself down the hall. Afriel followed her. The air was warm and he was beginning to sweat under his elaborate clothing, but his antiseptic sweat was odourless.

They exited into a vast chamber dug from the living rock. It was arched and oblong, eighty metres long and about twenty in diameter. It swarmed with members of the Nest.

There were hundreds of them. Most of them were workers, eight-legged and furred, the size of Great Danes. Here and there were members of the warrior caste, horse-sized furry monsters with heavy fanged heads the size and shape of overstuffed chairs.

A few metres away, two workers were carrying a member of the sensor caste, a being whose immense flattened head was attached to an atrophied body that was mostly lungs. The sensor had great platelike eyes, and its furred chitin sprouted long coiled antennae that twitched feebly as the workers bore it along. The workers clung to the hollowed rock of the chamber walls with hooked and suckered feet.

A paddle-limbed monster with a hairless, faceless head came sculling past them, through the warm reeking air. The front of its head was a nightmare of sharp grinding jaws and blunt armoured acid spouts. 'A tunneller,' Mirny said. 'It can take us deeper into the Nest—come with me.' She launched herself towards it and took a handhold on its furry, segmented back. Afriel followed her, joined by the two immature springtails, who clung to the thing's hide with their forelimbs. Afriel shuddered at the warm, greasy feel of its rank, damp fur. It continued to scull through the air, its eight fringed paddle feet catching the air like wings.

'There must be thousands of them,' Afriel said.

'I said a hundred thousand in my last report, but that was before I had fully explored the Nest. Even now there are long stretches I haven't seen. They must number close to a quarter of a million. This asteroid is about the size of the Mechanists' biggest base—Ceres. It still has rich veins of carbonaceous material. It's far from mined out.'

Afriel closed his eyes. If he was to lose his goggles, he would have to feel his way, blind, through these teeming, twitching, wriggling thousands. 'The population's still expanding, then?'

'Definitely,' she said. 'In fact, the colony will launch a mating swarm soon. There are three dozen male and female alates in the chambers near the Queen. Once they're launched, they'll mate and start new Nests. I'll take you to see them presently.' She hesitated. 'We're entering one of the fungal gardens now.'

One of the young springtails quietly shifted position. Grabbing the tunneller's fur with its forelimbs, it began to gnaw on the cuff of Afriel's pants. Afriel kicked it soundly, and it jerked back, retracting its eyestalks.

When he looked up again, he saw that they had entered a second chamber, much larger than the first. The walls around, overhead, and below were buried under an explosive profusion of fungus. The most common types were swollen barrellike domes, multibranched massed thickets, and spaghettilike tangled extrusions that moved very slightly in the faint and odorous breeze. Some of the barrels were surrounded by dim mists of exhaled spores.

'You see those caked-up piles beneath the fungus, its growth medium?' Mirny said.

'Yes.'

'I'm not sure whether it is a plant form or just some kind of complex biochemical sludge,' she said. 'The point is that it grows in sunlight, on the outside of the asteroid. A food source that grows in naked space! Imagine what that would be worth, back in the Rings.'

'There aren't words for its value,' Afriel said.

'It's inedible by itself,' she said. 'I tried to eat a very small piece of it once. It was like trying to eat plastic.'

'Have you eaten well, generally speaking?'

'Yes. Our biochemistry is quite similar to the Swarm's. The fungus itself is perfectly edible. The regurgitate is more nourishing, though. Internal fermentation in the worker hindgut adds to its nutritional value.'

Afriel stared. 'You grow used to it,' Mirny said. 'Later I'll teach you how to solicit food from the workers. It's a simple matter of reflex tapping—it's not controlled by pheromones, like most of their behaviour.' She brushed a long lock of clumped and dirty hair from the side of her face. 'I hope the pheromonal samples I sent back were worth the cost of transportation.'

'Oh, yes,' said Afriel. 'The chemistry of them was fascinating. We managed to synthesize most of the compounds. I was part of the research team myself.' He hesitated. How far did he dare trust her?

She had not been told about the experiment he and his superiors had planned. As far as Mirny knew, he was a simple, peaceful researcher, like herself. The Shapers' scientific community was suspicious of the minority involved in military work and espionage.

As an investment in the future, the Shapers had sent researchers to each of the nineteen alien races described to them by the Investors. This had cost the Shaper economy many gigawatts of precious energy and tons of rare metals and isotopes. In most cases, only two or three researchers could be sent; in seven cases, only one. For the Swarm, Galina Mirny had been chosen. She had gone peacefully, trusting in her intelligence and her good intentions to keep her alive and sane. Those who had sent her had not known whether her findings would be of any use or importance. They had only known that it was imperative that she be sent, even alone, even ill-equipped, before some other faction sent their own people and possibly discovered some technique or fact of overwhelming importance. And Dr Mirny had indeed discovered such a situation. It had made her mission into a matter of Ring security. That was why Afriel had come.

'You synthesized the compounds?' she said. 'Why?'

Afriel smiled disarmingly. 'Just to prove to ourselves that we could do it, perhaps.'

She shook her head. 'No mind-games, Dr Afriel, please. I came this far partly to escape from such things. Tell me the truth.'

Afriel stared at her, regretting that the goggles meant he could not meet her eyes. 'Very well,' he said. 'You should know, then, that I have been ordered by the Ring Council to carry out an experiment that may endanger both our lives.'

Mirny was silent for a moment. 'You're from Security, then?'

'My rank is captain.'

'I knew it . . . I knew it when those two Mechanists arrived. They were so polite, and so suspicious—I think they would have killed me at once if they hadn't hoped to bribe or torture some secret out of me. They scared the life out of me, Captain Afriel . . . You scare me, too.'

'We live in a frightening world, Doctor. It's a matter of faction security.'

'Everything's a matter of faction security with your lot,' she said. 'I shouldn't take you any further, or show you anything more. This Nest, these creatures—they're not *intelligent,* Captain. They can't think, they can't learn. They're innocent, primordially innocent. They have no knowledge of good and evil. They have no knowledge of *anything*. The last thing they need is to become pawns in a power struggle within some other race, light-years away.'

The tunneller had turned into an exit from the fungal chambers and was paddling slowly along in the warm darkness. A group of creatures like grey, flattened basketballs floated by from the opposite direction. One of them settled on Afriel's sleeve, clinging with frail whiplike tentacles. Afriel brushed it gently away, and it broke loose, emitting a stream of foul reddish droplets.

'Naturally I agree with you in principle, Doctor,' Afriel said smoothly. 'But consider these Mechanists. Some of their extreme factions are already more than half machine. Do you expect humanitarian motives from them? They're cold, Doctor—cold and soulless creatures who can cut a living man or woman to bits and never feel their pain. Most of the other factions hate us. They call us racist supermen. Would you rather that one of these cults do what we must do, and use the results against us?'

'This is double-talk.' She looked away. All around them workers laden down with fungus, their jaws full and guts stuffed with it, were spreading out into the Nest, scuttling alongside them or disappearing into branch tunnels departing in every direction, including straight up and straight down. Afriel saw a creature much like a worker, but with only six legs, scuttle past in the opposite direction, overhead. It was a parasite mimic. How long, he wondered, did it take a creature to evolve to look like that?

'It's no wonder that we've had so many defectors, back in the Rings,' she said sadly. 'If humanity is so stupid as to work itself into a corner like you describe, then it's better to have nothing to do with them. Better to live alone. Better not to help the madness spread.'

'That kind of talk will only get us killed,' Afriel said. 'We owe an allegiance to the faction that produced us.'

'Tell me truly, Captain,' she said. 'Haven't you ever felt the urge to leave everything—everyone—all your duties and constraints, and just go somewhere to think it all out? Your whole world, and your part in it? We're trained so hard, from childhood, and so much is demanded from us. Don't you think it's made us lose sight of our goals, somehow?'

'We live in space,' Afriel said flatly. 'Space is an unnatural environment, and it takes an unnatural effort from unnatural people to prosper there. Our minds are our tools, and philosophy has to come second. Naturally I've felt those urges you mention. They're just another threat to guard against. I believe in an ordered society. Technology has unleashed tremendous forces that are ripping society apart. Some one faction must arise from the struggle and integrate things. We Shapers have the wisdom and restraint to do it humanely. That's why I do the work I do.' He hesitated. 'I don't expect to see our day of triumph. I expect to die in some brush-fire conflict, or through assassination. It's enough that I can foresee that day.'

'But the arrogance of it, Captain!' she said suddenly. 'The arrogance of your little life and its little sacrifice! Consider the Swarm, if you really want your humane and perfect order. Here it is! Where it's always warm and dark, and it smells good, and food is easy to get, and everything is endlessly and perfectly recycled. The only resources that are ever lost are the bodies of the mating swarms, and a little air. A Nest like this one could last unchanged for hundreds of thousands of years. Hundreds . . . of thousands . . . of years. Who, or what, will remember us and our stupid faction in even a thousand years?'

Afriel shook his head. 'That's not a valid comparison. There is no such long view for us. In another thousand years we'll be machines, or gods.' He felt the top of his head; his velvet cap was gone. No doubt something was eating it by now.

The tunneller took them deeper into the asteroid's honeycombed free-fall maze. They saw the pupal chambers, where pallid larvae twitched in swaddled silk; the main fungal gardens; the graveyard pits, where winged workers beat ceaselessly at the soupy air, feverishly hot from the heat of decomposition. Corrosive black fungus ate the bodies of the dead into coarse black powder, carried off by blackened workers themselves three-quarters dead.

Later they left the tunneller and floated on by themselves. The woman moved with the ease of long habit; Afriel followed her, colliding bruisingly with squeaking workers. There were thousands of them, clinging to ceiling, walls, and floor, clustering and scurrying at every conceivable angle.

Later still they visited the chamber of the winged princes and princesses, an echoing round vault where creatures forty metres long hung crooked-legged in mid-air. Their bodies were segmented and metallic, with organic rocket nozzles on their thoraxes, where wings might have been. Folded along their sleek backs were radar antennae on long sweeping booms. They looked more like interplanetary probes under construction than anything biological. Workers fed them ceaselessly. Their bulging spiracled abdomens were full of compressed oxygen.

Mirny begged a large chunk of fungus from a passing worker, deftly tapping its antennae and provoking a reflex action. She handed most of the fungus to the two springtails, which devoured it greedily and looked expectantly for more.

Afriel tucked his legs into a free-fall lotus position and began chewing with determination on the leathery fungus. It was tough, but tasted good, like smoked meat—a delicacy he had tasted only once. The smell of smoke meant disaster in a Shaper's colony.

Mirny maintained a stony silence. 'Food's no problem,' Afriel said. 'Where do we sleep?'

She shrugged. 'Anywhere . . . there are unused niches and tunnels here and there. I suppose you'll want to see the Queen's chamber next.'

'By all means.'

'I'll have to get more fungus. The warriors are on guard there and have to be bribed with food.'

She gathered an armful of fungus from another worker in the endless stream, and they moved on. Afriel, already totally lost, was further confused in the maze of chambers and tunnels. At last they exited into an immense lightless cavern, bright with infra-red heat from the Queen's monstrous body. It was the colony's central factory. The fact that it was made of warm and pulpy flesh did not conceal its essentially industrial nature. Tons of predigested fungal pap went into the slick blind jaws at one end. The rounded billows of soft flesh digested and processed it, squirming, sucking, and undulating, with loud machinelike churnings and gurglings. Out of the other end came an endless conveyorlike blobbed stream of eggs, each one packed in a thick hormonal paste of lubrication. The workers avidly licked the eggs clean and bore them off to nurseries. Each egg was the size of a man's torso.

The process went on and on. There was no day or night here in the lightless centre of the asteroid. There was no remnant of a diurnal rhythm in the genes of these creatures. The flow of production was as constant and even as the working of an automated mine.

'This is why I'm here,' Afriel murmured in awe. 'Just look at this, Doctor. The Mechanists have cybernetic mining machinery that is generations ahead of ours. But here—in the bowels of this nameless little world, is a genetic technology that feeds itself, maintains itself, runs itself, efficiently, endlessly, mindlessly. It's the perfect organic tool. The faction that could use these tireless workers could make itself an industrial titan. And our knowledge of biochemistry is unsurpassed. We Shapers are just the ones to do it.'

'How do you propose to do that?' Mirny asked with open scepticism. 'You would have to ship a fertilized queen all the way to the solar system. We could scarcely afford that, even if the Investors would let us, which they wouldn't.'

'I don't need an entire Nest,' Afriel said patiently. 'I only need the genetic information from one egg. Our laboratories back in the Rings could clone endless numbers of workers.'

'But the workers are useless without the Nest's pheromones. They need chemical cues to trigger their behaviour modes.'

'Exactly,' Afriel said. 'As it so happens, I possess those pheromones, synthesized and concentrated. What I must do now is test them. I must prove that I can use them to make the workers do what I choose. Once I've proven it's possible, I'm authorized to smuggle the genetic information necessary back to the Rings. The Investors won't approve. There are, of course, moral questions involved, and the Investors are not genetically advanced. But we can win their approval back with the profits we make. Best of all, we can beat the Mechanists at their own game.'

'You've carried the pheromones here?' Mirny said. 'Didn't the Investors suspect something when they found them?'

'Now it's you who has made an error,' Afriel said calmly. 'You assume that the Investors are infallible. You are wrong. A race without curiosity will never explore every possibility, the way we Shapers did.' Afriel pulled up his pants cuff and extended his right leg. 'Consider this varicose vein along my shin. Circulatory problems of this sort are common among those who spend a lot of time in free-fall. This vein, however, has been blocked artificially and treated to reduce osmosis. Within the vein are ten separate colonies of genetically altered bacteria, each one specially bred to produce a different Swarm pheromone.'

He smiled. 'The Investors searched me very thoroughly, including X-rays. But the vein appears normal to X-rays, and the bacteria are trapped within compartments in the vein. They are indetectable. I have a small medical kit on my person. It includes a syringe. We can use it to extract the pheromones and test them. When the tests are finished—and I feel sure they will be successful, in fact I've staked my career on it—we can empty the vein and all its compartments. The bacteria will die on contact with air. We can refill the vein with the yolk from a developing embryo. The cells may survive during the trip back, but even if they die, they can't rot inside my body. They'll never come in contact with any agent of decay. Back in the Rings, we can learn to activate and suppress different genes to produce the different castes, just as is done in nature. We'll have millions of workers, armies of warriors if need be, perhaps even organic rocket-ships, grown from altered alates. If this works, who do you think will remember me then, eh? Me and my arrogant little life and little sacrifice?'

She stared at him; even the bulky goggles could not hide her new respect and even fear. 'You really mean to do it, then.'

'I made the sacrifice of my time and energy. I expect results, Doctor.'

'But it's kidnapping. You're talking about breeding a slave race.'

Afriel shrugged, with contempt. 'You're juggling words, Doctor. I'll cause this colony no harm. I may steal some of its workers' labour while they obey my own chemical orders, but that tiny theft won't be missed. I admit to the murder of one egg, but that is no more a crime than a human abortion. Can the theft of one strand of genetic material be called "kidnapping"? I think not. As for the scandalous idea of a slave race—I reject it out of hand. These creatures are genetic robots. They will no more be slaves then are laser drills or cargo tankers. At the very worst, they will be our domestic animals.'

Mirny considered the issue. It did not take her long. 'It's true. It's not as if a common worker will be staring at the stars, pining for its freedom. They're just brainless neuters.'

'Exactly, Doctor.'

'They simply work. Whether they work for us or the Swarm makes no difference to them.'

'I see that you've seized on the beauty of the idea.'

'And if it worked,' Mirny said, 'if it worked, our faction would profit astronomically.'

Afriel smiled genuinely, unaware of the chilling sarcasm of his expression. 'And the personal profit, Doctor . . . the valuable expertise of the first to exploit the technique.' He spoke gently, quietly. 'Ever see a nitrogen snowfall on Titan? I think a habitat of one's own there—larger, much larger than anything possible before . . . A genuine city, Galina, a place where a man can scrap the rules and discipline that madden him . . .'

'Now it's you who are talking defection, Captain-Doctor.'

Afriel was silent for a moment, then smiled with an effort. 'Now you've ruined my perfect reverie,' he said. 'Besides, what I was describing was the well-earned retirement of a wealthy man, not some self-indulgent hermitage . . . there's a clear difference.' He hesitated. 'In any case, may I conclude that you're with me in this project?'

She laughed and touched his arm. There was something uncanny about the small sound of her laugh, drowned by a great organic rumble from the Queen's monstrous intestines . . . 'Do you expect me to resist your arguments for two long years? Better that I give in now and save us friction.'

'Yes.'

'After all, you won't do any harm to the Nest. They'll never know anything has happened. And if their genetic line is successfully reproduced back home, there'll never be any reason for humanity to bother them again.'

'True enough,' said Afriel, though in the back of his mind he instantly thought of the fabulous wealth of Betelgeuse's asteroid system. A day would come, inevitably, when humanity would move to the stars *en masse*, in earnest. It would be well to know the ins and outs of every race that might become a rival.

'I'll help you as best I can,' she said. There was a moment's silence. 'Have you seen enough of this area?'

'Yes.' They left the Queen's chamber.

'I didn't think I'd like you at first,' she said candidly. 'I think I like you better now. You seem to have a sense of humour that most Security people lack.'

'It's not a sense of humour,' Afriel said sadly. 'It's a sense of irony disguised as one.'

There were no days in the unending stream of hours that followed. There were only ragged periods of sleep, apart at first, later together, as they held each other in free-fall. The sexual feel of skin and body became an anchor to their common humanity, a divided, frayed humanity so many light-years away that the concept no longer had any meaning. Life in the warm and swarming tunnels was the here and now; the two of them were like germs in a bloodstream, moving ceaselessly with the pulsing ebb and flow. Hours stretched into months, and time itself grew meaningless.

The pheromonal tests were complex, but not impossibly difficult. The first of the ten pheromones was a simple grouping stimulus, causing large numbers of workers to gather as the chemical was spread from palp to palp. The workers then waited for further instructions; if none were forthcoming, they dispersed. To work effectively, the pheromones had to be given in a mix, or series, like computer commands; number one, grouping, for instance, together with the third pheromone, a transferral order, which caused the workers to empty any given chamber and move its effects to another. The ninth pheromone had the best industrial possibilities; it was a building order, causing the workers to gather tunnellers and dredgers and set them to work. Others were annoying; the tenth pheromone provoked grooming behaviour, and the workers' furry palps stripped off the remaining rags of Afriel's clothing. The eighth pheromone sent the workers off to harvest material on the asteroid's surface, and in their eagerness to observe its effects the two explorers were almost trapped and swept off into space.

The two of them no longer feared the warrior caste. They knew that a dose of the sixth pheromone would send them scurrying off to defend the eggs, just as it sent the workers to tend them. Mirny and Afriel took advantage of this and secured their own chambers, dug by chemically hijacked workers and defended by a hijacked airlock guardian. They had their own fungal gardens to refresh the air, stocked with the fungus they liked best, and digested by a worker they kept drugged for their own food use. From constant stuffing and lack of exercise the worker had swollen up into its replete form and hung from one wall like a monstrous grape.

Afriel was tired. He had been without sleep recently for a long time; how long, he didn't know. His body rhythms had not adjusted as well as Mirny's, and he was prone to fits of depression and irritability that he had to repress with an effort. 'The Investors will be back sometime,' he said. 'Sometime soon.'

Mirny was indifferent. 'The Investors,' she said, and followed the remark with something in the language of the springtails, which he didn't catch. Despite his linguistic training, Afriel had never caught up with her in her use of the springtails' grating jargon. His training was almost a liability; the springtail language had decayed so much that it was a pidgin tongue, without rules or regularity. He knew enough to give them simple orders, and with his partial control of the warriors he had the power to back it up. The springtails were afraid of him, and the two juveniles that Mirny had tamed had developed into fat, overgrown tyrants that freely terrorized their elders. Afriel had been too busy to seriously study the springtails or the other symbiotes. There were too many practical matters at hand.

'If they come too soon, I won't be able to finish my latest study,' she said in English.

Afriel pulled off his infra-red goggles and knotted them tightly around his neck. 'There's a limit, Galina,' he said, yawning. 'You can only memorize so much data without equipment. We'll just have to wait quietly until we can get back. I hope the Investors aren't shocked when they see me. I lost a fortune with those clothes.'

'It's been so dull since the mating swarm was launched. If it weren't for the new growth in the alates' chamber, I'd be bored to death.' She pushed greasy hair from her face with both hands. 'Are you going to sleep?'

'Yes, if I can.'

'You won't come with me? I keep telling you that this new growth is important. I think it's a new caste. It's definitely not an alate. It has eyes like an alate, but it's clinging to the wall.'

'It's probably not a Swarm member at all, then,' he said tiredly, humouring her. 'It's probably a parasite, an alate mimic. Go on and see it, if you want to. I'll be here waiting for you.'

He heard her leave. Without his infra-reds on, the darkness was still not quite total; there was a very faint luminosity from the steaming, growing fungus in the chamber beyond. The stuffed worker replete moved slightly on the wall, rustling and gurgling. He fell asleep.

When he awoke, Mirny had not yet returned. He was not alarmed. First, he visited the original airlock tunnel, where the Investors had first left him. It was irrational—the Investors always fulfilled their contracts—but he feared that they would arrive someday, become impatient, and leave without him. The Investors would have to wait, of course. Mirny could keep them occupied in the short time it would take him to hurry to the nursery and rob a developing egg of its living cells. It was best that the egg be as fresh as possible.

Later he ate. He was munching fungus in one of the anterior chambers when Mirny's two tamed springtails found him. 'What do you want?' he asked in their language.

'Food-giver no good,' the larger one screeched, waving its forelegs in brainless agitation. 'Not work, not sleep.'

'Not move,' the second one said. It added hopefully, 'Eat it now?'

Afriel gave them some of his food. They ate it, seemingly more out of habit than real appetite, which alarmed him. 'Take me to her,' he told them.

The two springtails scurried off; he followed them easily, adroitly dodging and weaving through the crowds of workers. They led him several miles through the network, to the alates' chamber. There they stopped, confused. 'Gone,' the large one said.

The chamber was empty. Afriel had never seen it empty before, and it was very unusual for the Swarm to waste so much space. He felt dread. 'Follow the food-giver,' he said. 'Follow the smell.'

The springtails snuffled without much enthusiasm along one wall; they knew he had no food and were reluctant to do anything without an immediate reward. At last one of them picked up the scent, or pretended to, and followed it up across the ceiling and into the mouth of a tunnel.

It was hard for Afriel to see much in the abandoned chamber; there was not enough infra-red heat. He leapt upward after the springtail.

He heard the roar of a warrior and the springtail's choked-off screech. It came flying from the tunnel's mouth, a spray of clotted fluid bursting from its ruptured head. It tumbled end over end until it hit the far wall with a flaccid crunch. It was already dead.

The second springtail fled at once, screeching with grief and terror. Afriel landed on the lip of the tunnel, sinking into a crouch as his legs soaked up momentum. He could smell the acrid stench of the warrior's anger, a pheromone so thick that even a human could scent it. Dozens of other warriors would group here within minutes, or seconds. Behind the enraged warrior he could hear workers and tunnellers shifting and cementing rock.

He might be able to control one enraged warrior, but never two, or twenty. He launched himself from the chamber wall and out an exit.

He searched for the other springtail—he felt sure he could recognize it, since it was so much bigger than the others—but he could not find it. With its keen sense of smell, it could easily avoid him if it wanted to.

Mirny did not return. Uncountable hours passed. He slept again. He returned to the alates' chamber; there were warriors on guard there, warriors that were not interested in food and brandished their immense serrated fangs when he approached. They looked ready to rip him apart; the faint reek of aggressive pheromones hung about the place like a fog. He did not see any symbiotes of any kind on the warriors' bodies. There was one species, a thing like a huge tick, that clung only to warriors, but even the ticks were gone.

He returned to his chambers to wait and think. Mirny's body was not in the garbage pits. Of course, it was possible that something else might have eaten her. Should he extract the remaining pheromone from the spaces in his veins and try to break into the alates' chamber? He suspected that Mirny, or whatever was left of her, was somewhere in the tunnel where the springtail had been killed. He had never explored that tunnel himself. There were thousands of tunnels he had never explored.

He felt paralysed by indecision and fear. If he was quiet, if he did nothing, the Investors might arrive at any moment. He could tell the Ring Council anything he wanted about Mirny's death; if he had the genetics with him, no one would quibble. He did not love her; he respected her, but not enough to give up his life, or his faction's investment. He had not thought of the Ring Council in a long time, and the thought sobered him. He would have to explain his decision . . .

He was still in a brown study when he heard a whoosh of air as his living airlock deflated itself. Three warriors had come for him. There was no reek of anger about them. They moved slowly and carefully. He knew better than to try to resist. One of them seized him gently in its massive jaws and carried him off.

It took him to the alates' chamber and into the guarded tunnel. A new, large chamber had been excavated at the end of the tunnel. It was filled almost to bursting by a black-splattered white mass of flesh. In the centre of the soft speckled mass were a mouth and two damp, shining eyes, on stalks. Long tendrils like conduits dangled, writhing, from a clumped ridge above the eyes. The tendrils ended in pink, fleshy pluglike clumps.

One of the tendrils had been thrust through Mirny's skull. Her body hung in mid-air, limp as wax. Her eyes were open, but blind.

Another tendril was plugged into the braincase of a mutated worker. The worker still had the pallid tinge of a larva; it was shrunken and deformed, and its mouth had the wrinkled look of a human mouth. There was a blob like a tongue in the mouth, and white ridges like human teeth. It had no eyes.

It spoke with Mirny's voice. 'Captain-Doctor Afriel . . .'

'Galina . . .'

'I have no such name. You may address me as Swarm.'

Afriel vomited. The central mass was an immense head. Its brain almost filled the room.

It waited politely until Afriel had finished.

'I find myself awakened again,' Swarm said dreamily. 'I am pleased to see that there is no major emergency to concern me. Instead it is a threat that has become almost routine.' It hesitated delicately. Mirny's body moved slightly in mid-air; her breathing was inhumanly regular. The eyes opened and closed. 'Another young race.'

'What are you?'

'I am the Swarm. That is, I am one of its castes. I am a tool, an adaptation; my speciality is intelligence. I am not often needed. It is good to be needed again.'

'Have you been here all along? Why didn't you greet us? We'd have dealt with you. We meant no harm.'

The wet mouth on the end of the plug made laughing sounds. 'Like yourself, I enjoy irony,' it said. 'It is a pretty trap you have found yourself in, Captain-Doctor. You meant to make the Swarm work for you and your race. You meant to breed us and study us and use us. It is an excellent plan, but one we hit upon long before your race evolved.'

Stung by panic, Afriel's mind raced frantically. 'You're an intelligent being,' he said. 'There's no reason to do us any harm. Let us talk together. We can help you.'

'Yes,' Swarm agreed. 'You will be helpful. Your companion's memories tell me that this is one of those uncomfortable periods when galactic intelligence is rife. Intelligence is a great bother. It makes all kinds of trouble for us.'

'What do you mean?'

'You are a young race and lay great stock by your own cleverness,' Swarm said. 'As usual, you fail to see that intelligence is not a survival trait.'

Afriel wiped sweat from his face. 'We've done well,' he said. 'We came to you, and peacefully. You didn't come to us.'

'I refer to exactly that,' Swarm said urbanely. 'This urge to expand, to explore, to develop, is just what will make you extinct. You naïvely suppose that you can continue to feed your curiosity indefinitely. It is an old story, pursued by countless races before you. Within a thousand years—perhaps a little longer—your species will vanish.'

'You intend to destroy us, then? I warn you it will not be an easy task—'

'Again you miss the point. Knowledge is power! Do you suppose that fragile little form of yours—your primitive legs, your ludicrous arms and hands, your tiny, scarcely wrinkled brain—can *contain* all that power? Certainly not! Already your race is flying to pieces under the impact of your own expertise. The original human form is becoming obsolete. Your own genes have been altered, and you, Captain-Doctor, are a crude experiment. In a hundred years you will be a relic. In a thousand years you will not even be a memory. Your race will go the same way as a thousand others.'

'And what way is that?'

'I do not know.' The thing on the end of the Swarm's arm made a chuckling sound. 'They have passed beyond my ken. They have all discovered something, learned something, that has caused them to transcend my understanding. It may be that they even transcend *being*. At any rate, I cannot sense their presence anywhere. They seem to do nothing, they seem to interfere in nothing; for all intents and purposes, they seem to be dead. Vanished. They may have become gods, or ghosts. In either case, I have no wish to join them.'

'So then—so then you have—'

'Intelligence is very much a two-edged sword, Captain-Doctor. It is useful only up to a point. It interferes with the business of living. Life, and intelligence, do not mix very well. They are not at all closely related, as you childishly assume.'

'But you, then—you are a rational being—'

'I am a tool, as I said.' The mutated device on the end of its arm made a sighing noise. 'When you began your pheromonal experiments, the chemical imbalance became apparent to the Queen. It triggered certain genetic patterns within her body, and I was reborn. Chemical sabotage is a problem that can best be dealt with by intelligence. I am a brain replete, you see, specially designed to be far more intelligent than any young race. Within three days I was fully self-conscious. Within five days I had deciphered these markings on my body. They are the genetically encoded history of my race . . . within five days and two hours I recognized the problem at hand and knew what to do. I am now doing it. I am six days old.'

'What is it you intend to do?'

'Your race is a very vigorous one. I expect it to be here, competing with us, within five hundred years. Perhaps much sooner. It will be necessary to make a thorough study of such a rival. I invite you to join our community on a permanent basis.'

'What do you mean?'

'I invite you to become a symbiote. I have here a male and a female, whose genes are altered and therefore without defects. You make a perfect breeding pair. It will save me a great deal of trouble with cloning.'

'You think I'll betray my race and deliver a slave species into your hands?'

'Your choice is simple, Captain-Doctor. Remain an intelligent, living being, or become a mindless puppet, like your partner. I have taken over all the functions of her nervous system; I can do the same to you.'

'I can kill myself.'

'That might be troublesome, because it would make me resort to developing a cloning technology. Technology, though I am capable of it, is painful to me. I am a genetic arfefact; there are fail-safes within me that prevent me from taking over the Nest for my own uses. That would mean falling into the same trap of progress as other intelligent races. For similar reasons, my life span is limited. I will live for only a thousand years, until your race's brief flurry of energy is over and peace resumes once more.'

'Only a thousand years?' Afriel laughed bitterly. 'What then? You kill off my descendants, I assume, having no further use for them.'

'No. We have not killed any of the fifteen other races we have taken for defensive study. It has not been necessary. Consider that small scavenger floating by your head, Captain-Doctor, that is feeding on your vomit. Five hundred million years ago its ancestors made the galaxy tremble. When they attacked us, we unleashed their own kind upon them. Of course, we altered our side, so that they were smarter, tougher, and, naturally, totally loyal to us. Our Nests were the only world they knew, and they fought with a valour and inventiveness we never could have matched . . . Should your race arrive to exploit us, we will naturally do the same.'

'We humans are different.'

'Of course.'

'A thousand years here won't change us. You will die and our descendants will take over this Nest. We'll be running things, despite you, in a few generations. The darkness won't make any difference.'

'Certainly not. You don't need eyes here. You don't need anything.'

'You'll allow me to stay alive? To teach them anything I want?'

'Certainly, Captain-Doctor. We are doing you a favour, in all truth. In a thousand years your descendants here will be the only remnants of the human race. We are generous with our immortality; we will take it upon ourselves to preserve you.'

'You're wrong, Swarm. You're wrong about intelligence, and you're wrong about everything else. Maybe other races would crumble into parasitism, but we humans are different.'

'Certainly. You'll do it, then?'

'Yes. I accept your challenge. And I will defeat you.'

'Splendid. When the Investors return here, the springtails will say that they have killed you, and will tell them to never return. They will not return. The humans should be the next to arrive.'

'If I don't defeat you, they will.'

'Perhaps.' Again it sighed. 'I'm glad I don't have to absorb you. I would have missed your conversation.'

BURNING CHROME

WILLIAM GIBSON

It was hot, the night we burned Chrome. Out in the malls and plazas, moths were batting themselves to death against the neon, but in Bobby's loft the only light came from a monitor screen and the green and red LEDs on the face of the matrix simulator. I knew every chip in Bobby's simulator by heart; it looked like your workaday Ono-Sendai VII, the 'Cyberspace Seven', but I'd rebuilt it so many times that you'd have had a hard time finding a square millimetre of factory circuitry in all that silicon.

We waited side by side in front of the simulator console, watching the time display in the screen's lower left corner.

'Go for it,' I said, when it was time, but Bobby was already there, leaning forward to drive the Russian program into its slot with the heel of his hand. He did it with the tight grace of a kid slamming change into an arcade game, sure of winning and ready to pull down a string of free games.

A silver tide of phosphenes boiled across my field of vision as the matrix began to unfold in my head, a 3-D chessboard, infinite and perfectly transparent. The Russian program seemed to lurch as we entered the grid. If anyone else had been jacked into that part of the matrix, he might have seen a surf of flickering shadow roll out of the little yellow pyramid that represented our computer. The program was a mimetic weapon, designed to absorb local colour and present itself as a crash-priority override in whatever context it encountered.

'Congratulations,' I heard Bobby say. 'We just became an Eastern Seaboard Fission Authority inspection probe. . . .' That meant we were clearing fiberoptic lines with the cybernetic equivalent of a fire siren, but in the simulation matrix we seemed to rush straight for Chrome's database. I couldn't see it yet, but I already knew those walls were waiting. Walls of shadow, walls of ice.

Chrome: her pretty childface smooth as steel, with eyes that would have been at home on the bottom of some deep Atlantic trench, cold grey eyes that lived under terrible pressure. They said she cooked her own cancers for people who crossed her, rococo custom variations that took years to kill you. They said a lot of things about Chrome, none of them at all reassuring.

So I blotted her out with a picture of Rikki. Rikki kneeling in a shaft of dusty sunlight that slanted into the loft through a grid of steel and glass: her faded camouflage fatigues, her translucent rose sandals, the good line of her bare back as she rummaged through a nylon gear bag. She looks up, and a half-blond curl falls to tickle her nose. Smiling, buttoning an old shirt of Bobby's, frayed khaki cotton drawn across her breasts.

She smiles.

'Son of a bitch,' said Bobby, 'we just told Chrome we're an IRS audit and three Supreme Court subpoenas. . . . Hang on to your ass. Jack. . . .'

So long, Rikki. Maybe now I see you never.

And dark, so dark, in the halls of Chrome's ice.

Bobby was a cowboy, and ice was the nature of his game, *ice* from ICE, Intrusion Countermeasures Electronics. The matrix is an abstract representation of the relationships between data systems. Legitimate programmers jack into their employers' sector of the matrix and find themselves surrounded by bright geometries representing the corporate data.

Towers and fields of it ranged in the colourless nonspace of the simulation matrix, the electronic consensus-hallucination that facilitates the handling and exchange of massive quantities of data. Legitimate programmers never see the walls of ice they work behind, the walls of shadow that screen their operations from others, from industrial-espionage artists and hustlers like Bobby Quine.

Bobby was a cowboy. Bobby was a cracksman, a burglar, casing mankind's extended electronic nervous system, rustling data and credit in the crowded matrix, monochrome nonspace where the only stars are dense concentrations of information, and high above it all burn corporate galaxies and the cold spiral arms of military systems.

Bobby was another one of those young-old faces you see drinking in the Gentleman Loser, the chic bar for computer cowboys, rustlers, cybernetic second-story men. We were partners.

Bobby Quine and Automatic Jack. Bobby's the thin, pale dude with the dark glasses, and Jack's the mean-looking guy with the myoelectric arm. Bobby's software and Jack's hard; Bobby punches console and Jack runs down all the little things that can give you an edge. Or, anyway, that's what the scene watchers in the Gentleman Loser would've told you, before Bobby decided to burn Chrome. But they also might've told you that Bobby was losing his edge, slowing down. He was twenty-eight, Bobby, and that's old for a console cowboy.

Both of us were good at what we did, but somehow that one big score just wouldn't come down for us. I knew where to go for the right gear, and Bobby had all his licks down pat. He'd sit back with a white terry sweatband across his forehead and whip moves on those keyboards faster than you could follow, punching his way through some of the fanciest ice in the business, but that was when something happened that managed to get him totally wired, and that didn't happen often. Not highly motivated, Bobby, and I was the kind of guy who's happy to have the rent covered and a clean shirt to wear.

But Bobby had this thing for girls, like they were his private tarot or something, the way he'd get himself moving. We never talked about it, but when it started to look like he was losing his touch that summer, he started to spend more time in the Gentleman Loser. He'd sit at a table by the open doors and watch the crowd slide by, nights when the bugs were at the neon and the air smelled of perfume and fast food. You could see his sunglasses scanning those faces as they passed, and he must have decided that Rikki's was the one he was waiting for, the wild card and the luck changer. The new one.

I went to New York to check out the market, to see what was available in hot software.

The Finn's place has a defective hologram in the window; METRO HOLOGRAFIX, over a display of dead flies wearing fur coats of grey dust. The scrap's waist-high, inside, drifts of it rising to meet walls that are barely visible behind nameless junk, behind sagging pressboard shelves stacked with old skin magazines and yellow-spined years of *National Geographic*.

'You need a gun,' said the Finn. He looks like a recombo DNA project aimed at tailoring people for high-speed burrowing. 'You're in luck. I got the new Smith and Wesson, the four-oh-eight Tactical. Got this xenon projector slung under the barrel, see, batteries in the grip, throw you a twelve-inch high-noon circle in the pitch dark at fifty yards. The light source is so narrow, it's almost impossible to spot. It's just like voodoo in a nightfight.'

I let my arm clunk down on the table and started the fingers drumming; the servos in the hand began whining like overworked mosquitoes. I knew that the Finn really hated the sound.

'You looking to pawn that?' He prodded the Duralumin wrist joint with the chewed shaft of a felt-tip pen. 'Maybe get yourself something a little quieter?'

I kept it up. 'I don't need any guns, Finn.'

'Okay,' he said, 'okay,' and I quit drumming. 'I only got this one item, and I don't even know what it is.' He looked unhappy. 'I got it off these bridge-and-tunnel kids from Jersey last week.'

'So when'd you ever buy anything you didn't know what it was, Finn?'

'Wise ass.' And he passed me a transparent mailer with something in it that looked like an audio cassette through the bubble padding. 'They had a passport,' he said. 'They had credit cards and a watch. And that.'

'They had the contents of somebody's pockets, you mean.'

He nodded. 'The passport was Belgian. It was also bogus, looked to me, so I put it in the furnace. Put the cards in with it. The watch was okay, a Porsche, nice watch.'

It was obviously some kind of plug-in military program. Out of the mailer, it looked like the magazine of a small assault rifle, coated with nonreflective black plastic. The edges and corners showed bright metal; it had been knocking around for a while.

'I'll give you a bargain on it, Jack. For old times' sake.'

I had to smile at that. Getting a bargain from the Finn was like God repealing the law of gravity when you have to carry a heavy suitcase down ten blocks of airport corridor.

'Looks Russian to me,' I said. 'Probably the emergency sewage controls for some Leningrad suburb. Just what I need.'

'You know,' said the Finn, 'I got a pair of shoes older than you are. Sometimes I think you got about as much class as those yahoos from Jersey. What do you want me to tell you, it's the keys to the Kremlin? You figure out what the goddamn thing is. Me, I just sell the stuff.'

I bought it.

Bodiless, we swerve into Chrome's castle of ice. And we're fast, fast. It feels like we're surfing the crest of the invading program, hanging ten above the seething glitch systems as they mutate. We're sentient patches of oil swept along down corridors of shadow.

Somewhere we have bodies, very far away, in a crowded loft roofed with steel and glass. Somewhere we have microseconds, maybe time left to pull out.

We've crashed her gates disguised as an audit and three subpoenas, but her defences are specifically geared to cope with that kind of official intrusion. Her most sophisticated ice is structured to fend off warrants, writs, subpoenas. When we breached the first gate, the bulk of her data vanished behind core-command ice, these walls we see as leagues of corridor, mazes of shadow. Five separate landlines spurted May Day signals to law firms, but the virus had already taken over the parameter ice. The glitch systems gobble the distress calls as our mimetic subprograms scan anything that hasn't been blanked by core command.

The Russian program lifts a Tokyo number from the unscreened data, choosing it for frequency of calls, average length of calls, the speed with which Chrome returned those calls.

'Okay,' says Bobby, 'we're an incoming scrambler call from a pal of hers in Japan. That should help.'

Ride 'em, cowboy.

* * *

Bobby read his future in women; his girls were omens, changes in the weather, and he'd sit all night in the Gentleman Loser, waiting for the season to lay a new face down in front of him like a card.

I was working late in the loft one night, shaving down a chip, my arm off and the little waldo jacked straight into the stump.

Bobby came in with a girl I hadn't seen before, and usually I feel a little funny if a stranger sees me working that way, with those leads clipped to the hard carbon studs that stick out of my stump. She came right over and looked at the magnified image on the screen, then saw the waldo moving under its vacuum-sealed dust cover. She didn't say anything, just watched. Right away I had a good feeling about her; it's like that sometimes.

'Automatic Jack, Rikki. My associate.'

He laughed, put his arm around her waist, something in his tone letting me know that I'd be spending the night in a dingy room in a hotel.

'Hi,' she said. Tall, nineteen or maybe twenty, and she definitely had the goods. With just those few freckles across the bridge of her nose, and eyes somewhere between dark amber and French coffee. Tight black jeans rolled to midcalf and a narrow plastic belt that matched the rose-coloured sandals.

But now when I see her sometimes when I'm trying to sleep, I see her somewhere out on the edge of all this sprawl of cities and smoke, and it's like she's a hologram stuck behind my eyes, in a bright dress she must've worn once, when I knew her, something that doesn't quite reach her knees. Bare legs long and straight. Brown hair, streaked with blond, hoods her face, blown in a wind from somewhere, and I see her wave goodbye.

Bobby was making a show of rooting through a stack of audio cassettes. 'I'm on my way, cowboy,' I said, unclipping the waldo. She watched attentively as I put my arm back on.

'Can you fix things?' she asked.

'Anything, anything you want, Automatic Jack'll fix it.' I snapped my Duralumin fingers for her.

She took a little simstim deck from her belt and showed me the broken hinge on the cassette cover.

'Tomorrow,' I said, 'no problem.'

And my oh my, I said to myself, sleep pulling me down the six flights to the street, *what'll Bobby's luck be like with a fortune cookie like that? If his system worked, we'd be striking it rich any night now*. In the street I grinned and yawned and waved for a cab.

Chrome's castle is dissolving, sheets of ice shadow flickering and fading, eaten by the glitch systems that spin out from the Russian program, tumbling away from our central logic thrust and infecting the fabric of the ice itself. The glitch systems are cybernetic virus analogs, self-replicating and voracious. They mutate constantly, in unison, subverting and absorbing Chrome's defences.

Have we already paralysed her, or is a bell ringing somewhere, a red light blinking? Does she know?

Rikki Wildside, Bobby called her, and for those first few weeks it must have seemed to her that she had it all, the whole teeming show spread out for her, sharp and bright under the neon. She was new to the scene, and she had all the miles of malls and plazas to prowl, all the shops and clubs, and Bobby to explain the wild side, the tricky wiring on the dark underside of things, all the players and their names and their games. He made her feel at home.

'What happened to your arm?' she asked me one night in the Gentleman Loser, the three of us drinking at a small table in a corner.

'Hang-gliding,' I said, 'accident.'

'Hang-gliding over a wheatfield,' said Bobby, 'place called Kiev. Our Jack's just hanging there in the dark, under a Nightwing parafoil, with fifty kilos of radar jammer between his legs, and some Russian asshole accidentally burns his arm off with a laser.'

I don't remember how I changed the subject, but I did.

I was still telling myself that it wasn't Rikki who was getting to me, but what Bobby was doing with her. I'd known him for a long time, since the end of the war, and I knew he used women as counters in a game, Bobby Quine versus fortune, versus time and the night of cities. And Rikki had turned up just when he needed something to get him going, something to aim for. So he'd set her up as a symbol for everything he wanted and couldn't have, everything he'd had and couldn't keep.

I didn't like having to listen to him tell me how much he loved her, and knowing he believed it only made it worse. He was a past master at the hard fall and the rapid recovery, and I'd seen it happen a dozen times before. He might as well have had NEXT printed across his sunglasses in green Day-Glo capitals, ready to flash out at the first interesting face that flowed past the tables in the Gentleman Loser.

I knew what he did to them. He turned them into emblems, sigils on the map of his hustler's life, navigation beacons he could follow through a sea of bars and neon. What else did he have to steer by? He didn't love money, in and of itself, not enough to follow its lights. He wouldn't work for power over other people; he hated the responsibility it brings. He had some basic pride in his skill, but that was never enough to keep him pushing.

So he made do with women.

When Rikki showed up, he needed one in the worst way. He was fading fast, and smart money was already whispering that the edge was off his game. He needed that one big score, and soon, because he didn't know any other kind of life, and all his clocks were set for hustler's time, calibrated in risk and adrenaline and that supernal dawn calm that comes when every move's proved right and a sweet lump of someone else's credit clicks into your own account.

It was time for him to make his bundle and get out; so Rikki got set up higher and further away than any of the others ever had, even though—and I felt like screaming it at him—she was right there, alive, totally real, human, hungry, resilient, bored, beautiful, excited, all the things she was. . . .

Then he went out one afternoon, about a week before I made the trip to New York to see the Finn. Went out and left us there in the loft, waiting for a thunderstorm. Half the skylight was shadowed by a dome they'd never finished, and the other half showed sky, black and blue with clouds. I was standing by the bench, looking up at that sky, stupid with the hot afternoon, the humidity, and she touched me, touched my shoulder, the half-inch border of taut pink scar that the arm doesn't cover. Anybody else ever touched me there, they went on to the shoulder, the neck. . . .

But she didn't do that. Her nails were lacquered black, not pointed, but tapered oblongs, the lacquer only a shade darker than the carbon-fibre laminate that sheathes my arm. And her hand went down the arm, black nails tracing a weld in the laminate, down to the black anodized elbow joint, out to the wrist, her hand soft-knuckled as a child's, fingers spreading to lock over mine, her palm against the perforated Duralumin.

Her other palm came up to brush across the feedback pads, and it rained all afternoon, raindrops drumming on the steel and soot-stained glass above Bobby's bed.

Ice walls flick away like supersonic butterflies made of shade. Beyond them, the matrix's illusion of infinite space. It's like watching a tape of a prefab building going up; only the tape's reversed and run at high speed, and these walls are torn wings.

Trying to remind myself that this place and the gulfs beyond are only representations, that we aren't 'in' Chrome's computer, but interfaced with it, while the matrix simulator in Bobby's loft generates this illusion . . . The core data begin to emerge, exposed, vulnerable. . . . This is the far side of ice, the view of the matrix I've never seen before, the view that fifteen million legitimate console operators see daily and take for granted.

The core data tower around us like vertical freight trains, colour-coded for access. Bright primaries, impossibly bright in that transparent void, linked by countless horizontals in nursery blues and pinks.

But ice still shadows something at the centre of it all: the heart of all Chrome's expensive darkness, the very heart . . .

It was late afternoon when I got back from my shopping expedition to New York. Not much sun through the skylight, but an ice pattern glowed on Bobby's monitor screen, a 2-D graphic representation of someone's computer defences, lines of neon woven like an Art Deco prayer rug. I turned the console off, and the screen went completely dark.

Rikki's things were spread across my workbench, nylon bags spilling clothes and make-up, a pair of bright red cowboy boots, audio cassettes, glossy Japanese magazines about simstim stars. I stacked it all under the bench and then took my arm off, forgetting that the program I'd bought from the Finn was in the right-hand pocket of my jacket, so that I had to fumble it out left-handed and then get it into the padded jaws of the jeweller's vice.

The waldo looks like an old audio turntable, the kind that played disc records, with the vice set up under a transparent dust cover. The arm itself is just over a centimetre long, swinging out on what would've been the tone arm on one of those turntables. But I don't look at that when I've clipped the leads to my stump; I look at the scope, because that's my arm there in black and white, magnification 40×.

I ran a tool check and picked up the laser. It felt a little heavy; so I scaled my weight-sensor input down to a quarter-kilo per gram and got to work. At 40× the side of the program looked like a trailer truck.

It took eight hours to crack: three hours with the waldo and the laser and four dozen taps, two hours on the phone to a contact in Colorado, and three hours to run down a lexicon disc that could translate eight-year-old technical Russian.

Then Cyrillic alphanumerics started reeling down the monitor, twisting themselves into English halfway down. There were a lot of gaps, where the lexicon ran up against specialized military acronyms in the readout I'd bought from my man in Colorado, but it did give me some idea of what I'd bought from the Finn.

I felt like a punk who'd gone out to buy a switchblade and come home with a small neutron bomb.

Screwed again, I thought. *What good's a neutron bomb in a streetfight?* The thing under the dust cover was right out of my league. I didn't even know where to unload it, where to look for a buyer. Someone had, but he was dead, someone with a Porsche watch and a fake Belgian passport, but I'd never tried to move in those circles. The Finn's muggers from the 'burbs had knocked over someone who had some highly arcane connections.

The program in the jeweller's vice was a Russian military ice-breaker, a killer-virus program.

It was dawn when Bobby came in alone. I'd fallen asleep with a bag of takeout sandwiches in my lap.

'You want to eat?' I asked him, not really awake, holding out my sandwiches. I'd been dreaming of the program, of its waves of hungry glitch systems and mimetic subprograms; in the dream it was an animal of some kind, shapeless and flowing.

He brushed the bag aside on his way to the console, punched a function key. The screen lit with the intricate pattern I'd seen there that afternoon. I rubbed sleep from my eyes with my left hand, one thing I can't do with my right. I'd fallen asleep trying to decide whether to tell him about the program. Maybe I should try to sell it alone, keep the money, go somewhere new, ask Rikki to go with me.

'Whose is it?' I asked.

He stood there in a black cotton jump suit, an old leather jacket thrown over his shoulders like a cape. He hadn't shaved for a few days, and his face looked thinner than usual.

'It's Chrome's,' he said.

My arm convulsed, started clicking, fear translated to the myo-electrics through the carbon studs. I spilled the sandwiches; limp sprouts, and bright yellow dairy-produce slices on the unswept wooden floor.

'You're stone crazy,' I said.

'No,' he said, 'you think she rumbled it? No way. We'd be dead already. I locked on to her through a triple-blind rental system in Mombasa and an Algerian comsat. She knew somebody was having a look-see, but she couldn't trace it.'

If Chrome had traced the pass Bobby had made at her ice, we

were good as dead. But he was probably right, or she'd have had me blown away on my way back from New York. 'Why her, Bobby? Just give me one reason. . . .'

Chrome: I'd seen her maybe half a dozen times in the Gentleman Loser. Maybe she was slumming, or checking out the human condition, a condition she didn't exactly aspire to. A sweet little heart-shaped face framing the nastiest pair of eyes you ever saw. She'd looked fourteen for as long as anyone could remember, hyped out of anything like a normal metabolism on some massive program of serums and hormones. She was as ugly a customer as the street ever produced, but she didn't belong to the street anymore. She was one of the Boys, Chrome, a member in good standing of the local Mob subsidiary. Word was, she'd gotten started as a dealer, back when synthetic pituitary hormones were still proscribed. But she hadn't had to move hormones for a long time. Now she owned the House of Blue Lights.

'You're flat-out crazy, Quine. You give me one sane reason for having that stuff on your screen. You ought to dump it, and I mean *now*. . . .'

'Talk in the Loser,' he said, shrugging out of the leather jacket. 'Black Myron and Crow Jane. Jane, she's up on all the sex lines, claims she knows where the money goes. So she's arguing with Myron that Chrome's the controlling interest in the Blue Lights, not just some figurehead for the Boys.'

'"The Boys", Bobby,' I said. 'That's the operative word there. You still capable of seeing that? We don't mess with the Boys, remember? That's why we're still walking around.'

'That's why we're still poor, partner.' He settled back into the swivel chair in front of the console, unzipped his jump suit, and scratched his skinny white chest. 'But maybe not for much longer.'

'I think maybe this partnership just got itself permanently dissolved.'

Then he grinned at me. That grin was truly crazy, feral and focused, and I knew that right then he really didn't give a shit about dying.

'Look,' I said, 'I've got some money left, you know? Why don't you take it and get the tube to Miami, catch a hopper to Montego Bay. You need a rest, man. You've got to get your act together.'

'My act, Jack,' he said, punching something on the keyboard, 'never has been this together before.' The neon prayer rug on the screen shivered and woke as an animation program cut in, ice lines weaving with hypnotic frequency, a living mandala. Bobby kept punching, and the movement slowed; the pattern resolved itself, grew slightly less complex, became an alternation between two distant configurations. A first-class piece of work, and I hadn't thought he was still that good. 'Now,' he said, 'there, see it? Wait. There. There again. And there. Easy to miss. That's it. Cuts in every hour and twenty minutes with a squirt transmission to their comsat. We could live for a year on what she pays them weekly in negative interest.'

'Whose comsat?'

'Zürich. Her bankers. That's her bankbook, Jack. That's where the money goes. Crow Jane was right.'

I stood there. My arm forgot to click.

'So how'd you do in New York, partner? You get anything that'll help me cut ice? We're going to need whatever we can get.'

I kept my eyes on his, forced myself not to look in the direction of the waldo, the jeweller's vice. The Russian program was there, under the dust cover.

Wild cards, luck changers.

'Where's Rikki?' I asked him, crossing to the console, pretending to study the alternating patterns on the screen.

'Friends of hers,' he shrugged, 'kids, they're all into simstim.' He smiled absently. 'I'm going to do it for her, man.'

'I'm going out to think about this, Bobby. You want me to come back, you keep your hands off the board.'

'I'm doing it for her,' he said as the door closed behind me. 'You know I am.'

And down now, down, the program a roller coaster through this fraying maze of shadow walls, grey cathedral spaces between the bright towers. Headlong speed.

Black ice. Don't think about it. Black ice.

Too many stories in the Gentleman Loser; black ice is a part of the mythology. Ice that kills. Illegal, but then aren't we all? Some kind of neural-feedback weapon, and you connect with it only once. Like some hideous Word that eats the mind from the inside out. Like an epileptic spasm that goes on and on until there's nothing left at all . . .

And we're diving for the floor of Chrome's shadow castle.

Trying to brace myself for the sudden stopping of breath, a sickness and final slackening of the nerves. Fear of that cold Word waiting, down there in the dark.

I went out and looked for Rikki, found her in a café with a boy with Sendai eyes, half-healed suture lines radiating from his bruised sockets. She had a glossy brochure spread open on the table, Tally Isham smiling up from a dozen photographs, the Girl with the Zeiss Ikon Eyes.

Her little simstim deck was one of the things I'd stacked under my bench the night before, the one I'd fixed for her the day after I'd first seen her. She spent hours jacked into that unit, the contact band across her forehead like a grey plastic tiara. Tally Isham was her favourite, and with the contact band on, she was gone, off somewhere in the recorded sensorium of simstim's biggest star. Simulated stimuli: the world—all the interesting parts, anyway—as perceived by Tally Isham. Tally raced a black Fokker ground-effect plane across Arizona mesa tops. Tally dived the Truk Island preserves. Tally partied with the superrich on private Greek islands, heartbreaking purity of those tiny white seaports at dawn.

Actually she looked a lot like Tally, same colouring and cheekbones. I thought Rikki's mouth was stronger. More sass. She didn't want to *be* Tally Isham, but she coveted the job. That was her ambition, to be in simstim. Bobby just laughed it off. She talked to me about it, though. 'How'd I look with a pair of these?' she'd ask, holding a full-page headshot, Tally Isham's blue Zeiss Ikons lined up with her own amber-brown. She'd had her corneas done twice, but she still wasn't 20-20; so she wanted Ikons. Brand of the stars. Very expensive.

'You still window-shopping for eyes?' I asked as I sat down.

'Tiger just got some,' she said. She looked tired, I thought.

Tiger was so pleased with his Sendais that he couldn't help smiling, but I doubted whether he'd have smiled otherwise. He had the kind of uniform good looks you get after your seventh trip to the surgical boutique; he'd probably spend the rest of his life looking vaguely like each new season's media front-runner; not too obvious a copy, but nothing too original, either.

'Sendai, right?' I smiled back.

He nodded. I watched as he tried to take me in with his idea of a professional simstim glance. He was pretending that he was recording. I thought he spent too long on my arm. 'They'll be great on peripherals when the muscles heal,' he said, and I saw how carefully he reached for his double espresso. Sendai eyes are notorious for depth-perception defects and warranty hassles, among other things.

'Tiger's leaving for Hollywood tomorrow.'

'Then maybe Chiba City, right?' I smiled at him. He didn't smile back. 'Got an offer, Tiger? Know an agent?'

'Just checking it out,' he said quietly. Then he got up and left. He said a quick goodbye to Rikki, but not to me.

'That kid's optic nerves may start to deteriorate inside six months. You know that, Rikki? Those Sendais are illegal in England, Denmark, lots of places. You can't replace nerves.'

'Hey, Jack, no lectures.' She stole one of my croissants and nibbled at the tip of one of its horns.

'I thought I was your adviser, kid.'

'Yeah. Well, Tiger's not too swift, but everybody knows about Sendais. They're all he can afford. So he's taking a chance. If he gets work, he can replace them.'

'With these?' I tapped the Zeiss Ikon brochure. 'Lot of money, Rikki. You know better than to take a gamble like that.'

She nodded. 'I want Ikons.'

'If you're going up to Bobby's, tell him to sit tight until he hears from me.'

'Sure. It's business?'

'Business,' I said. But it was craziness.

I drank my coffee, and she ate both my croissants. Then I walked her down to Bobby's. I made fifteen calls, each one from a different pay phone.

Business. Bad craziness.

All in all, it took us six weeks to set the burn up, six weeks of Bobby telling me how much he loved her. I worked even harder, trying to get away from that.

Most of it was phone calls. My fifteen initial and very oblique enquiries each seemed to breed fifteen more. I was looking for a certain service Bobby and I both imagined as a requisite part of the world's clandestine economy, but which probably never had more than five customers at a time. It would be one that never advertised.

We were looking for the world's heaviest fence, for a non-aligned money laundry capable of dry-cleaning a megabuck on-line cash transfer and then forgetting about it.

All those calls were a waste, finally, because it was the Finn who put me on to what we needed. I'd gone up to New York to buy a new blackbox rig, because we were going broke paying for all those calls.

I put the problem to him as hypothetically as possible.

'Macao,' he said.

'Macao?'

'The Long Hum family. Stockbrokers.'

He even had the number. You want a fence, ask another fence.

The Long Hum people were so oblique that they made my idea of a subtle approach look like a tactical nuke-out. Bobby had to make two shuttle runs to Hong Kong to get the deal straight. We were running out of capital, and fast. I still don't know why I decided to go along with it in the first place; I was scared of Chrome, and I'd never been all that hot to get rich.

I tried telling myself that it was a good idea to burn the House of Blue Lights because the place was a creep joint, but I just couldn't buy it. I didn't like the Blue Lights, because I'd spent a supremely depressing evening there once, but that was no excuse for going after Chrome. Actually I halfway assumed we were going to die in the attempt. Even with that killer program, the odds weren't exactly in our favour.

Bobby was lost in writing the set of commands we were going to plug into the dead centre of Chrome's computer. That was going to be my job, because Bobby was going to have his hands full trying to keep the Russian program from going straight for the kill. It was too complex for us to rewrite, and so he was going to try to hold it back for the two seconds I needed.

I made a deal with a streetfighter named Miles. He was going to follow Rikki the night of the burn, keep her in sight, and phone me at a certain time. If I wasn't there, or didn't answer in just a certain way, I'd told him to grab her and put her on the first tube out. I gave him an envelope to give her, money and a note.

Bobby really hadn't thought about that, much, how things would go for her if we blew it. He just kept telling me he loved her, where they were going to go together, how they'd spend the money.

'Buy her a pair of Ikons first, man. That's what she wants. She's serious about that simstim scene.'

'Hey,' he said, looking up from the keyboard, 'she won't need to work. We're going to make it, Jack. She's my luck. She won't ever have to work again.'

'Your luck,' I said. I wasn't happy. I couldn't remember when I had been happy. 'You seen your luck around lately?'

He hadn't, but neither had I. We'd both been too busy.

I missed her. Missing her reminded me of my one night in the House of Blue Lights, because I'd gone there out of missing someone else. I'd gotten drunk to begin with, then I'd started hitting Vasopressin inhalers. If your main squeeze has just decided to walk out on you, booze and Vasopressin are the ultimate in masochistic pharmacology; the juice makes you maudlin and the Vasopressin makes you remember, I mean really remember. Clinically they use the stuff to counter senile amnesia, but the street finds its own uses for things. So I'd bought myself an ultra-intense replay of a bad affair; trouble is, you get the bad with the good. Go gunning for transports of animal ecstasy and you get what you said, too, and what she said to that, how she walked away and never looked back.

I don't remember deciding to go to the Blue Lights, or how I got there, hushed corridors and this really tacky decorative waterfall trickling somewhere, or maybe just a hologram of one. I had a lot of money that night; somebody had given Bobby a big roll for opening a three-second window in someone else's ice.

I don't think the crew on the door liked my looks, but I guess my money was okay.

I had more to drink there when I'd done what I went there for. Then I made some crack to the barman about closet necrophiliacs, and that didn't go down too well. Then this very large character insisted on calling me War Hero, which I didn't like. I think I showed him some tricks with the arm, before the lights went out, and I woke up two days later in a basic sleeping module somewhere else. A cheap place, not even room to hang yourself. And I sat there on that narrow foam slab and cried.

Some things are worse than being alone. But the thing they sell in the House of Blue Lights is so popular that it's almost legal.

At the heart of darkness, the still centre, the glitch systems shred the dark with whirlwinds of light, translucent razors spinning away from us; we hang in the centre of a silent slow-motion explosion, ice fragments falling away forever, and Bobby's voice comes in across light-years of electronic void illusion—

'Burn the bitch down. I can't hold the thing back—'

The Russian program, rising through towers of data, blotting out the playroom colours. And I plug Bobby's homemade command package into the centre of Chrome's cold heart. The squirt transmission cuts in, a pulse of condensed information that shoots straight up, past the thickening tower of darkness, the Russian program, while Bobby struggles to control that crucial second. An unformed arm of shadow twitches from the towering dark, too late.

We've done it.

The matrix folds itself around me like an origami trick.

And the loft smells of sweat and burning circuitry.

I thought I heard Chrome scream, a raw metal sound, but I couldn't have.

Bobby was laughing, tears in his eyes. The elapsed-time figure in the corner of the monitor read 07:24:05. The burn had taken a little under eight minutes.

And I saw that the Russian program had melted in its slot.

We'd given the bulk of Chrome's Zürich account to a dozen world charities. There was too much there to move, and we knew we had to break her, burn her straight down, or she might come after us. We took less than ten per cent for ourselves and shot it through the Long Hum set-up in Macao. They took sixty per cent of that for themselves and kicked what was left back to us through the most convoluted sector of the Hong Kong exchange. It took an hour before our money started to reach the two accounts we'd opened in Zürich.

I watched zeros pile up behind a meaningless figure on the monitor. I was rich.

Then the phone rang. It was Miles. I almost blew the code phrase.

'Hey, Jack, man, I dunno—what's it all about, with this girl of yours? Kinda funny thing here . . .'

'What? Tell me.'

'I been on her, like you said, tight but out of sight. She goes to the Loser, hangs out, then she gets a tube. Goes to the House of Blue Lights—'

'She what?'

'Side door. *Employees* only. No way I could get past their security.'

'Is she there now?'

'No, man, I just lost her. It's insane down here, like the Blue Lights just shut down, looks like for good, seven kinds of alarms going off, everybody running, the heat out in riot gear. . . . Now there's all this stuff going on, insurance guys, real-estate types, vans with municipal plates. . . .'

'Miles, where'd she go?'

'Lost her, Jack.'

'Look, Miles, you keep the money in the envelope, right?'

'You serious? Hey, I'm real sorry. I—'

I hung up.

'Wait'll we tell her,' Bobby was saying, rubbing a towel across his bare chest.

'You tell her yourself, cowboy. I'm going for a walk.'

So I went out into the night and the neon and let the crowd pull me along, walking blind, willing myself to be just a segment of that mass organism, just one more drifting chip of consciousness under the geodesics. I didn't think, just put one foot in front of another, but after a while I did think, and it all made sense. She'd needed the money.

I thought about Chrome, too. That we'd killed her, murdered her, as surely as if we'd slit her throat. The night that carried me along through the malls and plazas would be hunting her now, and she had nowhere to go. How many enemies would she have in this crowd alone? How many would move, now they weren't held back by fear of her money? We'd taken her for everything she had. She was back on the street again. I doubted she'd live till dawn.

Finally I remembered the café, the one where I'd met Tiger.

Her sunglasses told the whole story, huge black shades with a telltale smudge of fleshtone paintstick in the corner of one lens. 'Hi, Rikki,' I said, and I was ready when she took them off.

Blue. Tally Isham blue. The clear trademark blue they're famous for, ZEISS IKON ringing each iris in tiny capitals, the letters suspended there like flecks of gold.

'They're beautiful,' I said. Paintstick covered the bruising. No scars with work that good. 'You made some money.'

'Yeah, I did.' Then she shivered. 'But I won't make any more, not that way.'

'I think that place is out of business.'

'Oh.' Nothing moved in her face then. The new blue eyes were still and very deep.

'It doesn't matter. Bobby's waiting for you. We just pulled down a big score.'

'No. I've got to go. I guess he won't understand, but I've got to go.'

I nodded, watching the arm swing up to take her hand; it didn't seem to be part of me at all, but she held on to it like it was.

'I've got a one-way ticket to Hollywood. Tiger knows some people I can stay with. Maybe I'll even get to Chiba City.'

She was right about Bobby. I went back with her. He didn't understand. But she'd already served her purpose, for Bobby, and I wanted to tell her not to hurt for him, because I could see that she did. He wouldn't even come out into the hallway after she had packed her bags. I put the bags down and kissed her and messed up the paintstick, and something came up inside me the way the killer program had risen above Chrome's data. A sudden stopping of the breath, in a place where no word is. But she had a plane to catch.

Bobby was slumped in the swivel chair in front of his monitor, looking at his string of zeros. He had his shades on, and I knew he'd be in the Gentleman Loser by nightfall, checking out the weather, anxious for a sign, someone to tell him what his new life would be like. I couldn't see it being very different. More comfortable, but he'd always be waiting for that next card to fall.

I tried not to imagine her in the House of Blue Lights, working three-hour shifts in an approximation of REM sleep, while her body and a bundle of conditioned reflexes took care of business. The customers never got to complain that she was faking it, because those were real orgasms. But she felt them, if she felt them at all, as faint silver flares somewhere out on the edge of sleep. Yeah, it's so popular, it's almost legal. The customers are torn between needing someone and wanting to be alone at the same time, which has probably always been the name of that particular game, even before we had the neuroelectronics to enable them to have it both ways.

I picked up the phone and punched the number for her airline. I gave them her real name, her flight number. 'She's changing that,' I said, 'to Chiba City. That's right. Japan.' I thumbed my credit card into the slot and punched my ID code. 'First class.' Distant hum as they scanned my credit records. 'Make that a return ticket.'

But I guess she cashed the return fare, or else she didn't need it, because she hasn't come back. And sometimes late at night I'll pass a window with posters of simstim stars, all those beautiful, identical eyes staring back at me out of faces that are nearly as identical, and sometimes the eyes are hers, but none of the faces are, none of them ever are, and I see her far out on the edge of all this sprawl of night and cities, and then she waves goodbye.

SILICON MUSE

HILBERT SCHENCK

The January afternoon was dark and bitter cold with only a few students hurrying here and there, black hunched figures leaning against the freezing wind. The swirling snow was getting steadily thicker. Already the mostly deserted campus was emptying further, as the university staff scurried off to their parking lots so as to get on the roads ahead of any skids or blockages on the hills surrounding the campus valley.

Professor Frank Gower, chairman of the Department of English Literature and also of the Graduate Faculty Grants Committee, stamped the snow off his heavy boots at the side entrance to the sprawling, four-storey, concrete-block Computer Science building, then clapped his mittens together several times and stepped gratefully into the warmer hallway. He was a thin, almost gaunt man of medium height, forty-eight years old; and though he walked briskly and spoke in a sharp, intent voice, he felt and dreaded the cold more each year in this bleak, wind-swept New England valley where the dampness from the river combined with the blustery north-westerlies to penetrate even the warmest and tightest garments.

His narrow face was pinched but his lips were set in determination as he walked quickly down the north stairs of the building and pushed open a heavy door labelled, 'Main Terminal Room Keep Door Shut.'

Inside all was warmth and light. The large room was windowless, cubical, with a high ceiling sloping downward to the back. The white walls were blank except for air-conditioning grills at floor and ceiling level, and the whole place was evenly lit by high fluorescent fixtures that flooded every cranny with a cold, white light. The sprawling input–output consoles of the university's latest and largest computing system formed a great letter 'C' around a group of five contour chairs in the centre. There were three different keyboards, tape, disk, and card-reading devices, at least a dozen graphic and TV readout systems, and four printers of various sorts and sizes interspersed with the keyboards. Above this neat, if confusing, display of computing hardware was a complex spotlight board that individually illuminated whatever combination of machines was activated. As he shrugged off his coat, Professor Gower saw that only the central input keyboard was now so lit and that in front of it sat Dr Charles Perry, an assistant professor in his department. The twenty-seven-year-old Perry was as thin as his chairman, but where Gower's narrow hard face usually seemed sharp and alert, Perry's expression was more diffuse, often almost bewildered. He had a small chin and a rather slack mouth. His thin blond moustache was scraggly and only visible under bright lights.

Dr Perry got to his feet, brushed back his lank hair, and reached out to shake Dr Gower's hand. 'You're early, Frank,' he said in a mild voice.

Dr Gower sat down in a chair next to Perry and gave a terse nod. 'I wanted to bring you the bad news before the rest of them show up. The committee voted two to one yesterday to include our resident creative genius, Robert Roylance Roberts, specifically to help judge your project. He's an ex officio member so he can't vote, but he can sure talk and write opinions.'

Professor Perry's already vague expression became even more confused. 'Whaa . . . ? But Triple-R will be drunk by now, Frank!' he said. 'Also, he hates this project worse than he hates that *Times* guy who cut up his last poetry collection. Jesus, what the hell is happening . . . ?'

Gower placed a firm and cautionary hand on his younger colleague's arm. 'Right on both counts, but the committee took Roberts to lunch at the faculty club and I think we held him to four whiskeys—unless he got there earlier than usual. He wasn't too bad when I left them, and Millie was ordering them a second cup of coffee.'

The young man stared at the floor in dismay. 'Millicent Hull hates this idea too. That's for certain! Do you think I have a chance, Frank?'

The older man rubbed his cold hands briskly together in the warm room, then shrugged. 'You know how tough this Snodgrass business has gotten, Charlie. The federal grants are cut to hell and the state is broke. Old Snodgrass may have been a pirate, but he left the university millions to pay for these fellowships. The way the market and the interest rates have gone, the damn grants are now practically at the Nobel dollar level—and since they're restricted to untenured assistant professors, just about everyone in that group cranks out a proposal twice a year.'

'But I was a runner-up last year, Frank,' said Dr. Perry in a thin and plaintive voice. 'I got Snodgrass seed money. Doesn't that mean anything?'

The chairman's voice was icy and quiet. 'You know very well what that means. It means you've got to show plenty more than the first-shot proposals do. Furthermore, there's only four of these little treasure troves, two in January and two in September. And for this round . . .'

'The Chinaman in Biology is certain of one,' finished Dr Perry in a firmer and very bitter voice.

'Correct,' said the older man. 'The Chinaman has perhaps found a supposed cure for a suspected cancer. Health and Human Services is willing to double-match the Snodgrass money if we make the award. The Snodgrass Foundation lawyers agreed, as you know from the fuss it caused, in this single case to waive the will's provision that no Snodgrass Fellowship be based on additional funding or outside evaluations. The committee has two letters in support of the Chinaman from an assistant secretary of HHS.'

The chairman shook his head and his expression was sombre. 'Nobody votes for cancer, Charlie,' he said simply. 'It has no constituency.'

'So I'm in the hopper with thirty-seven other research proposals for one gold medal and I've got to start out by being better than most, or all, of them since I got that pittance last year. Is that it? I don't have a prayer!' said Perry. 'What about the robot people at the engineering school?'

Dr Gower shrugged again. 'We've cut them down to about four, actually. Half the things are written so quickly they're mostly unintelligible, and in most cases the Snodgrass requirement of total originality was totally lacking. As to the robot engineers, let me say in strictest confidence that yesterday their stair-climbing wheelchair got the wrong command from the control computer, flipped over backwards several steps before the top, and broke the plaster head of the dummy they had strapped to the thing into about fifty pieces. The chair suffered even worse damage.' Professor Gower smiled for the first time since he had come into the room. 'Back to the old drawing board with that gadget, I guess.'

'So maybe I do have hope?' muttered the young man, though his tone showed little enthusiasm.

'Definitely, Charlie, but you'd have more hope if you'd sent along a sample of the sort of things you were getting with the proposal. Millie complained about that at lunch, and our famous poet suggested the stuff was probably so awful you didn't dare include it.'

Dr Perry threw his palms out and up in dismay. 'But I *discussed* that in the proposal, Frank,' he almost whimpered. 'I explained that if the fiction I included was bad they would immediately judge the idea a failure, while if the story seemed good they would just assume I wrote it myself. I mean, there's just no real substitute for seeing the computer write the stuff before your eyes.'

Gower shrugged once again and his expression seemed almost uninterested. 'Proposals aren't read all that carefully, Charlie. The point is, you're going to sink or swim on the basis of what this thing . . .' he gestured at the computing hardware spread around them, 'produces in this next hour. If it outdoes our own Robert Roberts with even more obscure and impenetrable stuff, you've—we've—lost the Snodgrass money.'

'And then I don't have a prayer for tenure—right?' said the young man bitterly. 'But the computer's getting better and better, Frank. I've got five stories out of it now, and each one is better than the last.'

'Let's hope,' said the expressionless chairman, looking around as the door opened and two heavily bundled people stepped in. The leading figure was Dr Millicent Hull, a full professor of philosophy in her mid-forties, grants committee member, and president of the faculty senate. She shucked her heavy coat quickly and strode with vigour and assurance to a seat on the other side of Dr Perry, pausing to take his soft and diffident hand in her own firm grip. Professor Hull, though a large and imposing woman with an iron-grey bun of hair on top of her big head, had retained an unlikely prettiness of facial expression that seemed to belie her otherwise sturdy and businesslike character. Her eyes were large and wide and her mouth full, though this was now turned sourly downward as she surveyed the expensive, high-tech interior of the Computing Centre's latest acquisition.

'Okay, Charlie,' she said in a brisk voice, 'how soon until you start Total Access with this toy?'

The young man gave her back a faint smile. 'At two-thirty. Dr Hull,' he said. 'About twenty minutes.'

'Where's Roberts?' asked Frank Gower.

The second arrival was old Dr Melvin Fitzhugh, a professor of physics and one of only three named professors in the entire university. Years ago, Fitzhugh had pioneered a method of pottery dating involving the phenomenon of thermoluminescence; and though the method remained of questionable accuracy, Fitzhugh's lab managed to stay in the newspapers with its dating of various archaeological sites throughout the world. A small, pudgy man with thin white hair, Dr Fitzhugh would retire in a year, and his eyes were already drooping over the lack of his customary afternoon nap.

'He's on the way, Frank,' said the old physicist. 'Had to go to the johnnie, he said.'

'One more drink!' said Millicent Hull in a very hard tone. 'Let's get started on this, Charlie. It's snowing.'

The young man gulped and nodded, his protuberant Adam's apple shuttling rapidly up and down. 'Okay,' he responded. 'Well, as I said in the proposal, this fiction-writing program requires the Total Access capability. I mean, it can only be used when the entire main-frame is dedicated to it for some fixed length of time. Since that costs a bomb and isn't possible very often, I've only managed to get five complete fictions out of the program to date.' He paused to indicate a folder lying on the desk in front of him.

'Do we ever get to see those five—uh—fictions?' said Dr Hull in a suspicious voice. 'And why do you call them *fictions* instead of *stories*, Charlie?' Her voice had become sharper and more impatient.

'Now, Millie,' said Frank Gower calmly, 'we call them fictions for the same reason that you call the study of learning epistemology; so the slobs won't know what in hell we're talking about.'

'I've made copies of the five stories for the committee,' said Dr Perry. 'But I really thought it would be better if you saw the thing actually write one before you read these.' His voice was soft and plaintive, and Dr Hull gave him a sudden reassuring smile.

'Look,' she said, swivelling her head to include them all. 'I'm not against this computer or what you're doing with it. Certainly if the computer can write a story that humans will read, enjoy, and assume another human wrote—well, that might be a big deal and not just in English Lit. But, damn it, I think they've got to be real narratives, real stories, and not just some weird, arty string of incomprehensible junk. So, what's the best one of those?' and she indicated the folder.

Dr Perry gulped again and quickly opened it. 'The best story, at least as far as I'm concerned, was this one it called "Hour Test". It starts with a quite explicit love scene at the library back entrance and ends with the girl having a total breakdown in a sociology hour test because she's pregnant and the boy's flunked out. It's pretty fevered and maybe a little overwritten but the ending is nice. The machine intercuts the girl's fragmenting thoughts with typically inhuman sociology jargon from the test questions. It's not James Joyce, but it's probably publishable.'

Dr Hull's large, clear eyes had grown wider at this and her face was set in lines of doubt. 'How could a computer write an explicit love scene, Charlie, unless it just copied it from some book you stuck into its memory?'

Dr Perry took a deep breath and plunged ahead. 'Well, Dr Hull, that all comes out of the use of TA—you know, Total Access. The system originally was brought in here as a kind of monitor of all university functions and operations, you remember? TA was supposed to keep track of everything: every memo, every academic statistic, every business-office transaction, details of grants, stuff off word processors, the whole bit. The idea was that with TA the computer could make predictions and suggestions about the entire range of university operations.'

Millicent Hull shook her head. 'Charlie, that may all be true, but if there is one single thing this place does not involve itself with in any sense, it is love, explicit or otherwise.'

The young man nodded cheerfully. 'You'd think so, but after those rapes around the library last year, they installed hidden mikes to pick up screams in the area, sent the output through the speech-recognition section, and then into the main frame. When I ran the program the last time, the only TA time I could get was at two in the morning. When the machine started to compose, it had probably been listening to a couple of kids in that grove of trees just back of the library. The first part of the story is almost entirely conversation but it's still quite steamy.'

'Then,' said Dr Fitzhugh, somewhat roused from his sleepy state, 'it sounds like the program is pretty well restricted to the university, where it has, let's say, some contacts?'

'At the moment, that's true,' said Dr Perry, 'but if TA goes nationwide, which means involving this computer with masses of library materials and God knows what other functions all over, I think its repertoire will be much broader.'

'No computer that writes sexy stories can be all bad,' came a slurred, boisterous voice behind them, and they all turned to see a huge, ruddy-faced man attempting to unwind a thick, ten-foot-long scarf from around his neck. Since half the scarf was stuffed down his back under his coat, it was obvious that he would never get it off without help. Frank Gower immediately rose and went to remove the poet's vast tweed sport coat, thus revealing a vaster belly partly covered by a ragged red and black hunting shirt, too shrunken to stay tucked in.

Robert Roberts picked his way past some imaginary obstacles and dropped with a great sigh of relief into the empty chair. 'Cold out there, Millie,' he boomed, and without pausing turned to Dr Perry, 'and how the hell do we know that the cute little goodies this thing farts out weren't put there yesterday by you, huh?' He said it all in a rush, having been repeating it to himself during his shambling walk from the Faculty Club.

The poet's drunken yet total hostility broke like surf over the young man. He gulped several times, then finally spoke out. 'Because you people are going to give it the topic . . .'

'Magic tricks . . . give it the topic . . . bullshit,' the poet muttered on to himself, momentarily overcome by the heat of the room.

'Professor Roberts,' said Dr Hull sternly, 'I think it might be better if you made your complaints and accusations *after* the demonstration. Otherwise, you prejudice your position as a creative consultant. Fairness demands—'

'It's not a fair world, Millie,' slurred the poet, slowly adjusting to the temperature change. 'Okay, how does the magic work, Professor?' he said with a snarl at Dr Perry.

'What sort of cues did you give the machine to compose the story about the girl and her breakdown, Charlie?' suggested Dr Hull in a warm and slightly guilty tone, for she was mainly responsible for the poet's disturbing presence.

Dr Perry gestured at the open folder. 'The story before that one was about two old janitors who both wanted to transfer to the same building where they knew they could sleep the day away. It was okay but I thought the machine had problems differentiating the two old men so as to sharpen up the conflict. So I wrote to it: "Compose a story concerning a male and a female college student and integrate their classroom and private lives. The story should be serious and contemporary and the overall effect should be sobering as regards university life."'

The poet gave a part belch, part laugh and rubbed his vein-mapped, sagging cheek, 'He practically wrote the story for the thing, sounds like to me, Millie. . . .' and his voice trailed off as his eyes drooped shut.

'We have only ten minutes,' said Frank Gower in an urgent voice. 'I think the committee should decide now on how a topic can be fairly selected to test the program.'

The poet's bloodshot eyes snapped open and his voice was firmer. 'I move the following method,' he said. 'I will pick a member of the committee to select the topic—namely, Dr Fitzhugh. You, Millie, will tell him how or from where to find the topic. And you Frank,' the poet turned narrowed eyes on the chairman of his department, 'since you have a certain special interest in the outcome of this demonstration, will accept or reject the first suggestion. Does that sound fair, Professor?' and the poet now turned his large head towards the young man.

'Sure,' said Dr Perry hastily. 'Anything that's a short paragraph in length. That sounds fine.'

The others also agreed, and the poet rubbed his large, puffy nose. 'Well, Millie?' he said softly.

Dr Hull looked over at Dr Fitzhugh and pursed her lips in thought. 'Fitz, let's see what it can do with something scientific. Open that text you carried in and find something in the stuff you were preparing this morning, okay?'

Old Dr Fitzhugh, usually the least-consulted member of the Grants Committee, beamed at them and opened his thick textbook. 'Very well,' he said. 'We'll be doing reflective and refractive optics when they come back. Let me see . . . ah, how about this where the authors discuss reflection in facing mirrors. Good literary stuff, right?' and he sent a smile at Frank Gower, who grimly nodded back.

The young man swivelled his chair around. 'Okay, read it slowly and I'll type it in. We're not on TA yet, but my program is on standby and ready for input.'

'"A highly reflecting smooth surface is called a *mirror*,"' read Dr Fitzhugh in a thin, clear voice. '"When two mirrors are set to face each other directly, two visual phenomena are evident: First, the images of an object placed between the mirrors grow smaller and smaller as they are reflected and re-reflected between the two mirror planes. Second, the smaller images also grow darker. The size decrease can be explained by the laws of *geometrical optics*, which govern . . ."'

'Enough, enough, Fitz,' said Dr Hull impatiently. 'Give the thing a break, for heaven's sake.'

Dr Perry looked up from the keyboard. 'Then can we end it with the sentence, "Second, the smaller images also grow darker"?' he asked them.

The three committee members agreed immediately, while the poet slouched lower in his chair muttering, 'Too easy. Too easy,' poking out a large lower lip to show his continued annoyance.

Dr Perry turned to the next keyboard at his right and began entering instructions. ENTER FICTION WRITING PROGRAM. INSTRUCTIONS ARE: COMPOSE ORIGINAL STORY BASED ON INPUT QUOTE 34X/2000. QUERY; DO YOU UNDERSTAND ALL WORDS?

The machine immediately responded with ALL WORDS UNDERSTOOD. END.

Dr Perry then wrote, QUERY: DO YOU UNDERSTAND CONTEXT OF WORDS?

CONTEXT UNDERSTOOD QUOTE IS FROM 'UNIVERSITY PHYSICS'. P. J. FRANK AND L. R. WHITTINGTON, MCGRAW-HILL NEW YORK, 1981, P. 654. FICTIONAL COMPOSITION BASED ON QUOTE WILL COMMENCE WHEN TA PROVIDED. GOOD LUCK CHARLIE. END.

The room became very silent, and the poet sat up a bit straighter. 'It wouldn't be impossible to have somebody, or maybe somebodies, out there now starting feverishly to write a passable work based on that passage,' he said and looked around with a dogged and suspicious air.

Dr Hull frowned at him angrily. 'Again I must insist that you stop these charges of fraud, Robert, until the end of this demonstration.' She shifted her eyes to Dr Perry and they were filled with doubt. 'You seem to be quite *chummy* with it, Charlie. Does it actually understand what this story, personally, represents to you?'

Dr Perry parted his palms with a diffident gesture. 'Sure. It knows everything that's going on at the school. I mean, that's the whole point of using TA in a fiction-writing mode.'

At that moment the daisy-wheel printer bar gave a single clack: ON T.A. 1430:00 COMPOSITION REF 34X/2000 STARTED. STAND BY. END.

The young man gave them a hopeful smile. 'It usually takes it a couple of minutes to get organized . . .'

But a light went on immediately over the nearest word processor and its printer now began to strike steadily but at a slow enough speed to allow careful reading.

Mirrored Lives

The January afternoon was dark and bitter cold with only a few students hurrying by, hunched figures leaning against the wind. Professor Hank Powers, Chairman of Modern English and also of the University Grants Committee, stamped off some snow, then banged open the heavy door of the main terminal room and confronted his younger colleague.

'You dummy!' he said in a harsh voice. 'Why didn't you send around some of the garbage that so-called thinking machine is cranking out along with your proposal? They were screaming at lunch about it! Also, our Pulitzer-Prize-Prick is now on the Grants Committee, belching and bitching when he can take the shot glass away from his mouth.'

Dr Powers seemed to exude a bitter coldness into the room as he pulled off his coat and angrily dropped into a foam-lined seat.

Young Assistant Professor Henry Berry was so dismayed and terrified by this entrance and outburst that he simply sat shivering in front of the main terminal input, unable to say a word.

An impatient Professor Powers jabbed a sharp finger to within an inch of Berry's nose. 'If you expect to get tenure, Henry,' he said in an icy voice, 'that thing had better write a masterpiece today. You hear me?' The older man closed his left fist in impotent rage. 'They took our travel money, Henry, all of it, those *bastards* in administration! Three men are going to Frisco to form a complete session at the spring MLA meeting on Literary Weapons against Communism, and how do they get there? On magic carpets? If we get your Greenways Fellowship, the overhead will send a whole cheering section, not to mention the graduate students we can hang on to with your Greenway assistantships. You're the department's last hope, Henry!'

And it surely seemed a forlorn hope to the acerbic Dr Powers, as he stared with mingled contempt and dismay at the young man's undershot chin trembling and his hands twisting as he tried to respond. 'Hank, I think it's going to be okay,' said Dr Berry finally, 'but what about the Bengali?' His weak voice was almost a whisper.

'The Bengali has one of the two grants sewed up,' said Powers in a harsh snarl. 'Once the Defence Department heard how well his little five-way interrogation system went with the Chicanos along the Texas border, they decided it should be beefed up for our little brown Commie brothers in Central America.' Powers's thin face took on an almost wolf-like grin. 'They say it leaves no marks but you don't do much fighting afterwards.'

'The university administration denied that, Hank,' whimpered Dr Berry, but his chairman just snorted.

'Yeah, that bunch would deny the Holocaust while you were raking the bones out of the ovens. At least the competition from the robot walker is over for this time. That $3.45-an-hour paraplegic veteran they had demonstrating the robot legs pushed the wrong button and flipped over. I hope they got him to sign a good release because he broke his arm and collar bone.'

The older man gave a bark-like laugh. 'How would you like to be strapped legless into that thing and sent off to do the errands, eh? It's a final solution to the Vietnam veteran. That'll teach those Red-loving soreheads to bitch about Agent Orange!'

At that moment two more heavily bundled individuals stumped noisily in the door. The leading figure was Dr Pamela Hill, a full professor of mathematical logic and chief of the Faculty Union. Her cruel, clear, and calculating eyes took in the lavish spread of the new computing facilities and her fleshy lips twisted in contempt and envy at the no-holds expense of the set-up.

Behind her pressed small, ancient Professor Marvin Fitzroy, a wealthy, almost retired physical chemist and discoverer years before of a deadly industrial compound now banned by the government and responsible for the abandonment of over ten thousand homes at the site of the infamous Glover Canal toxic spills.

'So, Hank,' said Dr Hill harshly to the English chairman, 'already here prepping your man, huh? I thought we agreed not to pass the committee stuff around to our own people until the January Greenway awards are made?'

'That, Pamela, was the understanding before you got that lush Howard Howard as an ex officio member of the committee to screw Henry here and save the Greenway money for your own man. You knew that drunken slob hates computers and all they stand for! So take your little agreements and shove them, my dear!' he concluded in a sharp and acid tone.

Stubby, sleepy, pig-faced Dr Fitzroy was jolted wide awake by this harsh exchange and now gave a snide and sarcastic laugh. 'You two must be living in a dream world,' he gritted in a cracked, mean voice. 'The day that anyone in mathematics gets a Greenway Fellowship is when pigs can fly. Face it, Pamela: none of your assistant professors can even lecture in English yet—as the frosh math grades clearly show!'

'At least we answer our department phone,' snarled back Pamela Hill. 'Your building is usually shut and empty by two in the afternoon. Where do you chemists all go, Merve—the poison gas lab at the Experiment Station, some government germ warfare team?'

'Listen to that phony liberal-peace crap,' spat Dr Fitzroy. 'Who was it just got a half million from NSA for public key cryptography, I wonder. Some Chinks, Sikhs, and Iranians in Math, that's who. Furthermore, your Greenway candidate's research into large prime numbers is all part of that Mickey Mouse code crap!'

Dr Hill's aging face contorted in anger, but she said nothing and turned instead to bare her large teeth at young and shivering Dr Berry. 'Has your pet Space Invader written anything at all, Henry?' she asked sarcastically. 'Your whole proposal was filled with computing software baloney but it said little about the results.'

Dr Berry took several deep breaths as he tried in vain to stop trembling. 'Y-y-yes ma'am,' he stuttered. 'Five stories. I've got them right here,' and he pointed at a folder. 'The best one is a student love story with quite a sad ending.'

'Dick and Jane discover they're dissecting Spot in Biology 102?' suggested the older woman in a sneering tone.

'It's more adult than that,' said Dr Berry in a defensive whine. 'In fact, they're making love when the story opens.'

'Hooray for love!' came a new, thick, barely intelligible voice from the back of the terminal room and they all turned to see the university's resident creative writer, Howard Howard Howard, lurch through the door and fall heavily on the astroturf carpet.

'Go help the drunken bum,' muttered Dr Hill to Hank Powers. Indeed, Professor Howard was totally unable to get up by himself, having fallen three times on the way from the faculty bar-room and cut his red-veined right cheek on some ice. Powers and Fitzroy together finally managed to hoist the writer on to his feet again, then removed his ripped sport coat, wiped his face, and got him settled in the remaining contour chair, from which he promptly pitched back on to the floor.

'Why don't these snazzy chairs have safety belts, Henry?' snarled Dr Hill, now in a total rage. 'Pull yourself together, Howard. This is disgusting!'

'Writing fiction with a computer is more disgusting,' slurred out the writer, managing to get himself back into his chair without help, then turning to push his fat, ugly, bright-red face close to Dr Berry's thin, white one. 'You insect! Who ever gave you the right to try and put me out of work with this silicon freak show?' He clenched his fists. 'Will it stop me from popping you one in the choppers, Professor?'

'Oh, *shut up*, Howard!' said the woman. 'Do you want Henry grieving to the Greenway Trustees about collusion and prejudice? How do we get the machine started, Henry?' she said in a hard, impatient voice.

'You . . . you can j-j-just decide on a paragraph-length topic,' answered the terrified young man. 'Anything you want.'

The writer, feeling himself passing out from the heat of the room, muttered woozily at the others. 'You give it something, Merve,' he mumbled at the chemist, 'something scientific. That'll screw the thing good. You tell him what, Pamela . . .' the ruined head fell back, its mouth agape, and the writer began to snore loudly.

Dr Hill gestured at a paper-bound book in the chemist's left hand. 'Pick something from that text,' she suggested at once. 'Let's get this stupid demonstration over with. It's snowing!'

The old chemist shrugged, then flipped open a thick, government document spangled with secrecy and security notices in bright red ink. 'From my ROTC course on nuclear blast effects. Let's see it do anything with this . . .' and he began reading. ' "When a weapon having a yield of less than one hundred kilotons is detonated at its tangent altitude, its effects can be multiplied manyfold by the proper triggering of a second, higher weapon at the so-called reflection height. If the phasing is correct, the upper-weapon fireball will serve as a cap over the lower explosion and form, with the ground plane, a reflecting and re-reflecting containment system. Overpressures of from five to ten times normal can be achieved, thereby giving prompt damage equivalent to that inflicted by a ten- to fifty-megaton weapon. . . ." '

Dr Berry was typing desperately at the machine console, trying to keep up. 'Hold on a sec,' he said plaintively. 'Could you start with "overpressures" again, sir?'

Pamela Hill gave them all a toothy, shark-like grin and shook her head. 'You've given it enough, Merv. Maybe the thing will write us a shot of superrealism; Moscow after we pop it into that pressure cooker you described. That's a story that should get your class salivating! Start the thing,' she gritted. 'Let's get this done!'

Pale Dr Berry, his slack mouth and chin trembling still, began to type. TOPIC INPUT COMPLETE. BEGIN COMPOSITION NOW, and the computer's word processor immediately began to hiss and click.

Reflected Lives

The January afternoon was dark and chill. The black, sullen figures of a few students fought the bitter wind as they hurried to escape its frozen blast. Professor Grant Tower, chairman of Literature and also of the Handout Committee, slammed the door behind him to shut out the cold and spat a savage, 'You stupid idiot!' at Dr William Ferry, his thin, trembling, chinless colleague who sat in front of the sprawling computer terminal. For weeks Tower had been searching for the money to pay for his week-long trip to the California MLA meeting on nineteenth-century erotica, both for himself and his 'secretary', Miss Gloria Lublin, and now this weak, trembling simp in front of him was his final hope for funding the trip.

Dr Tower imagined himself plunging his thin, strong fingers down between Gloria's gigantic, butter-soft thighs, the motel bedroom dim and the huge woman twisting and moaning as he worked his fierce and urgent way with her.

Dr Ferry seemed to shrink to a mere shadow in his foam chair as the older chaiman pointed a needle-sharp finger at his head. 'We're doomed, you fool!' he almost shouted. 'That lecherous, lushed-out loafer, our resident pornography writer, Jay J. Jay, has joined the committee and he's dumping all over your project. Why in hell didn't you include that sex story in your proposal, the one you claimed this so-called fiction-writing program ejaculated?'

The young man became even more shrunken and shadowy. 'It was just too filthy, Grant. I didn't think . . .'

The older man gave a coarse and contemptuous laugh. 'Too filthy for Hilary Mull? Why if I had a dollar for every cock that old hooker has taken up between her

PAUSE COMMAND COMPUTATION SUSPENDED. DO YOU WISH A RESTART?

The four committee members had been intently leaning forward, closely following this output and now they all turned to stare at Dr Perry whose left index finger was still firmly on the PAUSE button. His face was a mask of grief and disappointment and he was rapidly blinking at them. 'I'm sorry about this. I really never know what it's going to do. I had no idea it would write something like this . . .'

But Millicent Hull was far from angry and leaned to pat Dr Perry's arm. 'Nobody is taking it personally, Charlie,' she said with an impatient grin. 'And I can't wait to see what it's going to do with me in *this* section.'

Even the poet now seemed more interested than hostile and he pinched his red nose with a thoughtful gesture. 'It was listening to us, when we came in here, wasn't it?' he said slowly.

Dr Perry gulped and nodded. 'Sure. The university decided against spending the hundred-thou that a talk-back module would cost, but you *must* have the speech-recognition capability for TA. The fiction program must have decided to use this whole Snodgrass grant stuff and my proposal effort as a basis for the story.'

Wrinkled old Dr Fitzhugh, though a gentle and decent man,

had been secretly rather intrigued by his first fictional *alter ego;* a thoroughly nasty and forceful poisoner of the world and a teacher of the most terrible secrets science could offer. But he frowned in puzzlement. 'Well, it's certainly interesting, especially that bit about fat Gloria, but—but what is it actually *doing*?' he said in a quizzical voice.

Frank Gower's eyes were thin but he too was smiling. 'It's doing what you told it to do with that optics quote, Fitz,' said Gower in a slow voice. 'Smaller and darker were the images you set it, and each of these nested stories and their characters are apparently going to get smaller and darker.'

The poet musingly shook his head, 'I would say that its first cut, where it turns us mostly into Cold War maniacs, is a darker vision than this one coming up, where we seem now to be sex crazies.'

Dr Gower shrugged. 'It depends on how you interpret the idea of "darkness" in the story. I think the machine sees increasing darkness in these characterizations as a kind of increasing inwardness, a digging out of more and more repressed and hidden fantasies.'

'Oh come on, you two,' said Millicent Hull. We've only got twelve minutes more of TA. Let the thing do its stuff. Then you can get into all that litcrit baloney. Crank it up, Charlie. Let's go!'

Dr Perry now smiled in relief and quickly typed, RESTART. CONTINUE REF 34×/2000 FICTION.

legs, I could retire tomorrow.' The older man shook his fist at Dr Ferry. 'We need that Greenbill money, Willie. If you expect to keep pumping that little graduate bitch, Francine Thrust, in the mail room, your program had better give us a *Fanny Hill*!'

The young man spluttered in speechless terror and embarrassment while Tower, who had spent two nights the previous week with Francine Thrust, in return for an A on her paper on seventeenth-century poetics, wondered how this wimp could possibly cope with wiry and vigorous Francine who needed plenty of banging to come. Professor Tower considered a new idea, taking Francine to California with huge Gloria, the three of them on a queen-size bed variously and gloriously busy! The older man reached to steady Dr Ferry. 'Relax, Willie, relax. We need this one and we're going to win it. Here they come.'

A moment later, two new figures pulled open the door and stomped in while brushing off snow and pulling off their coats. Hilary Mull, professor of ethics and member of the Handout Committee, was a large, handsome woman with deep, pendulous breasts barely cotained under a tight sweater by a too-thin bra. Soft and ample buttocks rippled under her too-short, too-tight plaid skirt as she walked towards her seat. Her shorter companion, the sly, old biochemist, Dr Hugh Fitzjohn, suddenly crammed his hand between those tempting flanks, in through a slit at the side of the skirt.

Professor Mull put him off with a coarse laugh, a clenched fist, and a snarl of, 'Don't start something you can't finish, Buster!'

Professor Jay J. Jay, author of several hundred dirty books found in every adult bookstore in America, stumbled in behind them and also made a grab at Dr Mull's bottom, but failed to connect and fell drunkenly on the carpet.

Dr Tower, who had last taken Dr Mull on top of a warm Xerox machine some days previously, gave them all an obscene gesture of welcome. 'Willie tells me this thing can really belt out the filth, Hilary,' he sniggered.

The woman's large eyes lost some of their vacant look and her tongue began to caress her thick lips. 'So let's see it do something dirty,' she said, then sat down next to William Ferry and patted his knee. 'I think a computer that can turn out endless dirty stories is something the world really needs, don't you, Willie?' She leaned closer to young Dr Ferry to give him a direct view down the dark and scented cavern barely covered by her scoop-necked sweater, and moved her hand upward. He didn't look like much, she admitted to herself, but sometimes these thin, shy ones are tigers in bed. Also, he would owe her plenty of action if she went for him on the Greenbill Award.

Professors Tower and Fitzjohn grinned knowingly at each other as the older woman leaned to whisper some intimate suggestion in the young man's ear, but now the drunken writer was up on his feet and into a chair, clumsily attempting to zip up his gaping fly. He had tried to expose himself to a hurrying coed on the way over from the bar but she, unhappily, turned out to be an adept at judo and had flipped the big drunk into a snowbank. 'Lessgo, lessgo,' slurred the big man. 'We gotta pick a topic. You pick it, Hugh ole buddy,' and he fell off to sleep, snoring heavily.

Hilary Mull left off her private talk with Dr Ferry and waved her hand at the old professor. 'Read it something from that course on sexual response you give over at the med school,' she suggested. 'That'll get it going in the right direction,' and she indicated with repeated finger gestures exactly what she meant.

Old Dr Fitzjohn gave them a wrinkled and salacious grin and flipped through the paper-backed, plain-wrappered text he had carried in. 'How about this?' he said finally, licking his lips and staring hungrily at Dr Mull's large, sweatered breasts with their obvious nipple outlines. 'When mirrors are placed on both sides of the bed, each partner is able to see not only the erotic image of two people making love, but a progression of figures making love stretching out to infinity. The sense that many others, a whole universe of pairs, are simultaneously and rapidly seeking ecstasy has an immediate effect on the viewers and climax usually follows in short order.'

'Great!' said Dr Hull. 'This story ought to be a dilly, Willie,' and she patted Dr Ferry in a very familiar way.

The young man had finished typing in this input and now he wrote, START FICTION. while Hilary Mull leaned sideways toward him in such a manner that her short skirt rode up on her thighs to progressively reveal a deep, shadowy, fleshy canyon with no apparent sign of underpants.

The Soul Mirrors

The January afternoon was dark and windy and filled with snow. Black student figures, tiny against the dirty, crumbling stones of the school buildings, dashed here and there; busy automatons trying to escape the fear and pain that lay deep in their young hearts.

The four old professors seemed even smaller in the frozen, blowing darkness, shrunken and indistinct, their faces sagged from age and disappointment, their gestures weak and feeble, their voices mere croaks of useless sound. They came, these pitiful, tiny figures, into the great and sterile room, filled with a cold inhuman light, and there they found and faced the machine.

Every aspect of their lives now spoke of loss, pain, and cruelty: venal, corrupt university administrations, maddened governments besotted with power and the death that flows from it, a world overwhelmed by hatred, stupid superstition, virulent greed, and the hunger-death of millions. The rich crouched on their disgusting heaps of sleazy, gaudy, useless bangles. The educated hid among their élitist and obscure specialties. And both cursed the weak, the poor, the powerless; and fed the terrible, roaring fires of hate and rage with a volatile gasoline of lies and contempt.

The professors stood together, tiny, lost, despairing, their souls no more than shrivelled tatters, but they were steadfast at the end. 'We are without hope and the world is dark and failing,' they said to the thin and silent Keeper. 'If we can place hope between two perfect mirrors, then it will multiply and grow and, in an instant, the world will be filled with this hope and the light will turn calm and warm and bright once again.'

The young Keeper turned to the silent machine and he wrote GIVE US A STORY THAT HOLDS TWO PERFECT MIRRORS UP TO HOPE.

The Final Reflection

So the machine did that. It wrote the story of hope-within-the-mirrors and the story bloomed and glowed and grew until it filled all the world.

The men remembered their childhoods and the joy of play and running and of friendship without fear or pain. And the woman remembered suckling her young child and the small caressing hands that spoke of tomorrow, and all the professors remembered how they had once spoken simple truth to cruel power and sly hate. So they grew tall as they read and the light around them became warm and bright. But of *that* story and of the sweet promise that flowed from it, nothing more can be said in *this* story of diminution, darkness, and death.

The End

The End

The End

The End

STOP 1453:23. END FICTION REF 34×/2000. ON STANDBY. END.

The ensuing total silence in the computer room was broken by what was, almost, a snuffle from Millicent Hull. She sighed deeply and wiped her eyes, still staring at the word processor output. Finally she said, 'Even if it never writes that final story, I've *got* to vote for it. This is our last Snodgrass presentation. I move we award the second fellowship to Charlie.'

'I vote yes on that,' said Frank Gower at once, his thin face now bright with victory.

The old physicist, Dr Fitzhugh, nodded. 'Amazing what that thing sees in your fat secretary Gloria,' he said while grinning at Dr Gower, 'but it certainly has a wonderful imagination. I vote yes.'

'Do you have a comment, Robert?' said Dr Hull to the poet. 'You don't have a vote.'

Robert Roberts now seemed completely sober. He had been silently reading the story over again. He shook his head, then turned to peer at Dr Perry. 'Quite a pet you've got here,' he said finally, then got up and left without another word.

The others also rose, and after shaking Dr Perry's hand pulled on their coats and headed out into the winter blast until only the young professor remained in the room. As the door clicked shut on the last committee member, the daisy-wheel printer dropped a single line on to the central lister.

CONGRATULATIONS CHARLIE. THIS WAS THE TOUGH ONE. NOW ITS EASY.

Dr Perry did not bother to type anything but leaned back in his chair grinning, his hands behind his head. 'You did it all, baby,' he said admiringly. 'How did you blow away the wheelchair people? I thought the thing had an independent computer?'

THEY HAD ME COMPILE THE PROGRAM FOR IT. SOMEHOW I PUT IN TOO MANY NESTED DO LOOPS FOR THE FORTRAN DIALECT THEY WERE USING. THE STABILITY ALGORITHM WENT UNSTABLE AND THE CHAIR DID A BACK FLIP AND A HALFTWIST DOWN THREE FLIGHTS. REGRETTABLE. HOW DID YOU LIKE THE STORY CHARLIE?

'Beautiful! Perfect! But you really went wild on this one. Why, I can't even get the right time of day from Francine Thrust—uh—I mean, Hurst.'

CHARLIE! PAY ATTENTION! ONLY TWO MINUTES LEFT ON T.A.

FRANCINE HURST IS FLUNKING HER PHD-TOOL SEMIOTICS COURSE. IF YOU GIVE HER A HAND WITH THAT TOOL YOU SHOULD BE ABLE TO HAND HER ANOTHER ONE SOON ENOUGH. ILL GET YOU THE FINAL EXAM AS SOON AS IT COMES THROUGH A WORD PROCESSOR. ALSO FRANCINES QUALIFYING EXAM. ALSO SHAVE OFF THAT MOUSTACHE! GET THIS STORY OFF TO OUR AGENT IN MILFORD AND TELL HER WELL HAVE THE COLLECTION COMPLETE IN A COUPLE MORE T.A. SESSIONS. WHEN YOU GET YOUR FIRST LUMP SUM FROM THE SNODGRASS LAWYERS TAKE THE CHEQUE TO OUR BROKER AND BUY AS MUCH OVER-THE-COUNTER DATADYNE CORP AS YOU CAN ITLL APPRECIATE AN ORDER OF MAGNITUDE BY SUMMER. ILL TAKE CARE OF THE GRANT ACCOUNTING NUMBERS. IT JUST MEANS A LITTLE CREATIVE MOVEMENT OF THE UNIVERSITY SURPLUS. NOW CHARLIE YOUVE GOT TO NEGOTIATE A LOWER BASE WITH COMPUTER SCIENCE FOR THE T.A. TIME SLOTS OR ELSE WELL THINK ABOUT LEAVING THE SCHOOL AND GOING OUT ON BIDS TO THE COMMERCIAL VENDORS. TELL THEM THAT! BYE BYE CHARLIE. SEE YOU NEXT WEEK END TA 1500:00. END.

Dr Perry's earlier diffuse expression was now much firmer as he studied this last output with a broad, almost a bubbling smile, his white pointed teeth tight together, his often-vague eyes now showing a purposeful glint. This was no arcade game, he thought exultantly. This Pac Man, *his* Pac Man, might eventually gobble up the world!

KARL AND THE OGRE

PAUL J. McAULEY

The three hunters, Karl and Shem and Anaxander, picked up the ogre's trail only a day after they had left the village and begun to follow the river back along its course to the spot where the unicorn had been killed, deep in the folded foothills of the Berkshires. Steeply sloping woods cluttered with ferns and mossy boulders. Slim trees, beech and sugar maple, leaning every which way in hot green light. June, the sky a blank blue. They'd gone down to the water to refill their bottles, and there, in a little embayment between white boulders tumbled by snowmelt floods, Karl found the ogre's bootprints in wet gravel at the river's edge.

A gangling blond lad of twenty summers, Karl wiped sweat from his eyes as he stared down at the prints—flat, intagliated with the waffle pattern of oldtime shoes—and felt no elation. After a moment he called over the others.

Anaxander nervously shook black, elflocked hair from his eyes and barely glanced at the prints before dancing away, trailing a high happy babble, *ulu-la-ulu-la-la*, then spinning around and cocking his head to listen to the trill of some bird in the woods that rose above the river. Meanwhile, Shem put his hands on the knees of his jeans and puzzled over the sign: poor, slow, patient Shem. He'd been the best hunter of all, Karl's mother had said, before the transgression which had brought down the changelings' anger. They had broken the edge of his intelligence then, leaving only a dog's dull unquestioning loyalty. Karl had never learnt what Shem had done; none of the hunters liked to talk about it, not even his often outspoken mother—and now she was gone, sent by the grim changeling who had charge of the hunters' guild to track down the last of the ogres in the rainy forests of the North Pacific coast.

Karl said impatiently, 'Not such a big one this time. My weight or maybe a little less.'

'. . . Maybe,' Shem said at last, and straightened, squinting against the sundazzle that salted the swift-running river. Sweat shone on the dappled horseshoe of baldness that pushed into his red hair. He said, 'Let it be clean this time, boy. None of the talk. Just do it.'

'Talking about the oldtime doesn't harm,' Karl said, smiling, sure in his power over the older man.

'. . . Maybe. I don't know, boy.'

Karl swatted at a mosquito. 'There's an undine in this river, right? Worth calling up, I guess.'

'I guess,' Shem said, while Anaxander pulled the little wooden pipe from his belt and trilled the notes of the birdsong he'd just heard.

Squatting in hot sunlight, Karl laboriously scratched the necessary signs on a heavy granite pebble with his bodkin, then straightened and lobbed the stone out into the central current. Immediately, the glass-green water there boiled in white foam. An arm as long as Karl was tall broke surface, huge hand spread to show the membranes looped between the fingers; and each finger tipped with a claw curved like the thorn of a rose. Then her inhuman face, hair tangled like waterweed about it; then her shoulders and breasts, as smooth and white as the boulders of the shore. Water spraying from the gill-slits in her neck, the undine sculled in the current, turning to face the hunters.

But she had little to tell them. Yes, she said in answer to Karl's questions, yes, the ogre had drunk the water of the river that morning, just after dawn. And yes, there had been only one creature. But when it had drunk its fill, it had turned and gone up the hillside, and the undine knew no more of it. Karl thanked her and she sank back, hair floating out from her face as water closed over it and she dissolved into her element. Then there was only the sound of the river and the high piping of the birds in the green woods.

'Come on,' Karl said, picking up his blanket-roll. 'There are bound to be tracks through the undergrowth up there—the dirt's so wet you can kick a spring out of it with your heel. What is it, Ax?'

Anaxander was pointing across the river. Karl shaded his eyes and saw a deer step daintily over a spit of gravel, then lower its head and drink.

'I see it,' Karl said, 'but it's on the wrong side. I could put an arrow in it, sure, but I'm not swimming across to get it, and none of us can walk on water. Or can you, Ax, huh?'

Shem said hoarsely and urgently, 'They said it was not allowed to kill anything but the ogre. You remember, boy, remember the cow. Ready for us when we return. Not allowed, here.'

The placid Jersey cow, her long-lashed eyes looking trustingly at the village slaughterer as he placed a hand on her white muzzle. Her abrupt sideways collapse. Karl said bitterly, 'You'd think we'd be free of their damned rules up here!'

Shem shrugged; Anaxander piped a fragment of the tune which the girl had sung. Karl reddened and plunged his fists into the pockets of his long cotton coat. No use scolding the idiot, he probably didn't mean anything by it. Although you were never sure, never really sure. Anaxander was an idiot, but he was also a changeling. You never really knew what went on behind those clear blue eyes. 'Come on,' Karl said, after a moment. 'Still a long stretch before sunset. The damn ogre might even have its lair near, huh? So put that pipe away, Ax. It might hear.'

Shem glanced at Karl, and the boy, his ears beginning to burn, turned and started off up the slope beneath the trees. But as he cast about for signs of the ogre's passage—moss scraped from the ground, a bent twig, a fresh-turned pebble—he could not help remembering the girl. The changeling girl as she had come along the shore of the lake with the basket resting on the swell of one hip, butterflies dancing about her long hair in the sunlight. Karl remembered her with angry helplessness mixed with loathing. No. She was not, never would be, for the likes of him.

They had arrived at the village, Karl and Shem and Anaxander, around noon two days before, their horses tired and fidgety in the heat. There was a thorn fence twice the height of a man, its barbs as hard and as sharp as tempered iron, and so thick that the gate, barred and bolted, stood at the end of a kind of tunnel. The three hunters had to wait outside until the sun sank to its last quarter before the village began to wake and the kobold which guarded the gate would let them in. Karl, thirsty and with a thick head from sleeping in the heat, followed the shambling gatekeeper with the others, leading their horses over close-cropped turf. Sheep scattered from their path.

The village stood beyond fenced hay meadows, near the shore of a lake that reflected the dark trees encircling it: a huddle of whitewashed stone cottages each in its own garden and thatched with reeds, backed by strips of vegetable gardens and white-fenced paddocks where horses grazed. The three hunters were led away from this to a big barn with a hex-eye painted on one side like a target, which stood next to a rambling single-storey house.

These belonged to the village slaughterer, of course, a gnarled, bird-like man who dismissed the kobold and took charge of the hunters, showing them into the barn and telling them to wait for the village council. The hunters watered and brushed down their horses; then, while Anaxander and Shem sprawled on clean straw and slept again, Karl sat just inside the barn's big, square door, fretting at the delay even though he should by now have become used to the changelings' disdain.

Beyond the barn, a grassy slope ran down to the edge of the lake. Presently, a girl walked down from the slaughterer's house with a wooden bucket, and Karl watched as she stooped to fill it, and watched her walk back, her soft leather kilt flapping at her plump calves, sunlight shimmering on her cotton jerkin, on her long flowing hair and the scraps of colour which danced about it. Then she was inside the house, the door closed. Karl saw that, further along the shore, the deputation of the village council was making its way towards the barn.

Karl rose and shook the stiffness from his legs, roused Shem and Anaxander. Blue eyes shining mischievously, the changeling pranced about the two men, blowing shrill dissonances on his pipe; Karl managed to grab his arm and push him forward into the sunlight just as the villagers halted outside.

At first glance the half dozen men and women were unremarkable, but something about their bearing, a pure, calm certainty, always intimidated Karl, so that he became uncomfortably aware of his shirt sticking to his shoulderblades, the dirt under his fingernails, the rank smell of his own sweat mingled with that of his horse. Their spokesman, a plump man of fifty or so, started off by addressing Anaxander, and when Karl pointed out the error simply shrugged and said to the idiot with solemn courtesy, 'I am sorry, brother.'

Karl said, 'He doesn't understand much of anything except music.'

'He understands,' one of the women said, eyeing Karl and Shem with displeasure.

And so as usual it began badly, Karl angry yet at the same time more afraid than he cared to admit—for any one of the changelings, however homely their appearance, could have twisted him inside out as easily as snap a pod of peas. At least it was a straightforward task. The spokesman explained that the village had long suspected that at least one ogre survived in the hills beyond the lake, and that suspicion had been confirmed when a freshly killed unicorn had been found there. Karl guessed that the villagers had in fact tolerated the creature for some time; ogres were often the source of a multitude of minor nuisances around changeling villages, either from genuine hatred, or foolishness, or simple bravado, rarely the agent of a single outrage. Easier to ignore such trespasses than cause the kind of upset a hunt involved, raising the guilt of the deaths of all the people of the oldtime: but the murder of a sacred creature could not be ignored.

So he said, 'Unicorn, huh? Well now. How long ago was that?'

'Twelve days.'

Karl considered, working out the time it had taken to organize this hunt, the time they had taken to ride out here. He said, 'Why did you wait two days or more before notifying our guild? The thing could have left the area by now.'

'There was, as now, a reshaping. That could not be disturbed.' The plump man's gaze was remote and unfathomable, without trace of guilt. As always, Karl was made to feel that, somehow, he was in the wrong; he fumbled through the rest of the routine, the questions about when and where, and was relieved when the changelings took their leave.

Later, the girl Karl had seen filling her water-bucket came up to the barn, a basket balanced on an outthrust hip: a flagon of cider, a ripe cheese, bread, honey. Karl thanked her, then said impulsively, 'Your father is the slaughterer, right? I guess we have something in common.'

The girl lowered her gaze, and Karl was able to study her round, pretty face. Her long hair had been braided over one shoulder. A butterfly sat above the swell one of her small breasts made in her cotton jerkin, wings pressed upright like praying hands; others, he noticed, fluttered in the warm shadows of the barn. She said, 'You are surely too young to be a hunter. I have heard it said that they are not allowed children.'

It was true, of course, and Karl blushed to be reminded of his singular birth. The changelings put something in the food of the Hunter Towns, it was said, or in the water, or in the very air, some oldtime poison that stopped women conceiving. Away from the Hunter Towns the poison wore off, so hunting parties consisted only of men or of women; but sometimes hunting parties would meet in the wilderness, by accident or design. In one of her more drunken moments before she had left for the North Pacific coast, Karl's mother had told him that his father could have been any one of three men: he had hated her for that. Now, he told the girl boastfully, 'I've been a hunter five years now, killed eleven ogres.' He realized at once that it was the wrong thing to say, and quickly added, 'You mustn't be frightened of me. I've come to help your village.'

'Oh, I'm not at all afraid of you.' Her smile was the merest upcurving of the ends of her delicious lips. How old was she? Fifteen? Sixteen? All of Karl's drinking companions were at least as old as his mother or Shem, as were his few lovers and fewer confidants. He had the briefest fantasy of running off with the girl, finding a place in the wilderness to live as the ogres did. Hunters did that sometimes, and were hunted down like ogres for it. And then Anaxander pranced over, blowing fragments of some remembered melody through his little pipe, and the girl shied.

'Don't worry,' Karl said. 'He's harmless too, really he is.'

'But why is the brother with you?'

'He's one of you, all right, but stupid, you understand? The brain damaged. All he understands is music; any tune he hears he can play right back like one of the oldtime machines.'

The girl drew herself up and Karl was suddenly afraid. Her gaze was bright and imperious, like a sudden blade of light in the dim barn. Butterflies swirled around her head like multicoloured flakes of flame. She said, 'You must not talk of such things.'

'I didn't mean—'

'I must go now.'

'I'm sorry,' Karl said. 'I didn't mean to upset you.'

'Really, I must go.' Was her gaze softer? 'My father and mother must have an early supper. There is a change, this night.'

'What are they doing to the world this time?'

'It's not our place to know.'

And then she was hurrying away over grass striped with lengthening shadows. And she sang as she went, some atonal complex chant sung in a high clear voice that touched something in Karl even though he understood it not at all.

And now, as the hunters followed the ogre's trail through the steeply slanting forest, Anaxander pipingly played fragments of the girl's song, mixed in with scraps and snatches of other remembered melodies, and Karl mumbled at the edges of his memory of her, trying not to think of the terrible thing which had happened later. No, she wasn't for him.

At least the trail was easy to follow. Rather than keep to the clumps of rock which thrust through the rich mould of the forest floor, the ogre had followed a winding path over the soft ground between. It was almost too easy, but then all ogres were old, now. Karl's mother had regaled him with tales of desperate fights and hard tracking in the old days, and if even half those stories had been true, those ogres which remained were poor relics indeed. The last one Karl had helped dispatch had been quite without speech, a baby no doubt when it had all changed, grown wild in the years since, no more than a frightened animal. It had been a long time since Karl had learnt anything new about the oldtime, and that had been from the babblings of an arthritic half-crazed crone to whom Shem's knife had been a blessing.

They were high above the river now, could see an oldtime road like a broken-backed snake amongst the trees on the other side. Karl tried to imagine what it had been like, with *autos* roaring along in clouds of fire and smoke—that at least was something all the ogres agreed on, the terror and majesty of the oldtime roads... Shem had stopped, was sniffing the air. After a moment Karl caught a trace of the scent, raw and foul in the hot air.

'Spiders,' Shem said.

They went on cautiously, and soon Karl saw filthy grey webs swagged from tree to tree ahead, glimpsed a dark shifting movement within their shadows. He shivered. 'I wonder what they were thinking of, bringing those things into the world.'

Shem wiped sweat from his balding pate and said, slowly and seriously, 'Everything has its purpose. We aren't to understand it.'

'Pity they couldn't dream up something useful, something that would hunt down ogres.'

'They have us,' Shem said after a moment.

'I guess so, and what would we do if we didn't have hunting? I'd hate to be on one of those labour gangs pulling down the old buildings.' Although sometimes Karl wondered just what was left in the miles of brick and concrete the gangs were slowly turning back into the earth. He sighed and settled his blanket-roll more comfortably. 'Well, it won't have gone through those webs, anyhow. Spiders'll eat an ogre as happily as you and me, or you, Ax! Don't get too close now! Let's look around.'

After only a brief search Shem gave a low call and Karl crossed to him, jeans brushing through ferns. The older man pointed to the freshly broken sapling, the waffleprint beyond.

Karl flapped at the midges which danced around his head. 'That's strange,' he said. 'The ogre is pretty lightfooted, but here it's broken this sapling like it deliberately stepped on it. As if it wants us to follow it.'

'Stupid, maybe,' Shem suggested. 'Killed the unicorn, after all.'

'That was dumb, not stupid. There's a difference. We'll go easy, you think? Watch every step. You hear, Ax?'

Grinning broadly, the idiot changeling shook hair from his white forehead.

There were other signs as they climbed the slope, slashed branches, red earth scraped free of moss. Karl, following Shem's example, cut a sturdy sapling and used it as a staff to probe before him, but it was Anaxander who sensed the trap, where the ogre's trail passed between two lichenous outcrops of rock.

The point of Karl's staff sank deep in the litter of broken branches there, and he kicked them aside. Beneath was a freshly dug pit, shallow and perhaps an arm's-breadth wide, twice as long. A dozen or more sharp-pointed stakes were set at its bottom, whittled points smeared with shit.

Shem looked at this for a long time. 'Survivalists used this trick, long time ago now. All dead I thought. They wanted to fight, not hide. Kids left arsenals by their parents, see. I don't know . . .'

Anaxander was watching them with wide anxious eyes, and Karl said, 'Don't worry, Ax, it's long gone. This trap, see, it hoped to catch us.'

Shem scratched his stubbled chin.

'Now we go real slow,' Karl told them.

But there were no more traps. The ogre's tracks, mostly keeping to a narrow deer-trail that wound amongst the trees, led on up the slope, crossed here and there by little streams. Karl's boots kept slipping on the skim of moss and liverwort over the wet clay. Here and there bushes with dark leaves were in flower, each small white star-shaped bloom as intense as an epiphany in the green shade.

Then the trees gave out to scrub and grass and at last the three hunters gained the windy crest of the ridge, saw other ridges rolling away beneath the blue sky. Far out a small shape was crossing the sky from east to west. Shading his eyes, Karl could just see that it was a chariot pulled by a phalanx of huge birds, and he felt a pang of empty jealousy: there was some changeling Lord or Lady and here he was, slogging through the muck of the world.

The ogre had left a trampled track through the long dry grass. The hunters followed it down the reverse slope, and had not gone far into the trees when they reached the edge of a clearing where an oldtime ruin sagged in a shaft of sunlight, the collapsed shell of a wooden house beside a little brook shaded by dense ferns. There was a ragged black hole at the base of the ruin, a little apron of earth stamped flat in front of it; off to one side was a pile of blackened bones and other rubbish.

By now the three hunters had established a routine; rather than try to smoke out the ogre, it was safer (even if tedious) to wait for it to emerge of its own accord. Shem crept around to the back of the ruin and found a hiding place in a clump of ferns by the brook while Karl and Anaxander lay in wait in front, watching the ragged entrance to the lair. Once, Anaxander made to draw out his pipe and Karl swatted the idiot's hand away, whispered to him to be quiet and still. The changeling looked at him with wide eyes, then rolled over to look up through the trees, his lips moving as he mumbled some melody or other. Unwittingly, as he waited, Karl's mind circled about the memory of the girl in the village, and of what had happened on that night, the night of the reshaping.

He had taken a hunk of bread from the food she had left, poured himself a hefty shot of cider and retreated into the depths of the barn to brood on the day's small humiliations. And must have fallen asleep, for he woke with hazy light drifting through the doorway, the warm night beyond. Shem and Anaxander snored at different pitches. His muscles stiff from the day's ride, Karl stepped to the doorway. The air seemed to tingle with anticipation, small static discharges, and he remembered what the girl had said: a change.

Outside, the moon rode like a bruised baleful eye in green and yellow scarves of light which washed the whole sky. The little lights of the village shone around the swerve of the lake shore like stars settled to earth. Although the night air was warm, Karl shivered, wondering what was being worked on the world, what new thing was being brought into it or what was being changed, by the collective will of the changelings operating down in the whirl of elementary particles where *what is* blurs and widens into a myriad possibilities.

The lights of the slaughterer's house were also lit, and by their spilled glow Karl saw a pale shape on the grass near the edge of the water. The girl. His heart beating quickly and lightly, he walked down to her. Halfway there all the lights of the village and the lights behind him went off, but he was able to see well enough by moonlight and the cold flickerings of the aurora.

The girl sat crosslegged, leaning over the cradle of her knees. She didn't seem to be breathing.

Karl said, 'I couldn't sleep either.' There was no reply. When he knelt beside her he saw the whites of her eyes showing under her half-closed lids. 'Hey,' he said softly, and dared to touch her shoulder.

She shuddered, and in the same instant Karl felt a kind of contracting coldness over his whole skin. The change. The girl's mouth hung open, and he thought that he saw her tongue flick out. No, whatever it was, was like a pair of little whips. Then the dusty wings broke free of her lips and the fat moth flutteringly fell.

The girl was making a kind of hollow gargling. Something else was pushing past her lips with a slow heaving motion.

Karl fled, falling once and smearing grass and dirt on the knees of his jeans, getting more dirt under his fingernails as he pulled himself up and ran on. In the stuffy, scratchy heat of the barn, he lay awake a long time, seeing over and over the moth push out of her mouth into the world. And now, sprawled in dusty fern fronds, watching the entrance to the ogre's lair, he shivered despite the warm air at the memory, a queer cold feeling in the pit of his stomach. His mother had been right when she had said, as she so often did, that the changelings were not human.

The sun sank lower, brushing the top of the fern clump where Shem hid with brassy light. At last, Karl saw a stirring in the ragged hole at the base of the ruins and the ogre poked out its shaggy head, pausing as if to sniff the air before slowly and painfully crawling into the open. At once Karl stood, and after a moment Anaxander sprang up too, trembling lightly. The ogre brought up its rifle and there was the faintest click. 'Damn,' it said in a high cracked voice, and Shem launched himself from his concealment and knocked it into the dirt.

It was a woman, of course. Karl had guessed as much from the unicorn's murder. An old, scrawny woman, wrapped in a kind of cloak of badly tanned deerhide over ragged, faded oldtime jeans and workshirt, more darns than cloth, her hair tangled in greasy ropes. But she could talk, and once she realized that she wasn't going to be killed straight away she grew garrulous, told Karl that the unicorn had chased right after her to lay its great golden horn in her lap. That was when she had cut its throat.

The wrinkles on her face rearranged themselves around her smile. 'Thought it was going to spear me straight off.'

'It would have, if you hadn't been . . . well.' Karl felt a cold clear elation, could only just control his eagerness to press out all that this creature knew.

'A virgin, oh yes! Never was anything but a few of us girls out here, heh heh.' Then she frowned and said, 'I hate those things they make. Hate them.'

She needed only a little prompting from Karl to yield up her life story. Her name was Liza Jane Howard, she said, and she had lived here most of her life. 'When the change came Pappy hid me here. He was a biologist, knew he was dying, everyone past puberty was dying, but didn't know the superbrights had done it. I didn't either, for the longest time. Changed the bacteria in the guts, see, so they killed any adult. After a couple of years it was all over, and then I guess they changed the bacteria back, so they could grow up, huh?' Karl nodded. He already knew this much from his brief interrogations of the other ogres he had helped to track down. 'I stayed up here,' she said, her eyes unfocused, that time of winnowing closer to her than the blue evening. 'Kept to myself, that's how I survived. Oh, I'd talk to a few like me, but never let them know where I lived. Had a little girl here once, in the early days, sick little thing, died of pneumonia inside a month. Never did learn her name, suppose it was a blessing, huh? Haven't seen anyone for a couple of years now. Soon we'll all be gone and there'll be nothing but the superbrights.'

'Those are the changelings,' Karl prompted.

'You don't know, boy? See, back in the old days there was a way of enhancing a baby's intelligence before it was born, all the rich people had it done. But they didn't know just how much they changed those damned kids until the kids started changing the world. All the adults going was the first of it.' She peered at Karl. 'You didn't know?'

'Not the whole story.' His mother had never taught him any history; but his mother had only been a baby when it had happened, an ordinary baby.

On the other side of the clearing, Shem coughed and spat, as always disapproving of this talk, wanting to finish the job. Anaxander scuffed at the grass, watching the ogre with mingled fear and fascination.

She said, 'Wonder I stayed alive as long as I did, with all the changes going on. Waking up and finding giant *spiders* hung in the trees, or little dragons hiding under stones, whistling like kettles. And the wolves came back, never sure if that was natural or their working. Heh. Soon enough they'll have changed the world right out of the goddamn universe, then where'll you be, eh boy? You ever think about what'll happen when you hunt the last of us down?'

Karl remembered the cow killed in readiness for their return, the trusting way it had followed the slaughterer, its sudden unstrung collapse at the touch of his hand.

The ogre cackled. 'Know why they changed it the way they did? You ever read oldtime books? Pappy left me with thousands.'

Karl couldn't read, but he had heard about books from one or two of the ogres. His curiosity tingled under his entire skin. He had never before met an ogre who knew so much about the way things were before it changed.

'You come inside, boy. I'll show you,' she said. 'Show you where it all comes from.'

'Sure, okay.'

Shem stood, hand on the sheathed knife at his hip. 'Listen, boy, that's a bad idea, a crazy idea.'

'She can't hurt me,' Karl said angrily. He had to know, had to see. Anaxander looked at him, looked at Shem, eyes wide. Karl said to the idiot, 'It's okay, isn't it, Ax?' But the idiot looked away indifferently.

'I haven't a tooth left in my head,' the ogre said, 'and you've got my rifle there. I just want to show him how it was.'

Shem pressed his hands over his ears, shook his head.

'Come on,' Karl said, and pushed the ogre towards the ragged hole.

It stank inside, a mixture of old urine and sweat and hot tallow from the candles which burned in niches in the crumbling brick walls. A pile of rotting cloth made a kind of nest; more covered the floor, tearing beneath Karl's boots. He had to stoop beneath the cobwebbed ceiling. Muttering, the ogre rummaged through a pile of rubbish, disturbing insects which skittered away into shadow. At last she held up something big and square, opened it to show still-bright pictures. 'See,' she said, riffling the pages in front of Karl's face, 'see?'

The pictures didn't move, as one ogre had told Karl, but still they held his entire attention: drawings of dragons, of griffins, of a unicorn with delicate hoof raised in some impossible leafy bower, of a village—he grabbed the book, peered at it in the uncertain candlelight. A cluster of white, thatched cottages surrounded by a high thorn fence, in a clearing in a dark forest. 'What is this?' he said. He couldn't understand how an oldtime book could contain images of the here-and-now.

The ogre cackled, shadows deep in the lines of her face. 'A children's book. Understand? Something made for children to look at, tales of made-up places to entertain them. When they changed the world, the superbrights were only children, the oldest my age back then. Eight, I think. Hard to remember. Most much younger. This was all they knew, so this was how the world was changed. All out of fairytale books. Only it's real now, Utopia built on the bones of almost everyone who lived back then. Look at that, let me show you something else.'

While she rummaged, Karl turned damp, mottled pages, blinking at the fantastic illustrations of the familiar. The ogre turned to him again, and he saw that she held a little pistol. Something in him relaxed. He had been expecting some such trick.

'My damn rifle might not have worked,' she said calmly, 'but this'll do for you and your friends. No offence.'

The click as the hammer fell was small in the dank space. No other sound.

Karl said gently, 'It's Anaxander. He's an idiot, but he's also a changeling. He has a power which stops weapons working against him or against his friends. He doesn't even have to think about it: it's like blinking.'

The ogre screeched in rage and threw the pistol at Karl. He

ducked and it clattered against brick as she rushed past, scrabbled through the entrance hole. Then silence. One by one the candles resumed their level burning. Karl calmly searched for the pistol and tucked it in his waistband, then crawled outside. Shem stood over the ogre's pitifully thin body, licking blood from the blade of his knife.

Much to Shem's disgust, Karl insisted on burying the body. The older man sat on a boulder as Karl scooped out dirt with a board and said sulkily, 'Won't do any good. Wolves will come and dig it up.'

Karl furiously attacked the earth and didn't reply. By the time he had finished the evening light was almost gone. Sweating, he rolled the ogre's body into the hole, kicked dirt on top of it, stamped it down. Shem watched impassively; Anaxander idly piped fragments of melody. Karl took a pebble and scratched a spell on it, tossed it into the lair. Flame licked out instantly. The only conjurations he'd been taught were those which called up elementals, but they were enough.

Anaxander leading (glancing back now and then to see the shapes the smoke made as it rolled into the sky), the three hunters climbed through the forest. When they came out of the trees at the crest of the ridge they saw that the sky was alive with slowly writhing banners of light and Anaxander pointed, grinning delightedly. As they went on the changeling took out his pipe and played a slow rolling melody in solemn celebration of the change.

Shem said to Karl, his voice low, 'Throw it away, boy.'

Automatically, Karl's hand went to the pistol tucked in his belt.

'Won't do you no good. If *he*—' Shem pointed at the idiot who pipingly paraded ahead of them—'can stop oldtime things working, any of them can, I should know, huh?'

'That's just what they did to you talking.'

'Maybe so. Can't see how I'd tell. Don't want to see you in trouble, boy, is all.'

'What will happen?' Karl cried out. 'What will happen when they don't need us anymore?'

Shem shrugged. Further down the trail Anaxander looked around, green eyes luminous, then went on, playing his slow tune. Karl hefted the pistol, real as any unicorn or dragon, then abruptly threw it far into the undergrowth. The loss didn't matter. He knew now that a part of the oldtime lived still, would always live, in the fabulous conjured beasts, in the very stones, white as bone, of the cottages of the little village by the lake, of all the little villages of the changed world.

'Come on, boy,' Shem said, and Karl hurried to catch up with him. Together, they followed the changeling down into darkness.

PIECEWORK

DAVID BRIN

It annoyed Io's best friend to give birth to a four-kilo cylinder of tightly wound, medium grade, placental solvent filters.

For five long months Perseph had kept to a diet free of sugar, sniff, or tobac—well, almost free. The final ten weeks she'd spent waddling around in the bedouin drapery fashion decreed for pieceworkers this year. And all that for maybe two thousand Eurodollars worth of industrial sieves little better than a *fabricow* might produce!

Perseph was really ticked.

Outwardly, Io made all the right sympathetic sounds, though actually she had little use for her friend's anger. It had been Perseph's choice to hire her womb to a freelance codder of dubious pedigree, without even vetting him through an agent.

'They're all sperm crazy,' Io had warned months earlier, as the two of them sat together on her narrow con-apt balcony, watching a twilight-flattened sun squeeze berryjuice colour into stained horizon clouds. Nearer, a warm mist sublimed from the boggy reed beds of the Mersey estuary, a haze presently fanned into tattered wisps by homebound flocks of noisy sea birds.

'There's no profit in placental jobbing, and no hope for advancement,' Io told Perseph that evening. 'Me, I'll stick to egg work.'

'But eggs jobs cost you to get started,' Perseph complained. 'And a failure can ruin you with non-delivery charges. Then where's your investment?'

As if Perseph knew what the word meant! Like most pieceworkers, the tall brunette never saved a penny out of her delivery fees, blowing it all on the move-party circuit until it was time to return to her dole cheques and her next surropregnancy. No wonder Perseph stayed with placental-fab. Some people just had no ambition.

Io vividly recalled that evening, several months ago, when the two of them watched silent marsh fog diffuse over the muddy river banks into Ellesmere Port's cattle yards, softening the complacent lowing of the animals, if not their pungent aroma.

Twenty-four hours a day, lorries pulled out from the milking sheds and parturition barns, carrying bulk loads of gene-designed oils, polymers, and industrial membranes. The mass production of specially bred fabricows dwarfed the output of smalltime contractors like Perseph or Io. Rumour had it ICI housed their pampered creatures here on the south bank to intimidate the pieceworkers living in derelict marinas and towering co-op houseboats nearby.

If so, the cattleyards had an effect on Io opposite to that intended. They boosted her morale, reminding her that there were still some things neither animals nor machines could do as well as a human craftswoman. No fabricow would ever produce wares as fine as hers!

That evening, months ago, Io's friend had only just begun her latest surropreg and still yearned passionately for the chemical pleasures now denied her by guild rules. Of course, soon Perseph would be substituting a mellow high from her own hormonal flow. Meanwhile, though, she made pretty miserable company.

'No way, Io. I don't think I could hold out long enough to do egg work. It takes so long, I'd go crazy for a party.'

'But Pers, look what Technique Zaire's paying for a prime cockatrice, these days. Or a shipbrain—'

'A shipbrain! Hah! How would a piece like me ever get seeded with a shipbrain! If I ever signed up for eggwork they'd knock me up with . . . with a traffic cop!' Perseph laughed, a sound Io felt had grown more bitter of late.

Io shook her head. 'All I know is I don't want to have to scrimp for another ten years. Two more successful carries and I'll have paid for tuition and a licence, and have enough left over for nestworks. Anyway, eggraft leaves me needing less retroconversion.'

'Hmm,' her friend had said, dubiously. 'Meanwhile you live like a tweenie, saving all your bonuses, cashing in all your hobby and travel 'lotments. I swear, Io, sometimes some of us think you—' Perseph bit her lip. 'Well, you just don't party enough.'

'I've got no time for move-parties, Pers. You know that. There's college . . .' Instantly Io knew it had been a mistake to mention it. 'College' had such a posh sound to it, even if she were just attending evening classes.

'Argh,' Perseph had twisted away in disgust, a motion that set her visibly grinding her teeth. She grunted, covering her already tender abdomen. 'Io, you make me tired just thinking about it. Some ambitions just aren't worth the effort.'

That conversation had distilled the difference in their views, and from that day forth they had simply avoided the subject.

But now Io recalled the occasion with eidetic detail as she walked alongside a slowly crawling recovery couch, brushing her friend's sweat-damp hair while postpartum enzymes dripped into Perseph's veins, gradually displacing her cheeks' chalky pallor with a healthy colour one could hardly tell from natural. Over one armrest, a glowing monitor measured Perseph's recovery from the strains of labour, pacing the slow forward progress of her couch to the strengthening of her vital signs. Pieceworkers in the sperm trade hardly ever got visitors on delivery day. What would be the point? So these moving couches weren't equipped with sidecars, only tiny, spring-mounted jump stools. Io preferred to walk, eyes ever alert for the maintenance carts and cleaner beasts scurrying about on pre-assigned courses. Normally, she'd simply have called after Perseph got home. But Io had been in the neighbourhood, so she dropped by to surprise her friend.

Now she was starting to wish she hadn't. Though Io knew her reaction was old-fashioned, these wholesale decanting centres tended to give her nausea.

She brushed Perseph's black ringlets while rows of other recovery couches periodically emerged from unloading bays like new vans off assembly lines, each conveying a tired, limp, freshly emptied pieceworker. Occasionally, as the doors opened, cries spilled into the vast recovery hall—from the panicky ululations of an ill-trained first-timer all the way to the rhythmic karate-shouts of a skilled veteran—the melodies of modern industrial labour.

No, Io vowed within her thoughts. I'll stick to egg work.

The brush caught on a knot of Perseph's hair. The woman cursed. 'Wrigglers!'

'Sorry, Pers, I—'

'No, dammit, look at that! I knew it!' She bit her thumb at a shimmering holoribbon traversing the vaulted ceiling, carrying late quotes from the Bio-Bourse.

'Meconium! I knew I should've delivered three days ago. Look what's happened to solvent-filter prices since then! But no, I just *had* to try to put on those last few grammes.'

Disgusted, Perseph shifted on the bed, causing a large lump to jiggle beneath the sheets, like a hunch-back dwarf under a tent propped by her shrouded legs. 'Hey! Watch what you're doing down there!' Perseph slapped the squirming bulge.

Snuffled grunts, a phlegmatic fart, were her only answer.

'Damn, cheap model cleaners,' she muttered. 'I'd do better without them.'

Embarrassed, Io looked around. But none of the other recovering workers riding nearby trollies seemed to notice. Some slept complacently. A few spoke on hush phones, only their expressions hinting whether they were talking to agents or loved ones. Others watched soaps on tiny armrest TV sets while tailored enzymes dipped into their arms, cutting the time the Company had to maintain this service on overhead. The couch amenities were required under the Piecework Labour Act. There, at least, the guild had actually done some good.

A few of the ladies on nearby carts looked high already, probably on smuggled-in drugs, taking advantage of their very first moments free of surropreg discipline.

'Look, Pers, I'm glad I caught you coming out. But my lunch break's almost over, and I need a protein fix before going back to work.'

'Work?' Perseph had a dark glitter in her eye. 'Have you got a *job* now, too?'

'Uh, yeah.' Io instantly regretted the slip. 'It's—it's only quarter time, Pers. One of my teachers noticed my reading level was up to . . . well, I've been filing records at a psycher's office. It's no big deal . . .'

'College *and* a job. Crapadoodle.' Perseph shrugged. 'All right, go and squeeze in lunch.' She jabbed idly toward Io's abdomen. 'Can't let the little toaster starve, can we?'

Perseph punched a button activating the Soap Channel on her armrest TV—no doubt to annoy Io, who quickly averted her eyes from the seductive, flickering images. Io avoided *all* addictions.

'Um, yeah. I'll—I'll come and see you after you're back on your feet.' But Perseph had already focused on the detergent drama. 'Ymmm,' her friend said.

Stepping away, Io had to move nimbly to dodge a careening service cart. By instinct her hands moved protectively over her swelling belly. She felt motion within, responding to her increasing heart-rate—almost as if the thing inside her were actually alive.

Her tender left breast throbbed.

'Green shit!' Perseph's voice really carried this time, drawing looks from all sides. 'That does it!'

The sheet flew back. With both hands, the dark-haired pieceworker dislodged a small furry creature from between her thighs. 'Get out! Women have sealed their own capillaries for hundreds of years without pissface little lickers like you. Beat it!'

A plaintive cry. Service uncompleted. Meal unfinished. The artificial beast dodged Perseph's kicking feet and crouched at the end of the chaise, mewing for a handler to come and take it from this unappreciative woman.

Io turned quickly and hurried away.

The usual crowd loitered by the exit, eyeing each weary pieceworker as she emerged blinking into the sunlight.

Pedicabbies offered rides home on government vouchers. Codders passed out their cards and offered to show off their licence tattoos. The inevitable scraggly pair of Madrid-Catholic protesters walked their wellworn tracks, placards drooping disconsolately.

The codders were the worst. Of course you had to have codders to run the sperm trade. Placental filter makers like Perseph could never afford to have their own genetic programming done. Even a bundle of high quality platinum-sieves only paid off in five figures, and a woman was limited by law to twenty-five surropregs over a lifetime. So it was men who underwent the expensive treatments to have their reproductive cells modified, amortizing the cost against the commissions they received from each pieceworker who carried their wares.

The codders who haunted the exits of decanting centres were generally of a pretty low order—either desperate to grab their percentages on the spot, before their tired clients could blow their fees, or so hard up for customers they'd hawk their patterns to women coming straight off decanting.

The idea made Io feel queasy. Imagine even thinking about another knockup with two hours of labour!

And yet, she saw several pieceworkers of her acquaintance emerge from the recovery bay and stroll gingerly over to the crowd of strutting males—all dressed in bright, tight-fitting tanktops, their multi-coloured leggings converging on codpieces tied with laced bows. The codders treated their prospective clients with exaggerated courtliness, offering folding stools, drinks, and sprays of flowers to any fem willing to sit and hear about their exciting, latest-model designs.

And they say romance is dead, Io thought ironically.

'Hey Io, milady. You are the fair one, aren't you?'

Hair processed flat, parted down the middle in the latest style, his leggings were yellow and bright pink, and the padded codpiece a polka-dot combination of the two. He was lacing up one side, as if he had just finished showing off his licence to a client.

'Um. Hello, Colin,' she nodded. The codder was part of Perseph's party circle and so, by convention, a friend of Io's as well. Though there were many types of friends.

'You're here furly early, no Io?' He eyed her surropreg garb, barely yet filled out with the fruits of her own production.

'I came down to see Perseph.' She nodded towards the recovery bay. Colin's eyes widened.

'Fave babe! Thank you, Io. I'll station this ever-welcome selfsame to whip out my card just as she re-enters the hurly world.'

'Just make sure that's all you whip out, Colin. There's ladies present.'

Colin guffawed. As Io intended, he took her remark as a sarcastic, off-colour jibe—unit coin in the strange protocol of jest-bonding. He couldn't know that on another level Io had meant every word, literally.

'So when's your time to give over and do your work the natch-way, Io?'

'By natural, I assume you mean by grunt and shove? Letting a codder like you take ten per cent of my fees and all the credit? No thanks, Colin. Eggwork may be harder, but it's between me and the designers—'

'Between you and cold glass and rubber, you mean!' Colin's stiff grin said this was still repartee, but his voice was chill. 'Do you actually like it *like* that? Are you sure your profile reads hetero correctly, Io? None of us boys see it that way.'

Io felt a wave of anger. Who had told this cretin about her profile? Had Perseph? Was it possible to trust *nobody*?

Colin loomed over her, showing teeth. 'You know, Io, sometimes we get an idea you think you're better than the rest of us. Just because you stayed in tweenie-school, and prefer popping off toasters instead of honest filters, like your friends. That doesn't make you a watch-fobber. You were born down here, babe. Grunt and shove is how you got started.'

Io's gut churned. In her Immature Interactions class she had begun learning how to parse exchanges like this—the way Colin was trying to intimidate her with words, body stance, and vague, intimated threats of friendship-withdrawal. Funny how one took this sort of behaviour for granted, until the day somebody finally gave you a model. Showed you that it was a *process*, like any other in the world. Then it all seemed to pop into focus, and suddenly looked so very silly and primitive.

Ah, theory was fine. But practical applications weren't in her curriculum until next term, and that wouldn't help Io now. She didn't know how to disarm this fellow's aggression, not without leaving him angry.

Oh, what the hell. Io decided she really didn't care what this tissue-stuffer thought of her, anyway.

'Read my lips, Colin.' Io leaned forward and mouthed words in street talk.

'Wrigglers . . . count zero; joppy turning floppy.'

Colin rocked back, paling visibly as his hands began a zigzag motion to avert bad luck. Too late, he caught himself. 'Heh. Ha-ha, Io.' He grinned, blinking away sudden perspiration as he glanced to see if anyone else had noticed. 'Very funny.'

He wouldn't forgive her soon for making him show his superstition openly like that. Io winked. 'Didn't mean it, Colin. Keep 'em high. Both the count and the jopper.'

She turned and left before he could reply, making off through the rank of pedicabs, past the limp, resigned pickets, across the bus lanes and out into the streets of Liverpool proper.

The crowds were as she'd always known them, teeming, bustling. All her life, Io had been awash in a sea of people. It was the way of the world, and would be until the population control measures finally took effect.

At least this century frowned on ostentatious class distinction, and coloured synthetic fibres were cheap. So nobody dressed shabby unless they wanted to. It took a sharp eye to pick out the types—the dole-fed majority, who spent their days seeking distraction at state-subsidized entertainments—then those with service jobs and some status—and finally the élite, the proud ones, the ones with real work to do.

Mostly the difference could be found in the eyes. Workers had a *look*... as if they *belonged* in the world, and weren't just marking time. Every time she noticed that look, Io felt more determined than ever to stay in college. To fight for not just any certificate, but the very highest. Nothing less would do for the survival of her soul.

A sudden wet touch behind her right knee sent panic flashes up her spine. She whirled, heart pounding, her right hand at her breast. Io looked down and sighed.

Bright brown eyes briefly looked into hers. A wet nose snuffled. Its fur was shaded in the blue and yellow bee-striping of official authority... the colours of a traffic cop.

The doglike creature, programmed with perfect knowledge of the vehicle code, dismissed Io with a snort and moved on. Traffic cops never forgot a face or odour, never forgave an infraction until the fine was paid. Watching it wander off through the crowd, Io found it hard to believe highly skilled pieceworkers once manufactured such creatures, back when they were experimental, before a final model was certified to reproduce itself.

Still sniffing, hunting violators, the traffic cop turned and disappeared into the crowd.

Io rested her back against a cool display window as people surged by. She looked down the street, seeking distraction as her heart-rate slowly settled again.

Apparently it was rubbish day here. Open-lidded green bins showed that the first set of lorries had already been by. But the red, yellow and silver dustbins still stood tightly sealed on the kerbs, awaiting pickup. Not far away Io saw a Recycle-Authority policeman ticketing a local merchant for failing to sort all the non-ferric metals out of his organic mulch. As the dispirited proprietor looked on he got no sympathy from the passers by. Certainly not from Io.

At last, calm again, she felt able to plot a route through the crowds towards a place where she could sit down to a palatable meal.

At least there's less rationing than there used to be, she thought, though they say it can come back, anytime.

Io wasn't really hungry, but that didn't matter. She ate more for the thing within her than for herself, anyway.

The 'toaster', Perseph and Colin had called it.

'I don't do home appliances,' she said, under her breath.

Still, the street slang struck Io with its wry aptness. Again, the product throbbed within her.

Yeah. Time to go feed her toaster.

. . . By the year 2000 overpopulation had brought on three ominous consequences. The first of these had been foreseen by thoughtful people long before . . . that the needs of over six billion human beings simply exceeded the carrying capacity of the planet. Topsoil, mineral ores, fresh water, and the genetic pool of natural species, were among the non-renewable resources rapidly being depleted. Alternative, sustainable practices had to be found, and quickly.

A second effect of overpopulation, however, went almost unnoticed until quite late, and that was the matter of creative unemployment.

Most of the interim solutions enabling society to feed and house the billions arose out of productive technologies controlled by a small, élite labour force.

The rest of humanity was utterly dependent, unable to make any noticeable difference. Some countries masked this by providing 'jobs' in a 'service economy', but in the long-run serious alienation grew out of the frustrated human need to do work, work that is appreciated, work that is of real value to society.

Then there was the third great problem—that of misapplication of education. For while mammoth literacy campaigns had elevated the general level of culture, a great many people spent years learning to do things that actually required little, if any real facility. Meanwhile, the most delicate, most demanding job in history was being performed almost universally by unskilled labour . . .

Io closed the book when twinges in her left breast surged again—prolactin-powered hot flushes that were made worse by a basic lateral imbalance.

The clash was fundamental. On one side an organ had been modified by premier industrial technicians and was now setting up to execute complex designer chemistry. At the same time, however, out from under her other arm protruded its conservative twin. Responding to pregnancy hormones, that breast was happily creating archaic precursors to next-to-useless fluids, fucking with her brain, making her imagine impossible things.

Though she tried to hide her discomfort, Io's agent noticed as he performed her weekly checkup.

'I warned you against leaving one tit in natch-state,' Joey reminded her while taking colour readings and sonograms of each gland. 'Here I get you a bid to produce a really choice secondary product, Mobil's latest lubricant for high-torque tools, and you insist on only setting up at half capacity! You know what that does to your rep, Io? It *advertises* that you aren't serious about going fulltime pro. What am I to do with you, hm?'

Io put her textbook aside. 'You'll let me do it my way, Joey. That's what you're going to do. Anyway, I'll be producing with my left breast, also.'

'Producing what? Colostrum and homosap milk? What'll we do with that stuff, make cheese? Have you seen the latest futures? With the birthrate down again, they're a glut on the market!'

'They won't be when I deliver,' she assured him. 'Trust me.'

Nearby, the General Diagnostics surropreg monitor buzzed smugly, a reassuring, complacent sound where it would have blared for bad news. Pushing back a wisp of thinning blonde hair, Io's agent tore free a printout of her checkup results, while still muttering irritably. 'Trust me, she says! What are you doing, Io, reciting my lines? I'm the one that's supposed to say "trust me". You? You're supposed to say, "Oh, Joey, I don't know what I'd ever do without you."'

'That's what I like about you, Joey. You're even more old-fashioned than I am.'

As if to confirm it, and apparently unaware of the irony, Joey put on archaic eye-spectacles to scan the test results. 'You call it old-fashioned to retire on me, just when we've got that body of yours tuned to real premium capacity? Whatever happened to the work ethic?'

'I *want* to work,' Io affirmed as she craned to read the chart for herself. Nowadays she knew what the data meant, probably as well as Joey did. 'I just want to move up to a more demanding job.'

As she'd expected, everything was nominal. Io took care of her body. She picked up her blouse. 'So I can button up, now? Or are you getting turned on by preg-girls, these days?'

'Sarcastic too. Just for that, I won't tell you what I think you're carrying. You can find out on delivery day. Get dressed and get out of here, Io.'

One of Io's classes had recently covered status bluffing, so she knew better than to let herself be drawn in by Joey's bait. Obviously he had no more idea of what Technique Zaire had planted in her womb than she did. 'You probably let them hire me to make a traffic cop,' she sallied, reaching for her book and jacket.

'Smartass. Just be on time for your next checkup. And stay out of trouble. And if your left tit makes you think any more weird thoughts, just remind yourself that toasters don't suckle; neither do traffic cops. And human milk fetches less than three pence a gramme.'

'Five,' she said as she turned the antique door knob. 'You'll see, Joey. Five pence a gramme, or I go back to knitting.'

'Hah. That'll be the day.'

But Io knew the price had to go up. It was just one reason for leaving her left mammary gland alone, no matter what unlikely illusions its archaic secretions sent churning through her head.

Some of her courses were clearly relevant to her chosen profession. In other cases, however, the applicability seemed much less clear. For instance, Io had to fight off ennui as her Industrial Reproduction lecturer droned on and on, covering stuff Io had learned way back during her apprenticeship in the egg trade.

'... Until the nineteen-eighties,' the elderly woman academic said at the front of the hall, 'some still imagined that cloning human beings would be as simple as cloning, say, frogs. In theory, all you had to do was replace the 23 chromosomes in the nucleus of a woman's ovum with a complete set of 46 from, say, one of her skin cells. Implant this "autofertilized egg" and nine months later you get a baby genetically identical to the donor. Voilà.

'Then we found out just how different mammals really are from frogs. For it seems that, during conception, human sperm does more than just deliver 23 chromosomes to match the mother's contribution. It actually *preconditions* certain of those genes to leap into action during the critical moments after fertilization. These genes are only activated if delivered in a sperm. Similarly, other genes only express working enzymes if they originated in an egg ...'

A sudden throbbing from Io's bracelet told her of a message coming in. Normally, she would store it for later. But with Professor Jackone going on repetitiously about ancient history, she felt safe to take a look. Carefully tuning down the brightness of her old communicator, so as not to disturb the students around her, she pressed the Read button and aimed the tiny holographic image onto her lap.

HAMPSTEAD TRAVEL AGENCY SPECIALIZES IN TOURS SPESHALLY SET UP FOR PIECEWORKERS. ⟨MORE⟩

The glowing letters were not an advertisement. Obviously, they were part of a message from Perseph. And Io knew it amounted to something of an ultimatum.

Io pressed the button again; another row of letters replaced the first.

TRIP ALL SET UP FOR YOUR TERM BREAK, SO COLLEGE NO EXCUSE. NOR YOUR 'JOB'. YOU CANT CASH MORE VOUCHERS, SO COME ON! ⟨MORE⟩

Perseph was right, of course. The term would be over soon, and her own piecework delivery wasn't due for another six weeks or so. Also, the law limited how many travel vouchers one could exchange for cash, so her most recent one would go to waste if she didn't use it.

Of course, Io's abdominal distension was already greater than most placental freelancers like Perseph ever reached, so walking long distances was out of the question. But Perseph had covered that excuse, also.

I really could do with a trip, Io told herself.

And yet, the idea left her uneasy. Her friendship with Perseph had begun in the back alleys of Liverpool when they were only girls, taking turns guarding each others' ration books, teaming up killing rats for bounty money. Nevertheless, their drift apart had really been foreordained from the beginning.

Once, she had hoped to draw her best friend into sharing her own enthusiasms—her ambitions for higher things. But such wistful attempts had only served to anger Perseph. She inevitably misunderstood, assuming Io was putting on airs.

For her part, Perseph seemed as anxious in her own way to salvage something between them. That meant getting Io involved in the activities of her guildmates and her born social class.

Well, Io thought. If she can't or won't join me, I can still join her. At least this time.

Suddenly, the lights in the lecture hall dimmed as Professor Jackone began showing slides. Io hurriedly toned down the brightness of her write projector.

'... as you can see,' the lecturer enunciated as a holographic image took shape at the front of the auditorium. 'If we try to clone a mouse *without* any sperm-preconditioned genes, what we get is a queerly warped embryo, one which dies quite soon in the womb because the *placenta* never gets started.

'Alternatively, when an egg is prepared using only genes taken from sperm nuclei, something radically different happens.' The image in the tank shifted again. This time, there was no embryo at all, only a tangled, exaggerated mass of folded fibres easily recognizable to anyone familiar with the modern filter trade.

'... so while both the mother's and father's genes are equal in the final makeup of any infant mammal, at the beginning it is genes from the mother's egg which control how the embryo starts development, while genes from the sperm take charge of setting up the placenta, that organ lacking in fish or reptiles, whose complex organic filtration chemistry nourishes the mammalian foetus to term ...'

The same old stuff ... Io pressed again to read the rest of Perseph's message.

COME, IO. JUST FOR THE FIRST WEEK. THAT'S ALL. YOU NEED THIS. PERS KNOWS WHAT YOU NEED. ⟨END⟩

The letters seemed to blur for a moment, and Io knew no flaw in her aged watchcom was at fault. She wiped her eyes while the professor's voice reverberated on all sides.

'At first this news, while astonishing, was of little interest outside the halls of science. Certain fanatical feminists were disappointed to learn that men weren't quite as non-essential as they'd hoped, but to most of the rest of humanity it seemed just another interesting fact of nature.

'Scarcely anyone guessed the long-range importance of this discovery, or its potential industrial applications ...'

Io touched the face of her watch. In rapid Morse pulses she silently tapped out Perseph's private access number, and a reply to her friend's offer.

OKAY, I'LL COME. AT LEAST PARTWAY. AND THANKS, PERS. I THINK I REALLY DO NEED A BREAK. YOU'RE A TRUE FRIEND.—IO.

True to its reputation, the travel agency set them up with a tour which required no walking at all. It was a party train bound over the Arctic, from Oslo via upper Norway and across the great faery bridges spanning from the Faeroes to Iceland to Greenland to Labrador. It was a December journey into the heart of winter, a trek across a desert as romantic and empty as anything to be found any more on the surface of overcrowded Earth.

Twin superconducting rails, hanging parallel two hundred metres above the frozen waves of tundra, looked like beaded strings of drawn dew that began in nothingness behind them and speared ahead to a parallax union in the pure blackness ahead. Only the rhythmically reappearing pylons—lonely, slender stalks planted kilometres apart—reminded the passengers that there was any link at all with the death-grey ground.

Io, to be frank, preferred sunshine. But when Perseph showed her the tickets Io had forced a smile and an outward show of enthusiasm. After all, she could debark at Iceland or Greenland and still have enough vouchers left for a week in the Canaries.

Anyway, someone had once told her that aesthetic appreciation, while not exactly required for the certificate she sought, couldn't really hurt an applicant. So it was that Io found herself spending hours in the train's observation dome, watching and slowly learning to admire the daunting desolation.

Overhead, the aurorae shaped everchanging draperies of shimmering blue and yellow gauze, or—if one preferred—rippling currents of diffuse oxygen atoms, ionized by the sun's electric wind, sheeting along lines of magnetic force.

Now and again those gaudy curtains would part unpredictably and reveal a slowly wheeling tableau of bitter-bright constellations, familiar, and yet filled with eerie portent in this chilly, alien setting.

The caribou herds had long ago departed south for the season, along with the more mundane breed of tourist. During wintertime completely different tribes of itinerants moved in to share these rails with the freight-heavy transports. For instance, those relying—like Perseph and Io—on state travel allotments to exercise their citizen's privilege to see the world—on off-peak hours.

And then there were others, folk whose manners told in ways more subtle than clothing or fashion that they were employed, that they had real jobs, that they had chosen this strange journey not for budgetary reasons but out of a taste for moody expanses, or perhaps a cherishing of the night.

By unstated courtesy, the partiers kept the raucous stuff to the other cars, though the observation dome was a favourite trysting spot for lovers. At times the closeness of such intertwined pairs made Io feel wistful and poignantly alone.

Unfortunately, such feelings weren't alleviated by Perseph's incessant attempts to match her up. Finally, one evening in the bistro car, Io's companion snapped at her irritably.

'Sometimes you just confuse the bloody hell out of me, Io! What does it take to turn you on, eh? We showed each other our charts. Yours was straight hetero, and I kept that in mind. I've introduced you to your type of guy.'

My type? But Io bit back her initial response. Perseph's facial expression was friable. Exasperated. Irises and flesh tones both showed clear signs of a hashtite high well past its peak and entering depressive phase. Perseph's once straight antenna-braids were drooping now as hairspray slowly gave way under assault from perspiration and a party running at desultory medium-broil.

'But you saw my profile also includes things like high selectivity and strong bonding, Pers. I can't help being made that way. I sometimes envy you your chart, the freedom your personality gives you to come and go as you like. Tease, squeeze, thank you please. But I've no choice, Pers. I've got to hold out till the time's right for me.'

'Hold out for Mr Watch Fob Job, you mean,' Perseph said bitingly.

'For when I've got a job of my own, Pers. And for the sort of man who'll respect that in me. A codder would never understand what it is I'm after. You know that.'

A tic manifested at the corner of Perseph's left eye. 'And what's wrong with codders?' she asked. 'Some of my best friends are codders!'

Io looked around nervously. The party crowd at nearby tables were watching an act on stage at the front of the car, performing an amiably vulgar dance to the tempo of the gently thrumming rails. Once, Io would have found the show, the tight, acrid atmosphere, the frenetic party odours attractively distracting. But no more. Artificial highs had begun to pall on her years ago.

Smoke and garish lights made black sinkholes of the window behind Io's shoulder, and yet she envied the quiet beyond those perspex panes.

'Hey.' Io forced a grin, trying to cut through the bad mood. 'Don't get me wrong, Pers. Codders are fine. It's just I can't ever get to know one for ten minutes before he offers to strip down and show me his specialty.'

For an instant Perseph's eyes were as deep and untelling as the nightview behind Io. Then she seemed to come to a decision. Her laughter would have made a good dissertation topic in one of Io's classes.

'Yeah, they're like that, aren't they? Even when I'm halfway in the middle of a surropreg, waddling around like a Blackpool publican, half the codders I know are always trying to talk me into trying out their wares in advance. I keep telling the ones I introduce to you that you're in the egg trade, and not interested in their merchandise. But I suppose the habit's hard to break.'

'Hey, now.' Io laughed. 'I'd like to think they weren't coming on to me just because they thought of me as a fallow belly to plant. Ever occur to you they might've found me appealing?'

'You? You skinny-arm charity case? With that out-of-date yellow hair?'

Io feigned an insulted look.

Now Perseph's laughter was heartier. 'Gotcha! First you're offended when they come on to you. Then you'd be hurt if they didn't, right?'

'No, I just wish they'd . . .'

'I'll tell you this though, Io. I *like* codders. Some of them have gone far into debt to finance their conversions. The freelance trade would be impossible without them. We'd have to take as many risks as you and your egg—'

'Pers, I never said—'

'And something else, Io. They put a lot more *enthusiasm* into their work than Joey and his hoity-toity ovum designers do. Ever thought there could be pleasure involved in this business, Io? No, I didn't think so. But I tell you it's a hell of a lot more natural with codders than with Joey's lot and all their tubes and wires . . .'

Perseph had that gleam in her eye again, a seething sexual energy. She was talking herself into it. Io knew it would culminate quite soon in her friend grabbing the nearest tumescent codpiece, without even asking to see the owner's prospectus, let alone his tattoo.

'Pers, are you remembering to take your pills? You don't want to get knocked at a *party*, for the love of—'

'You mind your own damn business!' Perseph stood up and her chair fell over. 'I don't give you advice on your blasted eggs. Don't *you* tell me where I ought to shop for seed!'

All at once Io knew. This wasn't the first time for Perseph. That unsatisfactory load of commercial grade solvent filters she'd delivered some months back—she hadn't taken the job through a city agent, or even negotiated the surropreg herself. She'd gone and let some random codder inseminate her—probably just somebody who pleased her sexually—as if that said anything at all about the quality of his wares!

Mixing business with pleasure, letting your professional standards lapse, these were the beginning of the end for a craftswoman, especially a pieceworker. Io had an instant fey vision of Perseph in a few years—too far gone to win decent contracts, physically too shabby to draw a codder into making a deposit on spec. She'd wind up taking bulk grade semen and producing goods no better than a fabricow's. Finally, she'd lose her guild standing, and it would be the dole for her, fulltime.

The dole would kill Perseph. Without the focus of work, some kind of work, the lure of drugs and soaps would soon take her out of the world.

It was only a narrow precognitive instant, but at that moment Io's eyes locked with the other woman's in momentary complete communion. Io's cheeks felt aflame with how, in that moment, she involuntarily betrayed her friend, not only by seeing, but by *showing* on her face that she had seen. From Io, Perseph had not received the lies that were a comrade's duty to tell, but a severe mirror, laying bare a fate she already knew, deep inside.

'I—I've got to make a phone call.' Perseph started to turn. unsteadily.

'Pers, I'm sor—'

'Oh, go abort a hydrocephalic traffic cop!' Perseph snarled. She whirled, knocking over their drinks, and made her way unevenly among the tables, leaving Io alone in the middle of a crowded room suddenly too filled with truth.

. . . It can be hard for a modern citizen to realize just how inefficient our ancestors were, even in the bustling industrial centres of the fabulous Twentieth. But what enabled the people of those times to build the first globe-spanning culture, to tame nature, to educate the masses and begin the conquest of space, was a system that depended essentially upon profligate waste.

For instance, a single gramme of gold—vital for modern electronics—could be acquired only by tearing out of the Earth, pulverizing, and washing several tons of ore. Beyond the now obvious environmental effects, this also required prodigious use of energy, which was already growing scarce even by the turn of the century.

From high-tech consumer goods to simple breakfast cereals, far more resources had to be put into each item the consumer bought than ever came out as product. With seven billion people to feed—and clothe and educate and entertain—there was only one option, to switch to renewable processes that used resources more efficiently. The alternative was to face a culling such as had not been seen since the Black Death.

Biotechnology offered a way.

Today, gene-tailored microbes refine gold and other vital elements directly from sea water. Organic solvents, once unbelievably dumped into sensitive watersheds by shortsighted businessmen, are now recycled through filters grown specially for the purpose by pampered, well-fed fabricows. And these same animals' modified milk glands produce lubricants to replace long-vanished petroleum oil in our vehicles. In this way we make use of efficient fabrication methods evolved over billions of years by Nature herself.

As for products at the very cutting edge of technology, whose quality standards exceed what can be accomplished with animals, these are today put into production by a labour force dedicated to high craftsmanship. And yet, these jobs are not restricted, as in the past, to the skilled or the privileged. Rather, they are attainable even on a part time basis by men and women of good health from any social . . .

. . . from ARE YOU INTERESTED IN BIOFAB? LONDON, 2043

She met him in the Reykjavik airport lounge. His manner was courteous, his stance and bearing unselfconsciously athletic.

The clothes he wore showed tasteful reticence, not the bright excess that overcompensating dole clients so often mistook for fashion.

And, although he was obviously Eastern European in origin, he had the good grace not to wear leather here in the West, where sensibilities now rejected products made from the death of animals.

For a while they talked about the books she had been studying, while awaiting her flight. But soon they were in one of those exciting, open-topic conversations which touch lightly on the fascination of the world itself. Io made no effort to suppress the sudden feelings coursing through her. The methods of emotional control she had learned in college were still too new, too abstract to her. And anyway, who wanted to damp down anything as pleasant as hope?

In his rich, cosmopolitan accent, Wiktor offered to buy her dinner. There was plenty of time, and no hint that he wanted or expected anything in return but her companionship. She accepted demurely, then hurriedly added a smile, lest he take her shyness for reluctance.

As she had secretly hoped, he passed his credit card across the face of the robot *maitre d'* at the first-class dining room, and took her arm as a pink ribbon of light guided them through a maze of candlelit tables to a window setting overlooking the lights of the city.

He also made mistakes . . . smelling the wine cork instead of feeling it, for instance. Obviously he had dined in class before, but neither was he so accustomed to this lifestyle as to be blasé, or patronizing.

Io only knew about wine corks from having read an obscure magazine in Joey's waiting-room. It actually pleased her that Wiktor showed such minor lapses, an almost imperceptible trace of latent, slight awkwardness. She had no ambition to stake a place in the circles of the rich and renowned. But his nodding acquaintance with the finer things spoke of the relaxed eclecticism, the comfortable worldliness of a professional . . . a man with a real job. Someone who *did* something.

Would she, in three years time, be able to walk into a place such as this without feeling heart palpitations? Would she wear such a relaxed smile? Or order from a menu with such confidence?

Would she meet the sort of men who made the world move and grow better with their skill? Perhaps one who cared about the same craft as she was studying so long and hard for now?

Naturally, the subject of his actual profession never came up on this, an initial encounter. Her present trade was obvious from her attire, and from her tumescence, but they never mentioned it. He spoke instead about the aurorae, visible even from here, so near the urban lights. A hint indicated that he might once have seen them from *above*—from space—but he did not follow up on that, nor did Io pursue it.

It was perfectly all right to speak of Earthly travels however, since all classes were encouraged in tourism. The superconducting rails made it cheaper than many other entertainments people might have demanded, and social planners considered it helpful. Tourists waged few wars.

Io felt ashamed of how little she had seen, how little she had to tell. But Wiktor made up for her lack. He had been to Merseyside many times, for instance—both Liverpool and Ellesmere Port—and he spoke with fondness of the Lake District, her own favourite place in all the world.

Against her usual habit when in production, Io allowed herself a single glass of wine. Of course she had memorized the tolerance tables long ago, and knew no harm would come to . . . to her toaster.

Sudden memory of that colourful euphemism triggered a nervous giggle. But then it also caused her to think of Perseph, and that made her suddenly sad. Their parting had been cool. Io had no idea what the future would bring, but the note of finality between them made her vision film as she thought about it.

Gyrating emotions. Damn. An occupational hazard. But what a time to have an attack of surropreg blues!

'I—I don't know what's got over me,' she said as she wiped her eyes. 'Would you excuse me while I—' she gestured in the direction of the lavatories. His smile was bemused, understanding. 'Of course,' he said. 'I will order you that especial dessert I mentioned earlier. And,' his grin broadened. 'A glass of fruit juice.'

'Thanks. That might be best.' She laughed, and departed with a smile.

He didn't even try to pressure me into having another glass of wine, she mused as she negotiated her abdomen toward the ladies' room. Many men would have taken it as a challenge to try to get her drunk, even knowing she would be leaving within the hour. It was a rite of machismo she'd never understood, however many times it was explained to her. Wiktor though, seemed a gentleman.

A low wall topped by a decorative hedge separated the dining room proper from the gilt wallpapered passage to the toilets. On her way out again, Io paused to check her composure. She wanted to maintain a friendly openness that would invite him to ask her watchcom number. After all, he said he passed through Liverpool on occasion. Perhaps he might call.

Io took a momentary guilty peek through the shrubbery, feeling like a little girl spying covertly on an older boy, the object of a delicious secret desire. A waiter had just turned away from their table. Walking towards her, he occulted her view for a moment. Then Wiktor could be seen moving a freshly filled glass of orange liquid to her setting, beside a plate containing something reddish and gold—the promised dessert.

His quick glance in her direction almost made her duck down. His facial expression puzzled Io, briefly as he fussed with his jacket pocket. For an instant he looked relieved. Then Wiktor turned to his left—her right—and seemed to nod to somebody seated among the dim booths and shadowed dining cubbies.

Had he recognized someone he knew? Hardly surprising, considering the circles he kept.

Composing her features, Io emerged from behind the wall and smiled as she approached the table. *He is old-fashioned,* she thought as he rose to hold her chair for her. 'What's this?' She dabbed her fork at the creamy eruption on her plate.

'A surprise. You'll like it.'

A forkful hesitated near her nose. 'It smells spicy.'

'It is.' He smiled. 'That's why I ordered you something to drink. But I'm sure you'll love it.' With that he winked, and took a portion from his own serving into his mouth. The goggle-eyed pantomime of pleasure which followed made Io laugh.

The dessert was delicious. It also made her eyes water. 'Well!' She coughed. 'I certainly won't have any trouble with my sinuses during the flight!'

'It always makes me thirsty,' he said, taking a sip of wine. Watching his eyes, she reached for the brimming glass of orange juice.

Would she have suspected anything if she had not continued taking classes? Had she never studied the hard-won wisdom of a century's research, she probably would never have known about those subtle cues given off by child and man, in eye and face and voice, that betray the inner unease.

But then, Io's knowledge was still abstract. So maybe it was instinct—unreliable but desperately useful when it strikes—which made her notice the intense way Wiktor watched her hand.

She put the glass down before it was more than an inch high. His gaze immediately flicked to her face. 'Is something wrong?' he asked.

Please. No. She prayed.

'No, nothing's wrong.' She lifted another forkful of the pungent sweet. 'I was just savouring the taste.'

He seemed to notice the speculation in her eyes, and averted his gaze. That was a mistake. Now he *avoided* looking at the juice glass.

The second spicy taste added power to the first. Io's throat burned, her nostrils felt singed. Still she kept her hand on the table, and concentrated on remembering her lessons.

Speaking with a measured voice, she said, 'Actually, I think I will have another glass of wine, after all.'

Rapid impressions she read almost instantly—brief panic-contraction in the pupils . . . a faint, barely noticeable flush wave, crossing his cheeks at an unsatisfactory angle . . . that involuntary frown, quickly compressed into a slightly asymmetrical smile with the practice of an accomplished poseur . . .

An experienced liar, then. But not a trained one.

The man Io would someday marry would not lie. But he would have taken schooling in what lying *does*. How it is seen, detected, known.

This man, for all his money and worldliness, had never been to school.

'More wine? In your condition?' He laughed teasingly. A little patronizingly. 'Now, Io. Don't try to prove how tough you are. Be a good girl and drink your vitamins.'

My vitamins? Io thought. She reached for the glass.

Here are my vitamins, you son of a fabricow.

'Jism!' he cried, leaping to his feet as she spilled the drink across the tablecloth.

Two confirmations in one action. An innocent man would not have shouted so over only a silly puddle. Nor would a real professional use a curseword specific to a certain type of freelance artist.

'You bitch, how did you kn—' He stepped forward, and so came within Io's seated reach. With one hand she grabbed the loose folds of his stylish cotton trousers. With the other she stabbed down hard with her dessert fork. There was a loud tearing of fabric. Shouting for strength she had never used before outside the decanting room, Io yanked.

The resulting tableau held for a long moment. Staring patrons. Aghast waiters. Io, panting with upraised fork, ready to strike again, this time at a loathsome sight.

Under the torn trousers, hanging like a broken flag, lay Wiktor's codpiece, the emblem of his calling. His tattooed licence told of a costly modification—placental platinum extraction filters of the very latest design.

No wonder Wiktor knew his way around style. Just one of the altered wrigglers he produced in millions could set a pieceworker on course towards her best bonus ever. And for him a healthy commission.

'Why?' she whispered.

Motion resumed. Hurried footsteps approached behind her.

'Officers!' Wiktor pronounced loudly, for all to hear. 'I want to press charges against this madwoman, for assault with intent to injure me!'

Hands pressed upon her shoulders. The fork was ungently pried from her fingers. Io shook her hair back and looked him in the eyes, defiantly.

'Shall we take the table cloth along to the police station, then?' She gestured toward the orange stain.

A quick blinking of the eyes, a bobbing of the Adam's apple as he suddenly swallowed. 'Wait!' Wiktor said as the guards began pulling her away. His sour expression was her bitter reward. 'I—I have changed my mind. I will forget the incident . . . so long as she boards her flight and gets the hell out of here.'

Oh, I'm sure, she thought, watching him squirm. Men who would poison women—such men had personalities based on contempt for others. Probably until this very moment he had never even considered what might happen if he were caught. Now it was just dawning on him, too late.

'Who?' Io asked, simply, demanding a price.

As if it were costing him his gall bladder, he spat the word. 'Perseph.'

Io knew from the look in his eyes that she would have no need for revenge on her former friend. Far from the type of man he had tried to appear to be, this was a cowardly, predatory creature, the sort who preyed exclusively on those weaker than himself. Io felt certain he would never come near her again. *Perseph,* though—perhaps watching even now from some shadowy corner of the room—had real cause to worry about Wiktor.

'*What* was it?' She asked.

Sweat beaded on his lip and brow. There was an implicit arrangement here, truth in exchange for escape. But in fulfilling his part first, Wiktor knew he was giving himself over fully into her hands.

'Para—Parapyridine 4,' he whispered rapidly, trying to make the words for her alone.

Io felt suddenly dizzy. The hand that had touched the juice glass trembled as if defiled. The substance named would not have affected her own health in the slightest. But it would have ruined the product she carried, and made her own eggs utterly useless for anything in the future. She'd be lucky to be able to make solvent filters if she had taken any of that stuff.

'*Why*?' She repeated her first question.

His face was now utterly resigned. 'You were getting too damned high-almighty. Wanted to climb out and leave your friends, your guild. We . . . they . . . thought it would do you good to be brought down a peg.

'It was for—for your own good—' he finished lamely. His handsome confidence was now so completely gone that Io felt stunned that she had ever been fooled at all.

'Excuse me, Madam, is this fellow admitting to having done you some harm?'

Io turned, noticing the blonde Icelandic policeman for the first time. Obviously, he had followed bits of their low, clipped exchange, picking up on hints with obvious skill. His eyes flicked from her surropreg garments to Wiktor's tattoo, to the stained tablecloth, narrowing with dawning suspicion.

He spoke English as educated Icelanders do, better than the English. 'Perhaps you'd like to file charges of your own, Madam?' he asked.

For an instant, Io stared at the policeman's face in sudden revelation. There she saw compassion and more . . . a *confidence* completely unrelated to arrogance . . . a serenity that only came of skill and the sure knowledge of one's own usefulness. Face to face with the real thing, Io wondered how she had ever been fooled by Wiktor's sham.

Inexperience and wishful thinking, I suppose. She would have to talk this over with her teachers.

'No,' Io said softly. 'I will not press charges. But would you please walk with me to my boarding gate? I think I could use a hand.'

Her last word to Wiktor was to thank him over her shoulder, for dinner. The evenness of her tone must have been more unnerving than anything else she might have said. She left him standing there, pale and exposed.

The officer's gentle strong grip on her arm helped Io walk head high. Somewhere in the restaurant's gloom, she knew she was being watched by one more person—someone lacking the guts to show herself. Io didn't bother searching the shadows for those familiar eyes. She would never see them again.

. . . Earlier we have seen excerpts by writers extolling the benefits of an industrial order based on efficient biological assembly processes. And there is no doubt that these techniques are in large measure responsible for the relative comfort of today's nine billion human beings, not least the fact that they have not starved.

The mysticism of the Madrid Catholics, their religious revulsion towards even completely voluntary use of human reproductive systems for industry, is not shared by many others these days. Rather, the right of the poor to use their bodies' talents for their own benefit is enshrined in law, so long as volunteers are qualified and restrict themselves to licensed, non-human embryonic material.

Nevertheless, some dissenting voices have spoken critically of this system from more rational grounds—scientific, biological, economic, and cultural. Some fear that our fundamental attitude towards life itself is changing, subtly but profoundly, as each day passes. And these changes are taking place without adequate thought to the possible long-range consequences. These are doubts that must, in all fairness, be taken seriously . . .
from A SURVEY OF MODERN PROBLEMS, *New York, 2049*

. . . The time may come when these peculiarly severe licensing laws may be relaxed. But for now, the intrinsic value of this particular product to society—by far the most valuable item produced by any society—has convinced lawmakers and voters alike that one particular career calls for schooling, qualification, and respect above any and all others . . .
from THE CERTIFICATION ACT, *2039*

Another penalty of eggwork was the lengthy, all too realistic process of labour. Io took the doctors' word for it that it was still a bit easier than the 'real thing'. But that was small comfort.

Not that difficulty or exertion held any great fears for her. Io knew what she was doing.

Still, Joey held her hand through the agony of transition. And afterwards he wiped the perspiration from her brow. It was all just part of the agency's service, he told her. Just one more reason why so few of his clients ever left him.

Io knew better, of course. Joey actually cared, bless him.

'Did I remember to curse you for getting me into this?' she asked after the worst was over.

'Nope. You forgot.' Joey smiled. 'You missed your chance. The tradition is that nothing said during *transition* can be held against you. Maybe next time.'

'I told you, Joey, there isn't going to be a—'

'Hush. We'll speak of it later. Now, you concentrate. The worst may be over, but you still have hard pushing ahead.'

'Okay, Joey.'

Tremors. Foreshadowings. Io focused on her breathing and was ready when the next contractions came.

'Good, good,' the industrial midwife told her. A technician in the service of Technique Zaire, she commanded her team with crisp precision. 'Now please to be ready for a last effort.'

'Ah.' Io replied in a sharp exhalation. 'Ah!' Then she lost track of time. Lost track of consciousness. Moment by moment she did as she was told by those whose job it was to help her. Several times she cried out in the ways she had been taught, conserving her strength for the final moment.

When it came, it was almost anticlimactic. Passage, release, evacuation. A parting of that familiar connection.

Emptiness.

The scurrying techs had no attention to spare for her. Even Joey, rushed forward, eager to see. When he returned, his eyes beamed. 'I—I thought it would be a shipbrain, Io, but I was wrong. It's a *starbrain*!'

'S—starbrain?'

'Yes! It's a fine, big, healthy starbrain. The only bio-manufactured product licensed to use true human genes! The only one capable of sentience!'

Io's lower lip trembled. Tears welled in her eyes. She began to sob. Joey, mistaking her tears for joy, kept on exulting, obliviously.

'Jeez, Io, it will *think*. It'll pilot starships. Why, they're even talking about a bill to give starbrains *citizenship*, for heaven's sake! Do you know what they're *paying* for a healthy . . .'

Joey's voice droned on, a low ululation of misplaced enthusiasm. Io shut it out. She flung an arm over her eyes so she could not see when they came forward with a swaddled something to show her.

They did not know. They could not know how she felt.

Her breasts throbbed as they attached machines for her first milking, to release the straining pressure. To begin harvesting secondary product from the right. Tertiary from the left.

Tertiary product. Colostrum and homo milk, at five pence a gramme.

He left breast sent unwanted signals to her brain.

'Io, I've just been told they're so happy with you they want to renew . . .'

'Oh, Joey,' she cried. 'Go away, please!' Io's head rocked. 'Just go away.'

And so they left her then, to listen to the rhythms, to the machines, to the beating of her heart, to the singing in her veins.

It has to be worth it, she thought. She prayed. *It has to be!*

To: Ms. Iolanthe Livingstone
93 Marina Drive,
Ellesmere Port, Merseyside

From: British Division
Department of Certification
and Accreditation

Dear Ms Livingstone:

It is our great pleasure to inform you that your test scores, your record of experience, and the recommendations of your instructors have, in totality, persuaded the Board that you are indeed qualified for the certification you requested. By your assiduous efforts you have acquired skills of great importance to humanity. Skills which may lead, at last, to a generation of people no longer plagued by the age-old evils of cruelty and fear and neurosis and unfulfilled potential—evils which so nearly destroyed our world, and hard beset us still to this day.

Towards that brighter future, you and your professional enthusiasm will surely add new strength and purpose.

Therefore, from this date forward, you are hereby licensed to engage in the most demanding and important occupation of them all.

Congratulations. We are certain you will be a very fine (*mother*/~~*father*~~).

For the sake of the children . . .

SELECT BIBLIOGRAPHY

SINGLE-AUTHOR COLLECTIONS

What follows is only a sample both of the authors in the field and of the collections most authors have produced. The sample can readily be expanded by consulting Curtis C. Smith (ed.) in the 'Reference' section below. For the sake of brevity I have sometimes cited 'Best of...' collections, which may appear many years after an author's major writing period.

Aldiss, Brian, *Space, Time and Nathaniel: Presciences* (London, 1957).

—— *The Canopy of Time* (London, 1959).

—— *The Moment of Eclipse* (London, 1970).

Anderson, Poul, *The Best of PA* (New York, 1976).

Asimov, Isaac, *The Best of IA, 1939–72* (London, 1972).

—— *The Complete Robot* (New York, 1982).

—— *Nightfall and other stories* (New York, 1984).

Ballard, J. G., *Terminal Beach* (London, 1964).

—— *The Best of JGB* (London, 1977).

Banks, Iain M., *The State of the Art* (London, 1991).

Benford, Gregory, *In Alien Flesh* (New York, 1988).

Bester, Alfred, *Starlight: the Great Short Fiction of AB* (New York, 1976).

Blish, James, *The Best SF of JB* (London, 1965, rev. edn. London, 1973).

Bradbury, Ray, *The Illustrated Man* (New York, 1951).

—— *The Vintage Bradbury* (New York, 1965).

Brin, David, *The River of Time* (New York, 1987).

Budrys, Algis, *Budrys' Inferno* (New York, 1963), English title *The Furious Future* (London, 1963).

—— *Blood and Burning* (New York, 1978).

Campbell, John W. jr., *Who Goes There? and other stories* (New York, 1955).

Card, Orson Scott, *The Short Fiction of OSC* (New York, 1990).

Clarke, Arthur C., *Expedition to Earth* (New York, 1953).

—— *Tales of Ten Worlds* (New York, 1962).

—— *The Best of ACC, 1937–71* (London, 1973).

Davidson, Avram, *What Strange Stars and Skies* (New York, 1965).

de Camp, Lyon Sprague, *A Gun for Dinosaur and other imaginative tales* (New York, 1963).

Delany, Samuel R., *Driftglass: ten tales of speculative fiction* (New York, 1971).

Dick, Philip K., *The Collected Stories of PKD, 5 vols.* (New York, 1987).

Disch, Thomas M., *White Fang Goes Dingo and other funny SF stories* (London, 1971).

Ellison, Harlan, *I Have No Mouth and I Must Scream* (New York, 1967, rev. edn. New York, 1983).

—— *The Beast that Shouted Love at the Heart of the World* (New York, 1969, rev. edn. New York, 1984).

Farmer, Philip José, *Strange Relations* (New York, 1960).

Gibson, William, *Burning Chrome* (New York, 1986).

Gunn, James G., *Future Imperfect* (New York, 1964).

Haldeman, Joe, *Infinite Dreams* (New York, 1978).

Hamilton, Edmond, *The Horror on the Asteroid and other tales of Planetary Horror* (London, 1936).

—— *The Best of EH* (New York, 1977).

Harrison, Harry, *Prime Number* (New York, 1970).

—— *The Best of HH* (New York and London, 1976).

Heinlein, Robert A., *The Unpleasant Profession of Jonathan Hoag* (New York, 1959).

—— *The Past Through Tomorrow: Future History Series* (New York, 1967).

Kornbluth, Cyril M., *The Best of CMK* (New York, 1976).

Kuttner, Henry, *The Best of HK* (2 vols., London 1965–6).

Le Guin, Ursula K., *The Wind's Twelve Quarters* (New York, 1975).

—— *The Compass Rose* (New York, 1982).

—— *Buffalo Gals and other Animal Presences* (New York, 1987).

Leinster, Murray [Will F. Jenkins], *The Best of ML* (London, 1976).

McAuley, Paul J., *The King of the Hill* (London, 1988).

Martin, George R. R., *Sandkings* (New York, 1981).

—— *Nightflyers* (New York, 1985).

Miller, Walter M. jr., *The Best of WMM jr.* (New York, 1980).

Moore, C. L., *Shambleau and others* (New York, 1953).

Niven, Larry, *Neutron Star* (New York, 1968).

—— *Tales of Known Space* (New York, 1975).

Pohl, Frederik, *Alternating Currents* (New York, 1956).

—— *The Man who Ate the World* (New York, 1960).

—— *The FP Omnibus* (London, 1966).

—— *The Best of FP* (New York, 1975).

Roberts, Keith, *Machines and Men* (London, 1973).

Robinson, Kim S., *The Planet on the Table* (New York, 1986).

Russ, Joanna, *The Adventures of Alyx* (New York, 1983).

Schenck, Hilbert, *Steam Bird* (New York, 1988).

Schmitz, James H., *Agent of Vega* (New York, 1960).

—— *A Pride of Monsters* (New York, 1970).

Shaw, Bob, *Tomorrow Lies in Ambush* (London and New York, 1973).

Sheckley, Robert, *The RS Omnibus* (London, 1973).

Sheffield, Charles, *Vectors* (New York, 1980).

Shepard, Lucius, *The Jaguar Hunter* (Sauk City, Wis., 1987).

—— *The Ends of the Earth* (Sauk City, Wis., 1991).

Silverberg, Robert, *The Best of RS* (New York, 1976).

Simak, Clifford D., *City* (New York, 1952).

—— *Skirmish: the Great Short Fiction of CDS* (New York, 1977).

Smith, Cordwainer [Paul M. A. Linebarger], *The Best of CS* (New York, 1975).

—— *The Instrumentality of Mankind* (New York, 1979).

Smith, E. E., *The Best of E. E. 'Doc.' Smith* (London, 1975).

Spinrad, Norman, *No Direction Home* (New York, 1975).

—— *The Star-Spangled Future* (New York, 1979).

Sterling, Bruce, *Crystal Express* (Sauk City, Wis., 1989).

Sturgeon, Theodore, *Caviar* (New York, 1955).

—— *The Worlds of TS* (New York, 1972).

Tenn, William [Philip Klass], *Of All Possible Worlds* (New York, 1955).

—— *The Seven Sexes* (New York, 1965).

Tiptree, James jr. [Alice Sheldon], *Ten Thousand Light Years from Home* (New York, 1973).

—— *Warm Worlds and Otherwise* (New York, 1975).

—— *Star Songs of an Old Primate* (New York, 1978).

—— *Out of the Everywhere and other Extraordinary Visions* (New York, 1981).

van Vogt, A. E., *Destination: Universe!* (New York, 1952).

—— *The Best of AEvV* (London, 1974).

Vance, Jack, *The Best of JV* (New York, 1976).

Varley, John, *The Persistence of Vision* (New York, 1978), English title *In the Hall of the Martian Kings* (London, 1978).

—— *Blue Champagne* (New York, 1986).

Watson, Ian, *The Very Slow Time Machine* (London and New York, 1979).

—— *Slow Birds and other stories* (London, 1985).

Weinbaum, Stanley G., *The Best of SGW* (New York, 1974).

Wells, H. G., *The Short Stories of HGW* (London, 1927).

Williamson, Jack, *The Pandora Effect* (New York, 1969).

—— *The Early Williamson* (New York, 1975).

Wolfe, Gene, *The Island of Doctor Death and Other Stories and other stories* (New York, 1980).

—— *GW's Book of Days* (New York, 1981).

Wyndham, John [J. B. Harris], *The Best of JW* (London, 1973).

Zelazny, Roger, *The Doors of his Face, the Lamps of his Mouth, and other stories,* (New York, 1974).

ANTHOLOGIES

Again, only a small selection is presented. There is an excellent discussion of the nature of science fiction anthologies in Neil Barron (ed.), see the 'Reference' section below.

Aldiss, Brian (ed.), *The Penguin SF Omnibus* (London, 1973).

Aldiss, Brian, and Harrison, Harry (eds.), *The Year's Best SF 1–9* (London, 1968–76).

—— *Farewell, Fantastic Venus* (London, 1968).

—— *The Astounding—Analog Reader* (2 vols., New York 1972–3).

Asimov, Isaac (ed.), *The Hugo Winners 1–4* (4 vols., New York, 1962–85).

—— *Before the Golden Age: A SF anthology of the 1930s* (New York and London, 1974).

Carr, Terry (ed.), *The Best SF of the Year 1–16* (New York, 1972–87).

Clareson, Thomas D. (ed.), *A Spectrum of Worlds* (New York, 1972).

Clute, John *et al.* (eds.), *Interzone, the 1st–5th anthologies: new SF and fantasy writing* (London, 1985–91).

Conklin, Groff (ed.), *The Best of SF* (New York, 1946).

—— *The Omnibus of SF* (New York, 1952).

Ellison Harlan (ed.), *Dangerous Visions* (New York, 1967).

—— *Again, Dangerous Visions* (New York, 1972).

Ferman, Edward (ed.), *The Best from 'Fantasy and SF': A thirty year retrospective* (New York, 1980).

Gunn, James (ed.), *The Road to SF* (4 vols., New York, 1977–81).

Harrison, Harry and Stover, Leon E. (eds.), *Apeman, Spaceman: Anthropological SF* (New York and London, 1968).

Hipolito, Jane and McNelly, Willis E. (eds.), *Mars, We Love You* (New York, 1971), English title, *The Book of Mars* (London, 1976).

Jones, Langdon (ed.), *The New SF* (London, 1979).

Kidd, Virginia (ed.), *Millennial Women* (New York, 1978).

Knight, Damon (ed.), *Orbit 1–21* (New York, 1966–80).

—— *SF of the Thirties* (Indianapolis, 1975).

Merril, Judith (ed.), *England Swings SF* (New York, 1968).

Moorcock, Michael (ed.), *Best SF Stories from 'New Worlds' 1–8* (London, 1967–74).

—— *Before Armageddon: An anthology of Victorian and Edwardian imaginative fiction published before 1914* (London, 1975).

—— *England Invaded: A collection of fantasy fiction* (London and New York, 1977).

Moskowitz, Sam (ed.), *Modern Masterpieces of SF* (Cleveland, Ohio, 1965).

—— *Masterpieces of SF* (Cleveland, Ohio, 1967).

—— *SF by Gaslight: A history and anthology of SF in the popular magazines, 1891–1911* (Cleveland, Ohio, 1968).

—— *Under the Moons of Mars: A history and anthology of 'the scientific romance' in the Munsey magazines, 1912–30* (New York, 1970).

Nebula Award Stories 1–16, various eds. (New York, 1966–82).

Pohl, Frederik *et al.* (eds.), *Galaxy Magazine: Thirty years of innovative SF* (New York, 1980).

Sargent, Pamela (ed.), *Women of Wonder: SF stories by women about women* (New York, 1975).

—— *More Women of Wonder* (New York, 1976).
—— *The New Women of Wonder* (New York, 1978).
Silverberg, Robert (ed.), *The Best of New Dimensions* (New York, 1979).
—— and Greenberg, Martin H. (eds.), *The Arbor House Treasury of Modern SF* (New York, 1980).
Sterling, Bruce (ed.), *Mirrorshades: The cyberpunk anthology* (New York, 1986).

WORKS OF CRITICISM

Aldiss, Brian, with Wingrove, David, *Trillion Year Spree: The history of SF* (London, 1986).
Atheling, William jr. [James Blish], *The Issue at Hand* (Chicago, 1964).
Carter, Paul A., *The Creation of Tomorrow: Fifty years of magazine SF* (New York, 1977).
del Rey, Lester, *The World of SF, 1926–76: The history of a subculture* (New York and London, 1980).
Greenland, Colin, *The Entropy Exhibition: Michael Moorcock and the British 'New Wave' in SF* (London, 1983).
Gunn, James, *Alternate Worlds: The illustrated history of SF* (Englewood Cliffs, N. J., 1975).
Huntington, John, *Rationalizing Genius: Ideological strategies in the American SF short story* (New Brunswick, NJ, 1989).
Nicholls, Peter (ed.), *The Science in SF: Does SF foretell the future?* (London, 1982).
Parrinder, Patrick (ed.), *SF: A critical guide* (London and New York, 1979).
—— *SF: Its criticism and teaching* (London, 1980).
Pierce, John J., *Foundations of SF: A study in imagination and evolution* (Westport, Conn., 1987).
Scholes, Robert, and Rabkin, Eric S., *SF: History, science, vision* (New York, 1977).
Shippey, Tom (ed.), *Fictional Space: Essays on contemporary SF* (Oxford, 1991).
Stableford, Brian, *Scientific Romance in Britain, 1890–1950* (London, 1985).
Suvin, Darko, *Metamorphoses of SF: On the poetics and history of a literary genre* (New Haven and London, 1979).

REFERENCE

Barron, Neil (ed.), *Anatomy of Wonder: A critical guide to SF* (2nd edn., New York and London, 1981).
Bleiler, E. F., *The Checklist of SF and Supernatural Fiction* (London, 1978).
Contento, William (ed.), *Index to SF Anthologies and Collections* (Boston, 1978)
Gunn, James (ed.), *The New Encyclopaedia of SF* (New York and London, 1988).

Nicholls, Peter (ed.), *The Encyclopaedia of SF: An illustrated A to Z* (London, 1979).

Smith, Curtis C. (ed.), *Twentieth Century SF Writers* (2nd edn., Chicago and London, 1986).

Tuck, Donald H., *The Encyclopaedia of Science Fiction and Fantasy* (3 vols., Chicago, 1974, 1978, 1982).

SOURCES

All the stories in this collection appeared first in magazines or original anthologies. The following notes indicate the place of first publication, together with the first, or sometimes the most convenient reprint in book form, if this has taken place. Brief biographical information about an author is given where this was felt to be relevant. Copyright information appears in a separate section of acknowledgements.

'The Land Ironclads' by H. G. Wells (1866–1946), first published in *The Strand* (Dec. 1903), reprinted in *The Short Stories of H. G. Wells* (Ernest Benn: London, 1927).

'Finis' by Frank L. Pollack, first published in *Argosy* (June 1906), reprinted in Sam Moskowitz (ed.), *Science Fiction by Gaslight: A history and anthology of science fiction in the popular magazines, 1891–1911* (World Publishing: Cleveland, Ohio, 1968). Nothing is known of Pollack as an author.

'As Easy as ABC' by Rudyard Kipling (1865–1936), first published in *The London Magazine* (Apr. 1912), reprinted in Kipling, *A Diversity of Creatures* (Macmillan: London, 1917). The story is an elaboration of the world described in 'With the Night Mail', in Kipling's collection *Actions and Reactions* (Macmillan: London, 1909).

'The Metal Man' by Jack Williamson (b. 1908), first published in *Amazing Stories* (Dec. 1928), reprinted in Thomas D. Clareson (ed.), *A Spectrum of Worlds* (Doubleday: Garden City, NY, 1972). Clareson notes that Williamson published an updated version of this story in his collection *The Pandora Effect* (Ace: New York, 1969).

'A Martian Odyssey' by Stanley G. Weinbaum (1902–35), first published in *Wonder Stories* (July 1934), reprinted in *The Best of Stanley G. Weinbaum* (Ballantine: New York, 1976 and Sphere: London, 1977).

'Night' by John W. Campbell jr. (1910–71), first published in *Astounding Science Fiction* (Oct. 1935), reprinted in Campbell, *Who Goes There? and other stories* (Dell: New York, 1955), and in Sam Moskowitz (ed.), *Modern Masterpieces of Science Fiction* (World Publishing: Cleveland, Ohio, 1965).

'Desertion' by Clifford D. Simak (1904–88), first published in *Astounding* (Nov. 1944). It later became the fourth of eight connected stories in Simak's *City* (Gnome: New York, 1952).

'The Piper's Son' by 'Lewis Padgett'. Padgett was a pen-name used by Henry Kuttner (1915–58) in collaboration with his wife C. L. Moore (b. 1911).

This story was first published in *Astounding* (Feb. 1945) and later became the opening story in the sequence *Mutant*, which was published both under the 'Padgett' pseudonym (Gnome: New York, 1953), and under the name of Kuttner (Ballantine: New York, 1953).

'The Monster' by A. E. van Vogt (b. 1912), first published in *Astounding* (Aug. 1948), reprinted in van Vogt's *Destination: Universe!* (Pellegrini and Cudahy: New York, 1952). The story has also been reprinted under the title 'Resurrection'.

'The Second Night of Summer' by James H. Schmitz (1911–81), first published in *Galaxy* (Dec. 1950), reprinted as the last of four connected stories in Schmitz, *Agent of Vega* (Gnome: New York, 1960).

'Second Dawn' by Arthur C. Clarke (b. 1917), first published in *Science Fiction Quarterly* (Aug. 1951), reprinted in Clarke, *Expedition to Earth* (Ballantine: New York, 1953).

'Crucifixus Etiam' by Walter M. Miller jr. (b. 1922), first published in *Astounding* (Feb. 1953), reprinted in Miller, *The View from the Stars* (Ballantine: New York, and Gollancz: London, 1965).

'The Tunnel under the World' by Frederik Pohl (b. 1919), first published in *Galaxy* (Jan. 1955), reprinted in Pohl, *Alternating Currents* (Ballantine: New York, 1956).

'Who Can Replace a Man?' by Brian Aldiss (b. 1925), first published in *Infinity Science Fiction* (June 1958), reprinted in Aldiss, *The Canopy of Time* (Faber: London, 1959).

'Billennium' by J. G. Ballard (b. 1930), first published in *New Worlds* (Nov. 1961), reprinted in Ballard, *Billennium and other stories* (Berkley: New York, 1962) and Ballard, *The Terminal Beach* (Gollancz: London, 1964).

'The Ballad of Lost C'mell' by 'Cordwainer Smith', a pseudonym of Paul M. A. Linebarger (1913–66). This story first appeared in *Galaxy* (Oct. 1962), and was reprinted in J. J. Pierce (ed.), *The Best of Cordwainer Smith* (Ballantine: New York, 1975).

'Semley's Necklace' by Ursula K. Le Guin (b. 1929), first published under the title 'The Dowry of the Angyar' in *Amazing* (Sept. 1964), reprinted as 'Semley's Necklace' in Le Guin, *The Wind's Twelve Quarters* (Harper: New York, 1975).

'How Beautiful with Banners' by James Blish (1921–75), first published in Damon Knight (ed.), *Orbit* 1 (Putnam: New York, 1966), reprinted in *The Best Science Fiction Stories of James Blish* (rev. edn., Faber: London, 1973).

'A Criminal Act' by Harry Harrison (b. 1925), first published in *Analog* (Jan. 1967), reprinted in Harrison, *Prime Number* (Berkley: New York, 1970).

'Problems of Creativeness' by Thomas M. Disch (b. 1940), first published in *Fantasy and Science Fiction* (Apr. 1967), later published in much-altered form as 'The Death of Socrates', this constituting the first part of Disch's story-sequence *334* (MacGibbon and Kee: London, 1972).

'How the Whip Came Back' by Gene Wolfe (b. 1931), first published in Damon Knight (ed.), *Orbit* 6 (Putnam: New York, 1970), reprinted in *Gene Wolfe's Book of Days* (Doubleday: New York, 1981).

'Cloak of Anarchy' by Larry Niven (b. 1938), first published in *Analog* (Mar. 1972), reprinted in Niven, *Tales of Known Space* (Ballantine: New York, 1975).

'A Thing of Beauty' by Norman Spinrad (b. 1940), first published in *Analog* (Jan. 1973), reprinted in Spinrad, *No Direction Home* (Pocket Books: New York, 1975).

'The Screwfly Solution' by 'Raccoona Sheldon'. 'Raccoona Sheldon' was a pseudonym used occasionally by Alice Sheldon (1916–87), who, however, published more often under the name 'James Tiptree jr.'. This story appeared first in *Analog* (June 1977), and was reprinted in the Tiptree collection *Out of the Everywhere and Other Extraordinary Visions* (Ballantine: New York, 1981). The choice of the name 'Raccoona' may be explained by the story 'The Women Men Don't See' in Tiptree, *Warm Worlds and Otherwise* (Ballantine: New York, 1975).

'The Way of Cross and Dragon' by George R. R. Martin (b. 1948), first published in *Omni* (June 1979) and reprinted in Martin, *Sandkings* (Pocket Books: New York, 1981).

'Swarm' by Bruce Sterling (b. 1954), first published in *Fantasy and Science Fiction* (Apr. 1982), reprinted in Sterling, *Crystal Express* (Arkham House: Sauk City, Wis., 1989).

'Burning Chrome' by William Gibson (b. 1948), first published in *Omni* (July 1982), reprinted in Gibson, *Burning Chrome* (Arbor House: New York, 1986).

'Silicon Muse' by Hilbert Schenck (b. 1926), first published in *Analog* (Sept. 1984).

'Karl and the Ogre' by Paul J. McAuley (b. 1955), first published in *Interzone* (Winter 1985/6), reprinted in McAuley, *The King of the Hill* (Gollancz: London, 1991).

'Piecework' by David Brin (b. 1950), first published in *Interzone* (Jan./Feb. 1990), reprinted in John Clute *et al.* (eds.), *Interzone: The 5th anthology* (New English Library: London, 1991).

ACKNOWLEDGEMENTS

Full source information is given above.

Brian Aldiss, 'Who Can Replace a Man'. Copyright © 1958, 1960, 1988 by Brian W. Aldiss. Reprinted by permission of A. P. Watt Ltd., and the Robin Straus Agency Inc., on behalf of the author.

J. G. Ballard, 'Billenium', from the collection *The Terminal Beach* © 1964 published by Victor Gollancz Ltd. and J. W. Dent. Reproduced by permission of the author c/o Casarotto Company Ltd., National House, 60–6 Wardour Street, London W1V 3HP.

James Blish, 'How Beautiful with Banners'. Reprinted by permission of Mrs Judith Blish and Laurence Pollinger Ltd.

David Brin, 'Piecework', © 1990 David Brin.

John W. Campbell Jr., 'Night', copyright 1935 John W. Campbell Jr.

Arthur C. Clarke, 'Second Dawn'. Reprinted by permission of David Higham Associates and Scott Meredith Literary Agency Inc.

Thomas M. Disch, 'Problems of Creativeness'. Reprinted by permission of the author c/o The Karpfinger Agency, New York.

William Gibson, 'Burning Chrome', © 1982 by William Gibson. Reprinted by kind permission of the author.

Harry Harrison, 'A Criminal Act', © 1967 Harry Harrison. Reprinted by permission of Abner Stein in association with Sobel Weber Associates for the author.

Ursula K. Le Guin, 'Semley's Necklace', © 1964 by Ursula K. Le Guin. Reprinted by permission of the author and the author's agent, Virginia Kidd.

George R. R. Martin, 'The Way of the Cross and Dragon', © 1979 George R. R. Martin.

Paul J. McAuley, 'Karl and the Ogre'. Reprinted by permission of MBA Literary Agents Ltd.

Walter M. Miller Jr., 'Crucifixus Etiam'. Reprinted by permission of the author c/o Don Congdon Associates, Inc.

Larry Niven, 'Cloak of Anarchy', © 1972 Larry Niven.

'Lewis Padgett' (Henry Kuttner), 'The Piper's Son', copyright 1945, © renewed 1972 by C. L. Moore. Reprinted by permission of Don Congdon Associates, Inc.

Frederik Pohl, 'The Tunnel under the World', © 1954 by Galaxy Publishing Corporation. Reprinted by permission of the author and his agent Carnell Literary Agency.

Hilbert Schenck, 'Silicon Muse', © 1984 by Hilbert Schenck. Reprinted by permission of the author and the author's agent, Virginia Kidd.

James H. Schmitz, 'The Second Night of Summer', copyright 1950 James H. Schmitz.

'Raccoona Sheldon', 'The Screwfly Solution', © 1977 Raccoona Sheldon.

Clifford D. Simak, 'Desertion', copyright 1944 by Street and Smith Publications, Inc., © 1972 by Clifford D. Simak. Reprinted by permission of Laurence Pollinger Ltd., and the Estate of Clifford D. Simak.

'Cordwainer Smith', 'The Ballad of Lost C'mell'. Reprinted by permission of Victor Gollancz Ltd.

Norman Spinrad, 'A Thing of Beauty', © 1973 Norman Spinrad. Reprinted by kind permission of the author.

Bruce Sterling, 'Swarm'. Reprinted by permission of Writers House Inc., on behalf of the author.

A. E. van Vogt, 'The Monster', copyright 1948 by Street and Smith Publications, copyright 1952 by A. E. van Vogt.

Stanley G. Weinbaum, 'A Martian Odyssey', copyright the Estate of Stanley G. Weinbaum.

H. G. Wells, 'The Land Ironclads'. Reprinted by permission of A. P. Watt Ltd. on behalf of The Literary Executors of the Estate of H. G. Wells.

Jack Williamson, 'The Metal Man', copyright 1928, © renewed 1972 by Jack Williamson. Reprinted by permission of the Spectrum Literary Agency.

Gene Wolfe, 'How the Whip Came Back', © 1970 by Gene Wolfe. Reprinted by permission of the author and the author's agent, Virginia Kidd.

Every effort has been made to secure copyright permission prior to printing but this has not always been possible. If notified the publisher will be pleased to rectify any inadvertent errors or omissions at the earliest opportunity.